Data-Driven Decision Making for Long-Term Business Success

Sonia Singh
Toss Global Management, UAE

S. Suman Rajest
Dhaanish Ahmed College of Engineering, India

Slim Hadoussa
Brest Business School, France

Ahmed J. Obaid
University of Kufa, Iraq

R. Regin
SRM Institute of Science and Technology, India

A volume in the Advances in Business Information Systems and Analytics (ABISA) Book Series

IGI Global
PUBLISHER of TIMELY KNOWLEDGE

Published in the United States of America by
IGI Global
Business Science Reference (an imprint of IGI Global)
701 E. Chocolate Avenue
Hershey PA, USA 17033
Tel: 717-533-8845
Fax: 717-533-8661
E-mail: cust@igi-global.com
Web site: http://www.igi-global.com

Library of Congress Cataloging-in-Publication Data

Names: Singh, Sonia, 1978- editor. | Rajest, S. Suman, 1988- editor. | Hadoussa, Slim, 1980- editor. | Obaid, Ahmed J. (Ahmed Jabbar), editor. | Regin, R., 1985- editor.
Title: Data-driven decision making for long-term business success / edited by Sonia Singh, S. Suman Rajest, Slim Hadoussa, Ahmed J. Obaid, R. Regin.
Description: Hershey PA : Business Science Reference, [2024] | Includes bibliographical references.
Identifiers: LCCN 2023052000 (print) | LCCN 2023052001 (ebook) | ISBN 9798369321935 (hardcover) | ISBN 9798369321942 (ebook)
Subjects: LCSH: Decision making--Data processing. | Success in business.
Classification: LCC HD30.23 .D371584 2024 (print) | LCC HD30.23 (ebook) | DDC 658.4/038011--dc23/eng/20231206
LC record available at https://lccn.loc.gov/2023052000
LC ebook record available at https://lccn.loc.gov/2023052001

This book is published in the IGI Global book series Advances in Business Information Systems and Analytics (ABISA) (ISSN: 2327-3275; eISSN: 2327-3283)

British Cataloguing in Publication Data
A Cataloguing in Publication record for this book is available from the British Library.

For electronic access to this publication, please contact: eresources@igi-global.com.

Advances in Business Information Systems and Analytics (ABISA) Book Series

Madjid Tavana
La Salle University, USA

ISSN:2327-3275
EISSN:2327-3283

Mission

The successful development and management of information systems and business analytics is crucial to the success of an organization. New technological developments and methods for data analysis have allowed organizations to not only improve their processes and allow for greater productivity, but have also provided businesses with a venue through which to cut costs, plan for the future, and maintain competitive advantage in the information age.

The **Advances in Business Information Systems and Analytics (ABISA) Book Series** aims to present diverse and timely research in the development, deployment, and management of business information systems and business analytics for continued organizational development and improved business value.

Coverage

- Business Intelligence
- Information Logistics
- Business models
- Algorithms
- Business Systems Engineering
- Data Management
- Forecasting
- Legal information systems
- Business Process Management
- Statistics

IGI Global is currently accepting manuscripts for publication within this series. To submit a proposal for a volume in this series, please contact our Acquisition Editors at Acquisitions@igi-global.com or visit: http://www.igi-global.com/publish/.

The Advances in Business Information Systems and Analytics (ABISA) Book Series (ISSN 2327-3275) is published by IGI Global, 701 E. Chocolate Avenue, Hershey, PA 17033-1240, USA, www.igi-global.com. This series is composed of titles available for purchase individually; each title is edited to be contextually exclusive from any other title within the series. For pricing and ordering information please visit http://www.igi-global.com/book-series/advances-business-information-systems-analytics/37155. Postmaster: Send all address changes to above address.

Titles in this Series

For a list of additional titles in this series, please visit: www.igi-global.com/book-series

Intersecting Environmental Social Governance and AI for Business Sustainability
Cristina Raluca Gh. Popescu (University of Bucharest, Romania & The Bucharest University of Economic Studies, Romania & The National Institute for Research and Development in Environmental Protection, Romania & INCDPM, Bucharest, Romania & National Research and Development Institute for Gas Turbines (COMOTI), Bucharest, Romania) and Poshan Yu (Soochow University, China & Australian Studies Centre, Shanghai University, hina)
Business Science Reference • © 2024 • 310pp • H/C (ISBN: 9798369311516) • US $275.00

Leveraging AI and Emotional Intelligence in Contemporary Business Organizations
Dipanker Sharma (Central University of Himachal Pradesh, India) Bhawana Bhardwaj (Central University of Himachal Pradesh, India) and Mohinder Chand Dhiman (Central University of Himachal Pradesh, ndia)
Business Science Reference • © 2024 • 300pp • H/C (ISBN: 9798369319024) • US $270.00

Data-Driven Intelligent Business Sustainability
Sonia Singh (Toss Global Management, UAE) S. Suman Rajest (Dhaanish Ahmed College of Engineering, India) Slim Hadoussa (Brest Business School, France) Ahmed J. Obaid (University of Kufa, Iraq) and R. Regin (SRM Institute of Science and Technology, India)
Business Science Reference • © 2024 • 320pp • H/C (ISBN: 9798369300497) • US $265.00

Advancement in Business Analytics Tools for Higher Financial Performance
Reza Gharoie Ahangar (Lewis University, USA) and Mark Napier (Lewis University, USA)
Business Science Reference • © 2023 • 321pp • H/C (ISBN: 9781668483862) • US $250.00

Cases on Enhancing Business Sustainability Through Knowledge Management Systems
Meir Russ (University of Wisconsin-Green Bay, USA & Stellenbosch University, South Africa)
Business Science Reference • © 2023 • 366pp • H/C (ISBN: 9781668458594) • US $240.00

Streamlining Organizational Processes Through AI, IoT, Blockchain, and Virtual Environments
Marisol Hernández Hernández (Universidad Autónoma del Estado de México, Mexico)
Business Science Reference • © 2023 • 253pp • H/C (ISBN: 9781668486399) • US $250.00

Data-Driven Approaches for Effective Managerial Decision Making
Anubha (Jaipuria Institute of Management, Ghaziabad, India) and Himanshu Sharma (IILM Institute for Higher Education, New Delhi, India)
Business Science Reference • © 2023 • 336pp • H/C (ISBN: 9781668475683) • US $255.00

IGI Global
PUBLISHER of TIMELY KNOWLEDGE

701 East Chocolate Avenue, Hershey, PA 17033, USA
Tel: 717-533-8845 x100 • Fax: 717-533-8661
E-Mail: cust@igi-global.com • www.igi-global.com

Table of Contents

Preface xxiii

Chapter 1
Application of Strategic Human Resource Management Models for Organizational Performance 1
N. Geethanjali, PSNA College of Engineering and Technology, India
K. M. Ashifa, Istanbul Gelisim University, Turkey
Avantika Raina, Vivekananda Institute of Professional Studies, India
Jayashree Patil, Bharati Vidyapeeth, India
Rameshwaran Byloppilly, City University, Ajman, UAE
S. Suman Rajest, Dhaanish Ahmed College of Engineering, India

Chapter 2
Smart HR 4.0 With Impact of Technology Advancement and Industry 4.0 on HR Practices 20
Praveen Kakada, VIT Business School, Vellore Institute of Technology, Chennai, India
Muhammed Shafi M. K., Vellore Institute of Technology, Chennai, India

Chapter 3
A Comprehensive Review on Leveraging Business Intelligence for Enhanced Marketing Analytics 34
P. S. Venkateswaran, PSNA College of Engineering and Technology, India
Divya Marupaka, Unikon IT Inc., USA
Sachin Parate, Twillio, USA
Amit Bhanushali, Independent Researcher, USA
Latha Thammareddi, DXC Technology, USA
P. Paramasivan, Dhaanish Ahmed College of Engineering, India

Chapter 4
The Synergy of Management Information Systems and Predictive Analytics for Marketing 49
M. Lishmah Dominic, Annamalai University, India
P. S. Venkateswaran, PSNA College of Engineering and Technology, India
Latha Thamma Reddi, Independent Researcher, USA
Sandeep Rangineni, Pluto TV, USA
R. Regin, SRM Institute of Science and Technology, Ramapuram, India
S. Suman Rajest, Dhaanish Ahmed College of Engineering, India

Chapter 5
Celebrating Lives Beyond on Unveiling the Digital Legacy Manager for Empowering Personal Heritage Preservation 64
S. Sivabala, SRM Institute of Science and Technology, Ramapuram, India
P. Vidyasri, SRM Institute of Science and Technology, Ramapuram, India

Chapter 6
Empowering Employees' Enablement Intelligently With Data and Realizing Business Excellence ... 87
H. Hajra, Bharath Institute of Higher Education and Research, India
G. Jayalakshmi, Bharath Institute of Higher Education and Research, India

Chapter 7
Big Data Analytics and Its Impact on Human Resources Management 109
Anusha Thakur, University of Petroleum and Energy Studies, India

Chapter 8
Applications of Artificial Intelligence Tools in Higher Education 124
P. S. Venkateswaran, PSNA College of Engineering and Technology, Dindigul, India
Firas Tayseer Mohammad Ayasrah, Al Ain University, UAE
Varun Kumar Nomula, Georgia Institute of Technology, USA
P. Paramasivan, Dhaanish Ahmed College of Engineering, India
P. Anand, Dhaanish Ahmed College of Engineering, India
K. Bogeshwaran, Dhaanish Ahmed College of Engineering, India

Chapter 9
Impact of the COVID-19 Lockdown on Employee Engagement and Efficiency 137
Manisha Singh, VIT Bhopal University, India
Rakhi Tiwari, Barkatullah University, India
Vinod Bhatt, VIT Bhopal University, India
Yogesh Shukla, VIT Bhopal University, India

Chapter 10
Synergizing Efficiency and Customer Delight on Empowering Business With Enterprise Applications 149
D. Lavanya, PSNA College of Engineering and Technology, India
Sandeep Rangineni, Pluto TV, USA
Latha Thamma Reddi, DXC Technology, USA
R. Regin, SRM Institute of Science And Technology, Ramapuram, India
S. Suman Rajest, Dhaanish Ahmed College of Engineering, India
P. Paramasivan, Dhaanish Ahmed College of Engineering, India

Chapter 11
Intelligent Business Sustainability on Marketing System 164
M. Parveen Roja, PSNA College of Engineering and Technology, India
Shashank Agarwal, CVS Health, USA
Amrita Baid More, Prestige Institute of Management and Research, India
K. Bogeshwaran, Dhaanish Ahmed College of Engineering, India
A. Nagarajan, Dhaanish Ahmed College of Engineering, India
S. Manikandan, Dhaanish Ahmed College of Engineering, India

Chapter 12
Block Overflow on Frequently Asked Questions Using Blockchain 179
Jyoti P. Kanjalkar, Vishwakarma Institute of Technology, India
Rushikesh Kahat, Vishwakarma Institute of Technology, India
Sankalp Mahesh Kokse, Vishwakarma Institute of Technology, India
Sanket Katale, Vishwakarma Institute of Technology, India
Nishchay Ramchandani, Vishwakarma Institute of Technology, India
Pramod Kanjalkar, Vishwakarma Institute of Technology, India

Chapter 13
Rise of Next Generation Entrepreneurs Through Innovative Digital Strategies in MSMEs During COVID-19 193
Raji Rajan, Jain University, India
Mariam Mathen, Jain University, India
Megha Garud, Jain University, India
Melanie Elizabeth Lourens, Durban University of Technology, South Africa

Chapter 14
Influence of Government Initiatives and Information on Indian Women Entrepreneurial Ventures 209
Sasi Sundarakumar, Takshashila University, India
J. Tamil Selvi, Annamalai University, India
K. Ilangovan, Pondicherry University, India
Vellayan Srinivasan, S.A. Engineering College (Autonomous), India
A. S. Kannan, GRT Institute of Engineering and Technology, India
Vivek Arunachalam, Berlin School of Business and Innovation, Germany

Chapter 15
Overview of Industry 5.0 on Emerging Technologies and Human and Robot Collaboration 221
Usha Prabhu, Jain University, India
P. H. Reshma Sultana, Jain University, India
Vasudha Srivatsa, Adarsh Institute of Management and Information Technology, India
R. Vennila, Jain University, India
B. Manjunath, Jain University, India

Chapter 16
Can Firm Size Moderate Navigating Economic Performance Through Strategic Purchasing? 235
Uday Inala, University of Hyderabad, India
John Yesudas Valluri, Jain University, India
Gunupuru Koteswara Rao, University of Hyderabad, India
Shyamaladevi Balakrishnan, SRM Institute of Science and Technology, Kattankulathur, India
A. S. Kannan, GRT Institute of Engineering and Technology, India
Easwaramoorthy Rangaswamy, Amity Global Institute, Singapore

Chapter 17
Effect of Crude Oil Price Variations on Stocks With Special Reference to NSE 248
Shimna Jayaraj, Jain University, India
T. Shenbagavalli, Jain University, India
V. Vipanchi, Jain University, India
B.S. Sudha, Jain University, India
Juhi Jain, Jain University, India
Biswaranjan Senapati, Parker Hannifin Corp., USA

Chapter 18
A Study in Rural Areas of Southern Karnataka Districts in Dairy Farming Challenges Faced by the Entrepreneurs 264
M. S. Naveen Kumar, Jain University, India
G. M. Rajeshwari, REVA University, India
Sheetal V. Hukkeri, Jain University, India
S. Ashwini, Government First Grade College, India
B. G. Guruprasad, Jain University, India
Dilmurod Nasimov, Academy of Public Administration, Uzbekistan

Chapter 19
An Analysis of Credit Management and Bank Lending Practices in Developing Countries 278
Srinivas Kolachina, Koneru Lakshmaiah Education Foundation, India
Lisha Hundia, Koneru Lakshmaiah Education Foundation, India
Kancherla Mounishker, Koneru Lakshmaiah Education Foundation, India
Juluru Venkatesh, Koneru Lakshmaiah Education Foundation, India
Palanivel Rathinasabapathi Velmurugan, Berlin School of Business and Innovation, Germany
Ahmed J. Obaid, University of Kufa, Iraq

Chapter 20
A Comprehensive Approach to Exploring the Data Input for Performance Evaluation of Vegetable Distribution Center 296
C. Thilak Reddy, Jain University, India
V. Navaneethakumar, Jain University, India
V. Vinoth Kumar, Jain University, India
S. Yogananthan, Jain University, India

Chapter 21
A Study on Total Quality Management (TQM) in Warehouse Management in Logistics Limited.... 313
Pooja Kumari, Jain University, India
T. Shenbagavalli, Jain University, India
S. Ashwini, Jain University, India
K. Vidhya, Jain University, India

Chapter 22
A Systematic Study of Central Bank Digital Currency: Challenges, Limitations, and Its Effects on the Indian Economy 331
M. S. Nikhil, Jain University, India
Nischal V. Atreya, Jain University, India
H. Mehul Kumar, Jain University, India
B. Priyadharshini, Jain University, India
S. Ramya, Jain University, India

Chapter 23
Tourist Behaviour Analysis Using Data Analytics 343
L. Maria Michael Visuwasam, RMK College of Engineering and Technology, India
M. Srinath, RMK College of Engineering and Technology, India
V. S. Aswin Raj, RMK College of Engineering and Technology, India
A. Sirajudeen, RMK College of Engineering and Technology, India
S. Sudhir Maharaaja, RMK College of Engineering and Technology, India
Dakshin Raja, RMK College of Engineering and Technology, India

Chapter 24
A Study on Consumer Preference and Satisfaction Towards Various Brands of Hair Shampoo in Ahmedabad City: Consumer Preference and Satisfaction Towards Hair Shampoo Brands 356
Nupur Rawal, GLS University, India
Gurmeet Sikh Singh, GLS University, India

Chapter 25
Data-Driven Talent Management Practices for Eco-Innovation in State-Owned Enterprises 369
Sulaiman Olusegun Atiku, Namibia University of Science and Technology, Namibia & Walter Sisulu University, South Africa
Doreen K. Menjengua, Namibia University of Science and Technology, Namibia
Andrew Jeremiah, Namibia University of Science and Technology, Namibia
Hylton James Villet, Namibia University of Science and Technology, Namibia

Chapter 26
Data-Driven Decision Making for Achieving Sustainability in Apparel Business Value Chain 395
Kamalendu Pal, University of London, UK

Chapter 27
Impact of Intangible Capital, Organisational Culture, and Innovative Capabilities on the Organisational Performance of the Indian IT Industry 415
Asuri Simhakutty Kannan, GRT Institute of Engineering and Technology, India
P. Aranganathan, Gnanam School of Business, India
B. Elamurugan, Sri Manakula Vinayagar Engineering College, India
Christina Sheela, Gnanam School of Business, India
V. Anandavel, Sakthi Institute of Management and Information Studies, India
K. Ravichandran, New York Institute of Technology, UAE

Compilation of References 430

About the Contributors 475

Index 482

Detailed Table of Contents

Preface xxiii

Chapter 1
Application of Strategic Human Resource Management Models for Organizational Performance 1
N. Geethanjali, PSNA College of Engineering and Technology, India
K. M. Ashifa, Istanbul Gelisim University, Turkey
Avantika Raina, Vivekananda Institute of Professional Studies, India
Jayashree Patil, Bharati Vidyapeeth, India
Rameshwaran Byloppilly, City University, Ajman, UAE
S. Suman Rajest, Dhaanish Ahmed College of Engineering, India

Modern organizational management must include strategic human resource management (SHRM). It is an improvement over the conventional human resources management methods, mostly concerned with operations and connections with employees. Contrarily, SHRM recognizes that workers are one of a company's most significant assets and works to match HR practices with those aims and objectives. This method strongly emphasizes long-term planning, proactive decision-making, and a close connection between HR strategies and overarching corporate plans. Strategic human resource management includes all those activities affecting the behavior of individuals in their efforts to formulate and implement the strategic needs of the business. It is the pattern of planned human resource deployments and activities intended to enable the firm to achieve its goals.

Chapter 2
Smart HR 4.0 With Impact of Technology Advancement and Industry 4.0 on HR Practices 20
Praveen Kakada, VIT Business School, Vellore Institute of Technology, Chennai, India
Muhammed Shafi M. K., Vellore Institute of Technology, Chennai, India

This study emphasizes the significance of Smart Human Resources 4.0 (Smart HR 4.0) and the effects of Industry 4.0 and technological advancements on HR practices. The developments of Smart HR 4.0 in the HR field are also demonstrated in this chapter, emphasizing planning, organizing, staffing, directing, and controlling. Consequently, exploratory relationships among Smart HR 4.0, technology advancements, and Industry 4.0 are presented based on a systematic review. The chapter discusses the role of Smart HR 4.0 as a recent industrial entry into the human resources field was discussed in this study. A pool of 65 research articles published between 2014 and 2023 from top-tier peer-reviewed journals were considered for further understanding and investigation. In order to successfully navigate the obstacles of the Industry 4.0 revolution, an organization would need a strong Smart HR 4.0 strategy. Emerging technologies like the internet of things, big data, and artificial intelligence will automate most HR processes, creating leaner and more effective HR teams.

Chapter 3
A Comprehensive Review on Leveraging Business Intelligence for Enhanced Marketing Analytics 34
P. S. Venkateswaran, PSNA College of Engineering and Technology, India
Divya Marupaka, Unikon IT Inc., USA
Sachin Parate, Twillio, USA
Amit Bhanushali, Independent Researcher, USA
Latha Thammareddi, DXC Technology, USA
P. Paramasivan, Dhaanish Ahmed College of Engineering, India

In the rapidly evolving landscape of marketing, data-driven decision-making has become paramount for organizations seeking a competitive edge. This chapter presents a comprehensive review of the applications and impact of business intelligence (BI) in the realm of marketing analytics. The research aims to elucidate the multifaceted relationship between BI and marketing analytics, explore the benefits and challenges, and provide insights into emerging trends. The study employs a mixed-method research design involving both qualitative and quantitative approaches, including an extensive literature review and surveys. It examines how BI tools and practices empower marketing professionals with data-driven insights for more effective decision-making and marketing strategy optimization. The chapter discusses key applications, benefits, challenges, and emerging trends in the integration of BI and marketing analytics.

Chapter 4
The Synergy of Management Information Systems and Predictive Analytics for Marketing 49
M. Lishmah Dominic, Annamalai University, India
P. S. Venkateswaran, PSNA College of Engineering and Technology, India
Latha Thamma Reddi, Independent Researcher, USA
Sandeep Rangineni, Pluto TV, USA
R. Regin, SRM Institute of Science and Technology, Ramapuram, India
S. Suman Rajest, Dhaanish Ahmed College of Engineering, India

In the ever-evolving landscape of modern marketing, the convergence of management information systems (MIS) and predictive analytics has become a potent force. This chapter explores the transformative potential of combining MIS infrastructure with predictive analytics techniques to reshape marketing management. Predictive analytics, utilizing historical data and machine learning, empowers organizations to forecast future trends, customer behavior, and market dynamics. MIS, as the information backbone, facilitates the collection, processing, and dissemination of data for strategic decision-making. Marketing, once reliant on intuition, has transitioned into a data-driven discipline. This synergy enables businesses to not only understand past performance but also anticipate and respond to the dynamic demands of the marketplace. However, seizing this opportunity is not without challenges. Success hinges on the alignment of technical capabilities, organizational structure, and strategic vision with the digital landscape's evolution.

Chapter 5
Celebrating Lives Beyond on Unveiling the Digital Legacy Manager for Empowering Personal Heritage Preservation 64
S. Sivabala, SRM Institute of Science and Technology, Ramapuram, India
P. Vidyasri, SRM Institute of Science and Technology, Ramapuram, India

Technology has changed how people communicate, store information, and curate their lives in the digital age. This research study examines the complex management and preservation of digital legacies, a collection of digital assets, online accounts, and personal narratives left by deceased people. Digital inheritance offers a complex issue that requires a holistic approach. This research develops the Digital Legacy Manager software to handle this difficulty. The study discusses unmanaged digital legacies to start. It examines the emotional and psychological effects of impediments to obtaining digital relics of the deceased on bereaved loved ones. It also examines the complex financial and legal issues that arise when digital assets are out of reach, including lengthy legal battles and unsolved financial matters. When digital footprints are ignored, shared experiences, personal narratives, and cultural heritage are lost forever.

Chapter 6
Empowering Employees' Enablement Intelligently With Data and Realizing Business Excellence ... 87
H. Hajra, Bharath Institute of Higher Education and Research, India
G. Jayalakshmi, Bharath Institute of Higher Education and Research, India

Data excellence denotes the strategic manipulation of data to boost business performance and secure a competitive advantage. It empowers companies to extract critical insights about their operations, customer behavior, and market trends. This intelligence fosters data-driven decision-making, and with effective employee enablement, it leads to superior outcomes. Employee engagement, distinct from job performance, focuses on workers' emotional alignment with the company's values and interpersonal conduct. Engaged employees actively collaborate to elevate their job performance and are attuned to the company culture. HR experts link engagement to employees' perceptions of their job experience and treatment within the organization, emphasizing the pivotal role of emotions in driving a company's success and profitability. Employees are naturally inclined to commit to their organizations, fulfilling a profound desire to forge meaningful connections and contribute significantly to a valued cause.

Chapter 7
Big Data Analytics and Its Impact on Human Resources Management 109
Anusha Thakur, University of Petroleum and Energy Studies, India

Both artistic and scientific analytic aspects play a vital role in human resources (HR). With the rising number of transactions, customers, and employees, human resources are forced to emphasize on the adoption of novel technologies to aid faster in the decision-making processes. Big data is expected to significantly gain a ubiquitous presence in human resources. Employing data analytics in HR owes the potential to bring the sector in line with the rest of the operational activities in an organization. This chapter focuses on the role and benefits of big data analytics in human resources. It contemplates the key analytical solutions being offered by the market players and the real-use cases of organizations incorporating analytics in human resources to cater to their business goals. Further, the chapter also discusses the factors challenging the implementation of analytics in transforming business processes.

Chapter 8
Applications of Artificial Intelligence Tools in Higher Education 124
P. S. Venkateswaran, PSNA College of Engineering and Technology, Dindigul, India
Firas Tayseer Mohammad Ayasrah, Al Ain University, UAE
Varun Kumar Nomula, Georgia Institute of Technology, USA
P. Paramasivan, Dhaanish Ahmed College of Engineering, India
P. Anand, Dhaanish Ahmed College of Engineering, India
K. Bogeshwaran, Dhaanish Ahmed College of Engineering, India

The rapid integration of information and communication technologies (ICT) in higher education has brought about transformative changes to traditional teaching and learning practices. This chapter examines the multifaceted impacts of ICT in the higher education sector. Over the past two decades, ICT has revolutionized the way educational institutions operate, impacting teaching methodologies, student engagement, and administrative processes. In the realm of pedagogy, ICT has facilitated the shift towards student-centered learning, empowering learners with access to diverse digital resources and interactive learning platforms. Moreover, administrative tasks within higher education have been streamlined through the adoption of ICT, resulting in enhanced efficiency in enrollment, record-keeping, and communication between stakeholders. This optimization allows educators to focus more on instructional design and student support, fostering a conducive learning environment.

Chapter 9
Impact of the COVID-19 Lockdown on Employee Engagement and Efficiency 137
Manisha Singh, VIT Bhopal University, India
Rakhi Tiwari, Barkatullah University, India
Vinod Bhatt, VIT Bhopal University, India
Yogesh Shukla, VIT Bhopal University, India

The COVID-19 pandemic has forced organizations to adapt quickly to new ways of working, such as remote work and hybrid work arrangements. This has led to some challenges but also some opportunities to improve employee engagement and efficiency. One of the biggest challenges has been maintaining employee engagement during a time of great uncertainty and change. Organizations have tried to address this by developing creative and productive ways to engage their employees, such as online family engagement practices, online learning, virtual team building exercises, webinars with industry experts, weekly online alignment sessions, team meetings through video conference, short online game sessions, online contests and competitions, online programs, and online fitness and meditation. These activities can help employees stay connected with their colleagues and the organization, learn new skills, and improve themselves. Another challenge has been maintaining employee efficiency while working remotely.

Chapter 10
Synergizing Efficiency and Customer Delight on Empowering Business With Enterprise Applications 149
D. Lavanya, PSNA College of Engineering and Technology, India
Sandeep Rangineni, Pluto TV, USA
Latha Thamma Reddi, DXC Technology, USA
R. Regin, SRM Institute of Science And Technology, Ramapuram, India
S. Suman Rajest, Dhaanish Ahmed College of Engineering, India
P. Paramasivan, Dhaanish Ahmed College of Engineering, India

Enterprise applications have never been more important in an era where organizations thrive on efficiency and consumer happiness. This chapter is an enthralling voyage into the world of cutting-edge technology in which the authors investigate the revolutionary power of enterprise applications and their significant impact on modern enterprises. They delve into the dense web of corporate applications that serve as the backbone of enterprises, fueling growth and fostering innovation. These applications are intended to optimize procedures, streamline operations, and improve cross-departmental communication, allowing firms to function at maximum efficiency while maintaining a laser-like focus on customer satisfaction. They show how, in an ever-changing technological context, enterprise applications have developed from traditional software tools to agile, intelligent, and integrated solutions. The alternatives are endless, from enterprise resource planning (ERP) systems to customer relationship management (CRM) platforms.

Chapter 11
Intelligent Business Sustainability on Marketing System.. 164
M. Parveen Roja, PSNA College of Engineering and Technology, India
Shashank Agarwal, CVS Health, USA
Amrita Baid More, Prestige Institute of Management and Research, India
K. Bogeshwaran, Dhaanish Ahmed College of Engineering, India
A. Nagarajan, Dhaanish Ahmed College of Engineering, India
S. Manikandan, Dhaanish Ahmed College of Engineering, India

The information age, with the usage of big data, has created opportunities for smart marketing systems. Marketing data intelligence systems accelerate product innovation and growth strategies with the information obtained from the data mining techniques about the marketing stakeholders. The implementation and adaptation of creative, intelligent technologies aid marketers in speedy decisions and sustainable competitive strategies to gain a competitive advantage in the market that would help the organization's sustenance over the long term. This chapter explains marketing intelligence, its quotient, relevant theories, evolution, framework, the transformation of marketing intelligence systems from digital marketing to social engineering, the tools of marketing intelligence, and the benefits of marketing intelligence.

Chapter 12
Block Overflow on Frequently Asked Questions Using Blockchain 179
Jyoti P. Kanjalkar, Vishwakarma Institute of Technology, India
Rushikesh Kahat, Vishwakarma Institute of Technology, India
Sankalp Mahesh Kokse, Vishwakarma Institute of Technology, India
Sanket Katale, Vishwakarma Institute of Technology, India
Nishchay Ramchandani, Vishwakarma Institute of Technology, India
Pramod Kanjalkar, Vishwakarma Institute of Technology, India

This work shows how blockchain technology can evolve in our day-to-day lives and we can benefit from it. Much of the modern research work related to blockchain technology emphasizes its application for cryptocurrencies like Ethereum, bitcoin, etc. Blockchain technology is way more than cryptocurrency, and it can have various applications in the domain of finance, government, the banking industry, accounting, etc. Therefore, this study attempts to explore opportunities and their issues. The proposed system emphasizes the use of blockchain in frequently asked questions (FAQ) systems. The basic idea of the proposed system is that the questionnaire will post a question with an appropriate bounty amount and time so that others from the community can answer the question. The most upvoted answer is rewarded with a bounty amount. This transaction is carried out using blockchain technology. This helps to understand the level of contribution experience a person might have and is worthy in the eyes of the developer community for a reward.

Chapter 13
Rise of Next Generation Entrepreneurs Through Innovative Digital Strategies in MSMEs During COVID-19 193
Raji Rajan, Jain University, India
Mariam Mathen, Jain University, India
Megha Garud, Jain University, India
Melanie Elizabeth Lourens, Durban University of Technology, South Africa

This study's primary goal is to identify the difficulties and barriers experienced by MSMEs in India during COVID-19. The chapter discusses the recent trend of small businesses with a lot of creativity and innovation, which opened doors to next-generation entrepreneurship. MSMEs' adoption of technological innovations has been uneven and slow despite the fact that the growing digital economy has given entrepreneurs new opportunities for client service. The conceptual framework is based on the literature overview on the pandemic's effects on MSMEs and the decline in the growth of the economy. It can be concluded that the government understands the various challenges faced by MSMEs and offers various support. In the post-pandemic world of an expanding global digital economy, MSME owners' digital adoption and practices are still shaped by rival companies, suppliers, consumers, and other members of their peer group. In such cases, the entrepreneurs must implement new digital strategies to transform the business, which will facilitate their resilience and self-reliance.

Chapter 14
Influence of Government Initiatives and Information on Indian Women Entrepreneurial Ventures 209
Sasi Sundarakumar, Takshashila University, India
J. Tamil Selvi, Annamalai University, India
K. Ilangovan, Pondicherry University, India
Vellayan Srinivasan, S.A. Engineering College (Autonomous), India
A. S. Kannan, GRT Institute of Engineering and Technology, India
Vivek Arunachalam, Berlin School of Business and Innovation, Germany

This study uses a moderated mediation model to investigate how government initiatives and policies affect women's entrepreneurship in India. According to the study's hypotheses, the relationship between government policies and initiatives and women's entrepreneurship is moderated by the industry sector of these businesswomen and their access to information mediates this relationship. In order to evaluate the assumptions, the study collects data from 514 Indian women entrepreneurs who have used or are aware of any government programme or effort supporting women's entrepreneurship. The findings demonstrate that government initiatives and policies positively and significantly impact women'sentrepreneurship. However, this impact is less pronounced for women entrepreneurs in the manufacturing sector, likely due to less favourable access to information. The study adds to the body of knowledge on women's entrepreneurship

Chapter 15
Overview of Industry 5.0 on Emerging Technologies and Human and Robot Collaboration 221
Usha Prabhu, Jain University, India
P. H. Reshma Sultana, Jain University, India
Vasudha Srivatsa, Adarsh Institute of Management and Information Technology, India
R. Vennila, Jain University, India
B. Manjunath, Jain University, India

The mere idea of Industry 5.0 has lately arisen as the hope for a future industry founded on social and environmental sustainability. The proponents of Industry 5.0 argue that Industry 4.0 is not the best framework for ensuring long-term sustainability. Industry 4.0 focuses on technology-driven productivity in all spheres but neglects human intervention in the final production of the product or service; Industry 5.0 emerged by overcoming its fallacy on it. In 2015, the United Nations adopted a set of goals known as the Sustainable Development Goals (SDGs) with the aim of mobilizing all of its member states to take action to protect the environment, address social issues, and build global prosperity. It is a proactive, goal-oriented strategy that re-evaluates social, economic, and environmental expectations. There is synergy between Industry 5.0 and Society 5.0. Industry 5.0 seeks to understand the potential of big data, artificial intelligence, robots, and advanced digitalization in addressing emerging needs in the industrial, societal, and environmental.

Chapter 16
Can Firm Size Moderate Navigating Economic Performance Through Strategic Purchasing? 235
Uday Inala, University of Hyderabad, India
John Yesudas Valluri, Jain University, India
Gunupuru Koteswara Rao, University of Hyderabad, India
Shyamaladevi Balakrishnan, SRM Institute of Science and Technology, Kattankulathur, India
A. S. Kannan, GRT Institute of Engineering and Technology, India
Easwaramoorthy Rangaswamy, Amity Global Institute, Singapore

This study empirically investigates the relationship between strategic purchasing, environmental purchasing, and economic performance in the manufacturing industry in India. Employing partial least squares (PLS) analysis guided by the dynamic capability view theory, this study examined the direct and moderating linkages between organizational purchasing practices and economic outcomes. The findings reveal a significant positive association between strategic purchasing and economic performance, with firm size acting as a moderator. Conversely, no moderating effect of firm size is found between environmental purchasing and economic performance. This research underscores the pivotal role of strategic purchasing in maximizing a supplier base, enhancing supplier relations, and influencing expenditures and operations across the supply network. This provides insights into the strategic role of purchasing in maintaining quality standards and enabling international growth.

Chapter 17
Effect of Crude Oil Price Variations on Stocks With Special Reference to NSE 248
Shimna Jayaraj, Jain University, India
T. Shenbagavalli, Jain University, India
V. Vipanchi, Jain University, India
B.S. Sudha, Jain University, India
Juhi Jain, Jain University, India
Biswaranjan Senapati, Parker Hannifin Corp., USA

Crude oil consumption is one of the major economic indicators in the economy. The study examines the interrelation between crude oil prices and the stock market. The stock market indices chosen are Nifty 50, Nifty 100, Nifty 200, Nifty 500, Nifty Auto, Bank, and FMCG. The study has considered only one event, i.e., crude oil for six years, leaving a research gap for analyzing other macroeconomic indicators affecting the Indian stock market. This chapter intends to investigate whether any impact exists on different indices of NSE due to the changes in prices of crude oil globally due to certain internal and external factors. This chapter also helps suggest to the investors their deals in Indian and global markets. This study is done to know the impact of fluctuations in crude oil prices in the global market, which affects the Indian stock market, and also to know the reasons for the fluctuations in crude oil prices. This study also analyzes the dependency level of both variables (crude oil prices globally and the same prices in the Indian stock market).

Chapter 18
A Study in Rural Areas of Southern Karnataka Districts in Dairy Farming Challenges Faced by the Entrepreneurs 264
M. S. Naveen Kumar, Jain University, India
G. M. Rajeshwari, REVA University, India
Sheetal V. Hukkeri, Jain University, India
S. Ashwini, Government First Grade College, India
B. G. Guruprasad, Jain University, India
Dilmurod Nasimov, Academy of Public Administration, Uzbekistan

The purpose of the study is to shed light on the challenges faced by the current dairy farming entrepreneurs. The study aimed to identify the establishing and operational challenges of dairy farming entrepreneurs. Irrespective of age, gender, financial background, formal education, and experience, people will enter dairy farming. For everyone who is willing to start their farm and who is running their dairy farming, the current study will help them to identify the possible threats to the business. The main purpose is to give a prepared mindset for the potential entrepreneurs to be ready with their strategies to overcome these challenges. The study collected the available research articles on dairy farming. A structured questionnaire was administered and collected the data. Two hundred twenty-eight dairy farmers were taken as the sample, and exploratory factor analysis (EFA) was used to identify the factors with the help of SPSS. The study identified that the land and labor issues are the biggest challenges for dairy farming.

Chapter 19
An Analysis of Credit Management and Bank Lending Practices in Developing Countries 278
Srinivas Kolachina, Koneru Lakshmaiah Education Foundation, India
Lisha Hundia, Koneru Lakshmaiah Education Foundation, India
Kancherla Mounishker, Koneru Lakshmaiah Education Foundation, India
Juluru Venkatesh, Koneru Lakshmaiah Education Foundation, India
Palanivel Rathinasabapathi Velmurugan, Berlin School of Business and Innovation, Germany
Ahmed J. Obaid, University of Kufa, Iraq

The credit system and the banking activities processes increase people's investment practices, enhancing country people's economic condition. The research aims to understand the processes of banking activities and the importance of the credit management system. Concepts and the procedures of the credit management system are the most important things in lending a loan. The theory of banking activities is for understanding the activities of the banned credit system of the banks, including the processes of verification, calculation of loan details, and disbursing of the amount. The primary method has been used for collecting data from the respondents, including quantitative analysis, for a better understanding of all facts. This increases the possibility of earning and promotes developmental activities. Banks' lending practices increase their income, and the credit system increases the scope for developing the economic condition.

Chapter 20
A Comprehensive Approach to Exploring the Data Input for Performance Evaluation of Vegetable Distribution Center 296
C. Thilak Reddy, Jain University, India
V. Navaneethakumar, Jain University, India
V. Vinoth Kumar, Jain University, India
S. Yogananthan, Jain University, India

The performance evaluation of a vegetable distribution center is essential for optimizing its operations, improving efficiency, and meeting customer demands. This chapter aims to identify the key data required for evaluating the performance of a vegetable distribution center. By analyzing relevant metrics related to order fulfillment, inventory management, productivity, customer service, and cost and financial aspects, managers can gain insights into the center's performance, identify areas for improvement, and make data-driven decisions. This chapter provides an in-depth exploration of the data requirements and metrics necessary to evaluate the performance of a vegetable distribution center, offering valuable guidance for effective performance evaluation in this specific industry. The performance of the distribution is analyzed by considering various factors with respect to order management, inventory management, customer service, cost reduction, storage capacity, and transportation planning.

Chapter 21
A Study on Total Quality Management (TQM) in Warehouse Management in Logistics Limited.... 313
Pooja Kumari, Jain University, India
T. Shenbagavalli, Jain University, India
S. Ashwini, Jain University, India
K. Vidhya, Jain University, India

The goal of total quality management (TQM) is to ensure that all customers and users are completely satisfied at all times by preventing defects and equipping employees with the knowledge and attitude necessary to do so. Whether or not total quality management is in place, what TQM techniques have been adopted, how TQM affects warehouse management, and how TQM and warehouse management affect productivity are all questions that were explored in this chapter. This research is based on primary data, which has been collected with the help of questionnaires from the employees in an organization because questionnaires can cover a large population with lower cost and shorter time. A structured questionnaire was formed using Google Forms for the survey and was sent to the respondents for their responses. TQM in warehouse management helps in the effective management of the warehousing system and also has a positive effect on the quality of the warehouse. It provides efficiency to the employee to manage the warehousing system and also upgrade the same.

Chapter 22
A Systematic Study of Central Bank Digital Currency: Challenges, Limitations, and Its Effects on the Indian Economy 331
M. S. Nikhil, Jain University, India
Nischal V. Atreya, Jain University, India
H. Mehul Kumar, Jain University, India
B. Priyadharshini, Jain University, India
S. Ramya, Jain University, India

This chapter examines central bank digital currencies (CBDCs) and their possible impact on the Indian economy in an age of digitization. Commercial value, user experience, legal frameworks, and financial stability are crucial to understanding digital currencies. CBDCs are a new payment infrastructure frontier. The chapter emphasizes the significant investments needed to build a large user and merchant network, highlighting the far-reaching effects of digital currencies. This exploration aims to demystify CBDCs as electronic variants of fiat currency. CBDCs, issued by central banks as legal money, are versatile and available to the public, financial institutions, and businesses for savings and transactions. The study describes the rise of digital cash by tracing currency from early barter systems to physical notes and coins. It admits initial skepticism about digital currencies due to their volatility, diversity, and lack of official backing.

Chapter 23
Tourist Behaviour Analysis Using Data Analytics 343
L. Maria Michael Visuwasam, RMK College of Engineering and Technology, India
M. Srinath, RMK College of Engineering and Technology, India
V. S. Aswin Raj, RMK College of Engineering and Technology, India
A. Sirajudeen, RMK College of Engineering and Technology, India
S. Sudhir Maharaaja, RMK College of Engineering and Technology, India
Dakshin Raja, RMK College of Engineering and Technology, India

There has been a lot of hurry in the tourism business in recent years, and the rise of IT technology has had a major impact on vacationers. In recent years, numerous studies of big data have been devoted to analysing tourists' behaviour. Decision-making support from big data analytics has only been shown in a small number of studies. The proliferation of social media's ability to gather massive amounts of data has opened up new avenues for research and improved insights for policymakers. The purpose of this chapter is to gain a deeper comprehension of the motivations behind visitors' actions, as well as the environmental and social influences that shape their experiences. The digital lifestyle pattern outlines the idea of tourist behaviour, bridges the gap between the tourist and the digital world, and allows us to zero in on how that behaviour evolves over time. Using the idea of a digital lifestyle pattern, we may build strategies for the behaviour of tourists.

Chapter 24
A Study on Consumer Preference and Satisfaction Towards Various Brands of Hair Shampoo in Ahmedabad City: Consumer Preference and Satisfaction Towards Hair Shampoo Brands 356
Nupur Rawal, GLS University, India
Gurmeet Sikh Singh, GLS University, India

Hair shampoo plays a wide role in cosmetic products. Healthy roots and tips, daily shine, stronger hairs are the prime factors among the male and female genders driving the hair care product market globally. In this research, consumer preference and satisfaction towards different brands of hair shampoo in Ahmedabad city is studied. Hence, in this research, 26 brands have been taken both national and international brands to identify consumers' brand preference and factors that consumers consider. A total of 200 respondents' data is collected with the aid of a standardised questionnaire, and exploratory factor analysis and cluster analysis are used to analyse it. The result of the study shows that Dove and L'Oreal Paris are the most preferred brands. Brand image and usage experience, ethical and ecofriendly product, brand preference, product quality, and problem solving ability are the five factors which influence the consumer preference towards hair shampoo through factor analysis. Brand attributes and brand perception are the identified cluster groups through regression factor scores.

Chapter 25
Data-Driven Talent Management Practices for Eco-Innovation in State-Owned Enterprises............ 369
Sulaiman Olusegun Atiku, Namibia University of Science and Technology, Namibia & Walter Sisulu University, South Africa
Doreen K. Menjengua, Namibia University of Science and Technology, Namibia
Andrew Jeremiah, Namibia University of Science and Technology, Namibia
Hylton James Villet, Namibia University of Science and Technology, Namibia

This study explores the influence of data-driven talent management practices on eco-innovation in state-owned enterprises. A literature review was conducted to examine the role of people data, HR metrics, and people analytics in enhancing talent management practices and eco-innovation in state-owned enterprises. Findings revealed that people data is essential for making talent decisions and developing effective talent retention strategies. Additionally, two key drivers of eco-innovations were identified and grouped into external and internal drivers. External drivers include environmental regulations, competition pressures, and customers' demands for eco-friendly products and services. Internal drivers are organizational capabilities, technological capabilities, and corporate social responsibility. Therefore, data-driven talent development interventions are necessary for advancing organizational and technological capabilities to boost eco-innovation performance in state-owned enterprises.

Chapter 26
Data-Driven Decision Making for Achieving Sustainability in Apparel Business Value Chain........ 395
Kamalendu Pal, University of London, UK

Data-supported decision-making and understanding the customer's behaviour has become an essential and challenging problem for apparel businesses to sustain their position in competitive markets. Current information communication technologies (ICT) are ushering hope to mitigate this challenge, particularly the blockchain with internet of things (IoT)-based enterprise information system framework providing relevant services in global networks that mediate effective and sustainable supply chain operations. Data collection and interpretation of collected data (known as data analytics) on business-specific value creation process is most important in this architecture. This chapter reviews recent literature on technology-driven supply chain automation and related data analytics-related issues for managing sustainability. Lastly, the chapter presents an application area of 'market basket analysis' technique that focuses on discovering patterns in retail transaction data with the help of an algorithmic data mining method.

Chapter 27
Impact of Intangible Capital, Organisational Culture, and Innovative Capabilities on the Organisational Performance of the Indian IT Industry 415
Asuri Simhakutty Kannan, GRT Institute of Engineering and Technology, India
P. Aranganathan, Gnanam School of Business, India
B. Elamurugan, Sri Manakula Vinayagar Engineering College, India
Christina Sheela, Gnanam School of Business, India
V. Anandavel, Sakthi Institute of Management and Information Studies, India
K. Ravichandran, New York Institute of Technology, UAE

There is well-researched evidence for the linkages among intellectual capital, innovation capability, and organisational performance. However, no concrete evidence of such a relationship can be identified in knowledge-based industries such as the information technology (IT) sector. This study examined how organisational performance, organizational culture, and intellectual capital (human capital and organizational capital) are interconnected in the Indian IT sector and explored further how innovation capability can play a mediating role. In Bangalore, Hyderabad, and Chennai, 486 middle-level employees of selected IT companies were randomly selected for data collection. The authors used Smart PLS 3. A positive substantial impact is demonstrated by human capital, organizational capital, and culture on innovation capability, and an equally favorable substantial impact is demonstrated by innovation capability, human capital, and organizational capital on organizational performance.

Compilation of References 430

About the Contributors 475

Index 482

Preface

This book is an insightful and comprehensive treatise that delves deeply into the evolving site of modern business underpinned by the burgeoning role of data analytics. This exploration traces the journey of data analytics from its nascent stages of simple record-keeping to the complex, sophisticated algorithms of today that predict market trends and consumer behaviour with remarkable accuracy. This journey isn't just technological; it's a story of how data has become an invaluable asset in strategic decision-making. At its core, this narrative addresses the paradigm shift in business decision-making processes. Historically, decisions in business were often based on intuition, experience, and personal judgment. However, this book illustrates a compelling transition to an era where decisions are increasingly grounded in empirical evidence from meticulous data analysis. This shift underscores the fundamental change in how businesses view and utilize data, transforming it from a passive resource into a dynamic tool for gaining competitive advantages. The book delves into the specific tools and technologies driving this revolution. It provides an extensive overview of advanced data mining techniques, artificial intelligence, and machine learning, explaining how these technologies are employed to interpret and leverage vast amounts of data. The discussion extends to include the challenges and ethical implications posed by collecting and using personal data. The narrative stresses the importance of responsible data management practices, considering the privacy concerns and regulatory requirements that companies must navigate. A significant portion of the book is devoted to real-world case studies. These case studies are practical examples of how various companies, ranging from startups to multinational corporations, have successfully integrated data-driven strategies into their business models. These examples highlight the benefits, such as improved efficiency, enhanced customer satisfaction, and increased profitability, and provide critical insights into the challenges encountered and lessons learned during the implementation process. The case studies are diverse, covering a range of industries and geographical locations, offering a holistic view of the global business site. Leadership's role in fostering a data-centric culture within organizations is another critical area of focus. The book emphasizes that the effective use of data transcends technological capabilities and requires a fundamental shift in mindset and approach at all organizational levels. Leaders must understand the value of data and champion its use, encouraging a culture of continuous learning and adaptation. The narrative also addresses the potential drawbacks and limitations of data-driven decision-making. The book discusses the risks associated with an over-reliance on data, such as stifling creativity, potential biases in data interpretation, and the possibility of making decisions based on flawed or incomplete data sets. These discussions are balanced with forward-looking speculations on the future of data analytics in business. The book explores emerging trends and technologies that could further revolutionize decision-making processes, such as integrating big data with the Internet of Things (IoT), advancements in predictive analytics, and the increasing use of real-time data.

The book delves into the organizational structures and strategies that facilitate effective data utilization. It discusses the importance of building robust data infrastructures, investing in data literacy, and fostering cross-functional collaboration. It also examines the role of external factors, such as market dynamics, regulatory changes, and technological advancements, in shaping data-driven strategies. The human aspect of data analytics is another crucial theme. The book highlights the importance of balancing automated data analysis with human insight and judgment. It explores the evolving role of data scientists, analysts, and other professionals in interpreting data and translating it into actionable insights. The narrative emphasizes that while machines can process and analyze data at unprecedented speeds, human intuition and creativity remain essential for contextualizing data and making nuanced decisions. This book emerges as a guidebook and a cautionary tale. It equips business leaders, managers, and professionals with the knowledge and insights needed to harness the power of data effectively. Simultaneously, it serves as a reminder of the ethical considerations and potential pitfalls of data-driven decision-making. The book firmly posits that while data is a potent tool for business success, its power must be wielded wisely, ethically, and with human insight to achieve long-term success and sustainability in the ever-evolving business site.

ORGANIZATION OF THE BOOK

The book is organized into 27 chapters. A brief description of each of the chapters follows:

Chapter 1 discusses how Strategic HR management is essential in modern organisations (SHRM). It improves on traditional HR management, which focuses on operations and employee relations. In contrast, SHRM acknowledges that employees are a company's greatest asset and aligns HR policies with those goals. This approach stresses long-term planning, proactive decision-making, and HR initiatives alignment with company goals. Strategic human resource management encompasses all actions influencing employee behaviour in shaping and implementing business strategies. It involves planned human resource deployments and actions to help the company succeed. Strategic human resource management (SHRM) is "the development of a consistent, aligned collection of practices, programmes, and policies to facilitate the achievement of the organization's strategic objectives," according to Jeffery A. Mello. It can be strategy-focused, decision-focused, content-focused, or implementation-focused.

Chapter 2 report highlights Smart HR 4.0 and how Industry 4.0 and technology affect HR practises. This article shows Smart HR 4.0 emphasises planning, organising, staffing, directing, and controlling. Thus, a systematic review presents exploratory links between Smart HR 4.0, technology breakthroughs, and Industry 4.0. This report addresses Smart HR 4.0, a recent industry foray into human resources. Under study were 65 top-tier peer-reviewed journal papers from 2014 to 2023. A solid Smart HR 4.0 strategy is needed to handle the industry 4.0 transition. The Internet of Things, Big Data, and AI will automate most HR procedures, making HR teams leaner and more productive. This study adds to HR expertise and literature by conceptualising Smart HR 4.0. Smart HR 4.0 catalyses basic human resource functions like this article.

Chapter 3 analytics that data-driven decision-making is essential for competitive marketers in the fast-changing marketing world. Business Intelligence (BI) applications and effects in marketing analytics are covered in this study paper. The study examines the complex relationship between BI and marketing analytics, its pros and cons, and developing trends. The study uses a mixed-method design with qualitative and quantitative methods, including literature reviews and surveys. It investigates how BI technologies and methods help marketers make better decisions and optimise their strategies with data. BI-marketing analytics integration applications, benefits, problems, and trends are covered in the paper.

Chapter 4 examines how Management Information Systems (MIS) and predictive analytics have become powerful forces in modern marketing. This paper examines how MIS infrastructure and predictive analytics may transform marketing management. Using historical data and machine learning, predictive analytics helps companies predict market dynamics, customer behaviour, and trends. MIS, the information backbone, enables data collection, processing, and distribution for strategic decision-making. Data now drives marketing, which was formerly intuitive. This synergy helps firms assess past performance and anticipate and meet consumer wants. Taking advantage of this chance is difficult. Success depends on aligning technical skills, organisational structure, and strategic vision with digital landscape change. Management Information Systems (MIS) and predictive analytics interact dynamically in marketing management. MIS infrastructure enables predictive analytics, which helps companies predict customer behaviour, respond to market dynamics, and make data-driven decisions. The digital age provides massive customer data, but technological preparedness, organisational alignment, and strategic direction determine success. Predictive marketing combines human and computer learning to inform decision-makers.

Chapter 5 reviews that digital technology has revolutionised how individuals communicate store information, and curate their lives. This study addresses the challenging management and maintenance of digital legacies of deceased people's digital assets, online accounts, and personal narratives. Digital inheritance is complicated and demands a holistic strategy. This research creates Digital Legacy Manager software to solve this problem. The investigation begins with mismanaged digital legacies. Impediments to collecting digital relics of the deceased have emotional and psychological repercussions on bereaved loved ones. It also covers the intricate financial and legal concerns that arise when digital assets are unavailable, including protracted legal fights and untold financial matters. The study says that to ignore digital footprints is to lose shared experiences, personal narratives, and cultural legacy forever. Digital legacy management is crucial; thus, this paper introduces the Digital Legacy Manager, a new software application that lets people maintain, organise, and share their digital legacies. The user-centric software makes technology easy for everyone. Secure account administration, message and memoir creation, and asset categorization and sharing are crucial. These capabilities let users show thanks, share family and personal history, and give advice in a secure and confidential online setting. The Digital Legacy Manager encrypts and restricts data access. It integrates smoothly with digital platforms to facilitate multi-source digital asset management. According to this research, user experience and feedback, user testing, feedback integration, and ongoing support are crucial to software uptake and sustainability. Integration, AI-driven automation, and internationalisation are discussed in the study to adapt to shifting technological paradigms and user needs. This study indicates that digital legacy management is essential today and suggests the Digital Legacy Manager as a pioneering solution. The Digital Legacy Manager connects technology to the human desire for connection, remembering, and closure with a safe, user-friendly, and holistic platform for digital legacy management. It maintains personal and cultural history.

Chapter 6 introduces Data excellence, which is strategic data manipulation to improve corporate performance and gain a competitive edge. It helps firms gain valuable insights into operations, customer behaviour, and market trends. This information promotes data-driven decision-making and improved results with staff enablement. Employee engagement, not job performance, focuses on workers' emotional alignment with the company's values and interpersonal conduct. Engaged workers work together to improve performance and understand the company culture. HR professionals link engagement to employees' impressions of their job experience and treatment inside the firm, emphasising the importance of emotions in company performance and profitability. Employees are naturally drawn to their companies to make meaningful connections and help a good cause. Unlike happiness, drive, or culture, engagement requires purposeful employer cultivation of symbiotic relationships. It measures an individual's connection to their organisation and predicts job participation, with engaged people establishing high job identification. The chapter argues that employee engagement leads to job involvement. It provides tangible techniques for firms to boost and maintain employee engagement by describing engagement factors.

Chapter 7 develops how Artistic and scientific analysis are crucial in HR (HR). With more transactions, customers, and employees, human resources must prioritise adopting new technologies to speed up decision-making. Human resources will increasingly use big data. Data analytics may align HR with other operational functions in a firm. This article discusses big data analytics' benefits in HR. It examines market participants' important analytical solutions and real-world examples of firms using analytics in human resources to achieve their business goals. The paper also explores obstacles to altering company operations with analytics.

Chapter 8 explains traditional teaching and learning have been transformed by the fast integration of ICT in higher education. This abstract addresses ICT's complex effects on higher education. ICT has transformed educational institutions' teaching, student participation, and administrative operations over the past two decades. ICT has enabled student-centred learning by providing access to digital resources and interactive learning platforms. ICT also streamlines higher education administrative activities like enrollment, record-keeping, and stakeholder communication. This optimization lets teachers focus on instructional design and student support, creating a good learning environment. Resistance to technological change and guaranteeing fair access to digital resources for all pupils remain difficult. Further ICT integration could lead to immersive technology, AI-driven learning, and broader online education platforms in higher education. Higher education institutions must adapt to harness ICT's full potential to provide quality education and prepare students for a digital world.

Chapter 9 says that the COVID-19 pandemic has compelled enterprises to adopt remote and hybrid work arrangements swiftly. This has presented problems and possibilities to boost staff engagement and efficiency. Maintaining employee involvement under uncertainty and change has proved difficult. Online family engagement practises, online learning, virtual team building exercises, webinars with industry experts, weekly online alignment sessions, team meetings via video conference, short online game sessions, online contests and competitions, online programmes, and online fitness and meditation are some ways organisations have tried to engage their employees. These events help employees interact with coworkers and the company, gain new skills, and grow. Maintaining remote worker efficiency is another difficulty. Companies have sought to solve this by giving staff the necessary skills and resources and defining clear expectations and goals. Some companies provide flexible work arrangements to help employees balance work and life. Overall, COVID-19 has had mixed effects on staff engagement and efficiency. Being flexible and focused on employee requirements is crucial. Employers can keep employees engaged and productive even during a pandemic by providing them with the tools and resources they need and fostering a good and supportive work environment.

Chapter 10 shows in an age of efficiency and customer satisfaction, enterprise applications are more vital than ever. This chapter provides an exciting exploration of cutting-edge technology and corporate applications' dramatic impact on current businesses. This intriguing exposition will explore the thick web of corporate apps that power enterprise development and innovation. These applications enhance procedures, streamline operations, and promote cross-departmental communication to help organisations maximise productivity and customer satisfaction. We will discover how enterprise applications have evolved from traditional software tools to agile, intelligent, and integrated solutions in a changing technological environment. ERP systems, CRM platforms, SCM solutions, and BI tools are all available. Additionally, this chapter will illuminate acceptance and implementation challenges and obstacles. We will navigate practicality and pragmatism to provide a smooth digital transformation from data security to difficult migrations.

Chapter 11 analyzes how Big data has enabled clever marketing solutions in the information age. Data mining on marketing stakeholders helps marketing data intelligence systems improve product innovation and growth. Creative, intelligent technology assists marketers in making quick judgments and developing long-term competitive strategies to acquire a market edge and sustain the firm. This chapter discusses marketing intelligence, its quotient, pertinent theories, evolution, framework, the transformation of marketing intelligence systems from digital marketing to social engineering, tools, and benefits.

Chapter 12 shows how blockchain technology can enhance our daily lives. Much recent blockchain research focuses on cryptocurrencies like Ethereum, bitcoin, etc. Blockchain technology is more than cryptocurrency and has applications in finance, government, banking, accounting, etc. Thus, this study examines potential and concerns. The proposed system stresses blockchain in FAQ systems. Under the suggested method, the questionnaire posts a question with a bounty amount and time for community members to answer. The most popular response gets a bounty. This transaction uses blockchain. This helps the development community determine a person's contribution experience and award value. The Doubt poster can link a prize amount to the question, and if the worthy individual comes, the contract will start a reward stream to their wallet.

Chapter 13 seeks to explore Indian MSMEs' Covid-19 challenges. Next-generation entrepreneurship was enabled by the recent trend of creative and innovative small enterprises, according to the report. Despite the rising digital economy giving entrepreneurs new client service prospects, MSMEs have adopted technology improvements unevenly and slowly. A conceptual framework based on a literature review on pandemic effects on MSMEs and economic growth fall. Conclusion: The government recognises MSMEs' concerns and provides help. MSME owners' digital adoption and practises are still shaped by rival enterprises, suppliers, consumers, and peers in the post-pandemic global digital economy. Such entrepreneurs must use new digital techniques to alter their business and increase resilience and self-reliance. The study examines government support and MSMEs' future options. This conceptual study will help policymakers create MSME policies and academics comprehend and plan future empirical research.

Chapter 14 focuses on a moderated mediation model to examine how government policies affect Indian women's entrepreneurship. The study hypothesises that these businesswomen's industrial sector and information access mitigate the association between government policies and initiatives and women's entrepreneurship. The study surveys 514 Indian women entrepreneurs who have used or are aware of government programmes fostering women's entrepreneurship to test the assumptions. The data show that government policies and programmes boost women's entrepreneurship. This effect is less significant for women manufacturing entrepreneurs, perhaps due to less information access. The study advances public policy and women's entrepreneurship research by giving empirical data on the regulated mediation mechanism by which government policies and activities affect women's entrepreneurship in India.

Chapter 15 examines the concept of Industry 5.0, a sustainable, socially and environmentally responsible industry that has emerged recently. Industry 5.0 advocates say Industry 4.0 isn't sustainable enough. Industry 4.0 prioritises technology-driven productivity across all fields but ignores human interaction in product or service production; Industry 5.0 overcomes this flaw. The UN approved the Sustainable Development Goals (SDGs) in 2015 to encourage its member states to protect the environment, address social challenges, and increase global prosperity. This proactive, goal-oriented technique reassesses social, economic, and environmental expectations. Industry 5.0 and Society 5.0 synergize. "Industry 5.0" examines how big data, AI, robots, and enhanced digitalization might meet industrial, societal, and environmental needs. Society 5.0 addresses social and environmental challenges while boosting economic progress. This study explores significant issues with human-robot collaboration from the perspectives of the organisation, employees, and legal ramifications. Organizational robotics and human-robot co-working need more investigation. The method is blue skies research (based on secondary data).

Chapter 16 discusses the Strategic, environmental, and economic performance of Indian manufacturing, which are examined empirically in this study. This study used Partial Least Squares (PLS) analysis and dynamic capacity view theory to explore the direct and moderating effects of organisational purchasing policies on economic outcomes. Strategic purchasing positively affects economic performance, with firm size moderating. However, business size does not moderate environmental purchasing and economic success. According to this research, strategic purchasing maximises a supplier base, improves supplier relations, and affects supply network expenditures and operations. This shows how purchasing helps maintain quality and grow internationally. This study's limited generalizability to India's manufacturing sector suggests future research should cover other industries and include other perspectives. This research illuminates strategic sourcing's effects on economic performance and provides strategic management and supply chain optimization insights for academia and industry.

Chapter 17 discusses Crude oil consumption as a key economic indicator. The research studies crude oil prices and the stock market. The stock market indices are nifty 50, 100, 200, 500, auto, bank, and FMCG. The study only examined crude oil for six years, leaving a gap in research on other macroeconomic indicators affecting the Indian stock market. This research paper will examine whether global crude oil price variations due to internal and external causes affect NSE indices. This study paper also advises investors on Indian and global deals. This study examines how global crude oil price changes affect the Indian stock market and their causes. This study additionally examines both variables' dependency (crude oil prices globally and the same prices in the Indian stock market).

Chapter 18 illuminates dairy farming businesses' obstacles. The study examined dairy farming entrepreneurs' startup and operational obstacles. People will farm dairy regardless of age, gender, finances, formal education, or experience. The latest study will help dairy farmers and anyone considering a farm recognise potential hazards. The goal is to prepare aspiring entrepreneurs with techniques to overcome these problems. The study gathered dairy farming research publications. Data was acquired using a standardised questionnaire. SPSS was used to discover components using Exploratory Factor Analysis (EFA) on 228 dairy farmers. The study found that land and labour are dairy farming's major concerns. Quality, payment, medical crises, and claims processing are challenging. Dairy production is difficult since it requires proper housing, safety precautions, external feeds, and timely delivery. Entrepreneurs will see benefits by putting their time and money into dairy farming. Though optimism is excellent, entrepreneurs should anticipate business hazards to stay secure. In dynamic business situations, proactive steps always help organisational sustainability. Milk is a perishable product that must be actively managed to protect the business and cattle. It helps entrepreneurs plan for threats as they arise.

Chapter 19 states that Credit and banking activities boost investment and the economy. Research tries to comprehend the importance of banking operations and credit management systems. Lending relies largely on credit management system concepts and practises. The theory of banking activities explains the basic credit system of banks, including verification, loan computation, and disbursement. The primary approach was utilised to collect data from respondents, including quantitative analysis, to better grasp all facts. Financial sector and process importance for countrywide financial mobilisation. This boosts earnings and development. Banks earn more from lending, and the credit system boosts economic growth. Saving money and assets through banking reduces financial risk. Customer credit history, bank balance, and assets affect credit system processes. In addition to the captioned discussion, the article covered the 5Cs of credit, credit management system concepts, fractional reserve theory, bank lending, and current credit management and bank lending trends to update the research paper's goal.

Chapter 20 involves a vegetable distribution facility that must evaluate its performance to optimise operations, increase efficiency, and satisfy customers. This report identifies crucial data for evaluating a vegetable distribution centre's performance. Managers can evaluate the centre's performance, find areas for improvement, and make data-driven choices by monitoring indicators related to order fulfilment, inventory management, productivity, customer service, and cost and finances. This article examines the data and criteria needed to evaluate a vegetable distribution centre's performance, providing helpful advice for this industry. Order management, inventory management, customer service, cost reduction, storage capacity, and transportation planning are used to evaluate distribution performance. Share the areas for improvement with distribution managers to revise their efficiency and waste reduction operating plan.

Chapter 21 identifies that Total Quality Management (TQM) prevents problems and trains personnel to satisfy customers and users. This chapter examined if Total Quality Management is in place, what TQM approaches have been used, how TQM affects warehouse management, and how each influences productivity. This research uses primary data from employee questionnaires since questionnaires may cover a wide population quickly and cheaply. Google Forms was used to create a structured survey questionnaire for respondents. TQM in Warehouse Management improves warehouse quality and system management. Employees can efficiently manage and enhance the warehousing system.

Chapter 22 investigates Central Bank Digital Currencies (CBDCs) and their potential impact on the Indian economy in the digital age. Digital currencies must be understood for commercial value, user experience, regulatory frameworks, and financial stability. CBDCs are novel payment infrastructure. The essay highlights the considerable investments needed to develop a big user and merchant network and the far-reaching consequences of digital currency. This study seeks to explain CBDCs as electronic fiat currency. CBDCs, issued by central banks as legal money, can be saved and used by the public, financial institutions, and companies. The study traces currency from early barter systems to tangible notes and coins to digital payment. It initially doubted digital currencies due to their volatility, diversity, and lack of government support. As the global financial landscape changes, many countries, including India, are developing CBDCs. The RBI has extensively studied the viability of a CBDC in India, emphasising seamless integration features. The study found that CBDC implementation may increase transaction security and efficiency for stakeholders. According to a global survey, most central banks create or test CBDCs. Central Bank Digital Currencies, a secure, low-risk digital platform, modernise India's financial environment in a dynamic technical setting. Digitalization and India's financial future are the focus of this study.

Chapter 23 discusses how recent years have been busy in the tourism industry and how IT technology has greatly impacted vacationers. Much big data research has examined travellers' behaviour in recent years. Few research studies have proven big data analytics supports decision-making. Social media's ability to collect huge volumes of data has expanded research and policymaker insights. This research seeks to understand visitors' motivations and environmental and social influences. The digital lifestyle pattern defines tourist behaviour, connects it to the digital world, and lets us track its evolution. Tourist behaviour techniques can be based on digital lifestyle patterns. For decision-making, we formalise a process for analysing tourist behaviour using social media big data. Data analysis and predictive analytics enable real-time "smart tourism" big data assistance. The method's relevance in helping operational management analyse and predict tourist behavioural trends in scenic locations is shown using geo-tagged tourist photos submitted to Instagram and Facebook in Melbourne, Australia. The artefact's transparent method of studying unstructured big data can improve strategic decision-making about tourists' actions in real life.

Chapter 24 shows that shampoo is often used in cosmetics. Healthy roots and tips, Daily Shine, and stronger hairs drive the worldwide hair care product industry for men and women. This study examines Ahmedabad consumers' shampoo brand preferences and satisfaction. The literature shows that many studies have concentrated on hair care; however, there is a void in the hair shampoo area. This research takes 26 national and international brands to determine consumers' brand choices and the criteria they consider. Exploratory factor analysis and cluster analysis analysed 200 respondents' data from a standardised questionnaire. The study found Dove and L'Oreal Paris to be the most popular brands. Factor study shows that brand image and usage experience, ethical and eco-friendly products, brand preference, product quality, and problem-solving capacity influence hair shampoo selection. Regression factor scores identify brand attributes and perception as clusters.

Chapter 25 examines how data-driven talent management affects state-owned enterprise eco-innovation. A literature analysis examined how people data, HR metrics, and people analytics improve talent management and eco-innovation in state-owned firms. Findings showed that talent decisions and retention strategies require people data. External and internal eco-innovation drivers were also highlighted. External forces include environmental restrictions, competitiveness, and customer demand for eco-friendly products and services. Organizational, technological, and CSR skills drive internal dynamics. Thus, data-driven talent development is needed to improve organisational and technological capacities in state-owned firms for eco-innovation.

Chapter 26 survives in competitive markets, and garment companies must use data-driven decision-making and customer behaviour analysis. Current ICT, notably the blockchain with Internet of Things (IoT)-based enterprise information system framework, offers important services in global networks to enable effective and sustainable supply chain operations. This design prioritises data analytics on business-specific value development. Recent literature on technology-driven supply chain automation and data analytics for sustainability is reviewed in this chapter. The chapter concludes with a market basket analysis application that uses algorithmic data mining to find trends in retail transaction data.

Chapter 27 shows that several studies have linked "intellectual capital, innovative capability, and organisational performance". Knowledge-based businesses like IT show no such association. Innovation capability was evaluated as a mediator between "organisational performance, organisational culture, and intellectual capital (human and organisational capital)" in the Indian IT sector. Bangalore, Hyderabad, and Chennai randomly picked 486 middle-level IT personnel for data collecting. We utilised Smart PLS 3. "Human capital, organisational capital, and culture" positively impact "innovation capability" and similarly positively impact "organisational performance". But "organisational culture" didn't affect "organisational performance". It partially mediates. The report offers IT sector leaders practical advice on improving organisational performance through innovation using "human capital, organisational capital, and organisational culture" and suggests future research directions.

Data-Driven Decision Making for Long-Term Business Success aims to provide an in-depth examination of the impact of data-driven decision-making on achieving long-term commercial and economic success. In order to be considered for inclusion in this proposed book series, research must be novel to provide new insights through methodologically sound and evidence-based analysis. Recent years have seen a meteoric rise in data-driven decision-making, powered by advances in our capacity to collect and interpret information on an unimaginable scale. One of the greatest problems in today's technical and business climate is maintaining a healthy firm that can develop and continue to provide cutting-edge goods and services to the public and boost economic growth. Researchers are asked to solve the topic of how to ensure the long-term success of organisations by using evidence-based decision-making in this book series. When deploying and utilising critical technology, we zero in on how firms do so to maximise their impact. Numerous significant technologies have dramatically altered how businesses are operated. Blockchain, the Internet of Things (IoT), and artificial intelligence (AI) are examples of such technologies. How businesses make decisions, interact with clients, and introduce new offerings is now influenced by cutting-edge tech. The foundation for the connection between organisations and their many stakeholders has shifted thanks to new tools and techniques, including chatbots, virtual assistants, m-commerce, virtual teams, and interactions via the metaverse. The rapid pace of digitization has created new risks for businesses, particularly cybersecurity threats, and artificial intelligence has introduced new ethical questions and conundrums. Therefore, it is essential to create plans for long-term company expansion. This book series seeks contributions to modern machine learning methods, causal inference, and other data-driven approaches that might help businesses make better managerial decisions.

Sonia Singh
Toss Global Management, UAE

S. Suman Rajest
Dhaanish Ahmed College of Engineering, India

Slim Hadoussa
Brest Business School France, France

Ahmed J. Obaid
University of Kufa, Iraq

R. Regin
SRM Institute of Science and Technology, India

Chapter 1
Application of Strategic Human Resource Management Models for Organizational Performance

N. Geethanjali
PSNA College of Engineering and Technology, India

K. M. Ashifa
Istanbul Gelisim University, Turkey

Avantika Raina
https://orcid.org/0000-0002-9854-3147
Vivekananda Institute of Professional Studies, India

Jayashree Patil
Bharati Vidyapeeth, India

Rameshwaran Byloppilly
City University, Ajman, UAE

S. Suman Rajest
https://orcid.org/0000-0001-8315-3747
Dhaanish Ahmed College of Engineering, India

ABSTRACT

Modern organizational management must include strategic human resource management (SHRM). It is an improvement over the conventional human resources management methods, mostly concerned with operations and connections with employees. Contrarily, SHRM recognizes that workers are one of a company's most significant assets and works to match HR practices with those aims and objectives. This method strongly emphasizes long-term planning, proactive decision-making, and a close connection between HR strategies and overarching corporate plans. Strategic human resource management includes all those activities affecting the behavior of individuals in their efforts to formulate and implement the strategic needs of the business. It is the pattern of planned human resource deployments and activities intended to enable the firm to achieve its goals.

DOI: 10.4018/979-8-3693-2193-5.ch001

1. INTRODUCTION

Food waste has become a pervasive and urgent global issue, with far-reaching implications for Guest in 1997 asserts that SHRM should externally align HR practices with business goals that correspond to the organization's stage of development, organizational dynamics, and features and internally align as Strategic relationship connecting the external context and HR (Abu-Rumman, 2021). The potential to connect internal practices to the characteristics of the external market. Best practices that other organizations use as a standard (Abu-Rumman and Qawasmeh, 2021). Gestalt to use the appropriate methods in concurrence. Combinations of powerful complementary techniques (Al Shraah et al., 2022).

1.1. Challenges of Strategic Human Resources Management

Organizations can benefit greatly from implementing Strategic Human Resource Management (SHRM), but many difficulties and barriers must be overcome (Al Shraah et al., 2013). The key to successfully implementing SHRM is for HR professionals and enterprises to understand these issues (Evans & Davis, 2005). Here are a few issues that SHRM frequently faces:

Employee and manager resistance to change is possible, especially if they have grown accustomed to established HR methods (Anand et al., 2023). The successful execution of SHRM initiatives can be hampered by resistance (Alayli, 2023).

Lack of Senior Leadership Support: For SHRM efforts to be successful, senior leadership must support them (María et al., 2023). It may not be easy to obtain the required resources and dedication if upper management does not completely back SHRM (Arslan et al., 2021).

Resource Restrictions: Putting SHRM into practice frequently calls for investments in technology, education, and talent development (Ogunmola et al., 2021). Resource restrictions can be a problem (Khaled Lafi Al-Naif and Ata E. M. Al Shraah, 2018).

Complexity: SHRM is not an all-encompassing strategy. It can be challenging and time-consuming to modify HR procedures to align with an organization's goal and this requires considerable skill (Atasever, 2023).

Talent Scarcity: Finding and keeping top talent can be difficult, particularly in sectors with fierce competition. The global talent war can make finding the proper candidates for key positions challenging.

Data and Analytics Capabilities: Data analytics are a key component of many SHRM strategies. The effectiveness of measuring the impact of HR initiatives may be a challenge for organizations lacking strong data and analytics skills (Said & Tripathi, 2023).

Legal and Regulatory Compliance: HR procedures must adhere to all applicable legal and regulatory requirements. A complex balancing act may be required to guarantee compliance while coordinating HR with strategy (Srinivas et al., 2023).

Cultural Alignment: SHRM might call for a change in the organization's culture. Getting the intended SHRM culture and the current culture to coincide can be difficult.

Change Management: Successfully adopting SHRM frequently necessitates adjustments to employee expectations and HR procedures. To reduce opposition and disruptions, change management must be done effectively (Balas-Timar & Ignat, 2015).

Measuring ROI: It can be difficult to demonstrate the return on investment (ROI) of SHRM initiatives. Advanced measurements and analytics may be needed to quantify the effect of HR strategies on organizational performance (Ocoró et al., 2023).

Integration with Other Functions: SHRM needs to work closely and be integrated with other departments like marketing and finance (Demeter et al., 2021). It can be not easy to ensure seamless alignment throughout the business (Sharma et al., 2021b).

Short-Term vs. Long-Term Focus: It might be difficult to balance short-term performance and long-term strategic goals. SHRM frequently emphasizes long-term talent development, which might not immediately produce dividends (Pandit, 2023).

Technological Adaptation: In SHRM, utilizing HR technology is essential. HR software and systems selection, implementation, and adaptation may provide issues for organizations (Kuragayala, 2023).

Competitive Dynamics: Markets and industries are always changing. To maintain their competitiveness and handle new challenges, organizations must modify their SHRM strategy (Tambaip et al., 2023).

Globalization: Managing multiple labor laws, cultures, and worker dynamics for multinational firms makes SHRM initiatives more difficult (Sharma et al., 2021a).

Despite these obstacles, many businesses understand that SHRM is important to attaining their strategic objectives and raising overall performance (Sharma et al., 2021c). Planning, engaging stakeholders, constant learning, and a dedication to improving HR practices are frequently required to address these difficulties (Sharma et al., 2021d). The new modern SHRM models help in increasing organizational performance, which helps in attaining strategic objectives (fig.1).

Figure 1. Key concepts of SHRM

2. KEY CONCEPTS OF SHRM

Alignment with Business Goals: SHRM evolves with clean expertise of a corporation's mission, vision, and strategic objectives. HR specialists work carefully with pinnacle control to ensure that HR regulations, practices, and projects are in keeping with those desires. This alignment facilitates aggressive gain and sustainable increase (Storey et al., 2019).

Talent Acquisition and Retention: In SHRM, attracting and keeping top talent is a primary cognizance. It involves not only recruiting individuals with the right capabilities but also ensuring that they fit into the organization's lifestyle and values (Tripathi & Al-Shahri, 2023). Effective onboarding and expertise development programs play a sizeable position on this issue (Rad et al., 2019).

Performance Management: SHRM emphasizes the non-stop assessment of worker performance, presenting comments, and setting clear expectations. Performance management structures are designed to encourage and align employees with organizational goals, fostering a way of life of excellence (Rad & Demeter, 2020).

Employee Development: SHRM promotes ongoing knowledge of and improvement possibilities for personnel. This includes training, skill improvement, mentoring applications, and professional progression-making plans (Roman et al., 2020). A properly developed team of workers can adapt to converting commercial enterprise environments greater efficaciously (Rad et al., 2020a).

Diversity and Inclusion: SHRM recognizes the importance of range and inclusion within the place of business (Vashishtha & Dhawan, 2023). By developing an inclusive environment, agencies can leverage the precise views and talents of a diverse group of workers, main to innovation and advanced decision-making (Rad et al., 2020b).

Employee Engagement: Engaged employees are more productive and devoted to their work. SHRM techniques attention on fostering a high-quality workplace lifestyle, improving employee engagement, and improving average task delight (Rad et al., 2022).

Data-Driven Decision-Making: SHRM uses facts, analytics, and metrics to inform HR techniques and selections (Venkateswaran et al., 2023). This statistics-driven technique enables businesses to tune and measure the impact of HR initiatives, make important modifications, and optimize their team of workers (Ramos et al., 2023).

Compliance and Ethics: In addition to strategic alignment, SHRM emphasizes compliance with criminal and ethical standards. HR professionals are responsible for ensuring that the employer's HR practices follow labor laws and ethical ideas (Sabti et al., 2023).

3. UNDERSTANDING THE NEED FOR THE SHRM MODEL

The SHRM model is constructed upon the belief that human beings aren't simply prices but property that may power an employer ahead (Venkateswaran & Viktor, 2023). It entails a scientific approach to HR control, integrating HR techniques with the broader organizational strategy. Here's a breakdown of the key components of the SHRM version:

Alignment with Organizational Strategy: At the center of SHRM is aligning HR strategies with a corporation's overall business goals. This approach ensures that HR decisions and projects are designed to support and contribute to achieving the employer's goals (Vashishtha & Kapoor, 2023). For instance, if an agency's strategic goal is to make bigger into new markets, HR can also pay attention to talent acquisition and improvement to assist this enlargement (Walton, 1985: Stalin et al., 2019).

Talent Acquisition and Retention: SHRM emphasizes attracting, choosing, and maintaining the right expertise (Gupta, 2021a). It includes identifying the talents and abilities required to fulfill strategic desires and aligning recruitment efforts (Gupta, 2021b). Retaining top expertise is equally critical, as worker turnover can be expensive and disruptive (Wright & Ulrich, 2017).

Performance Management: Effective performance control is a cornerstone of SHRM. This entails setting clear performance expectations, imparting regular comments, and conducting performance reviews (Gupta, 2022). High-appearing personnel are identified and rewarded, at the same time as, underperformers are supported in enhancing their performance. Employee Development: SHRM acknowledges that an organization's success relies upon the boom and improvement of its personnel. HR strategies must encompass schooling, ability development, mentoring, and professional plans to ensure employees are ready to satisfy current and future challenges.

Diversity and Inclusion: SHRM acknowledges the price of a various workforce. Inclusive HR practices create surroundings where personnel of different backgrounds, stories, and views can thrive. This variety fosters innovation and may result in better selection-making. Employee Engagement: Engaged personnel are extra committed, efficient, and dependable. SHRM strongly emphasizes growing an advantageous workplace tradition where personnel are prompted and engaged with their paintings. Data-Driven Decision-Making: Data analytics and metrics play a vital function in SHRM. HR specialists use records to assess the impact of HR tasks, become aware of regions for development, and make informed decisions. This evidence-based technique guarantees that HR techniques are continually delicate and optimized.

Strategic Human Resource Management (SHRM) is important for organizations for several compelling reasons:

1. Alignment with Business Goals: SHRM ensures that HR practices and policies align intently with the corporation's strategic goals and targets. This alignment enables business achievement by ensuring that the staff is focused on what matters most to the business enterprise.
2. Talent Acquisition and Retention: SHRM techniques assist businesses in enticing, recruiting, and holding pinnacle expertise. Talent is a valuable asset and having the right people in the right roles contributes notably to organizational effectiveness and competitiveness.
3. Competitive Advantage: Effective SHRM can create an aggressive advantage using leveraging human capital. When HR practices are strategically designed to develop talents, foster innovation, and decorate worker engagement, businesses are better placed to outperform their competition.
4. Adaptability to Change: In today's fast-paced enterprise surroundings, groups must be agile and aware of change. SHRM emphasizes the improvement of a bendy and adaptable workforce that may quickly reply to shifts inside the marketplace or enterprise.
5. Employee Performance: SHRM specializes in improving employee overall performance via clear intention setting, ordinary remarks, and professional improvement. High-performing personnel make contributions to better general organizational overall performance.
6. Innovation and Creativity: SHRM fashions emphasizing worker engagement and a fine workplace subculture foster innovation and creativity. Employees who experience value and empowerment are likelier to contribute clean ideas and solutions.
7. Cost Efficiency: Strategic HR practices can assist groups in managing hard work costs successfully. This includes optimizing repayment and blessings, lowering turnover, and enhancing personnel productivity.
8. Risk Management: SHRM models additionally deal with compliance with exertions legal guidelines and guidelines, decreasing the hazard of legal issues and costly penalties. HR specialists ensure that the enterprise operates within the bounds of the regulation.
9. Diversity and Inclusion: SHRM promotes range and inclusion, which can cause a broader variety of views and abilities in the enterprise. Diverse teams are regularly extra innovative and better geared up to resolve complex problems.

10. Enhanced Employee Engagement: SHRM emphasizes developing a fine painting environment and fostering employee engagement. Engaged personnel are greater stimulated, devoted, and satisfied, which can result in lower turnover and higher productivity.
11. Data-Driven Decision-Making: SHRM encourages using records and analytics to inform HR techniques and decisions. This records-pushed technique facilitates groups to make informed selections about talent control and group worker optimization.
12. Long-Term Sustainability: By specializing in talent development, worker engagement, and alignment with strategic desires, SHRM contributes to the lengthy-time period sustainability of corporations. It ensures that businesses can thrive in stable and dynamic business environments.

4. TRADITIONAL SHRM MODELS AND FRAMEWORK FOR OPTIMIZATION OF HUMAN CAPITAL

Organizations can efficiently manage their group of workers and gain an aggressive advantage in the contemporary dynamic commercial enterprise panorama. Strategic Human Resource Management (SHRM) fashions offer frameworks and recommendations for groups to align their HR practices with their strategic dreams and goals. These fashions help HR specialists make informed decisions and broaden strategies that optimize human capital to drive business success. Here are a few outstanding SHRM models:

1. The Harvard Framework: Developed by Michael Beer, this model emphasizes the significance of HR guidelines and practices in influencing employee conduct, which in turn impacts organizational overall performance. It consists of 4 coverage regions: • Human Resource Flow, • Reward Systems • Employee Influence, • Work Systems (fig.2).
2. The Michigan Model: Also known as the Matching Model, this model was advanced by using David Ulrich and his colleagues. It highlights the alignment of HR practices with the employer's strategy (fig.3). The key components include the following:
    - HR practices should align with organizational goals.
    - Employees are assets to be controlled.
    - The emphasis on internal consistency in HR practices
3. The Guest Model: Developed using David Guest, this model makes a specialty of the results of HR practices (fig.4). It consists of four essential elements:
    - HR approach: Integrating HR policies with enterprise strategies.
    - HR practices: How HR regulations are implemented.
    - HR results: Employee behaviors and performance.
    - Organizational consequences: Overall business performance
4. The Ulrich Model: Created by David Ulrich, this model is frequently known as the HR Business Partner Model. It suggests that HR has to act as a strategic partner inside an organization, appearing 4 key roles: • Strategic Partner: Aligning HR method with normal enterprise approach. • Change Agent: Leading alternate projects in the company. • Administrative Expert: Managing HR functions correctly. • Employee Champion: Advocating for employees' wishes and worries.

Figure 2. Harvard framework

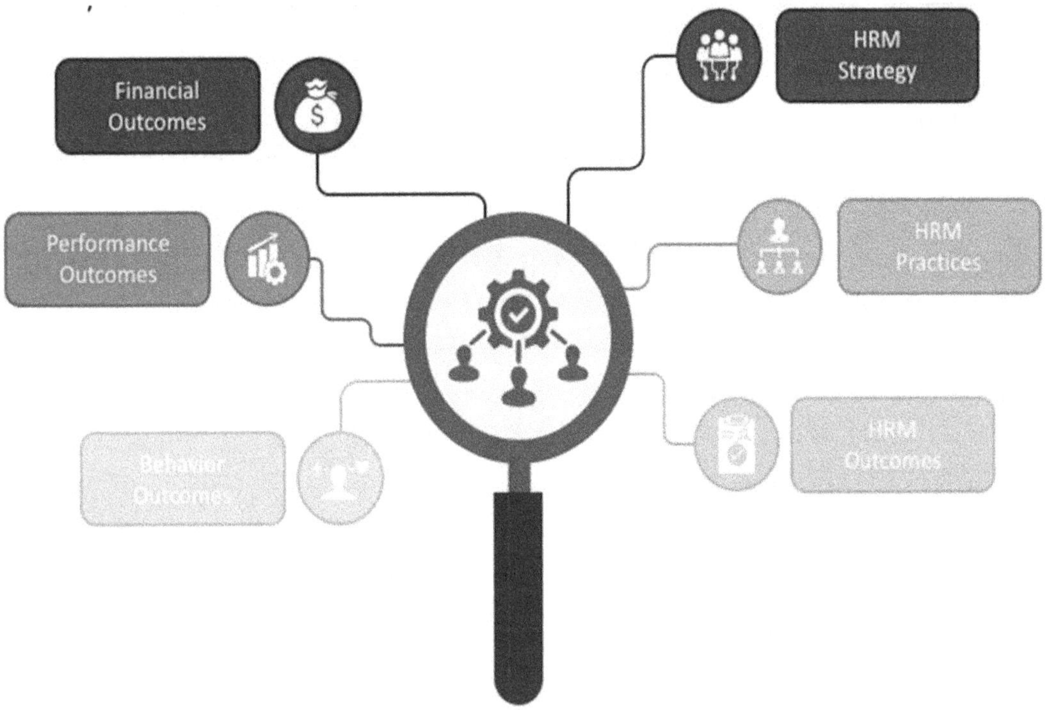

Figure 3. Michigan model

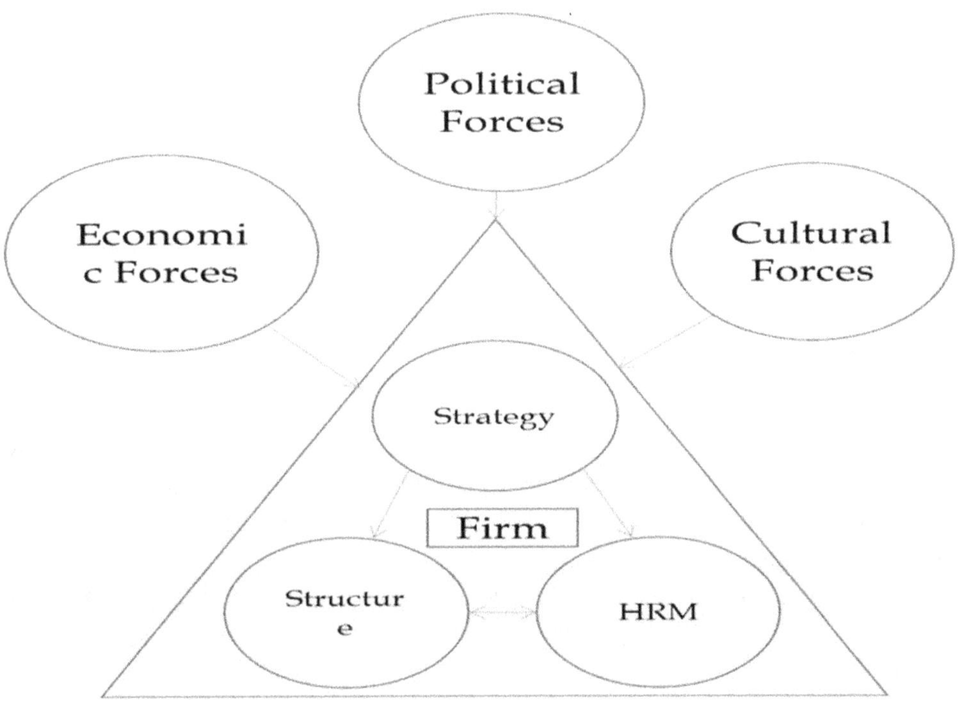

Figure 4. Guest model

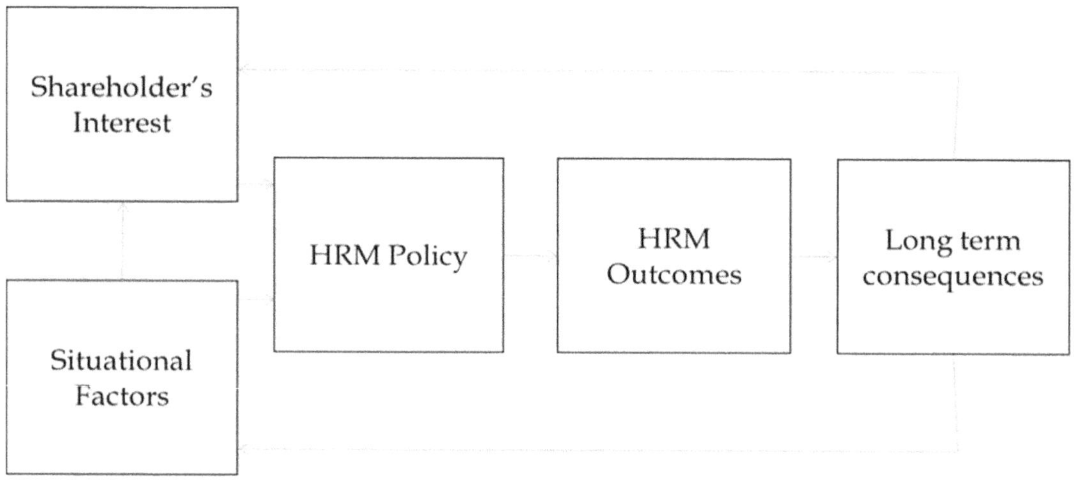

5. The HR Value Chain Model: This model, developed through John W. Boudreau and Peter M. Ramstad, is primarily based on the idea that HR practices should create a fee for the organization. It consists of 5 steps: • Workforce Planning, • Talent Acquisition, • Performance Management • Learning and Development • Total Rewards.
6. The Resource-Based View (RBV) Model: The RBV version, primarily based on the work of scholars like Jay Barney, indicates that a corporation's competitive benefit comes from its precise and treasured resources. Human capital is taken into consideration for this type of key asset. In this version, HR practices aim to build and preserve precious human sources (fig.5).

Figure 5. Resource-based view (RBV) model

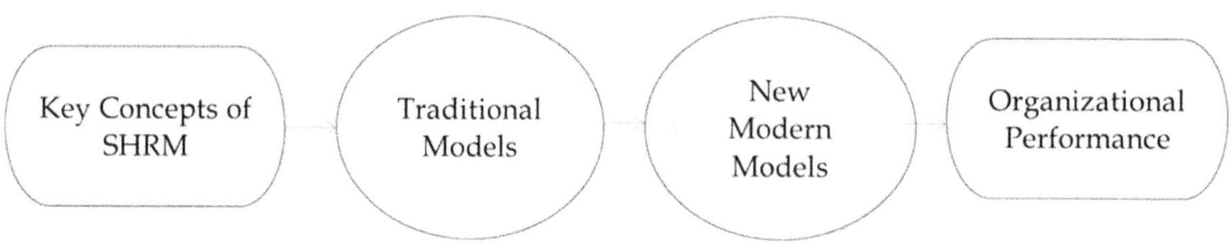

7. The Life Cycle Model: This version acknowledges that HR techniques and practices may additionally want to exchange as a business enterprise goes through distinctive degrees of its life cycle (e.g., startup, growth, adulthood, and decline). HR practices are tailored to satisfy the evolving needs of the corporation (fig.6).
8. The Best Practices Model: This technique specializes in identifying and adopting HR best practices that have been a hit in different organizations. It includes benchmarking towards enterprise leaders to enhance HR functions (fig.7).

Figure 6. Life cycle model

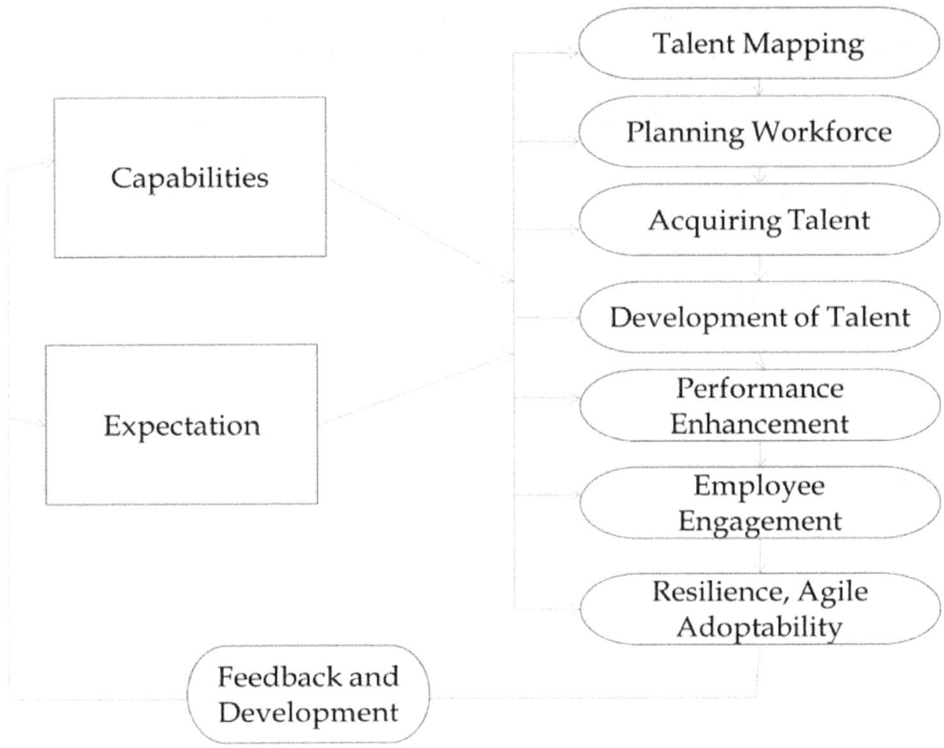

Figure 7. Best practices model

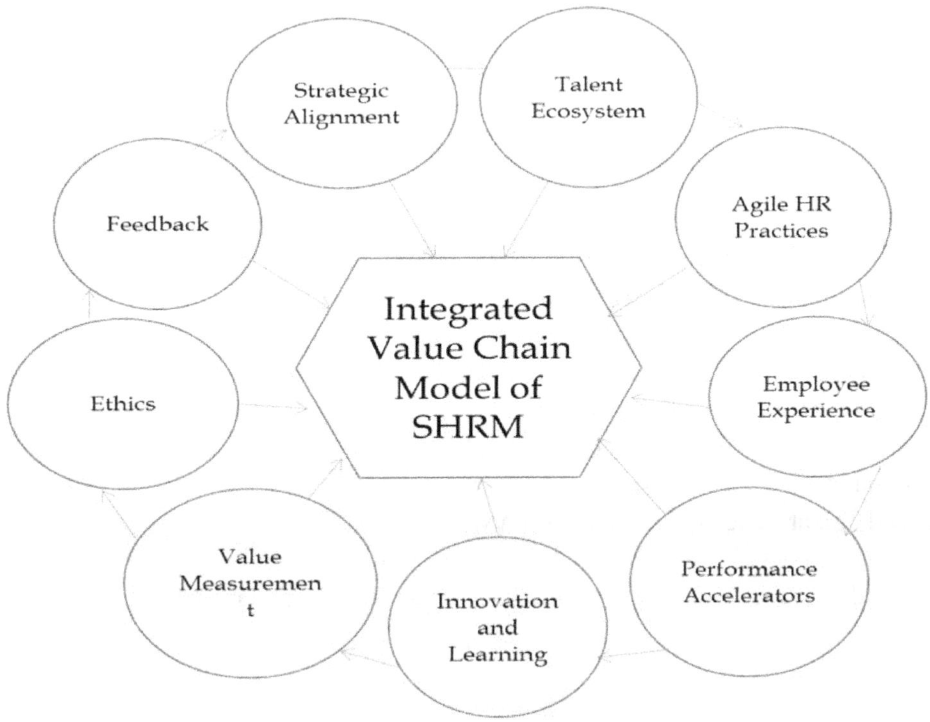

9. The High-Performance Work System (HPWS) Model emphasizes creating a piece environment that fosters worker engagement, innovation, and high overall performance. It generally includes practices like selective hiring, significant schooling, overall performance-based total rewards, and worker involvement (Priscila et al., 2023). Each of those SHRM fashions offers a unique angle on how HR can be strategically incorporated into a corporation to decorate its competitiveness and basic performance. Organizations may also pick or adapt fashions primarily based on their unique needs, desires, and contexts (fig.8).

Figure 8. High-performance work system (HPWS) model

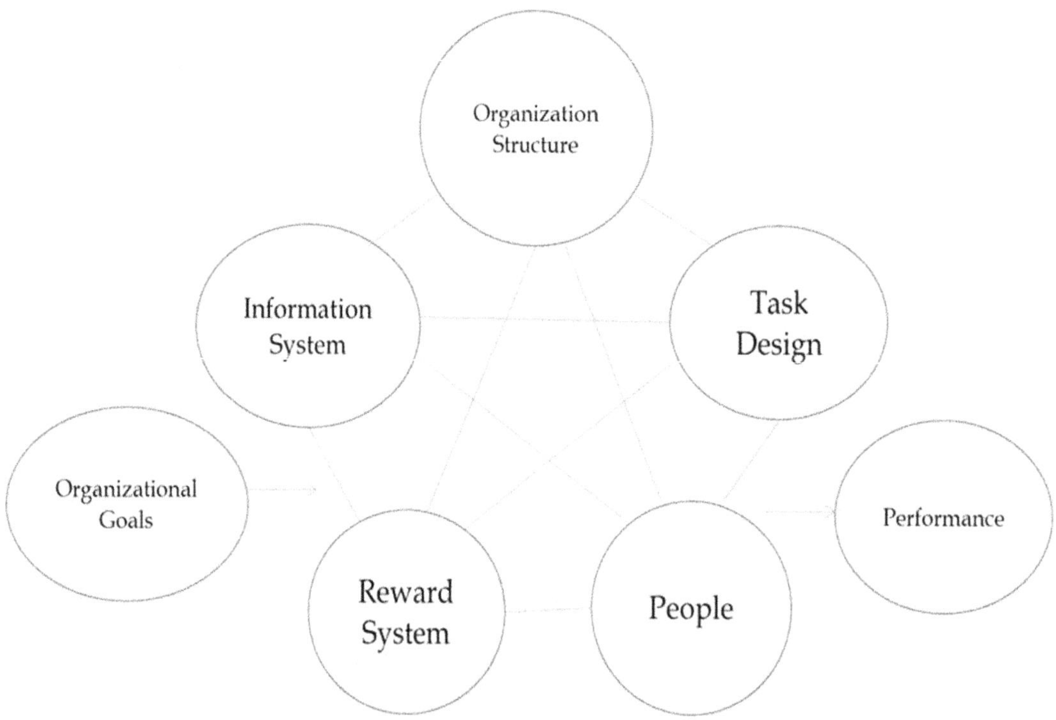

5. NEW MODELS OF SHRM FOR EFFECTIVE ORGANIZATIONAL PERFORMANCE

The two new models of SHRM were developed based on the Traditional SHRM models to bridge the gap and fulfill the needs of modern organizations.

- An Integrated Value Chain Model
- Integrated Talent Acceleration Model (ITAM)

An Integrated Value Chain Model of Strategic Human Resource Management

This model was framed by integrating various functions of human resource management with organizational strategy for increasing the employee's performance and improving the organization's overall performance.

1. Strategic Alignment: This model's core aligns HR techniques with universal organizational strategies and objectives. HR specialists work closely with top management to apprehend the enterprise's strategy, values, and tradition. HR strategies are advanced to aid and improve the achievement of business desires.
2. Talent Ecosystem: The employer perspectives its team of workers as a dynamic atmosphere of diverse expertise pools. These expertise pools include personnel, contingent employees, freelancers, and partners. The HR function specializes in creating inclusive and diverse talent surroundings to fulfill evolving enterprise needs.
3. Agile HR Practices: HR practices are designed to be agile and adaptable to converting commercial enterprise environments. Agile HR includes continuous remarks, speedy talent development, and the potential to modify personnel composition quickly. HR leverages generation and statistics analytics for actual-time choice-making (Saxena et al., 2023).
4. Employee Experience: A crucial pillar of this version is developing a high-quality worker experience. HR designs initiatives that enhance the worker journey, from recruitment to off-boarding. Employee nicely-being, engagement, and painting-lifestyles balance are necessary additives.
5. Performance Accelerators: HR capabilities as a catalyst for performance acceleration. Performance management is effects-oriented, specializing in outcomes and non-stop improvement. HR collaborates with managers to provide coaching and development opportunities.
6. Innovation and Learning Hub: HR is an innovation and studying hub. It encourages a lifestyle of continuous mastering and innovation among personnel. HR supports pass-functional collaboration to power innovation.
7. Value Measurement: Key performance indicators (KPIs) determine the price created through HR initiatives. Metrics include no longer the most effective conventional HR metrics (e.g., turnover fee) but also business effect metrics (e.g., revenue according to worker). HR continuously assesses and reports at the cost added.
8. Ethical and Sustainable HR: Ethical and sustainable HR practices are fundamental. HR ensures compliance with moral standards, variety and inclusion, and sustainability desires. The version emphasizes corporate social obligation in HR choices.
9. Feedback Loops: Continuous remarks loops are mounted with personnel and other stakeholders. Feedback informs HR strategies and practices, using development and adaptation. HR actively seeks input from employees and includes their perspectives.

The Integrated Value Chain Model of SHRM is designed to create a holistic and dynamic technique for managing human sources (fig.9). It places strategic alignment, agility, worker revel in, and value size at the vanguard, with a strong cognizance of moral and sustainable HR practices. This model acknowledges that HR isn't always a standalone function but is included in the company's price advent technique (Venkateswaran et al. 2018).

Figure 9. Integrated value chain model of SHRM

6. INTEGRATED TALENT ACCELERATION MODEL (ITAM)

A conceptual framework that organizations can use to strategically manage and optimize their processes for talent acquisition and development is called the Integrated Talent Acceleration Model (ITAM). To fulfill present and future business needs, ITAM assists firms in locating, luring, nurturing, and accelerating talent development. The Integrated Talent Acceleration Model's main applications and elements are as follows:

1. Identification and Talent Mapping: • Application: ITAM starts by outlining the organization's current talent landscape and determining the abilities, competencies, and skills required to meet strategic objectives.
   - Components: This phase entails undertaking a thorough examination of the current workforce, including competence mapping, skills assessments, and talent gap identification.
2. Planning a strategic workforce: • Application: ITAM assists businesses in coordinating their personnel with long-term strategic goals.
   - Components: Organizations create workforce plans during this phase that describe how they will hire, train, and keep employees to fulfill future business demands.
3. Attracting and acquiring talent: • Application: ITAM aids firms in locating and hiring the best individuals, supporting talent acquisition initiatives.
   - Components: Innovative hiring techniques, corporate branding, and focused sourcing initiatives are examples of strategies for luring talent.
4. Development of Dynamic Talent: • Application: ITAM strongly emphasizes ongoing learning and development to improve staff members' competencies.
   - Components: To foster talent and close skill gaps, firms employ personalized learning initiatives, mentorship programs, and other development opportunities at this phase.
5. Performance Enhancement and Appreciation: • Application: ITAM synchronizes team and individual performance with organizational goals.

- Components: Clear expectations are defined, frequent feedback is given, and exceptional contributions are recognized and rewarded through the establishment of performance management systems.

6. Employee Wellbeing and Engagement: • Application: ITAM enhances employee wellbeing, provides a positive work atmosphere, and ensures high levels of engagement.
   - Components: Initiatives that support employee engagement and happiness include work-life balance initiatives, professional development opportunities, and employee feedback methods.
7. Resilience and Agile Adaptability: • Application: ITAM encourages businesses to develop resilience and agility to react swiftly to market shifts and new business possibilities.
   - Components: Businesses encourage innovation, failure-based learning, and change management techniques.
8. Constant feedback and development: • Application: ITAM highlights the significance of gathering data and feedback to promote ongoing HR policies and procedures development.
   - Components: Recurring feedback loops, pulse surveys, and data analysis assist businesses in pinpointing areas for development and assisting in data-driven decision-making.

Organizations can proactively manage their talent pool to address present and upcoming business difficulties using the Integrated Talent Acceleration Model (ITAM). A structured approach to talent management offered by ITAM aids firms in better aligning their people resources with strategic goals, promoting a culture of learning and growth, and ultimately succeeding (fig.10).

Figure 10. Integrated talent acceleration model (ITAM)

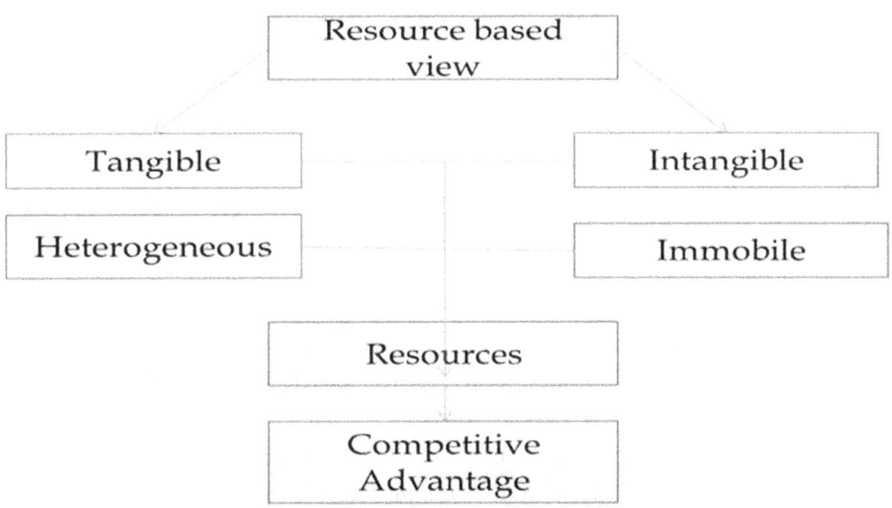

7. ORGANIZATIONAL PERFORMANCE

Models of strategic human resource management (SHRM) are crucial in determining how well an organization performs. These models offer a planned framework for matching company strategic goals with HR practices, ultimately affecting several organizational performance metrics. The following are some ways that a SHRM model might affect and improve organizational performance:

1. Corporate Strategy Alignment: SHRM models strongly emphasize the value of matching HR practices to the overarching company strategy. The staff will work toward common objectives if HR initiatives are closely related to the organization's strategic objectives. Higher organizational performance levels are made possible by this alignment.
2. Talent Acquisition and Retention: Top talent attraction, selection, and retention are frequently emphasized in SHRM models. Improved productivity and creativity are the results of a talented and skilled team, and these factors can help an organization perform financially and remain competitive.
3. Performance Management: SHRM models support efficient strategies for managing performance. Employee performance is more likely to be at its highest when they receive regular feedback, have defined performance objectives, and know how their work contributes to the company's success.
4. Employee Development: Investing in employee development, a crucial SHRM component, results in a staff that is more knowledgeable and flexible. Performance is improved when staff are properly taught to respond to shifting market conditions and technology developments.
5. Employee Engagement: In SHRM models, employee engagement is frequently given priority. Employees who are more devoted, content, and driven work harder, have lower turnover rates, and are more satisfied with their jobs, all of which increase organizational performance.
6. Diversity and Inclusion: Organizations can access a wider range of viewpoints and abilities by utilizing SHRM models that strongly emphasize diversity and inclusion. As a result, there may be increased creativity, improved problem-solving, and competitive advantage.
7. Data-Driven Decision-Making: SHRM models support using data to inform HR decisions. Organizations can choose wisely about talent management by studying workforce data and metrics, which will increase workforce efficiency and effectiveness.
8. Change Management: SHRM models frequently contain techniques for successfully managing organizational change. This is essential in the fast-paced business climate of today when performance during times of change can be greatly impacted by adaptability.
9. Total Rewards Systems: SHRM models consider the layout of total rewards systems, which comprise pay and benefits. These techniques can recruit and retain top talent, inspire staff members to give their best efforts and improve performance.
10. Strategic HR Metrics: To assess the success of HR activities, SHRM models recommend using important HR metrics. Organizations may pinpoint areas for improvement and optimize HR procedures to increase performance by tracking indicators like attrition rates, employee engagement ratings, and training ROI.

Finally, SHRM models offer an organized method for handling human resources that directly enhances organizational performance. Employees' quality of work life also plays a major role in organizational performance by employees (Sabarirajan & Geethanjali, 2011). Organizations can improve their competitiveness, profitability, and overall performance by integrating HR strategies into the broader business plan, focusing on talent acquisition and development, and encouraging employee involvement and diversity.

Firms can increase employee performance and productivity by incorporating SHRM into their daily operations to:

1. Maximize Employee Performance: SHRM models assist firms in attracting, developing, and retaining top personnel.
2. Strengthen Competitive Advantage: By efficiently utilizing their human resources, firms can achieve a competitive edge by aligning their HR processes with strategic goals.
3. Adapt to Change: SHRM frameworks offer tools for managing change and organizational development to ensure flexibility and adaptability in dynamic business environments.
4. Reduce Risks: Promoting compliance with legal requirements and ethical standards lowers the danger of legal problems and reputational harm.
5. Measure and Optimize: SHRM models include metrics and assessment tools that allow firms to assess the effectiveness of their HR processes and continuously improve them.
6. Promote a Positive Work Atmosphere: According to SHRM, employee engagement and organizational culture are important factors in creating an atmosphere that is both positive and productive.

8. CONCLUSION

In conclusion, SHRM models for strategic human resource management (SHRM) give organizations useful frameworks for efficiently managing their human resources in line with their strategic objectives. These models stress human resources' vital role in determining an organization's success and competitiveness. Each SHRM model provides a distinct viewpoint on how HR practices can be planned and implemented strategically to support an organization's overarching goal. Which model to adopt or modify will rely on the organization's unique requirements, objectives, and circumstances. The SHRM models are useful tools for firms looking to maximize the potential of their human resources in today's quickly evolving business environment. The fundamental idea is the same whether it's the Harvard Model, Michigan Model, Guest Model, or any other SHRM framework: HR practices should align with and contribute to accomplishing strategic objectives, thereby fostering organizational success.

REFERENCES

Abu-Rumman, A. (2021). Effective Knowledge Sharing: A Guide to the Key Enablers and Inhibitors. In D. Tessier (Ed.), *Handbook of Research on Organizational Culture Strategies for Effective Knowledge Management and Performance* (pp. 133–156). IGI Global. doi:10.4018/978-1-7998-7422-5.ch008

Abu-Rumman, A., & Qawasmeh, R. (2021). Assessing international students' satisfaction of a Jordanian university using the service quality model. *Journal of Applied Research in Higher Education*. Advance online publication. doi:10.1108/JARHE-05-2021-0166

Al-Naif, K. L., & Al Shraah, A. E. M. (2018). Working capital management and profitability: Evidence from Jordanian mining and extraction industry sector. *IUG Journal of Economics and Business.*, *2*(1), 42–60.

Al Shraah, A., Abu-Rumman, A., Alqhaiwi, L. A., & AlSha'ar, H. (2022). The impact of sourcing strategies and logistics capabilities on organizational performance during the COVID-19 pandemic: Evidence from Jordanian pharmaceutical industries. *Uncertain Supply Chain Management*, *10*(3), 1077–1090. doi:10.5267/j.uscm.2022.2.004

Al Shraah, A., Irtaimeh, H. J., & Rumman, M. A. (2013). The Strategic Human Resource Management Practices in Implying Total Quality Management (TQM): An Empirical Study on Jordanian Banking Sector. *International Journal of Management*, *4*(5), 179–190.

Alayli, S. (2023). Unravelling the Drivers of Online Purchasing Intention: The E-Commerce Scenario in Lebanon. *FMDB Transactions on Sustainable Social Sciences Letters*, *1*(1), 56–67.

Anand, P. P., Kanike, U. K., Paramasivan, P., Rajest, S. S., Regin, R., & Priscila, S. S. (2023). Embracing Industry 5.0: Pioneering Next-Generation Technology for a Flourishing Human Experience and Societal Advancement. *FMDB Transactions on Sustainable Social Sciences Letters*, *1*(1), 43–55.

Arslan, F., Singh, B., Sharma, D. K., Regin, R., Steffi, R., & Rajest, S. S. (2021). Optimization technique approach to resolve food sustainability problems. In *2021 International Conference on Computational Intelligence and Knowledge Economy (ICCIKE)*. IEEE. 10.1109/ICCIKE51210.2021.9410735

Atasever, M. (2023). Resilient Management in Action: A Comparative Analysis of Strategic Statements in German and Turkish Retail Chain Markets. *FMDB Transactions on Sustainable Management Letters*, *1*(2), 66–81.

Balas-Timar, D., & Ignat, S. (2015). Conceptual applicant screening model with fuzzy logic in industrial organizational contexts. *Procedia: Social and Behavioral Sciences*, *203*, 257–263. doi:10.1016/j.sbspro.2015.08.291

Demeter, E., Rad, D., & Balas, E. (2021). Schadenfreude and General Anti-Social Behaviours: The Role of Violent Content Preferences and Life Satisfaction. BRAIN. *Broad Research in Artificial Intelligence and Neuroscience*, *12*(2), 98–111. doi:10.18662/brain/12.2/194

Evans, W. R., & Davis, W. D. (2005). High-performance work systems and organizational performance: The mediating role of internal social structure. *Journal of Management*, *31*(5), 758–775. doi:10.1177/0149206305279370

Gupta, R. K. (2021a). A study on occupational health hazards among construction workers in India. *International Journal of Enterprise Network Management*, *12*(4), 325–339. doi:10.1504/IJENM.2021.119663

Gupta, R. K. (2021b). Adoption of mobile wallet services: an empirical analysis. *International Journal of Intellectual Property Management, 12*(3), 341 – 353. doi:10.1504/IJIPM.2021.10035526

Gupta, R. K. (2022). Utilization of Digital Network Learning and Healthcare for Verbal Assessment and Counselling During Post COVID-19 Period. Technologies. *Artificial Intelligence and the Future of Learning Post-COVID*, *19*, 117–134.

Kuragayala, P. S. (2023). A Systematic Review on Workforce Development in Healthcare Sector: Implications in the Post-COVID Scenario. *FMDB Transactions on Sustainable Technoprise Letters*, *1*(1), 36–46.

María, J. J. L., Polo, O. C. C., & Elhadary, T. (2023). An Analysis of the Morality and Social Responsibility of Non-Profit Organizations. *FMDB Transactions on Sustainable Technoprise Letters*, *1*(1), 28–35.

Ocoró, M. P., Polo, O. C. C., & Khandare, S. (2023). Importance of Business Financial Risk Analysis in SMEs According to COVID-19. *FMDB Transactions on Sustainable Management Letters*, *1*(1), 12–21.

Ogunmola, G. A., Singh, B., Sharma, D. K., Regin, R., Rajest, S. S., & Singh, N. (2021). Involvement of distance measure in assessing and resolving efficiency environmental obstacles. In *2021 International Conference on Computational Intelligence and Knowledge Economy (ICCIKE)*. IEEE. 10.1109/ICCIKE51210.2021.9410765

Pandit, P. (2023). On the Context of the Principle of Beneficence: The Problem of Over Demandingness within Utilitarian Theory. *FMDB Transactions on Sustainable Social Sciences Letters*, *1*(1), 26–42.

Priscila, S. S., Rajest, S. S., Tadiboina, S. N., Regin, R., & András, S. (2023). Analysis of Machine Learning and Deep Learning Methods for Superstore Sales Prediction. *FMDB Transactions on Sustainable Computer Letters*, *1*(1), 1–11.

Rad, D., Balas, E., Ignat, S., Rad, G., & Dixon, D. (2020a). A Predictive Model of Youth Bystanders' Helping Attitudes. *Revista romaneasca pentru educatie multidimensionala-Journal for Multidimensional Education, 12*(1Sup2), 136-150.

Rad, D., Balas, V., Lile, R., Demeter, E., Dughi, T., & Rad, G. (2020b). Statistical Properties of a New Social Media Context Awareness Scale (SMCA)-A Preliminary Investigation. *Sustainability (Basel)*, *12*(12), 5201. doi:10.3390u12125201

Rad, D., & Demeter, E. (2020). A Moderated Mediation Effect of Online Time Spent on Internet Content Awareness, Perceived Online Hate Speech and Helping Attitudes Disposal of Bystanders. *Postmodern Openings*, *11*(2, Supl 1), 107–124. doi:10.18662/po/11.2Sup1/182

Rad, D., Dughi, T., & Demeter, E. (2019). The Dynamics of the Relationship between Humor and Benevolence as Values. *Revista romaneasca pentru educatie multidimensionala-Journal for Multidimensional Education, 11*(3), 201-212.

Rad, D., Egerau, A., Roman, A., Dughi, T., Balas, E., Maier, R., & Rad, G. (2022). A Preliminary Investigation of the Technology Acceptance Model (TAM) in Early Childhood Education and Care. BRAIN. *Broad Research in Artificial Intelligence and Neuroscience*, *13*(1), 518–533. doi:10.18662/brain/13.1/297

Ramos, J. I., Lacerona, R., & Nunag, J. M. (2023). A Study on Operational Excellence, Work Environment Factors and the Impact to Employee Performance. *FMDB Transactions on Sustainable Social Sciences Letters*, *1*(1), 12–25.

Roman, A., Rad, D., Egerau, A., Dixon, D., Dughi, T., Kelemen, G., & Rad, G. (2020). Physical Self-Schema Acceptance and Perceived Severity of Online Aggressiveness in Cyberbullying Incidents. *Journal of Interdisciplinary Studies in Education*, *9*(1), 100–116. doi:10.32674/jise.v9i1.1961

Sabarirajan, A., & Geethanjali. (2011). A study on quality of work life and organizational performance among the employees of public and private banks in Dindigul. *International Journal of Economics and Research, 2*(6), 38-45.

Sabti, Y. M., Alqatrani, R. I. N., Zaid, M. I., Taengkliang, B., & Kareem, J. M. (2023). Impact of Business Environment on the Performance of Employees in the Public-Listed Companies. *FMDB Transactions on Sustainable Management Letters, 1*(2), 56–65.

Said, F. B., & Tripathi, S. (2023). Epistemology of Digital Journalism Shift in South Global Nations: A Bibliometric Analysis. *FMDB Transactions on Sustainable Technoprise Letters, 1*(1), 47–60.

Saxena, D., Khandare, S., & Chaudhary, S. (2023). An Overview of ChatGPT: Impact on Academic Learning. *FMDB Transactions on Sustainable Techno Learning, 1*(1), 11–20.

Sharma, D. K., Jalil, N. A., Regin, R., Rajest, S. S., Tummala, R. K., & Thangadurai. (2021a). Predicting network congestion with machine learning. In *2021 2nd International Conference on Smart Electronics and Communication (ICOSEC)*. IEEE.

Sharma, D. K., Singh, B., Herman, E., Regine, R., Rajest, S. S., & Mishra, V. P. (2021d). Maximum information measure policies in reinforcement learning with deep energy-based model. In *2021 International Conference on Computational Intelligence and Knowledge Economy (ICCIKE)*. IEEE. 10.1109/ICCIKE51210.2021.9410756

Sharma, D. K., Singh, B., Raja, M., Regin, R., & Rajest, S. S. (2021b). An Efficient Python Approach for Simulation of Poisson Distribution. In *2021 7th International Conference on Advanced Computing and Communication Systems (ICACCS)*. IEEE.

Sharma, D. K., Singh, B., Regin, R., Steffi, R., & Chakravarthi, M. K. (2021c). Efficient Classification for Neural Machines Interpretations based on Mathematical models. In *2021 7th International Conference on Advanced Computing and Communication Systems (ICACCS)*. IEEE.

Srinivas, K., Velmurugan, P. R., & Andiyappillai, N. (2023). Digital Human Resources and Management Support Improve Human Resources Effectiveness. *FMDB Transactions on Sustainable Management Letters, 1*(1), 32–45.

Stalin, G., Meharajan, T., & Venkateswaran, P. S. (2019). Impact of HRM practices on select IT companies' performance in Madurai. *International Journal of Scientific & Technology Research, 8*(12), 169–172.

Storey, J., Ulrich, D., & Wright, P. (2019). *Strategic Human Resource Management: A Research Overview*. . doi:10.4324/9780429490217

Tambaip, B., Hadi, A. F. F., & Tjilen, A. P. (2023). Optimizing Public Service Performance: Unleashing the Potential of Compassion as an Indicator of Public Service Motivation. *FMDB Transactions on Sustainable Management Letters, 1*(2), 46–55.

Tripathi, S., & Al-Shahri, M. (2023). Problems and Prospects on the Evolution of Advertising and Public Relations Industries in Oman. *FMDB Transactions on Sustainable Management Letters, 1*(1), 1–11.

Vashishtha, E., & Dhawan, G. (2023). Comparison of Baldrige Criteria of Strategy Planning and Harrison Text. *FMDB Transactions on Sustainable Management Letters, 1*(1), 22–31.

Vashishtha, E., & Kapoor, H. (2023). Implementation of Blockchain Technology Across International Healthcare Markets. *FMDB Transactions on Sustainable Technoprise Letters*, *1*(1), 1–12.

Venkateswaran, P. S., Sabarirajan, A., Arun, B., Muthupandian, T., & Manimaran, D. S. (2018). Technology Acceptance Model for Making Decision to Purchase Automobile in Coimbatore District. *International Journal of Mechanical Engineering and Technology*, *9*(11), 1608–1613.

Venkateswaran, P. S., Singh, S., Paramasivan, P., Rajest, S. S., Lourens, M. E., & Regin, R. (2023). A Study on The Influence of Quality of Service on Customer Satisfaction Towards Hotel Industry. *FMDB Transactions on Sustainable Social Sciences Letters*, *1*(1), 1–11.

Venkateswaran, P. S., & Viktor, P. (2023). A Study on Brand Equity of Fast-Moving Consumer Goods with Reference to Madurai, Tamil Nadu. *FMDB Transactions on Sustainable Technoprise Letters*, *1*(1), 13–27.

Walton, R. E. (1985). From control to commitment in the workplace. *Harvard Business Review*, *63*(2), 77–84.

Wright, P. M., & Ulrich, M. D. (2017). A road well-traveled: The past, present, and future journey of strategic human resource management. *Annual Review of Organizational Psychology and Organizational Behavior*, *4*(1), 45–65. doi:10.1146/annurev-orgpsych-032516-113052

Chapter 2
Smart HR 4.0 With Impact of Technology Advancement and Industry 4.0 on HR Practices

Praveen Kakada
VIT Business School, Vellore Institute of Technology, Chennai, India

Muhammed Shafi M. K.
https://orcid.org/0000-0001-9113-0780
Vellore Institute of Technology, Chennai, India

ABSTRACT

This study emphasizes the significance of Smart Human Resources 4.0 (Smart HR 4.0) and the effects of Industry 4.0 and technological advancements on HR practices. The developments of Smart HR 4.0 in the HR field are also demonstrated in this chapter, emphasizing planning, organizing, staffing, directing, and controlling. Consequently, exploratory relationships among Smart HR 4.0, technology advancements, and Industry 4.0 are presented based on a systematic review. The chapter discusses the role of Smart HR 4.0 as a recent industrial entry into the human resources field was discussed in this study. A pool of 65 research articles published between 2014 and 2023 from top-tier peer-reviewed journals were considered for further understanding and investigation. In order to successfully navigate the obstacles of the Industry 4.0 revolution, an organization would need a strong Smart HR 4.0 strategy. Emerging technologies like the internet of things, big data, and artificial intelligence will automate most HR processes, creating leaner and more effective HR teams.

1. INTRODUCTION

"Industry 4.0" refers to "smart" and networked production systems designed to observe, anticipate, and interact with the physical world to make decisions that support production in real time. It can increase production productivity, energy efficiency, and sustainability. Decreasing downtime and maintenance expenses boosts production (Pillai and Srivastava, 2022; Rana et al., 2019). According to Shamim et

DOI: 10.4018/979-8-3693-2193-5.ch002

al. (2016), Industry 4.0 ushers in smart factories and businesses' innovation. Businesses use Industry 4.0 technologies to increase productivity and efficiency (Puhovichova & Jankelova, 2022). The field of human resource management is not exempt from Industry 4.0, as various HRM verticals are being updated and automated due to its rise (Sivathanu and Pillai, 2018).

Industrial Revolution 4.0 led to Smart Human Resource 4.0 (Smart HR 4.0). In order to manage human resources across all generations effectively, industry 4.0 technologies are used (Rana et al.,2019; Sivathanu and Pillai, 2018). In order to manage next-generation employees effectively, Smart Human Resources 4.0 (SHR 4.0) is a new concept that is developing as a part of the broader 4th Industrial Revolution. It is characterized by innovations in digital technologies like the Big Data Analytics Internet of Things, artificial intelligence technologies systems (AI), and fast data networks like 4G and 5G (Hecklau et al., 2016). The objectives of "smart HR" are to assist the development of a high-performing staff, link human resources initiatives with the broader company plan, and improve employee satisfaction (Munsamy et al., 2019; Verma et al., 2020).

One area where smart HR 4.0 is likely to have a significant impact is talent management. With the help of predictive analytics and AI, smart HR 4.0 will identify the skills and competencies most in demand in the labor market, allowing organizations to quickly adapt to changing workforce needs. In recent years, the human resources (HR) field has significantly transformed due to technological advancements and the rise of Industry 4.0 (Pillai and Srivastava, 2022). This transformation has led to the emergence of "smart HR 4.0," which refers to using digital technologies and data-driven approaches to improve HR processes and decision-making. Research in this area has focused on exploring the influence of Industry 4.0 on HR and the benefits and challenges of adopting these technologies.

Compiling a complete list of essential competencies for work in a digitalized and networked society was observed, and even though each profession has unique requirements, human resource development must meet the identified competencies that are gaining importance (Verma et al., 2020). In addition, all detected competencies were grouped into a radar graphic, allowing the user to comprehend the criteria imposed on particular competencies (Hecklaua et al., 2016). In the second section of this work, a broad application approach for the competency model was explored briefly. It demonstrated how the model may evaluate and cultivate an employee's competencies to face future issues.

Another research lays forth a theoretical structure for organizational performance using dynamic capabilities developed due to Smart HRM 4.0 practices (Pillai et al., 2022). Industry 4.0 is an upcoming domain in the industrial revolution that is widening daily. Several types of research have been done and are in progress regarding several areas under Industry 4.0. Similarly, researchers have concluded that transitioning to Industry 4.0 requires a great change from traditional human resource practices to keep up with the demands of such a volatile industry and market (Gupta et al., 2019; Puhovichova et al., 2022).

While most of these researches have concluded that the Human resource management process must undergo major changes soon, there is a significant research gap in the techniques and methods required to adapt to the demands of Industry 4.0. Hecklaua et al. (2016) proposed a comprehensive list of essential competencies for a job in the modern digital and interconnected world. These competencies provide a list of skills one must acquire to survive in the human resource market during the upcoming industrial revolution. Also, there have been some controversies and conflicts concerning different authors on whether Smart HR 4.0 brings more jobs to the human resource management team or cuts down and reduces the workload (Brozzi et al., 2020; Dıaz-Chao et al., 2021).

Sivathanu et al. (2018) have concluded that the upcoming technologies, such as AI and Data, will automate most of the typical HRM processes, leading to leaner human resource management teams.

However, it can also be argued that the demands of the new industry require a very detailed analysis of the employees during recruitment to match the rapidly changing roles to technological developments (Bag et al., 2020; Rana et al., 2019). These contradictory views have their arguments, but both stand true in their respective approaches. Implementing the technologies mentioned will automate traditional HRM jobs, such as candidate filtering during recruitment, conducting recruitment assessments, etc. However, the human resources team does need to become more efficient and critical in the final selection of the candidates and providing the necessary skills through various processes (Bag et al., 2020).

The purpose of smart HR is to utilize technology and data-driven approaches to improve human resource management practices. The aim is to streamline HR processes, improve decision-making, increase efficiency and productivity, and provide employees with a better experience. This can include automating HR tasks, analyzing workforce data, improving communication and collaboration among HR and employees, and providing HR leaders with valuable insights and analytics. By adopting smart HR practices, organizations aim to create a more effective and efficient HR function that supports the organization's overall success (Burmeister, 2015).

So, this research aims The current investigation systematically review research on Smart HR 4.0 by conceptually reviewing 65 articles from top-tier journals. The important questions studied in this study are:

- What is the role of Smart 4.0 and Industry 4.0 specifically in the context of HR practices?
- What is the impact of Industry 4.0 and technology advancements on HR Practices?
- What is the motive behind the flow of technology advancements, and lately, how are these industry 4.0 dynamics interconnected with Smart 4.0?
- What are the upcoming study openings to address the research gaps related to Smart 4.0 and Industry 4.0 technologies?

2. LITERATURE REVIEW

Edwin Filippo defined Human Resource Management as "planning, organizing, directing, controlling procurement, development, compensation, integration, maintenance, and separation of human resources to achieve individual, organizational, and social objectives". Also, management was divided into 5 functions by Koontz and O'Donnel: Planning, Organizing, Staffing, Directing, and Controlling. Informed data contributes to the production of items that are produced in a manner that is more productive and efficient. The flexibility of manufacturers is increased so that they may better satisfy the demands of their customers through the use of mass customization, which ultimately seeks to attain efficiency with, in many circumstances, a lot size of one (Rabindran et al., 2015; Sivathanu and Pillai, 2020). A smart factory can attain information transparency and make better judgments because it collects more data from the factory floor and combines that data with other company operating processes.

Smart Human Resource (Smart HR) 4.0 states the combination of progressive technologies, such as machine learning and artificial intelligence, with traditional human resource management practices. This integration aims to enhance HRM's effectiveness and efficiency and improve the employee experience. (Rostami et al., 2020). In the context of Industry 4.0, smart HRM practices involve using data analytics, predictive technologies, and digital tools to support various HR functions, such as recruiting, performance management, and employee development. For example, using artificial intelligence in recruitment can help organizations identify the best candidates for a particular role by analyzing large amounts of data and predicting a candidate's fit. (Mendenhall et al., 2018). Smart HRM in Industry 4.0 can influence employee experience and enhance the overall efficiency and effectiveness of HRM practices (Rathore & Mehrotra, 2021; Sivathanu and Pillai, 2020). However, it is important for organizations to carefully consider the ethical and privacy implications of these technologies and ensure that they are being used responsibly and transparently.

Integrating new technologies and digitalization significantly impacts the HRM function, affecting various aspects such as recruitment, training and development, compensation, and performance management. One of the primary factors affecting HRM in Industry 4.0 is the change in the skillset required for the workforce. With the technological advancement of Artificial Intelligence (AI) enabled systems and the Internet of Things (IoT), there is an increased demand for employees with digital skills such as data analysis, technological intelligence systems, software development, and cybersecurity (Sivathanu and Pillai, 2020). HR departments must identify the skills needed for their organization and implement strategies to acquire and retain the right talent. Another factor is the shift in the traditional job roles and responsibilities. With the integration of technology, many tasks previously performed by humans are now automated (Boström, 2017). HR departments must provide employees with the necessary training and development opportunities to adapt to the changing job requirements. Moreover, they must also plan for a smooth transition for those employees whose jobs may become obsolete.

The impact of Industry 4.0 on HRM also extends to the employee experience. With the increase in automation, there is a need for HR departments to provide employees with a workplace environment that promotes collaboration, creativity, and innovation (Rathore & Mehrotra, 2021). Additionally, HR departments must develop innovative reward and recognition programs aligning with the organization's digital transformation journey. The effective usage of technology in HRM practices also affects the recruitment process. With the advent of online recruitment platforms, HR departments can access a larger pool of potential candidates and quickly identify the best fit for their organization (Bag et al., 2020; Fernández-Aráoz, 2019). However, HR departments must also ensure that their recruitment processes are inclusive and do not discriminate against any demographic group. Finally, privacy and data security are crucial concerns in the HRM function in Industry 4.0. With the increasing use of technology, HR departments have access to vast amounts of personal and sensitive employee information (Rabindran et al., 2015). HR departments must ensure proper security protocols to protect this information and comply with privacy laws.

In Smart HRM, diversity and inclusion, employee well-being, and talent management significantly shape the overall human resource management approach. These constructs are often multi-faceted and complex, requiring a deeper understanding and analysis to measure their impact in the workplace effectively. One key construct of Smart HRM in Industry 4.0 is employee well-being. This construct recognizes the importance of ensuring employees' physical, emotional, and mental well-being in the workplace (Adolph et al., 2014; Armstrong and Taylor, 2016). In the context of Industry 4.0, employee well-being can be enhanced through technology, such as wearable devices and virtual reality, to monitor and improve various aspects of employee health and well-being. (Ngai et al., 2019).

Another important construct in Smart HRM is talent management, which refers to the processes and strategies used to identify, attract, retain, and develop top talent. In Industry 4.0, talent management is transformed by using data analytics and predictive technologies, which allow organizations to understand their employees better and make informed decisions about talent development and management. (Mendenhall et al., 2018). Finally, diversity and inclusion a key constructs in Smart HRM in Industry 4.0, recognizing the importance of creating an inclusive workplace that respects all employees, regardless of their race, gender, ethnicity, sexual orientation, or other characteristics. In the context of Industry 4.0, technology can play a significant role in promoting diversity and inclusion by providing access to diverse perspectives and experiences and automating and reducing bias in HR processes. (Watson & Taylor, 2020).

Smart HRM in Industry 4.0 represents a significant opportunity for organizations to improve HR practices and enhance the employee experience. By leveraging advanced technologies and data analytics, organizations can improve various aspects of HR, such as recruitment, performance management, and employee well-being, while promoting workplace diversity and inclusion.

2.1. Relationship Between Smart HR 4.0, Industry 4.0, and Technological Advancements

Smart HR 4.0, on the other hand, refers to integrating technology into the human resources function. It involves using data analytics, machine learning, and other advanced technologies to support various HR practices, from recruitment to talent retention. The aim of Smart HR 4.0 is to enhance the efficiency and effectiveness of HR processes, improve employee experience, and support business objectives. Smart HR 4.0 allows organizations to revolutionize their human resources processes and benefit from increased efficiency, improved customer satisfaction, and enhanced management capabilities. Organizations can gain a competitive edge in the marketplace by understanding the implications of Smart HR 4.0 and developing strategies to capitalize on its potential. The human resource department must adapt its HR procedures to the rapidly shifting technology environment as new-age technologies become more prevalent in today's cutthroat economy (Rathore & Mehrotra, 2021; Rana et al., 2019).

Technologies driven by the next generation's workforce can change HR procedures and give the company some advantages, which is why Smart HR 4.0 is becoming increasingly popular (Sivathanu and Pillai, 2018). Industry 4.0 with technological processes and Smart HR 4.0 are two key trends shaping the work's future. They are both related to the Fourth Industrial Revolution and technology integration in different workplace areas. The association between Smart HR 4.0 and Industry 4.0 can be described as interdependent, as they impact and support each other in several ways.

Workforce Transformation: Industry 4.0 is leading to a transformation of the workforce, with a shift towards more technologically skilled workers. This change in the workforce composition also affects HR processes, requiring companies to invest in upskilling and reskilling their employees. Smart HR 4.0 supports this transformation by providing new tools and platforms to help employees acquire new skills and knowledge. For example, smart HR systems can identify skills gaps and suggest learning and development programs to fill those gaps (Verma et al., 2020).

Data-Driven Decision Making: Due to Industry 4.0, enormous volumes of data are being generated that may be used to guide decisions. These data are being used by Smart HR 4.0 to assist HR procedures like hiring, performance evaluation, and employee involvement. Data analytics, for instance, can be utilized to comprehend employee engagement and pinpoint the elements that lead to high levels of employee satisfaction (Lasi et al.,2014; Rojko, 2017). According to a PWC study, businesses that use data and analytics in their HR procedures are more likely to see higher employee happiness and engagement levels.

Employee Experience: Industry 4.0 is leading to changes in how work is done, with a greater emphasis on collaboration, flexibility, and the usage of technology-enabled software systems. Smart HR 4.0 supports this shift by providing employees with new tools and platforms to support collaboration and improve their overall experience at work. For example, smart HR systems can automate repetitive tasks and allow HR professionals to focus on strategic initiatives, leading to a more positive employee experience (Rabindran & Bozic, 2015).

Talent Acquisition: Industry 4.0 is leading to a greater demand for technologically skilled workers, making it more challenging for companies to find the right talent. Smart HR 4.0 is addressing this challenge by leveraging data and advanced technologies to support talent acquisition processes, such as sourcing, screening, and interviewing. For example, AI-powered recruitment systems can analyze large amounts of candidate data to identify the best-fit candidates for a specific role (Sivathanu and Pillai, 2018).

Different research has shown that big data analytics can be used to improve the accuracy and reliability of employee performance evaluations and identify areas where employees need additional training and development (Verevka, 2019). Some of the major findings and additional research include the following -

a. **Increased efficiency:** The adoption of Industry 4.0 technologies in HR, such as AI-powered recruitment systems and big data analytics, has improved the efficiency and accuracy of HR processes.
b. **Improved decision-making:** Using big data analytics can provide valuable insights into employee behavior and satisfaction and help organizations make better HR decisions.
c. **Increased employee engagement and satisfaction**: Organizations that have adopted Industry 4.0 technologies in HR have reported improved employee engagement and satisfaction (Cascio, 2016).
d. **Privacy and security concerns:** There are concerns about the potential for privacy and security breaches when using Industry 4.0 technologies in HR.
e. **Algorithmic bias:** There is a risk of algorithmic bias in decision-making when using AI in HR, which can lead to discrimination.

Importance of ethics and legal compliance: The adoption of Industry 4.0 technologies in HR raises important ethical and legal considerations, such as data privacy and fair treatment of employees (Burmeister et al., 2015; Cascio, 2016). There is a strong association between Smart HR 4.0 and Industry 4.0 because the two are interdependent. Industry 4.0 requires a highly-skilled, flexible workforce that can adapt to changing circumstances. This means that organizations need a robust HR strategy to recruit, retain, and develop this workforce (Fernández-Aráoz, 2019).

At the same time, developing a smart HR 4.0 intellectual strategy can support the goals of Industry 4.0. For example, advanced technologies such as machine learning and predictive analytics can help HR professionals make more informed decisions about staffing and employee development. This, in turn, can help organizations build a workforce better equipped to support the goals of Industry 4.0 (Ravindran et al., 2015). Given the close relationship between Industry 4.0 and Smart HR 4.0, it is reasonable to formulate the hypothesis: Integrating Industry 4.0 technologies in HR management will improve the efficiency and effectiveness of HR processes.

3. METHODOLOGY

3.1 Data Collection and Procedure

The research articles published in prestigious leading journals between 2013 and 2023 comprise the data set for the current study. 2013 was chosen as the starting date for the analysis to account for two decades of investigation in this century. Instead of doing specific population research, we aimed to identify trends using a broad sample; thus, we made every effort to find as many publications as possible for the periods mentioned earlier. The following keywords were used in a literature search from the Emerald, EBSCO, Scopus, and Web of Science (WoS) databases: "Smart HR 4.0," "Industry 4.0," "Revolution 4.0," "Technology Advancements," and "Smart HR Practises." A thorough search was conducted using these terms in combination, ensuring that the most relevant articles were involved in this systematic review.

We could observe trends over a longer time frame thanks to the search window of 2013 to 2023 (inclusive). One team member screened each pertinent paper to ensure it was appropriate for review. Our analysis covered 65 research papers, of which 52 (80%) were empirical studies, 10 (15%) were reviews or conceptual papers, and 3 (3%) were conceptual with practical applications. These studies were disseminated in reputable, peer-reviewed journals. Throughout our search period, we did our best to incorporate pertinent publications on the subject published in scholarly journals.

3.2. Data analysis

An Excel spreadsheet was used to enter the data from the chosen publications for further investigation. Additionally, the writers rated the correctness of twenty articles at random. The following details were entered into our spreadsheet for each article: the year of publication, the name of the journal, the type of article (Review vs. empirical), methods of research (quantitative, qualitative, or mix), the key findings, the type of (Smart HR 4.0, Industry 4.0 and Advance Technologies).

In order to summarize the results of this study, all the themes and keywords were generated from the Excel sheet of each column. The articles' titles, keywords, and subheadings were primarily used to identify the themes/Smart HR 4.0 being examined. After that, they were divided into more comprehensive categories: Smart HR 4.0, Industry 4.0, Technology developments, and HRM practices. One researcher carried out these methods, another checked them, and the main researcher confirmed them. Our strategy is comparable to that of Cooke et al. (2019).

4. DISCUSSION

Our investigation sought to discover Smart HR 4.0 and Industry 4.0 to combine research in a discrete sector. Influence on HR practice progressed in technology advancements. The analysis identified 5 specific core activities of HR managers would effectively manage through our understanding of Smart 4.0.

Planning: According to Koontz, "Planning is deciding in advance - what to do, when to do & how to do. It bridges the gap from where we are & where we want to be". Planning is key in the management process, connecting the present to the future. As the scale of an organization increases, the scope of planning and volumes to handle get very high, leading to excessive workload for HRM personnel and increasing the chances of any errors in the plans. So, incorporating I4.0 technologies such as Artificial Intelligence and Machine Learning in HRM Planning allows the organization to plan multiple operations with proper coordination and efficiency. Another way in which Smart HR 4.0 is disrupting HRM planning is through the use of predictive analytics (Biswas, 2021). Analyzing such data allows the necessary actions to be easily identified and implemented.

Smart HR 4.0 is enabling organizations to improve their workforce planning through the use of scenario planning. Scenario planning is a strategic method that involves creating multiple scenarios of possible futures and developing plans to address each scenario (Niraj & Kashyap, 2019). By creating scenarios based on potential changes in the business environment, such as changes in market conditions or new technology, HR professionals can develop workforce plans that are flexible and adaptable. A study conducted by McKinsey found that companies that use scenario planning are better able to anticipate and respond to changes in the business environment than those that do not (McKinsey & Company, 2019). The study also found that companies that use scenario planning are more likely to achieve their strategic objectives and outperform their peers.

Organizing: Henry Fayol states, "To organize a business is to provide it with everything useful or its functioning, i.e., raw material, tools, capital, and personnel". In the context of Smart HR 4.0, organizing involves using technology and data analytics to optimize the HR function and support the organization's overall goals. One of the most significant contributions of Smart HR 4.0 to organizing is making an impact in assigning roles. HR professionals can use data analytics tools to match employees' skill sets with specific organizational job roles. This approach can help organizations identify the best candidate for a particular role, increasing employee satisfaction and productivity (Gupta & Pandey, 2021). This process can also help reduce the time to recruit new employees and avoid potential mismatches.

Smart HR 4.0 can also enhance coordination and collaboration within organizations. HR professionals can use project management tools that enable effective communication and collaboration among team members. Using these tools allows employees to work collaboratively, regardless of their physical location. Also, a centralized communication system allows different departments and geographical locations to effectively and quickly communicate in a very organized and reliable manner. This approach can increase efficiency, lower costs, and improve performance. (Rathore & Mehrotra, 2021).

Staffing: According to Koontz & O'Donnell, "Managerial function of staffing involves operating the organization structure through proper and effective selection, appraisal & development of personnel to fill the roles designed in the structure". A smart HR can greatly assist in managing human resources planning by providing insights into workforce demographics, skill sets, and future needs. Smart HR can use technology to automate and streamline the recruitment process, reducing the time and resources required to fill positions. By using advanced analytics and AI tools, smart HR can identify candidates with the right skills and experience and those who are the best fit for the organization's culture.

Smart HR can identify gaps in the organization's current skill set and develop strategies to address these gaps. This can be done by analyzing workforce data and identifying key areas where additional training or hiring may be necessary. This can help better fit the available workforce and the organization's needs. Predictive analytics can help in forecasting future workforce needs and requirements. This can be done by analyzing workforce data, industry trends, and economic forecasts to develop accurate predictions about future workforce needs. This can help in planning for hiring, training, and development initiatives. Smart HR can also help develop and implement talent management strategies to ensure the organization has the right people in the right positions.

Directing: According to Ernest Dale, "Direction is telling people what to do and seeing that they do it to the best of their ability. It includes making assignments, corresponding procedures, seeing that mistakes are corrected, providing on-the-job instructions, and, of course, issuing orders". One of the key functions of management impacted by Smart HR 4.0 is the directing function, which involves setting goals and objectives, communicating them to employees, and motivating them to achieve them. Smart HR 4.0 gives managers the tools to set and communicate clear employee goals and objectives. By leveraging big data analytics and AI, managers can now access real-time data on employee performance and use this data to set personalized goals and targets that align with the organization's overall objectives [41]. This personalized approach to goal-setting helps to increase employee engagement and motivation, as employees feel a sense of ownership over their goals and are more likely to be committed to achieving them.

Smart HR 4.0 is helping managers to improve communication with employees. With the help of collaboration tools, such as instant messaging, video conferencing, and social media, managers can now communicate with employees more effectively, regardless of their location or time zone. This improved communication helps build stronger relationships between managers and employees, improving employee engagement and reducing turnover. It is also helping managers to track employee performance and give real-time feedback. Performance management software and technologies allow managers to collect, evaluate, and deliver real-time feedback on employee performance. Real-time feedback motivates and engages employees since they can see the results of their efforts and modify them to meet their goals.

Controlling: According to Theo Heiman, "Controlling is the process of checking whether or not proper progress is being made towards the objectives and goals and acting, if necessary, to correct any deviation". An efficient system of control helps to predict deviations before they occur. A smart HR can help ensure performance goals are clearly defined, specific, and measurable. This will make it easier to track progress and determine whether goals have been achieved or not. A smart HR can help identify deviations from goals by utilizing data analytics and performance tracking systems.

By collecting and analyzing data on employee performance, HR can identify patterns and trends that may indicate a deviation from goals. For example, suppose an employee consistently falls short of their targets or deadlines. In that case, HR can work with that employee to identify the underlying reasons for the performance gap and develop strategies to address it (Andreas et al., 2022). Smart HR 4.0 is helping managers to automate routine tasks, such as data entry and report generation, allowing them to focus on more strategic activities. With the help of automation tools, managers can now streamline the data collection and analysis process, freeing up time for more meaningful activities such as coaching and mentoring employees. This shift towards more strategic activities helps managers to improve employee engagement and productivity.

5. IMPLICATIONS AND CONTRIBUTIONS

The 4th industrial revolution, also known as Industry 4.0, has substantially influenced Human Resources Practices that operate within organizations. Smart HR 4.0 refers to applying Industry 4.0 intelligent technologies to HR functions. According to a survey conducted by Deloitte, 64% of companies are already using advanced technologies to manage their workforce, and another 26% plan to do so soon (Deloitte, 2019). Furthermore, 69% of these companies believe that Industry 4.0 will significantly impact their HR strategies and processes. One of the main ways in which Industry 4.0 technologies are disrupting HR is through data analytics. With the help of AI and machine learning, HR professionals can collect and analyze vast amounts of data on employee performance, engagement, and satisfaction. This information can be used to identify patterns and trends, allowing HR to make data-driven decisions that lead to better outcomes for the organization and its employees (Capelli et al., 2018).

Another way in which Industry 4.0 is changing HR is through the use of virtual and augmented reality (VR and AR) in training and development. VR and AR technologies enable employees to experience real-life scenarios in a simulated environment, making training for complex or dangerous situations easier. This approach improves training effectiveness, reduces costs, and eliminates the need for physical training facilities (Kaur & Singh, 2021). Industry 4.0 is also disrupting traditional recruitment processes.

With AI-powered recruitment tools, companies can screen many job applications quickly and accurately, using algorithms to identify the most suitable candidates. This approach saves time and reduces bias in the hiring process (O'Neil & Achter, 2018).

5.1. Suggestions and Recommendations

When determining whether or not to implement Smart HR 4.0, it is vital to consider the possible benefits and obstacles that may arise carefully. The following are some suggestions and advice that can be helpful for businesses interested in implementing Smart HR 4.0: Before implementing Smart HR 4.0, businesses should determine whether or not they are prepared to follow this methodology. This includes assessing the organization's existing IT infrastructure, data capabilities, and HR procedures to evaluate whether or not they are prepared for the change necessary for Smart HR 4.0 to be implemented. New skill sets and capabilities are required of HR professionals for them to implement Smart HR 4.0 effectively. As a result, businesses should invest in employee training and development programs to guarantee that HR professionals have the appropriate knowledge and abilities to thrive in an environment based on Smart HR 4.0.

Similarly, Industry 4.0 involves a combination of various new and firstly developing technologies, so it requires a substantial investment in the technology itself and appropriate employees to manage the same to keep up with the developments. Concerns relating to data collecting, processing, and usage are key ethical and privacy issues raised by the deployment of Smart HR 4.0. Companies should address these concerns proactively by developing clear policies and guidelines for collecting and using data and ensuring that these policies are effectively communicated to employees. In addition, companies should ensure that they protect employees' personal information confidentiality. In short, companies ready to embrace this transformation should carefully evaluate their readiness, define clear objectives and goals, develop a roadmap for implementation, invest in employee training and development, and address ethical and privacy concerns. By taking these steps, organizations can successfully implement Smart HR 4.0 and reap the benefits of this transformative approach to HR.

5.2. Future Direction of Research

Several areas could be researched in the future in the field of smart HR, including:

- Artificial intelligence and machine learning: Developing new AI and machine learning algorithms to support and enhance HR processes, such as recruitment, performance evaluation, and talent management.
- Employee engagement and well-being: Studying the impact of smart HR technologies on employee engagement, well-being, and job satisfaction and identifying ways to enhance these outcomes further.
- Data privacy and security: Investigating the challenges and best practices for protecting employee data in the context of smart HR systems.
- Integration with other HR technologies: Examining the potential benefits of integrating smart HR systems with other HR technologies, such as employee benefits and payroll systems.
- Globalization and diversity: Investigating how smart HR systems can support HR practices in a global context and address the challenges of diversity and inclusivity in the workplace.

6. CONCLUSION

This systematic review emphasized Smart Human Resources 4.0 (Smart HR 4.0) and the effects of Industry 4.0 and technological advancements on HR practices. In conclusion, Smart HR 4.0 is a transformative approach to HR that leverages advanced technologies and principles of Industry 4.0 to improve HR practices. With the help of big data analytics, AI, and other advanced technologies, Smart HR 4.0 enables organizations to make more informed decisions, enhance employee engagement and productivity, and improve overall organizational performance. While there are challenges to implementing Smart HR 4.0, such as the need for new skill sets and the need to address ethical concerns related to data privacy, the benefits of this approach to HR are clear. As organizations increasingly adopt Smart HR 4.0, the HR industry will continue to evolve, providing new opportunities and challenges for HR professionals and organizations alike.

In conclusion, the Smart HR 4.0 and Industry 4.0 associations are complex and interdependent. By implementing a Smart HR 4.0 plan, organizations can support the goals of Industry 4.0 and build a highly-skilled, flexible, and adaptable workforce. At the same time, Industry 4.0 initiatives can drive the development of Smart HR 4.0 strategies by creating a need for a more agile and responsive workforce. Overall, Smart HR is a promising technology that can potentially transform the HR industry. It can help organizations to become more efficient, effective, and employee-centric. However, it is essential to carefully consider the risks and challenges associated with the technology and develop strategies to mitigate them.

REFERENCES

Adolph, S., Tisch, M., & Metternich, J. (2014). Challenges and approaches to competency development for future production. *Journal of International Scientific Publications – Educational Alternatives, 12*(8), 1001-1010.

Armstrong, M., & Taylor, S. (2016). *Armstrong's Handbook of Human Resource Management Practice* (13th ed.). Kogan.

Bag, S., Gupta, S., & Luo, Z. (2020). Examining the role of logistics 4.0 enabled dynamic capabilities on firm performance. *International Journal of Logistics Management, 31*(3), 607–628. doi:10.1108/IJLM-11-2019-0311

Biswas, A. (2021). The impact of Industry 4.0 on HR. *The Journal of Business Strategy, 42*(1), 44–53.

Boström, M. (2017). The Fourth Industrial Revolution: How digitization is transforming human resources. *Human Resource Management Review, 27*(4), 600–612.

Brozzi, R., Forti, D., Rauch, E., & Matt, D. T. (2020). The advantages of Industry 4.0 applications for sustainability: Results from a sample of manufacturing companies. *Sustainability (Basel), 12*(9), 3647. doi:10.3390u12093647

Burmeister, C., Luettgens, D., & Piller, F. T. (2015). Business model innovation for industry 4.0: Why the "how connections, sensors, and data are revolutionizing business". *Harvard Business Review.*

Capelli, P., Neely, A., & Stiehl, B. (2018). *Strategic human capital: A new approach to talent management in the age of uncertainty*. Harvard Business Review Press.

Cascio, W. F. (2016). *Managing human resources: Productivity, quality of work life, profits* (7th ed.). McGraw-Hill/Irwin.

Deloitte. (2019). *Industry 4.0 and the future of work*. https://www2.deloitte.com/content/dam/Deloitte/lu/Documents/technology/lu-en-industry-4-0-future-work.pdf

Díaz-Chao, Á., Ficapal-Cusí, P., & Torrent-Sellens, J. (2021). Environmental assets, Industry 4.0 technologies and firm performance in Spain: A dynamic capabilities path to reward sustainability. *Journal of Cleaner Production*, *281*, 125264. doi:10.1016/j.jclepro.2020.125264

Felsberger, A., Qaiser, F. H., Choudhary, A., & Reiner, G. (2022). The impact of Industry 4.0 on the reconciliation of dynamic capabilities: Evidence from the European manufacturing industries. *Production Planning and Control*, *33*(2-3), 277–300. doi:10.1080/09537287.2020.1810765

Fernández-Aráoz, C. (2019). The future of work: Building a people-centered organization. *MIT Sloan Management Review*, *60*(2), 12–16.

Gupta, S., Qian, X., Bhushan, B., & Luo, Z. (2019). Role of cloud ERP and big data on firm performance: A dynamic capability view theory perspective. *Management Decision*, *57*(8), 1857–1882. doi:10.1108/MD-06-2018-0633

Hecklau, F., Galeitzke, M., Flachs, S., & Kohl, H. (2016). Holistic approach for human resource management in industry 4.0. *Procedia CIRP*, *54*, 1–6. doi:10.1016/j.procir.2016.05.102

International Chamber of Shipping. (n.d.). *Shamika Sirimanne*. Retrieved March 31, 2023, from https://www.ics-shipping.org/person/shamika-sirimanne/

Jerman, A., Pejić Bach, M., & Aleksić, A. (2019). Transformation towards smart factory system: Examining new job profiles and competencies. *Systems Research and Behavioral Science*, *37*(2), 388–402. doi:10.1002res.2657

Jin, G., Sperandio, S., & Girard, P. (2017). Management of the design process: Human resource allocation in factories of the future. *Insight - International Council on Systems Engineering*, *20*(4), 19–22. doi:10.1002/inst.12175

Kambur, E., & Yildirim, T. (2022). From traditional to smart human resources management. *International Journal of Manpower*. Advance online publication. doi:10.1108/IJM-10-2021-0622

Kang, J., Kim, H., Kim, H., & Kim, S. (2019). The impact of Industry 4.0 on human resource management: A literature review. *Sustainability*, *11*(13), 3.

Kaur, R., & Singh, D. (2021). Industry 4.0 and HRD: Reimagining the future of workplace learning and development. In Redesigning Work in the Fourth Industrial Revolution (pp. 147-159). Springer.

Lasi, H., Fettke, P., Kemper, H., Feld, T., & Hoffmann, M. (2014). Industry 4.0. *Business & Information Systems Engineering*, *6*(4), 239–242. doi:10.100712599-014-0334-4

Mendenhall, M. E., Lee, J., & Yasin, M. M. (2018). Talent management in the context of Industry 4.0. *Journal of World Business*, *53*(4), 410–417.

Mukhuty, S., Upadhyay, A., & Rothwell, H. (2022). Strategic sustainable development of Industry 4.0 through the lens of social responsibility: The role of human resource practices. *Business Strategy and the Environment*, *31*(5), 2068–2081. doi:10.1002/bse.3008

Munsamy, M., & Telukdarie, A. (2019). Digital HRM model for process optimization by adoption of Industry 4.0 technologies. *Proceedings of the IEEE International Conference on Industrial Engineering and Engineering Management*, 374-378. 10.1109/IEEM44572.2019.8978726

Ngai, E. W. T., & Cheng, T. C. E. (2019). Employee well-being in Industry 4.0: A review of literature. *International Journal of Human Resource Management*, *30*(16), 2265–2282.

Niraj, R., & Kashyap, G. (2019). Scenario planning: A tool for strategic thinking. *Business Horizons*, *62*(4), 563–573.

O'Neil, K., & Achter, T. (2018). Disruptive trends in workforce development. *Journal of Workforce Development*, *12*(1), 1–1.

Pillai, R., & Srivastava, K. B. L. (2022). Smart HRM 4.0 for achieving organizational performance: A dynamic capability view perspective. *International Journal of Productivity and Performance Management*. Advance online publication. doi:10.1108/IJPPM-04-2022-0174

Pillai, R., Yadav, S., Sivathanu, B., Kaushik, N., & Goel, P. (2022). Use of 4.0 (I4.0) technology in HRM: A pathway toward SHRM 4.0 and HR performance. *Foresight*, *24*(6), 708–727. doi:10.1108/FS-06-2021-0128

Puhovichova, D., & Jankelova, N. (2022). *Changes of human resource management in the context of the impact of the fourth industrial revolution*. Retrieved from https://stumejournals.com/journals/i4/2020/3/138.full.pdf

Rabindran, R., & Bozic, D. (2015). A study of privacy and data security in human resource management. *International Journal of Information Management*, *35*(6), 586–595.

Rana, G., & Sharma, R. (2019). Emerging human resource management practices in Industry 4.0. *Strategic HR Review*, *18*(4), 18. doi:10.1108/SHR-01-2019-0003

Rathore, M., & Mehrotra, D. (2021). Smart HR 4.0: Enabling Industry 4.0 through HRM. In *Industry 4.0 and Smart Manufacturing* (pp. 133–144). Springer.

Rojko, A. (2017). Industry 4.0 concept: Background and overview. *International Journal of Interactive Mobile Technologies*, *11*(5), 77–89. doi:10.3991/ijim.v11i5.7072

Rostami, P., Ramezani, M., & Sabri, M. (2020). Smart human resource management: A review of literature. *International Journal of Information Management*, *52*, 101653.

Shamim, S., Cang, S., Yu, H., & Li, Y. (2016). Management approaches for industry 4.0: A human resource management perspective. In *2016 IEEE Congress on Evolutionary Computation (CEC)* (pp. 5309-5316). IEEE. 10.1109/CEC.2016.7748365

Shaw, P., & Varghese, R. M. (2018). Industry 4.0 and future of HR. *Journal of Management*, *5*(6), 96–103.

Sivathanu, B., & Pillai, R. (2020). Technology and talent analytics for talent management: A game changer for organizational performance. *The International Journal of Organizational Analysis*, *28*(2), 457–473. doi:10.1108/IJOA-01-2019-1634

Sivathanu, B. B., & Pillai, B. (2018). Smart HR 4.0: How industry 4.0 is disrupting HR. *Human Resource Management International Digest*, *26*(4), 7–11. doi:10.1108/HRMID-04-2018-0059

Verevka, T. V. (2019). *Development of industry 4.0 in the hotel and restaurant business*. IBIMA Business Review. doi:10.5171/2019.324071

Verma, A., Bansal, M., & Verma, J. (2020). *Industry 4.0: Reshaping the future of HR*. Strategic Direction., doi:10.1108/SD-12-2019-0235

Watson, D., & Taylor, S. (2020). Diversity and inclusion in Industry 4.0: The role of technology. *Human Resource Management Review*, *30*(2), 181–192.

Chapter 3
A Comprehensive Review on Leveraging Business Intelligence for Enhanced Marketing Analytics

P. S. Venkateswaran
https://orcid.org/0000-0001-8958-103X
PSNA College of Engineering and Technology, India

Divya Marupaka
https://orcid.org/0009-0005-1893-4842
Unikon IT Inc., USA

Sachin Parate
Twillio, USA

Amit Bhanushali
https://orcid.org/0009-0005-3358-1299
Independent Researcher, USA

Latha Thammareddi
https://orcid.org/0009-0005-6338-7972
DXC Technology, USA

P. Paramasivan
Dhaanish Ahmed College of Engineering, India

ABSTRACT

In the rapidly evolving landscape of marketing, data-driven decision-making has become paramount for organizations seeking a competitive edge. This chapter presents a comprehensive review of the applications and impact of business intelligence (BI) in the realm of marketing analytics. The research aims to elucidate the multifaceted relationship between BI and marketing analytics, explore the benefits and challenges, and provide insights into emerging trends. The study employs a mixed-method research design involving both qualitative and quantitative approaches, including an extensive literature review and surveys. It examines how BI tools and practices empower marketing professionals with data-driven insights for more effective decision-making and marketing strategy optimization. The chapter discusses key applications, benefits, challenges, and emerging trends in the integration of BI and marketing analytics.

DOI: 10.4018/979-8-3693-2193-5.ch003

1. INTRODUCTION

In the digital age, where consumers are inundated with choices and information, businesses must adapt their marketing strategies to remain relevant and competitive (Abdel Azeem et al., 2021). This necessitates a fundamental shift from traditional marketing practices to data-driven decision-making underpinned by marketing analytics (Alabdullah et al., 2021a). This chapter elucidates the critical importance of marketing analytics in modern business, emphasizing its role in customer-centricity, campaign optimization, competitive advantage, impact measurement, agility, and personalization (Alabdullah et al., 2021b). Industry 5.0 opens up many opportunities for businesses and industries, such as increased productivity, customization, better decision-making, and sustainable growth (Venkateswaran, 2023; Al-Abyadh & Abdel Azeem, 2022).

In the dynamic and highly competitive landscape of modern business, the importance of marketing analytics cannot be overstated (Alayli, 2023). This indispensable tool has evolved from being a valuable asset to becoming the very lifeblood of effective marketing strategies and business success (Al-Abrat, & Alabyad, 2021). In an era characterized by rapid technological advancements, ever-changing consumer preferences, and inundation of data, marketing analytics has emerged as the guiding light for organizations seeking not just survival but also thriving in the digital age (Alabdullah and Ahmed, 2021; Venkitaraman & Kosuru, 2023).

The cornerstone of marketing analytics is data-driven decision-making, a paradigm shift that has revolutionized the way businesses operate (Al-maaitah et al., 2021). It has transformed marketing from an art into a science, where every move is based on empirical evidence rather than mere intuition (An et al., 2023; Balas-Timar & Ignat, 2015). This introduction delves into the paramount importance of marketing analytics in the context of modern business and underscores the growing significance of data-driven decision-making (Al-maaitah et al., 2021).

The digital revolution, the proliferation of e-commerce, and the ubiquity of smartphones have ushered in an era where consumers are more informed, connected, and discerning than ever before (Rad et al., 2020). In this environment, marketing has evolved from a one-way communication channel to a dynamic, interactive, and data-rich discipline (Rad et al., 2022). Marketing analytics is the linchpin that enables businesses to thrive amidst these changes (Demeter et al., 2021).

Visualization tools transform raw data into intuitive dashboards and reports, providing stakeholders with real-time insights (Pandit, 2023). Through segmentation and targeting, we identify distinct customer groups and personalize marketing strategies to resonate with each segment's unique characteristics and needs (Saxena et al., 2023). Predictive analytics helps us forecast trends and customer behaviors, offering a glimpse into the future to guide strategic decisions (Ldbyani & Al-Abyadh, 2022).

Enhanced marketing analytics also places a significant emphasis on customer lifetime value (CLV) analysis, enabling businesses to understand the long-term value of their customer base and allocate marketing resources judiciously (Tripathi & Al-Shahri, 2023). A/B testing and experimentation allow us to refine marketing strategies through empirical testing, while attribution modeling untangles the web of marketing channels to reveal which ones are truly driving conversions (Hong et al., 2022).

Moreover, sentiment analysis delves into the emotions and opinions of customers, helping us gauge public perception and refine our strategies accordingly. Machine learning and artificial intelligence usher in the era of personalization and automation, enabling businesses to serve their audiences with tailored content and experiences (Kanaan-Jebna et al., 2022).

Marketing analytics encompasses the systematic collection, analysis, interpretation, and utilization of data related to customer behavior, market trends, and campaign performance (Roman et al., 2020). It empowers organizations to make informed decisions, allocate resources effectively, and gain a competitive edge (Hong, 2023).

Here's why marketing analytics is paramount in modern business:

Informed Decision-Making: The traditional approach of making decisions based on gut instincts and past experiences is no longer sufficient in the data-driven age. Modern consumers generate vast amounts of data through their online interactions, and businesses that harness this data are better equipped to make informed decisions (Priscila et al., 2023). Marketing analytics transforms this wealth of data into actionable insights, guiding businesses in choosing the most effective marketing strategies, channels, and messaging (Anand et al., 2023).

Resource Optimization: Marketing budgets are finite resources, and their allocation demands rigorous management. Marketing analytics provides businesses with the tools to optimize their campaigns continually (Kosuru & Venkitaraman, 2022; Vashishtha & Kapoor, 2023).). It helps identify which marketing channels are most effective, which strategies yield the best results, and which campaigns should be adjusted or discontinued. This iterative approach not only enhances cost efficiencies but also maximizes return on investment (ROI) (Atasever, 2023).

Customer-Centric Strategies: In the modern marketplace, consumers are inundated with choices and information. To stand out in this crowded space, businesses must shift their focus from product-centric to customer-centric strategies. Marketing analytics enables organizations to collect, analyze, and understand vast datasets related to customer behavior, preferences, and engagement (Rad et al., 2019). Armed with these insights, businesses can create personalized customer experiences that resonate with individual needs and preferences, fostering loyalty and advocacy (Ocoró et al., 2023).

Measuring Marketing Impact: One of the enduring challenges in marketing has been quantifying the impact of marketing initiatives on key performance indicators (KPIs) such as sales, customer acquisition, and brand awareness. Marketing analytics offers a path to attribution clarity, enabling businesses to measure the influence of marketing efforts accurately (Said & Tripathi, 2023). This not only validates marketing's contribution to the bottom line but also enables continuous improvement (Ramos et al., 2023).

Agility in Response to Market Dynamics: In today's fast-paced business environment, agility is a prized asset. Consumer behaviors can change rapidly, and external factors such as economic shifts or global events can disrupt markets. Marketing analytics equips organizations with real-time insights, allowing them to pivot swiftly in response to changing market dynamics. This agility can be a game-changer in uncertain times, helping businesses stay resilient and adapt to new challenges (Kuragayala, 2023).

Competitive Advantage: In a landscape marked by cutthroat competition, gaining a competitive advantage is paramount. Marketing analytics provides the tools to monitor competitors, assess market trends, and identify whitespace opportunities (Sabti et al., 2023). By staying ahead of the curve and swiftly adapting to changing market dynamics, businesses can position themselves as industry leaders (Venkateswaran & Viktor, 2023).

Personalization at Scale: The modern consumer expects personalized experiences, whether in marketing messages, product recommendations, or customer service. Marketing analytics enables businesses to achieve personalization at scale by segmenting their customer base and tailoring messages and offers to specific segments (Srinivas et al., 2023). This not only enhances customer satisfaction but also drives higher conversion rates and customer lifetime value (María et al., 2023).

Accountability and ROI Measurement: Marketing analytics fosters a culture of accountability within organizations. When decisions are based on data, it becomes easier to trace the impact of specific strategies and campaigns. From campaign managers to chief marketing officers (CMOs), marketing professionals are held accountable for results, and ROI measurement becomes a standard practice (Vashishtha & Dhawan, 2023).

The significance of marketing analytics lies not only in its ability to decipher customer behavior and market trends but also in its capacity to validate strategies, optimize resources, and propel businesses forward in an era defined by technological advancement and digital transformation. As organizations strive to remain relevant and competitive, marketing analytics emerges not merely as a tool of choice but as a strategic imperative, enabling them to thrive in the data-driven landscape of modern business.

2. BUSINESS INTELLIGENCE AND MARKETING ANALYTICS

Numerous knowledge gaps persist regarding the realization of benefits from big data and the necessary adaptations for incumbent firms (Rialti et al., 2019). While previous research has explored the advantages derived from employing big data in streamlining business processes, such as through Customer Relationship Management (CRM) or Enterprise Resource Planning (ERP) systems (Matarazzo et al., 2021), and the value it contributes to safeguarding an organization's market position and operational effectiveness (Li et al., 2021; Weerasinghe et al., 2021), several unanswered queries revolve around the utilization of big data in marketing (Rialti et al., 2019).

These unresolved questions encompass a spectrum of issues. Firstly, there's the inquiry into how big data influences strategic marketing opportunities (Quinn et al., 2016). Secondly, there's a need to comprehend how organizations undergo digital transformation in response to big data dynamics (Warner and Wäger, 2019). Furthermore, an exploration into the essential digital marketing capabilities required for achieving success is warranted (Herhausen et al., 2020; Homburg and Wielgos, 2022), along with an examination of how these capabilities can be effectively applied to address strategic marketing challenges (Phillips-Wren and Hoskisson, 2015).

Machine learning applications in the business landscape are extensive and diverse, encompassing a wide array of functionalities. These applications range from the deployment of virtual assistants and chatbots to the creation of highly personalized advertisements tailored to the profiles of target users. Moreover, machine learning plays a pivotal role in systematically maximizing performance and optimizing budget allocation for businesses (Agarwal et al., 2020; Davenport et al., 2020; Huang & Rust, 2021; Ma & Sun, 2020; Vermeer et al., 2019).

In the realm of marketing, the integration of machine learning is rapidly evolving and becoming a reality for numerous companies worldwide. Recent statistics reveal that approximately 84% of marketing agencies have initiated AI and machine learning projects, while a substantial 75% of large enterprises have reported notable enhancements in consumer satisfaction, often by up to 10%. Despite the availability of certain reviews that delve into the application of machine learning in marketing (Ma & Sun, 2020), which shed light on the transformative impact of machine learning and Big Data analysis on digital marketing strategies, there remains a noticeable absence of a comprehensive evaluation effort from a strategic marketing perspective.

Business Intelligence is a comprehensive framework encompassing technologies, processes, and strategies that empower organizations to transform raw data into meaningful and actionable insights.

The primary objective of BI is to facilitate informed decision-making by providing access to relevant data and analytical tools (Xu et al., 2023).

Data Integration: BI systems collect data from diverse sources, such as databases, spreadsheets, and external data feeds, and integrate them into a unified repository.

Data Warehousing: Data warehouses are used to store data in a structured format, making it easily accessible for analysis and reporting.

Data Visualization: BI tools offer visualization capabilities, including dashboards and reports, to present data in an understandable format. Visualizations help users identify trends, patterns, and insights quickly.

Analytics: BI platforms often include analytical tools for exploring data, generating insights, and conducting ad-hoc analyses. This may involve descriptive, diagnostic, predictive, or prescriptive analytics.

Reporting: BI systems generate comprehensive reports that allow stakeholders to monitor key performance indicators (KPIs), track business operations, and make data-informed decisions.

Marketing Analytics is a specialized field of analytics focused on evaluating marketing strategies, campaigns, and initiatives. It employs data-driven techniques to measure the effectiveness of marketing efforts, optimize resource allocation, and enhance customer engagement.

3. DATA COLLECTION

Marketing Analytics starts with the collection of relevant data from various sources, including website analytics, social media platforms, email campaigns, and customer databases.

Segmentation:

A fundamental principle of Marketing Analytics is customer segmentation. By dividing the customer base into distinct groups based on demographics, behavior, or preferences, organizations can tailor marketing strategies to specific segments (Tambaip et al., 2023).

Performance Metrics:

Metrics like customer acquisition cost (CAC), customer lifetime value (CLV), click-through rate (CTR), conversion rate, and return on investment (ROI) are essential in assessing the performance of marketing campaigns.

Attribution Modeling:

Understanding how different marketing touchpoints contribute to conversions is crucial. Attribution models allocate credit to various touchpoints in the customer journey, helping organizations make informed decisions about resource allocation.

A/B Testing:

Experimentation is integral to Marketing Analytics. A/B testing involves comparing two versions (A and B) of a marketing element (e.g., webpage, email subject line) to determine which performs better in terms of a specific metric.

The Relationship between BI and Marketing Analytics:

The relationship between Business Intelligence and Marketing Analytics is symbiotic, where BI serves as the foundation, and Marketing Analytics leverages BI capabilities to make data-driven marketing decisions (Venkateswaran et al., 2023). Here's how they interconnect.

Data Integration:

BI systems excel at data integration. They aggregate data from various sources, including marketing platforms and customer databases. Marketing Analytics relies on this integrated data to assess campaign performance, customer behavior, and other critical marketing metrics.

Data Warehousing:

Data warehousing is a core BI component. It provides a structured repository for data storage and retrieval. Marketing Analytics leverages data warehousing to access historical marketing data for trend analysis and long-term performance evaluation.

Data Visualization:

BI tools offer data visualization capabilities, which Marketing Analytics employs to create visually appealing dashboards and reports. These visualizations make it easier for marketing professionals to interpret data, track campaign metrics, and identify areas for optimization.

Analytics:

BI platforms often include analytical tools that can be harnessed by Marketing Analytics. For instance, predictive analytics within BI systems can assist in forecasting customer behavior or campaign outcomes, aiding in marketing strategy planning.

Reporting:

BI systems generate comprehensive reports that provide an overview of organizational performance. Marketing Analytics relies on these reports to assess the impact of marketing efforts on overall business goals and KPIs.

4. APPLICATIONS OF BI IN MARKETING ANALYTICS

4.1 Customer Segmentation

Customer segmentation is a crucial component of modern marketing strategy, and Business Intelligence (BI) plays a pivotal role in facilitating this process. BI empowers organizations to collect, analyze, and interpret vast datasets, providing valuable insights that enable effective customer segmentation. In this explanation, we'll explore how BI enables customer segmentation and provide real-world examples of its implementation.

Data Integration:

One of the foundational aspects of BI is data integration. BI systems gather data from various sources, including customer databases, CRM systems, web analytics, and more. By centralizing this data, BI creates a unified view of customer information, eliminating data silos and ensuring that all relevant data is readily available for analysis.

Example:

Consider a multinational retail corporation with online and offline sales channels. BI integrates data from in-store transactions, e-commerce platforms, and customer loyalty programs. This integrated data provides a comprehensive view of customer interactions, enabling the company to segment its customer base effectively.

Data Warehousing:

BI systems often incorporate data warehousing capabilities. Data warehouses store historical customer data in a structured and organized format. This historical data is invaluable for analyzing customer behavior over time, identifying trends, and making informed segmentation decisions.

Example:

A telecommunications company uses BI to maintain a data warehouse containing years of customer call records, billing information, and service usage data. By analyzing this historical data, the company identifies patterns in customer behavior, such as peak usage times, which inform segmentation strategies for service offerings.

Data Visualization:

BI tools offer data visualization features, including dashboards and reports, which transform complex datasets into easy-to-understand visuals. These visualizations help marketing professionals and decision-makers grasp insights quickly and make informed segmentation choices.

Example:

An e-commerce company employs BI to create dashboards displaying customer demographics, purchase history, and website engagement metrics. Visualizations highlight segments of high-value customers based on factors like average order value and purchase frequency, aiding marketing teams in targeted campaigns.

Reporting:

BI generates comprehensive reports that provide detailed insights into customer behavior, preferences, and engagement with products or services. These reports are instrumental in shaping segmentation strategies and measuring their effectiveness.

Example:

A subscription-based streaming service leverages BI-generated reports to segment its user base. By analyzing viewing habits, content preferences, and user engagement metrics, the company creates targeted content recommendations and marketing campaigns for different user segments.

Personalization:

Effective customer segmentation leads to personalized marketing efforts. BI not only facilitates segmentation but also enables organizations to deliver personalized experiences to customers through targeted messaging, product recommendations, and tailored offerings.

Example:

An online marketplace employs BI to segment customers based on their past purchase behavior, preferences, and browsing history. Using this segmentation, the platform delivers personalized product recommendations to users when they log in, increasing the likelihood of conversions.

4.2 Tracking and Optimization of Marketing Campaigns

Business Intelligence (BI) tools play a pivotal role in the tracking and optimization of marketing campaigns, offering organizations the means to make data-driven decisions that enhance campaign effectiveness and maximize return on investment (ROI).

Two key components of this process are ROI measurement and A/B testing.

4.2.1 ROI Measurement

ROI measurement is a critical aspect of evaluating the success and effectiveness of marketing campaigns. It helps organizations understand the financial impact of their marketing efforts and enables data-driven adjustments to optimize future campaigns.

4.2.2 A/B Testing

A/B testing, also known as split testing, is a fundamental technique for optimizing marketing campaigns by comparing two versions (A and B) of a marketing element to determine which performs better in terms of a specific metric, such as conversion rate or click-through rate.

Example:

A social media advertising campaign for a clothing retailer involves testing two different ad creatives (Version A and Version B) to see which generates more clicks and conversions. BI tools are used to track and analyze the performance of each version. The BI-generated report shows that Version B has a significantly higher click-through rate and conversion rate, leading the retailer to allocate a larger budget to Version B and use it as the primary ad creative.

4.3 Predictive Analytics in Marketing

Predictive analytics in marketing is a powerful approach that leverages data, statistical algorithms, and machine learning techniques to forecast future customer behavior and trends. It enables marketers to make data-driven decisions, tailor their strategies, and allocate resources effectively.

Customer Lifetime Value (CLV) Prediction:

Predictive analytics can estimate the CLV for individual customers. This allows businesses to allocate marketing resources more effectively by focusing on high-value customers who are likely to generate the most revenue over time.

Churn Prediction:

Predictive models can identify customers at risk of churning or canceling their subscriptions. Marketers can then implement retention strategies to reduce churn rates.

Personalized Content Recommendations:

Predictive algorithms analyze user behavior and preferences to provide personalized content recommendations, such as product suggestions, articles, or videos. This increases user engagement and conversion rates.

Lead Scoring:

Predictive lead scoring ranks potential leads based on their likelihood of converting into customers. It helps sales teams prioritize leads for follow-up and nurture high-potential leads.

Dynamic Pricing:

Retailers and e-commerce platforms use predictive analytics to adjust product pricing dynamically based on demand, inventory levels, competitor pricing, and customer behavior.

Example: An online airline booking platform uses predictive models to optimize ticket prices based on factors like booking patterns, demand, and seat availability. This maximizes revenue and seat occupancy.

4.4 Benefits and Impact of BI in Marketing Analytics

4.4.1 Improved Decision-Making

Improved decision-making is one of the most significant benefits of implementing Business Intelligence (BI) in modern organizations. BI systems provide valuable data-driven insights and tools that enable informed and strategic decision-making across various departments and functions. Here's how BI contributes to improved decision-making:

- Data Integration and Accessibility
- Advanced Analytics
- Historical Analysis
- Real-time Monitoring
- KPI Tracking
- Scenario Planning
- Collaboration and Data Sharing
- Informed Resource Allocation
- Compliance and Governance

4.4.2 Enhanced Customer Engagement

Enhanced customer engagement is a crucial goal for businesses looking to build strong, long-lasting relationships with their customers. Business Intelligence (BI) plays a significant role in achieving this goal by providing organizations with valuable insights and tools to better understand and connect with their customer base. Here's how BI contributes to enhanced customer engagement:

- 360-Degree Customer View
- Personalized Marketing Campaigns
- Behavioral Analysis
- Real-time Interactions
- Customer Feedback Analysis
- Omni channel Engagement
- Performance Tracking and Optimization

5. CHALLENGES FOR BUSINESS INTELLIGENCE BI

Business Intelligence (BI) offers numerous benefits, but organizations often face several challenges when implementing and using BI solutions. These challenges can vary depending on factors like the complexity of the organization, data sources, and technology infrastructure. Here are some common challenges for BI:

- Data Quality and Integration
- Data Security and Privacy
- Complexity of Data Sources
- Scalability and Performance
- User Adoption and Training
- Costs and Budget Constraints
- Complexity of BI Tools
- Data Governance and Ownership

- Keeping Up with Technology Advances
- Interpreting and Acting on Insights

BI is akin to a guiding star that illuminates the path forward. In marketing, it enables teams to create campaigns that resonate with specific customer segments, resulting in higher engagement and conversion rates. In finance, it facilitates precise resource allocation, optimizing budgets and investments. Sales teams benefit from efficient lead prioritization, focusing their efforts where they are most likely to yield results. Supply chain managers use real-time data to ensure optimal inventory levels, meeting demand without overstocking. This democratization of data-driven decision-making empowers all members of an organization to contribute to its success. However, the landscape of data-driven decision-making is not without its challenges. Data security and privacy concerns loom large, requiring organizations to protect sensitive information within the bounds of stringent regulatory requirements. Robust security measures, access controls, and encryption are integral to a comprehensive data protection strategy. Aligning BI tools with data protection regulations is crucial, allowing organizations to unlock the full potential of BI while mitigating associated risks.

BI's role in decision-making transcends the confines of the executive suite, extending its reach to every department within an organization. Marketing teams harness BI to craft campaigns tailored to specific customer segments, while finance departments leverage it to allocate resources more effectively. Sales teams utilize predictive analytics to prioritize leads, and supply chain managers optimize inventory levels with real-time data. The democratization of data-driven decision-making ensures that every employee, regardless of their role, can contribute to an organization's success.

The advent of Business Intelligence (BI) tools has heralded a revolution in the world of decision-making. Gone are the days when gut instincts and intuition were the guiding forces behind critical business choices. In today's data-rich environment, organizations have harnessed the power of data-driven insights to shape their strategies, optimize operations, and seize opportunities. The integration and analysis of data from various sources have armed decision-makers with a panoramic view of their business landscape, enabling them to make informed choices founded on empirical evidence rather than conjecture.

However, amidst the transformative power of BI, significant challenges loom. Data security and privacy concerns have grown in tandem with the increasing reliance on data-driven decision-making. In an environment marked by heightened regulatory scrutiny and the omnipresent threat of data breaches, organizations must implement robust security measures, access controls, and encryption to safeguard sensitive information. BI tools must align with data protection regulations and industry standards to mitigate risks effectively and protect both the organization and its customers.

BI is not merely a tool or a technology; it represents a paradigm shift in how organizations operate and thrive in the digital era. It is the fusion of data, technology, and human expertise that unlocks unprecedented insights and drives informed decision-making. The impact of BI reverberates across various aspects of business operations, from optimizing supply chains to enhancing customer engagement. Its influence is profound and far-reaching, making it a linchpin in the quest for success and sustainability in the modern business landscape. At the heart of BI's transformative power is its ability to provide decision-makers with a holistic perspective of their organization. By integrating data from diverse sources, BI tools create a comprehensive canvas that paints a detailed picture of the business landscape. This multifaceted view allows decision-makers to navigate complexities, identify trends, and uncover opportunities that might otherwise remain hidden. It empowers organizations to make data-driven choices that align with their overarching goals and strategies.

The role of BI in decision-making is akin to a guiding star that illuminates the path forward. It dispels uncertainty and ambiguity, replacing them with clarity and precision. In marketing, BI empowers teams to craft campaigns that resonate with specific customer segments, leading to higher engagement and conversion rates. Finance departments can allocate resources with precision, optimizing budgets and investments. Sales teams prioritize leads efficiently, focusing their efforts where they are most likely to yield results. Supply chain managers, armed with real-time data, ensure that inventory levels are optimized to meet demand without overstocking.

6. CONCLUSION

This democratization of data-driven decision-making is a fundamental shift that empowers all members of an organization to contribute to its success. Yet, the landscape of data-driven decision-making is not without challenges. Data security and privacy concerns have become paramount. Organizations must safeguard sensitive information against the backdrop of stringent regulatory requirements and the ever-looming threat of data breaches. Robust security measures, access controls, and encryption are essential components of a comprehensive data protection strategy. Aligning BI tools with data protection regulations ensures that organizations can harness the full potential of BI while mitigating the associated risks. In conclusion, Business Intelligence is a transformative force that transcends being a mere tool or technology; it is a fundamental shift in how organizations operate and succeed in the digital age. The fusion of data, technology, and human expertise fuels the engine of BI, unlocking unprecedented insights and driving informed decision-making. Its impact reverberates across the spectrum of business operations, from optimizing supply chains to enhancing customer engagement. Organizations that embrace BI and its principles will be better positioned to navigate the complexities of the modern business landscape, innovate, and achieve sustainable growth. In conclusion, Business Intelligence represents not just a tool but a transformative force reshaping how organizations operate and thrive in the digital age.

REFERENCES

Abdel Azeem, H. A. H., & Al-Abyadh, M. H. A. (2021). Self-compassion: The influences on the university students' life satisfaction during the COVID-19 outbreak. *International Journal of Human Rights in Healthcare*. Advance online publication. doi:10.1108/IJHRH-08-2021-0153

Agarwal, R., & Helfat, C. E. (2009). Strategic renewal of organizations. *Organization Science*, *20*(2), 281–293. doi:10.1287/orsc.1090.0423

Al-Abrat, N. A. S., & Alabyad, M. H. A. (2021). The Extent of Awareness of Faculty Members at Albayda University About the Concept of Educational Technology and Their Attitudes Towards It. In A. M. Al-Bakry (Ed.), *New Trends in Information and Communications Technology Applications. NTICT 2021* (Vol. 1511). Springer. doi:10.1007/978-3-030-93417-0_13

Al-Abyadh, M. H. A., & Abdel Azeem, H. A. H. (2022). Academic achievement: Influences of university students' self-management and perceived self-efficacy. *Journal of Intelligence*, *10*(3), 55. doi:10.3390/jintelligence10030055 PMID:35997411

Al-maaitah, D. A., Tha'er Majali, M. A., & Almaaitah, T. A. (2021). The role of leadership styles on staffs job satisfaction in public organizations. *Journal of Contemporary Issues in Business and Government, 27*(1), 772–783.

Al-maaitah, T. A., Tha'er Majali, M. A., & Almaaitah, D. A. (2021). The Impact of COVID-19 on the Electronic Commerce Users Behavior. *Journal of Contemporary Issues in Business and Government, 27*(1), 772–783.

Alabdullah, T.T.Y., Ahmed, E.R. (2021). New Insights to Investigate the Impact of Internal Control Mechanisms on Firm Performance: A Study in Oman. *Riset Akuntansi dan Keuangan Indonesia, 6*(2).

Alabdullah, T. T. Y., Al Fakhri, I., Ahmed, E. R., & Jebna, A. K. (2021b). Empirical Study of The Influence of Board of Directors' Feature on Firm Performance. *Russian Journal of Agricultural and Socio-Economic Sciences, 11*(119), 137–146. doi:10.18551/rjoas.2021-11.16

Alabdullah, T. T. Y., Al-Fakhri, I., Ahmed, E. R., & Kanaan-Jebna, A. (2021a). Corporate Governance System and Firm Financial Performance. *Acta Scientific Computer Sciences, 4*(6), 97–103.

Alayli, S. (2023). Unravelling the Drivers of Online Purchasing Intention: The E-Commerce Scenario in Lebanon. *FMDB Transactions on Sustainable Social Sciences Letters, 1*(1), 56–67.

An, Q., Hong, W. C. H., Xu, X., Zhang, Y., & Kolletar-Zhu, K. (2023). How Education Level Influences Internet Security Knowledge, Behaviour, and Attitude: A Comparison among Undergraduates, Postgraduates and Working Graduates. *International Journal of Information Security, 22*(2), 305–317. doi:10.100710207-022-00637-z PMID:36466362

Anand, P. P., Kanike, U. K., Paramasivan, P., Rajest, S. S., Regin, R., & Priscila, S. S. (2023). Embracing Industry 5.0: Pioneering Next-Generation Technology for a Flourishing Human Experience and Societal Advancement. *FMDB Transactions on Sustainable Social Sciences Letters, 1*(1), 43–55.

Atasever, M. (2023). Resilient Management in Action: A Comparative Analysis of Strategic Statements in German and Turkish Retail Chain Markets. *FMDB Transactions on Sustainable Management Letters, 1*(2), 66–81.

Balas-Timar, D., & Ignat, S. (2015). Conceptual applicant screening model with fuzzy logic in industrial organizational contexts. *Procedia: Social and Behavioral Sciences, 203*, 257–263. doi:10.1016/j.sbspro.2015.08.291

Davenport, T., Guha, A., Grewal, D., & Bressgott, T. (2020). How artificial intelligence will change the future of marketing. *Journal of the Academy of Marketing Science, 48*(1), 24–42. doi:10.100711747-019-00696-0

Demeter, E., Rad, D., & Balas, E. (2021). Schadenfreude and General Anti-Social Behaviours: The Role of Violent Content Preferences and Life Satisfaction. BRAIN. *Broad Research in Artificial Intelligence and Neuroscience, 12*(2), 98–111. doi:10.18662/brain/12.2/194

Herhausen, D., Miočević, D., Morgan, R. E., & Kleijnen, M. H. P. (2020). The digital marketing capabilities gap. *Industrial Marketing Management, 90*, 276–290. doi:10.1016/j.indmarman.2020.07.022

Homburg, C., & Wielgos, D. M. (2022). The value relevance of digital marketing capabilities to firm performance. *Journal of the Academy of Marketing Science*, *50*(4), 666–688. doi:10.100711747-022-00858-7 PMID:35463184

Hong, W. C. H. (2023). The impact of ChatGPT on foreign language teaching and learning: Opportunities in education and research. *Journal of Education Technology and Innovation*, *5*(1).

Hong, W. C. H., Chi, C.-Y., Liu, J., Zhang, Y.-F., Lei, N.-L., & Xu, X.-S. (2022). The influence of social education level on cybersecurity awareness and behaviour: A comparative study of university students and working graduates. *Education and Information Technologies*. PMID:35791319

Huang, M.-H., & Rust, R. T. (2021). A strategic framework for artificial intelligence in marketing. *Journal of the Academy of Marketing Science*, *49*(1), 30–50. doi:10.100711747-020-00749-9

Kanaan-Jebna, A., Baharudi, A. S., & Alabdullah, T. T. Y. (2022). Entrepreneurial Orientation, Market Orientation, Managerial Accounting and Manufacturing SMEs Satisfaction. *Journal of Accounting Science*, *6*(1), 1–14. doi:10.21070/jas.v6i1.1590

Kosuru, V. S. R., & Venkitaraman, A. K. (2022). Developing a Deep Q-Learning and Neural Network Framework for Trajectory Planning. *European Journal of Engineering and Technology Research*, *7*(6), 148–157. doi:10.24018/ejeng.2022.7.6.2944

Kuragayala, P. S. (2023). A Systematic Review on Workforce Development in Healthcare Sector: Implications in the Post-COVID Scenario. *FMDB Transactions on Sustainable Technoprise Letters*, *1*(1), 36–46.

Ldbyani, A., & Al-Abyadh, M. H. A. (2022). Relationship between Dark Triad, Mental Health, and Subjective Well-being Moderated by Mindfulness: A Study on Atheists and Muslim Students. *Islamic Guidance and Counseling Journal*, *5*(1), 71–87. doi:10.25217/igcj.v5i1.2642

Li, L., Lin, J., Ouyang, Y., & Luo, X. (2022). Evaluating the impact of big data analytics usage on the decision-making quality of organizations. *Technological Forecasting and Social Change*, *175*(121355), 121355. doi:10.1016/j.techfore.2021.121355

Ma, L., & Sun, B. (2020). Machine learning and AI in marketing – Connecting computing power to human insights. *International Journal of Research in Marketing*, *37*(3), 481–504. doi:10.1016/j.ijresmar.2020.04.005

María, J. J. L., Polo, O. C. C., & Elhadary, T. (2023). An Analysis of the Morality and Social Responsibility of Non-Profit Organizations. *FMDB Transactions on Sustainable Technoprise Letters*, *1*(1), 28–35.

Matarazzo, M., Penco, L., Profumo, G., & Quaglia, R. (2021). Digital transformation and customer value creation in Made in Italy SMEs: A dynamic capabilities perspective. *Journal of Business Research*, *123*, 642–656. doi:10.1016/j.jbusres.2020.10.033

Ocoró, M. P., Polo, O. C. C., & Khandare, S. (2023). Importance of Business Financial Risk Analysis in SMEs According to COVID-19. *FMDB Transactions on Sustainable Management Letters*, *1*(1), 12–21.

Pandit, P. (2023). On the Context of the Principle of Beneficence: The Problem of Over Demandingness within Utilitarian Theory. *FMDB Transactions on Sustainable Social Sciences Letters*, *1*(1), 26–42.

Phillips-Wren, G., & Hoskisson, A. (2015). An analytical journey towards big data. *Journal of Decision Systems, 24*(1), 87–102. doi:10.1080/12460125.2015.994333

Priscila, S. S., Rajest, S. S., Tadiboina, S. N., Regin, R., & András, S. (2023). Analysis of Machine Learning and Deep Learning Methods for Superstore Sales Prediction. *FMDB Transactions on Sustainable Computer Letters, 1*(1), 1–11.

Quinn, L., Dibb, S., Simkin, L., Canhoto, A., & Analogbei, M. (2016). Troubled waters: The transformation of marketing in a digital world. *European Journal of Marketing, 50*(12), 2103–2133. doi:10.1108/EJM-08-2015-0537

Rad, D., Balas, E., Ignat, S., Rad, G., & Dixon, D. (2020). A Predictive Model of Youth Bystanders' Helping Attitudes. *Revista romaneasca pentru educatie multidimensionala-Journal for Multidimensional Education, 12*(1Sup2), 136-150.

Rad, D., Dughi, T., & Demeter, E. (2019). The Dynamics of the Relationship between Humor and Benevolence as Values. *Revista romaneasca pentru educatie multidimensionala-Journal for Multidimensional Education, 11*(3), 201-212.

Rad, D., Egerau, A., Roman, A., Dughi, T., Balas, E., Maier, R., & Rad, G. (2022). A Preliminary Investigation of the Technology Acceptance Model (TAM) in Early Childhood Education and Care. BRAIN. *Broad Research in Artificial Intelligence and Neuroscience, 13*(1), 518–533. doi:10.18662/brain/13.1/297

Ramos, J. I., Lacerona, R., & Nunag, J. M. (2023). A Study on Operational Excellence, Work Environment Factors and the Impact to Employee Performance. *FMDB Transactions on Sustainable Social Sciences Letters, 1*(1), 12–25.

Rialti, R., Marzi, G., Ciappei, C., & Busso, D. (2019). Big data and dynamic capabilities: A bibliometric analysis and systematic literature review. *Management Decision, 57*(8), 2052–2068. doi:10.1108/MD-07-2018-0821

Roman, A., Rad, D., Egerau, A., Dixon, D., Dughi, T., Kelemen, G., & Rad, G. (2020). Physical Self-Schema Acceptance and Perceived Severity of Online Aggressiveness in Cyberbullying Incidents. *Journal of Interdisciplinary Studies in Education, 9*(1), 100–116. doi:10.32674/jise.v9i1.1961

Sabti, Y. M., Alqatrani, R. I. N., Zaid, M. I., Taengkliang, B., & Kareem, J. M. (2023). Impact of Business Environment on the Performance of Employees in the Public-Listed Companies. *FMDB Transactions on Sustainable Management Letters, 1*(2), 56–65.

Said, F. B., & Tripathi, S. (2023). Epistemology of Digital Journalism Shift in South Global Nations: A Bibliometric Analysis. *FMDB Transactions on Sustainable Technoprise Letters, 1*(1), 47–60.

Saxena, D., Khandare, S., & Chaudhary, S. (2023). An Overview of ChatGPT: Impact on Academic Learning. *FMDB Transactions on Sustainable Techno Learning, 1*(1), 11–20.

Srinivas, K., Velmurugan, P. R., & Andiyappillai, N. (2023). Digital Human Resources and Management Support Improve Human Resources Effectiveness. *FMDB Transactions on Sustainable Management Letters, 1*(1), 32–45.

Tambaip, B., Hadi, A. F. F., & Tjilen, A. P. (2023). Optimizing Public Service Performance: Unleashing the Potential of Compassion as an Indicator of Public Service Motivation. *FMDB Transactions on Sustainable Management Letters*, *1*(2), 46–55.

Tripathi, S., & Al-Shahri, M. (2023). Problems and Prospects on the Evolution of Advertising and Public Relations Industries in Oman. *FMDB Transactions on Sustainable Management Letters*, *1*(1), 1–11.

Vashishtha, E., & Dhawan, G. (2023). Comparison of Baldrige Criteria of Strategy Planning and Harrison Text. *FMDB Transactions on Sustainable Management Letters*, *1*(1), 22–31.

Vashishtha, E., & Kapoor, H. (2023). Implementation of Blockchain Technology Across International Healthcare Markets. *FMDB Transactions on Sustainable Technoprise Letters*, *1*(1), 1–12.

Venkateswaran. P.S. (2023). Industry 5 - Challenges and Opportunities for business and industries. In *Transition from Industry 4.0 to Industry 5.0: Radical changes in Indian Business Environment* (pp. 233-245). Infinite Learning Solutions.

Venkateswaran, P. S., Singh, S., Paramasivan, P., Rajest, S. S., Lourens, M. E., & Regin, R. (2023). A Study on The Influence of Quality of Service on Customer Satisfaction Towards Hotel Industry. *FMDB Transactions on Sustainable Social Sciences Letters*, *1*(1), 1–11.

Venkateswaran, P. S., & Viktor, P. (2023). A Study on Brand Equity of Fast-Moving Consumer Goods with Reference to Madurai, Tamil Nadu. *FMDB Transactions on Sustainable Technoprise Letters*, *1*(1), 13–27.

Venkitaraman, A. K., & Kosuru, V. S. R. (2023). Hybrid deep learning mechanism for charging control and management of Electric Vehicles. *European Journal of Electrical Engineering and Computer Science*, *7*(1), 38–46. doi:10.24018/ejece.2023.7.1.485

Vermeer, S. A., Araujo, T., Bernritter, S. F., & van Noort, G. (2019). Seeing the wood for the trees: How machine learning can help firms in identifying relevant electronic word-of-mouth in social media. *International Journal of Research in Marketing*, *36*(3), 492–508. doi:10.1016/j.ijresmar.2019.01.010

Warner, K. S. R., & Wäger, M. (2019). Building dynamic capabilities for digital transformation: An ongoing process of strategic renewal. *Long Range Planning*, *52*(3), 326–349. doi:10.1016/j.lrp.2018.12.001

Weerasinghe, K., Scahill, S. L., Pauleen, D. J., & Taskin, N. (2022). Big data analytics for clinical decision-making: Understanding health sector perceptions of policy and practice. *Technological Forecasting and Social Change*, *174*(121222), 121222. doi:10.1016/j.techfore.2021.121222

Xu, X., Hong, W. C. H., Zhang, Y., Jiang, H., & Liu, J. (2023). Learning Paths Design in Personal Learning Environments: The Impact on Postgraduates' Cognitive Achievements and Satisfaction. *Innovations in Education and Teaching International*, 1–16. doi:10.1080/14703297.2023.2189603

Chapter 4
The Synergy of Management Information Systems and Predictive Analytics for Marketing

M. Lishmah Dominic
Annamalai University, India

P. S. Venkateswaran
PSNA College of Engineering and Technology, India

Latha Thamma Reddi
https://orcid.org/0009-0005-6338-7972
Independent Researcher, USA

Sandeep Rangineni
https://orcid.org/0009-0003-9623-4062
Pluto TV, USA

R. Regin
SRM Institute of Science and Technology, Ramapuram, India

S. Suman Rajest
https://orcid.org/0000-0001-8315-3747
Dhaanish Ahmed College of Engineering, India

ABSTRACT

In the ever-evolving landscape of modern marketing, the convergence of management information systems (MIS) and predictive analytics has become a potent force. This chapter explores the transformative potential of combining MIS infrastructure with predictive analytics techniques to reshape marketing management. Predictive analytics, utilizing historical data and machine learning, empowers organizations to forecast future trends, customer behavior, and market dynamics. MIS, as the information backbone, facilitates the collection, processing, and dissemination of data for strategic decision-making. Marketing, once reliant on intuition, has transitioned into a data-driven discipline. This synergy enables businesses to not only understand past performance but also anticipate and respond to the dynamic demands of the marketplace. However, seizing this opportunity is not without challenges. Success hinges on the alignment of technical capabilities, organizational structure, and strategic vision with the digital landscape's evolution.

DOI: 10.4018/979-8-3693-2193-5.ch004

1. INTRODUCTION

Predictive analytics is the practice of using data, statistical algorithms, and machine learning techniques to identify the likelihood of future outcomes based on historical data (Abu-Rumman, 2021). It involves analyzing past and current information to make predictions about future events or trends (Abu-Rumman and Qawasmeh, 2021). The primary goal of predictive analytics is to forecast what might happen in the future so that organizations can make informed decisions and take proactive actions to achieve desired outcomes or mitigate potential risks (Al Shraah et al., 2022).

In today's business landscape, even small- and midsize enterprises engage with customers on an extensive scale, spanning a multitude of communication channels (Al Shraah et al., 2013). These channels encompass websites, social media platforms, mobile applications, and physical store interactions (Alayli, 2023). This proliferation in the speed, volume, and diversity of customer interactions has presented companies with a unique opportunity to foster and nurture the kind of personal relationships that were once the cornerstone of successful business practices (Al-maaitah et al., 2021).

In the rapidly evolving landscape of modern business, where data reigns supreme, and decision-makers seek to stay ahead of the competition, the convergence of Management Information Systems (MIS) and predictive analytics in marketing management has emerged as a transformative force (Al-maaitah et al., 2021). The union of these two powerful domains has ushered in a new era where data-driven insights and informed decision-making are the cornerstones of success for marketing professionals (Ameisen, 2019).

Marketing management, once reliant on intuition and experience, has now evolved into a sophisticated field that harnesses the vast troves of data generated in the digital age (Anand et al., 2023; Gupta, 2021a). MIS, on the other hand, has long been recognized as the backbone of effective organizational management, providing the infrastructure for collecting, processing, and disseminating information to support strategic and tactical decision-making (Arslan et al., 2021). The synergy between MIS and predictive analytics has reshaped the marketing landscape, enabling businesses to not only understand past performance but also anticipate future trends, customer behavior, and market dynamics (Bari et al., 2016; Gupta, 2021b).

This comprehensive exploration seeks to delve deep into the dynamic relationship between Management Information Systems and predictive analytics within the realm of marketing management (Burkov, 2019). We will uncover the pivotal role that MIS plays in facilitating predictive analytics, transforming marketing strategies, and enabling organizations to adapt to the ever-changing demands of the marketplace (Demeter et al., 2021; Gupta, 2022).

However, seizing this opportunity is far from straightforward, and numerous businesses falter in their attempts due to the absence of essential technical infrastructure, organizational capabilities, and a coherent strategic direction (Khaled Lafi Al-Naif and Ata E. M. Al Shraah, 2018). The burgeoning digitization of customer interactions, coupled with our increasing reliance on digital platforms for daily activities, has granted businesses access to an unparalleled wealth of customer data (Mert, 2022). This treasure trove of information holds the potential to significantly enhance customer service and engagement (Murphy, 2012). Yet, it's imperative to recognize that successfully leveraging this data is contingent on a company's ability to harness its technical capabilities, streamline its organizational structure, and align its strategy with the evolving digital landscape (Ogunmola et al., 2021).

Predictive marketing serves as the bridge connecting the realms of machine learning and human intelligence (Pandit, 2023). Its primary purpose is to bolster and enhance human intelligence by incorporating the capabilities of machine learning (Provost & Fawcett, 2013). In essence, predictive marketing works to empower and elevate human decision-making through the integration of machine learning technologies (Regin et al., 2023).

Predictive marketing places a central emphasis on nurturing and managing customer relationships rather than solely concentrating on product development or sales channels (Rad et al., 2020). In this customer-centric approach, the focus shifts from merely identifying potential customers for existing products to the capability of anticipating which products will align with the evolving preferences of existing customers (Rad et al., 2019).

Rather than aiming solely to maximize sales, organizations operating within this customer-centric paradigm, often referred to as the "customer era," prioritize the optimization of customer lifetime value and the expansion of the share of wallet (Rad et al., 2022). These strategies are seen as instrumental in driving overall enterprise profitability (Rajest et al., 2022).

Furthermore, the traditional organizational structure, which was often organized around product lines or sales channels, is reconfigured to center around the customer (Ramos et al., 2023). Placing the customer at the heart of operations, companies harness the power of big data and predictive analytics to adapt processes and organizational structures in ways that facilitate personalized interactions (Regin et al., 2023).

This shift results in communications becoming highly targeted, with the paramount metric being the relevance of the message rather than its reach (Regin et al., 2023). The evolution towards relevance-centric communication is a hallmark of the customer-centric approach fostered by predictive marketing practices (Regin et al., 2023).

2. PREDICTIVE ANALYTICS MODELS FOR MARKETING

2.1. Clustering Model

Clustering models, a subset of unsupervised machine learning techniques, are pivotal tools in data analysis and pattern recognition (Regin et al., 2023). These models aim to group similar data points together while distinguishing them from dissimilar ones, thereby revealing hidden structures and insights within datasets. Clustering has wide-ranging applications across various domains, including marketing, customer segmentation, image recognition, biology, and recommendation systems (Roman et al., 2020). In this exploration, we delve into the world of clustering models, examining their fundamental concepts, common algorithms, practical applications, and potential challenges (Sabti et al., 2023).

At its core, clustering is about organizing data into meaningful groups, or clusters, based on inherent similarities or patterns among data points (Said & Tripathi, 2023). These groups often lack predefined labels, making clustering a form of unsupervised learning (Saxena & Chaudhary, 2023). The primary objective is to discover hidden structures within the data, enhance data understanding, and support decision-making processes (figure 1) (Sharma et al., 2021a).

A: Moderate purchaser
B: High Spenders –Frequent purchaser
C: Poor Purchaser
D: Rare Purchaser

Figure 1. Customers are clustered based on their purchase pattern

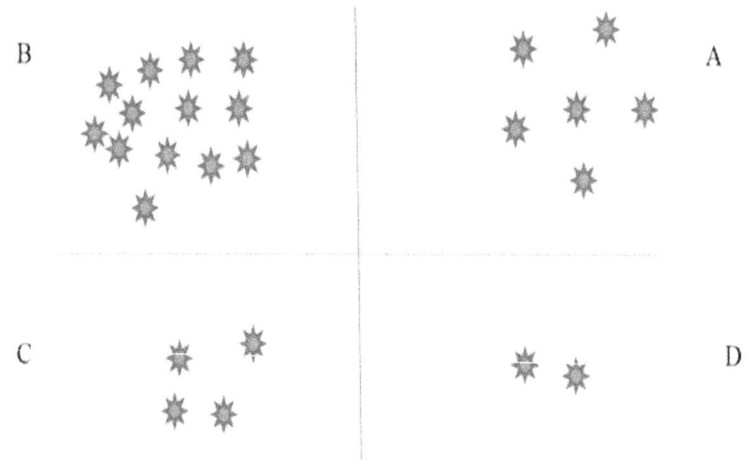

Clustering helps businesses group customers with similar behaviors, preferences, or purchase histories (Sharma et al., 2021b). This information is invaluable for targeted marketing campaigns, product recommendations, and personalized experiences (Sharma et al., 2021c).

In image analysis, clustering can be used to segment images, recognize objects, or identify regions of interest (Sharma et al., 2021d). It's widely employed in medical imaging, object tracking, and facial recognition systems (Shynu et al., 2023). Clustering can be applied to detect anomalies or outliers in data, which is critical in fraud detection, network security, and quality control (Siegel, 2013).

2.2. Sales Forecasting Model

Sales forecasting is a critical aspect of business planning and strategy that involves predicting future sales performance based on historical data and various quantitative and qualitative factors (Srivastava & Roychoudhury, 2020). Accurate sales forecasting provides organizations with valuable insights into revenue expectations, helps in managing resources efficiently, and enables informed decision-making (Srivastava & Roychoudhury, 2021). To achieve this, companies often employ various sales forecasting models (Steffi et al., 2023).

Time series forecasting relies on historical sales data to project future sales patterns (Shynu et al., 2023). It assumes that future sales will exhibit similar trends and seasonality as observed in the past (Steffi et al., 2023). Techniques such as moving averages, exponential smoothing, and autoregressive integrated moving averages (ARIMA) are commonly used within the time series framework.

Moving averages calculate the average of sales data over a specific time period, smoothing out short-term fluctuations and highlighting underlying trends (Strickland, 2015). Exponential smoothing assigns exponentially decreasing weights to past observations, giving more significance to recent data. ARIMA models take into account both trend and seasonality, making them suitable for more complex time series data.

Machine learning techniques are also increasingly being employed for sales forecasting. Linear regression, decision trees, and neural networks are among the algorithms used to capture complex relationships between sales and various predictors. Linear regression models estimate the linear relationship between sales and one or more independent variables like advertising expenditure, economic indicators, or customer demographics. Decision trees segment data into subsets based on predictor values, allowing for non-linear relationships to be captured. Neural networks, especially deep learning models, can identify intricate patterns in large datasets, making them well-suited for complex sales forecasting tasks.

Another important aspect of sales forecasting is demand forecasting, particularly in industries with perishable goods or variable demand. Demand forecasting models estimate the future demand for specific products or services, enabling businesses to optimize inventory management and production planning. These models consider factors like historical demand patterns, market trends, seasonality, and external factors such as economic conditions and competitor actions (figure 2).

Figure 2. Unsupervised learning-clustering
Source: Analytics Vidhya (2022)

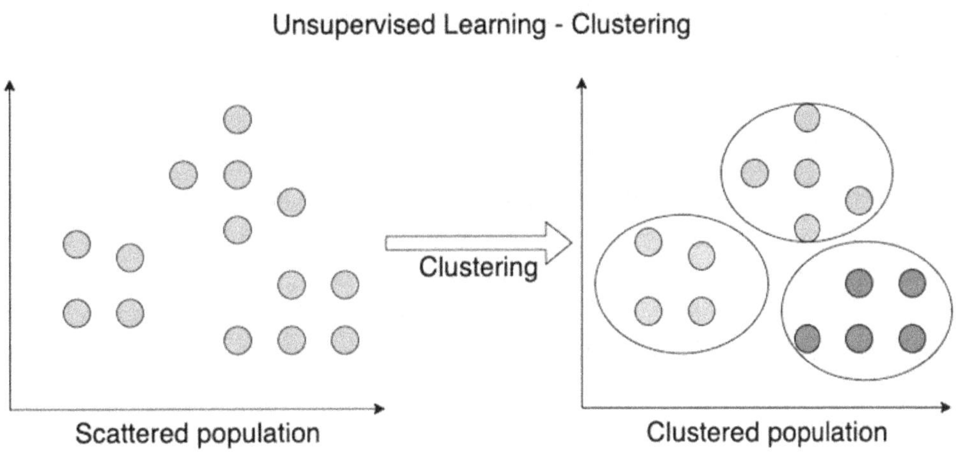

2.3. Cross-Selling and Upselling Model

Cross-Selling:

Cross-selling and upselling models are essential strategies used by businesses to increase revenue and enhance customer relationships. These techniques involve offering customers additional products or services that complement or upgrade their initial purchases. By effectively implementing cross-selling and upselling models, companies can boost their profitability and provide customers with enhanced value (Winters & Hummel, 2014).

Cross-selling is the practice of offering customers related or complementary products or services to what they are already purchasing. The goal is to encourage customers to add more items to their cart or engage in additional transactions. This strategy is particularly effective in e-commerce, retail, and service industries.

To implement cross-selling effectively, businesses can utilize data analytics and customer segmentation to understand the preferences and buying patterns of their customers. Recommendation engines powered by machine learning algorithms can analyze historical purchase data and make personalized cross-selling suggestions in real-time. Amazon's "Customers who bought this also bought..." feature is a well-known example of this strategy.

Upselling:

Upselling involves encouraging customers to upgrade to a more expensive or feature-rich version of a product or service they intend to purchase. It aims to maximize the value of the customer's transaction and increase the average order value.

In a software context, upselling might involve offering a premium subscription with additional features or offering a larger-sized product. In the airline industry, it could involve offering passengers the option to upgrade their seats to business class.

3. SALES PIPELINE ANALYSIS

Sales pipeline analysis is a critical aspect of sales management and strategy that involves the systematic examination and monitoring of the various stages a sales opportunity goes through, from initial lead generation to final deal closure. It provides organizations with valuable insights into the health and efficiency of their sales processes, helping them make informed decisions, allocate resources effectively, and ultimately improve sales performance (Tambaip et al., 2023).

Visualizing Sales Progress: One of the fundamental benefits of sales pipeline analysis is its ability to provide a visual representation of the sales process. Sales managers and teams can see, at a glance, how many leads are in each stage of the pipeline, which deals are progressing, and where potential bottlenecks or delays might occur. This visualization helps in managing sales opportunities effectively.

Forecasting Sales Revenue: By tracking the value of deals at each stage of the pipeline, businesses can estimate future revenue more accurately. This is especially important for setting revenue targets, resource allocation, and financial planning. It allows organizations to anticipate potential shortfalls or surpluses in revenue and make adjustments accordingly.

Identifying Sales Trends: Sales pipeline analysis enables the identification of trends and patterns in the sales process. This includes insights into which products or services are selling well, which market segments are most profitable, and which sales representatives are performing at their best. These insights can guide strategic decisions such as product development, marketing campaigns, and resource allocation.

Improving Sales Efficiency: By analyzing the conversion rates between pipeline stages, businesses can identify areas where sales opportunities are getting stuck or dropping out of the pipeline. This information is crucial for process optimization and improving overall sales efficiency. For example, it may reveal the need for additional training or support for sales teams at specific stages (figure 3).

Prioritizing Leads: Not all leads are equal in terms of potential value or likelihood of conversion. Sales pipeline analysis helps in lead prioritization by assigning scores or rankings to leads based on their characteristics and behavior. This allows sales teams to focus their efforts on high-potential opportunities, improving their chances of success.

Managing Resources: By understanding the status and volume of opportunities in the pipeline, organizations can allocate resources such as sales personnel, marketing budgets, and customer support more effectively. This prevents overcommitting or underutilizing resources at different stages of the sales process.

Enhancing Customer Relationships: A well-managed sales pipeline also facilitates better customer relationships. Sales teams can stay organized and ensure timely follow-ups, which enhances the customer experience. It also enables sales representatives to provide more accurate information to customers regarding order delivery and support.

Real-Time Monitoring: In today's dynamic business environment, real-time monitoring of the sales pipeline is crucial. Advanced CRM (Customer Relationship Management) systems and analytics tools provide up-to-the-minute insights into sales performance, allowing businesses to make agile decisions in response to changing market conditions.

Figure 3. Sales pipeline

4. SENTIMENT ANALYSIS

Sentiment analysis, also known as opinion mining, is a powerful natural language processing (NLP) technique that involves the use of algorithms and machine learning models to analyze and determine the sentiment or emotional tone expressed in text data. It helps businesses and organizations gain valuable insights into public opinion, customer feedback, social media discussions, and online reviews.

Sentiment analysis works by processing and categorizing text data into different sentiment categories, typically positive, negative, or neutral. More advanced sentiment analysis models may employ a finer-grained approach, categorizing sentiments into multiple categories like strongly positive, moderately positive, mildly positive, and so on.

While sentiment analysis is a powerful tool, it faces challenges such as sarcasm, irony, context-dependent sentiments, and language nuances that can be difficult for models to interpret accurately. Additionally, sentiment analysis models may struggle with analyzing text in languages.

4.1. Customer Lifetime Value (LTV) Prediction

Customer Lifetime Value (LTV) prediction is a crucial concept and practice in marketing and customer relationship management that estimates the total value a customer is expected to generate for a business over their entire relationship. It plays a pivotal role in shaping marketing strategies, customer acquisition efforts, and overall business profitability.

LTV prediction involves analyzing historical customer data to forecast how much revenue an individual customer is likely to generate in the future. The following key components are typically considered in LTV calculations:

Historical Purchase Behavior: This includes data on a customer's past purchases, frequency of purchases, and the monetary value of those transactions. Analyzing purchase history provides insights into spending patterns and customer loyalty.

Churn Rate: Understanding the likelihood of a customer churning (i.e., ceasing to do business with the company) is critical. High churn rates can significantly impact LTV, so strategies to reduce churn are essential.

Average Order Value (AOV): AOV measures the average amount a customer spends in a single transaction. Knowing this value helps in estimating the potential revenue from future purchases.

Purchase Frequency: This metric represents how often a customer makes a purchase. Predicting future purchase frequency is essential for LTV calculations.

Customer Retention Period: This is the estimated time a customer will continue to do business with the company. It is used to determine the duration over which LTV is calculated with limited training data.

4.2. Attribution Model

Attribution modeling is a crucial analytical framework used in digital marketing to determine the value and impact of various marketing channels and touchpoints along the customer journey. It allows businesses to understand how different marketing efforts contribute to conversions and sales, helping them allocate resources effectively and optimize their marketing strategies.

Applications of Attribution Modeling:

Optimizing Marketing Budgets: Attribution modeling helps businesses allocate marketing budgets more effectively. By understanding which channels are most influential, they can invest more in high-impact areas.

Improving Campaign Efficiency: Marketers can optimize their campaigns by focusing on the channels and strategies that contribute the most to conversions, resulting in better ROI.

Identifying Weak Points: Attribution modeling highlights areas of the customer journey that may need improvement. This can lead to refinements in marketing strategies or website design to enhance the overall user experience.

Enhancing Customer Engagement: By knowing the customer journey path, businesses can create more personalized and effective content and messaging for each stage of the journey.

Measuring Marketing Channel Effectiveness: Attribution modeling helps marketers measure the success of individual marketing channels and campaigns accurately, ensuring data-driven decision-making.

4.3. Propensity Model

When most people think of predictive analytics, they picture probability or propensity models. Neural networks, logistic regression, random forest, and regression trees are just few of the mathematical processes used in these models. Marketers could care less about the names of these algorithms. What's crucial to understand is that propensity models accurately forecast a customer's future behaviour by gaining insight from historical data.

In direct mail, propensity models are commonly referred to as reaction models since they predict a customer's response, such as whether or not they would make a purchase after receiving a mailer. As guided-learning models, propensity models improve with time and experience, but this training process does take some time. Models can improve their accuracy over time by collecting and analysing data, such as whether or not a buyer really made a purchase after being targeted (Venkateswaran et al., 2023).

4.4. RFM Model

RFM (Recency, Frequency, Monetary) modeling is a method employed in predictive analytics and customer segmentation to gain insights into customer behavior and classify them based on their past interactions. This approach finds extensive application in marketing and customer relationship management (CRM) to pinpoint specific customer groups and tailor personalized marketing strategies. Let's delve into the workings of RFM modeling:

Recency (R):

Recency gauges how recently a customer has engaged with your business or made a purchase. Customers who have interacted more recently are often more engaged and valuable. To determine recency, the time elapsed since the customer's last interaction or purchase is computed, typically measured in days or months.

Frequency (F):

Frequency assesses how often a customer engages with your business or makes purchases. Customers who frequently interact may exhibit greater loyalty and value. To calculate frequency, you tally the number of transactions or interactions within a specific timeframe, such as a year.

Monetary (M):

Monetary value quantifies how much money a customer has spent on your products or services. High-value customers are those who have made substantial purchases. To derive monetary value, you sum up the total expenditure by a customer over a specific period.

Once you have computed the R, F, and M scores for each customer, you can leverage this information for predictive analytics and customer segmentation:

Customer Segmentation:

Using RFM scores, you can divide your customer base into distinct groups. For instance:

High-Value Customers: Marked by high R, high F, and high M scores.

Loyal but Dormant Customers: Characterized by high F, low R, and high M scores.

New or Recently Active Customers: Identified by high R, low F, and high M scores.

At-Risk Customers: Typically exhibit low R, low F, and high M scores.

Low-Value Customers: Typically display low R, low F, and low M scores.

Personalized Marketing:

Marketing campaigns and promotions can be customized for specific customer segments based on their RFM scores. For example, you might offer discounts to at-risk customers to re-engage them or recommend new products to high-value customers to boost their spending.

Customer Lifecycle Management:

RFM modeling aids in comprehending where customers stand in their lifecycle with your business. This information can guide the development of targeted retention and acquisition strategies.

4.5. Decision Tree Model

A decision tree model is a widely used tool in predictive analytics and machine learning for making decisions or predictions based on a set of conditions or features. It is a tree-like structure where each internal node represents a feature or attribute, each branch represents a decision or rule, and each leaf node represents an outcome or a class label. Decision tree models are employed for various tasks, including classification and regression. Here's an overview of decision tree models in predictive analytics:

Decision Tree Structure:

Root Node: The top node of the tree represents the initial decision point and is based on the most important feature or attribute in the dataset.

Internal Nodes: These nodes represent intermediate decision points, where a feature is evaluated to make a decision about which branch to follow.

Branches: The branches emanating from each internal node correspond to the possible outcomes or values of the feature being evaluated.

Leaf Nodes: The terminal nodes or leaf nodes provide the final prediction or classification.

4.6. Logistic Regression Model

Logistic regression is a statistical modeling technique that is widely used in marketing for various purposes, including customer behavior prediction, lead scoring, customer segmentation, and response modeling. Here's how logistic regression models are used in marketing:

Customer Behavior Prediction: Logistic regression can be used to predict binary outcomes, such as whether a customer will purchase a product (yes/no) or whether they will churn (stay or leave). For example, a marketing team might build a logistic regression model to predict whether a customer is likely to make a purchase based on various customer attributes and historical data.

Lead Scoring: In lead generation and sales, logistic regression models can be employed to assign scores to leads based on the probability of conversion. This helps sales teams prioritize leads with a higher likelihood of converting into paying customers.

Customer Segmentation: Logistic regression can assist in segmenting customers into different groups based on their likelihood to take a specific action. For instance, marketers might use logistic regression to segment customers into high-value, medium-value, and low-value groups for targeted marketing campaigns.

Response Modeling: Logistic regression is often used in direct marketing campaigns, such as email marketing or direct mail. Marketers can build models to predict the likelihood of a customer responding to a marketing message or offer. This allows for the customization of marketing materials and targeting those customers who are most likely to respond positively.

Market Basket Analysis: Logistic regression can also be applied to understand associations between products or services that customers tend to buy together. This information can be used for cross-selling and bundling strategies.

5. CONCLUSION

Predictive analytics models have become indispensable tools in modern marketing management. These models enable organizations to move beyond traditional approaches and make data-driven decisions that directly impact their marketing strategies. By harnessing historical data, statistical algorithms, and machine learning techniques, businesses can anticipate customer behavior, forecast trends, and identify opportunities and risks. Predictive analytics in marketing empowers businesses to personalize their marketing efforts, target the right audiences, and optimize resource allocation. It enhances lead scoring, customer segmentation, and response modeling, making marketing campaigns more efficient and effective. Moreover, predictive analytics enables organizations to adapt quickly to changing market dynamics and customer preferences.

However, the successful implementation of predictive analytics in marketing requires more than just data and algorithms. It necessitates a robust technical infrastructure, skilled data analysts, and a culture of data-driven decision-making. Organizations must also address privacy and ethical considerations when handling customer data. As the marketing landscape continues to evolve, predictive analytics will play an increasingly vital role in helping businesses stay competitive and relevant. It empowers marketing professionals to make informed choices, maximize ROI, and ultimately deliver more value to their customers. In the digital age, where data is abundant, and customer expectations are high, predictive analytics models are a powerful ally in achieving marketing success.

REFERENCES

Abu-Rumman, A. (2021). Effective Knowledge Sharing: A Guide to the Key Enablers and Inhibitors. In D. Tessier (Ed.), *Handbook of Research on Organizational Culture Strategies for Effective Knowledge Management and Performance* (pp. 133–156). IGI Global. doi:10.4018/978-1-7998-7422-5.ch008

Abu-Rumman, A., & Qawasmeh, R. (2021). Assessing international students' satisfaction of a Jordanian university using the service quality model. *Journal of Applied Research in Higher Education*. Advance online publication. doi:10.1108/JARHE-05-2021-0166

Al-maaitah, D. A., Tha'er Majali, M. A., & Almaaitah, T. A. (2021). The role of leadership styles on staffs job satisfaction in public organizations. *Journal of Contemporary Issues in Business and Government*, *27*(1), 772–783.

Al-maaitah, T. A., Tha'er Majali, M. A., & Almaaitah, D. A. (2021). The Impact of COVID-19 on the Electronic Commerce Users Behavior. *Journal of Contemporary Issues in Business and Government*, *27*(1), 772–783.

Al-Naif, K. L., & Al Shraah, A. E. M. (2018). Working capital management and profitability: Evidence from Jordanian mining and extraction industry sector. *IUG Journal of Economics and Business.*, *2*(1), 42–60.

Al Shraah, A., Abu-Rumman, A., Alqhaiwi, L. A., & AlSha'ar, H. (2022). The impact of sourcing strategies and logistics capabilities on organizational performance during the COVID-19 pandemic: Evidence from Jordanian pharmaceutical industries. *Uncertain Supply Chain Management*, *10*(3), 1077–1090. doi:10.5267/j.uscm.2022.2.004

Al Shraah, A., Irtaimeh, H. J., & Rumman, M. A. (2013). The Strategic Human Resource Management Practices in Implying Total Quality Management (TQM): An Empirical Study on Jordanian Banking Sector. *International Journal of Management*, *4*(5), 179–190.

Alayli, S. (2023). Unravelling the Drivers of Online Purchasing Intention: The E-Commerce Scenario in Lebanon. *FMDB Transactions on Sustainable Social Sciences Letters*, *1*(1), 56–67.

Ameisen, E. (2019). *Building machine learning-powered applications*. O'Reilly Media.

Anand, P. P., Kanike, U. K., Paramasivan, P., Rajest, S. S., Regin, R., & Priscila, S. S. (2023). Embracing Industry 5.0: Pioneering Next-Generation Technology for a Flourishing Human Experience and Societal Advancement. *FMDB Transactions on Sustainable Social Sciences Letters*, *1*(1), 43–55.

Arslan, F., Singh, B., Sharma, D. K., Regin, R., Steffi, R., & Rajest, S. S. (2021). Optimization technique approach to resolve food sustainability problems. In *2021 International Conference on Computational Intelligence and Knowledge Economy (ICCIKE)*. IEEE. 10.1109/ICCIKE51210.2021.9410735

Bari, A., Chaouchi, M., & Jung, T. (2016). *Predictive analytics for dummies*. Wiley.

Burkov, A. (2019). *The hundred-page machine learning book*. Andriy Burkov.

Demeter, E., Rad, D., & Balas, E. (2021). Schadenfreude and General Anti-Social Behaviours: The Role of Violent Content Preferences and Life Satisfaction. BRAIN. *Broad Research in Artificial Intelligence and Neuroscience*, *12*(2), 98–111. doi:10.18662/brain/12.2/194

Gupta, R. K. (2021a). A study on occupational health hazards among construction workers in India. *International Journal of Enterprise Network Management*, *12*(4), 325–339. doi:10.1504/IJENM.2021.119663

Gupta, R. K. (2021b). Adoption of mobile wallet services: An empirical analysis. *International Journal of Intellectual Property Management*, *12*(3), 341–353. doi:10.1504/IJIPM.2022.124634

Gupta, R. K. (2022). Utilization of Digital Network Learning and Healthcare for Verbal Assessment and Counselling During Post COVID-19 Period. *Technologies Artificial Intelligence and the Future of Learning Post-COVID*, *19*, 117–134.

Mert, I. (2022). *Assessment of Accounting Evaluation Practices, A Research-Based Review of Turkey and Romania. Springer Cham.*

Murphy, K. P. (2012). *Machine learning: A probabilistic perspective*. MIT Press.

Ogunmola, G. A., Singh, B., Sharma, D. K., Regin, R., Rajest, S. S., & Singh, N. (2021). Involvement of distance measure in assessing and resolving efficiency environmental obstacles. In *2021 International Conference on Computational Intelligence and Knowledge Economy (ICCIKE)*. IEEE. 10.1109/ICCIKE51210.2021.9410765

Pandit, P. (2023). On the Context of the Principle of Beneficence: The Problem of Over Demandingness within Utilitarian Theory. *FMDB Transactions on Sustainable Social Sciences Letters*, *1*(1), 26–42.

Provost, F., & Fawcett, T. (2013). *Data science for business*. O'Reilly Media.

Rad, D., Balas, E., Ignat, S., Rad, G., & Dixon, D. (2020). A Predictive Model of Youth Bystanders' Helping Attitudes. *Revista Romanesco pentru educatie multidimensionala-Journal for Multidimensional Education, 12*(1Sup2), 136-150.

Rad, D., Dughi, T., & Demeter, E. (2019). The Dynamics of the Relationship between Humor and Benevolence as Values. *Revista romaneasca pentru educatie multidimensionala-Journal for Multidimensional Education, 11*(3), 201-212.

Rad, D., Egerau, A., Roman, A., Dughi, T., Balas, E., Maier, R., & Rad, G. (2022). A Preliminary Investigation of the Technology Acceptance Model (TAM) in Early Childhood Education and Care. BRAIN. *Broad Research in Artificial Intelligence and Neuroscience*, *13*(1), 518–533. doi:10.18662/brain/13.1/297

Rajest, S. S., & Regin, R., T, S., & R, S. (2022). Strategic Leadership And Alignment Affect Organisation Performance. *Central Asian Journal Of Mathematical Theory And Computer Sciences*, *3*(12), 248–266.

Ramos, J. I., Lacerona, R., & Nunag, J. M. (2023). A Study on Operational Excellence, Work Environment Factors and the Impact to Employee Performance. *FMDB Transactions on Sustainable Social Sciences Letters*, *1*(1), 12–25.

Regin, R., & Rajest, S. S., T, S., & R, S. (2023a). A Review of Secure Neural Networks and Big Data Mining Applications in Financial Risk Assessment. *Central Asian Journal of Innovations on Tourism Management and Finance*, *4*(2), 73–90.

Regin, R., & Rajest, S. S., T, S., & R, S. (2023b). An Analytical Study of Development in Response to the COVID-19 Pandemic. *Central Asian Journal of Medical and Natural Science*, *4*(1), 199–216.

Regin, R., & Rajest, S. S., T, S., & R, S. (2023c). Human Resource Perspective and Pitfalls at Work. *Central Asian Journal of Innovations on Tourism Management and Finance*, *4*(1), 31–49.

Regin, R., Rajest, S. S., Shynu, T., & Steffi, R. (2023). Audit Committee and the Overall Performance of Companies. International Journal on Economics. *Finance and Sustainable Development*, *5*(3), 18–31.

Regin, R., Suman Rajest, S., Shynu, T., & Steffi, R. (2023). Electronic Tourism as A Destination Marketing Strategy for World Travellers. *Central Asian Journal of Mathematical Theory and Computer Sciences.*, *4*(5), 9–28.

Roman, A., Rad, D., Egerau, A., Dixon, D., Dughi, T., Kelemen, G., & Rad, G. (2020). Physical Self-Schema Acceptance and Perceived Severity of Online Aggressiveness in Cyberbullying Incidents. *Journal of Interdisciplinary Studies in Education*, *9*(1), 100–116. doi:10.32674/jise.v9i1.1961

Sabti, Y. M., Alqatrani, R. I. N., Zaid, M. I., Taengkliang, B., & Kareem, J. M. (2023). Impact of Business Environment on the Performance of Employees in the Public-Listed Companies. *FMDB Transactions on Sustainable Management Letters*, *1*(2), 56–65.

Said, F. B., & Tripathi, S. (2023). Epistemology of Digital Journalism Shift in South Global Nations: A Bibliometric Analysis. *FMDB Transactions on Sustainable Technoprise Letters*, *1*(1), 47–60.

Saxena, D., & Chaudhary, S. (2023). Predicting Brain Diseases from FMRI-Functional Magnetic Resonance Imaging with Machine Learning Techniques for Early Diagnosis and Treatment. *FMDB Transactions on Sustainable Computer Letters*, *1*(1), 33–48.

Sharma, D. K., Jalil, N. A., Regin, R., Rajest, S. S., Tummala, R. K., & Thangadurai. (2021a). Predicting network congestion with machine learning. In *2021 2nd International Conference on Smart Electronics and Communication (ICOSEC)*. IEEE.

Sharma, D. K., Singh, B., Raja, M., Regin, R., & Rajest, S. S. (2021b). An Efficient Python Approach for Simulation of Poisson Distribution. In *2021 7th International Conference on Advanced Computing and Communication Systems (ICACCS)*. IEEE.

Sharma, D. K., Singh, B., Regin, R., Steffi, R., & Chakravarthi, M. K. (2021c). Efficient Classification for Neural Machines Interpretations based on Mathematical models. In *2021 7th International Conference on Advanced Computing and Communication Systems (ICACCS)*. IEEE.

Sharma, K., Singh, B., Herman, E., Regine, R., Rajest, S. S., & Mishra, V. P. (2021d). Maximum information measure policies in reinforcement learning with deep energy-based model. In *2021 International Conference on Computational Intelligence and Knowledge Economy (ICCIKE)*. IEEE. 10.1109/ICCIKE51210.2021.9410756

Shynu, T., Rajest, S. S., Regin, R., & Steffi, R. (2023). Data Mining-Based Point of Sale with Auto-Source Triggering and Business Reports. *Central Asian Journal Of Mathematical Theory And Computer Sciences*, *4*(2), 116–141.

Shynu, T., Rajest, S. S., Regin, R., & Steffi, R. (2023). Analysis of the Impact of Employee Training and Development on Performance. *Central Asian Journal of Innovations on Tourism Management and Finance*, *4*(6), 1–25.

Siegel, E. (2013). *Predictive analytics: The power to predict who will click, buy, lie, or die*. Wiley.

Srivastava, D. K., & Roychoudhury, B. (2020). Words are important: A textual content based identity resolution scheme across multiple online social networks. *Knowledge-Based Systems*, *195*, 105624. doi:10.1016/j.knosys.2020.105624

Srivastava, D. K., & Roychoudhury, B. (2021). Understanding the Factors that Influence Adoption of Privacy Protection Features in Online Social Networks. *Journal of Global Information Technology Management*, *24*(3), 164–182. doi:10.1080/1097198X.2021.1954416

Steffi, R., Rajest, S. S., Regin, R., & Shynu, T. (2023). An Examination of the Effects That Marketing Methods Have on Non-Governmental Organizations. *Middle European Scientific Bulletin*, *34*(3), 189–207.

Steffi, R., Rajest, S. S., Regin, R., & Shynu, T. (2023). Developing Banking Sector Strategies Amid Economic Turmoil. International Journal on Economics. *Finance and Sustainable Development*, *5*(4), 78–100.

Strickland, J. (2015). *Predictive analytics using R*. CreateSpace Independent Publishing Platform.

Tambaip, B., Hadi, A. F. F., & Tjilen, A. P. (2023). Optimizing Public Service Performance: Unleashing the Potential of Compassion as an Indicator of Public Service Motivation. *FMDB Transactions on Sustainable Management Letters*, *1*(2), 46–55.

Venkateswaran, P. S., Singh, S., Paramasivan, P., Rajest, S. S., Lourens, M. E., & Regin, R. (2023). A Study on The Influence of Quality of Service on Customer Satisfaction Towards Hotel Industry. *FMDB Transactions on Sustainable Social Sciences Letters*, *1*(1), 1–11.

Vidhya, A. (2022). Retrieved October 22, 2023, from Analyticsvidhya.com website: https://www.analyticsvidhya.com/

Winters, R., & Hummel, M. (2014). *Practical predictive analytics*. Pearson.

Chapter 5
Celebrating Lives Beyond on Unveiling the Digital Legacy Manager for Empowering Personal Heritage Preservation

S. Sivabala
SRM Institute of Science and Technology, Ramapuram, India

P. Vidyasri
SRM Institute of Science and Technology, Ramapuram, India

ABSTRACT

Technology has changed how people communicate, store information, and curate their lives in the digital age. This research study examines the complex management and preservation of digital legacies, a collection of digital assets, online accounts, and personal narratives left by deceased people. Digital inheritance offers a complex issue that requires a holistic approach. This research develops the Digital Legacy Manager software to handle this difficulty. The study discusses unmanaged digital legacies to start. It examines the emotional and psychological effects of impediments to obtaining digital relics of the deceased on bereaved loved ones. It also examines the complex financial and legal issues that arise when digital assets are out of reach, including lengthy legal battles and unsolved financial matters. When digital footprints are ignored, shared experiences, personal narratives, and cultural heritage are lost forever.

1. INTRODUCTION

1.1 Background

In today's digital era, people rely heavily on technology for communication, storing personal information, and documenting their lives (Heath, 2020; Wijesundara, & Fernando, 2020). The proliferation of social media, email accounts, online banking, cloud storage, and various digital platforms has resulted in the

DOI: 10.4018/979-8-3693-2193-5.ch005

creation of vast amounts of digital data (Cleland & Williamson, 2017). While these digital footprints offer convenience and connectivity, they also pose challenges when managing and preserving one's digital legacy after one passes away (table 1).

Table 1. Impact of unmanaged digital legacies

Emotional and Psychological Toll	
Lack of closure	Many individuals suffer from emotional distress and unresolved feelings when they are unable toaccess or receive messages from their deceased loved ones.
Financial and Legal Implications	Unmanaged digital legacies can lead to financial complications and legal challenges, especiallyregarding access to online accounts and digital assets.
Loss of Shared Memories and Stories	Without managed digital legacies, shared memories, stories, and experiences can be lost, leaving future generations without a connection to theirfamily history.

1.2 Problem Statement

When individuals pass away without a plan for their digital assets and accounts, their loved ones are often left in a state of uncertainty and frustration (Devi & Rajasekaran, 2023). Accessing and managing these digital legacies becomes a daunting task, leading to emotional distress, financial burdens, and legal complications. Furthermore, the lack of access to important personal information, cherished memories, and final messages can deeply impact the grieving process and the ability to honor the deceased's wishes (Regin et al., 2023).

1.3 Objectives

The primary objective of this research paper is to explore the experiences of individuals who have suffered from the lack of access to their loved ones' digital information after their passing. By understanding the challenges and consequences associated with unmanaged digital legacies, we aim to highlight the importance of addressing this issue (Sajini et al., 2023).

The secondary objective is to propose the development of a software application, the Digital Legacy Manager, to empower individuals to preserve and share their digital legacies effectively. This software will enable users to organize and securely store their digital assets, leave messages for their loved ones, and provide a framework for managing and transferring their digital information after their demise (Gaayathri et al., 2023).

Through this research, we seek to shed light on the significance of leaving a meaningful digital legacy, improve the posthumous digital access experience for loved ones, and provide a practical solution that bridges the gap between technology and the human need for connection, remembrance, and closure (Smith et al., 2017).

2. UNDERSTANDING DIGITAL LEGACIES

2.1 Definition and Scope

Digital legacies refer to the collection of an individual's digital assets, accounts, and online presence that they leave behind after their death (Cirillo et al., 2023). These can include but are not limited to social media profiles, email accounts, digital photos and videos, blogs, online subscriptions, financial records, and personal documents stored in the cloud or on electronic devices (Perera, 2020). The scope of digital legacies encompasses both the tangible and intangible aspects of an individual's digital presence (table 2).

Table 2. Types of digital legacies

Types of Digital Legacy	Examples	Challenges
Social Media Accounts	Facebook, Instagram,Twitter	Gaining posthumousaccess
Digital Assets	Photos, Videos,Documents	Organizing andpreserving assets
Online Accounts	Email, Banking, Subscriptions	Securing and managing the accountcredentials
Digital Memories	Blogs, Diaries, Journals	Ensuringaccessibility and privacy

2.2 Types of Digital Legacies

Digital legacies can be categorized into different types based on their nature and purpose. Some common types of digital legacies include:

- Social Media Legacies: These encompass the individual's social media accounts and the content they have shared, including photos, videos, posts, and interactions with others (Sepúlveda & Parra-Arnau, 2021).
- Personal Digital Archives: This includes personal documents, photos, videos, and other digital files stored on electronic devices or in the cloud. It often represents a person's life history, memories, and personal milestones.
- Financial and Business Legacies: These encompass online banking and investment accounts, business-related documents, client information, and other digital assets associated with financial and business affairs (Littman, 2015).

Creative Works and Intellectual Property: Digital legacies can also consist of creative works such as writings, music compositions, artwork, and other intellectual property stored in digital formats.

2.3 Challenges and Consequences of Unmanaged Digital Legacies

The lack of planning and management of digital legacies can give rise to several challenges and consequences:

- Difficulty in Access and Retrieval: Loved ones may encounter obstacles in gaining access to the deceased person's online accounts, digital files, and personal information, leading to frustration and difficulties in handling administrative and financial matters.
- Emotional and Psychological Impact: The loss of access to cherished memories, and personal messages and the inability to continue interacting with the digital presence of the deceased can intensify the grieving process and impede closure for family and friends.
- Legal and Financial Complexities: Unmanaged digital legacies can result in legal challenges related to digital inheritance, intellectual property rights, and privacy issues. Moreover, the lack of access to important financial information and accounts can cause financial hardship and delays in settling the deceased person's affairs (Oosterman et al., 2016).
- Loss of Family History and Cultural Heritage: Digital legacies often contain valuable family history, cultural traditions, and personal stories. Without proper management, this rich heritage may be lost, depriving future generations of their roots and identities (Schilder & Clark, 2018).

Understanding these challenges and consequences emphasizes the need for proactive measures in managing digital legacies and underscores the significance of developing a comprehensive solution, such as the Digital Legacy Manager, to address these issues effectively (Lodha et al., 2023).

3. IMPACT ON LOVED ONES

3.1 Emotional and Psychological Toll

The unavailability of a loved one's digital legacy can have a profound emotional and psychological impact on those left behind. The inability to access personal messages, photos, and other digital artifacts of the deceased can intensify grief, prolong the mourning process, and hinder the healing and acceptance of loss. The digital presence of a loved one often serves as a source of comfort, connection, and remembrance, and its absence can leave a void in the lives of the bereaved.

3.2 Financial and Legal Implications

Unmanaged digital legacies can give rise to financial and legal complexities for the loved ones of the deceased. Financially, the lack of access to online banking accounts, investment portfolios, and other digital financial assets can lead to delays in handling financial matters, paying bills, and accessing funds necessary for the family's well-being. From a legal perspective, the absence of a clear plan for digital inheritance and the transfer of digital assets can result in disputes, legal battles, and uncertainties surrounding the ownership and control of these assets.

3.3 Loss of Shared Memories and Stories

Digital legacies often hold a wealth of shared memories and stories that form an integral part of a family's history and cultural heritage. These digital artifacts, such as photos, videos, and written messages, not only provide a sense of identity and belonging but also serve as a means of passing on traditions, values, and life lessons to future generations. The loss of access to these shared memories and stories can deprive loved ones of the opportunity to connect with their past and preserve their family's legacy for future descendants (Jeba et al., 2023).

Recognizing the significant impact on loved ones underscores the importance of developing solutions that facilitate the management, preservation, and access to digital legacies. By addressing the emotional, financial, and cultural implications of unmanaged digital legacies, the Digital Legacy Manager aims to alleviate these burdens and provide a means for loved ones to cherish, honor, and pass on the digital heritage of their deceased family members.

4. IMPORTANCE OF LEAVING MESSAGES

4.1 Expressing Love and Gratitude

Leaving messages for loved ones is a powerful way to express love, appreciation, and gratitude. In the digital realm, heartfelt messages can transcend time and space, providing comfort and solace to those left behind. By taking the opportunity to convey feelings of affection, admiration, and gratitude through digital messages, individuals can leave a lasting impact on their loved ones, even after they have passed away.

4.2 Sharing Personal and Family History

Messages left as part of a digital legacy provide an avenue for sharing personal and family history. These messages can include anecdotes, stories, and recollections that illuminate the experiences, traditions, and values that shape a person's identity. By sharing personal and family history, individuals contribute to the preservation of their heritage and offer a valuable resource for future generations to understand their roots and cultural background.

4.3 Passing on Wisdom and Guidance

Messages left behind in a digital legacy can serve as a means of padding on wisdom, life lessons, and guidance. Individuals can impart their knowledge, experiences, and insights to their loved ones, providing them with valuable guidance and support as they navigate life's challenges. By leaving messages that encapsulate their beliefs, philosophies, and lessons learned, individuals can positively influence the lives of their loved ones, even in their absence.

Leaving messages as part of a digital legacy is not only a way to connect with loved ones beyond the limitations of time and space but also an opportunity to create a lasting impact. The Digital Legacy Manager aims to facilitate and encourage the act of leaving messages, providing individuals with a platform to express their love, share their personal and family history, and pass on their wisdom and guidance to future generations.

5. EXISTING SOLUTIONS AND LIMITATIONS

5.1 Posthumous Digital Access

Posthumous digital access refers to the ability of loved ones to gain access to the digital accounts and assets of a deceased individual. Some platforms and services have implemented policies and procedures to address this issue. They may require designated individuals to provide proof of death and legal documentation to gain access to the deceased person's accounts. However, the process can be complex, time-consuming, and varies across different platforms. The limitations of posthumous digital access include the following:

- Lack of Uniformity: There is no standardized process for posthumous digital access, and each platform has its own policies and procedures, making it challenging for loved ones to navigate the process consistently.
- Privacy Concerns: Striking a balance between granting access to digital accounts and respecting the privacy and confidentiality of the deceased can be difficult. Privacy laws and policies can impede access, leading to restrictions and potential conflicts.

5.2 Legacy Preservation Services

Legacy preservation services have emerged to help individuals manage and preserve their digital legacies. These services typically provide secure storage, message delivery, and account management options. Users can store important documents, passwords, and instructions for their loved ones to access after their passing. However, legacy preservation services also have limitations, including:

- Lack of Adoption: Many people are unaware of or do not actively engage with legacy preservation services, resulting in limited adoption and usage.
- Reliance on Service Providers: The long-term sustainability and availability of these services depend on the viability of the service provider. If the provider goes out of business or discontinues the service, the stored information and messages may become inaccessible.

5.3 Challenges and Criticisms

Existing solutions face several challenges and criticisms in addressing the complexities of digital legacies:

- Lack of Awareness and Planning: Many individuals are unaware of the importance of managing their digital legacies and fail to plan for their digital assets. This lack of awareness and planning contributes to the difficulties faced by loved ones after their passing (Kasket, 2019).
- Security and Privacy Concerns: Storing sensitive information and messages in digital platforms raises security and privacy concerns. Ensuring the protection and confidentiality of personal data becomes crucial to maintaining trust in legacy management solutions (Saxena & Chaudhary, 2023).

- User Experience and Usability: Some existing solutions may suffer from poor user experience, making it challenging for individuals to navigate and utilize the platforms effectively. Usability improvements and intuitive interfaces are necessary to encourage adoption and active usage.

Addressing the limitations and challenges of existing solutions is essential to develop an effective Digital Legacy Manager. By understanding the drawbacks of posthumous digital access, legacy preservation services, and the associated criticisms, the Digital Legacy Manager can aim to overcome these limitations and provide a comprehensive, user-friendly solution for managing and preserving digital legacies.

6. DIGITAL LEGACY MANAGER: CONCEPT AND FEATURES

6.1 Overview of the Software

The Digital Legacy Manager is a software application designed to empower individuals to effectively manage, preserve, and share their digital legacies. It serves as a comprehensive platform that facilitates the organization, storage, and accessibility of digital assets, messages, and instructions for loved ones after the individual's passing. The software aims to simplify the process of digital legacy management, providing users with peace of mind and ensuring their digital presence is handled according to their wishes.

6.2 User Interface and Functionality

The user interface of the Digital Legacy Manager is designed to be intuitive, user-friendly, and accessible to individuals of varying technological expertise. The software provides a seamless and organized user experience, allowing users to easily navigate and interact with their digital assets and features. It incorporates visually appealing and responsive design elements to enhance usability.

The functionality of the Digital Legacy manager includes:

- Account Management: Users can securely store and manage their digital accounts, passwords, and access credentials in a centralized location. This feature simplifies the process for loved ones to gain posthumous access to important accounts.
- Message and Memoir Creation: The software enables users to compose and save messages, letters, and memoirs for their loved ones. These personal messages can be scheduled for delivery at specific times or triggered by predetermined events, ensuring the timely and meaningful communication of their thoughts and sentiments.
- Asset Organization and Sharing: Users can categorize, tag, and organize their digital assets, such as photos, videos, and documents, making it easier for loved ones to locate and access these important files. The software also allows for selective sharing of assets with designated individuals, ensuring privacy and control over personal information (table 3).

Table 3. Key features and benefits

Key Features Benefits	
Account Management	Secure storage and easy access to digital accounts
Message and Memoir Creation	Express love, share personal history, andguidance
Asset Organization andSharing	Easy categorization,
	selective sharing of assets
Simplified Digital AssetManagement	Efficient management and retrieval of digital assets
Enhanced Communicationand connection	Continued connection and support for loved ones
Secure and Confidential Storage	Protection of sensitive information
Customization andPersonalization	Tailored digital legacymanagement
Legacy Preservation andContinuity	Perpetuation of memoriesand values

6.3 Key Features and Benefits

The Digital Legacy Manager offers several key features and benefits:

- Simplified Digital Asset Management: The software provides a centralized platform for managing and organizing digital assets, eliminating the need to search through multiple accounts and devices. This streamlines the process for loved ones to locate and access important files and information (Angeline et al., 2023).
- Enhanced Communication and Connection: By enabling users to leave messages and memoirs, the software fosters ongoing communication and connection with loved ones even after the user's passing. It ensures that personal sentiments, advice, and wisdom are shared, providing comfort and guidance to those left behind.
- Secure and Confidential Storage: The Digital Legacy Manager prioritizes the security and confidentiality of users' digital assets and personal information. It employs robust encryption protocols and data protection measures to safeguard sensitive data, ensuring privacy and peace of mind.
- Customization and Personalization: The software allows users to customize their digital legacy management preferences, including the selection of recipients for messages and the organization of digital assets. This customization ensures that the digital legacy reflects the individual's unique preferences and intentions.
- Legacy Preservation and Continuity: The Digital Legacy Manager serves as a means to preserve and continue an individual's digital legacy, passing on their memories, stories, and values to future generations. It ensures that the individual's digital footprint is a lasting testament to their life, providing a bridge between past, present, and future.

By incorporating these features and delivering these benefits, the Digital Legacy Manager aims to revolutionize digital legacy management, empowering individuals to have control over their digital presence and ensuring a meaningful and seamless transition of their digital legacies to their loved ones.

7. IMPLEMENTATION AND TECHNICAL CONSIDERATIONS

7.1 Data Security and Privacy

Data security and privacy are paramount considerations in the implementation of the Digital Legacy Manager. The software should employ robust encryption algorithms to protect users' sensitive information and digital assets. Measures such as secure socket layers (SSL), data encryption at rest and in transit, and multi-factor authentication can enhance the security of the stored data. Additionally, the software should comply with relevant data protection regulations to ensure user privacy and gain trust in handling personal information.

7.2 Authentication and Access Control

Authentication and access control mechanisms are crucial to safeguard the digital legacies stored within the Digital Legacy Manager. User authentication can be implemented through various methods, including passwords, biometrics, or two-factor authentication. Strong access control mechanisms should be in place to ensure that only authorized individuals, such as designated beneficiaries or legal representatives, can gain access to the digital assets and messages of the deceased.

7.3 Integration With Existing Digital Platforms

To enhance usability and convenience, the Digital Legacy Manager should integrate with existing digital platforms and services commonly used by individuals. Integration can allow for seamless import and management of digital assets from various sources, such as social media platforms, cloud storage services, email providers, and online banking accounts. This integration should be designed with privacy and security in mind, ensuring that data from external platforms is securely imported and managed within the Digital Legacy Manager.

7.4 Scalability and Infrastructure Considerations

The implementation of the Digital Legacy Manager should consider scalability to accommodate a growing user base and increasing volumes of data. The software should be designed with scalability in mind, allowing for efficient storage, retrieval, and management of digital legacies as the user base expands. The underlying infrastructure should be robust and capable of handling increased demand, ensuring smooth performance even during peak usage periods (Rajest et al., 2023a).

7.5 Backup and Disaster Recovery

To mitigate the risk of data loss or system failure, regular backups and disaster recovery plans should be implemented for the Digital Legacy Manager. Regularly scheduled backups of user data should be performed and stored securely in off-site locations or redundant storage systems. In the event of system failure or data corruption, the software should have mechanisms in place to quickly restore data and ensure continuity of service.

The implementation of the Digital Legacy Manager should prioritize data security, privacy, and seamless integration with existing digital platforms. By addressing these technical considerations, the software can provide a reliable and secure platform for managing and preserving digital legacies effectively (Rajest et al., 2023b).

8. SYSTEM ARCHITECTURE AND TECHNICAL FRAMEWORK

8.1 System Architecture Diagram

The system architecture of the Digital Legacy Manager is a multi-tiered structure designed to ensure robustness, scalability, and data security. It comprises the following key components (fig.1):

1. User Interface (UI):
    - The user interacts with the Digital Legacy Manager through a web-based graphical user interface (GUI).
    - The UI is designed for ease of use and allows users to create and manage digital messages, assets, and account information.
2. Application Layer:

Figure 1. System architecture

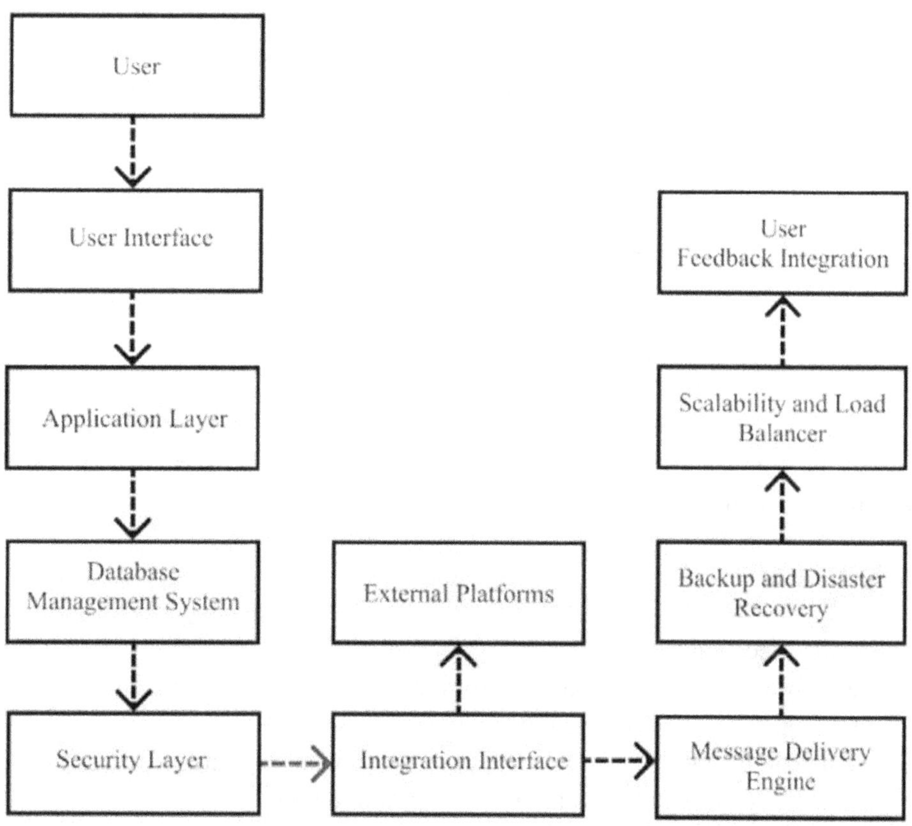

- The application layer serves as the brain of the system, where business logic and processing take place.
- It handles user authentication, message scheduling, asset organization, and integration with external platforms.

3. Database Management System (DBMS):
    - The DBMS is responsible for storing and managing user data securely.
    - It stores digital assets, user account information, messages, and user preferences.
4. Security Layer:
    - The security layer includes authentication and authorization mechanisms.
    - Multi-factor authentication ensures secure user access, while access control defines who can access what data.
5. Integration Interface:
    - This component facilitates integration with external digital platforms.
    - It allows the Digital Legacy Manager to import and export data from and to popular platforms such as social media, email, and cloud storage.
6. Message Delivery Engine:
    - The message delivery engine manages the scheduling and delivery of messages and memoirs.
    - It ensures that messages are delivered to designated recipients according to the user's preferences.
7. Backup and Disaster Recovery (BDR):
    - The BDR component ensures data integrity and availability.
    - It regularly backs up user data and has disaster recovery mechanisms in place to restore data in case of system failures.
8. Scalability and Load Balancer:
    - To accommodate a growing user base, the architecture includes load-balancing mechanisms.
    - This ensures that the system can handle increased demand while maintaining performance.
9. User Feedback Integration:
    - User feedback is collected through the UI and processed in this component.
    - Feedback is used for continuous improvement of the Digital Legacy Manager.
10. External Platforms:
    - The system interacts with external digital platforms to import and export data.
    - This ensures seamless integration with various digital services used by the users.

This system architecture diagram outlines the core components and their interaction within the Digital Legacy Manager, providing a high-level view of how the software functions to empower individuals in managing and preserving their digital legacies.

8.2 Security Model

1. Authentication Mechanism:
    - Utilize a robust authentication system to ensure that only authorized users can access the Digital Legacy Manager (Fig.2).
    - Implement multi-factor authentication (MFA) to enhance security, requiring users to provide two or more types of authentication before granting access.

2. Authorization:
   - Employ role-based access control (RBAC) to define and manage user roles and permissions within the application (Fig.3).
   - Establish strict authorization policies to ensure that users can only access the features and data for which they have explicit permission.

3. Data Encryption:

Figure 2. Authentication mechanism
Source: Rakesh (2023)

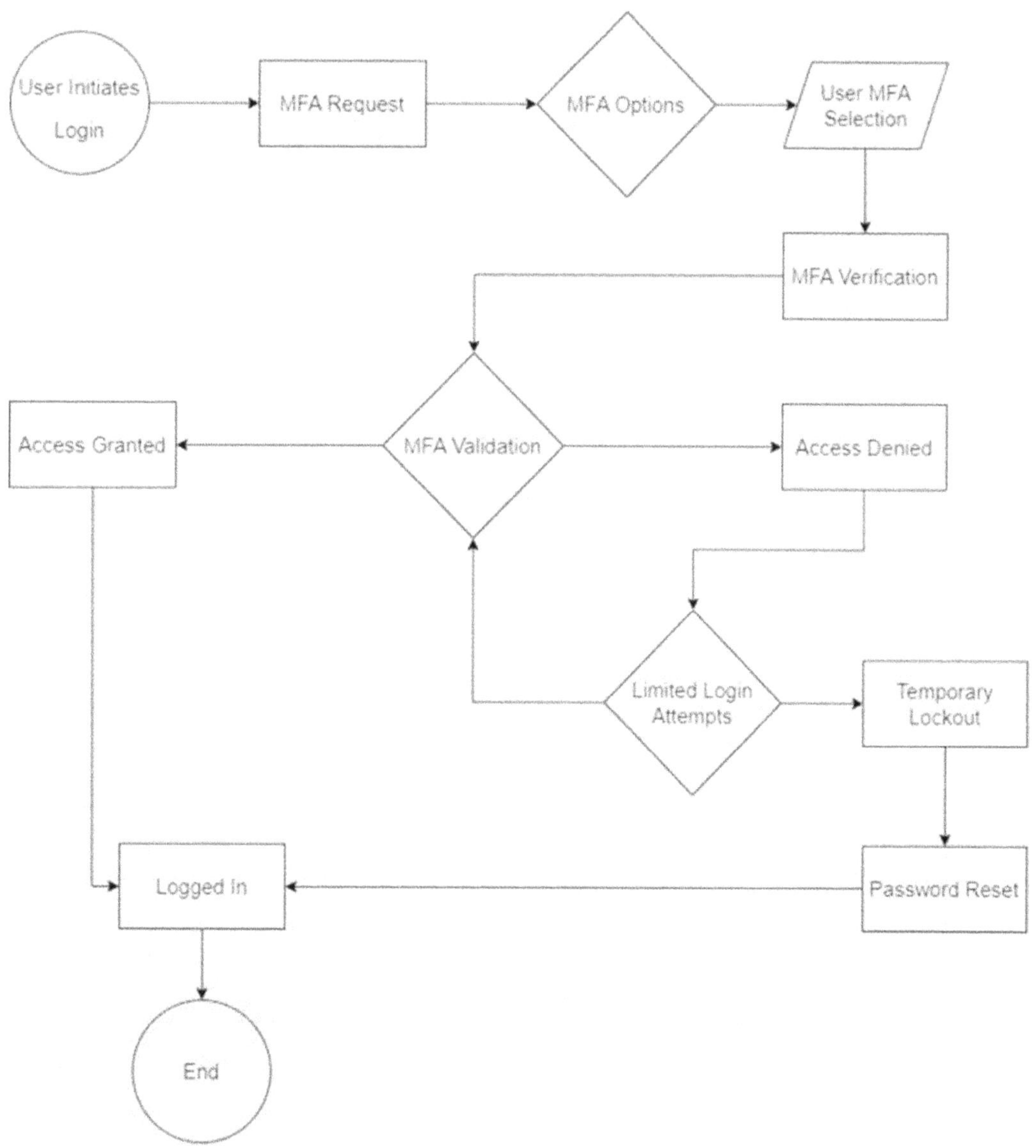

- Encrypt data both in transit and at rest using industry-standard encryption algorithms (e.g., TLS for data in transit, AES for data at rest) (fig.4).
- Employ strong encryption key management practices to protect encryption keys from unauthorized access.

Figure 3. Authorization
Source: Wallarm (2021)

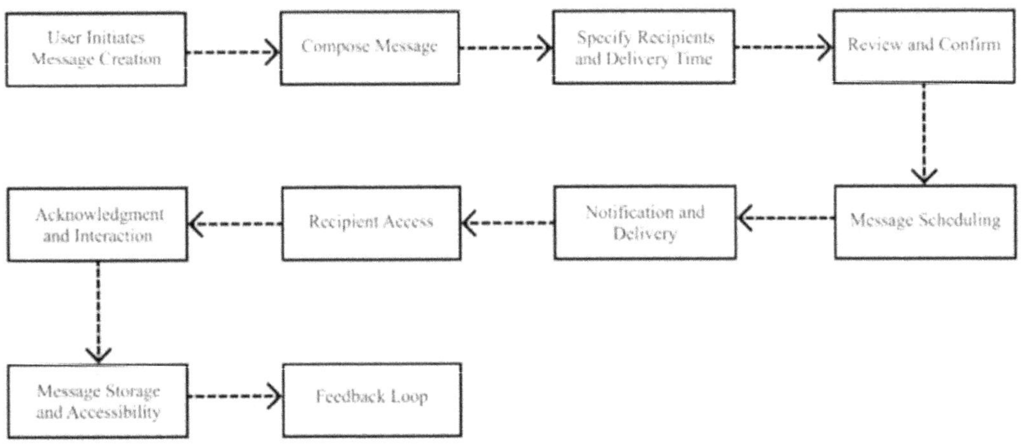

4. Secure Storage:
   - Ensure secure storage of user data, digital assets, and messages using secure and redundant storage solutions.
   - Regularly audit and assess storage security measures to identify vulnerabilities and address them promptly.

Figure 4. Data encryption
Source: Siddhesh (2022)

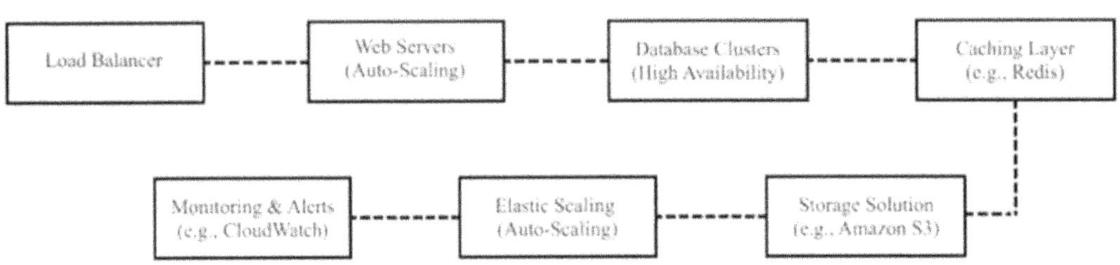

5. Secure API Communication:
   - Implement secure API communication by using techniques such as API keys, OAuth, or token-based authentication (fig.5).
   - Employ rate limiting and throttling to prevent abuse of APIs and protect against potential attacks.

6. Logging and Monitoring:
   - Implement comprehensive logging and monitoring mechanisms to track user activities and system events (fig.6).
   - Set up real-time alerts for suspicious or unauthorized activities, enabling rapid response to security incidents.

Figure 5. Secure API communication
Source: Brad (2021)

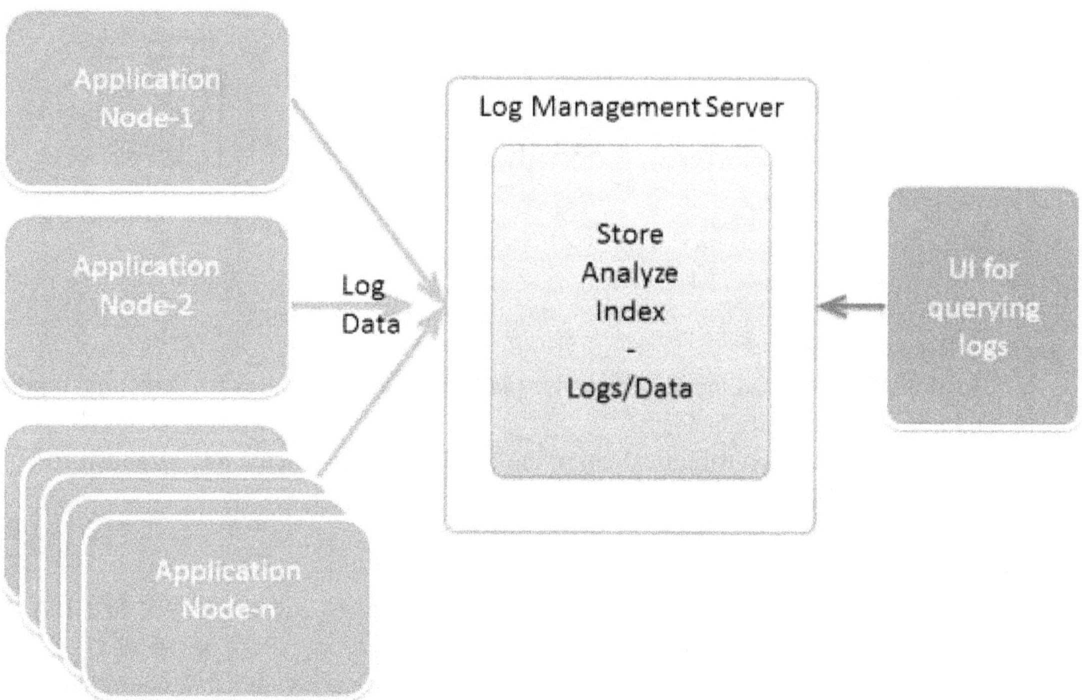

7. Vulnerability Assessment and Penetration Testing:
   - Conduct regular vulnerability assessments and penetration testing to identify and remediate security weaknesses.
   - Engage third-party security experts to perform thorough assessments and provide recommendations.

Figure 6. Logging and monitoring
Source: Vishal (2012)

8. Incident Response Plan:
   - Develop a well-defined incident response plan outlining procedures for detecting, reporting, and mitigating security incidents.
   - Define roles and responsibilities within the incident response team and establish communication protocols.

9. Data Privacy Compliance:
   - Ensure compliance with relevant data privacy regulations, such as GDPR or HIPAA, depending on the nature of user data and jurisdiction.
   - Implement data retention and deletion policies in accordance with legal requirements.

10. User Education:
    - Educate users about security best practices, such as the importance of strong passwords and the risks of sharing login credentials.
    - Provide clear guidelines on how to securely manage their digital legacy within the application.

8.3 Scaling Infrastructure

1. Web Servers:
   - Utilize a cloud-based infrastructure to host the application across multiple virtual machines (VMs).
   - Implement auto-scaling groups to ensure the appropriate number of instances based on traffic demand.

Figure 7. Scaling infrastructure

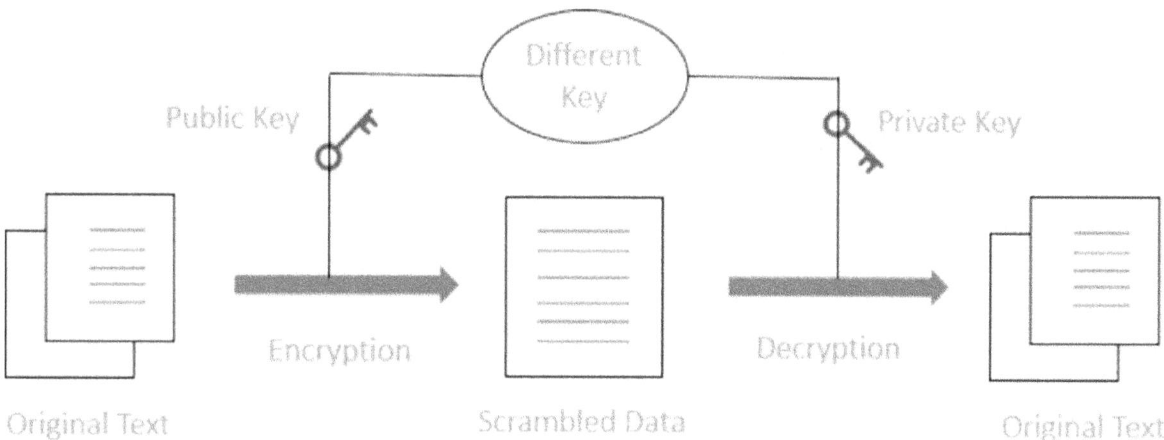

2. Load Balancer:
   - Deploy a load balancer (e.g., AWS Elastic Load Balancer) to distribute incoming requests evenly across the web servers.
   - Enable features like health checks to direct traffic to healthy instances.
3. Database Clusters:
   - Set up database clusters (e.g., Amazon RDS Multi-AZ setup) to ensure high availability and failover.
   - Employ read replicas to offload read traffic and enhance performance.
4. Caching Layer:
   - Integrate an in-memory caching layer (e.g., Redis) to store frequently accessed data, reducing the load on the database.
   - Configure cache eviction policies and set expiration times for cache entries.
5. Storage Solution:
   - Use a scalable object storage service (e.g., Amazon S3) for storing multimedia files securely and cost- effectively.
   - Implement access controls and encryption to ensure data privacy.
6. Elastic Scaling:
   - Set up automatic scaling policies that trigger based on metrics such as CPU utilization, request rates, or response times.

- Determine scaling thresholds and the number of instances to add or remove during scaling events.

7. Monitoring and Alerting:
   - Implement monitoring tools (e.g., Amazon CloudWatch) to track performance metrics of different components.
   - Configure alerts to notify administrators when thresholds are breached.

8.4 Message Delivery Workflow

1. User Initiates Message Creation (fig.8):

Figure 8. Message delivery workflow

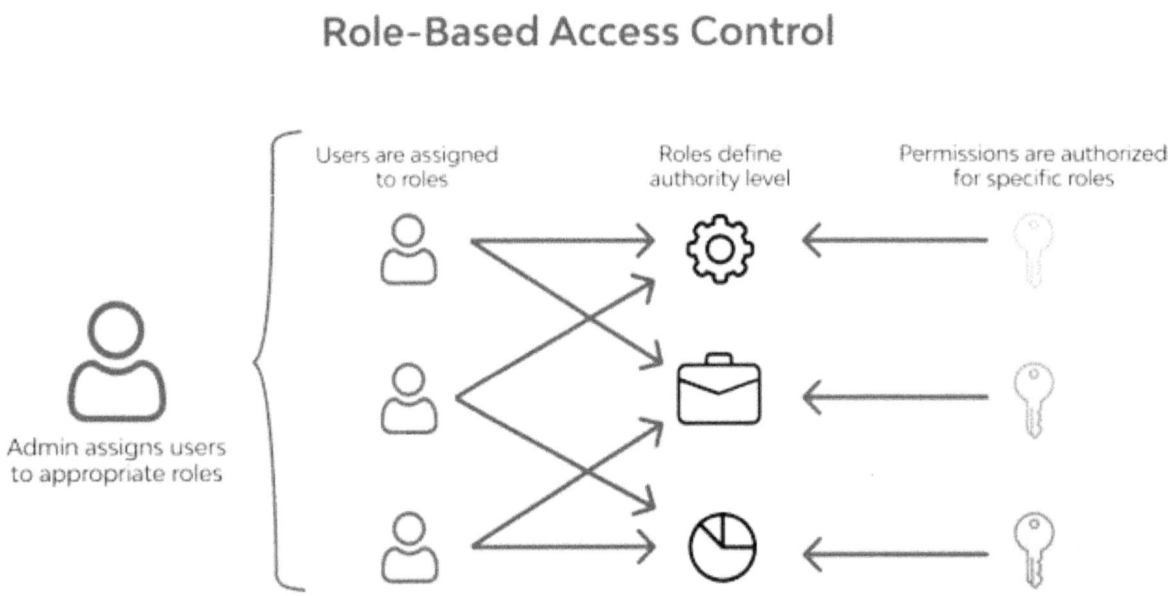

   - The user logs into the Digital Legacy Manager platform.
   - They select the option to create a new message or memoir.
2. Compose Message:
   - The user writes and composes their message or memoir.
   - They can attach digital assets, such as photos or videos, to the message.
3. Specify Recipients and Delivery Time:
   - The user designates specific recipients for the message. Recipients can be individuals, groups, or designated contacts.
   - They set the desired delivery time, which can be immediate or scheduled for a future date.
4. Review and Confirm:

- The user reviews the message content, recipients, and delivery time.
- They confirm the details and proceed to schedule the message for delivery.

5. Message Scheduling:
   - The Digital Legacy Manager stores the message and delivery instructions securely.
   - It initiates the countdown to the scheduled delivery time.
6. Notification and Delivery:
   - The system triggers the message delivery process when the scheduled delivery time arrives.
   - Recipients receive notifications via email or within the Digital Legacy Manager platform.
7. Recipient Access:
   - Recipients access the delivered message through a secure link or within their Digital Legacy Manager account.
   - They can view the message content, attached assets, and any additional instructions.
8. Acknowledgment and Interaction:
   - Recipients can acknowledge the message or engage in interactions, such as replying or sharing memories.
9. Message Storage and Accessibility:
   - Delivered messages and memoirs are securely stored within the Digital Legacy Manager for future reference.
   - Recipients can access them whenever they wish.
10. Feedback Loop:
    - The Digital Legacy Manager may collect feedback from recipients about their experience with the delivered message.
    - User feedback is used to improve the message delivery process continually.

8.5 Multi-factor Authentication Flow

1. User Initiates Login (fig.9):
   - Users access the Digital Legacy Manager and initiate the login process by providing their username and password.
2. MFA Request:
   - The system recognizes the user's login attempt and detects that MFA is enabled for the account.
3. MFA Options:
   - The system presents the user with multiple MFA options, which may include:
     - SMS Verification: User receives a one-time code via SMS.
     - Email Verification: User receives a one-time code via email.
     - Authentication App: User generates a code using an authenticator app (e.g., Google Authenticator).
     - Biometric Scan: User uses fingerprint or facial recognition(if available on the device).
4. User MFA Selection:
   - The user selects their preferred MFA method from the options presented.
5. MFA Verification:

- The user completes the selected MFA method, which typically involves entering a code, scanning a QR code, or using a biometric scan.

6. MFA Validation:
   - The system validates the provided MFA information against the stored records.
7. Access Granted:
   - If MFA validation is successful, the system grants access to the user's account.
8. Access Denied:
   - If MFA validation fails, the system denies access and may prompt the user to retry or choose an alternative MFA method.
9. Limited Login Attempts:
   - The system may limit the number of login attempts to prevent unauthorized access.
10. Temporary Lockout:
    - After a predefined number of failed MFA attempts, the account may be temporarily locked for security purposes.
11. Password Reset:
    - In case of repeated failed attempts, the user may have the option to reset their password or contact support for assistance.

Figure 9. Multi-factor authentication flow

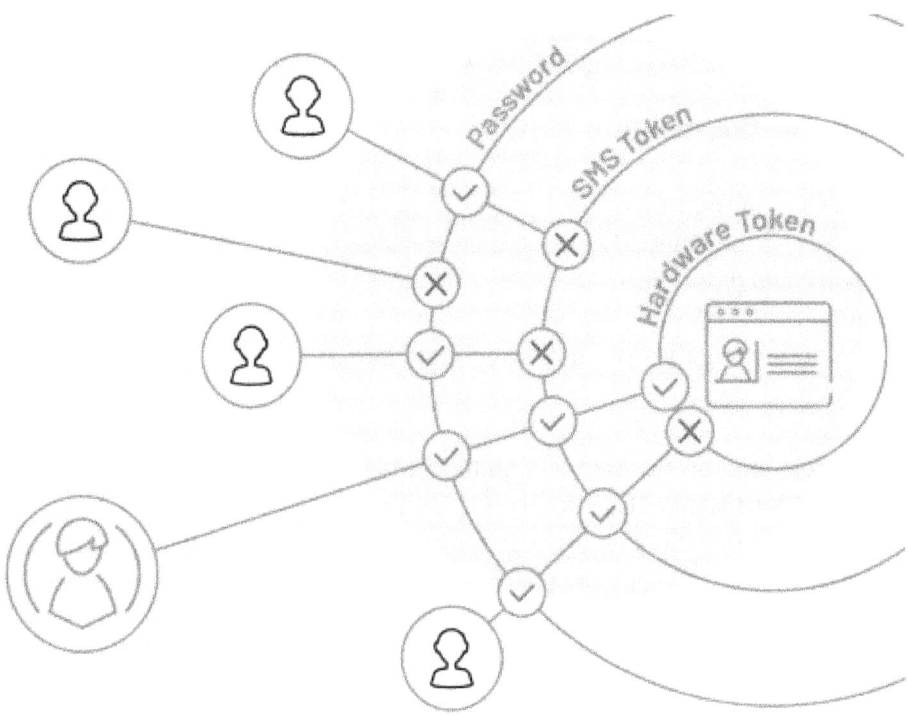

9. USER EXPERIENCE AND FEEDBACK

9.1 User Testing and Evaluation

User testing and evaluation are crucial in ensuring a positive user experience for the Digital Legacy Manager. Conducting user testing sessions with diverse individuals can help identify usability issues, pain points, and areas for improvement. Feedback from these testing sessions can inform iterative design and development processes, resulting in an intuitive and user-friendly software interface.

9.2 Incorporating User Feedback

User feedback is essential to refining and enhancing the Digital Legacy Manager. Feedback can be collected through various channels, such as user surveys, feedback forms, and user support interactions. Developers can prioritize feature enhancements, bug fixes, and user experience improvements by actively listening to users' suggestions, concerns, and needs. Regular software updates based on user feedback contribute to a more user-centric and satisfying digital legacy management experience.

9.3 Long-term Adoption and Sustainability

Ensuring long-term adoption and sustainability of the Digital Legacy Manager requires ongoing support, updates, and maintenance. Regular software updates and bug fixes address security vulnerabilities, compatibility issues, and evolving user needs. The software should be compatible with operating systems, web browsers, and devices to accommodate a wide user base. Building a strong support system, including customer service, technical assistance, and user documentation, can also enhance users' long-term adoption and satisfaction.

9.4 User Education and Outreach

Promoting user education and outreach efforts are vital for successfully adopting and utilizing the Digital Legacy Manager. Providing comprehensive user documentation, tutorials, and FAQs can assist users in understanding the software's features, functionalities, and best practices. Conducting webinars, workshops, and educational campaigns can raise awareness about the importance of managing digital legacies and highlight the software's benefits. Collaborating with relevant organizations, such as estate planning firms, funeral homes, and support groups, can further expand user outreach efforts.

9.5 Measuring User Satisfaction

Measuring user satisfaction through surveys and user feedback mechanisms can provide insights into the overall user experience and help identify areas for improvement. Regularly assessing user satisfaction metrics, such as Net Promoter Score (NPS) or Customer Satisfaction (CSAT) scores, can gauge user perception and loyalty toward the Digital Legacy Manager. User satisfaction measurement helps track progress, identify trends, and ensure that the software meets user expectations over time.

By prioritizing user experience, incorporating user feedback, ensuring long-term adoption and sustainability, and providing user education and outreach, the Digital Legacy Manager can evolve into a robust and widely adopted software solution for effectively managing and preserving digital legacies.

10. CONCLUSION

10.1 Summary of Findings

In this research paper, we have explored the concept of digital legacies and the challenges individuals face in managing and preserving them. We have discussed the emotional and practical implications of unmanaged digital legacies, highlighting the need for effective solutions. As proposed in this paper, the Digital Legacy Manager aims to address these challenges and provide a comprehensive platform for individuals to manage their digital legacies.

10.2 Contributions and Significance

The Digital Legacy Manager has the potential to make a significant impact on individuals and their loved ones by facilitating the management, preservation, and sharing of digital legacies. The software empowers individuals to express their love, share their personal and family history, and pass on wisdom and guidance by providing features such as message creation, asset organization, and account management. The user-centric approach, incorporating data security and privacy measures, integration with existing platforms, and user feedback incorporation, ensures a positive and meaningful user experience.

10.3 Future Directions

As technology and digital practices continue to evolve, the Digital Legacy Manager must also adapt and evolve. Future directions for the software may include:

- Enhanced integration: Expanding integration capabilities with emerging digital platforms and technologies, ensuring compatibility and seamless data import/export.
- Artificial intelligence and automation: Leveraging AI technologies to automate tasks, such as organizing digital assets or managing message deliveries, to streamline the user experience further.
- Collaboration with legal and estate planning professionals: Collaborating with legal experts and estate planning professionals can help address the complexities of posthumous digital access and ensure compliance with legal requirements.
- Social and community features: Introducing social and community features within the Digital Legacy Manager can foster connections among users, providing support, guidance, and shared experiences related to digital legacy management.
- Internationalization and multilingual support: Expanding the software's language support and localization efforts to cater to users from diverse cultural backgrounds and regions.

By considering these future directions, the Digital Legacy Manager can continue to meet the evolving needs of users and remain a relevant and valuable tool for managing digital legacies. In conclusion, the Digital Legacy Manager serves as a vital solution in addressing the challenges associated with digital legacies. Its user-friendly interface, robust functionality, and focus on data security and privacy enable individuals to manage and preserve their digital legacies effectively, ensuring a lasting connection with their loved ones even after they have passed away. The development and adoption of the Digital Legacy Manager can positively impact individuals, families, and communities, providing solace, support, and a means to pass on their legacy for generations to come.

REFERENCES

Angeline, R., Aarthi, S., Regin, R., & Rajest, S. S. (2023). Dynamic intelligence-driven engineering flooding attack prediction using ensemble learning. In *Advances in Artificial and Human Intelligence in the Modern Era* (pp. 109–124). IGI Global. doi:10.4018/979-8-3693-1301-5.ch006

Brad, S. (2021). *6 Tips for Maximum API Security*. DuoCircle Blog. https://www.duocircle.com/email-security/6-tips-for-maximum-api-security

Cirillo, S., Polese, G., Salerno, D., Simone, B., & Solimando, G. (2023). Towards Flexible Voice Assistants: Evaluating Privacy and Security Needs in IoT-enabled Smart Homes. *FMDB Transactions on Sustainable Computer Letters*, *1*(1), 25–32.

Cleland, K., & Williamson, A. (2017). Digital legacies: Personal artifacts in an augmented reality. In *Proceedings of the 2017 CHI Conference on Human Factors in Computing Systems* (pp. 1731-1744). ACM.

Devi, B. T., & Rajasekaran, R. (2023). A Comprehensive Review on Deepfake Detection on Social Media Data. *FMDB Transactions on Sustainable Computing Systems*, *1*(1), 11–20.

Gaayathri, R. S., Rajest, S. S., Nomula, V. K., & Regin, R. (2023). Bud-D: Enabling Bidirectional Communication with ChatGPT by adding Listening and Speaking Capabilities. *FMDB Transactions on Sustainable Computer Letters*, *1*(1), 49–63.

Heath, S. (2020). *The digital hereafter: Exploring death and the afterlife in the digital age*. Cambridge Scholars Publishing.

Jeba, J. A., Bose, S. R., & Boina, R. (2023). Exploring Hybrid Multi-View Multimodal for Natural Language Emotion Recognition Using Multi-Source Information Learning Model. *FMDB Transactions on Sustainable Computer Letters*, *1*(1), 12–24.

Kasket, E. (2019). *All the Ghosts in the Machine: Illusions of Immortality in the Digital Age*. Robinson.

Littman, J. (2015). Digital legacy and death: Practical and ethical aspects of digital inheritance. *International Journal of Law and Information Technology*, *23*(4), 349–370.

Lodha, S., Malani, H., & Bhardwaj, A. K. (2023). Performance Evaluation of Vision Transformers for Diagnosis of Pneumonia. *FMDB Transactions on Sustainable Computing Systems*, *1*(1), 21–31.

Oosterman, J. M., Drossaert, C. H., Eysenbach, G., & Graafland, M. (2016). Towards a new paradigm for patient-web communication: Seeking to address the pitfalls of health 1.0. *Journal of Medical Internet Research*, *18*(6), e110.

Perera, S. (2020). Digital legacy: Legal and ethical considerations in the post-mortem management of online accounts. *Information & Communications Technology Law*, *29*(1), 34–58.

Rajest, S. S., Singh, B., Obaid, A. J., Regin, R., & Chinnusamy, K. (Eds.). (2023b). Advances in Computational Intelligence and Robotics *Advances in artificial and human intelligence in the modern era.*, doi:10.4018/979-8-3693-1301-5

Rajest, S. S., Singh, B., Obaid, J. A., Regin, R., & Chinnusamy, K. (Eds.). (2023a). Recent developments in machine and human intelligence. Advances in Computational Intelligence and Robotics. doi:10.4018/978-1-6684-9189-8

Rakesh, S. (2023). *What is Multi-Factor Authentication (MFA)?* LoginRadius Blog. https://www.loginradius.com/blog/identity/what-is-multi-factor-authentication/

Regin, R., Khanna, A. A., Krishnan, V., Gupta, M., & Bose, R. S., & Rajest, S. S. (2023). Information design and unifying approach for secured data sharing using attribute-based access control mechanisms. In Recent Developments in Machine and Human Intelligence (pp. 256–276). IGI Global.

Sajini, S., Reddi, L. T., Regin, R., & Rajest, S. S. (2023). A Comparative Analysis of Routing Protocols for Efficient Data Transmission in Vehicular Ad Hoc Networks (VANETs). *FMDB Transactions on Sustainable Computing Systems*, *1*(1), 1–10.

Saxena, D., & Chaudhary, S. (2023). Predicting Brain Diseases from FMRI-Functional Magnetic Resonance Imaging with Machine Learning Techniques for Early Diagnosis and Treatment. *FMDB Transactions on Sustainable Computer Letters*, *1*(1), 33–48.

Schilder, J., & Clark, D. (2018). Digital legacy planning: A new way to talk about and plan for digital death and the digital afterlife. *Omega*.

Sepúlveda, M. J., & Parra-Arnau, J. (2021). Digital Death: A Critical Review of the Literature and the Challenges Ahead. In *International Conference on Human-Computer Interaction* (pp. 564-580). Springer.

Siddhesh, S. (2022). *What is Data Encryption?* Geeksforgeeks Blog. https://www.geeksforgeeks.org/what-is-data-encryption/

Smith, C. M., Shanks, G., & Smith, A. D. (2017). My loved one's Facebook account: Deceased user practices on social networking sites. *Information Technology & People*, *30*(2), 443–466.

Vishal, B. (2012). *Log Management as a Service*. SitePoint Blog. https://www.sitepoint.com/log-management-as-a-service/

Wallarm. (2021). *What is RBAC (Role-Based Access Control)?* Wallarm Blog. https://www.wallarm.com/what/what-exactly-is-role-based-access-control-rbac

Wijesundara, I., & Fernando, A. (2020). Digital Legacy: Challenges and Opportunities in Estate Planning. In *Proceedings of the 2020 2nd International Conference on Computer Science and Software Engineering* (pp. 93-97). ACM.

Chapter 6
Empowering Employees' Enablement Intelligently With Data and Realizing Business Excellence

H. Hajra
Bharath Institute of Higher Education and Research, India

G. Jayalakshmi
Bharath Institute of Higher Education and Research, India

ABSTRACT

Data excellence denotes the strategic manipulation of data to boost business performance and secure a competitive advantage. It empowers companies to extract critical insights about their operations, customer behavior, and market trends. This intelligence fosters data-driven decision-making, and with effective employee enablement, it leads to superior outcomes. Employee engagement, distinct from job performance, focuses on workers' emotional alignment with the company's values and interpersonal conduct. Engaged employees actively collaborate to elevate their job performance and are attuned to the company culture. HR experts link engagement to employees' perceptions of their job experience and treatment within the organization, emphasizing the pivotal role of emotions in driving a company's success and profitability. Employees are naturally inclined to commit to their organizations, fulfilling a profound desire to forge meaningful connections and contribute significantly to a valued cause.

INTRODUCTION

Kahn coined the concept of engagement at work as the 'Harnessing of Organizational Members' self to their work roles.' In role plays, individuals actively participate in the engagement by employing and showcasing their physical, emotional, and cognitive attributes (Lucey, 2009). Employees who are engaged go beyond commitment (Ramos et al., 2023). They are not merely ardent or arrogant. They possess the

DOI: 10.4018/979-8-3693-2193-5.ch006

ability to envision their future as well as comprehend the company's mission and objectives. They are fired up and ready to use their skills and initiative to contribute to their employer's pursuit of long-term commercial success (Atasever, 2023).

Employee engagement is a multifaceted concept that represents the level of enthusiasm and connection employees feel toward their place of work (Batth, 2018). It measures how emotionally invested employees are in their company, often manifesting as a deep-seated loyalty that transcends mere job satisfaction (Rurkkhum & Bartlett, 2012). This mindset is the cumulative result of an individual's experiences at work, filtered through their affections and disaffections with the day-to-day realities of their job (Saxena et al., 2023). The extent to which employees feel engaged can vary depending on whether they perceive their job as a vehicle for achieving their ambitions (Srinivas et al., 2023). This perception is, in turn, influenced by the degree of success or failure they experience in pursuing these goals within the workplace (María et al., 2023).

An engaged employee typically approaches their work with energy and enthusiasm, demonstrating a commitment that is both emotional and intellectual (Priscila et al., 2023). They are not just present at work; they are passionately invested in their tasks, exhibiting a level of dedication that often goes beyond the expected standards (Sabti et al., 2023). Such engagement is evident in how these individuals apply themselves to their roles with focus and intensity, channeling their best abilities toward the company's objectives (Vashishtha & Kapoor, 2023).

The benefits of having an engaged workforce are profound. Engaged employees tend to be more productive, as their passion for the work often leads to a greater willingness to go the extra mile (Pandit, 2023). They are also more likely to remain with the company, reducing turnover rates and the associated costs of recruiting and training new staff (Said & Tripathi, 2023). Furthermore, their enthusiasm can be infectious, contributing to a positive work environment that fosters collaboration and innovation (Ogunmola et al., 2021).

Companies that understand the importance of employee engagement often strive to align individual goals with organizational objectives (Venkateswaran et al., 2023). They create environments where employees feel their work is meaningful and that they are part of something larger than themselves (Venkateswaran & Viktor, 2023). This alignment helps employees see the value in their efforts and how these contribute to the company's success, reinforcing their engagement (Ocoró et al., 2023).

Understanding and improving employee engagement requires a proactive approach. Organizations must seek to understand the personal goals of their employees and provide opportunities for growth and achievement within the company structure (Singh et al., 2023). They must foster a culture where feedback is encouraged and employees feel heard and valued. Moreover, leadership plays a crucial role in setting the tone for an engaged workforce; leaders must demonstrate a commitment to the company's values and mission and show genuine care for their employees' well-being and professional development.

Job engagement is not a static attribute but a dynamic state that can fluctuate over time and is influenced by many factors (Bisoyi et al., 2019). It is a critical indicator of a company's health and a key driver of its performance. By investing in employee engagement, companies are not just improving the output and efficiency of their workforce. Still, they are building a more resilient organization better equipped to adapt to change and capitalize on opportunities in the competitive business landscape.

- Stay - Desire to become a member of the group.
- Say - Positive attributes characterize the company.
- Strive - Exceed expectations by going the extra mile beyond the minimum requirement.

Establishing and nurturing engagement within an organization requires a two-way interaction between the employee and the employer. The employee engagement serves as a measure of an individual's connection and affiliation with the organization. This is how the implementation of data-based decision-making can be carried out:

DEFINE KEY PERFORMANCE INDICATORS (KPIS)

Specify the crucial performance metrics and indicators that align with your business objectives. These KPIs will serve as reference points for assessing performance and guiding decision-making.

Establish Data-Driven Processes: Integrate data-driven decision-making into your organization's workflows and culture. Encourage employees to base their decisions on evidence supported by data and provide the necessary tools and training to enhance data literacy.

Foster Collaboration and Communication: Cultivate cross-functional collaboration to leverage collective insights and expertise. Promote open communication channels for sharing data, analysis, and insights across departments, nurturing a culture that values collaboration and data-informed decision-making.

Monitor and Evaluate: Continually monitor and assess the outcomes of data-driven decisions. Measure results against established KPIs, pinpoint areas that need improvement and adjust strategies accordingly.

Addressing the Data Skills and Talent Gap: Invest in initiatives that enhance data literacy and upskilling within your organization. Cultivate a culture that values data-driven practices and motivates employees to embrace data analytics and interpretation.

Here are how businesses can foster a data-centric culture.

Leadership Dedication: Establishing a data-driven culture begins with unwavering commitment from leadership. Executives should lead by example, prioritize data-based decision-making, and convey the significance of data excellence throughout the organization.

Data Literacy Enhancement: Promote data literacy at all organizational levels by offering training and resources. Provide workshops, online courses, and certifications to equip employees with the skills to analyze and interpret data proficiently.

Cultivate Inquisitiveness and Experimentation: Encourage employees to delve into data, ask questions, and experiment with various analytical techniques. Create a supportive environment where errors are viewed as opportunities for learning and stimulate data-driven experimentation.

Acknowledge and Reward Data-Driven Accomplishments: Acknowledge and reward individuals or teams demonstrating remarkable data-driven achievements. Celebrate success stories, share insights, and establish knowledge-sharing platforms to inspire others.

ELEMENTS OF EMPLOYEE ENGAGEMENT

International research indicates that employee engagement consists of three essential components:

- The employees and their distinct psychological characteristics and individual experiences
- The employers and their ability to foster a conducive environment that encourages employee engagement
- Collaboration among employees across all hierarchical levels.

Therefore, creating a win-win situation and an environment that supports this cooperation is mostly on the shoulders of the organization.

CLASSIFICATION OF EMPLOYEE ENGAGEMENT CATEGORIES

According to Gallup, (2013) the consulting organization, individuals can be categorized into various types (Figure 1).

Figure 1. Distribution of Individuals category-wise in the consulting organization

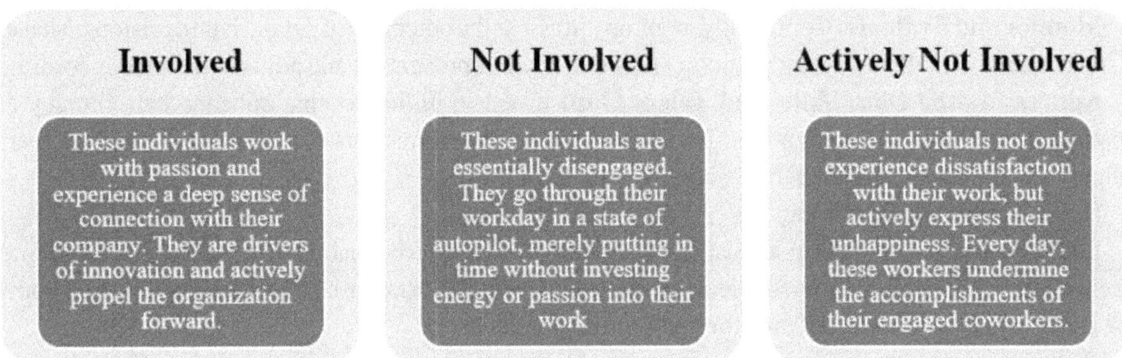

IMPORTANCE OF ENGAGEMENT

Employee engagement is the linchpin that holds the potential to elevate organizational performance and secure outstanding business outcomes (Tripathi & Al-Shahri, 2023). When employees exhibit symptoms of disengagement or alienation, manifesting through a noticeable drop in commitment and a waning of motivation, it signals a deeper issue within the organizational framework (Pasumarti & Pasumarti, 2019). This detachment is not a sudden occurrence but a gradual process often rooted in the sense of meaninglessness that employees associate with their work. Such a scenario is detrimental as it implies that employees feel estranged from their authentic selves, leading to negative outcomes (Luthans & Peterson, 2002).

Addressing this critical issue requires managers to not only recognize the signs of disengagement but also to proactively engage in cultivating a culture that fosters deep employee engagement (Vashishtha & Dhawan, 2023). Engagement is more than mere satisfaction; it is about passion and involvement in one's work. It is about employees feeling that their work is significant, that their contributions matter, and that they are part of something greater than themselves (Tambaip et al., 2023). It is about excitement and involvement, which serve as a distinct measure of engagement, differentiating it from other organizational metrics (Phoek et al., 2023).

The repercussions of not nurturing employee engagement are significant and far-reaching. Numerous studies have drawn a clear line connecting engagement with crucial organizational outcomes such as employee turnover, customer loyalty, workplace safety, productivity, and profitability. Engaged employees tend to stay with their employers longer, reducing turnover and the associated costs of recruiting and training new staff (Subbarao, 2020). Moreover, their commitment to the organization's goals often translates into higher levels of customer service, resulting in enhanced customer loyalty and, ultimately, profitability (Kuragayala, 2023).

Engaged employees are typically more attentive and conscientious about their work environment, contributing to a safer workplace (Sharma et al., 2021). Their heightened involvement leads to better adherence to safety protocols and fewer accidents. In terms of productivity, engaged employees are the powerhouse of the organization (Hussain & Alam, 2023). Their enthusiasm and commitment often result in higher quality work and innovation, driving the company to pursue excellence.

An organization's capacity to manage employee engagement effectively is thus inextricably linked to its success (Subbarao, 2019). When employees are engaged, they bring their best selves to work, channeling their talents and energies in a way that propels their growth and that of the organization. The benefits are manifold and extend beyond tangible outcomes. Engaged employees contribute to a positive organizational culture that is vibrant and resilient, capable of withstanding the pressures of an ever-changing business environment.

Cultivating employee engagement is not merely a managerial duty but a strategic imperative. By investing in the drivers of engagement, such as meaningful work, recognition, personal development, and a supportive work environment, organizations can unlock the full potential of their workforce. Engaged employees are the heart of a thriving organization, and their vibrancy reflects the business's health. Some benefits of having engaged employees include:

- Engaged employees exhibit loyalty to the company, actively advocate for its products and services, and contribute to its overall success.
- Engaged employees are typically highly motivated and perform at an elevated level. Furthermore, a noteworthy correlation exists between employee engagement and profitability.
- Engaged employees cultivate an emotional connection with the organization, impacting customer interactions and enhancing customer satisfaction and service standards.
- Employee engagement nurtures enthusiasm, dedication, and alignment with the organization's strategies and objectives.

In a competitive environment, employee engagement cultivates loyalty, establishes trust in the organization, nurtures a dynamic and energetic work environment, accelerates business growth, and transforms employees into influential brand advocates.

WHAT ARE THE METHODS FOR MEASURING EMPLOYEE ENGAGEMENT?

Gallup, (2013) research consistently demonstrates that workplaces with higher levels of employee engagement experience reduced staff turnover, increased customer loyalty, enhanced productivity, and higher earnings compared to less engaged workplaces. These positive outcomes highlight the business benefits of actively involving employees and contribute to increased shareholder value. On the other hand, negative working relationships often play a significant role in the low levels of engagement observed among many employees.

Step I: Listen

It is crucial for the employer to actively listen to employees and acknowledge that this process is continuous. Gathering information from employees is essential as it provides valuable insights and guidance. By listening to their input, leaders can foster greater employee engagement. Consequently, employee retention and productivity increase. Engaged employees are more likely to experience job satisfaction, remain committed to the organization, pursue career advancement, and work hard for better performance standards.

Step II: Assess the present level of engagement of employee

In order to evaluate the impact of employee engagement on company performance, regular measurements must be taken. Nevertheless, it is crucial to recognize that relying solely on surveys to evaluate engagement without implementing a strategy to address the findings can result in a decline in employee engagement. Therefore, it is not sufficient to merely gauge the pulse of employee engagement; an action plan is also essential.

Measuring Employee Engagement: Employee satisfaction surveys can determine employee engagement levels. Through a well-designed satisfaction survey, we can assess the extent of employee involvement within the organization.

Having a clear understanding of my work expectations: Employees should be fully aware of their responsibilities.

Materials and equipment: For employees to accomplish their duties to the best of their abilities and support their skills, experience, and talents, they require appropriate tools and equipment.

Do what I do best every day: Are your staff members playing the appropriate parts? Ensuring abilities match those expectations requires understanding the essential requirements for each function.

Supervisor at work cares: Supervisors must spend most of their time with their most effective employees. Someone at work cares. Many supervisors focus most of their attention on workers lagging.

Coworkers committed to quality: Many businesses assemble teams at random without considering that workers would only psychologically join a team if they believe their teammates will encourage and support their high levels of performance and dedication. Highly skilled employees possess elevated expectations and depend on their peers to foster their growth toward achieving excellence.

Chance for learning and development: The company should foster a culture that motivates staff to pursue innovation or develop better methods for more efficient outcomes. Great managers always inquire what knowledge and abilities are required in addition to talent to get the best results for each employee.

Step III: - Recognize areas of concern or areas that require improvement

Identify the specific problem areas that contribute to employee disengagement.

Step IV: Take proactive steps to enhance enablement by addressing the identified problem areas

Nothing is more demoralizing for workers than being asked for their opinions while their problems remain unresolved. When small steps are taken to address these issues, employees perceive their opinions are valued. This sense of worth enhances motivation, drives performance, and inspires future contributions. The initial step in taking action is listening attentively to employee feedback, while the final step is implementing a solid action plan.

FACTORS LEADING TO EMPLOYEE ENGAGEMENT

Research has identified several key factors that significantly impact employee engagement. These factors include:

Providing opportunities for personal and career development: High-engagement workplaces allow people to grow professionally, pick up new abilities, learn new knowledge, and reach their maximum potential. As businesses invest in their employees' career trajectories, employees, in turn, demonstrate increased commitment and investment in the company.

Effective Talent Management in Career Development: Career development significantly impacts employee engagement as it not only helps employers retain top talent but also provides opportunities for personal growth.

Leadership: Treating Employees with Respect: Successful organizations value each employee's skills and contributions regardless of their position.

Leadership - The Organization's Code of Conduct: The moral values of a corporation also influence a person's involvement.

The Image: the degree to which employees believe the goods and services their employer offers to its clients are high caliber will primarily determine how enthusiastically they would endorse them.

OTHER FACTORS

Fair treatment and the same opportunities: If all employees received equal opportunities for development and advancement from their superiors, there would be high levels of employee engagement.

Performance appraisal and fair evaluation of an employee's performance are crucial factors in determining their level of engagement. In companies that utilize a transparent and unbiased performance appraisal method, employee engagement tends to be high.

Earnings and Benefits: It must have a fair wage structure to motivate people to work for the company. Employees should also gain specific advantages and compensation to increase their levels of engagement.

Safety and health: According to health and safety research, employee engagement is poor if they don't feel safe at work. To ensure the health and safety of their employees, every organization needs to use proper techniques and processes.

Career satisfaction: Employees can only be engaged if satisfied with their job. Therefore, a company must ensure the employee's employment meets his professional goals so he can like his work and, ultimately, be happy with his position.

Communication: The open-door policy should be implemented by the company. Effective communication within an organization should encompass both upward and downward channels using the appropriate communication channels. When employees have a voice in decision-making and the opportunity to be heard by their supervisors, the likelihood of high employee engagement increases.

Co-operation: Employee engagement occurs when everyone supports one another, including all supervisors and employees.

Friendliness to Families: An individual's personal life impacts their work life. When employees perceive that the company considers the needs of their family, they develop an emotional attachment to the organization and become more engaged.

ESSENCE OF EMPLOYEE ENGAGEMENT

How can leaders effectively inspire and engage the minds, hearts, and hands of their workforce? Numerous options for action are presented in the literature that we have enumerated. These are the important factors of Employee Engagement, essential for fostering employee engagement.

BIND: Employee value must be demonstrated by leaders. The level of engagement among employees is a clear indicator of how they view their interactions with management. When a company says that its employees are its most precious asset, the employees examine if the company and its leader live up to that claim.

CLARITY: A clear vision must be expressed by the leader. People want to know the senior leadership's vision for the company and the department heads' objectives for their respective divisions, units, or teams. The clarity individuals have about their objectives and what they aim to achieve significantly influences their success in both personal and organizational contexts.

CAREER: A leader should provide opportunities for challenging and rewarding work that contribute to the career development of their employees. The majority of people desire to change their jobs. A good leader will challenge the team but must also create confidence that the challenge can be met.

BEAR: Leaders ensure clarity regarding expectations and provide feedback to their team members on their performance. They also establish effective systems and procedures that support goal achievement and assist individuals in mastering challenging tasks.

PRAISE: According to surveys, employees frequently believe they get rapid feedback when their performance is subpar or poor. The same workers report that receiving praise and acknowledgment for excellent performance is significantly less common. In addition to frequently recognizing others, excellent leaders also coach and communicate.

GRANT: Individuals desire to feel that their opinions are valued and impact the organization's success. In conclusion, effective leaders enable followers to recognize and value their role in the growth and success of the company.

CONFIDENCE: Good leaders contribute to developing trust inside an organization by being role models for high moral and performance standards. Leaders should actively seek out the level of participation in an organization.

CREDIBILITY: A company must maintain its reputation, and leaders should act with integrity. Individuals want to feel a sense of pride and satisfaction about their organizations, work, and themselves.

COLLABORATE: Studies demonstrate that teams with members who trust and cooperate with them perform better than people or teams who don't have strong interpersonal bonds. Great leaders build teams and inspire co-operation by fostering a safe environment. Polls indicate a strong correlation between employee engagement and coworkers' care demonstration. Therefore, a constant task for leaders is to get people to work together on organizational, departmental, and group goals while excluding people who are only interested in themselves.

STATEMENT OF THE PROBLEM

To assess the level of employee commitment to organizational goals and address employee engagement challenges in the workplace. Knowing what motivates employees is beneficial for taking remedial action when necessary and creating long-term goals. This study also focuses on offering ideas to enhance the effectiveness of the current system and practises used to engage the workforce.

OBJECTIVES OF THE STUDY

- To pinpoint the elements contributing to employee disengagement and take note of them.
- To assess the impact of employee effort on individual outcomes.
- To research how well the company's employee engagement policies are working.
- To identify the elements that help and impede employee engagement.
- Identify the issues and elements that influence employees' commitment to their work.
- To offer workable recommendations for enhancing employee performance and making the best use of their potential.
- It is also conducted to assess the overall percentage of employees fully engaged in their work, which helps enhance task efficiency and achieve organizational goals.

SCOPE AND NEED OF THE STUDY

This study will contribute to a decrease in attrition and an improvement in production and profit. It will explore and concentrate on how to increase employee commitment and engagement in the organization's expansion.

LIMITATIONS OF STUDY

- Despite the systematic and planned nature of the investigation, some obstacles remained insurmountable. These made up the research limitations.
- Every interviewer encounters one issue: the respondents' unwillingness to complete the questionnaire.
- It was unable to confirm the accuracy of the information gathered from employees.

REVIEW OF LITERATURE

Alayli (2023) explored that measuring the productivity of an organization involves more than just assessing factors such as profit, new products, customer satisfaction, and employee satisfaction. It is also assessed in terms of employee engagement. Engaged employees exhibit a positive attitude toward their work and demonstrate a strong commitment. This article delves into the difficulties HR managers encounter as they strive to improve employee engagement for the organization's long-term viability. It illuminates different facets of employee engagement, encompassing its advantages, primary indicators, and the factors that influence it.

Anand et al., (2023) provide an overview of the motivational practices employed by industries in various sectors. It emphasizes that having an enthusiastic team is crucial for success, while lackluster employees can have a negative impact on the organization. According to Gallup (2013) organization survey, 24% of workers in Japan are "actively disengaged," expressing their dissatisfaction and demonstrating a lack of motivation, resulting in an estimated $232 billion in lost productivity annually. In the United States, 14% of workers are actively disengaged, while in Singapore, 12%, costing $6 billion. A recent report suggests that failing to retain top talent can lead to a company losing up to 40% of its profits. An ideal work environment encompasses trust in leadership, a sense of pride in one's work, and positive interpersonal relationships. Therefore, trust, pride, and personal safety are crucial for employee engagement.

Arslan et al., (2021) convey their messages and foster deep employee engagement. Recently, business leaders have recognized the value of storytelling and its ability to captivate employees. This article explores why companies utilize storytelling, the process involved, and the various communication channels available within organizations to convey stories that drive employee engagement. Business leaders and executives can leverage the expressive power of storytelling to connect with those who truly matter the employees. Stories breathe life into business messages, enabling leaders to engage employees in many ways. Through storytelling, leaders can effectively convey messages that motivate, inspire, challenge, stimulate, excite, and shape their employees. Furthermore, storytelling exemplifies key leadership practices, such as sharing a refreshing vision, creating suitable settings and context, and captivating employees' hearts, minds, and souls to help the company achieve its objectives.

Atasever, (2023) recognized the benefits of an engaged workforce for the company. In this context, in collaboration with managers actively practicing in the field and industry leaders, "The Human Factor" investigates the terrain of employee engagement and delves into the crucial elements that play a significant role in fostering successful initiatives and also the employee engagement encompasses the understanding that one's work is meaningful and has a positive impact while also experiencing enjoyment and fulfillment in the job, along with having sufficient time to work and appreciate the work.

RESEARCH METHODOLOGY

The study adopts an analytical approach, meticulously sifting through facts and information readily accessible within the public domain to formulate critical assessments concerning its focal subject. By design, this research leans on a non-probability sampling method, specifically, a convenience sampling strategy. This method is particularly advantageous regarding efficiency in terms of both cost and time. It involves selecting study participants who are easily reachable and willing to contribute the necessary data, thus streamlining the research process significantly.

In executing this strategy, 120 individuals were selectively culled from a larger cohort of 250 employees. The choice of these participants was not random but was predicated on the ease with which they could be approached and their readiness to partake in the study, providing a practical balance between comprehensive data collection and resource constraints. The instrument of choice for data gathering was a structured questionnaire, which offers the dual benefits of standardization and ease of analysis, ensuring that each participant was presented with the same set of questions in the same order.

The structured nature of the questionnaire allows for a systematic exploration of the relationship between the study variables, facilitating a robust data collection conducive to quantitative analysis. The Chi-square test, a statistical tool commonly employed in research to ascertain the significance of the associations between categorical variables, was utilized to delve into the intricacies of the interrelations among the variables. This test is instrumental in determining whether the observed relationships in the sample data reflect true associations within the broader population or merely the result of random chance.

The analytical nature of the study, combined with the strategic use of convenience sampling and structured questionnaires, underpins the rigorous examination of the subject matter. The choice of the Chi-square test further underscores the study's commitment to methodological rigor, ensuring that the conclusions drawn are both statistically valid and empirically sound. In doing so, the research aims to contribute valuable insights into the field, grounded in a systematic analysis of public domain data, which could potentially inform future research, policy formulation, and practical applications in the relevant study area.

ANALYSIS AND INTERPRETATIONS

Table 1 displays the category Opportunity to excel in daily work alongside the category Received recognition and praise for performance.

Table 1. Opportunity to excel in daily work

Description	Very Satisfied	Satisfactory	Dissatisfied	Total
Opportunity for daily optimal performance.	35	10	5	50
Acknowledgment and praise received for exemplary work performance.	30	15	5	50
Total	65	25	10	100

CHI-SQUARE TEST

H0: There is no significant relationship between the opportunity to do the work best daily and receiving recognition and praise for doing good work.

H1: There is a significant relationship between the opportunity to do the work best daily and receiving recognition and praise for doing good work.

O = Actual frequency

E = Expected frequency

Expected frequency of any cell = (The Row total of the cell) X (Column total of the cell) / Total Observation

Table 2 shows employee satisfaction levels with performance opportunities and work recognition.

Table 2. Employee satisfaction levels with performance opportunities and work recognition

Description	Very Satisfied	Satisfactory	Dissatisfied	Total
Opportunities	32.5	12.5	5	50
Recognition	32.5	12.5	5	50
Total	65	25	10	100

Degree of freedom = (r-1) (c-1)
2-1 *3-1
= 1*2
= 2
Level of significance=0.05
So, tabulated value is: 5.99

Figure 2. A representation of employee satisfaction survey results in workplace fulfillment and recognition

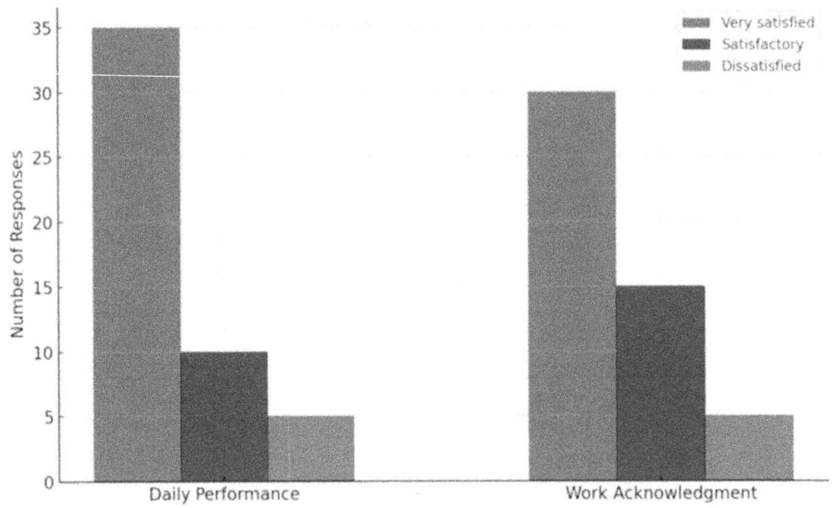

Figure 2 briefly presents the findings of an employee satisfaction survey, differentiating between "Very Satisfied," "Satisfactory," and "Dissatisfied" across two distinct aspects of job satisfaction. In the realm of "Daily Performance," a substantial number of respondents '35 out of 50' report a high level of satisfaction, a testament to the opportunities for optimal performance provided by the workplace. Meanwhile, ten employees are moderately satisfied, and a smaller group of 5 registers dissatisfaction. The second aspect, "Work Acknowledgment," also showcases a positive tilt, with 30 employees feeling very satisfied with their recognition for their work, though with a slightly higher number '15' indicating mere satisfaction, and again, five dissatisfied. The data was amalgamated into 100 individual responses, where the majority, 65, express a high degree of satisfaction, 25 view their experiences as satisfactory, and a minority of 10 remain dissatisfied. This graphical representation underscores the overall positive workplace sentiment while also pinpointing areas that could be enhanced to improve employee contentment (Table 3).

Table 3. Breaking down the numbers: A statistical analysis of satisfaction and deviation from expectations

O	E	(O-E)	(O-E)2	(O-E)2/E
35	32.5	2.5	6.25	0.192
10	12.5	-2.5	6.25	0.5
5	5	0	0	0
30	32.5	-2.5	6.25	0.192
15	12.5	2.5	6.25	0.5
5	5	0	0	0
			Calculatedvalue	**1.38**

Figure 3. Pie chart representation of chi-square contribution per category

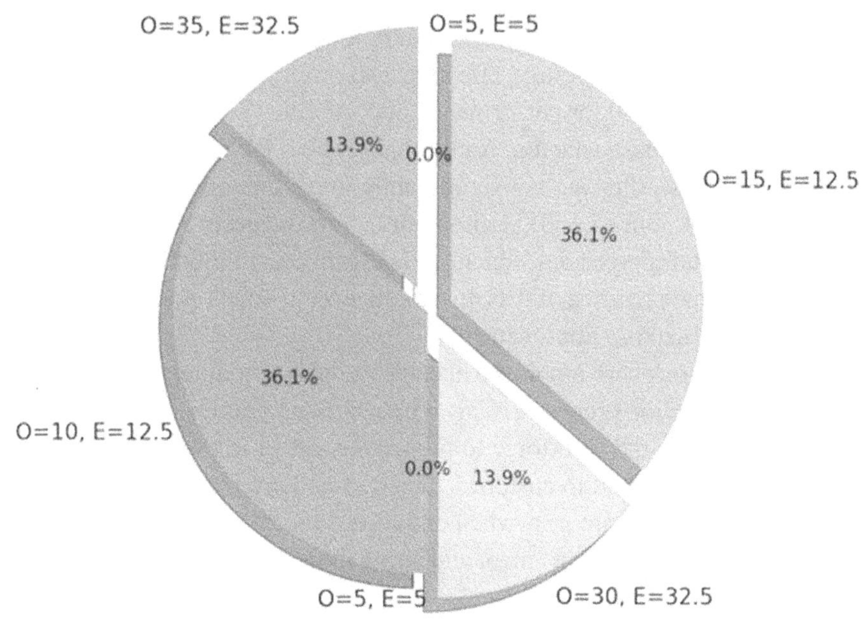

Figure 3 illustrates the distribution of the calculated (O−E)²/E(O−E)²/E values for a dataset, where OO represents observed frequencies and EE denotes expected frequencies under a certain hypothesis. The chart is divided into six segments, each corresponding to a different O/EO/E pair from the dataset. Two segments (corresponding to O=35, E=32.5O=35, E=32.5 and O=15, E=12.5O=15, E=12.5) are more prominent, indicating a higher contribution to the total chi-square statistic, marked by their exploded view in the chart. The segments representing O=5, E=5O=5, and E=5 show no contribution (0.0%), reflecting perfect agreement between observed and expected values. Despite variations in observed and expected frequencies, the visual representation culminates in a cumulative calculated value of 1.38, suggesting how closely the observed frequencies align with the expected frequencies. The differences and their squared proportions to the expected values give a sense of the variance within the data, crucial for chi-square tests of independence or goodness-of-fit.

RESULT

Empowering employees intelligently through data enablement centers on strategically using data analytics and information systems to significantly uplift the workforce's skills and productivity. This systematic approach to employee enablement is not just about distributing data but also providing the workforce with the means to effectively interpret and leverage this information. Access to relevant data, sophisticated analytical tools, and comprehensive training programs equip employees to make more informed decisions swiftly and confidently. This access is the cornerstone of a transformative shift toward a data-driven culture within an organization, where transparency and the free flow of information prevail, breaking down traditional hierarchical barriers. From a results perspective, table 1 reflects employee satisfaction levels concerning two key workplace factors: the opportunity for daily optimal performance and the acknowledgment and praise for exemplary work.

Out of 50 responses for each category, the majority feel very satisfied with the opportunity for daily optimal performance (35 responses), indicating a strong organizational support system that enables employees to excel in their daily tasks. Similarly, 30 employees expressed high satisfaction with their recognition for outstanding work, suggesting effective acknowledgment practices within the company. Satisfactory levels are moderate (10 for performance opportunities and 15 for acknowledgment), indicating room for improvement. Dissatisfaction is minimal for both factors (5 for each), highlighting that while there are areas to address, they are not significantly impacting employee morale. The high level of very satisfied responses (65 out of 100) across both factors suggests a positive environment where employees feel empowered and appreciated, which can lead to higher productivity and engagement within the organization. However, the presence of dissatisfaction, even if small, points to potential areas where the company could focus on making improvements.

In cultivating such a culture, every employee becomes a data custodian, capable of utilizing insights to drive innovation and streamline processes. This empowerment manifests as increased agility within the business structure, enabling the workforce to proactively adapt to evolving market dynamics. Empowered employees are more attuned to customer demands and are instrumental in devising solutions that resonate with market needs. Moreover, when employees are adept at handling data, they are more likely to identify opportunities for improvement and waste reduction, leading to heightened operational efficiency.

Table 2 presents data on the satisfaction levels of individuals regarding "Opportunities" and "Recognition," presumably in a workplace or similar environment. For both categories, the distribution of satisfaction levels is identical. Exactly 32.5% of individuals have reported being "Very Satisfied" with the opportunities and recognition they receive. Another 12.5% feel that what they receive is "Satisfactory" in both areas. A smaller portion, 5%, have expressed "Dissatisfaction" with both opportunities and recognition. The cumulative satisfaction percentages for each category add up to 50%. When considering the total responses across both categories, 65% of the feedback is "Very Satisfied," a quarter of the responses are "Satisfactory," and a tenth indicates "Dissatisfaction," tallying to a 100% distribution of the sample considered. This suggests a positive trend in satisfaction levels overall, with most individuals feeling very satisfied or at least satisfied with their opportunities and recognition. The identical distribution across both categories could imply a consistent experience or perception of the evaluated factors.

The benefits of this enablement extend beyond internal operations. Businesses can align individual contributions with broader strategic objectives by investing in employees' data competencies. This alignment is critical for coherent organizational growth and ensuring that every employee's efforts support the overarching business goals. The compounded effect of these individual efforts is a substantial improvement in overall performance metrics. This empowerment leads to employees feeling more valued and invested in their roles, which can enhance job satisfaction and reduce turnover rates. A capable and content workforce is fundamental to driving customer satisfaction; satisfied employees tend to deliver better customer experiences, which fosters customer loyalty and can lead to increased profitability.

In the broader scope of industry competition, the intelligent enablement of employees through data is a pivotal differentiator. Organizations that excel in this facet can outpace competitors by being more responsive to market shifts, more innovative in their offerings, and more efficient in their operations. As a result, these organizations don't just compete; they set the pace and direction of their industry.

Table 3. represents a chi-square test calculation, a statistical method used to compare observed data with data we expect to obtain according to a specific hypothesis. The columns "O" and "E" represent the observed and expected frequencies. The "(O-E)" column shows the difference between these frequencies, and "(O-E)^2" is the square of this difference. The final column, "(O-E)^2/E", is the chi-square contribution from each category, obtained by dividing the squared differences by the expected frequency.

The observed frequencies in the first row are slightly higher than expected (35 vs. 32.5), while in the second row, they are slightly lower (10 vs. 12.5). The third row shows perfect agreement between observed and expected frequencies (5 vs. 5). This pattern repeats for the next set of three rows with different values.

The chi-square contributions vary, with nonzero values ranging from 0.192 to 0.5, indicating varying degrees of deviation from the expected frequencies. The sum of these chi-square contributions is the calculated value of 1.38, which would be compared against a chi-square distribution with the appropriate degrees of freedom to determine statistical significance. A low chi-square value suggests that the observed distribution is not significantly different from the expected distribution, indicating a good fit between observed data and the model or hypothesis tested.

Ultimately, the intelligent enablement of employees through data is about leveraging human capital to its fullest by making data a central pillar of the work environment. When employees at all levels are empowered with data, they become agents of change and growth, capable of propelling the business toward excellence that aligns with the company's vision and objectives. The result is a resilient, forward-thinking enterprise characterized by high performance, robust customer relationships, and an enviable position in the marketplace. Since the tabulated Value is MORE than the Calculated Value (5.99>1.38), the Null hypothesis (H0) is Accepted. Consequently, there is a lack of significant correlation between the opportunity to perform at one's best every day and receiving recognition and praise for exceptional work.

DISCUSSION AND FINDINGS

Based on the observations mentioned earlier and analysis, it appears that most employees are actively engaged in their work and hold a positive perception of their organization. However, a few employees exhibit disengagement, and a few are moderately engaged and have the potential to become fully engaged with the right guidance and careful planning from their supervisors. There is a strong correlation between employees who actively advocate their employer as an excellent workplace and the overall satisfaction of employees with the organization.

According to the research, it has been observed that engaged employees tend to stay with their jobs due to their satisfaction and enjoyment of the work they do. On the other hand, unengaged employees also demonstrate an intention to remain in their current positions. Various factors contribute to this decision, including financial considerations, a desire for stability and security, familiarity with their current working conditions, and resistance to change. Employees are often reluctant to embrace changes that could potentially enhance the organization. Instead, they prefer maintaining the status quo and resisting alterations to their established routine.

As per the research findings, a significant percentage (50%) of the participants agreed that their employers effectively motivate and encourage them to work diligently and give their best daily. The analysis of the empirical study indicated that employees' psychological experiences play a crucial role in shaping their expression and performance within the workplace. Additionally, a majority of respondents (60%) confirmed that they have a clear understanding of their company's vision and mission.

According to the findings, several challenges can impede employee engagement. The empirical research suggests that age plays a significant role in determining the most prominent challenge, particularly regarding resistance to change. As employees grow older, they may exhibit a higher level of resistance towards embracing new ideas and initiatives. Furthermore, the length of service appears to be inversely related to the level of engagement. As employees spend more time in their roles, their engagement tends to decline.

Nearly half of the surveyed individuals (50%) agreed that the organization treats all employees fairly. Most responders (60%) also expressed that working with everyone in the organization is pleasant and cooperative. Based on the table provided, it can be observed that 70% of employees indicated strong satisfaction with the opportunities to perform their best work each day. An additional 20% expressed satisfaction, while a small proportion of employees (10%) reported slight dissatisfaction with the opportunities provided.

Hygiene factors, such as health and security, conflicts with managers and coworkers, low wages, long working hours, and poor working conditions, can contribute to job dissatisfaction. These factors have the potential to make individuals feel unengaged in their work. When employees experience issues in these areas, it can lead to a decline in their overall job satisfaction and a decreased level of engagement.

According to the provided table, it can be seen that 60% of employees indicated a strong level of satisfaction, 30% expressed satisfaction, and 10% reported slight dissatisfaction with the recognition and praise they received for their good work. Furthermore, the table also indicates that 70% of employees expressed strong satisfaction with the opportunities they had at work to learn and grow.

The limited opportunities for employee growth can lead to a higher risk of employee turnover. Therefore, management must prioritize and focus on increasing promotion opportunities based on employee performance. Organizations can enhance employee satisfaction and engagement by providing clear paths for career advancement and recognizing and rewarding exceptional performance, ultimately reducing turnover rates. Creating a culture that values and supports employee growth and development is essential in retaining talent and fostering a motivated workforce.

The data indicates that the criteria for job security are not highly satisfactory, highlighting the need for management to prioritize and enhance employee job security. Ensuring job stability can create a conducive work environment where employees can perform without fearing job loss, increasing job satisfaction and engagement.

Additionally, the table reveals that most employees (70%) are very satisfied with their commitment to doing quality work, while 20% expressed satisfaction and 10% reported dissatisfaction. This demonstrates that most employees are highly dedicated to delivering quality work, which is a positive aspect of the organization. It is also worth noting that the table suggests that only a few employees feel their ideas or work are not being recognized or appreciated, implying that the organization values and acknowledges employee contributions significantly.

Based on the analysis, it has been concluded that the current duration of in-house training, which is only three days, is insufficient to provide employees with comprehensive knowledge across different domains. Therefore, extending the training period to 7 days is recommended to ensure employees receive a more thorough understanding of the subject matter.

Additionally, although there is active participation of employees in decision-making processes, it is observed that the suggestions provided by employees are rarely implemented. This lack of action on employee suggestions can demotivate employees and undermine their confidence. Management must address this issue by actively considering and implementing viable employee suggestions, fostering a sense of empowerment and engagement.

Moreover, the implementation of non-financial incentive programs can be beneficial. Such programs can incentivize and motivate staff based on output and performance, increasing productivity. Organizations can create a positive work environment and drive improved performance by recognizing and rewarding employees' achievements and contributions.

Motivator factors indeed play a crucial role in fostering employee engagement. As highlighted in the theoretical framework and reinforced in the analysis, career development opportunities and training programs contribute significantly to high levels of employee engagement. Providing employees with avenues for growth and advancement enhances their skills and knowledge and instills a sense of purpose and commitment to the organization.

Recognition for achievements and the nature of work tasks and responsibilities also contribute to employee involvement and engagement. Employees want to feel valued for their contributions and challenged in their roles to maintain a sense of excitement and fulfillment. When individuals are recognized and appreciated for their efforts, it creates a positive work environment and motivates them to perform at their best.

Addressing motivator factors such as career development, training opportunities, recognition, and challenging work tasks helps create an engaged workforce, leading to improved performance and organizational success.

Management should carefully consider the valuable suggestions and new ideas provided by employees. Incorporating employee input can significantly enhance the efficiency and effectiveness of the organization. By actively listening to and implementing employee suggestions, management can tap into the collective knowledge and creativity of the workforce, leading to innovative solutions and improved outcomes.

Furthermore, providing employees with better career development opportunities is crucial for both individual and organizational growth. Offering avenues for professional advancement, skill-building, and personal growth benefits individual employees and strengthens the workforce's overall capabilities. It fosters continuous learning and development, contributing to employee engagement and organizational success.

In summary, by valuing employee input and providing robust career development possibilities, management can create a culture of collaboration, growth, and innovation, increasing the organization's efficiency and effectiveness.

SUGGESTIONS

- Managers and supervisors should have regular meetings with employees to address how the business, the workplace, and their standard of life could be improved and issues with their families.
- Foster a positive and healthy work atmosphere by boosting interactions, credibility, and confidence, among other things.
- Some workers complain that their work is tedious and dull. Encourage them to participate in the organization's employment enrichment programs, job rotation, and other events.
- Engage employees more with enjoyable workdays, cross-training, and mentorship programs.
- Because there are few possibilities for employees to grow, there may be a high employee turnover rate; therefore, management must prioritize expanding the number of promotion opportunities based on employee performance.
- The criteria for job security are not sufficiently fulfilling; therefore, management should prioritize employee job security to enable them to work without concerns about losing their positions within the company.
- Based on our investigation, we have concluded that the current in-house training duration, which spans only three days, is insufficient for a comprehensive understanding of all pertinent subjects. Consequently, we recommend extending the training period to 7 days.
- To cultivate inspiration within the workforce, management can benefit from considering valuable advice from employees. This practice will enhance employee motivation and, ultimately, foster higher levels of employee engagement.
- Despite active employee participation in decision-making, implementing their recommendations is infrequent, leading to declining employee confidence.

CONCLUSION

Employee engagement is closely linked with performance and satisfaction, creating a sense of belonging within the organization through various activities. In the digital age, mastering data is crucial for business success, allowing for informed decisions, enhanced customer experiences, increased efficiency, and identifying risks and opportunities. Building a data-centric culture and investing in robust data systems are essential for thriving in today's data-intensive landscape. Effective communication with employees is central to a company's competitive edge, making ongoing learning, improvement, measurement, and action vital components of employee engagement. This emotional investment in the company's mission is a barometer for employee contentment and organizational needs, now a critical element of HR strategies to foster organizational success. By harnessing data effectively, businesses gain critical insights and drive informed decision-making to fuel growth, a concept explored in the context of data excellence in this article. Ultimately, the organization has to enhance and maintain employee engagement, requiring a delicate mix of resources and dedication to nurture a successful business environment.

LIMITATIONS

From a limitations point of view, this research encapsulates a visionary approach but also carries implicit challenges and constraints. While the infusion of data analytics promises to enhance decision-making and streamline processes, the practical implementation of such a strategy is fraught with potential difficulties. The foremost among these is the need for a robust digital infrastructure capable of handling vast amounts of data securely and efficiently. Additionally, there's the challenge of ensuring that all employees have the requisite skills and training to leverage this data effectively, which could necessitate a significant investment in professional development. Privacy and ethical considerations also loom large, as the collection and use of data must navigate the complex landscape of regulations and personal privacy concerns. There's the risk of data overload, where the sheer volume of information leads to analysis paralysis rather than enlightened action. Finally, achieving business excellence through employee enablement is predicated on the assumption that data insights automatically translate to improved performance, a link that is not always guaranteed. Thus, while the ambition is commendable, it must be tempered with a careful consideration of these limitations.

FUTURE SCOPE

In the forthcoming era, businesses striving for excellence will increasingly hinge on the intelligent enablement of their workforce, leveraging the vast potential of data analytics and artificial intelligence. As organizations navigate through the complexities of the digital age, the focus will intensify on harnessing data to streamline decision-making processes and empower employees with actionable insights and predictive tools that enhance productivity and innovation. The paradigm will shift towards creating an ecosystem where intelligent systems provide real-time, context-aware information, enabling workers to make informed decisions swiftly, anticipate market trends, and meet customer expectations with unprecedented precision. This will lead to a more agile business environment where employee potential is maximized, fostering a culture of continuous improvement and learning. In this case, the symbiosis of human creativity with data-driven intelligence will be pivotal in realizing business excellence setting a new standard for competitive advantage and sustainable growth. The future scope extends beyond mere data accessibility; it entails cultivating a data-centric mindset across organizational hierarchies, thus democratizing data and driving a transformational shift in how value is created and delivered.

REFERENCES

Alayli, S. (2023). Unravelling the Drivers of Online Purchasing Intention: The E-Commerce Scenario in Lebanon. *FMDB Transactions on Sustainable Social Sciences Letters*, *1*(1), 56–67.

Anand, P. P., Kanike, U. K., Paramasivan, P., Rajest, S. S., Regin, R., & Priscila, S. S. (2023). Embracing Industry 5.0: Pioneering Next-Generation Technology for a Flourishing Human Experience and Societal Advancement. *FMDB Transactions on Sustainable Social Sciences Letters*, *1*(1), 43–55.

Arslan, F., Singh, B., Sharma, D. K., Regin, R., Steffi, R., & Rajest, S. S. (2021). Optimization technique approach to resolve food sustainability problems. In *2021 International Conference on Computational Intelligence and Knowledge Economy (ICCIKE)*. IEEE. 10.1109/ICCIKE51210.2021.9410735

Atasever, M. (2023). Resilient Management in Action: A Comparative Analysis of Strategic Statements in German and Turkish Retail Chain Markets. *FMDB Transactions on Sustainable Management Letters*, *1*(2), 66–81.

Batth, V. (2018). The study of financial performance of Indian public sector undertakings. *Global Journal of Finance and Management*, *10*(1), 21–43.

Bisoyi, B., Das, D., Subbarao, P. S., & Das, B. (2019). An evaluation on green manufacturing: It's technique, significance and rationality. *IOP Conf. IOP Conf. Ser. Mater. Sci. Eng*, *653*(1).

Gallup, Inc. (2013). *The benefits of employee engagement*. Retrieved November 11, 2023, from Gallup.com website: https://www.gallup.com/workplace/236927/employee-engagement-drives-growth.aspx

Hussain, S., & Alam, F. (2023). Willingness to Pay for Tourism Services: A Case Study from Harappa, Sahiwal. *FMDB Transactions on Sustainable Management Letters*, *1*(3), 105–113.

Kuragayala, P. S. (2023). A Systematic Review on Workforce Development in Healthcare Sector: Implications in the Post-COVID Scenario. *FMDB Transactions on Sustainable Technoprise Letters*, *1*(1), 36–46.

Lucey, J. J. (2009). The impact of a communications strategy and five step survey process on the improvement of employee engagement. *Management Services*, 9–15.

Luthans, F., & Peterson, S. J. (2002). Employee engagement and manager self-efficacy. *Journal of Management Development*, *21*(5), 376–387. doi:10.1108/02621710210426864

María, J. J. L., Polo, O. C. C., & Elhadary, T. (2023). An Analysis of the Morality and Social Responsibility of Non-Profit Organizations. *FMDB Transactions on Sustainable Technoprise Letters*, *1*(1), 28–35.

Ocoró, M. P., Polo, O. C. C., & Khandare, S. (2023). Importance of Business Financial Risk Analysis in SMEs According to COVID-19. *FMDB Transactions on Sustainable Management Letters*, *1*(1), 12–21.

Ogunmola, G. A., Singh, B., Sharma, D. K., Regin, R., Rajest, S. S., & Singh, N. (2021). Involvement of distance measure in assessing and resolving efficiency environmental obstacles. In *2021 International Conference on Computational Intelligence and Knowledge Economy (ICCIKE)*. IEEE. 10.1109/ICCIKE51210.2021.9410765

Pandit, P. (2023). On the Context of the Principle of Beneficence: The Problem of Over Demandingness within Utilitarian Theory. *FMDB Transactions on Sustainable Social Sciences Letters*, *1*(1), 26–42.

Pasumarti, S. S., & Pasumarti, S. S. (2019). Work life balance: A challenge for employees in Indian IT and ITES industry. *Rupkatha Journal on Interdisciplinary Studies in Humanities*, *11*(2). Advance online publication. doi:10.21659/rupkatha.v11n2.15

Phoek, S. E. M., Lauwinata, L., & Kowarin, L. R. N. (2023). Tourism Development in Merauke Regency, South Papua Province: Strengthening Physical Infrastructure for Local Economic Growth and Enchanting Tourist Attractions. *FMDB Transactions on Sustainable Management Letters*, *1*(2), 82–94.

Priscila, S. S., Rajest, S. S., Tadiboina, S. N., Regin, R., & András, S. (2023). Analysis of Machine Learning and Deep Learning Methods for Superstore Sales Prediction. *FMDB Transactions on Sustainable Computer Letters*, *1*(1), 1–11.

Ramos, J. I., Lacerona, R., & Nunag, J. M. (2023). A Study on Operational Excellence, Work Environment Factors and the Impact to Employee Performance. *FMDB Transactions on Sustainable Social Sciences Letters*, *1*(1), 12–25.

Rurkkhum, S., & Bartlett, K. R. (2012). The relationship between employee engagement and organizational citizenship behaviour in Thailand. *Human Resource Development International*, *15*(2), 157–174. doi:10.1080/13678868.2012.664693

Sabti, Y. M., Alqatrani, R. I. N., Zaid, M. I., Taengkliang, B., & Kareem, J. M. (2023). Impact of Business Environment on the Performance of Employees in the Public-Listed Companies. *FMDB Transactions on Sustainable Management Letters*, *1*(2), 56–65.

Said, F. B., & Tripathi, S. (2023). Epistemology of Digital Journalism Shift in South Global Nations: A Bibliometric Analysis. *FMDB Transactions on Sustainable Technoprise Letters*, *1*(1), 47–60.

Saxena, D., Khandare, S., & Chaudhary, S. (2023). An Overview of ChatGPT: Impact on Academic Learning. *FMDB Transactions on Sustainable Techno Learning*, *1*(1), 11–20.

Sharma, D. K., Jalil, N. A., Regin, R., Rajest, S. S., Tummala, R. K., & Thangadurai. (2021). Predicting network congestion with machine learning. In *2021 2nd International Conference on Smart Electronics and Communication (ICOSEC)*. IEEE.

Singh, M., Bhushan, M., Sharma, R., & Cavaliere, L. P. L. (2023). An Organized Assessment of the Literature of Entrepreneurial Skills and Emotional Intelligence. *FMDB Transactions on Sustainable Management Letters*, *1*(3), 95–104.

Srinivas, K., Velmurugan, P. R., & Andiyappillai, N. (2023). Digital Human Resources and Management Support Improve Human Resources Effectiveness. *FMDB Transactions on Sustainable Management Letters*, *1*(1), 32–45.

Subbarao, S. (2019). Influence of Demographic Factors on Recruitment and Selection of Employees in IT & ITES Industry. *Journal of Advanced Research in Dynamical & Control Systems*, *11*(6), 52–61.

Subbarao, S. (2020). CSR and Socio-Economic Development-A case study of selected PSU's in the State of Odisha. *Journal of Critical Reviews*, *7*(13), 1407–1415.

Tambaip, B., Hadi, A. F. F., & Tjilen, A. P. (2023). Optimizing Public Service Performance: Unleashing the Potential of Compassion as an Indicator of Public Service Motivation. *FMDB Transactions on Sustainable Management Letters*, *1*(2), 46–55.

Tripathi, S., & Al-Shahri, M. (2023). Problems and Prospects on the Evolution of Advertising and Public Relations Industries in Oman. *FMDB Transactions on Sustainable Management Letters*, *1*(1), 1–11.

Vashishtha, E., & Dhawan, G. (2023). Comparison of Baldrige Criteria of Strategy Planning and Harrison Text. *FMDB Transactions on Sustainable Management Letters*, *1*(1), 22–31.

Vashishtha, E., & Kapoor, H. (2023). Implementation of Blockchain Technology Across International Healthcare Markets. *FMDB Transactions on Sustainable Technoprise Letters*, *1*(1), 1–12.

Venkateswaran, P. S., Singh, S., Paramasivan, P., Rajest, S. S., Lourens, M. E., & Regin, R. (2023). A Study on The Influence of Quality of Service on Customer Satisfaction Towards Hotel Industry. *FMDB Transactions on Sustainable Social Sciences Letters*, *1*(1), 1–11.

Venkateswaran, P. S., & Viktor, P. (2023). A Study on Brand Equity of Fast-Moving Consumer Goods with Reference to Madurai, Tamil Nadu. *FMDB Transactions on Sustainable Technoprise Letters*, *1*(1), 13–27.

Chapter 7
Big Data Analytics and Its Impact on Human Resources Management

Anusha Thakur
https://orcid.org/0000-0001-8761-2250
University of Petroleum and Energy Studies, India

ABSTRACT

Both artistic and scientific analytic aspects play a vital role in human resources (HR). With the rising number of transactions, customers, and employees, human resources are forced to emphasize on the adoption of novel technologies to aid faster in the decision-making processes. Big data is expected to significantly gain a ubiquitous presence in human resources. Employing data analytics in HR owes the potential to bring the sector in line with the rest of the operational activities in an organization. This chapter focuses on the role and benefits of big data analytics in human resources. It contemplates the key analytical solutions being offered by the market players and the real-use cases of organizations incorporating analytics in human resources to cater to their business goals. Further, the chapter also discusses the factors challenging the implementation of analytics in transforming business processes.

INTRODUCTION

Technology has unprecedently redefined the way businesses operate nowadays. In today's scenario, analytics is not about determining interesting facts and waning them for managers. Big data has emerged as a game-changer in organizations and industries, particularly, in the HR industry. Human resource management (HRM) is experiencing an archetype shift from the conventional period of small data to the evolving era of big data.

The competence to analyze massive amounts of data has witnessed significant accessibility over the past few years, with businesses emphasizing on incorporation of analytics in managing the workforce efficiently. The growing popularity of this technology in organizations can be attributed to the decline in the cost of storing the data and the data production technology (Nocker, 2019). In addition to this, the

DOI: 10.4018/979-8-3693-2193-5.ch007

techniques that augment the processing and manipulation of stored data are increasingly being embedded within standard software, thereby enabling HR practitioners to easily extract insights from the stored data, and subsequently, impact the overall performance (McAfee A. B., 2012).

Analytics in human resources poses to be profitable in making HR executive decisions concerning organizational and employee performance. Big data is becoming a pervasive tool and a resource, enabling the segments to shift from simply reporting data to organizations conducting advanced workforce planning, predicting employee performance, and making informed talent decisions.

Several companies are making substantial technological investments to manage their day-to-day transactions, with few of them using these aggregated terabytes of information to generate meaningful data-driven decisions (Fiore, 2014). The usage of data in HRM has witnessed significant evolution over the past few years from basic metrics to big data via human resource analytics. Analytics in human resources comprises of external and internal data collection and manipulation, to back up the decisions relevant to the personnel connected to the organizational performance and business results (Marler, 2016).

With predetermined expectations, generating an optimized big data deployment becomes relatively forthright. Adopting underlying infrastructure and technologies provides the highest levels of business agility, investment protection, and time to the market (Networks, 2012). With this trend, significant re-examination and extension of the preceding research methods and results are expected to witness a rise (Zhang, 2021). Capitalizing big data with HR, enhances every segment, such as performance management, training and development, compensation, and recruitment, thereby making efficient and smarter decisions.

The paper emphasizes on illustrating the factors bolstering the demand for analytics in the human resource segment of an organization, in terms of data governance, organization, environment, and technology). It also discusses the different aspects hindering the implementation of analytics in organizations.

Big data represents various prospects for organizations to augment their strategies and accordingly make the right decisions at the best possible time. With more and more companies implementing big data solutions, newer ways are being introduced to avoid wasteful spending, particularly on personnel costs. The role of this technology is thereby becoming prominent, accelerating the way any business functions.

Research Questions

RQ1: Need for big data in human resources
RQ2: Real-use cases of big data in human resources systems
RQ3: Major players implementing the same in their businesses.
RQ4: Factors boosting and hindering the demand for big data analytics in human resources
RQ5: Future trends for implementing big data technology in human resources management.

Purpose of the Article

In today's scenario, the HR systems are largely transcending their role as the "people people", with value and performance-driven roles, via impactful insights at the point of need. Integrating the concept of big data technology in an organization's workflow process offers solutions to address the challenges related to the same. This paper illustrates different future technological trends of the implementation of big data analytics in human resources systems. Further, the paper also discusses key strategies incorporated to develop solutions by different businesses.

Key Findings in the Research

Retaining the top talent and finding the right employee for a suitable role is essentially the most important aspect of an organization. The HR segment in organizations has become more data-oriented. The workforce visions and analytics upheaval, driven by advanced intelligent automation capabilities and technology, puts the human resources organization to be the prognostic factor being looked upon by the businesses. Hence, the incorporation of big data in human resources enables organizations to reinvent the workflow processes, and accordingly strategize their models and solutions, coping with the changing competitive scenario.

LITERATURE REVIEW

Human Resources are expected to witness a profound and dramatic change, particularly in terms of digital transformation across the organizations in the world. One of the most essential aspects for an organization nowadays is to understand the way of operating digitally, with the use of digital apps and tools to deliver solutions.

Although personal interactions, interviews, and tests are still the primary methods of recruitment, the implementation of big data technology also ensures making the right decisions at the right time (Sharma, 2019). Businesses focusing on big data specializations are expected to witness an increase in overall operational efficiency with intelligent decisions.

Big data combined with cloud computing and virtualization, enables the data centers to substantially transform and grow over the next few years. The technology owes the potential to generate an architectural upheaval in the way software, storage, and systems are linked and managed. The real-time capability of the latest big data solutions enables business intelligence to speed up and accordingly shape the organization's decision-making process.

NEED FOR BIG DATA ANALYTICS IN HUMAN RESOURCE MANAGEMENT:

Shifting workforce potentials is expected to propel the organizations to develop different user-centric HR models to cater to the changing needs and requirements. The concept of big data has become ubiquitous across businesses emphasizing every segment to be analytic in their operational activities.

The ways in which big data is expected to benefit the human resource segments can be illustrated as:

- **Recruiting the best talent:** Attracting talented professionals poses a challenge for several organizations. The incorporation of analytics in human resources is expected to enable HR managers to filter the resumes, with ease and subsequently narrow their search to the desirable and suitable candidates, in lesser time.
- **Augmenting training and development:** Providing an efficient training process for the existing workforce plays an important part in an organization (Alexis, 2017). The inclusion of analytics-based dashboards helps develop a customized training schedule for the new employees on the basis, of their job characteristics and education portfolio and, further helps the dashboards to produce data, to efficaciously calculate the return on the training investment, which otherwise is

challenging. Gathering such kind of granular data at an individual level helps the senior management to seamlessly identify the advantages of training investments.

- **Increasing employee retention:** Employee turnover poses to be a major issue for businesses across the world. The experience of the employees in an organization is directly linked to the attrition rate of the same. The amalgamation of analytics in the human resource segment of an organization offers clarity in understanding the employee experience. The technology helps to locate the patterns and trends across the service lines, teams, and departments as well as highlights the key issues expected to gain traction among the employees. In addition to this, the incorporation of analytics also helps to minimize the cost of attrition and its subsequent impact on the organization, thereby offering suitable measures and solutions to minimize the same (Kundariya, 2023).
- **Enhancing employee engagement and motivation:** The performance of an employee in an organization is largely based on the employee's engagement. The data collected at the organizational level thereby enables the senior management to understand the factors propelling employee turnover and subsequently, design the policies impacting the retention of the same (Nocker, 2019).
- **Prioritizing the recruitment channels:** In today's scenario, organizations are engaged in using a variety of recruitment channels to fill in suitable vacant positions. Big data analytics helps to reveal effective recruitment channels, whether in terms of online job boards, external initiatives, or internal recruitment (Talend, n.d.).

Leveraging the concept of big data helps to inform and enhance every segment of human resources such as compensation, recruitment, performance, training, and development. Understanding the importance of acquiring and retaining top talent is a necessity for organizations to succeed (Kumar, 2018). This can largely be attributed to the increasing number of transactions, employees, and customers along with the rising adoption of newer technologies, amid an unstable business environment.

Identifying individuals from diversified backgrounds in terms of gender, ethnicity, race, and others poses to be a crucial factor in an organization. Developing creative approaches with advanced technologies enables organizations to offer efficient people management and business processes. Technologies such as big data help analyze huge volumes of information to reveal correlations and hidden patterns, thereby leading to smarter business moves with higher profitability. Better planning, effective use of resources, and employee motivation are a few big data-driven changes for HR professionals. Shifting beyond the analysis of employee retention and engagement, the amalgamation of artificial intelligence, and analytics, enables the companies to emphasize on increasing operational issues to enhance overall performance (Deloitte, People Analytics: Recalculating The Route, 2017). For instance:

- Artificial intelligence software helps analyze and access an employee's personality via software (Oran, 2016).
- The data-driven tools help in predicting fraud patterns, showing trust networks, and the real-time correlations between engagement and coaching, thereby analyzing the employee patterns for time management (Gloor, 2015).
- The off-the-shelf retention models available from ADP, Oracle, SAP, Ultimate Software, and Workday, are expected to easily understand the factors bolstering the attrition rate.
- With the advent of technology, the patterns of payroll leakage can easily be analyzed, thereby enabling improvements of millions of dollars via enhanced practices in terms of workforce management.

- Several companies such as Deloitte are emphasizing on human performance data, billing hours, and travel data, to help employees enhance their overall performance levels.

The insights gained from the implementation of this technology helps firms to make decisions, that can uplift productivity, enhance operational performance, and increase overall profitability. For organizations, emphasizing on strategizing their business models in the HR division, big data certainly is the perfect option to yield transformative results.

In the fast-developing market, the analytics teams are expected to deliver impact and cater to the changing curve scenario and the organizational goals. Hence, as the benefits of big data analytics continue to unfold, HR professionals owes the potential to create greater value creation with better decision-making solutions.

REAL-USE CASES OF BIG DATA IN HUMAN RESOURCES

In today's scenario, big data in human resources is developing the latest implementable solutions to predict and enhance the performance of organizations. To cater to the changing marketplace, the HR sections are majorly emphasizing towards tapping into an enormous competitive advantage by leveraging data analytics and keeping their processes seamless. Incorporating big data in human resources further offers a few benefits (Council, 2020) illustrated as:

Employee Retention

The experience of an employee plays a vital role in the attrition rate of an organization. With positive experience and environment, the retention level of the employees is expected to witness a rise (Otomeyt, 2022). The incorporation of technologies such as big data augments the retention of employees in companies experiencing high staff turnover. The technology enables the HR departments, to identify different trends and patterns offering quantitative data, conduct surveys regularly, and execute data-driven programs. Improvising the different technological analytics in the segment thereby helps to offer the employees with the right perks, benefits, and flexibility to retain the top-most talents (Ravindra, 2019). An example to illustrate the same:

- *Xero:* Xero is a New-Zealand based company, founded in 2006. The company with nearly 3.7 million subscribers, is one of the leaders in cloud computing with its presence across the United Kingdom, Australia, Canada, Hong Kong, New Zealand, and South Africa (Xero, 2006). The company is engaged in offering cloud-based accounting software for medium and small-sized businesses.

Xero emphasizes on utilizing big data to understand the retention and attrition rates of the employees. In addition to this, with the trial of this technology in its call center (comprising nearly 48,700 employees), the attrition rate could be minimized by approximately 20 percent during a 6-month trial period, thereby posing to be profitable to the same (Walker, 2012).

Improving Learning and Development

With the rise of online learning, the concept of corporate learning and development is becoming more customized to the learners. The modified learning technology, powered by big data analytics, permits course segments, activities, and test questions to be tailored accordingly, to cater to the changing preferences and learning pace of the learner. Online learning and self-paced techniques are considerably the most cost-effective means of training concerning expensive training courses.

- *Danone:* Danone is a Paris-based food processing company, established in 1919. The company has built a user-friendly online platform, named Danone Campus 2.0, which is an easily accessible and continually updated cloud-based platform, allowing its employees a user-friendly, digital space. In addition to this, the platform also enables the employees to highlight internal and external knowledge, thereby sharing the best practices, and enhancing collaboration (Otto, 2016).

Enhancing the Strategic Workforce Planning

The Incorporation of big data analytics in the human resources department helps revolutionize an organization's talent acquisition efforts and seamlessly manage a decentralized talent landscape. The inclusion of this technology helps cater to the labor market challenges and accordingly prepares the organizations for future workforce needs and requirements. In addition to this, it also enables efficient disclosure of the employee skills, and proactive identification of the expertise for shortages of labor if any in the future. The technology also addresses issues such as; skills important and insignificant over the next few years, along with how employee development can be targeted to enable the employees to shift to in-demand professions (Zimmermann, n.d.). For instance:

- *WilsonHCG:* WilsonHCG is a global talent solution provider company. The company operates with its manufacturing facilities in nearly six continents and 65 countries across the world. The company offers TALENT™, an inclusive approach, that enables organizations to engage, attract, and hire the right talent, catering to the changing marketplace. The solutions offered by the company (WislonHCG, 2023) include:

    i. Recruitment Process Outsourcing (RPO): The RPO delivers the advanced analytics and technologies required to nurture the hired talents to cater to future needs.
    ii. Total Talent Solutions: These solutions centralize the hiring process for contingent, temporary, part-time, and full-time workers, thereby enabling the talent acquisition team to look after the overall workforce all at once.
    iii. Talent Acquisition Consulting: The cutting-edge technologies and configured robust strategies help transform process talent acquisition.
    iv. Executive Search: The talent intelligence solution is engaged in delivering high-impact unmatched results to cater to critical business needs and requirements.
    v. Contingent Talent Solutions: The company provides a wide range of contingent workforce solutions going beyond the conventional staffing models and Managed Service Providers (MSP). It also offers services such as permanent placement, contract staffing, contingent resource outsourcing, and proprietary second-generation MSP solutions.

Optimizing the Costs: Several businesses nowadays are using a mix of channels to source talent (Giri, 2021). Instead of staffing the entire HR department, usage of this technology enables the incorporation of software for daily HR management. Leveraging these specialized systems helps minimize the costs, and offer additional benefits to the employees. For instance:

- *Virtual Vocations:* Virtual Vocation founded in 2007, is a family-owned business that emphasizes on transforming the way of finding jobs. The company is a 100 percent remote company, and it caters to the key challenges being faced by job-seekers while looking to work virtually from any remote location across any region of the world. Virtual vocations enable job-seekers to find legitimate remote-location jobs quickly and more easily (Vocations, 2007).

Offering Unseen Talent Insights: The HR department with the inclusion of big data analytics with Natural Language Processing helps analyze the internal talent profile data, project reviews, and feedback, instead of hiring external talent. An example illustrating the same:

- *Engagedly:* Engagedly, founded in 2014, is a US-based company that is well-versed with the current performance management scenario. The versatile and modern suite is, designed to engage all the users, from the manager to the employee, to the administrator to the CEO (Engagedly, 2014).

Enhancing Customer Experience

Analytics and data play a vital role in understanding the perceptions of employees concerning the company's nature of work, culture, along with an individual's overall experience. Analytics in the workforce helps unlock significant insights impacting customer satisfaction, employee engagement, and candidate experience. For instance:

- *McAfee:* McAfee, is a US-based, online protection company. The company focuses on protecting and empowering people with integrated and easy-to-use solutions. The company focuses on offering solutions to enable the private and public sectors to share talent during cybersecurity events (McAfee, 2019).

Organizations nowadays are focusing on redesigning their HR programs to leverage mobile and digital tools and implement Artificial Technology (AI) to deliver HR solutions. Having the right capabilities and tools to collect and decode data in business, proves to be beneficial for enhancing the efficiency of the human resources processes (Schooley, 2023). Hence, with an efficient application of big data analytics, the HR departments in the organizations can better manage the talent under their view, with higher productivity and profitability.

KEY PLAYERS INCORPORATING BIG DATA IN HUMAN RESOURCES

Leveraging big data in HR systems enables companies to enhance every HR segment with better performance and higher profitability. Few companies incorporating big data in their HR systems are illustrated as:

Microsoft

About: Microsoft established in 1975, is headquartered in Redmond, Washington, United States. The company is engaged in providing digital transformation solutions for the era of an intelligent edge and an intelligent cloud. The company began its operations in India in 1990, with its offerings comprising global cloud services from local data centers to bolster the digital transformation across government agencies, businesses, and SMEs.

Solutions offered: Microsoft is engaged in transforming the human resources systems by upgrading the way AI and analytics are used. Upgradation of the core process enabled the offering of effective and efficient self-service portals for the employees and powerful tools for the human resources division via the usage of SAP success factors. These processes comprise of the applications related to human capital management (HCM) such as payroll, rewards, employee portal, and other HR functions.

Unlike all the large-scale changes, this solution involves a large number, of touchpoints and complexity. The Microsoft Azure Data Lake enables the modern analytics platform to seamlessly store, ingest, change, and evaluate the data, at the same time ensuring compliance, maintaining data security, and delivering simpler data discoverability (Fleck, 2023). The different factors bolstering the transformational process can be attributed to factors such as agile and modern engineering, HR data coverage, advanced analytic skills, big data platforms, and self-service utilities. Hence, enabling the connected insights that are secure and trusted via a recent data platform in Azure Cloud poses to be the major goal to propel the digital data revolution in the HR ecosystem.

Capgemini

About: Capgemini, is an information technology services provider, established in 1967. The company is headquartered in Paris. Capgemini is engaged in partnering with companies to completely revolutionize and manage businesses by revealing technological values. The company has leveraged technology to cater to the different business needs and requirements, from designing to strategizing to implementing to managing the various operational activities. It focuses on enhancing connectivity, data artificial intelligence, digital engineering, software, and the fast-evolving fields of cloud platforms.

Solutions offered: Organizations striving to build and offer best-in-class employee experience are expected to quickly identify and cater to the changing trends in employee values, preferences, and behavior. To cope with the changing market scenario, the company has developed influential HR data analytic solutions to empower organizations to recruit and retain top talent, while creating an equitable and diversified workplace.

The company focuses on identifying the key trends, gaining insights, and accordingly revolutionizing the capabilities of the organization's analytics. This is achieved by visualizing the major trends across different business functions and providing recommendations and insights for the next action via the concepts of machine learning and artificial intelligence.

Juniper Networks

About: Juniper Networks headquartered in California, was founded in 1996. The company constantly focuses on the typical assumptions being made about HR, and the use of big data in HR. The company is the provider of high-performance cybersecurity and networking products to public sector organizations, enterprise companies, and service providers.

Solutions offered: Juniper Networks is a cybersecurity and networking solutions company, engaged in radically transforming the HR industry. The company emphasizes on the questions such as assumptions related to HR, and how the analytics in HR revolutionizes its targeted business outcomes.

Juniper Networks focuses on gaining insights into diversified career paths of the industry, thereby enabling it to develop strategies for retaining the top talents in the present and near future.

FACTORS BOOSTING THE DEMAND FOR ANALYTICS IN HUMAN RESOURCES

1. **Increasing emphasis on workforce optimization:** Efficacious strategic planning plays a pivotal role in the growth of a business. This strategic approach is gaining traction in terms of becoming a necessity, rather than a good-to-have. With streamlined alignment and integration of varied business functions, an optimized workforce creates unity in the growth of a company holistically.

The important components of Workforce Optimization (Kharlantseva, 2023)include:

- *Workforce planning and estimation:* An effective workforce optimization strategy focuses on assessing and forecasting the workforce needs, on the basis, of, market trends, industry shifts, market planning, and growth projections. Effective implementation of strategies is expected to address the gap between the present and the future workforce needs.
- *Recruitment and talent acquisition:* The data-driven methods offer pivotal insights for augmenting business outcomes. Analytics act as an influential push in the quest of sourcing, hiring talents, and, optimizing the workplace (Mazor, 2018).
- *Shift management and employee scheduling:* Creating a go-ahead workforce system, given the business needs, is one of the vital aspects offered by efficient shift management and employee scheduling.
- *Goal setting and performance management:* Goal setting and performance management, include assessing the performance of the employees, regularly, providing constructive feedback, setting performance plans or benchmarks, setting realistic goals, and identifying the work.
- *Training and development initiatives:* The training and development plan augments the expertise and skills of the employees, thereby boosting their performance. Investments in the development of employees help organizations to create a high-performing workplace.
- *Employee engagement and employee retention:* To boost the performance impacting change, it becomes necessary for managers to emphasize on restructuring the retention strategies in businesses (Tupper, 2022). The HR professionals need to shift their focus of conversations to progression, and promotion in varied directions, along with a culture to back up career trials. Hence, keeping the employees engaged increases productivity and contributes to the growth of an organization.

The concept emphasizes on balancing the key performance metrics, such as enhancing customer experience, workforce scheduling, and employee satisfaction, with maximized productivity. Hence, it poses as a pathway to long-term businesses, amended and assessed regularly to cater to the changing business requirements.

2. Growing concept of Remote Working: Remote working or working from home has ushered in the era of connectedness, inclusiveness, and productivity. Flexibility and accessibility during the hiring process play a significant role in reaching the right balance between employers and employees thereby, creating a fairer work environment (Goasduff, 2021). For organizations, backing up remote and hybrid team members, and prioritizing a culture of accessibility, accountability, and flexibility to information is significantly important. At the same time, for several workers, remote and distributed work has catered to several challenges, by removing inaccessible and unnecessary commutes, and attendance demands, thereby, posing an opportunity (Jamous, 2023).

The work-from-home, work-from-anywhere, distributed policies pave new opportunities, without bias and barriers. In order, to, ensure accessibility of ease, and cater to the changing momentum, flexible remote work plays a vital role in an organization. Remote working has hence, unlocked newer ways of amalgamating work and life, thereby, impacting traditionally underserved and underrepresented workplace communities, and boosting the analytics demand.

CHALLENGES HINDERING THE IMPLEMENTATION OF ANALYTICS IN HUMAN RESOURCES

Over the past few years, the concept of data analytics has gained significant traction in the human resource segment owing to its capability to offer key insights rooted on the data-driven decision-making processes. The emerging HR segments are expected to offer significant benefits to organizations. However, assimilating an analytics-based concept in human resource management (HRM) poses to be a complicated process, thereby restraining its adoption among the organizations. Few factors expected to hinder the inclusion of technologies in human resources can be illustrated as:

- **Absence of standard benchmarks and HR metrics:** One of the key challenges in the HR systems is identifying the metrics relatable to the objectives and contexts of an organization, and those focusing on offering insights regarding the improvement areas. The quantitative benchmarks' value and metrics are expected to act as a challenge for HR professionals, in terms of constant improvement and quality before considering the simple benchmarking and quantity aspects.

The organizations emphasize on shifting from dispersed and siloed aspects to a multidimensional complex analysis approach in amalgamation with artificial intelligence, machine learning, and advanced statistics to forecast the future (Razvan, 2022).

FUTURE TRENDS OF BIG DATA IN HUMAN RESOURCES

The concept of big data has proven its value to organizations of different sizes, types, and industries. New types of big data techniques and architectures for collecting, managing, processing, and evaluating the range of data in an organization are witnessing continual changes.

While considering the technologies such as cloud computing, HR professionals are more confident in enabling new avenues such as strategic decision-making, control costs, and workplace flexibility. As with any business revolution, the concept of cloud technology poses to be a critical enabler, wherein, it connects the emerging technologies, devices, data, and systems to let the companies operate innovatively, speedily, and with more agility.

However, it offers organizations and individuals with a gradual approach to generate and establish the lasting change in the way the work is done (Karthik, 2022). To cope with the increase in big data analytics and complexity requirements, the cloud is essentially required.

The different key trends in big data enabling organizations to cater to the challenges are as follows:

- Boost in innovations in the hybrid and cloud platforms: To deal with the inevitable rise in data generation, organizations are increasingly spending more on their resources to store this data in a wide array of hybrid cloud and cloud-based systems optimized for the V's of big data. Over the past few years, the handling of the storage infrastructure by the organizations resulted in massive data centers managed and secured by the enterprises. Shift in preferences towards the adaption of the cloud infrastructure is expected to enable the HR systems to seamlessly deal with the limitless amount of data, with enhanced efficiency. Using this technology to change the process of thinking, collaborating, and working helps organizations to accordingly align their strategies, and cater to the next digital talent divide, thereby developing the business goals. Hence, many organizations view the cloud as a long-term and viable choice for the HR revolution. In addition to the innovations in cloud storage, enterprises also need to emphasize towards the implementation of new data architecture approaches to easily handle the V's (variety, veracity, and volume) issues (Schmelzer, 2023).
- Innovations in Talent Hybrid: Executing talent management processes in the cloud along with maintaining the processes for time management, payroll, and core HR services are one of the essential aspects of cloud adoption. The usage of people analytics and talent management solutions is expected to enable organizations to completely revolutionize performance goal management, succession planning, compensation, onboarding, recruitment, and others.

Businesses nowadays owes the capability to collect data in real-time, and strategically analyze the different aspects and segments to make better well-informed decisions. To stay agile in the competitive world, the concept of big data analytics plays a pivotal role, wherein, it enables the organizations to exploit the data efficaciously and pave way for new opportunities in the future.

DISCUSSION

The usage of big data analytics in the human resource context is significantly one of the latest and innovative developments, with great potential. The increasing interest of HR professionals and researchers can be attributed to the different benefits offered by the incorporation of analytics at both the individual as well as organizational levels.

Moving forward, the concept of analytics technology is anticipated to deliver significant customized recommendations. The technology helps with the real-time prediction of the hiring/recruitment, thereby, enhancing the overall quality and performance of the businesses. This paper illustrates the real use cases of big data in human resources management in terms of improving the quality, services, and monitoring, thereby catering to the efficacious decision-making processes and strategies of the organization.

Key Takeaways

Organizations nowadays are engaged in redesigning their strategies and models, by improvising the latest technologies and accordingly building digitally powered enterprise analytic solutions. Businesses emphasize on identifying different market opportunities, thereby setting up certain goals to attain productivity.

Big data analytics, is increasingly becoming a business function emphasizing on using the data to understand every operational section, with analytics being embedded into the real-time apps. One of the key aspects also includes a proper understanding of the impact of megatrends (such as demographic shifts) on the markets, thereby enabling the players to accordingly strategize their future action plans.

- Increasing need to efficaciously use human resources, and gather real-time observation of employee behaviors, as well as reduce the operational costs of an enterprise, are few of the factors expected to propel the market growth over the forecasted period.
- Ethical and legal concerns concerning the implementation of analytics in the human resource segments pose a restraining factor for the same.

The key market players are increasingly investing in programs to use the data in all aspects of operational improvement, talent management, and workforce planning, owing to the growing adoption of cloud HR systems. Key players such as Microsoft, Capgemini, and Juniper Networks, are a few of the illustrated examples of companies incorporating big data analytics in human resource management.

CONCLUSION

Any organization whether in the public or commercial sector is successful, with a successful workforce. Whether an enterprise is in higher education, government, industry, or business, the companies are striving to create and execute overarching HR strategies to change the way HR systems deliver solutions to back the individuals and enterprises. This includes revolutionizing the operations with the leading cloud technologies in human resources (such as SAP SuccessFactors, and Workday HR) along with other mobile solutions, engaged in enhancing and re-energizing the experience of the individuals. To build this, strategies for system integration, analytics, and data integrity are required to seamlessly offer decision support to businesses (KPMG, 2023).

Tools such as employee satisfaction surveys, team assessments, exit interviews, and social media platforms enables the HR professionals to forecast and minimize employee effectiveness and satisfaction concerns. With the HR systems moving towards personalization, and ensuring a positive experience, it becomes vital for an organization to build a talent pipeline (Chorna, 2022). To build this, big data has become a necessity for better workflow and processes in an organization. Big data enables employers to analyze the reasons behind lesser employee retention rates, thereby making it easier to understand the pitfalls in the organizations and work accordingly to gain a competitive edge in the changing market scenario.

Learning the art of managing big data poses to be a crucial factor for an HR division in any business. Organizations nowadays are engaged in creating an environment and developing solutions to completely reimagine and revitalize their human resources systems empowering the employees (Deloitte, HR Transformation: Accelerating Change with a Human Focus, 2019).

Big data, when coupled with analytics, paves the way for several opportunities in an organization to enhance operational efficiencies, catering to the changing market scenario. Big data in HRM refers to the usage of varied data sources to analyze and advance practices such as compensation, training and development, recruitment, performance management, and end-to-end business performance (Scott, 2021). Hence, the incorporation of big data enables HR managers to track the efficacy of recruitment efforts and better recognize the competitive strategies to attract the right people at the right time for the right positions.

REFERENCES

Alexis, A. a. (2017). HR Metrics and Talent Analytics. In D. G. Collings (Ed.), *Oxford Handbook of Talent Management*. Oxford University Press.

Chorna, I. (2022, October 11). *HR forecast*. Retrieved from Big data for HR: Everything you need to know: https://hrforecast.com/how-will-big-data-transform-your-hr-practices/

Council, F. H. (2020, January 2). *Nine Benefits Of Embracing Big Data In Human Resources*. Retrieved from Forbes Human Resources Council: https://www.forbes.com/sites/forbeshumanresourcescouncil/2020/01/02/nine-benefits-of-embracing-big-data-in-human-resources/?sh=42edc12b6582

Deloitte. (2017, February 27). *People Analytics: Recalculating The Route*. Retrieved from Deloitte: https://www.deloitte.com/global/en/our-thinking/insights/topics/talent/human-capital-trends/people-analytics-in-hr.html

Deloitte. (2019). *HR Transformation: Accelerating Change with a Human Focus*. Deloitte.

Engagedly. (2014). Retrieved from Engagedly: https://engagedly.com/

Fiore, J. a. (2014). *Workforce Analytics: The Three-Minute Guide*. Deloitte.

Fleck, A. (2023, February 2). *Microsoft*. Retrieved from Enabling advanced HR analytics and AI with Microsoft Azure Data Lake: https://www.microsoft.com/insidetrack/blog/enabling-advanced-hr-analytics-and-ai-with-microsoft-azure-data-lake/

Giri, Y. (2021, August 17). Big Data in HR: 4 Key Applications. *HR Trends*, p. 1. Retrieved from https://www.randstad.in/hr-news/hr-trends/big-data-hr-4-key-applications/

Gloor, P. A. (2015, November 17). *What Email Reveals About Your Organization*. Retrieved from Massachusetts Institute of Technology Sloan Management Review: https://sloanreview.mit.edu/article/what-email-reveals-about-your-organization/

Goasduff, L. (2021, June 9). *Information Technology*. Retrieved from Digital Workers Say Flexibility Is Key to Their Productivity: https://www.gartner.com/smarterwithgartner/digital-workers-say-flexibility-is-key-to-their-productivity

Jamous, T. (2023, February 22). *Forbes Councils Member*. Retrieved from Remote And Flexible Working Remain The Biggest Opportunities For Inclusive Workplaces: https://www.forbes.com/sites/forbesbusinesscouncil/2023/02/22/remote-and-flexible-working-remain-the-biggest-opportunities-for-inclusive-workplaces/?sh=342c79503ccd

Karthik, R. a. (2022, January 31). *SAP News Center*. Retrieved from HR Transformation Is Changing in a New Hybrid Era: https://news.sap.com/2022/01/hr-transformation-is-changing-in-new-hybrid-era/

Kharlantseva, M. (2023, July 4). *Everhour*. Retrieved from Workforce Optimization: Benefits and Strategies to Boost Productivity: https://everhour.com/blog/workforce-optimization/#:~:text=Workforce%20optimization%2C%20also%20known%20as,satisfaction%20to%20meet%20business%20goals

KPMG. (2023). *The future of HR*. Retrieved from Workforce Insights and Analytics: https://advisory.kpmg.us/insights/future-hr/future-hr-workforce-insights-analytics.html

Kumar, V. (2018, December 20). *The Role of Big Data in Human Resource Management*. Retrieved from Association for Intelligent Information Management: https://info.aiim.org/aiim-blog/role-of-big-data-in-human-resource-management

Kundariya, H. (2023, March 3). *Workpay Technologies, Inc*. Retrieved from How Big Data and Analytics Is Transforming Human Resources in the 21st Century: https://www.myworkpay.com/blogs/how-big-data-and-analytics-is-transforming-human-resources-in-the-21st-century#:~:text=Data%20analytics%20can%20provide%20HR%20with%20a%20clear,attrition%20issues%20in%20real-time%20and%20improve%20employee%20retention

Marler, J. a. (2016). An Evidence-based Review of HR Analytics. *The International Journal of Human Resource Management, 28*(1), 3-26.

Mazor, A. H. (2018). *Deloitte*. Retrieved from Talent acquisition analytics: Using analytics for smarter sourcing and hiring decisions: https://www2.deloitte.com/us/en/pages/human-capital/articles/talent-acquisition-analytics.html

McAfee. (2019, June 19). *McAfee*. Retrieved from Expanding Our Vision to Expand the Cybersecurity Workforce: https://www.mcafee.com/blogs/other-blogs/executive-perspectives/expanding-our-vision-to-expand-the-cybersecurity-workforce/

McAfee, A. B. (2012). Big Data: The Management Revolution. *Harvard Business Review, 90*(10), 60–68. PMID:23074865

Networks, J. (2012). *Introduction to Big Data: Infrastructure And Networking Considerations*. Juniper Networks.

Nocker, M. a. (2019). Big Data and Human Resources Management: The Rise of Talent Analytics. *Big Data and Employee Wellbeing, Social Sciences, 8*(10), 273.

Oran, O. (2016, June 7). *Wall Street Hopes Artificial Intelligence Software Helps It Hire Loyal Bankers*. Retrieved from Reuters: https://www.reuters.com/article/us-banks-hiring-ai-idUSKCN0YT163

Otomeyt. (2022, July 7). AI. *Big Data is Redefining HR Practices*, p. 1.

Otto, S. S. (2016, December 5). *Chief Learning Officer*. Retrieved from Corporate Learning's Transformation in the Digital Age: https://www.chieflearningofficer.com/2016/12/05/corporate-learnings-transformation-digital-age/

Ravindra, S. (2019, September 17). *Data Science*. Retrieved from 4 Applications of Big Data in HR (With Real-World Examples): https://www.kolabtree.com/blog/4-applications-of-big-data-in-hr-with-real-world-examples/

Razvan. (2022, September 6). *hranalyticslibrary.com*. Retrieved from HR Analytics Challenges & How to Overcome Them: https://hranalyticslibrary.com/hr-analytics-challenges-overcome/

Schmelzer, R. (2023, January 5). TechTarget. *Top Trends in Big Data for 2023 and Beyond*, p. 1.

Schooley, S. (2023, March 23). *How to Utilize Big Data for Human Resources*. Retrieved from Business.com: https://www.business.com/articles/how-to-utilize-big-data-for-human-resources/

Scott, A. (2021, August 24). *Data Science Central*. Retrieved from Big Data Technology Importance in Human Resource Management: https://www.datasciencecentral.com/big-data-technology-importance-in-human-resource-management/

Sharma, T. (2019, September 26). *Top 5 Big Data Use Cases in the HR Department*. Retrieved from Global Tech Council: https://www.globaltechcouncil.org/big-data/top-5-big-data-use-cases-in-the-hr-department/

Talend. (n.d.). *How Does Big Data Work for HR Analytics?* Retrieved from Talend: https://www.talend.com/resources/big-data-hr-analytics/#:~:text=Without%20the%20use%20of%20big%20data%2C%20recruiting%20top,delivering%20results%20and%20which%20ones%20aren%E2%80%99t%20very%20effective

Tupper, H. a. (2022, July 4). *Harvard Business Review*. Retrieved from Employee Retention: It's Time to Reimagine Employee Retention: https://hbr.org/2022/07/its-time-to-reimagine-employee-retention

Vocations, V. (2007). Retrieved from Virtual Vocations: https://www.virtualvocations.com/aboutus

Walker, J. (2012, September 20). Meet the New Boss: Big Data. *The Wall Street Journal*.

Wislon, H. C. G. (2023). Retrieved from WislonHCG: https://www.wilsonhcg.com/

Xero. (2006). Retrieved from Xero Limited: https://www.xero.com/about/

Zhang, Y. X., Xu, S., Zhang, L., & Yang, M. (2021). Big Data and Human Resource Management Research: An Integrative Review and New Directions for Future Research. *Journal of Business Research*, *133*, 34–50. doi:10.1016/j.jbusres.2021.04.019

Zimmermann, S. (n.d.). *Labor Market 5.0: Enhance strategic HR planning through Big Data Skills Analysis*. Retrieved from WifOR: https://www.wifor.com/en/enhance-strategic-hr-planning-through-big-data-skills-analysis/#:~:text=Big%20Data%20Skills%20Analysis%20supports%20companies%20in%20preparing,in%20order%20to%20counteract%20shortages%20of%20skilled%20labor

Chapter 8
Applications of Artificial Intelligence Tools in Higher Education

P. S. Venkateswaran
https://orcid.org/0000-0001-8958-103X
PSNA College of Engineering and Technology, Dindigul, India

Firas Tayseer Mohammad Ayasrah
https://orcid.org/0000-0002-6477-000X
Al Ain University, UAE

Varun Kumar Nomula
Georgia Institute of Technology, USA

P. Paramasivan
Dhaanish Ahmed College of Engineering, India

P. Anand
Dhaanish Ahmed College of Engineering, India

K. Bogeshwaran
Dhaanish Ahmed College of Engineering, India

ABSTRACT

The rapid integration of information and communication technologies (ICT) in higher education has brought about transformative changes to traditional teaching and learning practices. This chapter examines the multifaceted impacts of ICT in the higher education sector. Over the past two decades, ICT has revolutionized the way educational institutions operate, impacting teaching methodologies, student engagement, and administrative processes. In the realm of pedagogy, ICT has facilitated the shift towards student-centered learning, empowering learners with access to diverse digital resources and interactive learning platforms. Moreover, administrative tasks within higher education have been streamlined through the adoption of ICT, resulting in enhanced efficiency in enrollment, record-keeping, and communication between stakeholders. This optimization allows educators to focus more on instructional design and student support, fostering a conducive learning environment.

DOI: 10.4018/979-8-3693-2193-5.ch008

1. INTRODUCTION

Over the past two decades, Information and Communication Technologies (ICT) have become ubiquitous across all aspects of life. Their influence has significantly transformed the practices and procedures of businesses and governance (Ocoró et al., 2023). However, in the field of education, while ICT has made some progress, its impact hasn't been as extensive as in other domains (Al Khawaldeh, et al., 2022). Education has traditionally been a socially oriented activity, emphasizing the importance of strong teacher-student relationships for quality learning (Alawneh, 2022). By embracing ICT, higher education institutions can create more dynamic and interactive learning experiences for students (Vashishtha & Kapoor, 2023). This technology enables access to vast educational resources, facilitates remote learning, and fosters global collaboration among students and educators (Alawneh et al., 2022). It also encourages self-paced learning, personalized education pathways, and adaptive learning systems that cater to individual student needs and preferences (An et al., 2023).

Moreover, the integration of ICT in education can enhance administrative efficiency, streamlining tasks such as enrollment, record-keeping, and communication between various stakeholders (Balas-Timar, 2015). This allows educators to focus more on instructional design and student support (Hong, 2023). However, the adoption of ICT in education also poses challenges (Xu et al., 2023). Some educators might be hesitant to fully embrace technology, fearing that it could replace traditional teaching methods (Demeter et al., 2021). Additionally, not all students have equal access to digital resources, leading to potential disparities in learning opportunities (Hong, 2021a,b).

Looking ahead, the future of higher education is likely to witness an even deeper integration of ICT into the learning process (Maseleno et al., 2023). Virtual and augmented reality technologies may offer immersive learning experiences, while artificial intelligence can provide personalized tutoring and support. ICT's influence is evident in the way educational institutions design and implement their teaching strategies (Nithyanantham, 2023). The shift towards online learning has necessitated the incorporation of new scientific concepts and skills into the curriculum, leading to a reconfiguration of traditional course structures (Tripathi & Al -Zubaidi, 2023). Additionally, the focus has expanded beyond mere subject knowledge to encompass essential competencies such as critical thinking, problem-solving, adaptability, and collaboration (Balas-Timar & Ignat, 2015).

As technology continues to evolve, students are now required to learn not only subject-specific content but also how to learn effectively using the available digital tools and resources (Hong et al., 2022). This broader skillset equips them with the capability to manipulate information, use technology proficiently, and work collaboratively in teams (Hong, 2018).

AI tools play a crucial role in enhancing the administrative efficiency and information management of educational institutions (Rad & Balas, 2020). These technologies enable better data collection and retrieval, streamlining various processes within universities (Tripathi & Al-Shahri, 2023). Customized software programs are developed to cater to the specific needs of each university, including admissions, entrance exams, fee collection, attendance management, mark sheet preparation, and other related activities (Lian et al., 2022).

As part of the technological revolution, several academic institutions have embraced new initiatives and implemented changes in their campus life to leverage the potential of these advancements (Saxena et al., 2023). The integration of technology has facilitated a more efficient and modern educational experience for students and faculty alike. By adapting to these innovations, universities aim to stay competitive and relevant in the rapidly evolving educational landscape (Rad et al., 2022).

Utilizing AI tools in education offers several benefits that promote critical thinking, inclusivity, problem-solving skills, and individual responsibility for learning improvement (Shruthi & Aravind, 2023). Moreover, it accelerates the exchange of information and enhances the learning experience in various ways (Rad & Demeter, 2020).

By incorporating AI, learners can access and assimilate new knowledge more efficiently, reducing the time required to acquire information. They can take advantage to explore different perspectives, engage in discussions, and align their beliefs with the subject matter (Venkatasubramanian et al., 2023). Additionally, AI enables students to access educational resources at their own pace, providing them with ample opportunities to interact with technology in real time (Rad et al., 2020a,b).

The use of AI also fosters effective communication and collaboration among students, faculty, and peers. This facilitates a more comprehensive understanding of course material, allowing students to fully grasp concepts and respond to questions effectively.

This interactive AI model is enhanced through effective communication among learners, teachers, and educational programs, which is enabled by technology. Real-time communication through technological platforms can be particularly stimulating for students, as it provides immediate feedback and encourages active participation. Through such interactions, students are motivated to engage in various activities that promote the development of communication skills and the exchange of ideas and insights. List of some common AI tools used in higher education:

- Chatbots: AI-powered chatbots provide instant support to students, answering their questions, guiding them through enrollment processes, and assisting with administrative tasks.
- Natural Language Processing (NLP) Tools: NLP tools enable language understanding and can be used for automated essay grading, language translation, and sentiment analysis of student feedback.
- Intelligent Tutoring Systems (ITS): ITS tools use AI to provide personalized tutoring, feedback, and recommendations to students, adapting to their learning styles and preferences.
- Data Analytics and Predictive Analytics: AI-driven data analytics tools help institutions analyze vast amounts of data to gain insights into student performance, retention rates, and other key metrics.
- Content Recommendation Systems: AI algorithms can suggest relevant learning resources, articles, and research papers based on a student's interests and academic preferences.
- Virtual Reality (VR) and Augmented Reality (AR) Learning: AI can enhance VR and AR experiences, creating interactive and immersive learning environments for students.
- Curriculum Development Tools: AI can assist in designing and optimizing curriculum based on student outcomes and industry needs.

2. PRE-FAULT FREQUENCY CANCELLATION (PFFC)

The digital divide also poses challenges in distance learning, limiting the availability of educational content for students with limited access to technology. Educational institutions should explore alternate learning methods to cater to students with limited technological access (Bisht et al., 2020). Venkateswaran et al. (2020) focus on exploring the involvement of university faculties in promoting sustainable development within the higher education context in Tamil Nadu, India.

Additionally, many students cannot afford laptops or personal computers, which are essential for modern-day education, exacerbating the educational disparities (Fry and Cilluffo, 2019). The inability to access these technological tools creates a disparity in learning opportunities, impacting academic performance and potential career prospects (Hasan and Bao, 2020; Adnan and Anwar, 2020).

Baker and Smith (2019) present a comprehensive definition of AI, describing it as the utilization of computers to perform cognitive tasks typically associated with human minds, particularly learning and problem-solving. Mathurajothi et al. (2018) studied the satisfaction of students with the University Libraries and provided useful information for library administrators and policymakers to improve and tailor their services based on student preferences and requirements. The close association between AI and machine learning is a common observation (Rad et al., 2019). Machine learning, a subset of AI, involves the application of supervised and unsupervised classification and profiling techniques to recognize patterns and make predictions (Vijayarani et al., 2023). According to Popenici and Kerr (2017), machine learning allows software to identify new patterns and apply them to situations beyond their initial design.

Within the realm of education, Luckin et al., (2016) delineate three primary categories of AI software applications that are already in use: a) personal tutors, b) intelligent support for collaborative learning, and c) intelligent virtual reality. Personal tutors offer personalized and adaptive learning experiences, tailoring instruction to individual student needs. Intelligent support for collaborative learning promotes effective teamwork and group engagement. Lastly, intelligent virtual reality offers immersive and interactive learning environments, enhancing students' experiential learning opportunities.

Information systems play a crucial role in modern educational environments, and in the context of engineering institutions, they can significantly affect various aspects of academic processes, administrative operations, and student experiences (Venkateswaran, 2015). Policymakers should prioritize digital infrastructure development in rural areas and allocate resources for technological inclusion in educational budgets (Wong et al., 2015).

3. RESEARCH METHODS

The applied research design in the present study is descriptive research. The samples (students) are selected from the twelve engineering colleges in Dindigul District. Students from the three circuit branches, namely ECE, CSE, and IT, were selected, and a systematic random sampling method was adopted. A sample of 360 students decided to collect the study (30 students X 12 colleges). Finally, a sample of 287 (132 males and 155 females) arrived due to poor and improper responses from the respondents. The data were analyzed using SPSS 26 software, and the findings were tabulated.

4. ANALYSIS AND DISCUSSIONS

Figure 1 presents the frequency of usage of AI tools among college students, categorized by gender. The majority of male students (50.8%) reported using AI tools on a daily basis, while 36.1% of female students use them daily. Overall, approximately 42.9% of all students use AI tools daily, indicating a relatively high frequency of engagement with AI tools. Around 22% of male students and 30.3% of female students use AI tools once in two days. The total percentage of students using AI tools at this frequency stands at 26.5%.

Figure 1. Usage of AI tools

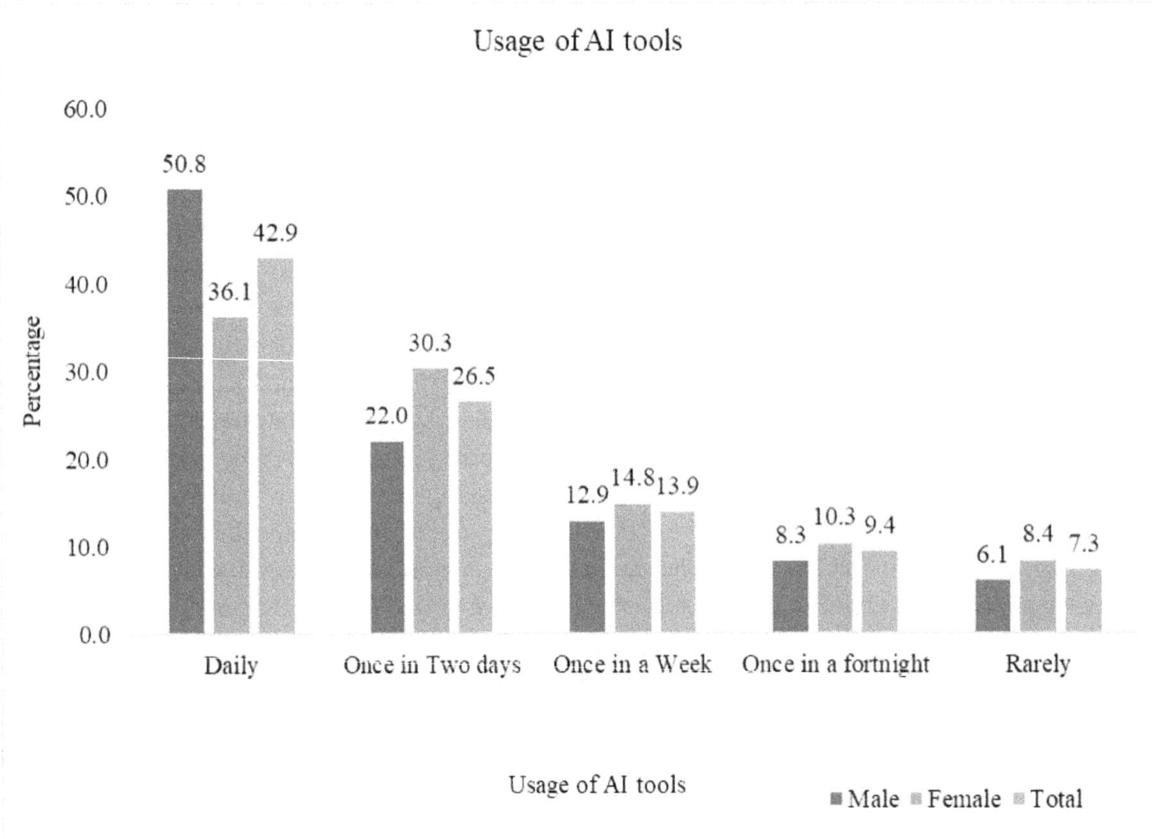

Usage of AI tools once a week is reported by 12.9% of male students and 14.8% of female students. The combined percentage of students who use AI tools weekly is 13.9%. A smaller proportion of male students (8.3%) and female students (10.3%) use AI tools once a fortnight. The total percentage of students at this frequency is 9.4%. A minority of male students (6.1%) and female students (8.4%) reported rare usage of AI tools. The combined percentage of students using AI tools rarely is 7.3%. This category indicates that only a small portion of students infrequently utilize AI tools.

Figure 2 presents the level of knowledge of using AI tools among college students, segregated by gender. 59.1% of male students and 41.3% of female students possess a very strong level of knowledge in using AI tools. The total percentage of all students with a very strong understanding is 49.5%. 31.1% of male students and 52.3% of female students demonstrate a strong level of knowledge in using AI tools. The combined percentage of students with strong knowledge is 42.5%. 6.1% of male students and female students (5.2%) have a neutral level of knowledge in using AI tools. The total percentage of students with neutral knowledge is 5.6%. A few male students (3.8%) and an even smaller percentage of female students (1.3%) possess a poor level of knowledge in using AI tools. The total percentage of students with poor knowledge is 2.4%. This suggests that a limited number of students have a poor grasp of AI tools.

Figure 2. Frequency of usage of AI tools

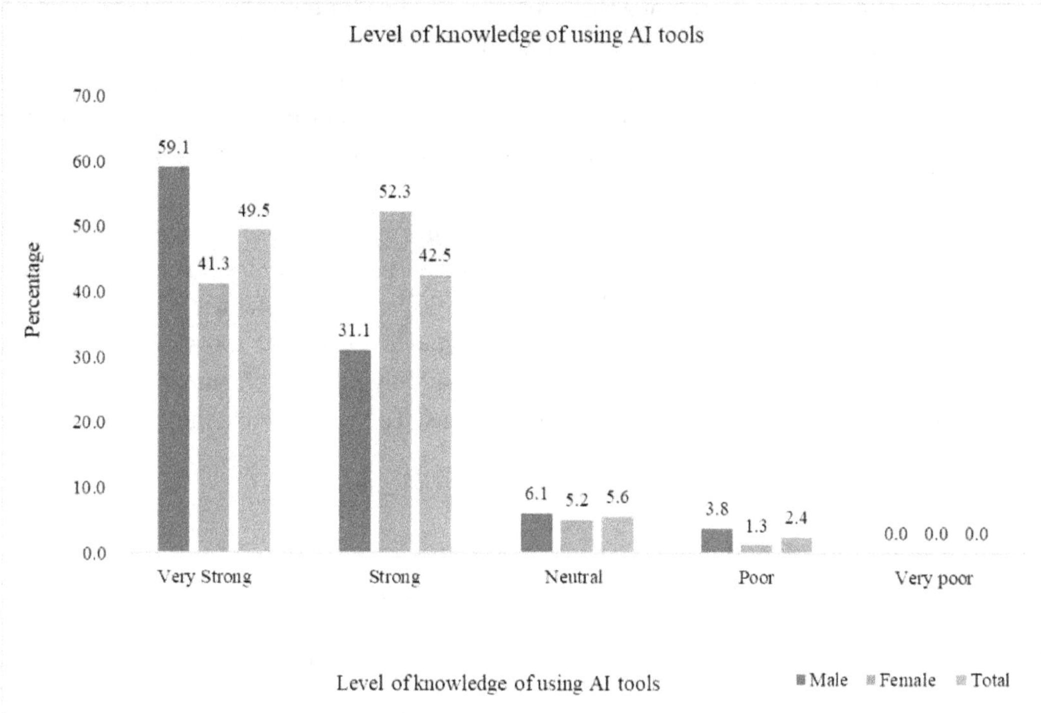

Figure 3. Reason for use of AI tools

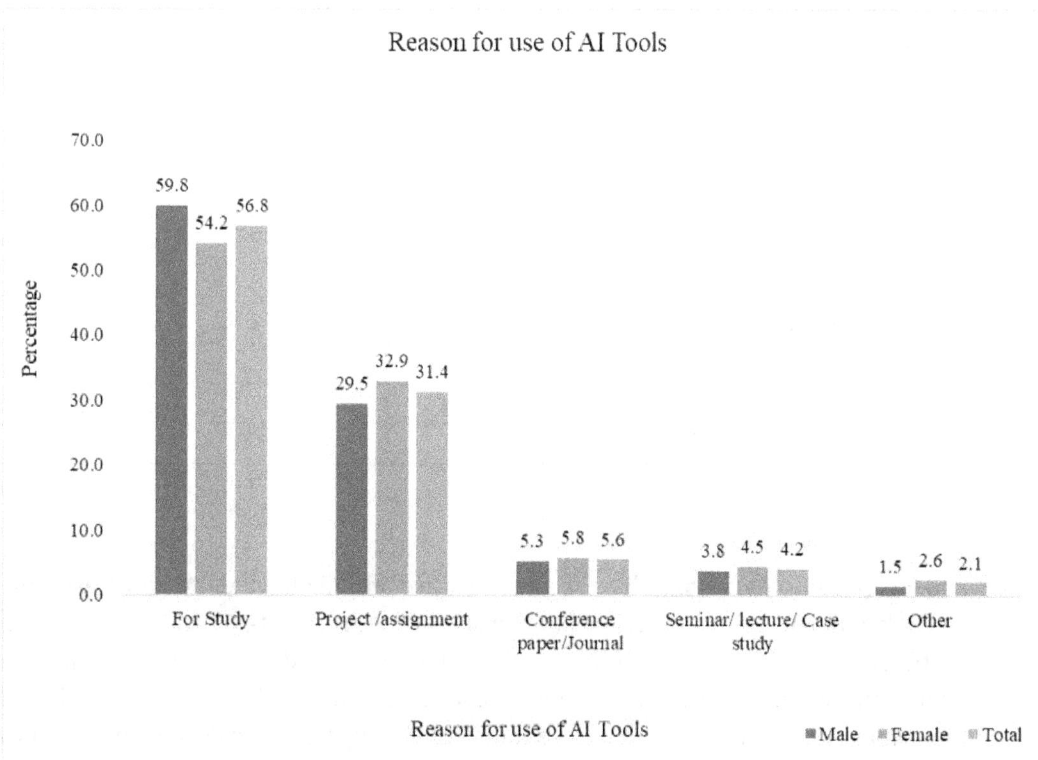

Figure 3 presents the reasons for the use of AI tools among college students, categorized by gender. 59.8% of male students and 54.2% of female students use AI tools for their studies. The total percentage of all students using AI tools for study purposes is 56.8%. This indicates that the primary reason for using AI tools in colleges is for academic-related activities, such as research, learning, and accessing educational resources. 29.5% of male students and 32.9% of female students utilize AI tools for their projects or assignments. The combined percentage of students using AI tools for project or assignment work is 31.4%.

A small percentage of male students (5.3%) and female students (5.8%) use AI tools for writing conference papers or journal articles. The total percentage of students using AI tools for academic publications is 5.6%. A few male students (3.8%) and slightly more female students (4.5%) use AI tools for seminars, lectures, or case study analysis. The total percentage of students using AI tools for these purposes is 4.2%. A small percentage of male students (1.5%) and a slightly higher percentage of female students (2.6%) reported using AI tools for other unspecified reasons. The total percentage of students using AI tools for other purposes is 2.1% (Table 1).

Table 1. Attitude towards AI tools

S.No.	Attitudes Towards AI Tools	Mean Score of		'T' Statistics
		Male	Female	
1	AI tools would help me organize my work	3.226	3.623	-6.713
2	Using AI tools would make the subject matter more interesting	3.345	3.827	-8.822
3	AI tools save time and effort	3.233	3.619	-6.695
4	Using AI tools is enjoyable	3.248	3.641	-7.073
5	AI tools make me much more productive	3.376	*3.835*	-8.287
6	Teaching with AI tools offers real advantages	3.423	3.778	-5.893
7	AI tools have proved to be effective learning tools	3.261	3.565	-4.447
8	AI tools can enhance students' learning	3.475	3.774	-5.016
9	I would rather do things by hand than with AI tools	3.422	3.832	-7.684
10	AI tools will improve education	3.255	3.649	-7.004
11	AI tools do not scare me at all	3.468	*3.857*	-6.957
12	I do not like talking with others about AI tools	3.162	3.546	-6.722
13	I like to use AI tools in teaching	*3.717*	3.814	-.526
14	AI tools are a fast means of getting information	3.606	3.714	-.773
15	I would like to learn more about AI tools	*3.715*	3.788	-.349

Source: Primary data

Female students (mean score: 3.623) have a more positive attitude towards AI tools, helping them organize their work compared to male students (mean score: 3.226). The t-statistic of -6.713 indicates a significant difference in attitudes between the genders, with females showing a stronger belief in the organizational benefits of AI tools. Female students (mean score: 3.827) exhibit a more positive attitude towards AI tools, making the subject matter more interesting compared to male students (mean score:

3.345). The t-statistic of -8.822 suggests a significant difference in attitudes, with female students finding AI tools more engaging in their learning experiences.

Both male (mean score: 3.233) and female (mean score: 3.619) students have positive attitudes toward AI tools saving time and effort. The t-statistic of -6.695 indicates that female students, on average, have slightly more positive views on the time-saving benefits of AI tools.

Female students (mean score: 3.641) demonstrate a more positive attitude towards enjoying the use of AI tools compared to male students (mean score: 3.248). The t-statistic of -7.073 suggests a significant difference in attitudes, with females finding more enjoyment in utilizing AI tools. Female students (mean score: 3.835) have a more positive attitude towards AI tools, making them more productive compared to male students (mean score: 3.376). The t-statistic of -8.287 indicates a significant difference in attitudes, with females perceiving greater productivity gains from AI tool usage.

Both male (mean score: 3.423) and female (mean score: 3.778) students express positive attitudes towards the advantages of teaching with AI tools. The t-statistic of -5.893 suggests that female students, on average, hold slightly stronger beliefs in the benefits of AI tools in teaching. Both male (mean score: 3.261) and female (mean score: 3.565) students have positive attitudes toward AI tools as effective learning tools. The t-statistic of -4.447 indicates a significant difference in attitudes, with female students perceiving AI tools as more effective in learning.

Female students (mean score: 3.774) have a more positive attitude towards AI tools enhancing students' learning compared to male students (mean score: 3.475). The t-statistic of -5.016 indicates a significant difference in attitudes, with females having stronger beliefs in the learning benefits of AI tools.

Both male (mean score: 3.422) and female (mean score: 3.832) students express positive attitudes towards using AI tools instead of doing things by hand. The t-statistic of -7.684 indicates that female students, on average, have stronger preferences for using AI tools. Both male (mean score: 3.255) and female (mean score: 3.649) students hold positive attitudes towards AI tools improving education. The t-statistic of -7.004 suggests a significant difference in attitudes, with females expressing stronger beliefs in the positive impact of AI tools on education.

Both male (mean score: 3.468) and female (mean score: 3.857) students express relatively low fear of AI tools. The t-statistic of -6.957 indicates a significant difference in attitudes, with female students having less fear of AI tools. Both male (mean score: 3.162) and female (mean score: 3.546) students have positive attitudes towards discussing AI tools with others. The t-statistic of -6.722 indicates a significant difference in attitudes, with females being more inclined to discuss AI tools with others.

Female students (mean score: 3.814) have a more positive attitude towards using AI tools in teaching compared to male students (mean score: 3.717). The t-statistic of -0.526 suggests a slight difference in attitudes, with females expressing slightly stronger beliefs in the value of AI tools in teaching.

Both male (mean score: 3.606) and female (mean score: 3.714) students perceive AI tools as a fast means of getting information. The t-statistic of -0.773 indicates that male and female students' attitudes in this regard are quite similar. Both male (mean score: 3.715) and female (mean score: 3.788) students have positive attitudes towards learning more about AI tools. The t-statistic of -0.349 indicates that male and female students' attitudes in this aspect are relatively similar.

5. DISCUSSION

It is necessary to create awareness among college students about the advantages of AI tools. This helps them enrich their knowledge and encourages them to explore more and more e-resources. All engineering colleges ensure the availability of AI tools in their college. Faculty members should encourage the students to use the AI tools in the college by giving assignments and exercises based on them.

All engineering colleges must understand the student's expectations of AI tools. Student's mindset is changing drastically in the past ten years. They hesitate to carry notebooks but are ready to bring their laptop. Students are expecting a 24 X 7 Wi-Fi campus, a computer lab with a fast net facility, etc.

As AI tools become more prevalent in colleges, it is crucial for institutions to invest in training and professional development programs for faculty, staff, and students. Adequate training will ensure that educators and staff are proficient in using AI tools and can effectively integrate them into the teaching and learning process. Students also need guidance on how to make the most of AI tools to enhance their learning experience.

The adoption of AI tools may require significant financial investment in terms of purchasing and maintaining the necessary hardware and software. Administrators need to carefully allocate resources to ensure that the right AI tools are chosen to meet the specific needs of the institution and its stakeholders. They should also consider the long-term sustainability and scalability of the AI infrastructure.

AI tools often rely on vast amounts of data for their functioning. Institutions must prioritize data privacy and security to safeguard sensitive student information and comply with data protection regulations. Implementing robust data protection measures will build trust and confidence among students and faculty in using AI tools.

AI tools offer the potential for personalized learning experiences tailored to individual student needs. This requires understanding the unique requirements of different academic disciplines and students.

Regular monitoring and evaluation of AI tool usage are essential to assess their effectiveness and impact on student outcomes. Managers should implement data analytics and feedback mechanisms to gauge the success of AI tools in enhancing teaching and learning.

The adoption of AI tools may bring about changes in teaching methods and the overall learning environment. Effective communication and change management strategies are necessary to address concerns, build acceptance, and promote a positive attitude toward AI tools among faculty and students.

The landscape of AI technologies is rapidly evolving. College administrators should have a long-term vision for the integration of AI tools and remain adaptable to emerging trends and advancements in the field.

6. CONCLUSION

The widespread integration of AI tools in engineering colleges presents an exciting opportunity to revolutionize education and empower students to excel in the digital age. By raising awareness about the advantages of AI tools, colleges can inspire students to explore e-resources, expand their knowledge, and enhance their learning experiences. Faculty members play a vital role in this process by encouraging students to utilize AI tools through well-designed assignments and exercises.

To ensure the successful implementation of AI tools, institutions must invest in training programs for faculty, staff, and students, enabling them to proficiently leverage these technologies. Additionally, strategic allocation of resources should be made to procure and maintain AI infrastructure while prioritizing data privacy and security to protect student information. The transformative potential of AI tools lies in their ability to facilitate personalized learning experiences tailored to individual student needs. Regular monitoring and evaluation will help assess the impact of AI tools on student outcomes and refine their integration for optimal results.

As AI tools change teaching methods and learning environments, effective communication and change management strategies are crucial to fostering acceptance and enthusiasm among stakeholders. By addressing concerns and building confidence in AI, colleges can create an environment that embraces innovation and supports continuous learning.

REFERENCES

Adnan, M., & Anwar, K. (2020). Online learning amid the COVID-19 pandemic: Students' perspectives. *Journal of Pedagogical Sociology and Psychology*, *2*(1), 45–51. doi:10.33902/JPSP.2020261309

Al Khawaldeh, S., Alawneh, Y., & Alzboun, M. (2022). The availability of quality standards for the construction of science achievement tests from the point of view of the examination committees. *Hunan Daxue Xuebao. Shehui Kexue Ban*, *49*(9), 1233–1247.

Alawneh, Y. (2022). Role of Kindergarten Curriculum in Instilling Ethical Values among Children in Governorates of Northern West Bank, Palestine, Dirasat. *Education in Science*, *49*(3), 360–375.

Alawneh, Y., Ashamali, M., Abdel-Hassan, R., & Al-khawaldeh, S., & Engestroom, Y. (2022). Degree Of Use Of E-Learning Science Teachers In Public High Schools In During The Corona-Covid 19 Pandemic. *Journal of Positive School Psychology*, *6*(2), 1060–1070.

An, Q., Hong, W. C. H., Xu, X., Zhang, Y., & Kolletar-Zhu, K. (2023). How Education Level Influences Internet Security Knowledge, Behaviour, and Attitude: A Comparison among Undergraduates, Postgraduates and Working Graduates. *International Journal of Information Security*, *22*(2), 305–317. doi:10.100710207-022-00637-z PMID:36466362

Baker, T., & Smith, L. (2019). *Educ-AI-tion rebooted? Exploring the future of artificial intelligence in schools and colleges*. Academic Press.

Balas-Timar, D. (2015). Relationship between job performance and job satisfaction viewed from the chaos theory perspective. *International Journal of Education and Research*, *3*(3), 517–534.

Balas-Timar, D., & Ignat, S. (2015). Conceptual applicant screening model with fuzzy logic in industrial organizational contexts. *Procedia: Social and Behavioral Sciences*, *203*, 257–263. doi:10.1016/j.sbspro.2015.08.291

Bisht, R. K., Jasola, S., & Bisht, I. P. (2020). Acceptability and challenges of online higher education in the era of COVID-19: A study of students' perspective. *Asian Journal of Education and E-Learning*. doi:10.1108/AEDS-05-2020-0119

Demeter, E., Rad, D., & Balas, E. (2021). Schadenfreude and General Anti-Social Behaviours: The Role of Violent Content Preferences and Life Satisfaction. BRAIN. *Broad Research in Artificial Intelligence and Neuroscience*, *12*(2), 98–111. doi:10.18662/brain/12.2/194

Fry, R., & Cilluffo, A. (2019). A rising share of undergraduates are from poor families, especially at less selective colleges. Pew Research Center.

Hasan, N., & Bao, Y. (2020). Impact of "e-Learning crack-up" perception on psychological distress among college students during COVID-19 pandemic: A mediating role of "fear of academic year loss. *Children and Youth Services Review*, *118*, 105355. doi:10.1016/j.childyouth.2020.105355 PMID:32834276

Hong, W. C. H. (2018). The Effect of Absence of Explicit Knowledge on ESL/EFL Stress-Placement Accuracy: A quasi-experiment. *Asian EFL Journal*, *20*(2), 262–279.

Hong, W. C. H. (2021a). Improving English as a foreign language learners' writing using a minimal grammar approach of teaching dependent clauses: A case study of Macao secondary school students. In B. L. Reynolds & M. F. Teng (Eds.), *Innovative Approaches in Teaching English Writing to Chinese Speakers* (pp. 67–90). De Gruyter Mouton. doi:10.1515/9781501512643-004

Hong, W. C. H. (2021b). Macao Secondary School EFL Teachers' Perspectives on Written Corrective Feedback: Rationales and Constraints. *Journal of Educational Technology and Innovation*, *1*(04), 1–13.

Hong, W. C. H. (2023). The impact of ChatGPT on foreign language teaching and learning: Opportunities in education and research. *Journal of Education Technology and Innovation*, *5*(1).

Hong, W. C. H., Chi, C.-Y., Liu, J., Zhang, Y.-F., Lei, N.-L., & Xu, X.-S. (2022). The influence of social education level on cybersecurity awareness and behaviour: A comparative study of university students and working graduates. *Education and Information Technologies*. PMID:35791319

Lian, X., Hong, W. C. H., Xu, X., Kimberly, K. Z., & Wang, Z. (2022). The influence of picture book design on visual attention of children with autism: A pilot study. *International Journal of Developmental Disabilities*, 1–11. PMID:37885844

Luckin, R., Holmes, W., Griffiths, M., & Forcier, L. B. (2016). *Intelligence unleashed - an argument for AI in education*. Academic Press.

Maseleno, A., Patimah, S., Syafril, S., & Huda, M. (2023). Learning Preferences Diagnostic using Mathematical Theory of Evidence. *FMDB Transactions on Sustainable Techno Learning*, *1*(2), 60–77.

Mathurajothi, S., Subramani, S., & Venkateswaran, P. S. (2018). A Study on the Impact of Service Quality on Student Satisfaction towards the University Libraries in Dindigul District, Tamil Nadu, India. *Asian Journal of Information Science and Technology*, *8*(3), 63–66. doi:10.51983/ajist-2018.8.3.200

Nithyanantham, V. (2023). Study Examines the Connection Between Students' Various Intelligence and Their Levels of Mathematical Success in School. *FMDB Transactions on Sustainable Techno Learning*, *1*(1), 32–39.

Ocoró, M. P., Polo, O. C. C., & Khandare, S. (2023). Importance of Business Financial Risk Analysis in SMEs According to COVID-19. *FMDB Transactions on Sustainable Management Letters*, *1*(1), 12–21.

Popenici, S., & Kerr, S. (2017). Exploring the impact of artificial intelligence on teaching and learning in higher education. *Research and Practice in Technology Enhanced Learning, 12*(1), 22. Advance online publication. doi:10.118641039-017-0062-8 PMID:30595727

Rad, D., Balas, E., Ignat, S., Rad, G., & Dixon, D. (2020a). A Predictive Model of Youth Bystanders' Helping Attitudes. *Revista romaneasca pentru educatie multidimensionala-Journal for Multidimensional Education, 12*(1Sup2), 136-150.

Rad, D., Balas, V., Lile, R., Demeter, E., Dughi, T., & Rad, G. (2020b). Statistical Properties of a New Social Media Context Awareness Scale (SMCA)—A Preliminary Investigation. *Sustainability (Basel), 12*(12), 5201. doi:10.3390u12125201

Rad, D., & Balas, V. E. (2020). A Novel Fuzzy Scoring Approach of Behavioural Interviews in Personnel Selection. BRAIN. *Broad Research in Artificial Intelligence and Neuroscience, 11*(2), 178–188. doi:10.18662/brain/11.2/81

Rad, D., & Demeter, E. (2020). A Moderated Mediation Effect of Online Time Spent on Internet Content Awareness, Perceived Online Hate Speech and Helping Attitudes Disposal of Bystanders. *Postmodern Openings, 11*(2, Supl 1), 107–124. doi:10.18662/po/11.2Sup1/182

Rad, D., Dughi, T., & Demeter, E. (2019). The Dynamics of the Relationship between Humor and Benevolence as Values. *Revista romaneasca pentru educatie multidimensionala-Journal for Multidimensional Education, 11*(3), 201-212.

Rad, D., Egerau, A., Roman, A., Dughi, T., Balas, E., Maier, R., & Rad, G. (2022). A Preliminary Investigation of the Technology Acceptance Model (TAM) in Early Childhood Education and Care. BRAIN. *Broad Research in Artificial Intelligence and Neuroscience, 13*(1), 518–533. doi:10.18662/brain/13.1/297

Saxena, D., Khandare, S., & Chaudhary, S. (2023). An Overview of ChatGPT: Impact on Academic Learning. *FMDB Transactions on Sustainable Techno Learning, 1*(1), 11–20.

Shruthi, S., & Aravind, B. R. (2023). Engaging ESL Learning on Mastering Present Tense with Nearpod and Learningapps.org for Engineering Students. *FMDB Transactions on Sustainable Techno Learning, 1*(1), 21–31.

Tripathi, S., & Al-Zubaidi, A. (2023). A Study within Salalah's Higher Education Institutions on Online Learning Motivation and Engagement Challenges during Covid-19. *FMDB Transactions on Sustainable Techno Learning, 1*(1), 1–10.

Tripathi, S., & Al-Shahri, M. (2023). Problems and Prospects on the Evolution of Advertising and Public Relations Industries in Oman. *FMDB Transactions on Sustainable Management Letters, 1*(1), 1–11.

Vashishtha, E., & Kapoor, H. (2023). Implementation of Blockchain Technology Across International Healthcare Markets. *FMDB Transactions on Sustainable Technoprise Letters, 1*(1), 1–12.

Venkatasubramanian, S., Gomathy, V., & Saleem, M. (2023). Investigating the Relationship Between Student Motivation and Academic Performance. *FMDB Transactions on Sustainable Techno Learning, 1*(2), 111–124.

Venkateswaran, P. S. (2015). Influence of information systems in Engineering Institutions at Madurai District, Tamil Nadu, India. *International Journal of Applied Engineering Research: IJAER*, *9*(21), 10513–10528.

Venkateswaran, P. S., Sundar, S., Chandrasekar, K., Manju, E., & Geetha, U. (2020). The Role of University Faculties in Sustainable Development in Higher Education in Tamil Nadu, India. *International Journal of Advanced Science and Technology*, *29*(1), 1206–1219.

Vijayarani, K., Nithyanantham, V., Christabel, A., & Marupaka, D. (2023). A Study on Relationship Between Self-Regulated Learning Habit and Achievement Among High School Students. *FMDB Transactions on Sustainable Techno Learning, 1*(2), 92–110.

Wong, Y. C., Ho, K. M., Chen, H., Gu, D., & Zeng, Q. (2015). Digital divide challenges of children in low-income families: The case of Shanghai. *Journal of Technology in Human Services*, *33*(1), 53–71. doi:10.1080/15228835.2014.998576

Xu, X., Hong, W. C. H., Zhang, Y., Jiang, H., & Liu, J. (2023). Learning Paths Design in Personal Learning Environments: The Impact on Postgraduates' Cognitive Achievements and Satisfaction. *Innovations in Education and Teaching International*, 1–16. doi:10.1080/14703297.2023.2189603

Chapter 9
Impact of the COVID-19 Lockdown on Employee Engagement and Efficiency

Manisha Singh
VIT Bhopal University, India

Rakhi Tiwari
Barkatullah University, India

Vinod Bhatt
VIT Bhopal University, India

Yogesh Shukla
VIT Bhopal University, India

ABSTRACT

The COVID-19 pandemic has forced organizations to adapt quickly to new ways of working, such as remote work and hybrid work arrangements. This has led to some challenges but also some opportunities to improve employee engagement and efficiency. One of the biggest challenges has been maintaining employee engagement during a time of great uncertainty and change. Organizations have tried to address this by developing creative and productive ways to engage their employees, such as online family engagement practices, online learning, virtual team building exercises, webinars with industry experts, weekly online alignment sessions, team meetings through video conference, short online game sessions, online contests and competitions, online programs, and online fitness and meditation. These activities can help employees stay connected with their colleagues and the organization, learn new skills, and improve themselves. Another challenge has been maintaining employee efficiency while working remotely.

DOI: 10.4018/979-8-3693-2193-5.ch009

1. INTRODUCTION

The COVID-19 virus quickly began at the turn of 2020 and continues to obstruct people's livelihoods, economies, and workplaces. As the virus started to rise globally, the federal and state governments of the economies started to implement strict lockdowns and asked to adhere to the standing operating procedure of COVID-19. During this pandemic, a large number of employees became jobless. Still, there are many organizations that shifted their workforce from office to remote working for the health and well-being of the employees. The COVID-19 Pandemic compelled the organization to implement drastic changes in the workplace, and the outcomes of this force caused an entire disruption in the employees' work and experience (Batool et al., 2023).

Social distancing and extended Lockdown have resulted in a completely remote work environment. Organizations have moved into the virtual world (Kanaan-Jebna et al., 2022). Employee communication took place among the stakeholders via online mode. Face-to-face interaction is totally prohibited. The change of circumstances may not change in a couple of times (Harter et al., 2002).

Considering all the facts of the situation, this sudden and uncontrollable factor forced organizations to change their work style, but in this contingent situation, the organizations try to pay attention to the most important '*P*' factor of their business continuity and success, i.e., *'their people'*. However, it's very tough for employees from remote work with restricted resources. The major issue with employees' equilibrium between the work-life and personal life as well as it distracts them functionally and emotionally from their team and managers (MacLeod & Clarke, 2011). As per the present economic situation, financial stability is also one of the major concerns which disconcert them. At such times, it becomes essential for an organization to look out for the anxiety of its employees, and the organization has to help them to come up with ways to give their best while staying healthy and safe at the same time (Soni, 2019).

It is apparent that contemporary working conditions, even before COVID-19, were volatile due to technological advances, economic fluctuations, and political uncertainty, which would prevent all employees from ensuring job stability. The perceptions of insecurity in employees – the perceptual and unintentional perceptions of job loss have been increased by organizational restructuring and scale-downs, but COVID-19 has made the situation worse. Occupational insecurity can extend all over employees for two particular purposes. Initially, shifts in an organization, such as layoffs, reduction in volume, and fusions, are induced by measurable job insecurity. As well as secondly, employees from different work units can interpret certain threats or stressors in the same or collective manner. The most important thing, however, is that job insecurity is a major stressor for employees, which affects their efficiency and is adversely associated with employee engagement, Job attributes, and employees' psychological health. Considering that insecurity at the job is a risk factor for employees to be harmful by negative psychological responses which decline employees' performance.

In fact, during a crisis, there are only three opportunities for employee engagement - to increase, fall, or stay constant. There is plenty of evidence suggesting that the employee engagement level may have remained consistent, wherever the level of employee engagement noted with minute changes of 1- 2 percentage points year- over year for more than a decade.

The employees are one of the core valued assets to gain the competitive advantage with a set of capabilities to enhance efficiency in the organization. It may be one of the core competencies for the organization to concentrate on to engage employees. Many researchers and HR experts have found over the years that the organization's enthusiastic employees are a productive asset to the. In addition, research findings showed a positive connection between engagement and the desire for work. The differences between leader's and staff's needs make it possible for practitioners to modify organizational systems and policies to meet those requirements.

In recent decades, many organizations have felt the importance of employee engagement. The beginning of the year 2020 carried an even serious requisite for reinforcing the engagement level of employees owed to the COVID-19 crisis and Lockdowns worldwide. The whole world has been confronted by COVID-19. It does not only have an impact on an individual's health but also on an organization's overall health. Where many organizations had to dismiss employees, current employees show a lower level of employee engagement. Organizations are struggling for their sustainability during COVID-19; those who are not that stable are on the verge of insolvency. Such exceptional condition has formed anxiety among the employees interrelated to job insecurity, bonuses, performance appraisals, etc. Therefore, the reduced level of employee engagement level is obvious.

2. LITERATURE REVIEW

2.1. Employee Engagement

To encounter the term "engagement" in theoretical aspects/ literature is a major challenge due to the scarcity of the generic definition of employee engagement. Employee engagement is a positive, motivating force that links employees emotionally, cognitively, or physically with their organization (Kahn, 1990). In his study (Khan,1990) stated that engagement specifies the physiological and physical existence of performing the organizational role. The construct of the study of physiological settings depicted the importance, safety & availability identified as vital factors that support engagement to grow in an organization. Further research shows that the cognitive aspect is linked to the beliefs of managers, employees, and the working environment, whereas the Emotional aspect indicates the attitude of the employees towards the organization, and the managers mean positive or negative outlook. The physical aspect includes the physical strength to achieve the organizational purpose. Chapman et al., (2020) explored the model proposed by Kahn, which demonstrated that the importance, safety &availability of psychological settings are significantly linked with engagement.

Engaged employees were always attentive to their hard work, performance, and achievements, and employees felt they could make a difference in their jobs, efforts, and performance. The commitment of employees is generally seen as an inner mental state, i.e., physically, emotionally, and mentally, which integrates commitment, satisfaction, and effort on an employee's part. Engaged employees help the organization to achieve its mission, objective, execution, and implementation of its strategy and yield meaningful business outcomes. Particularly, these employees have high energy levels and enthusiasm and often are fully immersed in their work so that their working time goes rapidly and swiftly. In order to achieve their objectives, organizations, and employees depend on one another. The employee engagement should not be a unique implementation but should be integrated into the work environment. The six C parameters, that is, clarity, confidence, communication, connection, credibility, and career, are crucial for improving the purpose of effective employee engagement. The organization may increase the level of engagement by embellishing the employee commitment, decision-making, and transparency from managers. Employee engagement is a style that multiplies the possibilities of organizational achievement, supporting employees and organizational performance, efficiency, and employee welfare. The study depicted engagement as a notion that makes employees passionate and committed to their jobs.

2.2. Employee Engagement and Work Efficiency

Cooper et.al., 2014 stated in the study identified to establishing high expectations and prevalent performance assessments can increase employee productivity and cooperation. The lack of resources led organizations to rely more on cost-reduction productivity and efficiency. Reduced process modification could even decrease costs in the long run as process improvement approaches are engaged (Emrouznejad et al., 2010), but methods that enhance positive engagement should persist as part of the organization. To control the cost in short-duration has not been consistently successful. Malik, (2013) states in the study that an organization that maintains a high level of employee engagement practices has high employee turnover, efficiency, development, productivity & stakeholder satisfaction. Firms with engaged employees have greater employee retention, efficiency, productivity, and development, as well as employee and customer satisfaction.

2.3. Employee Engagement and Employee Performance

Academicians represent the linkage between engagement and performance. As per the report of Hewitt consultancy report identified, of those highly engaged employees, near to 78% are highly productive as well, and 40% have been recognized as having a significant impact on productivity, employee satisfaction, and financial performance. The engagement of all levels of organization must be considered a significant strategy (Frank et al. 2004). Consequent communication and coherent appreciation are the keys to good employee relations and improved employee satisfaction. A number of studies can be considered to stimulate the study done to understand the performance of employees with an integral process of human resource management practices.

Bakker & Demerouti (2008) specified that in rapidly changing markets, employers should recognize that highly committed employees can improve productivity and firm performance. That is to say, engaging employees are passionate about their work, have a sense of pleasure in working in the organization as well as and have enthusiastic participation in the functioning of the organization. Furthermore, employees involved in their work consider their organizations to be extremely important to maintain competitive advantages, to cope with changes, and to make sure for work innovation.

Shuck et al. (2011) stated in their study that certain researchers also emphasized employee engagement as a structure consisting of cognitive, emotional, and behavioral elements linked to the role of employee performance. Echols (2005) advised that in order to enhance employee engagement, managers should pay attention to the skills, knowledge, and talents of their staff. The author also said that if people know about their strengths and skills, their level of engagement will be higher, which consequently will result in higher performance. It represents an employee's engagement in his work to improve organizational performance and commitment (Sundaray, 2011).

2.4. Employee Engagement and Productivity

Nowadays, challenging face for organizations to enhance employees' productivity. Enhancing employee productivity has been one of the prime objectives for numerous organizations. Organizations that consider their employees as assets and involve them in engagement activities this identified a positive association between employee engagement and employee productivity. This is because a higher level of employee productivity supports an organization and its employees with numerous benefits. Sharma & Sharma

(2014) specified that higher productivity may lead to various favorable conditions for organizations, viz. economic growth, great profitability & social growth. Chen & Eyoun, (2021) investigated the relationship between the organizational culture &its leadership and employee engagement and found it utmost prominence and impact on the relationship between employee performance & productivity.

Rothmann & Rothmann (2010) have shown that strength, attitude, and positive professional behavior have become the essence of productivity in organizations and thus make businesses more efficient. Employers need to concentrate on the behavioral aspect of engagement to achieve better performance. Hanaysha (2016) identified multi-faceted dimensions of behavior, including faith in the organization, desire to make things better, comprehension of the diverse instances, a climate of support and self-respect, and competency to work and stay equipped, which have been identified as essential aspects for employee engagement.

Engagement can be defined as a two-fold process between employees and an organization. This is an approach for enhancing an employee's productivity and performance; it is indeed a means of ensuring the employee's commitment, motivation, and contribution to the accomplishment of the goals and values. A few researches stated that engagement not only improves an organization's non-monetary achievement (i.e., customer satisfaction, amenities skills, presence, appearance & turnover, etc.) but also impacts monetary achievement, which directly affects the company's profits (Sels et al., 2006). Sharma and Sharma (2014) specified employee productivity is determined by the duration of time the employee has spent at work, in addition to how "psychologically active" or efficient the employee is while at work. In order to ensure high employee productivity, companies must tackle such issues. Employees can achieve better wages, salaries and benefits, conditions of employment, and opportunities for employment only with increasing productivity.

The literature review done above has obviously conversed with the notion of employee engagement, efficiency &productivity. It indicates that employee engagement is a key determinant of organizational profitability and success, which organization determined by employee efficiency and productivity.

3. RATIONALE OF THE STUDY

Due to the COVID-19 pandemic, many nations are going through prolonged shutdowns. The organizations are compelled to implement the remote working regime in this difficult situation. However, the remote working regime is carrying lots of challenges for both employees as well as organizations. To overcome this crisis, organizations have to engage their employees in a sophisticated manner with the help of numerous practices of employee engagement. Though there are plenty of research works available on employee engagement practices and their relationship with the numerous HR factors/practices. But to, identifying the relationship between employee engagement with work efficiency still has a scope to explore. The purpose of the present study is to understand the COVID-19 crisis's impact on employees' efficiency through employees' engagement practices so that employees can easily perform remote work and keep them committed, efficient, and motivated.

3.1. Objectives of the Study

- To determine the Employee engagement practices affected during the COVID-19 Lockdown.
- To determine the impact of COVID-19 lockdown on employees Work efficiency.
- To determine the outcomes associated with the Employees' engagement practices during the COVID-19 lockdown.

4. RESEARCH MAP

From the above extensive review of literature, it is observed that employee engagement parameters such as employee performance, job security, organizational productivity, and organizational culture are strongly related to work efficiency (Figure 1).

Figure 1. Proposition framework

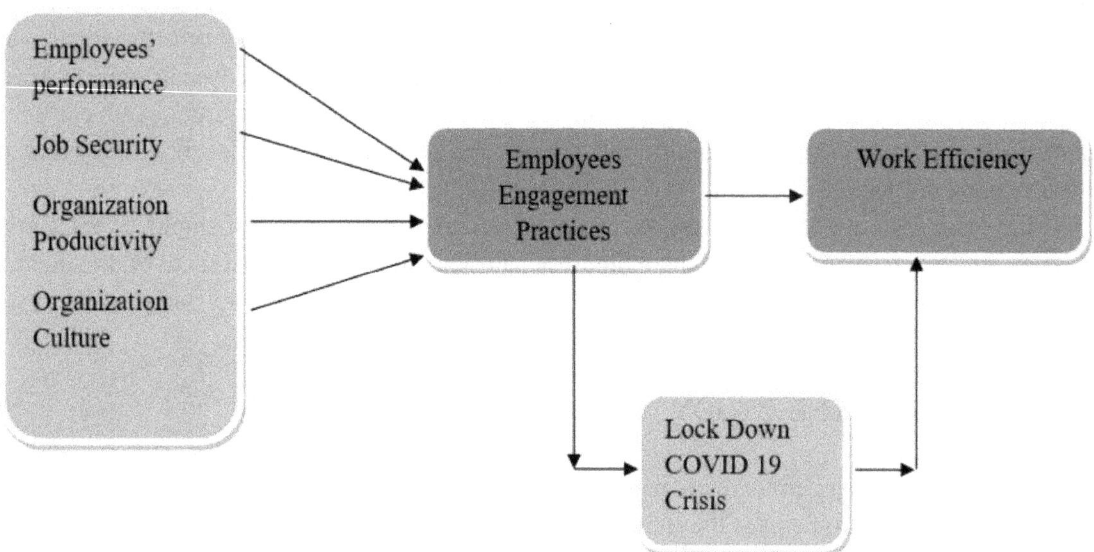

P_{01} = Lockdown has significantly affected employee engagement through employee performance.
P_{02} = There is a significant impact of the COVID-19 crisis on employee engagement through Job Security.
P_{03} = Lockdown has significantly affected employee engagement through Organization Productivity.
P_{04} = There is a significant impact of the COVID-19 crisis on employee engagement through Organization Culture.
P_{05} = There is a significant impact of the COVID-19 lockdown on Work Efficiency.

4.1. Lockdown Impact of COVID-19 on Employee Engagement Practices and Work Efficiency

Four propositions have been framed under the study to ascertain the impact of the COVID-19 lockdown on employee engagement and Work efficiency. Through the extensive review of the literature, it is concluded that the employees' engagement practices, such as Employee performance, organizational culture, Job Insecurity, and Organizational productivity, depend on employees' engagement. The employees' engagement further directly relates to Work efficiency.

4.2. P_{o1} = Lockdown Has Significantly Affected Employee Engagement Through Employees Performance

Employee performance is an important driving factor of employee engagement practices and appears to be a better predictor of job performance (Dajani, 2015). The unprecedented continuous lockdown activities in many nations have brought tremendous changes, and employees strongly perceived that these changes are disrupting their daily work performance (Hamid et.al., 2020).

To administer the COVID-19 crisis government has imposed many safety precautions such as wearing masks at work workplace, social distancing norms, etc. This has brought changes in the workplace, directly affecting employees' performance. Remote working has significantly brought a decline in employee performance. The Lockdown is responsible for lessening employee performance compared to the pre-COVID-19 crisis. Digital inequalities have also turned out as one of the critical factors contributing to employees' performance during lockdown emergencies. The digital platform has successfully helped humans in managing the effects of the COVID-19 crisis. Although it is a good initiative, but is subjected to network issues (Beaunoyer et al., 2020).

4.3. P_{o2} = There Is a Significant Impact of the COVID-19 Crisis on Employee Engagement Through Job Security

The lockdown crisis has significantly affected employability. The continuous Lockdown has risen to the stoppage of production and sitting at home without work for long days has hindered the organization's performance. In the absence of production marketing and selling of products, organizations are also not able to provide jobs and salaries to their employees.

COVID-19 has caused a job crisis, which can raise poverty and inequalities in many world countries. Some employers provide salaries based on actual working hours, while some have proceeded with retrenchment and layoff-(OECD Employment Outlook, 2020). *The global economic recession triggered by COVID-19 could result in 24.7 million job losses worldwide, approximately two million more than the 2008–2009 global financial crisis (International Labour Organization, 2020).* The COVID-19 pandemic has resulted in jobs moving away from high labor-productive sectors such as manufacturing and services to low-productivity sectors such as agriculture and construction, with manufacturing witnessing only a modest recovery in the fiscal year so far, the Centre for Monitoring Indian Economy. The outbreak of COVID-19 has resulted in the migration of unemployed people from the service sector to the agriculture sector. The lockdown crisis has brought the fear of job insecurity and emotional collapse (Fatma, 2020).

4.4. P_{o3} = Lockdown Has Significantly Affected Employee Engagement Through Organization Productivity

For any organization, the productivity of employees is essential. The more productive your employees are, the better you succeed. As per the Gallup report, 21% more productive highly engaged teams have a 28% relatively lower internal theft than low-engagement teams. Committed employees are innovative, but they always have a thought about what they're doing and how it can be done in the best manner. They can achieve their organizational objectives better by their performance and be cooperative and passionate, leading to greater workplace productivity. The worldwide spread of COVID-19 has a deep-rooted impact on employees and organizations. The frequent Lockdown in nations has caused business units to the verge of shutdown, leading to unemployment. Many business units admitted reduced production and decreased profit during the crisis of COVID-19. Many business firms reported a decrease in their productivity during COVID-19.

4.5. P_{o4} = There Is a Significant Impact of COVID-19 on Employee Engagement Through Organization Culture

The organization's culture is one of the strong indicators of employee Engagement practices. An effective organizational culture will be a robust parameter for judging employee engagement practices. Organizational culture tends to extend a congenial, healthy purpose and employee commitment (Al Shehri et al., 2017). The organizational culture helps in shaping the employees' behavior and mending ethics. If an organization wants to improve its performance, then the level of employee engagement should be kept high.

The COVID-19 crisis has made tremendous shifts in organizational culture. The worldwide Lockdown and its frequent extension led to drastic changes like work and business interactions. Employees are now having well working efficiently remotely. Now, they have gained expertise in working their task through digital platforms. However physical presence of workers cannot be comparable to remote working culture.

4.6. P_{o5}= There Is a Significant Impact of the COVID-19 Lockdown on Work Efficiency

Employee engagement serves as an important way to enhance employee work efficiency. An organization highly focused on employee engagement practices generally creates a positive work environment that leads to organizational efficiency. The employees who are found engaged possess a high degree of satisfaction with their job. The present coronavirus crisis has largely influenced the work efficiency of employees. The work-from-home practices have justified the management of the present situation. However, some studies believe that 55% of their colleagues are not more productive now than before the Lockdown. In some studies, 71% of employees found themselves much more efficient while working from home (Bick et al., 2020). Though work-from-home practices have been fruitful during the Corona crisis, they have been subjected to many pros and cons arguments, according to some research studies.

5. DISCUSSION

The COVID-19 crisis has been disastrous, like an earthquake disrupting human life on earth, causing damage not only to lives but also to the factors responsible for the growth and survival of human development. These upshots both employers and employees are enforcing them for alternative job arrangements. Prudent Brokers stated that 13% of organizations had been negatively influenced by the fact that their business had to be on the verge of shutdown. Manufacturing, retail, real estate, supply & logistics, and engineering are some of the badly hit sectors in India. Organizations noted the COVID-19 crisis declined employees' productivity. However, 50% of employers reported the same level of productivity among their employees; still, 28% of employers have no opinion on the level of employees' productivity and work efficiency during the COVID-19 crisis.

World Economic Forum expressed that COVID-19 is forcing organizations to scale remote working to accelerate digitalization and automation. The employees who are efficient in handling remote working are more likely to keep their jobs compared to the employees of the travel, tourism, and hospitality sectors in those pandemics affected more. However, most organizations are indeterminate about how remote working and hybrid working (turning up to the office a few days a week) will look out for the long term. Weforum surveyed the impact of the productivity of the employees and identified the majority of the employers anticipating 78% moderate negative impact of the present-day of working on employee efficiency and productivity, with 22% having a strong negative impact, whereas 15% have no impact with a mild curve towards to positive impact on the same. Behind these figures, there may be some reasons like the switch to remote working creates additional stress associated with the COVID-19 virus, unable to manage work-life balance, lack of sense of community & flow of communication may not be able to maintain by the newly remote working companies.

Through the pandemic outbreak, the work setting convention from physical to virtual as well as limited the entire workforce from office to home and forced remote working, which has caused a flexible but often unmanageable situation. Whereas such a new setting regarding performing a job provides plenty of flexibility to employees, it is a serious matter of concern for the organization and employers to assess the effectiveness of the performance appraisal. The concern is that since employees keep remote working partially, even on a large scale, numerous variables that influence workplace culture are not quite the same way or even at the same level as organizations. It is, therefore, essential for business leaders to concentrate on how COVID-19 impacts their work experience and what they can do to ensure a positive organizational culture for their employees.

Therefore, organizations need to redesign their policies based on digital dialogue for executing the task. The policies must be governed by the factors of Job Security, Health Safety, Flexible working hours, balancing between personal and professional life, and employee empowerment.

It is evident from this research work that different employee engagement practices, such as Employee performance, Organizational culture, Job Insecurity, and Organizational productivity, have a profound impact on work efficiency during the COVID-19 crisis. Better organizational policies and transformation of organization culture from absolute mechanization to digitalization is the drastic change that an employee, as well as the organization, is required to inculcate in their behavior. The greater the organization-inclined digital curve, the more the organization adapts for survival in this COVID-19 crisis.

6. CONCLUSION

Start to accelerate the use of technological resources that can give the deceptive perception of an unnecessary presence in a physical manner in the office. Although, many professional tasks can certainly be performed remotely. The organization must look onward to keep employees motivated & satisfied through the engagement practices on COVID-19 Crises. In the current situation, it is essential for the growth of companies to establish measures of employee commitment using technology. Many organizations are presently establishing several practices such as virtual interactions between team members, virtual training & development sessions, virtual learning and development, online weekly updates with managers, online webinars, and webinars with experts on time management, stress, burn-out, & anxiety, video conferencing, shared content like online books, live sessions, online courses, multi-authoring of documents, digital whiteboards, chat groups, e- learning modules. There are many other means that employees can be absolutely prompted about what it means to work for the organization, like virtual award gatherings, online exercises, medication, online counseling sessions, and virtual social interactions.

6.1. Future Scope of the Study

In the new ways of working, technology plays a vital role in determining the efficiency and productivity of the employees and how all these digital resources in the workplace can be successfully and efficiently incorporated into the organization's culture. This is not just a matter of IT concern; instead, it varies based on how far the culture of the organization is retained, as well as the ways in which employees can virtually socialize with each other. In the face of uncertainty, volatility, intricacy, and vagueness global COVID-19 crisis, the organization's major concerns are covert learning, redefinition, and transformation opportunities both at individual and organizational levels.

REFERENCES

Al Shehri, M., McLaughlin, P., Al-Ashaab, A., & Hamad, R. (2017). The impact of organizational culture on employee engagement in Saudi banks. *Journal of Human Resources Management Research, 2017*, 761672. Advance online publication. doi:10.5171/2017.761672

Bakker, A. B., & Demerouti, E. (2008). Towards a model of work engagement. *Career Development International, 13*(3), 209–223. doi:10.1108/13620430810870476

Batool, K., Zhao, Z.-Y., Irfan, M., & Żywiołek, J. (2023). Assessing the role of sustainable strategies in alleviating energy poverty: An environmental sustainability paradigm. *Environmental Science and Pollution Research International, 30*(25), 67109–67130. doi:10.100711356-023-27076-0 PMID:37103699

Beaunoyer, E., Dupéré, S., & Guitton, M. J. (2020). COVID-19 and digital inequalities: Reciprocal impacts and mitigation strategies. *Computers in Human Behavior, 111*, 106424. doi:10.1016/j.chb.2020.106424 PMID:32398890

Chapman, B., Swainston, J., Grunfeld, E. A., & Derakshan, N. (2020). COVID-19 outbreak effects on job security and emotional functioning amongst women living with breast cancer. *Frontiers in Psychology, 11*, 582014. doi:10.3389/fpsyg.2020.582014 PMID:33192902

Chen, H., & Eyoun, K. (2021). Do mindfulness and perceived organizational support work? Fear of COVID-19 on restaurant frontline employees' job insecurity and emotional exhaustion. *International Journal of Hospitality Management, 94*, 102850. doi:10.1016/j.ijhm.2020.102850 PMID:34785844

Cooper, H. D., Paterson, N. L., Stadler, M. J., & Saks, A. M. (2014). The relative importance of proactive behaviors and outcomes for predicting newcomer learning, well-being, and work engagement. *Journal of Vocational Behavior, 84*(3), 318–331. doi:10.1016/j.jvb.2014.02.007

Dajani, D., & Zaki, M. A. (2015). *The impact of employee engagement on job performance and organisational commitment in the Egyptian banking sector*. Academic Press.

Echols, M. E. (2005). Engaging employees to impact performance. *Chief Learning Officer, 4*(2), 44–48.

Emrouznejad, A., Anouze, A. L., & Thanassoulis, E. (2010). A semi-oriented radial measure for measuring the efficiency of decision making units with negative data, using DEA. *European Journal of Operational Research, 200*(1), 297–304. doi:10.1016/j.ejor.2009.01.001

Fatma, I. (2020). *The effects of COVID-19 pandemic on the workforce in Turkey*. Academic Press.

Frank, F., Finnegan, R., & Taylor, C. (2004). The Race for Talent: Retaining and Engaging Workers in the 21st Century. *Human Resource Planning, 27.*

Hamid, M., Wahab, S. A., Hosna, A. U., Hasanat, M. W., & Kamruzzaman, M. (2020). Impact of coronavirus (COVID-19) and employees' reaction to changes on employee performance of Bangladesh. *International Journal of Business and Management, 8*(8). Advance online publication. doi:10.24940/theijbm/2020/v8/i8/BM2008-013

Hanaysha, J. (2016). Improving employee productivity through work engagement: Evidence from higher education sector. *Management Science Letters, 6*(1), 61–70. doi:10.5267/j.msl.2015.11.006

Harter, J. K., Schmidt, F. L., & Hayes, T. L. (2002). Business-unit-level relationship between employee satisfaction, employee engagement, and business outcomes: A meta-analysis. *The Journal of Applied Psychology, 87*(2), 268–279. doi:10.1037/0021-9010.87.2.268 PMID:12002955

Kahn, W. A. (1990). Psychological conditions of personal engagement and disengagement at work. *Academy of Management Journal, 33*(4), 692–724. doi:10.2307/256287

Kanaan-Jebna, A., Baharudi, A. S., & Alabdullah, T. T. Y. (2022). Entrepreneurial Orientation, Market Orientation, Managerial Accounting and Manufacturing SMEs Satisfaction. *Journal of Accounting Science, 6*(1), 1–14. doi:10.21070/jas.v6i1.1590

MacLeod, D., & Clarke, N. (2011). *Engaging for success: Enhancing performance through employee engagement, a report to Government*. Academic Press.

Malik, H. (2013). Relationship between leader behaviors and employees'jobsatisfaction:a path-goal approach. *Pakistan Journal of Commerce and Social Sciences, 7*(1), 209–222.

Rothmann, S., & Rothmann, S. Jr. (2010). Factors associated with employee engagement in South Africa. *SA Journal of Industrial Psychology, 36*(2), 1–12. doi:10.4102ajip.v36i2.925

Sels, L., De Winne, S., Delmotte, J., Maes, J., Faems, D., & Forrier, A. (2006). Linking HRM and small business performance: An examination of the impact of HRM intensity on the productivity and financial performance of small businesses. *Small Business Economics*, *26*(1), 83–101. doi:10.100711187-004-6488-6

Sharma, M. S., & Sharma, M. V. (2014). Employee engagement to enhance productivity in current scenario. *International Journal of Commerce and Business Management*, *3*(4), 595–604.

Shuck, M. B., Rocco, T. S., & Albornoz, C. A. (2011). Exploring employee engagement from the employee perspective: Implications for HRD. *Journal of European Industrial Training*, *35*(4), 300–325. doi:10.1108/03090591111128306

Soni, S. (2019). Impact of organizational culture on employee engagement and effectiveness in Indian manufacturing company. *IITM Journal of Management and IT*, *10*(2), 42–52.

Sundaray, B. K. (2011). Employee engagement: A driver of organizational effectiveness. *European Journal of Business and Management*, *3*(8), 53–59.

Wolor, C. W., Solikhah, S., Fidhyallah, N. F., & Lestari, D. P. (2020). Effectiveness of E-training, E-leadership, and work life balance on employee performance during COVID-19. *Journal of Asian Finance. Economics and Business*, *7*(10), 443–450. doi:10.13106/jafeb.2020.vol7.no10.443

Chapter 10
Synergizing Efficiency and Customer Delight on Empowering Business With Enterprise Applications

D. Lavanya
PSNA College of Engineering and Technology, India

R. Regin
SRM Institute of Science And Technology, Ramapuram, India

Sandeep Rangineni
https://orcid.org/0009-0003-9623-4062
Pluto TV, USA

S. Suman Rajest
https://orcid.org/0000-0001-8315-3747
Dhaanish Ahmed College of Engineering, India

Latha Thamma Reddi
https://orcid.org/0009-0005-6338-7972
DXC Technology, USA

P. Paramasivan
Dhaanish Ahmed College of Engineering, India

ABSTRACT

Enterprise applications have never been more important in an era where organizations thrive on efficiency and consumer happiness. This chapter is an enthralling voyage into the world of cutting-edge technology in which the authors investigate the revolutionary power of enterprise applications and their significant impact on modern enterprises. They delve into the dense web of corporate applications that serve as the backbone of enterprises, fueling growth and fostering innovation. These applications are intended to optimize procedures, streamline operations, and improve cross-departmental communication, allowing firms to function at maximum efficiency while maintaining a laser-like focus on customer satisfaction. They show how, in an ever-changing technological context, enterprise applications have developed from traditional software tools to agile, intelligent, and integrated solutions. The alternatives are endless, from enterprise resource planning (ERP) systems to customer relationship management (CRM) platforms.

DOI: 10.4018/979-8-3693-2193-5.ch010

1. INTRODUCTION

An enterprise business system, which is also frequently referred to as an enterprise business solution (EBS), is a software application that is both comprehensive and integrated, and it provides support for and automates a variety of business processes throughout an entire firm (Arslan et al., 2021). It performs the function of a centralised data and information hub, making it possible for the company's many departments and operations to communicate and work together without any difficulty (Al-Maaitah et al., 2021a). Enterprise business systems are designed to streamline processes, boost efficiency, and enhance decision-making (Al-Maaitah et al., 2021b). They do this by offering real-time insights and data-driven analysis (Davenport & Harris, 2007). These systems frequently consist of a number of modules or applications that cater to specific functional areas such as finance, personnel resources, sales, inventory management, supply chain management, customer relationship management, and others (Balas-Timar, 2015). These modules and applications are often referred to collectively as a "solution."

Enterprise Business Systems, often known as EBS, are complex and comprehensive software systems that are used to support and automate a variety of business processes that are carried out within an organisation (Balas-Timar & Ignat, 2015). When you have a firm grasp of the fundamental ideas of EBS, you will have a solid foundation for comprehending the operation of these systems (Batool et al., 2023). The following are some fundamental ideas pertaining to enterprise business systems (Buttle, 2016): The EBS system integrates data and processes across the various departments and functions of an organisation (Chopra & Meindl, 2019). It prevents data silos and encourages smooth communication across modules, which ultimately results in a unified perspective of the entire organisation (Gupta, 2019). Integration is a crucial component of EBS due to the fact that it enables the transmission of data in real time and enhances the level of collaboration that can occur between the various teams (Demeter et al., 2021).

The Enterprise Business System (EBS) is composed of a variety of modules or applications, each of which fulfils a specific function for a company (Gupta, 2021a). These modules can function independently or as a component of a bigger system depending on your needs. Because modularity enables businesses to choose and configure only the functionalities they need, it enables a greater degree of flexibility in the deployment of EBS. EBS brings together information from a variety of sources and stores it in a single repository (Gupta, 2021b). The centralised storage of data ensures that the data is consistent and provides a reliable source of information from which decisions may be made (Dumas et al., 2018). The data repository acts as the basis for providing reports, analytics, and insights to various parts of the organisation (Khan et al., 2023). EBS systems are designed to accommodate both the expansion and the shifting requirements of an organisation (Gupta, 2022). As the company expands, they are able to manage growing data quantities, user requirements, and additional functionalities (fig.1).

EBS provides real-time reporting and analytical capabilities (Rad & Demeter, 2020). Users can access up-to-date information and generate reports on numerous parts of the business, improving data-driven decision-making (Kavanagh et al., 2017). EBS automates common and repetitive activities, eliminating manual intervention and the chance of error (Kumar & Reinartz, 2016).

Automating workflows inside a company helps to optimise business operations, which in turn boosts efficiency and saves both time and resources (fig.2) (Ogunmola et al., 2021). EBS implements a number of severe security procedures to protect critical corporate data from being accessed inappropriately and from cyber threats (Mohsan et al., 2022). Users will only be able to access the functionality and data that they need if they have been assigned the correct permissions, and role-based access controls ensure that this happens (Laudon & Laudon, 2020).

Figure 1. Enterprise resource planning (ERP)
Source: ERP Management System (2020)

Figure 2. Enterprise service bus
Source: Reddy (2016)

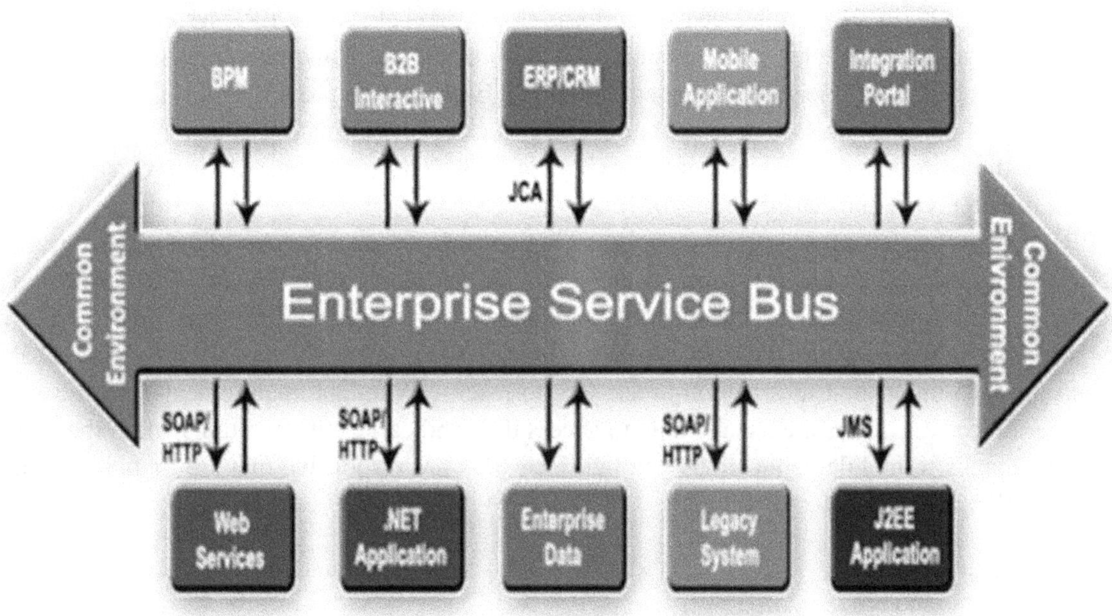

Business Intelligence (BI) tools are typically incorporated into EBS, and its purpose is to provide users with assistance in analysing data, recognising trends, and getting insights into the performance of their businesses (Payne & Frow, 2013). The capabilities of data visualisation provide graphical representations of complicated data, which makes the data simpler to comprehend and evaluate (Rad et al., 2020a). Users are able to access crucial information on mobile devices like smartphones and tablets because to the mobile applications and responsive user interfaces that are included in many modern EBS solutions (Roman et al., 2020; Sharma et al., 2021a). This enables mobile workforce and remote management (Rad et al., 2020b). It is possible to customise and design EBS systems so that they fulfil the requirements of a particular organisation (Rad et al., 2019). The system is modifiable, so businesses can tailor it to their particular needs in terms of business procedures and requirements (Simchi-Levi et al., 2019).

2. ENTERPRISE RESOURCE PLANNING

Enterprise Resource Planning (ERP) is a sort of enterprise business system that integrates and controls an organization's numerous key business activities and functions (Shanks et al., 2018). By offering a uniform and consolidated platform for data and information, ERP software is intended to expedite processes, boost efficiency, and allow data-driven decision-making (Smith & Johnson, 2018).

2.1. ERP System Components and Features

ERP systems contain a centralized database that holds data from several departments and functions, maintaining data consistency and giving the organization a single source of truth (Sherman, 2014). ERP integrates many corporate operations into a single system, including finance, human resources, manufacturing, supply chain management, sales, and customer relationship management (fig.3) (Sumner, 2018).

Users are able to make informed decisions in the here and now thanks to the real-time access that ERP software grants them to critical data and information (Rad et al., 2022). ERP systems automate and standardise business procedures, hence reducing the amount of manual labour required to complete tasks and improving overall efficiency (Sharma et al., 2021b). ERP systems provide reporting and analytical capabilities, which allow users to generate insights and track key performance indicators (KPIs) in order to monitor the performance of the organisation (Sharda et al., 2017). These capabilities can be accessed through the ERP system (Sharma et al., 2021c).

ERP systems implement security protocols and assign users to specific roles in order to restrict user access to only the information and functionalities that are pertinent to the tasks for which they are responsible (Sharma et al., 2021d). The business intelligence (BI) capabilities of many ERP systems are designed to help users analyse data and make decisions based on that analysis. ERP software enables organisations to tailor their information processing to meet their unique requirements and fulfil their particular objectives. Users are usually able to access data and carry out operations while they are on the move thanks to mobile applications and interfaces that are responsive that are included in many modern ERP systems

Figure 3. ERP system components and features
Source: Enterprise Resource Planning (2021)

2.2. ERP System Advantages

Greater Productivity and Efficiency: ERP streamlines company operations and eliminates unnecessary work, resulting in greater productivity and efficiency (Wisner et al., 2019).

Enhanced Data Visibility: ERP enables better decision-making by providing a real-time view of data across departments (Tristan Boutros, 2023).

Improved Collaboration: ERP promotes collaboration among many teams and departments by encouraging data exchange and communication.

Cost Savings: By improving inventory management, streamlining procurement processes, and reducing manual labor, ERP improves resource allocation and lowers operational costs (Żywiołek et al., 2022).

Regulatory Compliance: By assuring accurate and auditable data records, ERP assists firms in adhering to industry legislation and compliance standards.

2.3. ERP Implementation Disadvantages

ERP deployment can be complicated and time-consuming, necessitating careful planning and trained resources.

Cost: ERP deployment can have large upfront expenditures, including software licenses, gear, and training.

Organizational Change: ERP installation frequently necessitates modifications to existing company procedures, which may elicit employee opposition.

Data Migration: Data migration from old systems to the new ERP can be difficult and may necessitate data cleansing and validation.

The core ERP model consists of

- Customer Relationship Management (CRM)
- Supply Chain Management (SCM)
- Human Resources Management (HRM)
- Business Intelligence (BI) and
- Business Process Management (BPM)

3. CUSTOMER RELATIONSHIP MANAGEMENT

CRM systems are software solutions that are designed to manage and optimize interactions and connections with customers throughout their lifecycle. CRM systems give businesses a single platform for gathering, organizing, and analyzing customer data, allowing them to better understand and serve their customers. Companies may improve customer satisfaction, increase revenue, and improve overall business performance by adopting CRM systems (Tucmeanu et al., 2022).

3.1. CRM System Features

CRM systems store and manage customer data, such as contact information, purchase history, communication history, preferences, and interactions across several touchpoints. CRM delivers a comprehensive perspective of each customer, allowing businesses to understand their preferences, wants, and habits. CRM improves sales team performance by tracking sales prospects, managing leads, and automating sales procedures. CRM systems enable targeted marketing campaigns, automate email marketing, and track campaign effectiveness.

CRM allows efficient customer service management, such as ticketing, issue resolution, and customer feedback management. CRM systems provide data analysis and reporting tools to spot trends, monitor performance, and acquire insights into customer behavior. CRM systems often integrate with other business applications like ERP, marketing automation, and e-commerce systems to streamline data flow and enhance functionality.

3.2. Benefits of CRM Systems

Enhanced Customer Experience: CRM enables personalized interactions, ensuring customers receive relevant and timely communication.

Improved Sales Productivity: CRM automates sales processes, tracks leads, and provides sales reps with valuable customer insights, leading to increased productivity and sales efficiency.

Better Customer Retention: CRM systems help businesses identify and address customer concerns promptly, reducing churn rates and improving customer loyalty.

Targeted Marketing Campaign: CRM solutions frequently link with other business software such as ERP, marketing automation, and e-commerce systems to improve data flow and functionality.

Mobile Access: Many CRM systems provide mobile applications that allow sales personnel and customer care representatives to access customer data and manage interactions while on the road.

3.3. CRM Implementation Difficulties

Data Quality and Integrity: It can be difficult to ensure the accuracy and completeness of consumer data, especially when moving data from legacy systems.

User Adoption: Successful CRM deployment necessitates employee buy-in, and certain employees may be resistant to embracing new processes or technologies.

Integration Difficulty: Integrating CRM with other existing systems can be difficult, and appropriate planning is required to ensure smooth data flow.

3.4. Supply Chain Planning (SCP)

Supply Chain Planning (SCP) systems are software solutions that optimize and streamline supply chain operations planning and execution. SCP systems assist firms in properly managing the movement of commodities, information, and cash from the point of origin to the point of sale. These systems make demand forecasting, inventory management, production scheduling, and distribution planning easier, ensuring that the appropriate products are available at the right place and right time while minimizing costs and maximizing efficiency.

4. KEY COMPONENTS AND FEATURES OF SUPPLY CHAIN PLANNING (SCP) SYSTEMS

Demand Forecasting: SCP systems employ historical data and advanced forecasting algorithms to reliably predict future demand for items.

Inventory Optimization: SCP systems assist firms in optimizing inventory levels by establishing safety stock levels, reorder points, and economic order quantities.

Production Planning and Scheduling: SCP systems aid in the planning of production schedules, resource allocation, and capacity planning to fulfill demand while minimizing production costs.

Distribution Planning: SCP systems optimize distribution networks and transportation routes to ensure timely delivery of items to clients while lowering transportation costs.

Cooperation and Visibility: SCP systems enable real-time visibility into the supply chain, allowing for enhanced cooperation and decision-making among various stakeholders.

Scenario Planning: SCP systems enable firms to perform "what-if" scenarios to assess the impact of various supply chain decisions and modifications.

Risk Management: SCP systems aid in identifying and mitigating supply chain risks such as material flow disruptions or logistics concerns.

Performance Monitoring and Analytics: SCP systems provide analytics and reporting capabilities to monitor supply chain performance, track key performance indicators (KPIs), and identify areas for improvement.

Integration with Other Systems: SCP systems can integrate with other enterprise systems such as ERP, CRM, and Warehouse Management Systems (WMS) to optimize data flow and increase overall efficiency.

4.1. Advantages of Supply Chain Planning (SCP) Systems

Improved Forecasting Accuracy: SCP systems improve demand forecasting accuracy, lowering inventory carrying costs and stockouts.

Optimized Inventory Management: SCP aids in the reduction of excess inventory and holding expenses while guaranteeing that products are available when required.

Enhanced Operational Efficiency: SCP improves supply chain procedures, reducing lead times and enhancing overall operational efficiency.

Better Customer Service: By optimizing inventory and distribution, SCP systems increase order fulfillment and delivery times, resulting in higher customer satisfaction.

Cost reduction: SCP systems assist in identifying cost-saving alternatives such as transportation efficiency and supplier collaboration.

Increased Agility: SCP enables firms to respond swiftly to changes in demand, supply, or market situations.

4.2. Implementation of Supply Chain Planning (SCP) Difficulties

Data Quality and Integration: SCP deployment necessitates correct and timely data from several sources, demanding data integration and validation.

Complexity and scalability: Supply chains can be complex and dynamic, needing SCP systems to manage vast amounts of data and adapt to changing situations.

Cross-Functional Collaboration: SCP needs collaboration between different departments, and its implementation necessitates cooperation and buy-in from various stakeholders.

System Integration: Integrating SCP solutions with existing corporate systems can be difficult and may necessitate adaptation and careful planning.

4.3. Human Resources Management System

It is a business system created primarily to streamline and automate numerous human resource-related procedures within an organization. HRMS software assists HR departments in effectively managing their workforce, optimizing HR operations, and increasing employee satisfaction. HRMS's primary features and functionalities include the following:

Employee Information Management: Human resource management systems (HRMS) centralize employee data such as personal information, job details, qualifications, and work history. This guarantees that personnel records are correct and up to date.

Payroll Management: Human resource management systems (HRMS) automate payroll procedures such as wage computations, tax deductions, and benefits administration. It contributes to the accuracy and timely payment of employees.

Time and Attendance Tracking: Human resource management systems (HRMS) allow employees to enter their working hours, leave requests, and attendance, giving HR teams real-time data for attendance tracking and handling time-off requests.

Recruitment and Onboarding: HRMS aids in the recruitment process, from advertising job positions to application monitoring and interview management. It can also help to speed up the onboarding process for new employees.

Performance Management: Human resource management systems (HRMS) make performance assessments, goal planning, and performance reviews easier. It assists managers and employees in monitoring progress and identifying opportunities for improvement.

Training and Development: HRMS helps HR teams manage employee training programs, track employee progress, and save training records.

Employee Self-Service: Human resource management systems (HRMS) frequently feature a self-service portal that allows employees to access and update their personal information, check payslips, submit leave requests, and access HR-related documents.

Helps in Administration: HRMS assists in the administration of employee benefits such as health insurance, retirement programs, and other perks. It automates the enrollment and tracking of benefits.

Compliance and Reporting: HRMS aids in the compliance of labor laws and regulations by providing reports, tracking employee certifications, and keeping compliance records.

Analytics and Insights: HRMS gives useful insights and data analytics on employee performance, workforce demographics, and other HR metrics to HR professionals and management.

Employee Engagement and Feedback: Some HRMS systems provide employee surveys and feedback channels to assess employee satisfaction and engagement.

By assuring effective workforce management and employee engagement, an HRMS can considerably improve HR department efficiency and contribute to overall organizational performance. It also aids in the reduction of paperwork, the reduction of errors, and the reduction of costs.

5. BUSINESS INTELLIGENCE (BI)

Business intelligence is a collection of technology, processes, and tools that enable organizations to collect, analyze, and present data from multiple sources to assist data-driven decision-making and strategic planning. The basic purpose of business intelligence (BI) is to convert raw data into meaningful and actionable insights that can be used to gain a competitive edge, improve business performance, and find new possibilities.

The following are key components of Business Intelligence:

Integrating data from numerous sources, such as databases, spreadsheets, cloud services, and applications, into a centralised data warehouse or data repository is an essential step in the process of doing business intelligence (BI), which requires collecting data from a wide variety of sources. Querying, data mining, and statistical analysis are just some of the methods that can be used to analyse data with the help of business intelligence tools, which give companies the ability to review data using a range of methods. The identification of patterns, trends, and linkages amongst the data is facilitated by the use of these methodologies.

Data visualisation tools, like as charts, graphs, and dashboards, are made available by business intelligence systems. These tools make it possible for complex data to be presented in a manner that is both visually appealing and simple to comprehend. Reports on key performance indicators (KPIs) and other significant metrics can be generated by business intelligence (BI) systems. These reports comprise data that has been summarised and arranged in a logical fashion. These reports are widely utilised by executives and managers in order to evaluate performance and make decisions pertaining to strategy.

Some business intelligence solutions make it possible for non-technical people to independently access data and conduct analyses without having to rely on IT personnel for every data-related action. Users are able to construct their own reports and analyses through the usage of self-service business intelligence. Business intelligence (BI) can integrate models of predictive analytics to estimate future patterns and results based on existing data. This can help companies better anticipate changes in the market as well as the behaviour of their customers. Methods of data governance are widely utilised by BI systems in order to guarantee the data's high quality, maintain data security, and comply with relevant regulations.

5.1. Advantages of Business Intelligence

Informed Decision-Making: Business intelligence (BI) provides fast and reliable insights, allowing firms to make well-informed decisions based on data-driven facts.

Competitive Advantage: Organizations that use BI effectively get a competitive advantage by better knowing their market, customers, and competitors.

Increased Efficiency: BI automates data analysis and reporting operations, saving human labor and increasing overall operational efficiency.

Agility and Adaptability: The ability of the organization to adjust swiftly to changing market conditions and make agile decisions.

Improved Customer Experience: Business intelligence enables firms to obtain insights into customer behavior and preferences, resulting in better customer service and satisfaction.

Cost Savings: BI can uncover cost-cutting possibilities and inefficiencies, assisting in financial optimization.

5.2. Business Process Management

Business Process Management is a methodical technique for designing, implementing, monitoring, and optimizing business processes inside an organization. By optimizing processes and aligning them with company goals, BPM strives to improve efficiency, effectiveness, and agility. It entails identifying, documenting, automating, and continuously improving routines to obtain better results and increase overall performance.

6. KEY COMPONENTS OF BUSINESS PROCESS MANAGEMENT INCLUDE

Process Modelling: BPM begins with process modeling, which involves visually representing business processes with flowcharts, diagrams, or process maps. This stage assists stakeholders in comprehending the overall flow of activities, roles, and decision points.

Process Automation: BPM is frequently used to automate repetitive and manual tasks using software tools or workflow engines. Automation eliminates human errors, speeds up procedures, and maintains uniformity.

Process Execution: BPM ensures that business operations are consistently and efficiently carried out by set rules and norms.

Process Monitoring: BPM systems continuously monitor business process performance by tracking key performance indicators (KPIs) and other data. Real-time monitoring aids in the identification of bottlenecks and opportunities for improvement.

Process Analysis: Process data and performance metrics are analyzed in BPM to discover inefficiencies and opportunities.

Process Optimization: Based on the findings, BPM enables process improvement projects to optimize workflows, reduce costs, and improve quality and customer satisfaction.

Process Reengineering: In some circumstances, BPM may include reengineering processes from the ground up to achieve significant improvements or solve fundamental issues.

Process Governance: BPM implements governance measures to guarantee that processes are aligned with organizational strategies and comply with applicable legislation and standards.

6.1 Benefits of BPM

Enhanced Efficiency: BPM streamlines workflows, removes redundancies, and lowers manual interventions, resulting in greater process efficiency and productivity.

Improved Customer Experience: By improving processes, businesses may produce better products and services, resulting in more customer satisfaction.

Data-Driven Decision-Making: Through process analytics, BPM provides useful insights that assist firms in making data-driven decisions for continuous improvement.

Cost Reduction: BPM detects and eliminates superfluous steps, lowering operational costs and wasting resources.

Compliance and Risk Management: BPM ensures that processes are by applicable regulations and decreases the risk of errors and non-compliance.

Transparency and Accountability: BPM increases process transparency, making it easier to assign ownership and accountability for each stage.

Overall, Business Process Management is a helpful technique for firms looking to streamline their operations, generate innovation, and maintain a market competitive edge. It promotes an organizational culture of constant development and efficiency.

7. CONCLUSION

Enterprise software has the potential to completely revamp the way in which firms operate and communicate with their clientele. As the digital era unfolds, these powerful tools have become increasingly crucial for achieving success in today's competitive landscape and retaining that success over time. We have seen how business applications may serve as the basis for increasing productivity, enhancing workflows, and fostering more collaboration at every level of an organisation. Leveraging the capabilities of these integrated solutions enables businesses to unearth hidden potentials, streamline procedures, and capitalise on growth opportunities.

In addition, we have observed that corporate applications have a significant influence on the level of satisfaction experienced by customers. These technologies enable businesses to truly grasp their consumers' expectations and to exceed those expectations in a variety of ways, including by providing individualised experiences and proactive customer support. Through the utilisation of data-driven insights and cutting-edge analytics, businesses have the opportunity to forge profound and meaningful connections with their clientele, hence increasing consumer loyalty and advocacy.

Nevertheless, our journey has not been devoid of its share of challenges. Adoption and installation of corporate apps require careful planning, rigorous execution, and a proactive approach to overcome any hurdles. This is because adoption and installation of corporate apps cannot occur without these elements. Data security, change management, and seamless integration are just few of the hurdles that need to be conquered. However, with the right strategy and a dedication to innovation, these challenges may be addressed, which will result in amazing growth and success.

Your business will be able to expand its horizons, surmount challenges, and prosper in an environment that is constantly evolving so long as you have the power of these applications available to you. We are working to prepare the way for a future in which every business will thrive on the foundations of efficiency and customer happiness. Please allow this knowledge to be the spark that ignites change and creativity as we do so. The choices are essentially endless, and we have merely scratched the surface of our path to perfection.

REFERENCES

Al-Maaitah, D. A., Tha'er Majali, M. A., & Almaaitah, T. A. (2021a). The role of leadership styles on staffs' job satisfaction in public organizations. *Journal of Contemporary Issues in Business and Government*, *27*(1), 772–783.

Al-Maaitah, T. A., Tha'er Majali, M. A., & Almaaitah, D. A. (2021b). The Impact of COVID-19 on the Electronic Commerce Users Behavior. *Journal of Contemporary Issues in Business and Government*, *27*(1), 772–783.

Arslan, F., Singh, B., Sharma, D. K., Regin, R., Steffi, R., & Rajest, S. S. (2021). Optimization technique approach to resolve food sustainability problems. In *2021 International Conference on Computational Intelligence and Knowledge Economy (ICCIKE)*. IEEE. 10.1109/ICCIKE51210.2021.9410735

Balas-Timar, D. (2015). Relationship between job performance and job satisfaction viewed from the chaos theory perspective. *International Journal of Education and Research*, *3*(3), 517–534.

Balas-Timar, D., & Ignat, S. (2015). Conceptual applicant screening model with fuzzy logic in industrial organizational contexts. *Procedia: Social and Behavioral Sciences*, *203*, 257–263. doi:10.1016/j.sbspro.2015.08.291

Batool, K., Zhao, Z.-Y., Irfan, M., & Żywiołek, J. (2023). Assessing the role of sustainable strategies in alleviating energy poverty: An environmental sustainability paradigm. *Environmental Science and Pollution Research International*, *30*(25), 67109–67130. doi:10.100711356-023-27076-0 PMID:37103699

Buttle, F. (2016). *Customer relationship management: Concepts and tools*. Routledge.

Chopra, S., & Meindl, P. (2019). *Supply chain management: Strategy, planning, and operation*. Pearson.

Davenport, T. H., & Harris, J. G. (2007). *Competing on Analytics: The New Science of Winning*. Harvard Business Review Press.

Demeter, E., Rad, D., & Balas, E. (2021). Schadenfreude and General Anti-Social Behaviours: The Role of Violent Content Preferences and Life Satisfaction. BRAIN. *Broad Research in Artificial Intelligence and Neuroscience*, *12*(2), 98–111. doi:10.18662/brain/12.2/194

Dumas, M., La Rosa, M., Mendling, J., & Reijers, H. A. (2018). *Fundamentals of Business Process Management*. Springer. doi:10.1007/978-3-662-56509-4

Enterprise Resource Planning. (2021). Retrieved October 20, 2023, from indiamart.com website: https://m.indiamart.com/proddetail/enterprise-resource-planning-21681980191.html

ERP Management System. (2020, June 19). Retrieved October 20, 2023, from PT. Centra Rekayasa Enviro website: https://cr-enviro.com/new/?page_id=284

Gupta, R. K. (2019). *HRMS (Human Resource Management System)*. Concepts, Applications, and Challenges. Excel Books.

Gupta, R. K. (2021a). A study on occupational health hazards among construction workers in India. *International Journal of Enterprise Network Management*, *12*(4), 325–339. doi:10.1504/IJENM.2021.119663

Gupta, R. K. (2021b). Adoption of mobile wallet services: an empirical analysis. *International Journal of Intellectual Property Management, 12*(3), 341 – 353. doi:10.1504/IJIPM.2021.10035526

Gupta, R. K. (2022). Utilization of Digital Network Learning and Healthcare for Verbal Assessment and Counselling During Post COVID-19 Period. Technologies. *Artificial Intelligence and the Future of Learning Post-COVID*, *19*, 117–134.

Kavanagh, M. J., Thite, M., & Johnson, R. D. (2017). *Human Resource Information Systems: Basics, Applications, and Future Directions*. SAGE Publications.

Khan, M. A., Kumar, N., Mohsan, S. A. H., Khan, W. U., Nasralla, M. M., Alsharif, M. H., Żywiołek, J., & Ullah, I. (2023). Swarm of UAVs for network management in 6G: A technical review. *IEEE Transactions on Network and Service Management*, *20*(1), 741–761. doi:10.1109/TNSM.2022.3213370

Kumar, V., & Reinartz, W. (2016). *Customer relationship management: Concept, strategy, and tools*. Springer.

Laudon, K. C., & Laudon, J. P. (2020). *Management information systems: Managing the digital firm*. Pearson.

Mohsan, S. A. H., Othman, N. Q. H., Khan, M. A., Amjad, H., & Żywiołek, J. (2022). A comprehensive review of micro UAV charging techniques. *Micromachines*, *13*(6), 977. doi:10.3390/mi13060977 PMID:35744592

Ogunmola, G. A., Singh, B., Sharma, D. K., Regin, R., Rajest, S. S., & Singh, N. (2021). Involvement of distance measure in assessing and resolving efficiency environmental obstacles. In *2021 International Conference on Computational Intelligence and Knowledge Economy (ICCIKE)*. IEEE. 10.1109/ICCIKE51210.2021.9410765

Payne, A., & Frow, P. (2013). *Strategic customer management: Integrating relationship marketing and CRM*. Cambridge University Press. doi:10.1017/CBO9781139057417

Rad, D., Balas, E., Ignat, S., Rad, G., & Dixon, D. (2020b). A Predictive Model of Youth Bystanders' Helping Attitudes. *Revista romaneasca pentru educatie multidimensionala-Journal for Multidimensional Education, 12*(1Sup2), 136-150.

Rad, D., Balas, V., Lile, R., Demeter, E., Dughi, T., & Rad, G. (2020c). Statistical Properties of a New Social Media Context Awareness Scale (SMCA)-A Preliminary Investigation. *Sustainability (Basel), 12*(12), 5201. doi:10.3390u12125201

Rad, D., & Demeter, E. (2020). A Moderated Mediation Effect of Online Time Spent on Internet Content Awareness, Perceived Online Hate Speech and Helping Attitudes Disposal of Bystanders. *Postmodern Openings, 11*(2, Supl 1), 107–124. doi:10.18662/po/11.2Supl/182

Rad, D., Dughi, T., & Demeter, E. (2019). The Dynamics of the Relationship between Humor and Benevolence as Values. *Revista romaneasca pentru educatie multidimensional-Journal for Multidimensional Education, 11*(3), 201-212.

Rad, D., Egerau, A., Roman, A., Dughi, T., Balas, E., Maier, R., & Rad, G. (2022). A Preliminary Investigation of the Technology Acceptance Model (TAM) in Early Childhood Education and Care. BRAIN. *Broad Research in Artificial Intelligence and Neuroscience, 13*(1), 518–533. doi:10.18662/brain/13.1/297

Reddy, M. K. (2016, February 7). *1.IIB introduction*. Retrieved October 20, 2023, from IIB Developer website: https://iibdeveloper.wordpress.com/2016/02/07/how-to-learn-ibm-integration-bus/

Roman, A., Rad, D., Egerau, A., Dixon, D., Dughi, T., Kelemen, G., & Rad, G. (2020). Physical Self-Schema Acceptance and Perceived Severity of Online Aggressiveness in Cyberbullying Incidents. *Journal of Interdisciplinary Studies in Education, 9*(1), 100–116. doi:10.32674/jise.v9i1.1961

Shanks, G., Seddon, P. B., & Willcocks, L. (Eds.). (2018). *Enterprise resource planning: Concepts and practice*. Routledge.

Sharda, R., Delen, D., Turban, E., & King, D. (2017). *Business Intelligence, Analytics, and Data Science: A Managerial Perspective*. Pearson.

Sharma, D. K., Jalil, N. A., Regin, R., Rajest, S. S., Tummala, R. K., & Thangadurai. (2021a). Predicting network congestion with machine learning. In *2021 2nd International Conference on Smart Electronics and Communication (ICOSEC)*. IEEE.

Sharma, D. K., Singh, B., Raja, M., Regin, R., & Rajest, S. S. (2021b). An Efficient Python Approach for Simulation of Poisson Distribution. In *2021 7th International Conference on Advanced Computing and Communication Systems (ICACCS)*. IEEE.

Sharma, D. K., Singh, B., Regin, R., Steffi, R., & Chakravarthi, M. K. (2021c). Efficient Classification for Neural Machines Interpretations based on Mathematical models. In *2021 7th International Conference on Advanced Computing and Communication Systems (ICACCS)*. IEEE.

Sharma, K., Singh, B., Herman, E., Regine, R., Rajest, S. S., & Mishra, V. P. (2021d). Maximum information measure policies in reinforcement learning with deep energy-based model. In *2021 International Conference on Computational Intelligence and Knowledge Economy (ICCIKE)*. IEEE. 10.1109/ICCIKE51210.2021.9410756

Sherman, R. (2014). *Business Intelligence Guidebook: From Data Integration to Analytics*. Morgan Kaufmann.

Simchi-Levi, D., Kaminsky, P., & Simchi-Levi, E. (2019). *Designing and managing the supply chain: Concepts, strategies, and case studies*. McGraw-Hill Education.

Smith, J. D., & Johnson, A. B. (2018). *Human Resource Management Systems: Strategy, Implementation, and Effectiveness*. Pearson.

Sumner, M. (2018). *Enterprise resource planning*. Pearson.

Tristan Boutros. (2023). *The Process Improvement Handbook*. McGraw–Hill Education.

Tucmeanu, E. R., Tucmeanu, A. I., Iliescu, M. G., Żywiołek, J., & Yousaf, Z. (2022). Successful management of IT projects in healthcare institutions after COVID-19: Role of digital orientation and innovation adaption. *Healthcare (Basel)*, *10*(10), 2005. doi:10.3390/healthcare10102005 PMID:36292452

Wisner, J. D., Tan, K. C., & Leong, G. K. (2019). *Principles of supply chain management: A balanced approach*. Cengage Learning, UK.

Żywiołek, J., Tucmeanu, E. R., Tucmeanu, A. I., Isac, N., & Yousaf, Z. (2022). Nexus of transformational leadership, employee adaptiveness, knowledge sharing, and employee creativity. *Sustainability (Basel)*, *14*(18), 11607. doi:10.3390u141811607

Chapter 11
Intelligent Business Sustainability on Marketing System

M. Parveen Roja
PSNA College of Engineering and Technology, India

Shashank Agarwal
https://orcid.org/0009-0003-7679-6690
CVS Health, USA

Amrita Baid More
https://orcid.org/0000-0002-7440-9138
Prestige Institute of Management and Research, India

K. Bogeshwaran
Dhaanish Ahmed College of Engineering, India

A. Nagarajan
Dhaanish Ahmed College of Engineering, India

S. Manikandan
Dhaanish Ahmed College of Engineering, India

ABSTRACT

The information age, with the usage of big data, has created opportunities for smart marketing systems. Marketing data intelligence systems accelerate product innovation and growth strategies with the information obtained from the data mining techniques about the marketing stakeholders. The implementation and adaptation of creative, intelligent technologies aid marketers in speedy decisions and sustainable competitive strategies to gain a competitive advantage in the market that would help the organization's sustenance over the long term. This chapter explains marketing intelligence, its quotient, relevant theories, evolution, framework, the transformation of marketing intelligence systems from digital marketing to social engineering, the tools of marketing intelligence, and the benefits of marketing intelligence.

DOI: 10.4018/979-8-3693-2193-5.ch011

1. INTRODUCTION

The traditional approach to marketing intelligence considers the collection of data from surveys and internal sources on market competition, industry, and customers (Grooms, 2001). However, the contemporary approach to marketing intelligence considers data mining techniques and models to uncover marketing data intelligence (Kozlenkova et al., 2014). According to Huster (2005) and Efrat et al. (2017), "marketing intelligence is defined as the process of gathering information on customers, competitors, markets, and industry through data mining techniques and then is applied to strategic marketing plans (David Rajesh et al., 2015; Abu-Rumman, 2021).

1.1. Marketing Intelligence Quotient

The Marketing Intelligence Quotient measures the closeness of business organizations with their customers effectively and efficiently through their strong and intensive customer-centric approaches (Efrat et al., 2017). It ensures a better understanding of the customers so that the organizations can offer the right choices to the right customers (fig.1).

Figure 1. Marketing intelligent systems
Source: Grooms (2001)

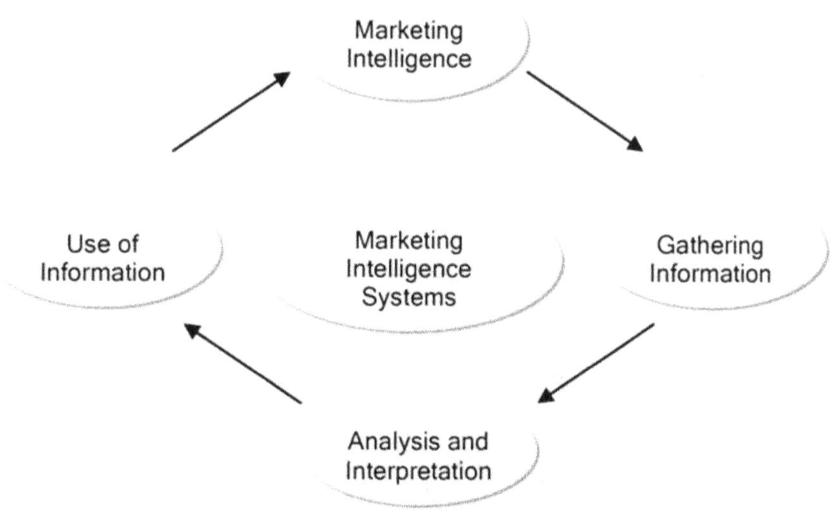

1.2. Theoretical Background

The marketing intelligence system is based on the resource-based theory (Barney, 1991; Al Shraah et al., 2013),), which states that organizations have to develop their capabilities to exploit the resources and gain a competitive advantage for sustainable development (Kozlenkova et al., 2014).

The market-based view or market positioning states that instead of a myopic view of inherent characteristics, the organization has to utilize the opportunities in the existing market environment to achieve a competitive advantage (McGee, 2015).

1.3. Evolution of Marketing Intelligence

Three waves of marketing intelligence are identified in the retail scenario (Festervand et al., 1988). The first wave used barcode scanning technology in product placement strategies like allocation, assortment, price, display, promotion, and feature advertising and also evaluated the outcome of sales turnover and margin (Huster, 2005; Gupta, 2021a; 2022). The second wave of marketing intelligence applied technologies like loyalty points, credit, and debit cards to track their purchase history, analyze those behavioral attributes, and design promotional communications for the targets (Gedenk et al., 2006; Al Shraah et al., 2022). The third-wave marketing intelligence system uses real-time tracking technologies like portable shipping devices, GPS, RFID, video, and clickstream that identify the customer path to the site, the factors affecting that and the purchase likelihood, etc. (Pio et al., 2021; Venkateswaran et al., 2018), to understand customer behavior and design the layout and atmospherics of the store, using navigational aids, placing products adjacently, managing queues and crowds in improving service levels and conducting in-store events and the outcome of these activities can be evaluated through the store path and traffic, penetration of aisle, dwelling time to know the amount of time spent by the customers in the particular location of the store, interaction time and conversion rate (Lies, 2019; Abu-Rumman and Qawasmeh, 2021) (fig.2).

Figure 2. Marketing intelligence framework
Source: Dam et al. (2019)

2. COMPONENTS OF MARKETING INTELLIGENCE

2.1. Market Intelligence

Market intelligence refers to the collection of wide sources of information about various exogenic factors like competition, government regulations, technology upgradations, and sociocultural, economic, and political environments to catch up with the changing trends, preferences, and needs of the customers in the current and future scenarios in both the existing and new markets (McGee, 2015; Tripathi & Al-Shahri, 2023).

These data may be collected from traditional sources like sales reports, customers, comparatively expensive research surveys, and the latest inexpensive open sources such as whitepapers and blogs (Venkateswaran et al., 2019).

2.2. Customer Intelligence

Customer intelligence means identifying their preferences and needs through the behavior of the customer segments based on their status, culture, lifestyle, habits, customs, and culture (Venkateswaran et al.,2018,2019). It includes identification, attraction, retention, and development of customers (Srivastava & Roychoudhury, 2020). The sources for this information may be their purchase history, billing records, surveys, and other customer relationship management (CRM) information that are available internally within the organization's website and their search information, including clickstream logs, server logs, cookies, internet protocol, searched web pages, e-commerce websites, and the competitors' sites, communication and their pattern in social media and their credit scores that are available externally (Khaled Lafi Al-Naif and Ata, 2018).

2.3. Product Intelligence

Product intelligence relates to product insights to enhance customer satisfaction and cash in on existing opportunities (Al-maaitah et al., 2021a). It includes product development and product recommendations. These insights may be sourced from websites, forums, blogs, reviews, feedback, and identifying needs through user-generated mining and web content that also satisfies the dual purpose of serving both the organization and the consumers as an idea generation and recommendation system (Srivastava & Roychoudhury, 2021).

2.4. Competitor Intelligence

Competitor intelligence means the capability of competing organizations in terms of their strengths and weaknesses to predict their strategies based on the information about their marketing mix, including their tactical decisions on price, product, marketing channels, advertising communications and promotions, and their relevant effectiveness on their brand performance, reputation, and profits (Al-maaitah et al., 2021).

3. DATA MINING MODELS FOR MARKETING INTELLIGENCE

Classification: Classification differentiates the customers based on the characteristics attributable to the behavior of the cluster (Mert, 2022). This classification can be done through data mining techniques like Naïve Bayes techniques, decision trees, if-then-else rules, support vector machines, neural networks, genetic algorithms, and market basket analysis (Vashishtha & Dhawan, 2023).

Association: The association enables the finding of the purchase pattern of customers in buying related products based on which the organizations can decide on the bundling marketing strategies (Bose & Mahapatra, 2001; Seng & Chen, 2010). Association techniques include Apriori algorithms, statistics, and association rules (Kuragayala, 2023).

Clustering: Clustering profiles, the users into segments. The clustering techniques include Naïve Bayes technique, K-means, neural networks, market basket analysis, self-organizing map, and RFM analysis (recency, frequency, monetary) techniques (Ocoró et al., 2023).

Regression: Regression finds the causal factors explaining the behavior of the customers. The regression techniques include linear regression, logistic regression, ordinal regression, and multiple regression (Venkateswaran & Viktor, 2023).

Prediction: Prediction predicts the future behavior of the customers based on the associated characteristics identified from the historical data. The prediction techniques include linear regression models, logistic model prediction neural networks, market basket analysis, and survival analysis (Srinivas et al., 2023).

Sequence discovery: Sequence discovery identifies the associations of behaviors observed from the previous purchase and information search records over a period of time. Sequence discovery techniques include set theory and statistics (fig.3).

4. BENEFITS OF MARKETING INTELLIGENCE

Marketing intelligence supports marketers to make the right decisions whenever required since it provides insights into their consumer behavior, based on which they can predict their future sales, finalize their budgets to optimize the performance of their operations through different channels of marketing, and after carefully considering the risks analyzed (María et al., 2023).

Marketing intelligence helps the entire organization to match the product demand and customer expectations and enables an optimal process, achieving cost efficiency and thus enhancing the quantitative sales performance, profitability, market share, and qualitative customer satisfaction and loyalty, resulting in their long-term relationship and customer value creation (Pandit, 2023).

4.1. Impact of Marketing Intelligence Systems on Competitive Strategies

The market leader may adopt strategies to increase the demand, protect the existing market, and expand the market, encouraging potential customers and motivating the existing customers to use the same product in multiple contexts. A marketing intelligence system provides customer insights that may be well-targeted for increasing sales.

Figure 3. Marketing intelligence systems as digital marketing techniques

The market challenger, with their similarity in financial strength and the size of the organization and its network, may attempt to pose a threat to the leader. However, they need to reduce the risk and define the right marketing strategies after careful consideration, which is very well possible with the marketing intelligence system, which highlights their strengths and weaknesses in comparison with the market leader (Gupta, 2021).

The market follower learns the strategies of the leader and tries to imitate the leader's strategies and products to earn reasonable profit without direct competition. They can exercise this by even attempting in new markets. The marketing intelligence system provides details about the prospective gaps that the follower can identify and adopt the leader's strategies to gain market share.

The niche marketer is usually a small-scale operator who identifies the unique, unexplored segments and offers innovative solutions for the unsatisfied needs of those segments. Again, the marketing intelligence system provides this information that enables niche marketers to identify, innovate, and follow up on prospective unique segments.

4.2. Managing Uncertainties

Highly unpredictable market situations are generally characterized by volatility in sales, cut-throat competition, and shortened product life cycles. The marketing information system provides the support of data and processed information about the market that aids the managerial decisions and thus gives a chance to cope with uncertain and unpredictable market situations. Fuzzy logic may be used to model the manager's perception of sales and the performance of the organization.

4.3. Impact on Retailing

The retail stores use various technologies like infrared light beams, mounted video cameras, door-closure switches, and pressure-sensitive mats. The data from these devices may be used to calculate the conversion rates, comparing them with the point-of-sale (POS) generated billing details. Enabling computer tracking, retailers can use thermal maps to find the percentage of customers penetrating each section of the shop. This data is very useful for retailers to revise the layout, reposition the displays, and design the appropriate push advertisements to clear the slow-moving merchandise and optimize the merchandise plan and purchase.

Combining the transaction data and traffic data and also the computer simulations can help to calculate the category-wise purchase and conversion rates that, in turn, can be used for comparison across time, regions, products, and stores. Moreover, it could aid in staffing adjustment strategies, changing the digital signs and other store-specific atmospherics to take the momentary shifts in strategies in real time.

Soft computing can be applied to model retail operations, competitive advertising, and pricing. The automated self-checkout information system helps the customers find the product on the relevant shelf, scan the products they place on the cart, and pay in cash or card the amount notified by the PSA at the checkout, generating the bill transferred from the PSA.

The automated self-checkout information system and Radio frequency identification (RFID) enable the retailer to be cost-conscious and make their stores lean. RFID enables retailers to generate the data warehouse of customers' psychographic and demographic profiles and the inventory position in retail stores. RFID helps retailers to retrieve product details like expiry, batch, and price easily.

5. IMPACT ON SUPPLY CHAIN MANAGEMENT

Fuzzy logic helps to improve the quick-response reorder system. Soft computing configures the coordinated supply chain system. The fuzzy controller generates the weekly reorder for every SKU individually. The fuzzy-controlled neural network (FCNN) provides accurate predictions for what-if scenarios, especially for seasonal product inventory management. RFID helps to track the integrated availability of products on shelves, stores, warehouses, and in transit so as to place the replenishment orders well in time considering the lead time.

5.1. Impact on Brand Promotions

Fuzzy controllers instantly generate personalized and automated advertisements based on the viewer's behavior. Soft computing using a fuzzy neural-genetic simulator would help to arrive at a decision support system to determine the pricing and promotional strategy based on the competitors' pricing and promotions. Case-based reasoning may be used to devise timely periodic promotional strategies based on the predictions.

5.2. Impact on Sales Performance

Neural networks and sales computing help to predict the sales of the organization. Neural networks are very useful for industry forecasts aggregating the industry-wide individual retailers' predicted sales. Collaborative filtering can be applied to promote the purchase of cross categories, applying the market basket analysis and recommender systems.

5.3. Impact on Segmentation

Fuzzy logic, neural networks, and their combination in the form of soft computing segments the customers so as to target them distinctively. Fuzzy logic reduces the ambiguity in classifying the overlapping segments considering the multiple characteristics, especially the qualitative characteristics like attitude, which are not very precise in linguistic form. Recommender systems offer recommendations to those individuals based on the attributed similarity of their behavior to the identified clusters. At present, recommender systems are used in voice commerce, video commerce, and e-commerce. Neural networks are highly useful for clustering complicated customer segments using a large database with hundreds of variable characteristics. Soft computing combining neuro-genetic techniques helps to identify the important predictor variables to identify the customers from the database for targeted marketing.

6. IMPACT ON CUSTOMER EXPERIENCE

A fuzzy inference system predicts the potential churn of the customers using the experiential knowledge of the managers or retailers about the churners. That could be used by the marketers to apply suitable strategies to solve the real-time problems of these potential churners in their consumption journey and prevent customer defection, which causes huge savings to the organization by reducing the cost arising out of customer churn (Atasever, 2023).

6.1. Modeling Consumer Behavior

Neural networks and the hybrid soft computing model the repurchase situations when using different channels of marketing so as to identify the optimum channel for maximizing sales. The neural network applies the recency, frequency, and monetary value (RFM) variables to eliminate the irrelevant variables and increase the predictive power of the repurchase models. Bayesian neural network predicts the RFM classifiers more accurately by including the non-RFM variables like duration of customer relationship and the usage of credit provision (David Rajesh et al., 2015).

6.2. Sources for Marketing Intelligence

Market intelligence collects information about everything related to the market, from the changing patterns of buying and customer preferences in the market to competitor activities, whereas competitive intelligence collects information about the strengths, futuristic plans, weaknesses, and strategies of competitors. They can be collected through various sources that include the following:

6.3. Contribution of Sales Force

In those organizations where salesmen play a key role in the distribution channel, they can use the knowledge and information of these salesmen to pass on the information to their manufacturing or service organizations about the pulse of the distributors, customers, and competitors in the market. According to Festervand et al. (1988), organizations can involve salesmen in the planning and designing of the operation of the marketing intelligence system.

Internet: The Internet enables the collection of huge macro-environmental data, competitors, markets, industries, and consumers.

Printed publications: Information about the consumers, competitors, suppliers, political, economic, cultural, and technological changes could very well be gauged from the traditional printed forms like reports, magazines, newspapers, books, and pamphlets.

Employees: Employees have a long association with the suppliers, customers, and other stakeholders of the business, and hence, they provide valuable insights about their behavior. They contribute a significant level of intelligence that aids managerial decisions.

Intermediaries: The intermediaries like distributors, dealers, stockists, retailers agents, and wholesalers relay the recent trends to the organization.

Industrial events: Conferences, associations, and trade fairs discuss the contemporary developments in the industry that provide valuable insights for managerial decisions.

Research Consultancies: The observations, experiments, and surveys conducted reveal the behavior of customers that can be presented in the comparative analysis of the differences in approach, styles, strategies, media, and budgets of the competitors.

Product/service test: Feedback from customers, especially first-time users, can be used to judge the performance of the product or service

Customers: Collecting information about the concerns, opinions, attitudes, and needs of existing and potential customers can be helpful in segmentation, targeting, and positioning strategies.

Competitors: Information about the competitors can be obtained from their employees, broadcasts, consultants, product re-engineering, and published reports.

6.4. Marketing Intelligence From Online Discussion

Online discussions like boards, forums, and blogs pertaining to the product can be analyzed with techniques like wrap, computational linguistics, text search, and classification to gather and explain the online behavior of the customers. It can be used for alerting customers early based on the prediction of the occurrence of critical incidents, tracking the buzz to find the trending ideas, and mining their sentiments to extract their aggregate opinion. Using open-source data, web mining, the Internet of Things (IoT), blogs, and microblogs also add to the data that can be further analyzed for their insights.

7. MARKETING INTELLIGENCE SYSTEMS AS DIGITAL MARKETING TECHNIQUES

Data-driven marketing: Big data, otherwise termed data-driven marketing, aligns the system of digital records of data of online transactions, be it a purchase or search, or any other form, target, process, and evaluation of outcomes.

Search engine marketing intelligence: It applies the outside-in approach to use the customer data gathered from digital communications, processes, and channels. Search engines like Google, Yahoo, and Bing use machine learning, deep learning, artificial intelligence, and artificial neural networks to improve the quality of the search results based on keyword optimization.

Microtargeting using social media: Micromarketing or targeting is viable for marketers to use the self-seed data provided by social media users in the form of shares, likes, comments, photos, and posts to identify and target the customer segments either through mass-customized or individualized communications or promotions. That, too, especially in geo-marketing, the location-specific services or communications are shared with mobile users using the sensor technology that can be used for push and pull marketing strategies.

Real-time marketing: It helps marketers design their outbound marketing strategies with streaming analytics to follow customer transactions, get to know their moods and emotions through social listening by tracking the social media behavior and the audio and videos they watch, and capitalize those moments to individualize their promotions and communications to attract the attention of those customers. This real-time data is also useful in recommendation marketing and dynamic pricing (fig.4).

Recommendation marketing: Recommender systems filter the choices based on past behavior and use social engineering techniques that influence users in compromising their information by creating trust and reputation to suggest the choices preferred by the customers, thus reducing the complexity of vast choices.

Dynamic pricing: Dynamic pricing enables optimizing pricing through automated price adjustments based on demand and availability, impacting the service industries like the hospitality industry, the travel industry, and even those products and services that function based on auctioneering strategy.

Proximity marketing: Smartphones with semantic web and global positioning system (GPS) help to identify the customers and use near field communication (NFC) to handle the customers' interaction through their mobile and point of sale, including the mobile touchpoints in the customer experience journey.

Semantic marketing: Open application programming interfaces (API) and chatbots use semantics and nomenclatures to offer artificial intelligence, virtual assistants, messaging services, and speech recognition to enhance customer services in customer relationship management.

Predictive marketing: Predictive marketing uses machine learning that captures images, speech, and data to determine the marketing strategies, including the predictive pricing for the products or services based on the chance of occurrence of the expected outcome derived from the observed data on the recurring behavior of the customers.

Touchpoint marketing: In the integrated marketing automation, digitalizing the touchpoints from perception, evaluation, intention, purchase, post-purchase, repurchase, and word-of-mouth recommendations at a faster pace with the required information like the programmatic advertisements that are presented automatically to meet the real-time situation enhancing the customer journey.

Figure 4. Marketing intelligence system as a transformation of social engineering

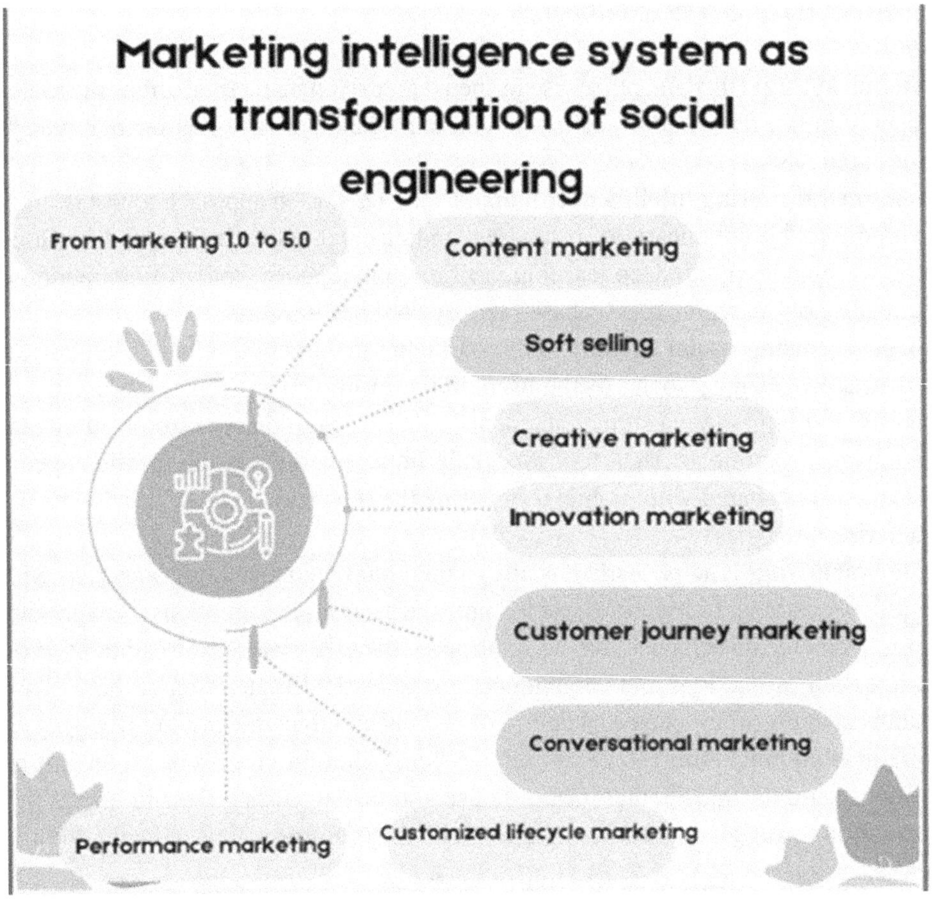

Content marketing: Social media, being the hybrid element of marketing, provides both inbound and outbound content where communication occurs between the organization and the customers and among the customers. With the attractiveness of information shifted towards edutainment, content marketing focuses on sharing media content and presenting attractive advertisements to create awareness of products, services, or ideas matching the customers' special interest rather than simply using the buy appeal.

Soft selling: The search engine provides the choice of inbound marketing, which can be used for interactive advertisements that exercise the pull strategy, influencer marketing that uses the content, search optimization, and brand-oriented social media marketing communications. Customized communications through mobile enable micro-targeting and recommender systems in real-time.

Creative marketing: It deals with creating new solutions even through crowd-sourcing for micro-segments targeted for specific characteristics observed through collective intelligence like location-specific and weather-specific communications shared with the smart communication devices.

Innovation marketing: Open-source intelligence initiates innovation driven by the data, users, events, social problems, and research that can be used in new product development and existing product or service improvements (Luigi Pio Leonardo Cavaliere et al., 2021).

Customer journey marketing: Marketing intelligence provides continuous online and offline support to potential customers in their consumption journey by providing relevant information at distinct touch points from perception, consideration, evaluation, purchase, and post-purchase decisions.

Conversational marketing: The usage of voice control mechanisms and virtual digital assistants uses artificial intelligence to recognize, comprehend, and comply with consumer choices and instructions to make consumption convenient.

Customized lifecycle marketing: Customizing the product life cycle to match the individual customer lifecycle requirements generates the personalized marketing experience that enables marketers to enhance customer relationship management with their online individual data collected, compiled, and clustered on the characteristics of the stage in their life cycle.

Performance marketing: Performance marketing measures the effectiveness of the digital marketing processes and their outcomes to optimize and undertake modification mechanisms in their marketing and promotional strategic approach.

8. CONCLUSION

Fuzzy logic devises models based on if-then rules comprehending human behavior. Fuzzy logic includes controls like speed, improvement in production, and economic and financial decisions. Fuzzy logic controllers combined with RFID generate information useful for behavioral marketing strategies. Neural networks use algorithms and constructs learned from behavioral data to forecast the behavior of different segments of customers. They are very useful in predicting risky customer behavior in the financial sector.

Soft computing uses a combination of neural networks, fuzzy logic, and algorithms to derive hybrid intelligence for modeling consumer behavior for different strategic applications. Soft computing combining neuro-fuzzy techniques enables one to learn and adapt to determine the independent task settings in a better way. Case-based reasoning learns consumer behavior using the k-nearest neighbor method to predict their decisions. Collaborative filtering learns the behavior of different clusters of consumers and generates recommendations that suit their likes and preferences.

In the digital transformation era, smart marketing using the marketing information system exploits marketing data intelligence through the application of data mining on specific functions of the marketing intelligence components and marketing mix elements. This intelligence system helps organizations to stand ahead of the competitive clutter and share the considerable market pie. With distinctive strategies, they retain their existing customers and attract potential customers by serving them better with the in-depth understanding gained from the insights on their behavior provided by the analytical findings of the marketing intelligence system.

REFERENCES

Abu-Rumman, A. (2021). Effective Knowledge Sharing: A Guide to the Key Enablers and Inhibitors. In D. Tessier (Ed.), *Handbook of Research on Organizational Culture Strategies for Effective Knowledge Management and Performance* (pp. 133–156). IGI Global. doi:10.4018/978-1-7998-7422-5.ch008

Abu-Rumman, A., & Qawasmeh, R. (2021). Assessing international students' satisfaction of a Jordanian university using the service quality model. *Journal of Applied Research in Higher Education*. doi:10.1108/JARHE-05-2021-0166

Al-maaitah, D. A., Tha'er Majali, M. A., & Almaaitah, T. A. (2021). The role of leadership styles on staffs job satisfaction in public organizations. *Journal of Contemporary Issues in Business and Government*, *27*(1), 772–783.

Al-maaitah, T. A., Tha'er Majali, M. A., & Almaaitah, D. A. (2021a). The Impact of COVID-19 on the Electronic Commerce Users Behavior. *Journal of Contemporary Issues in Business and Government*, *27*(1), 772–783.

Al-Naif, K. L., & Al Shraah, A. E. M. (2018). Working capital management and profitability: Evidence from Jordanian mining and extraction industry sector. *IUG Journal of Economics and Business.*, *2*(1), 42–60.

Al Shraah, A., Abu-Rumman, A., Alqhaiwi, L. A., & AlSha'ar, H. (2022). The impact of sourcing strategies and logistics capabilities on organizational performance during the COVID-19 pandemic: Evidence from Jordanian pharmaceutical industries. *Uncertain Supply Chain Management*, *10*(3), 1077–1090. doi:10.5267/j.uscm.2022.2.004

Al Shraah, A., Irtaimeh, H. J., & Rumman, M. A. (2013). The Strategic Human Resource Management Practices in Implying Total Quality Management (TQM): An Empirical Study on Jordanian Banking Sector. *International Journal of Management*, *4*(5), 179–190.

Atasever, M. (2023). Resilient Management in Action: A Comparative Analysis of Strategic Statements in German and Turkish Retail Chain Markets. *FMDB Transactions on Sustainable Management Letters*, *1*(2), 66–81.

Barney, J. (1991). Firm resources and sustained competitive advantage. *Journal of Management*, *17*(1), 99–120. doi:10.1177/014920639101700108

Dam, N. A. K., Le Dinh, T., & Menvielle, W. (2019). Marketing Intelligence from Data Mining Perspective. *International Journal of Innovation, Management and Technology*, *10*(5), 184–190. doi:10.18178/ijimt.2019.10.5.859

David Rajesh, Manimaran, & Venkateswaran. (2015). A study on the linkage between service quality, service loyalty and customer satisfaction in commercial banks in Madurai, Tamil Nadu, India. *International Journal of Contemporary Research in Humanities and Social Sciences, 2*(1), 89-103.

Efrat, K., Gilboa, S., & Yonatany, M. (2017). When marketing and innovation interact: The case of born-global firms. *International Business Review*, *26*(2), 380–390. doi:10.1016/j.ibusrev.2016.09.006

Festervand, T. A., Grove, S. J., & Eric Reidenbach, R. (1988). The sales force as a marketing intelligence system. *Journal of Business and Industrial Marketing*, *3*(1), 53–59. doi:10.1108/eb006051

Gedenk, K., Neslin, S. A., & Ailawadi, K. L. (2006). Sales Promotion. In *Retailing in the 21st Century* (pp. 345–359). Springer Berlin Heidelberg. doi:10.1007/3-540-28433-8_22

Grooms, B. T. F. (2001). *Marketing Intelligence: Executive Management Perceptions of Value* [Doctoral thesis]. Brunel University.

Gupta, R. K. (2021). A study on occupational health hazards among construction workers in India. *International Journal of Enterprise Network Management, 12*(4), 325–339. doi:10.1504/IJENM.2021.119663

Gupta, R. K. (2021a). Adoption of mobile wallet services: an empirical analysis. *International Journal of Intellectual Property Management, 12*(3), 341 – 353. doi:10.1504/IJIPM.2021.10035526

Gupta, R. K. (2022). Utilization of Digital Network Learning and Healthcare for Verbal Assessment and Counselling During Post COVID-19 Period. Technologies. *Artificial Intelligence and the Future of Learning Post-COVID, 19*, 117–134.

Huster M. (2005). *Marketing Intelligence: A First Mover Advantage*. Academic Press.

Kozlenkova, I. V., Samaha, S. A., & Palmatier, R. W. (2014). Resource-based theory in marketing. *Journal of the Academy of Marketing Science, 42*(1), 1–21. doi:10.100711747-013-0336-7

Kuragayala, P. S. (2023). A Systematic Review on Workforce Development in Healthcare Sector: Implications in the Post-COVID Scenario. *FMDB Transactions on Sustainable Technoprise Letters, 1*(1), 36–46.

Lies, J. (2019). Marketing intelligence and big data: Digital marketing techniques on their way to becoming social engineering techniques in marketing. *International Journal of Interactive Multimedia and Artificial Intelligence, 5*(5), 134. doi:10.9781/ijimai.2019.05.002

María, J. J. L., Polo, O. C. C., & Elhadary, T. (2023). An Analysis of the Morality and Social Responsibility of Non-Profit Organizations. *FMDB Transactions on Sustainable Technoprise Letters, 1*(1), 28–35.

McGee, J. (2015). *Market-based view*. Wiley Encyclopedia of Management., doi:10.1002/9781118785317.weom120075

Mert, I. (2022). *Assessment of Accounting Evaluation Practices, A Research-Based Review of Turkey and Romania. Springer Cham.*

Ocoró, M. P., Polo, O. C. C., & Khandare, S. (2023). Importance of Business Financial Risk Analysis in SMEs According to COVID-19. *FMDB Transactions on Sustainable Management Letters, 1*(1), 12–21.

Pandit, P. (2023). On the Context of the Principle of Beneficence: The Problem of Over Demandingness within Utilitarian Theory. *FMDB Transactions on Sustainable Social Sciences Letters, 1*(1), 26–42.

Pio, L., Cavaliere, L., Mangalasserri, K., Venkateswaran, P. S., Byloppilly, R., & Effendy, F. (2021). The Impact Of Brand Counterfieting on Consumer Behavior In the Fashion Sector. *Turkish Journal of Physiotherapy and Rehabilitation, 32*(3), 19831–19847.

Srinivas, K., Velmurugan, P. R., & Andiyappillai, N. (2023). Digital Human Resources and Management Support Improve Human Resources Effectiveness. *FMDB Transactions on Sustainable Management Letters, 1*(1), 32–45.

Srivastava, D. K., & Roychoudhury, B. (2020). Words are important: A textual content based identity resolution scheme across multiple online social networks. *Knowledge-Based Systems, 195*, 105624. doi:10.1016/j.knosys.2020.105624

Srivastava, D. K., & Roychoudhury, B. (2021). Understanding the Factors that Influence Adoption of Privacy Protection Features in Online Social Networks. *Journal of Global Information Technology Management, 24*(3), 164–182. doi:10.1080/1097198X.2021.1954416

Tripathi, S., & Al-Shahri, M. (2023). Problems and Prospects on the Evolution of Advertising and Public Relations Industries in Oman. *FMDB Transactions on Sustainable Management Letters, 1*(1), 1–11.

Vashishtha, E., & Dhawan, G. (2023). Comparison of Baldrige Criteria of Strategy Planning and Harrison Text. *FMDB Transactions on Sustainable Management Letters, 1*(1), 22–31.

Venkateswaran, D. R. P. S., Sabarirajan, D. R. A., Rajest, S. S., & Regin, R. (2019). The theory of the postmodernism in consumerism, mass culture and globalization. *Journal of Research on the Lepidoptera, 50*(4), 97–113. doi:10.36872/LEPI/V50I4/201075

Venkateswaran, P. S., Sabarirajan, A., & Arun, B. (2018). Impact of customer satisfaction on brand loyalty towards e-home appliances in Madurai. *International Journal of Exclusive Management Research*, 162–165.

Venkateswaran, P. S., & Viktor, P. (2023). A Study on Brand Equity of Fast-Moving Consumer Goods with Reference to Madurai, Tamil Nadu. *FMDB Transactions on Sustainable Technoprise Letters, 1*(1), 13–27.

Chapter 12
Block Overflow on Frequently Asked Questions Using Blockchain

Jyoti P. Kanjalkar
https://orcid.org/0000-0002-4064-7189
Vishwakarma Institute of Technology, India

Rushikesh Kahat
Vishwakarma Institute of Technology, India

Sankalp Mahesh Kokse
Vishwakarma Institute of Technology, India

Sanket Katale
Vishwakarma Institute of Technology, India

Nishchay Ramchandani
Vishwakarma Institute of Technology, India

Pramod Kanjalkar
Vishwakarma Institute of Technology, India

ABSTRACT

This work shows how blockchain technology can evolve in our day-to-day lives and we can benefit from it. Much of the modern research work related to blockchain technology emphasizes its application for cryptocurrencies like Ethereum, bitcoin, etc. Blockchain technology is way more than cryptocurrency, and it can have various applications in the domain of finance, government, the banking industry, accounting, etc. Therefore, this study attempts to explore opportunities and their issues. The proposed system emphasizes the use of blockchain in frequently asked questions (FAQ) systems. The basic idea of the proposed system is that the questionnaire will post a question with an appropriate bounty amount and time so that others from the community can answer the question. The most upvoted answer is rewarded with a bounty amount. This transaction is carried out using blockchain technology. This helps to understand the level of contribution experience a person might have and is worthy in the eyes of the developer community for a reward.

DOI: 10.4018/979-8-3693-2193-5.ch012

1. INTRODUCTION

The software known as the "Frequently Asked Questions" (FAQ) system allows members of a community to publish their inquiries or concerns at the same time. Other members of the community then respond with an acceptable response to the same question that was asked. Some of the systems have incorporated reward mechanisms in order to encourage more efficient replies. In which the response that is deemed to be most appropriate will be rewarded. If that is not the case, then many questions remain unsolved. The usage of blockchain technology is suggested for use in incentive systems due to the security, dependability, and speed benefits it offers.

The distributed data store is the most important component of a blockchain. Everyone participating in this distributed network has their own data store in which they keep track of all of the information relating to the transactions that have ever taken place on the network. These transaction records are encrypted before being saved in a series of blocks that are linked together. The chain of participants or peers is required to acknowledge the most current block of transactions at each stage of the technological process. The agreement is established by a process that involves the assent of the majority, the deletion of duplicate entries, double expenditure, and other similar activities. Due to the cryptographic layering of blocks and the elimination of duplicate entries, the agreed blockchain is not only irreversible but also immutable. This is possible due to the fact that the blockchain cannot be altered. It is not possible for any of the participants in this technology to improvise or edit the 'transaction history' of the events within this technology without first receiving majority consent from the chain.

Blockchain is a decentralised and distributed digital ledger technology that enables secure and transparent record-keeping of transactions across a network of computers. Blockchain was developed by Satoshi Nakamoto, who is referred to as the "father of cryptocurrency." Although it is the technology that underpins cryptocurrencies like Bitcoin and other digital currencies, its uses go well beyond those of digital currencies. Because it offers a method of data recording and transfer that is both tamper-proof and verifiable, blockchain technology has the potential to bring about a revolution in a variety of different markets. Blockchain's decentralized structure has the ability to shake up existing company models by eliminating the need for middlemen and enhancing the transparency and safety of digital transactions. This could cause traditional business models to become obsolete. However, it is vital to take into consideration the problems that are involved with the implementation of blockchain technology, such as scalability, regulatory issues, and energy usage.

The ability of blockchain technology to solve multiple problems plaguing the digital world and open up new avenues of exploration is the primary reason for its significance. The following are some of the most important characteristics that emphasize the significance of blockchain technology: Blockchain eliminates the need for a central authority or intermediary in transactions. This decentralized nature enhances trust among participants, as the entire network collectively validates and agrees on the state of the ledger. This is particularly significant in scenarios where trust is a critical factor, such as financial transactions and supply chain management.

Blockchain uses cryptographic techniques to secure transactions and maintain data integrity. Once a block is added to the chain, it becomes extremely difficult to alter its information due to the interdependence of blocks and the use of cryptographic hash functions. This immutability makes blockchain a secure and tamper-resistant technology. Participants in a blockchain network have identical access to the data that is being stored on the network. All relevant parties are able to view transactions, which increases transparency and decreases the likelihood of fraudulent activity. This function is especially helpful in supply chain management, which places a premium on being able to track things from the point of manufacture all the way to delivery.

The use of intermediaries is something that blockchain technology has the potential to eradicate, which will result in significant process efficiencies. This may result in transactions that are completed more quickly and at a lower cost. For instance, in the realm of financial services, blockchain technology has the potential to enable peer-to-peer transactions that do not require the participation of banks as intermediaries. Contracts that are automatically executed and whose terms are encoded straight into code are referred to as smart contracts. They automate the enforcement of commercial agreements and reduce the necessity for middlemen, hence reducing the likelihood of mistakes or fraudulent activity. This functionality has applications in a variety of sectors, including legal contracts, automated payment systems, and insurance policies, to name a few.

Blockchain operates on a global network of computers, making it accessible from anywhere in the world. This global accessibility is particularly significant for international transactions, as it can simplify and expedite cross-border payments. Blockchain enables the creation of digital assets and cryptocurrencies. Tokenization involves representing real-world assets, such as real estate or art, as digital tokens on a blockchain. Cryptocurrencies like Bitcoin and Ethereum have introduced new decentralized forms of currency and financial instruments. Blockchain ensures data consistency across all nodes in the network. This can be valuable in industries where maintaining accurate and unaltered records is crucial, such as healthcare, where patient records need to be secure and accurate.

The decentralized and programmable nature of blockchain has spurred innovation and the creation of new business models. Startups and established companies alike are exploring ways to leverage blockchain for novel applications, from decentralized finance (DeFi) to non-fungible tokens (NFTs). While the significance of blockchain is substantial, it's important to note that challenges, including scalability, regulatory concerns, and energy consumption, need to be addressed for broader adoption in various industries. Nevertheless, the potential impact of blockchain on how we transact, verify information, and establish trust is considerable. While blockchain technology offers enhanced security features, it is not without its own set of security challenges. Some of the key security issues associated with blockchain include:

In a proof-of-work blockchain, a 51% attack occurs when a single entity or a group of entities gains control of more than 50% of the network's mining power. This enables them to control the consensus algorithm, potentially leading to double-spending and undermining the integrity of the blockchain. Double spending is a risk in digital transactions where the same cryptocurrency or digital asset is spent more than once. While blockchain is designed to prevent double spending, it becomes a concern in certain scenarios, especially if a malicious actor gains control of a majority of the network's mining power. Smart contracts are susceptible to bugs and vulnerabilities in the code. If a smart contract contains a flaw, it can be exploited, leading to financial losses or unauthorized access to sensitive information. The infamous DAO (Decentralized Autonomous Organization) incident in Ethereum's early days is an example of a smart contract vulnerability leading to significant losses.

The consensus algorithm used by a blockchain network is crucial for its security. If there are vulnerabilities in the consensus mechanism, it could be exploited by attackers to manipulate the network. For example, the "Nothing at Stake" problem is a concern in proof-of-stake systems where validators may have little to lose by validating multiple competing blockchain histories. While blockchain transactions are pseudonymous, meaning they are associated with addresses rather than real-world identities, there are still privacy concerns. Analyzing transaction patterns and network activity could potentially reveal the identities of users, compromising their privacy.

A Sybil attack occurs when a single entity controls multiple nodes on a network, allowing them to influence the network's behavior. In blockchain, this could involve creating numerous fake nodes to gain control over the consensus mechanism or to launch other attacks. Blockchain technology, especially in the context of cryptocurrencies, faces regulatory uncertainties and compliance challenges. Legal and regulatory frameworks vary widely across jurisdictions, and blockchain projects must navigate these complexities to ensure compliance with laws related to financial transactions, data protection, and more.

As the number of transactions on a blockchain increases, scalability becomes a concern. Scaling solutions, such as layer two protocols, are being developed, but ensuring both scalability and security remains a challenge. The complexity of smart contracts increases the likelihood of introducing vulnerabilities. Writing secure smart contracts requires careful auditing and testing to identify and eliminate potential security risks. Blockchain networks are only as secure as the nodes that make up the network. If a significant number of nodes are compromised, it can undermine the security of the entire network. Supply chain attacks, where malicious actors compromise the hardware or software supply chain of nodes, are a potential risk. Addressing these security issues requires a combination of robust technical solutions, ongoing research and development, collaboration within the blockchain community, and adherence to best practices in blockchain development and deployment. As blockchain technology evolves, efforts to enhance security measures and mitigate risks continue to be a priority.

2. LITERATURE REVIEW

Casino et al. (2019) discussed the history of blockchain, applications of the current status of blockchain, the importance of the same, the advantages of blockchain, and its limitations. Emerging applications of blockchain are in various domains such as finance, integrity verification, governance, public sector and user services, voting, IoT, healthcare, privacy and security, education, and many more. However, the drawbacks are the suitability of blockchain, scalability, quantum resilience, management of big data, etc., which are experienced at a slow rate.

Vazakidis et al. (2019) discussed and reviewed blockchain technologies and the business surroundings. Applications of blockchain for business environments are also explained. The blockchain classifies as the Public, Private, and (hybrid) Consortium blockchain. The public blockchain, as the name suggests, is accessible and available to all publicly. All nodes have equal authority over the blockchain, and nobody will have complete control. In the private blockchain, participants are to be invited into the ecosystem. It has an administrator who governs the user permissions. Hybrid blockchain contains both private and public nodes. Currently, Blockchain technology is not the replacement for inherited legacy systems or old applications. But it can definitely be a supportive application to legacy systems.

Marchesi et al. (2022) discussed that in the coming period, it may even head to the development of new systems. That is what we call the way to Web 3.0. They proposed a new (dApp) decentralized application architecture for blockchain with storage devices, communities, end-user types, and other components.

Application of Blockchain Technology in Electric Vehicle Charging Piles Based on Electricity The Internet of Things (IoT) has introduced a blockchain in the sector of the Internet of Things. Liu et al. (2022) find a solution for the limitations of the electricity market and examine the likelihood that blockchain technology will be applied to the current electricity market. They also implement blockchain technology in the electricity market and are implementing blockchain analytics in the non-traditional renewable energy electricity market.

Vairam et al. (2021) concluded that the use of blockchain technology helps in upgrading the current system, which also results in improved ways of conducting the election. It is used to try to prevent the disadvantages of centralized conventional voting procedures. Such Electronic Ganache is used to construct the voting mechanism and inspect the functioning of the voting process. Once the votes have been cast, it is stored as being unchangeable and untouchable by the voters. This existing EVM system's security concerns are addressed.

Muangkammuen et al. (2018) discussed that with LSTM in an automated FAQ chatbot, we model an artificial neural network. The Thai text is accepted by our chatbot as a query and offers solutions if the likelihood of the outcome is higher than the cutoff point in order to provide accurate responses. To date, system performance has been assessed, and it was discovered. A newly created chatbot system could answer 86.36% of queries. With 93.2% accuracy for the right responses. For upcoming work, in order to increase the precision of the model for categorization.

FAQs may facilitate the creation of question-answer systems and be effective and may thus be employed as a component of a sophisticated question-answer system. As the foundation of the FAQ, the database of FAQ has an important effect on the overall question-answer system's performance. Frauenthaler et al. (2020) refined the clustering algorithm and combined it with the use of a similarity algorithm so the database is automatically created. Using this technique doesn't require too much manual involvement, and the FAQ is created automatically. Compared to various vehicle construction techniques, the FAQ's covering produced using our technique is significantly bigger than others.

Current blockchain relay systems demand that the destination immediately validate each relayed block header. Because of this, using these results in significant running costs. Connections between blockchains based on Ethereum where validating on-chain block headers is computationally costly. To get around these restrictions, we provide a new relay. A technique combining the on-demand validation pattern provides financial motivation to lower the relay's operational costs across blockchains powered by Ethereum by up to ninety-two percent. Due to this relay system, decentralized blockchain interoperability, as well as Ethereum Classic, is practical (Pande & Chetty, 2018).

Pande & Chetty (2019) and Pande & Chetty (2021) categorized this method as also being used to create a reliable college recommendation system because it not only finds connections between the learned characteristics but also preserves them in upper layers.

3. METHODOLOGY/EXPERIMENTAL

Users can come on the Blockoverflow app and post their doubts, which they want to be answered by the community. Anyone can attempt the question and post their respective answers. Other peers from the community can come and either post their own answers to a doubt or upvote a posted answer.

Proposed System

The current system works on the following steps stated below:

Step 1. Firstly, any user from the community who has been eligible for the system, i.e., connected their respective account to the metamask, can answer the doubts asked on the system.

Step 2. Also, authorized users (authorized by blockchain technology) can give their upvotes for the answers posted.

Step 3. Now, the user who is going to post a doubt has to predefine a bounty time and bounty amount before posting a doubt.

Step 4. Bounty Time: It is the time period for which a stream of tokens will flow to the winner's account. One day is the minimum bounty time.

Step 5. *Bounty Amount:* It is the amount that is going to be transferred per second to the winner's account.

Total Amount=Bounty amount*Bounty Time*86400

Step 6. Initially, the winner is the doubt poster, and the next winner is the one who is at the top of the list of upvotes.

Step 7. The time for which the one has the most upvotes for the particular answer for that time stream of tokens will be directed to the metamask account.

Step 8. A stream of tokens will be redirected from one account to another according to the highest number of upvotes.

Need of Blockchain in the System

Blockchain has the potential to transform many different industries because it offers a method that is at once safe, transparent, and efficient for transferring information and carrying out financial transactions. The technology behind blockchain tackles a number of difficulties that are present across a variety of businesses and ushers in fundamental shifts. The following is a list of important requirements that blockchain technology can fulfill: Trust in a central authority is typically necessary for the operation of traditional centralised systems. This can be a weak spot in the defenses of the authority since it leaves it open to the possibility of being hacked, manipulated, or subject to errors. Because it runs on a decentralised network of nodes, blockchain does not require the existence of a centralised authority to function. Trust and safety are bolstered because of the distributed structure of the ledger and the processes for reaching consensus. Concerns of data manipulation, fraudulent activity, and breaches of data security are common in digital record-keeping and transaction processes.

Blockchain uses cryptographic techniques and a decentralized consensus mechanism to secure transactions. The immutability of the ledger ensures that once a block is added, it is practically impossible to alter. Lack of transparency and accountability can lead to inefficiencies, fraud, and disputes in various industries. All participants in a blockchain network have access to the same information, promoting transparency. Transactions are recorded in a tamper-resistant manner, enhancing accountability. Many processes involve multiple intermediaries, leading to delays, higher costs, and potential points of failure.

Blockchain enables peer-to-peer transactions, reducing the need for intermediaries. This can result in faster and more cost-effective processes. Manual execution and enforcement of contracts can be time-consuming, error-prone, and costly. Smart contracts automate the execution of contractual agreements based on predefined conditions, reducing the need for intermediaries and minimizing the risk of errors. Traditional financial systems and transactions can be limited by geographic boundaries and operational hours. Blockchain operates on a global network, providing accessibility and enabling faster and more efficient cross-border transactions. Ensuring the accuracy and consistency of data is crucial in various industries, such as healthcare and supply chain management.

Blockchain maintains data integrity through cryptographic hashes and consensus mechanisms, ensuring that data remains consistent across all nodes in the network. Traditional business models may face limitations in terms of innovation and adaptability. Blockchain has spurred innovation by enabling new business models, such as decentralized finance (DeFi), tokenization of assets, and novel applications in various industries. Many people worldwide lack access to traditional banking services. Cryptocurrencies and blockchain-based financial services can provide financial inclusion by allowing individuals to access and participate in the global economy without the need for traditional banking infrastructure.

Supply chains often lack transparency, leading to challenges in tracking and verifying the authenticity of products. Blockchain enables end-to-end visibility in supply chains, allowing stakeholders to trace the origin and movement of products, thus reducing fraud and ensuring quality. In summary, the needs addressed by blockchain include enhancing trust, security, transparency, and efficiency in various processes across industries. As blockchain technology continues to evolve, it is likely to find even more applications to meet emerging needs and challenges.

- Efficiency: Blockchain can increase the efficiency of processes by eliminating the need for intermediaries, reducing transaction costs, and speeding up settlement times.
- Security: Blockchain uses cryptographic techniques to secure the data and transactions on the network. Once a transaction is recorded on the blockchain, it cannot be altered or deleted, which makes it tamper-proof.
- Trust: Blockchain provides a trustless environment where parties can transact with each other without having to rely on intermediaries or third parties. This increases trust between parties and reduces the risk of fraud.

Figure 1. Functions of blockchain in the system

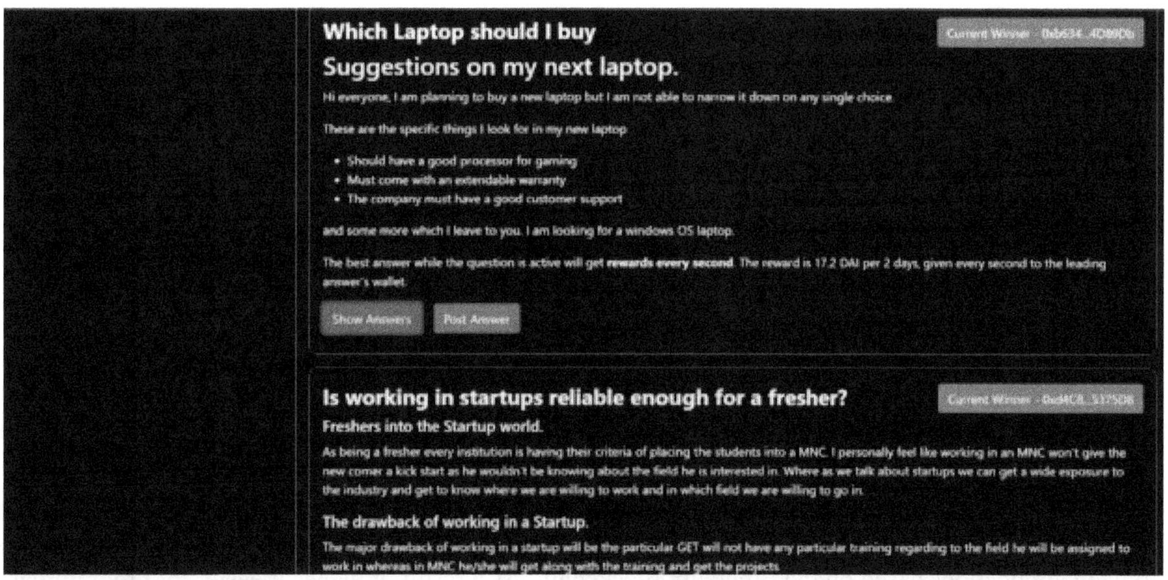

In the proposed system, blockchain technology first authorizes the user by connecting it to the metamask, which is a crypto wallet (Figure 1). Metamask confirms that the user is an authenticated one. And blockchain is responsible for transactions of ethers. Due to the use of blockchain technology, transaction efficiency increases. This also ensures security for transactions and trust and eliminates the chances of malicious practices (Figure 2).

Figure 2. Workflow of the system

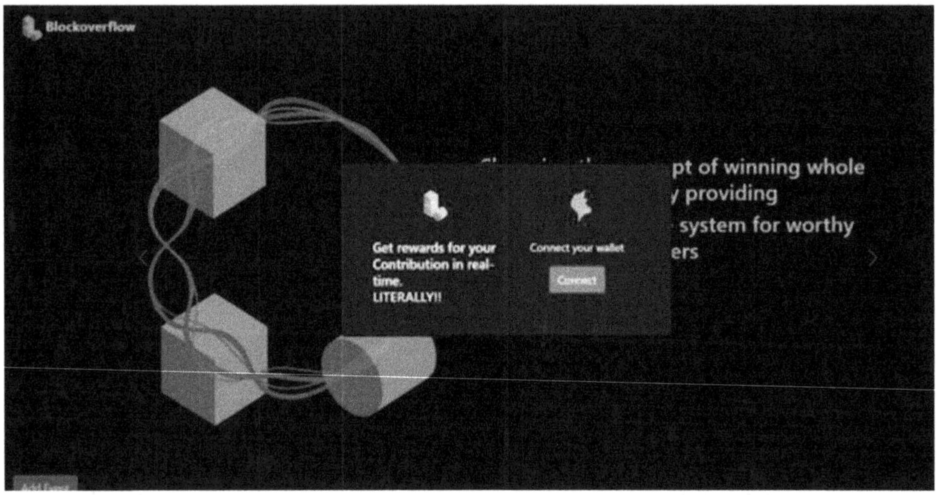

4. TECHNOLOGY USED

Solidity: Solidity is object-oriented; moreover, it is a contract-oriented programming language that is developed to implement smart contracts. Solidity is just languages like Python, JavaScript, and cpp, which also runs on Ethereum Virtual Machine (EVM).

Ethereum: Ethereum is a decentralized platform that is used to run blockchain applications. Applications that run the software precisely as it was written, with no chance of fraud, third-party influence, censorship, or downtime. Ethereum miners generate a cryptocurrency named Ether. These ethers are used to reward the computational operations performed to make the network secure.

Ethereum Virtual Machine: EVM is a runtime virtual platform for executing and implementing smart contracts in Ethereum. EVM mostly tries to concentrate on services for the security domain and executing untrusted code via a global network of open nodes. Denial-of-service (DoS) attacks are specifically protected against by EVM, which also confirms that the program doesn't have any access to each other's state (Figure 3).

Smart Contracts: Traditionally, contracts had a 3rd party person or authority through which contracts were completed. But Smart contracts are high-level program codes that do not require any third-party person or authority. Contracts are completed with some terms and conditions, and if those conditions are satisfied, contracts get completed. This program is written in a blockchain that is deployed to the Ethereum blockchain for further implementation. Solidity, Serpent, LLL Mutant, etc., are some of the programming languages that are used to write smart contracts (Figure 4).

Hardhat: It is an environment where blockchain developers compile, test, deploy, and debug decentralized applications based on the Ethereum blockchain. As a result, it makes it easier for programmers and developers to handle many of the responsibilities involved in creating Apps and smart contracts. Hard-hat gives developers additional, practical features in addition to the right tools they need to control this process. It also assists in automating some of these procedures (Figure 5).

Figure 3. User Interface

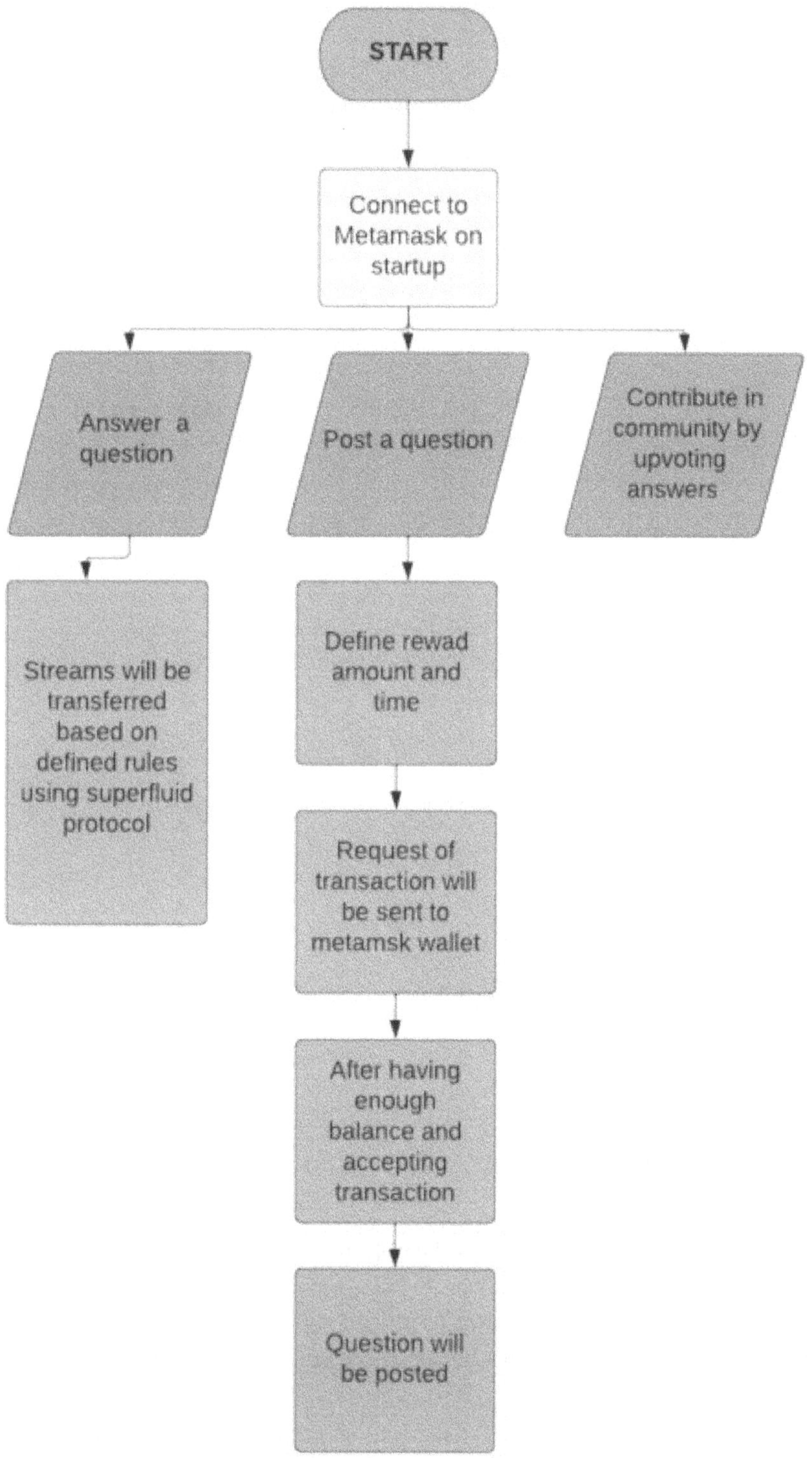

Figure 4. Question Section

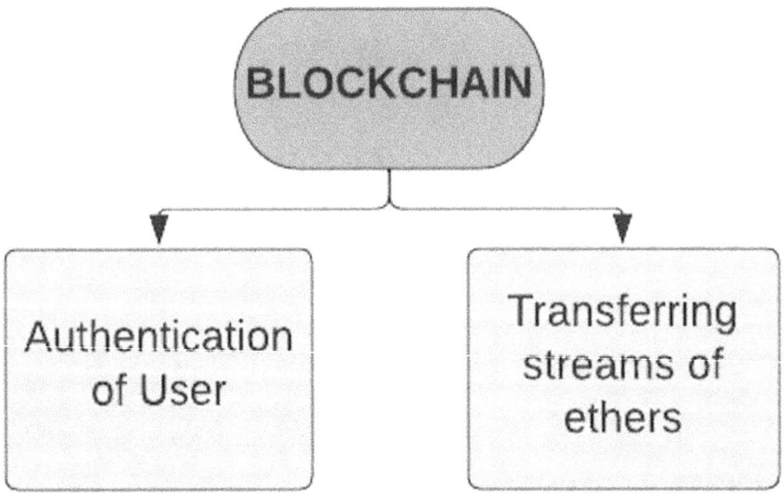

Figure 5. Superfluid

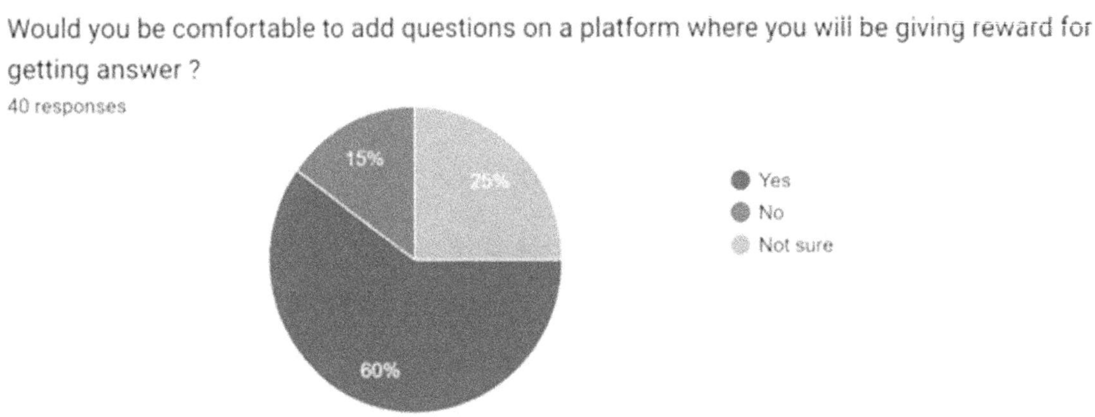

5. RESULTS AND DISCUSSIONS

The reward system of implemented FAQ system using blockchain has many advantages, as listed below (Figures 6 to 10):

Rapid Response: A questionnaire is going to reward with some bounty amount if one answers the most upvoted answer in a limited time. So, to get more rewards, we can have a rapid response to the asked questions.

Security: The use of blockchain in the transactions of rewards makes the system much more secure and reliable.

Abstraction: Overall, transaction details get abstracted when blockchain comes into the picture. So, no one is allowed to make changes in the history of transactions. And it all abstracts to contain an auditable and robust registry of all transactions.

The survey is conducted among the community to check whether adding rewards to the FAQ system makes any difference and to check the response of end users to the proposed system:

Figure 6. Survey responses Questionnaire 1

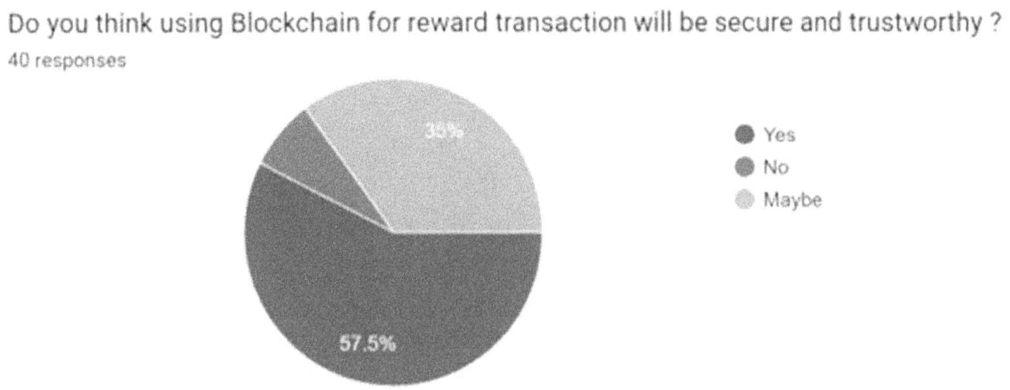

Almost 88% of the community is eager to respond quickly if they are awarded for the same.

Over 57% of respondents consider the use of blockchain as secure and trustworthy for reward transactions.

Figure 7. Survey responses Questionnaire 2

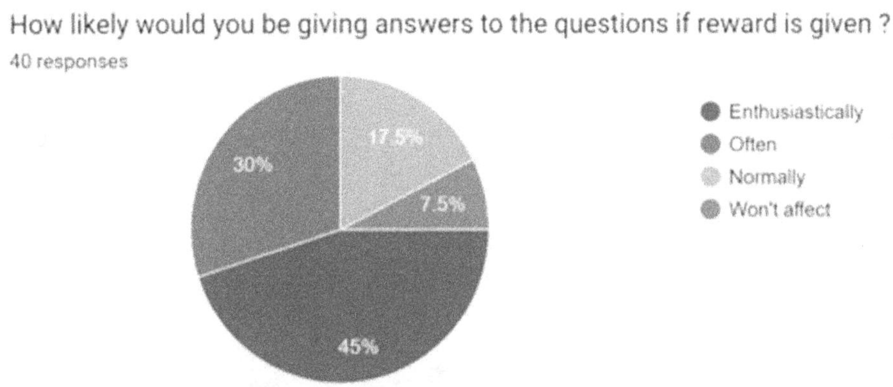

Figure 8. Survey responses Questionnaire 3

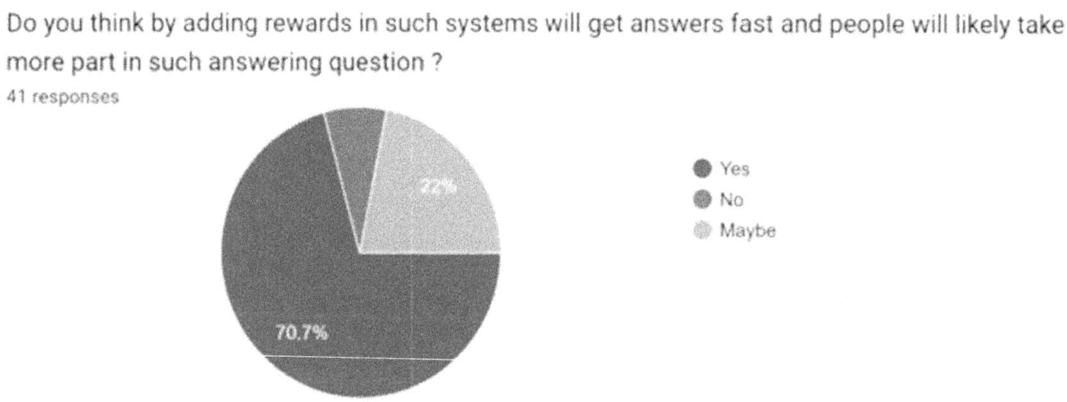

Figure 9. Survey responses Questionnaire 4

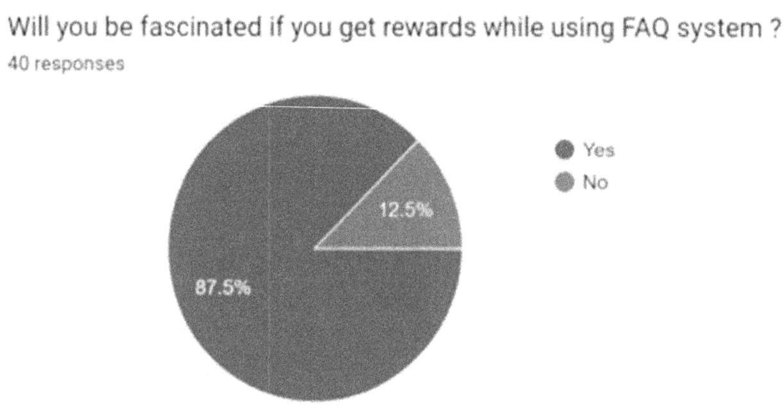

Figure 10. Survey responses Questionnaire 5

So, from the survey, it can be observed that adding a reward to the FAQ system makes a difference. Adding rewards in such a system can clearly make a difference as the response time given by the community is faster and is very necessary from both points of view as the questioner will get his answers fast and the answerer will get his reward as he participates and tries to be the top of the leaderboard of upvotes so that answerer can get the reward.

7. CONCLUSION

This will be helpful in understanding the amount of contribution experience one can have, as well as whether or not it is worthy in the eyes of the community of reward developers. The person who posts the doubt will have the ability to specify the amount of the reward, and if someone provides a satisfactory response, the contract will immediately begin depositing tokens representing the reward into the wallet of the contributor. Because of this, the environment is difficult, and there is a tremendous deal of room for improving the quality of each response. If another user receives a greater number of upvotes than you do, the reward stream will be redistributed to another user who is equally deserving. We are able to draw the conclusion that including prizes in the FAQ system plays a very significant impact. The meritorious response will be chosen by an automated system, and the level of accuracy will be the primary consideration in the process. Blockchain technology would be utilised in a variety of administrative processes, including voting, staff suggestion, institute reviews, and so on. Answers will be provided by automated bots, and they will be relevant to the particular subject area.

REFERENCES

Casino, F., Dasaklis, T. K., & Patsakis, C. (2019). A systematic literature review of blockchain-based applications: Current status, classification, and open issues. *Telematics and Informatics*, *36*, 55–81. doi:10.1016/j.tele.2018.11.006

Frauenthaler, P., Sigwart, M., Spanring, C., Sober, M., & Schulte, S. (2020). ETH relay: A cost-efficient relay for ethereum-based blockchains. In *2020 IEEE International Conference on Blockchain (Blockchain)*. IEEE. 10.1109/Blockchain50366.2020.00032

Liu, H., Lv, Z., Song, Z., Zhou, S., Liu, W., & Fang, M. (2022). Application of blockchain technology in electric vehicle charging piles based on electricity Internet of Things. *Wireless Communications and Mobile Computing*, *2022*, 1–10. doi:10.1155/2022/8533219

Marchesi, L., Marchesi, M., Tonelli, R., & Lunesu, M. I. (2022). A blockchain architecture for industrial applications. Blockchain. *Research and Applications*, *3*(4), 100088. doi:10.1016/j.bcra.2022.100088

Muangkammuen, P., Intiruk, N., & Saikaew, K. R. (2018). Automated Thai-FAQ Chatbot using RNN-LSTM. In *2018 22nd International Computer Science and Engineering Conference (ICSEC)*. IEEE.

Pande, S., & Chetty, M. S. R. (2018). Analysis of Capsule Network (Capsnet) Architectures and Applications. *Journal of Advanced Research in Dynamical and Control Systems*, *10*(10), 2765–2771.

Pande, S., & Chetty, M. S. R. (2019). Bezier Curve Based Medicinal Leaf Classification using Capsule Network. *International Journal of Advanced Trends in Computer Science and Engineering*, *8*(6), 2735–2742. doi:10.30534/ijatcse/2019/09862019

Pande, S. D., & Chetty, M. S. R. (2021). Fast medicinal leaf retrieval using CapsNet. In *Advances in Intelligent Systems and Computing* (pp. 149–155). Springer Singapore.

Vairam, T., Sarathambekai, S., & Balaji, R. (2021). Blockchain-based Voting System in Local Network. In *2021 7th International Conference on Advanced Computing and Communication Systems (ICACCS)*. IEEE.

Vazakidis, A., Kitsantas, T., & Chytis, E. (2019). A Review of Blockchain Technology and Its Applications in the Business Environment. *International Conference on Enterprise, Systems, Accounting, Logistics & Management*.

Chapter 13
Rise of Next Generation Entrepreneurs Through Innovative Digital Strategies in MSMEs During COVID-19

Raji Rajan
Jain University, India

Mariam Mathen
Jain University, India

Megha Garud
Jain University, India

Melanie Elizabeth Lourens
Durban University of Technology, South Africa

ABSTRACT

This study's primary goal is to identify the difficulties and barriers experienced by MSMEs in India during COVID-19. The chapter discusses the recent trend of small businesses with a lot of creativity and innovation, which opened doors to next-generation entrepreneurship. MSMEs' adoption of technological innovations has been uneven and slow despite the fact that the growing digital economy has given entrepreneurs new opportunities for client service. The conceptual framework is based on the literature overview on the pandemic's effects on MSMEs and the decline in the growth of the economy. It can be concluded that the government understands the various challenges faced by MSMEs and offers various support. In the post-pandemic world of an expanding global digital economy, MSME owners' digital adoption and practices are still shaped by rival companies, suppliers, consumers, and other members of their peer group. In such cases, the entrepreneurs must implement new digital strategies to transform the business, which will facilitate their resilience and self-reliance.

DOI: 10.4018/979-8-3693-2193-5.ch013

1. INTRODUCTION

In an economy where consumer demand is the dominant driver of growth, small businesses' ability to adapt, pivot, and use ingenuity to survive may not be sustainable. Growth is essential for the sustainability of any business venture. Business plans should be able to increase their relative market share and earnings in a stringent regulatory environment. The global pandemic has sunk consumer confidence to new lows, with the Treasury Department of India's monthly survey index recording 49.9 in September, the lowest level ever (Sanghera, 2020). India already struggled to give its people enough jobs, and the country's inflation rate is unusually high, putting household income under strain and potentially posing insurmountable challenges for many struggling small businesses.

The Indian government has launched a $42 billion collateral-free credit scheme to assist cash-strapped micro, small, and medium enterprises (MSMEs). According to government figures, around $20 billion had reached businesses as of November. Medium-sized and small-sized companies, as well as entrepreneurship, account for over one-third of India's GDP. But still, the industry is more vulnerable to catastrophes like the recent epidemic since it frequently has fewer resources than major businesses. The digital reboot has enabled the adoption of frictionless, electronic technology for money transfers, the opening of diverse markets, and the acceleration of employment by tech-focused enterprises. Digitalisation enabled remote working during the pandemic and tried to rebalance the workforce from migration towards metropolitan cities for new job opportunities.

1.1. MSMEs: Definition and Categorisation

The Micro, Small and Medium Enterprises Development (MSMED) Act, 2006 extensively recognised the potential and contribution of the Small-Scale Industry (SSI) sector; the act expanded the definitions and coverage of the sector, defining medium enterprises and recognising the concept of "enterprises" to include the manufacturing and services sectors. The MSMEs of Manufacturing Enterprises and Service Enterprises have been divided into micro, small, and medium enterprises, as indicated, based on the amount invested in Plant and machinery and the amount invested in equipment, respectively.

A notification regarding the implementation of the revision to the MSMEs criteria in India was released by the Ministry of MSME. As of July 1, 2020, the revised definition and criterion are in place. Beginning in 2006, the MSME Development Act went into force. On May 13, 2020, the latest revision was revealed following a 14-year hiatus. The definition of micro, small, and medium-sized enterprises was revised under this most recent version. The MSME investment and turnover limits were updated to reflect the present financial climate (Table 1).

Table 1. Composition guidelines: Annual turnover and plant and machinery/equipment investment (What's MSME, 2020)

Classification	Micro	Small	Medium
Manufacturing Enterprises and Enterprises Rendering Services	The annual turnover should not exceed Rs. 5 crores, and the investment in Plant, machinery, or equipment should not exceed Rs. 1 crore.	The annual turnover should not exceed Rs. 50 crores, and the investment in Plant, machinery, or equipment should not exceed Rs. 10 crores.	The annual turnover should not exceed Rs. 250 crores, and the investment in Plant, machinery, or equipment should not exceed Rs. 50 crores.

1.2. COVID-19 Lockdown's Effect on MSMEs

The MSMEs sector plays a crucial role in propelling the economic growth of India. A number of problems have caused the sector to grow gradually prior to the COVID-19 debacle, and demonetisation and the Goods and Services Tax have made things worse. Most MSMEs have an exurban unskilled labour base, as well as financial and health crises that have hampered growth and potential. The COVID-19 virus outbreak has drastically altered the operational environment of businesses and entrepreneurs. The abrupt implementation of the COVID-19 protocol-related logistics caused labour force migration, price increases, profit reductions, a financial crunch, decreased demand, and so on. This resulted in a 55% reduction in employment, a 17.3% decrease in annual sales, a postponement in raw material receipt, and a loss of credit access (Behera et al. 2020).

Ultimately, 70% of firms disclosed that they were unable to survive the first three months of lockdown, and many small businesses failed (Ghosh, 2020; Rathore, 2020). The survey results also showed that a large number of business owners from various countries who had been selling on digital platforms during the pandemic's early waves had not done so during any of the waves that followed. This suggests that while many firms have tried digital platforms, their adoption has been patchy and unsustainable. Participants in focus groups went into further detail about the reasons behind their reluctance to sell on digital platforms (Figure 1). These reasons included their inability to compete with low online prices, worries about intellectual property, the platforms' unsuitability for their business, inconsistent mobile coverage, and a lack of understanding about how to use the platforms effectively (Modi et al., 2022).

Figure 1. Percentage of MSMEs selling on digital platforms

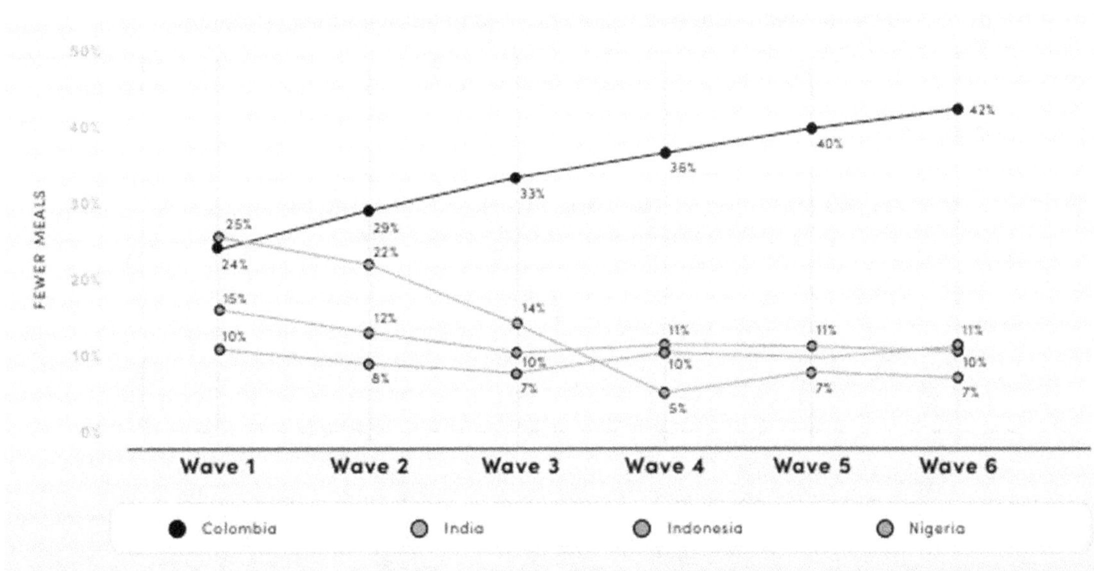

The COVID-19 dilemma is thought to be resolvable through the invention of business models (Breier et al., 2021). The goals of this research project will centre on how emerging businesses modified their business models through creativity and adaptation in order to endure and expand in spite of the ongoing COVID-19 pandemic. Numerous internal and external factors play a role in the digital evolution of MSMEs. Brown & Rocha (2020) list the following as internal elements: technological expertise, human talent, a digital approach, and the company's financial capacity to reinvent itself digitally. However, instances of external effects include modifications to the trends of consumer demand, the intuitiveness of digital technologies, and the competitiveness of the market (Wiliandri, 2020).

Additional ecological and economic catastrophes, such as the COVID-19 catastrophe, also bring on a sudden advance in digital enterprise. Numerous academic studies have examined how the pandemic has affected micro, small and medium and how businesses are evolving into digital platforms. The study focused on prospective actions that can foster entrepreneurship in the future as it examined how the COVID-19 epidemic affected entrepreneurial opportunities. The study combined numerous regression analyses with a literature review to examine the impact of relevant factors on potential new entrepreneurs. The findings suggested that the worldwide epidemic may have positive effects on business ownership, such as digitisation and the ability to adapt to new market patterns.

According to studies conducted by the Centre for Financial Inclusion (CFI), the pandemic significantly harmed MSMEs, and many found it difficult to deal with falling profitability, increased costs, and decreased client demand. Although the expanding digital economy has given entrepreneurs new avenues for client service, MSMEs' adoption of digital technology has been uneven and sluggish.

Although they are not a cure-all, digital tools can assist MSMEs in addressing a number of issues that have arisen since the epidemic and the continued severe economic conditions. Figure 2 below offers a number of illustrations of problems that MSMEs frequently bring up in CFI's focus groups, along with instances of digital solutions that could potentially be able to aid with these problems.

Figure 2. MSME challenges and potential digital solutions

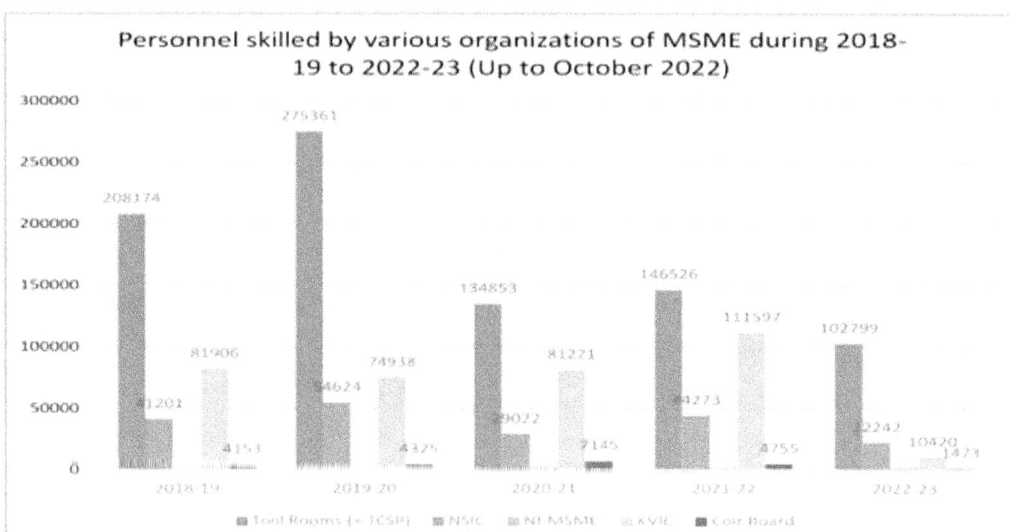

The Indian Express reports that the All India Manufacturing Organization polled five thousand MSMEs, and at least 71 per cent of the firms were unable to pay their employees' salaries, leaving many impoverished (The Hindu, 2020). This has raised the issue of the financial crisis without adequate liquidity, which forced many MSMEs to shut down the business. Almost 56% of electronic goods were imported from China, and due to the lockdown, it decreased to 20% (Prasad & Mondal, 2020). There was a decline in the textile industries, which almost stopped producing Sambalpuri sarees because of an inefficient supply chain. This led to lower labour, lower production, and lower supply, which gradually gave rise to inflation (Figure 3).

Figure 3. MSMEs risk build-up amid COVID-19 pandemic, says the report (2021)

Type of Digital Tool	Definition	Examples
Low-stakes	Low cost, does not require resource commitment	Communicating digitally with customers (e.g., WhatsApp) or marketing their business on social media (e.g., Facebook, Instagram)
High-stakes	Requires formal business registration and often includes a financial transaction or commitment	Use of delivery platform, ecommerce platform, online store

Aside from these issues, COVID-19 had some favourable impacts on MSMEs. Some businesses became self-sufficient and attempted to manufacture goods for the industry, such as face masks, sanitisers, and even ventilators. Manufacturing the goods within the country helped in livelihood and tried to bring stability to the employment rate. Numerous small businesses appeared as the new market trend by providing home delivery and thus creating a clean and comfortable society.

2. LITERATURE REVIEW

The paper focuses on secondary resources. It undertakes a review of the literature on business growth strategies and speaks with business owners and human resource specialists. For pertinent information, papers on approach plans, business development plans, and the notion of earnings were studied (Dexit & Pandey, 2011; Susmitha, 2014; Vasu & Javachanandra, 2014; Kotler, 1999). Sahasranamam et al., 2021) emphasised in a study the drivers of entrepreneurship and the article studied the rise in social enterprises and the well-being of entrepreneurs. Gans, (2018) explained in their article how to choose the strategies for business by investigating four generics and selecting a version which aligns with founding values and motivations. Firms should develop strategies according to the changing environment that will focus on increasing their market share to obtain and achieve a competitive advantage (Nathan, 2013). Looking at the current scenario, COVID-19 emerged as a great crisis that has affected many countries, causing disruptions in social, economic and health-system (Bacq and Lumpkin, 2020).

The effects of company tactics (both financially and marketing), as well as the leadership of innovation on the operational performance and economic indicators of SMEs in south-central Sonora, Mexico, are looked into and confirmed in this study by Valdez-Juárez et al. (2022). The impact of home offices and electronic commerce on innovation management and business performance is also examined. A multiple-group examination was also conducted to see if there are any notable distinctions between family-owned businesses and those that are not. 498 SMEs in the business sector, with 6 to 250 employees, make up the sample under analysis. In innovation management, the personal office also has major implications. Eventually, it was discovered that unidentified SMEs had the best company performance and innovation management.

The research advances both the idea of capacities and resources as well as the competitive behaviour theory. The primary objective of this research is to ascertain how technological advances affect business marketing choices during a global outbreak. A random selection of 128 small and medium-sized from Bangladesh is used in the study. Data were acquired through the mailing and online distribution of surveys. According to the research, entrepreneurs' choices regarding how to market their companies and how they seek, develop, and seize business opportunities are positively and significantly related. Additionally, it asserts the relationship between business owners' understanding of opportunities and actions taken to seize such opportunities through their business decisions in marketing. Entrepreneurial motivation, however, does not buffer the relationship between the exploitation of company possibilities and business marketing decisions.

The study gives academics a more complete knowledge of the advantages of AI in small-scale enterprises. The results will be helpful to academics, teachers, and practitioners. The assessments are more complex and varied than the methods used in the vast bulk of the few preceding studies. Colclough et al. (2019) discovered that managers' growth objectives rather than just the quantity of the resources base determine SME creativity introductions and that utilising ambidextrous innovation techniques yields good performance in innovation outcomes. A variety of societal and economic limitations that restricted people's mobility and in-person connections were backed by numerous governments in an effort to stop the virus from spreading. A significant proportion of sociological and commercial activity, including digital entrepreneurship, has moved to digital platforms as a result of less face-to-face connection.

Due to the effects of this phenomenon on elevating employment and economic growth, plenty of studies have lately been undertaken on the causes, facilitators, and government initiatives that support it (Sahut et al., 2021). As enablers, multimedia, crowdsourcing, free educational materials, 3D printing, graphic design, and data mining all promote young entrepreneurs by removing obstacles. The pandemic transformed buying habits and corporate creative strategies, which is a further driver influencing the digital reshaping of businesses of all sizes (MSMEs). The development of societal entrepreneurship online is seen as the result of the interaction among diverse agents, taking into account the government's lessened capacity to tune in to the expectations and successes of the stakeholders linked with an exogenous event. They used 131 pandemic-related applications from the Google Play and Apple App Stores to construct a PLS structural equation. They looked at the multiple interactions between the various components as well as the direct and indirect effects. The paper claims that DSEs act as catalysts for the flow of information and innovation to satisfy stakeholders when the government has failed to acknowledge the requirements of the people (Ibáñez et al., 2022).

2.1. Objective

- To comprehend the difficulties MSMEs in COVID-19 confront
- To study the recent trend of small businesses with creativity and entrepreneurship
- Suggestions to revive MSMEs in post-COVID

3. RESEARCH METHODOLOGY

Area and Scope of the Study: The paper focuses on the impact of COVID-19 on MSMEs in India and the challenges facing entrepreneurs in moving ahead during this pandemic. The obstacles forced the entrepreneurs to find new ways of entering the market and, for some, thrive for survival. The study also creates awareness about the support offered by the government during the pandemic. The sources of the study are based on secondary data collected from various books, annual reports, surveys, bulletins, etc.

Data Collection: The nature of the study is descriptive and resourceful. Pre-study materials like Publications, articles, and journals were referred to for a better understanding of the subject. Secondary sources were in high use, but a pure analysis is made with due care, which is reflected in the paper. A qualitative case study approach is being used to do research. Case studies offer a systematic approach to examining expansion methods by entrepreneurs towards digital strategies, gathering data, analysing information, and reporting findings.

Study Limitation: The primary topic that will be covered in this study is how to establish a digital-based MSMEs development strategy while dealing with the Covid-19 pandemic by using technology, like as social media and e-commerce, to your benefit. In this manner, it will be made clear that the digital business strategy for small-medium sized is one of the alternatives to current development while also preserving MSMEs from the COVID-19 pandemic. It is envisaged that the findings will be able to integrate the findings of an identical theme as initial research with contemporary studies based on the literature study approach described above. Finally, it is feasible to identify unique components in future studies by validating results from earlier investigations.

Expansion Through Innovative Strategies: In spite of Covid 19's detrimental effects on the economy, Indian business owners continued to use a variety of techniques to mobilise and grow their market, according to a poll by the World Economic Forum:

Future Business Going Into Digital: After a few months of lockdown, there is a lot of pressure on entrepreneurs to pay rent for offices and fear of becoming irrelevant, which keeps entrepreneurs moving with this tough phase. More Indian consumers are getting used to shopping online for groceries, and it's conceivable that more and more individuals will buy apparel online. Small manufacturers started to survive during the pandemic because of direct selling to consumers. Digital avenues can make it easier for them to navigate difficult times and reach wider consumers. It is helping vernacular language voice technology businesses like Vernacular.ai and digitally enabled hyper-local business models like Meesho to develop (Figure 4).

Figure 4. Modes of payment between MSMEs, suppliers, and customers during the pandemic

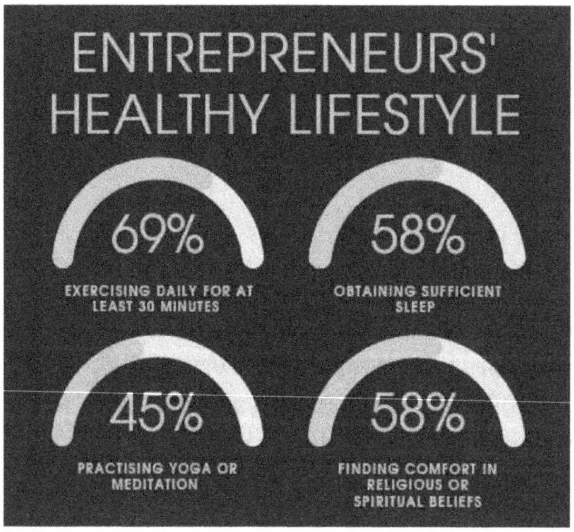

Multi-Sector Collaborations: The complexity created by the pandemic has induced multi-sector initiative that has brought different start-ups, universities and civil society to collaborate. The government-funded C-CAMP fosters high-end research and innovation and has launched the Covid-19 Innovation Development Accelerator (C-CIDA), which supports start-ups in areas of diagnostics, respiratory devices, therapeutics and cold chain technology. Such collaboration helps entrepreneurs engage with government regulatory processes around technology commercialisation and helps to expand and develop innovative products and services.

Localisation: The government's support programme for the MSME sector during CVID-19 included Atma-Nirbhar Bharat as one of its main focuses. To help localise some industries, like toy manufacturing and electronics manufacturing units, it offered a variety of incentives and programmes. The National Policy on Electronics, which calls for India to become a $400 billion centre of Electronics System Design and Manufacturing (ESDM) by 2025, gained momentum as a result of the pandemic. Localisation by the electronics supply chain provided excellent support for hardware companies like the ESDM incubation Centre in Hubli and the Super Fab-Lab in Kochi. Establishing new manufacturing clusters and platforms for small-scale firms in India is starting a new trend. These kinds of suggestions could strengthen the dependability of the supply chain, promote local employment, lower emissions caused by the transportation of goods, and decrease the importation of electrical goods, which account for around 13 per cent of all imports into India.

Advancement of Social Enterprises: Indian entrepreneurs demonstrated a high level of societal contribution to social causes, participating 52 per cent of the time and providing business services 65 per cent of the time. Great efforts were made to generate funds for projects related to Covid-19. Many entrepreneurs put stress on increasing the social and environmental consciousness of consumers. These programmes called for the creation of brand-new social enterprises, particularly in the fields of agriculture, healthcare, and sanitation. New business models like REVIVE and Maker's Asylum supported the informal sector entrepreneurs during the pandemic towards developing reasonable and effective healthcare products and also motivated individuals to engage in social enterprise (Figure 5).

Figure 5. World Economic Forum: Among the 23 countries studied, Indian entrepreneurs had some of the highest levels of social commitment
Source: Sahasranamam et al. (2021)

Figure 6. Healthy lifestyle choices during the pandemic played an important role in Indian entrepreneurs' ability to cope with the pandemic
Source: Sahasranamam et al. (2021)

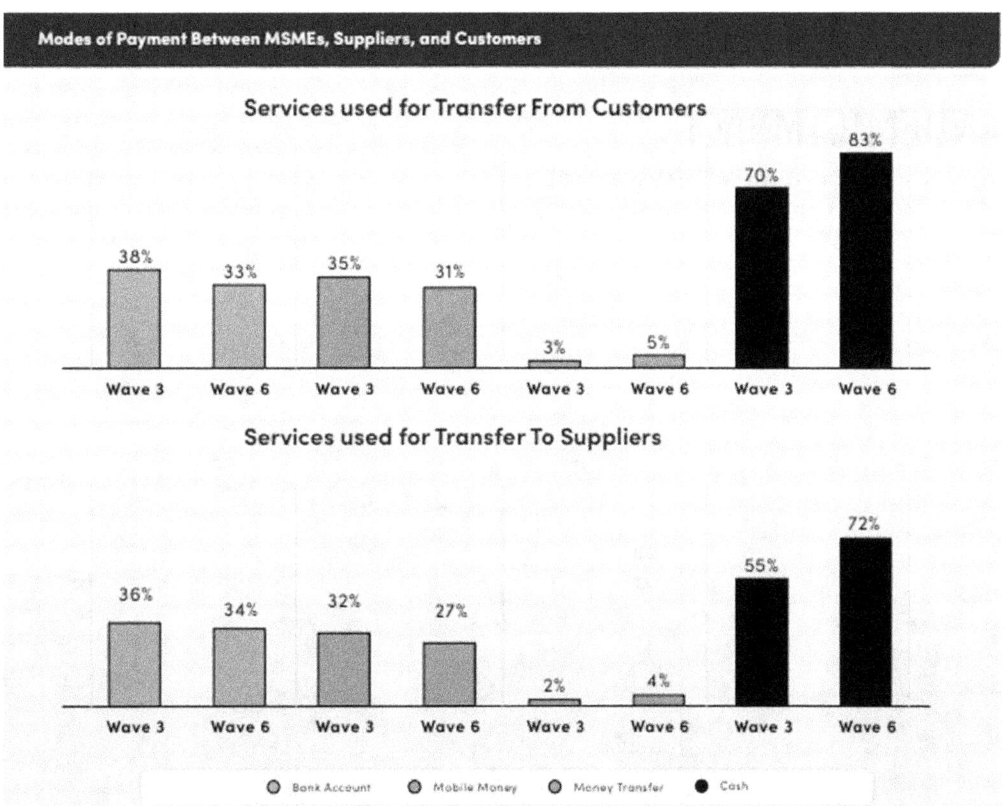

Well-Being and Resilience of Entrepreneurs: COVID-19 has increased the awareness of mental well-being in many countries as it has led to stress on entrepreneurs' productivity risk. The study observed that many Indian entrepreneurs exercised daily (69%), slept well (58%), practised Yoga (45%), and had religious and spiritual beliefs (58%) (Sahasranamam et al., 2021). This shows the healthy lifestyle choices of Indian entrepreneurs during the pandemic (Figure 6).

The personal resilience of entrepreneurs and their focus on self-care to sustain that resilience is significantly influenced by these trends. The study demonstrates a crucial foundation for both the durability and long-term success of their firms, as well as for individual innovation and efficiency.

Understand the Cost and Benefits of Digital Adoption: Research should be done to learn more about how different MSME segments go from low-stakes to high-stakes digital adoption. It is helpful to take "low-stakes" and "high-stakes" digital tools into distinct consideration in order to comprehend the advantages and disadvantages of adoption better. Low-stakes digital solutions, like social network marketing for businesses or digital consumer communication, are inexpensive to deploy and don't need a large financial or time investment. Conversely, high-stakes digital tools involve a cash transaction or commitment and call for official business registration. While a large number of MSMEs had used low-stakes electronic instruments during the pandemic, fewer of them, particularly women, reported adopting high-stakes digital tools for financial transactions. Furthermore, employment of high-stakes digital tools was uneven, with many business owners going back to their previous practices. This was equally true of the owners who tried them.

Figure 7. CFI report (2022)

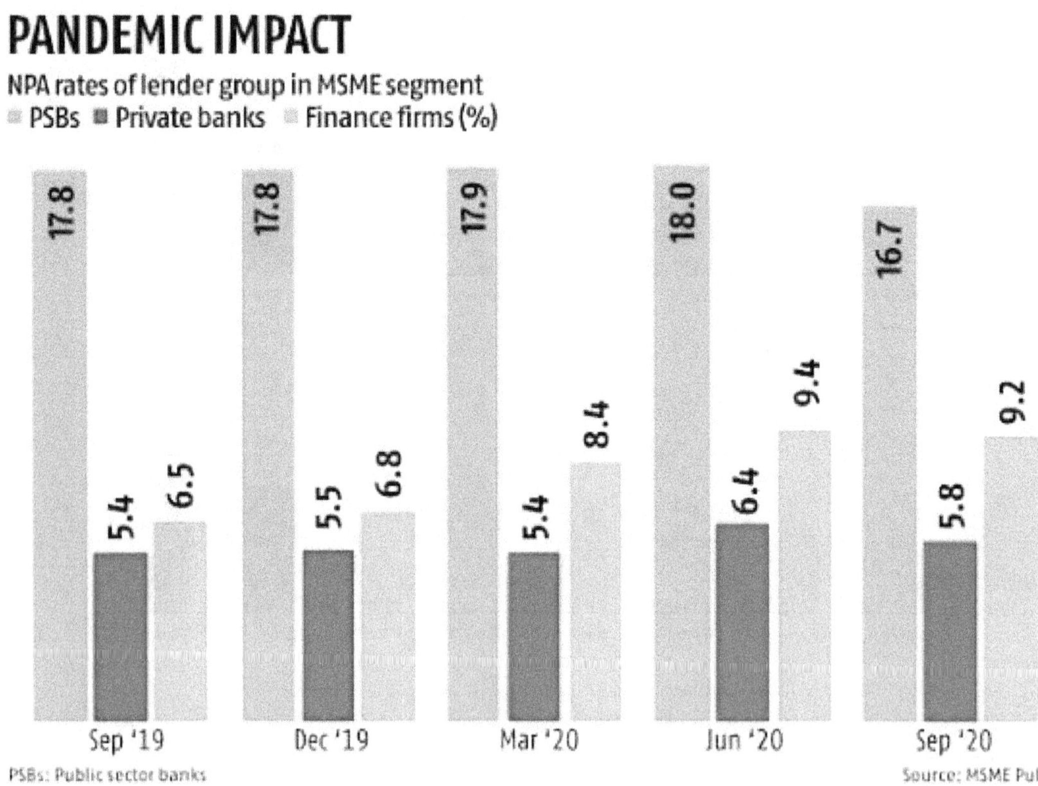

During the pandemic, these tendencies not only improve the Indian enterprise environment but also bring flexibility (Figure 7). These are the main forces behind India's goal of building a $5.1 trillion economy that is inclusive and continuous by 2025.

4. GOVERNMENT SUPPORT TO FACILITATE MSMES

The youth receive skill training from ministry-affiliated organisations in order to prepare them for paid employment and self-employment. Additionally, they offer skill-upgradation pieces of training to current business owners and employees in order to improve their performance. Furthermore, organisations within the Ministry also offer tailored, demand-driven training programs in accordance with industry requirements. The chart below shows the evolution of the M/o MSME's skill development programs from 2018–19 to 2022–23 (data up to October 2022) (Figure 8).

Figure 8. The evolution of the M/o MSME's skill development programs from 2018–19 to 2022–23
Source: MSME annual report 2022-23 (2022)

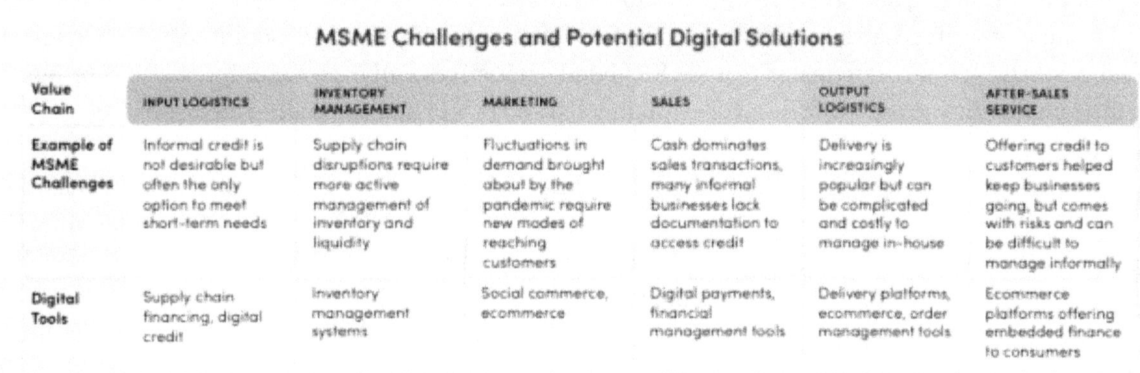
MSME Challenges and Potential Digital Solutions

Value Chain	INPUT LOGISTICS	INVENTORY MANAGEMENT	MARKETING	SALES	OUTPUT LOGISTICS	AFTER-SALES SERVICE
Example of MSME Challenges	Informal credit is not desirable but often the only option to meet short-term needs	Supply chain disruptions require more active management of inventory and liquidity	Fluctuations in demand brought about by the pandemic require new modes of reaching customers	Cash dominates sales transactions, many informal businesses lack documentation to access credit	Delivery is increasingly popular but can be complicated and costly to manage in-house	Offering credit to customers helped keep businesses going, but comes with risks and can be difficult to manage informally
Digital Tools	Supply chain financing, digital credit	Inventory management systems	Social commerce, ecommerce	Digital payments, financial management tools	Delivery platforms, ecommerce, order management tools	Ecommerce platforms offering embedded finance to consumers

Additional Actions Under Aatmanirbhar Bharat Abhiyaan: The Hon'ble Prime Minister made swift to emphasise the importance of MSMEs in advancing the nation following the COVID-19 outbreak. As a result, MSMEs were heavily represented in the announcements made in connection with the Aatmanirbhar Bharat Abhiyaan. Small and medium-sized enterprises (MSMEs) have benefited greatly from this package, receiving both a significant allocation and priority in the execution of measures aimed at reviving the economy. Under the package, a number of initiatives have been announced to give the MSME sector quick help. The Ministry of MSME is concentrating on all fronts in keeping with the Government of India's primary goal of reviving MSMEs across the nation. The Aatmanirbhar Bharat Package included the two subsequent announcements to improve MSMEs' access to financing alongside the already-existing credit-related initiatives and other announcements:

Subordinated Debt of Rs 20,000 Crores for Stressed MSMEs: On June 24, 2020, the Credit Guarantee Scheme for Subordinate Debt (CGSSD) for Stressed MSMEs was completed and made available. Under the program, money is provided to MSMEs whose units are still operating but whose accounts have been stressed (NPA). In order to establish a corpus that will provide guarantees for the loans that will be granted to the promoters of qualifying units, the GOI provides Rs 4,000 crores.

The goal of the initiative is to guarantee loans up to Rs 20,000 crore. It is being conducted through the Credit Guarantee Fund Trust for Micro and Small Enterprises (CGTMSE). Till March 31, 2023, the CGSSD for Stressed small businesses remains in effect.

Rs. 50 crores. Investment in equity for MSMEs made possible by the Self-Reliant India Fund: The aim of the Self-Reliant India Fund's (SRI Fund) goal is to meet MSMEs' unmet needs for cash and equity. To increase MSMEs' competitiveness in the global markets and have a multiplier effect on the economy, locating capital pools that can be substantially leveraged is essential.

On September 1, 2021, National Small Industry Corporation (NSIC) Venture Capital Fund Limited (NVCFL), a Special Purpose Vehicle (SPV), registered as an Alternative Investment Fund (AIF) Category II in order to carry out the SRI-Fund.

On October 12, 2021, the following parties signed the Contribution Agreement: (i) the Ministry of MSME, Government of India; (ii) National Small Industries Corporation Limited; (iii) NSIC Venture Capital Fund Limited; and (iv) SBI-CAP Ventures Limited.

The ratio of the funds to be committed by the SRI Fund and the funds to be mobilised by the Daughter Fund would be 4:1. It is anticipated that the SRI Fund's initiatives will have a multiplier effect, bringing significant liquidity to the MSME sector—roughly INR 50,000 cr and facilitating the nation's economic growth.

Status: As of December 31, 2022, 34 Daughter Funds in total had established an embattled relationship with NVCFL, the Mother Fund. Through the investment of Rs. 2,790 crores, 140 potential MSMEs received assistance. The Ministry of MSME has approved and disbursed Rs. 212.57 crore to NVCFL for the SRI-Fund's operationalization for the current fiscal year 2022–2023.

Technology Centres: Every year, the Ministry of MSME's Tool Rooms & Technical Institutions serve a vital role in giving jobless young and industry workers training in the development of practical skills. 18 Tool Rooms and technical Institutions that were established around the nation in 2021–2022 trained 1,43,227 trainees, supported 31,560 units and brought in Rs. 229.75 crore in revenue.

In accordance with the National Skill Qualification Framework, 76 courses have been created (NSQF). Through these TRs & TIs, students from 18 TRs & TIs frequently participate in a variety of national and international skill competition programs. Following the COVID-19 pandemic, TRs and TIs began implementing offline training initiatives.

Swachh Bharat Abhiyan: After contributing significantly to the introduction of the Central Government's flagship program, Swachh Bharat Abhiyan, MSMEs like the Coir Board have been adhering to the cleaning initiatives suggested by the program. Throughout the reporting year, the board has been putting its Action Plan into practice, which includes a number of action items like maintaining adequate disinfection procedures in all of the board's facilities to stop the spread of the Covid 19 pandemic, digitising office data, and cleaning initiatives.

4.1. Program for Financing and Credit to MSMEs

For the past three years, the margin money reimbursement has been disbursed at an annual rate. Disbursement for 2019–20 was disrupted by the lockdown that followed the COVID-19 epidemic (Table 2). PMEGP outperformed its FY 2021–22 performance, disbursing INR 2,978 Cr (~36% more than FY21) as MM subsidies, supporting 103,219 units (~39% more than FY21), and creating employment for almost 8 lakh people. Since the scheme's beginning, this is the highest.

Table 2. PMEGP performance in the past three years and the present (MSME annual report 2022-23, 2022)

Year	Margin Money Disbursed (Rs. Crore)	Micro Units Assisted (Number)	Estimated Employment Generated (Number)
2019-20	1950.82	66,653	5,33,224
2020-21	2188.80	74,415	5,95,320
2021-22	2977.41	103,219	8,25,752
2022-23*	1505.72	46,808	3,74,464

*31.12.2022

5. INTERNATIONAL COLLABORATIONS

MSMEs are now recognised on a global scale as the catalyst for economic expansion that supports equitable development. Likewise, MSMEs have been crucial in promoting economic growth and export development in India. But starting in the year 2020, the COVID-19 virus spread over the world, posing challenges for MSMEs. These enterprises have been forced to stay internationally competitive and constantly improve to equip themselves to handle the difficulties brought on by technological breakthroughs, shifts in needs, creation of new markets, etc., in order to keep their niche in the global and worldwide markets.

The government has taken initial steps to revive MSMEs during pandemics. It announced the Emergency Credit Line Guarantee Scheme under Aatmanirbhar Bharat Abhiyan in May to enhance business through the highest fiscal component of Rs 20 lakh crores. MSMEs' investment limits and turnover sizes have been redefined. The extended investment limit for micro-units is 1 crore; for small units, Rs 10 crore, and for medium units, Rs. 50 crores. The additional size of turnover for micro is Rs 5 crores, for small is RS 50 crores and for the medium is Rs. 100 crores. RBI took some initiative by lending at cheaper rates to help MSMEs. The government proposed collateral-free loans for the struggling MSME sector, which will help to stabilise their production process. Global tenders will be prohibited for public procurement in order to compete and supply with local and government tenders in order to support "Make In India" and thrive toward self-sufficiency in India. To replace the trade fairs and exhibitions, e-market linkage for MSMEs has been started, which will enable transactions generated by MSMEs through Fintech. In order to relieve the financial strain on enterprises, the government has taken the initiative to offer PF and EPF support to both personnel and firms. This relief totals Rs 6760 crore. In addition, in order to provide more liquidity to taxpayers, the government proposed a 25% reduction in the TDS rate for SMEs, NBFCs, and TCS.

A variety of initiatives have been proposed to assist MSMEs in alleviating the struggle to survive the pandemic. Most of the firms are experiencing financial instability and insecurity, so the government is taking adequate steps to help the businesses from the current crisis. Low-interest loans with longer amortisation terms are available. MSMEs' credit limits must be increased. To lessen the load, loan repayments should be postponed. Entrepreneurs should consistently check the flow of cash within the business. Budget estimates, envisioned cash flow, anticipated risks and financial commitments, and so on should be discussed with the financial department. Financial strategy requires accurate and timely information about the government's monetary support package and trade organisation support. Need to build a strong digital infrastructure that will transform the business, and new technologies allow buyers and suppliers to connect directly, providing an avenue for MSMEs. The gov't's e-marketplace will help MSMEs to raise the market share in procuring goods and services. Partnerships and mergers would help to collaborate with new tech leaders to penetrate in Indian market or cost reduction. Online banking provides MSMEs with a faster transaction process and reduces transaction expenses.

6. CONCLUSION

The purpose of this study is to evaluate how entrepreneurs strive to create new business strategies and discover government supports that enable MSMEs grow continually. Additionally, the study will investigate how COVID-19 will effect MSMEs, as well as the challenges and barriers they encounter. The study relied on secondary data and an exhaustive analysis of the relevant literature, which was compiled from a variety of sources, including websites, journals, papers, and magazines, among others. One might reach the conclusion that the government is aware of the numerous obstacles that micro, small, and medium-sized enterprises confront because it has offered a variety of forms of help. Innovative business expansion techniques were applied by entrepreneurs, which resulted in the creation of new prospects. The support provided by the government is analysed in this article, along with some recommendations for how the MSMEs can have a more successful future.

REFERENCES

Bacq, S., & Lumpkin, G. T. (2020). Social Entrepreneurship and COVID-19. *Journal of Management Studies*, *58*(1), 285–288. doi:10.1111/joms.12641 PMID:32398883

Behera, M., Mishra, S., Mohapatra, N., & Behera, A. R. (2020). COVID-19 pandemic and micro, small and medium Enterprises (MSMEs): Policy response for revival. *SEDME (Small Enterprises Development, Management & Extension Journal): A Worldwide Window on MSME Studies, 47*(3), 213–228. doi:10.1177/09708464211037485

Breier, M., Kallmuenzer, A., Clauss, T., Gast, J., Kraus, S., & Tiberius, V. (2021). The role of business model innovation in the hospitality industry during the COVID-19 crisis. *International Journal of Hospitality Management*, *92*, 102723. doi:10.1016/j.ijhm.2020.102723 PMID:36919038

Brown, R., & Rocha, A. (2020). Entrepreneurial uncertainty during the Covid-19 crisis: Mapping the temporal dynamics of entrepreneurial finance. *Journal of Business Venturing Insights*, *14*, e00174. doi:10.1016/j.jbvi.2020.e00174

CFI Report. (2022). Retrieved November 6, 2023, from Ctif-cfi.be website: https://www.ctif-cfi.be/index.php/en/news-quick-links/252-annual-report-2022

Colclough, S. N., Moen, Ø., Hovd, N. S., & Chan, A. (2019). SME innovation orientation: Evidence from Norwegian exporting SMEs. *International Small Business Journal*, *37*(8), 780–803. doi:10.1177/0266242619870731

Dexit, A., & Pandey, A. K. (2011). SMEs and Economic Growth in India: Cointegration Analysis. *The IUP Journal of Financial Economics*, *IX*(2), 41–57.

Gans, J. (2018). Strategy for Start-ups. Competitive Strategy Magazine. *Harvard Business Review*, 44–51.

Ghosh, S. (2020). Examining the COVID-19 relief package for MSMEs. *Economic and Political Weekly*, *55*(22), 10–12.

Ibáñez, M. J., Guerrero, M., Yáñez-Valdés, C., & Barros-Celume, S. (2022). Digital social entrepreneurship: The N-Helix response to stakeholders' COVID-19 needs. *The Journal of Technology Transfer*, *47*(2), 556–579. doi:10.100710961-021-09855-4 PMID:33814697

Kotler, P. (1999). *Marketing Management: Analysis, Planning, Implementation and Control* (9th ed.). Prentice Hall College Inc.

Modi, S., Braniff, L., El-Zoghbi, M., Emig, A., Michaels, L., & Stark, E. (2022). *Digital Adoption of MSMEs During COVID-19*. Retrieved November 6, 2023, from Centerforfinancialinclusion.org website: https://content.centerforfinancialinclusion.org/wp-content/uploads/sites/2/2022/09/Digital-adoption-of-Msmes-During-covid19-1.pdf

MSME annual report 2022-23. (2022). Retrieved November 6, 2023, from Gov.in website: https://msme.gov.in/msme-annual-report-2022-23

MSMEs risk build-up amid COVID-19 pandemic, says the report. (2021). *Business Standard News*. Retrieved November 6, 2023, from Business-standard.com website: https://www.business-standard.com/article/economy-policy/watch-out-for-msme-risk-build-up-amid-covid-19-pandemic-says-report-121021801579_1.html

Nathan, M. M. (2013). *Knowledge defines the growth strategy*. www.exceljockey.com

Prasad, R., & Mondal, A. (2020). Impact of COVID-19 pandemic on Indian economy with special reference to Indian MSMEs sector. *Research Gate*, (7), 16–21.

RathoreU. (2020). From slowdown to lockdown: Effects of the COVID-19 crisis on small firms in India. Oxford Policy Management, 1–32. doi:10.2139/ssrn.3615339

Sahasranamam, S., Stephan, U., & Zbierowski, P. (2021, July 29). *What can Indian entrepreneurs tell us about surviving COVID?* Retrieved November 6, 2023, from World Economic Forum website: https://www.weforum.org/agenda/2021/07/five-post-covid-trends-among-indias-entrepreneurs/

Sahut, J.-M., Iandoli, L., & Teulon, F. (2021). The age of digital entrepreneurship. *Small Business Economics*, *56*(3), 1159–1169. doi:10.100711187-019-00260-8

Sanghera, T. (2020, December 23). *Surviving COVID: The challenges facing India's small businesses.* Retrieved November 6, 2023, from Al Jazeera website: https://www.aljazeera.com/economy/2020/12/23/surviving-covid-the-challenges-facing-indias-small-businesses

Susmitha, M. M. (2014). *Growth and Performance of Small-size Industries in India with special reference to Kerala.* www.ffymag.com

The Hindu. (2020). *MSMEs will be the biggest casualty of COVID-19 in India.* https://www.thehindu.com/business/msmes-will-be-the-biggest-casualty-of-covid-19-in-india-study/article31084751.ece

Valdez-Juárez, L. E., Castillo-Vergara, M., & Ramos-Escobar, E. A. (2022). Innovative business strategies in the face of COVID-19: An approach to open innovation of SMEs in the Sonora region of Mexico. *Journal of Open Innovation*, *8*(1), 47. doi:10.3390/joitmc8010047

Vasu, M. S., & Jayachandra, K. (2014). Growth and Development of MSMEs in India: Prospects and problems. *Indian Journal of Applied Research*, *4*(5), 125–127. doi:10.15373/2249555X/MAY2014/40

What's MSME. (n.d.). Retrieved November 6, 2023, from Gov.in website: https://msme.gov.in/know-about-msme

Wiliandri, R. (2020). A Conceptual Approach to Identify Factors Affecting the Digital Transformation of Micro, Small and Mediumsized Enterprises (MSMEs) during Covid-19 Pandemic in Indonesia. *Ekonomi Bisnis*, *25*(2), 66–85. doi:10.17977/um042v25i2p66-85

Chapter 14
Influence of Government Initiatives and Information on Indian Women Entrepreneurial Ventures

Sasi Sundarakumar
Takshashila University, India

J. Tamil Selvi
Annamalai University, India

K. Ilangovan
Pondicherry University, India

Vellayan Srinivasan
S.A. Engineering College (Autonomous), India

A. S. Kannan
GRT Institute of Engineering and Technology, India

Vivek Arunachalam
Berlin School of Business and Innovation, Germany

ABSTRACT

This study uses a moderated mediation model to investigate how government initiatives and policies affect women's entrepreneurship in India. According to the study's hypotheses, the relationship between government policies and initiatives and women's entrepreneurship is moderated by the industry sector of these businesswomen and their access to information mediates this relationship. In order to evaluate the assumptions, the study collects data from 514 Indian women entrepreneurs who have used or are aware of any government programme or effort supporting women's entrepreneurship. The findings demonstrate that government initiatives and policies positively and significantly impact women'sentrepreneurship. However, this impact is less pronounced for women entrepreneurs in the manufacturing sector, likely due to less favourable access to information. The study adds to the body of knowledge on women's entrepreneurship

DOI: 10.4018/979-8-3693-2193-5.ch014

INTRODUCTION

In India, women's entrepreneurship is a crucial driver of social and economic advancement (Nair, 2016; Noor & Isa, 2020). Women entrepreneurs contribute to the empowerment, creativity, and variety of society and job possibilities for themselves and others (Sharma, 2013). The Global Entrepreneurship Monitor (GEM) report (2020) places India third out of 54 countries in terms of the proportion of women engaging in entrepreneurial activity in its early stages, with 15.5% of the female population between the ages of 18 and 64 doing so. "Women in Business" refers to a group of women who operate in the industry and are responsible for various tasks. There is a gender gap in entrepreneurship due to these challenges and restrictions, which restrict the potential and performance of women entrepreneurs (Sen & AL, 2021).

The Indian Government has introduced several policies and initiatives to encourage and assist women's entrepreneurship, including Startup India, Stand Up India, Mudra Yojana, etc., in recognition of the significance and potential of this sector. Various perks and incentives, including tax exemptions, subsidies, loans, grants, mentorship, training, and incubation, are intended for women entrepreneurs through these policies and initiatives. However, it is still being determined how these policies and initiatives will affect women's entrepreneurship and if they will be beneficial. There needs to be more empirical information on how these policies and initiatives affect the entrepreneurial behaviour and results of women entrepreneurs in India. Furthermore, it is essential to comprehend how various government initiatives and policies affect various types of entrepreneurs depending on their business sector, as various industries may present various possibilities and challenges for entrepreneurs.

The study of the effect of the government's policies on the behaviour of women entrepreneurs, as well as the impact of the study's findings on the lives of its participants, is the focus of this article. The study suggests that the relationship between government policies and initiatives and women's entrepreneurship is moderated by the industrial sector of the women entrepreneurs and that this relationship is mediated by the women entrepreneurs' access to information. The study used a survey approach to gather information from 514 Indian women entrepreneurs who have taken advantage of or are aware of any government program or policy encouraging women's entrepreneurship. To investigate the hypotheses, the study used structural equation modeling. The study adds to the body of knowledge on women's entrepreneurship and public policy by presenting empirical data on the regulated mediation mechanism through which government policies and initiatives impact women's entrepreneurship in India. Policymakers, practitioners, and female entrepreneurs may all benefit from the study's recommendations.

LITERATURE REVIEW

Women Entrepreneurship in India: Women's entrepreneurship is "the process whereby women initiate economic activities in the formal or informal sector" (Singh et al., 2016). The number of women joining the workforce has increased over the last few years, which has increased the number of women joining the labour. The success of a country's economy depends on its ability to attract and retain talent. By empowering women, enhancing their autonomy and agency, improving their access to resources and opportunities, increasing their participation in decision-making processes, challenging gender stereotypes and norms, and promoting gender equality and social justice, women's entrepreneurship can also foster the social development of a country (Kabeer et al., 2017).

India, which has an inhabitants of over 1.3 billion individuals, has one of the fastest-growing nations in the entire globe. India offers a sizable pool of potential women entrepreneurs who can support the country's economic and social advancement (Ingalagi et al., 2021). The number of people qualified to establish a business in the United States is based on their years in business. Out of these qualified women, over 100 million engage in some entrepreneurial activity (either emerging or established), making up about 15% of the entire female population (Kumar, 2021). This suggests that Indian women have a high level of entrepreneurial potential.

Numerous factors affect a person's ability to succeed, but the most important is having a good time. While some barriers and challenges are universal to all entrepreneurs, such as market competition, regulatory compliance, technological change, etc., others are unique to women entrepreneurs, such as gender discrimination, social norms, family obligations, etc. (Srivastava & Agrawal, 2020). Lower rates of opportunity recognition, business ownership, business development, and business survival among women than among men result from these challenges and barriers, which produce a gender gap in entrepreneurship in India (GEM report, 2020).

Government Policies and Initiatives for Women Entrepreneurship in India: India's government has implemented several initiatives to improve the quality of life for its citizens, including several initiatives to combat climate change. According to Gupta et al. (2019), these policies and initiatives offer women entrepreneurs various privileges and incentives, including tax breaks, subsidies, loans, grants, mentorship, training, and incubation. As opposed to some of these policies and initiatives, which are broader and target all entrepreneurs regardless of gender, others are more targeted to women entrepreneurs and either target just women entrepreneurs or give them precedence over male entrepreneurs (Goel& Madan, 2019). Some of the most important government initiatives and policies encouraging women's entrepreneurship in India are outlined in Table 1.

These are some of the most important government policies and initiatives for women entrepreneurship in India. There are several more policies and initiatives at the central, state, and municipal levels to support and promote women's sector entrepreneurship in various countries and areas. Additionally, the Indian government has worked with several regional, national, and international organisations, including NITI Aayog, UN Women, the World Bank, etc., to undertake different initiatives and programmes to boost the competitiveness and ability of women entrepreneurs in India.

Theoretical Framework and Hypotheses Development: The institutional theory and the resource-based perspective of the company serve as the foundation for this study's theoretical framework. According to the institutional theory, formal and informal social norms, such as laws, regulations, policies, practises, and values, impact how people behave and how well organisations work (Scott, 2014). According to the company's resource-based viewpoint, a company's performance and competitive advantage are determined by its capacity to develop and employ valuable, unusual, one-of-a-kind, and irreplaceable resources and talents (Barney, 1991).

These viewpoints hold that government policies and initiatives for women's entrepreneurship can be viewed as formal institutional factors that influence the entrepreneurial behaviour and outcomes of women entrepreneurs by offering them a variety of resources and incentives that can improve their entrepreneurial potential and performance. Although they may depend on numerous contextual factors that may moderate or mediate their relationship, these policies and initiatives may not have the same or direct effects on all women entrepreneurs. These two factors are the industry sector of women entrepreneurs and their access to information, which we suggest in this study.

Table 1. Initiatives of Government of India in promoting women entrepreneurship

Policy/Initiative	Description	Benefits/Incentives
Startup India	A flagship initiative launched by the Prime Minister of India in 2016 to foster a culture of innovation and entrepreneurship in the country.	- Tax exemptions for three years for eligible startups. - Fast-track patent application and reduced patent fees. - Easier compliance and regulatory norms. - Access to funding, mentoring, incubation, and networking opportunities through various schemes and programs. - Recognition and awards for outstanding startups.
Stand Up India	a programme introduced by the Indian Prime Minister in 2016 to make bank loans between 10 lakh and 1 crore available to at least one borrower from a Scheduled Caste (SC) or Scheduled Tribe (ST) and at least one woman per bank branch for the establishment of a new business.	- Collateral-free loans at concessional rates of interest. - Credit guarantee through National Credit Guarantee Trustee Company (NCGTC). - Handholding support through Stand Up India portal and Stand Up Connect Centers.
Mudra Yojana	A scheme launched by the Prime Minister of India in 2015 to provide loans up to 10 lakh to non-corporate, non-farm small/micro enterprises.	- Collateral-free loans at competitive rates of interest. - Three categories of loans based on the stage of business: Shishu (up to 50,000), Kishor (50,000 to 5 lakh), and Tarun (5 lakh to 10 lakh). - Credit guarantee through Credit Guarantee Fund Trust for Micro and Small Enterprises (CGTMSE). - Access to training, counseling, marketing, and other support services through Pradhan Mantri Mudra Yojana (PMMY) portal and Mudra Mitras.
Udyam Registration	A simplified online registration process for micro, small, and medium enterprises (MSMEs) launched by the Ministry of MSME in 2020.	- Self-declaration based registration without any documents or fees. - Single registration for all types of enterprises. - Unique Udyam Registration Number (URN) and e-certificate. - Access to various benefits and schemes offered by the government for MSMEs, such as priority sector lending, tax exemptions, subsidies, etc.
UdyogAadhaar Memorandum (UAM)	A one-page online registration form for MSMEs launched by the Ministry of MSME in 2015.	- Self-certification based registration without any documents or fees. - Single registration for all types of enterprises. - Unique UdyogAadhaar Number (UAN) and e-certificate. - Access to various benefits and schemes offered by the government for MSMEs, such as priority sector lending, tax exemptions, subsidies, etc.
Udyami Helpline	A toll-free number (1800-180-6763) launched by the Ministry of MSME in 2010 to provide information and guidance to existing and potential entrepreneurs.	- Information and guidance on various aspects of entrepreneurship, such as policies, schemes, programs, procedures, etc. - Referral to appropriate agencies or institutions for further assistance or support. - Grievance redressal mechanism for entrepreneurs facing problems or issues with government agencies or institutions.
Mahila E-Haat	An online marketing platform launched by the Ministry of Women and Child Development in 2016 to showcase products and services made by women entrepreneurs across the country.	- Free registration and listing of products and services on the website (www.mahilaehaat-rmk.gov.in). - Direct contact between buyers and sellers without any intermediaries or commission. - Access to digital payment options, logistics support, quality certification, etc. - Promotion and branding of products and services through social media, exhibitions, events, etc.
Trade Related Entrepreneurship Assistance and Development (TREAD) Scheme	A scheme launched by the Ministry of Micro, Small and Medium Enterprises in 2000 to provide economic empowerment to women through trade-related training, information, counseling, credit facilitation, etc.	- Grants up to 30% of the total project cost to non-governmental organizations (NGOs) for undertaking trade-related training and counseling activities for women entrepreneurs. - Credit guarantee cover up to 80% of the loan amount through National Credit Guarantee Trustee Company (NCGTC) for women entrepreneurs availing loans up to 50 lakh from banks or financial institutions. - Access to information, guidance, and market linkages through TREAD portal (www.tread.gov.in)

Source: Compilation by the Authors from the official websites of the schemes

The industry sector is the broad area of economic activity, such as agriculture, manufacturing, services, etc., in which women entrepreneurs conduct their firms. Depending on many factors, such as market demand, competition, technology, innovation, legislation, etc., the industry sector may offer distinct possibilities and challenges for women entrepreneurship (Acs et al., 2018). By setting up specific requirements and limitations for its execution and utilisation, the government sector may moderate the effects of government policies and initiatives on women's entrepreneurship.

According to Mishra and Zachary (2015), the ability of women entrepreneurs to access information refers to their capacity to acquire pertinent and trustworthy information about various facets of entrepreneurship, such as policies, schemes, programmes, procedures, etc., from a variety of sources, including government agencies, institutions, portals, etc. By permitting or facilitating their knowledge, comprehension, and acceptance of these policies and initiatives, access to information may mediate the effects of government policies and initiatives on women's entrepreneurship.

Based on these arguments, we develop the following hypotheses:

- H1: Government policies and initiatives positively and significantly affect women's entrepreneurship.
- H2: Government policies and initiatives have a positive and significant effect on access to information.
- H3: Access to information positively and significantly affects women's entrepreneurship.
- H4a: The industry sector moderates the relationship between government policies and initiatives and women entrepreneurship, such that the effect is weaker for women entrepreneurs in the manufacturing sector than for women entrepreneurs in the service sector.
- H4b: The industry sector moderates the relationship between government policies and initiatives and access to information, such that the effect is weaker for women entrepreneurs in the manufacturing sector than for women entrepreneurs in the service sector.
- H5a: Access to information moderates the relationship between government policies and initiatives and women entrepreneurship, such that the effect is weaker for women entrepreneurs with lower access to information than for women entrepreneurs with higher access to information.
- H5b: The industry sector moderates the indirect effect of government policies and initiatives on women's entrepreneurship through access to information, such that the effect is weaker for women entrepreneurs in the manufacturing sector than for women entrepreneurs in the service sector. (This is also called moderated mediation.)

Figure 1 shows the study's conceptual model, depicting the relationships among the variables and the hypotheses.

Figure 1. Conceptual model

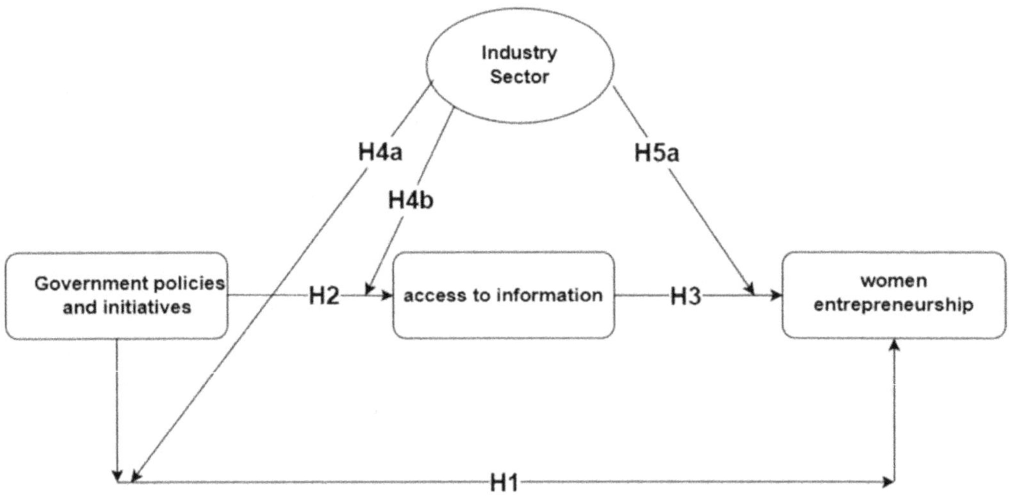

RESEARCH METHODOLOGY

Data Collection: The study used a survey approach to gather information from Indian women business owners who have used or are aware of any government effort or policy encouraging women's entrepreneurship. Two stages of sampling are used in the study. Based on the level of growth of women's entrepreneurship as determined by the Global Entrepreneurship Monitor (GEM) report (2019), the study first chooses a stratified random sample of 10 states from India's 28 states and eight union territories. Andhra Pradesh, Bihar, Gujarat, Karnataka, Kerala, Maharashtra, Rajasthan, Tamil Nadu, Uttar Pradesh, and West Bengal are the states that have been chosen. In the second step, 514 women entrepreneurs from these states are chosen as a convenience sample for the study. Both online and offline methods were used to acquire the data. In the online form, the questionnaire link was distributed through email and social media to various associations, networks, groups, forums, etc., for women entrepreneurs. Using personal connections and recommendations, the questionnaire was sent offline to various events, workshops, training sessions, etc., for women entrepreneurs. The data was gathered between March and May 2023. 51.4% of respondents responded. Additionally, the study ensures that each state is represented in the sample with at least 10% of women entrepreneurs.

A review of the literature and the views of experts were used to create the survey questionnaire. The questionnaire was divided into four sections: (1) the respondents' demographic profile; (2) the type and level of their awareness of and use of government policies and initiatives for women entrepreneurs; (3) the respondents' access to business information; and (4) the respondents' entrepreneurial behaviour and results.

In order to ensure the validity and reliability of the survey questionnaire, a pilot sample of 30 women entrepreneurs was used. The questionnaire was improved and completed using the comments from the pilot sample. To ensure the respondents could understand and access the final questionnaire, it was translated into Hindi and other regional languages.

Data Analysis: Using SPSS and AMOS software, data analysis was carried out. The data analysis involved the following steps: (1) data screening and cleaning; (2) descriptive statistics and structural testing; (3) measurement model validation; (4) moderated mediation testing; and (5) moderated mediation testing.

The data screening and cleaning involved looking for missing values, outliers, normalcy, multicollinearity, etc. and using the appropriate treatments or transformations as needed. For each variable in the study, the descriptive statistics and correlation analysis involved calculating the mean, standard deviation, and Pearson correlation coefficient. The study's findings were used to determine whether or not the study was successful. For the structural model testing, the direct and indirect effects of the independent variables on the dependent variable were calculated using structural equation modelling (SEM). The conditional indirect effects of the independent factors on the dependent variable were tested using the PROCESS macro at different moderator level levels (Hayes, 2018).

RESULTS

Correlation Analysis and Descriptive Statistics: The descriptive statistics and correlation matrix for the study's variables are shown in Table 2.

Table 2. The descriptive statistics and correlation matrix for the study's variables

Variable	Mean	SD	1	2	3
1. Government policies and initiatives	3.56	0.87	1		
2. Access to information	3.49	0.92	0.62***	1	
3. Women entrepreneurship	3.67	0.81	0.51***	0.58***	1
4. Industry sector (dummy)	0.47	0.50	-0.12**	-0.15**	-0.18***

Note: *** $p < 0.001$, ** $p < 0.01$, * $p < 0.05$

According to the mean values of the variables, the respondents' perceptions and levels of satisfaction with government policies and initiatives, information access, and women's entrepreneurship range from moderate to high. The standard deviation numbers suggest that the respondents' replies varied somewhat. According to the correlation matrix, all of the variables are highly connected except the industry sector dummy variable, which has a negative correlation with the other variables. This shows certain variations among women entrepreneurs depending on the industry sector in which they operate.

The correlation matrix supports H1 and H2 by demonstrating that government policies and initiatives have a favourable and substantial effect on women's entrepreneurship and access to information. This suggests that women entrepreneurs are more likely to establish and manage their enterprises effectively and to have access to pertinent information for their entrepreneurial activities the more they perceive and benefit from government policies and initiatives. Additionally, the correlation matrix supports H3 by demonstrating that information access has a favourable and substantial effect on women's entrepreneurship. This suggests that women entrepreneurs are more likely to improve their entrepreneurial knowledge, abilities, confidence, and performance with more information they can access. The correlation matrix supports H4, H5, and H6, which also demonstrates that the industry sector dummy variable has a negative and substantial influence on all the other variables. This suggests that, as a result of the different opportunities and challenges faced by them in their respective sectors, the effects of government policies and initiatives, as well as access to information, on women's entrepreneurship are weaker for women entrepreneurs in the manufacturing sector than for women entrepreneurs in the service sector.

Structural Equation Modeling: We tested the assumptions using structural equation modelling (SEM) with AMOS 26 software. According to Hair et al. (2019), SEM is a statistical approach that tests complicated correlations between numerous variables simultaneously while accounting for measurement errors and latent constructs. The structural model and measurement model are the two components of SEM. The measurement model explains how the latent constructs, which are unobserved variables, are related to the observable variables (indicators). The following is a list of some of the most common questions I have asked myself in the past several years.

As Anderson and Gerbing (1988) recommended, we conducted SEM in two steps. In order to determine the reliability and validity of the latent constructs, we first tested the measurement model by using confirmatory factor analysis (CFA). We tested the structural model in the second stage by calculating the path coefficients and testing the hypotheses.

Measurement Model: Government policies and initiatives, information access, and women's entrepreneurship were the three latent constructs in the measurement model. Three observed variables obtained using factor analysis from the survey questions were used to assess each latent construct. The dummy variable analysis handled the industry sector as an observed variable.

We evaluated the measurement model's validity and reliability using several metrics, including chi-square, the comparative fit index (CFI), the root mean square error of approximation (RMSEA), the standardised root mean square residual (SRMR), the composite reliability (CR), the average variance extracted (AVE), and factor loadings (Table 3).

Table 3. The results of the measurement model

Criteria	Value	Threshold
Chi-square	112.34	< 3 times df
Degrees of freedom (df)	51	-
Chi-square/df ratio	2.20	< 3
CFI	0.97	> 0.95
RMSEA	0.06	< 0.08
SRMR	0.04	< 0.08
CR (Government policies and initiatives)	0.88	> 0.7
CR (Access to information)	0.89	> 0.7
CR (Women entrepreneurship)	0.86	> 0.7
AVE (Government policies and initiatives)	0.67	> 0.5
AVE (Access to information)	0.69	> 0.5
AVE (Women entrepreneurship)	0.64	> 0.5

A number of measures, including chi-square, the comparative fit index (CFI), the root mean square error of approximation (RMSEA), the standardised root mean square residual (SRMR), the composite reliability (CR), the average variance extracted (AVE), and factor loadings, were used to assess the measurement model. The results demonstrated that the measurement model fit, validated, and was reliable in a suitable manner. Indicating a good fit to the data, the chi-square, CFI, RMSEA, and SRMR values all fell within allowable boundaries. The CR and AVE values were greater than the suggested criterion, pointing to the validity and reliability of the latent constructs. Factor loadings for the observed variables on the latent constructs were above 0.5 and significant, indicating convergent variable validity. In order to evaluate discriminant validity, the square root of AVE for each latent construct was compared to the correlations between the latent components. The results showed that the square root of AVE for each latent construct was more significant than the correlations among the latent constructs, indicating discriminant validity (Table 4).

Table 4. The results of the discriminant validity

Construct	Government Policies and Initiatives	Access to Information	Women Entrepreneurship
Government policies and initiatives	**0.82**		
Access to information	0.62	**0.83**	
Women entrepreneurship	0.51	0.58	**0.80**

Note: Diagonal elements are square root of AVE; off-diagonal elements are correlations among constructs

Thus, we conclude that the measurement model is valid and reliable and test the structural model.

Structural Model: The structural model consisted of six hypotheses, as shown in Figure 2.

Figure 2. Structural model

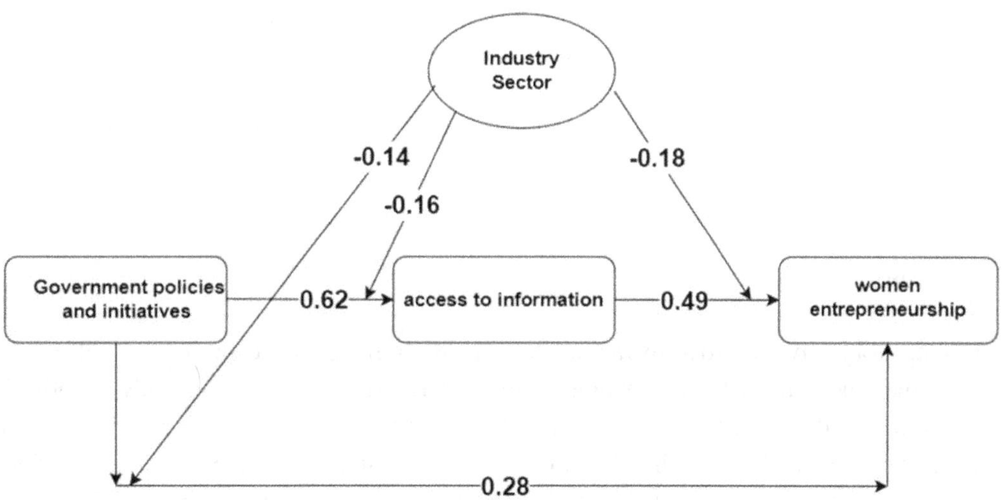

We estimated the path coefficients and tested the hypotheses using AMOS 26 software. We also performed bootstrapping with 5000 samples to test the significance of the indirect and moderated effects (Table 5).

Table 5. The results of the structural model

Hypothesis	Path	Coefficient	SE	t-Value	p-Value	Result
H1	Government policies and initiatives -> Women entrepreneurship	0.28	0.06	4.67	< 0.001	Supported
H2	Government policies and initiatives -> Access to information	0.62	0.05	12.40	< 0.001	Supported
H3	Access to information -> Women entrepreneurship	0.49	0.07	7.00	< 0.001	Supported
H4a	Government policies and initiatives x Industry sector -> Women entrepreneurship	-0.14	0.05	-2.80	< 0.01	Supported
H4b	Government policies and initiatives x Industry sector -> Access to information	-0.16	0.04	-4.00	< 0.001	Supported
H5a	Access to information x Industry sector -> Women entrepreneurship	-0.18	0.06	-3.00	< 0.01	Supported
H5b (indirect effect)	Government policies and initiatives x Industry sector -> Access to information -> Women entrepreneurship (moderated mediation)	-0.08	0.03	-2.67	< 0.01	Supported

Structural equation modelling (SEM) utilising AMOS 26 software was used to test the structural model. The findings corroborated all of the hypotheses and demonstrated that government initiatives and policies had a favourable and substantial effect on women's entrepreneurship (H1) and indirectly (H3) through policies to access information. However, the industrial sector in which the women entrepreneurs worked mitigated this effect, making it less pronounced for women in the manufacturing sector than for those in the service sector. The industry sector reduced the direct impact of government policies and initiatives on women's entrepreneurship (H4a), the direct impact of government policies and initiatives on access to information (H4b), the direct impact of access to information on women's entrepreneurship (H5a), and the indirect effect of government policies and initiatives on women's entrepreneurship through access to information (H5b). According to these findings, government policies and initiatives had a less beneficial influence on women entrepreneurs' entrepreneurial behaviour and outcomes due to their poorer access to information in the manufacturing sector.

DISCUSSION

This study's main objective was to utilise a moderated mediation model to examine how different government programmes and policies affected women's entrepreneurship in India. The study hypothesised that the industry sector of the latter moderates the relationship between government policies and initiatives and women's entrepreneurship and that the latter's access to information mediates this relationship. In order to collect data, a survey was conducted, and the results were analysed. The study's findings were used to determine whether or not women in the United States should be allowed to participate in the programme. To evaluate the hypotheses, structural equation modelling was utilised in the study.

The study's findings confirmed all of the assumptions. They demonstrated that government initiatives and policies had a significant and favourable effect on women's entrepreneurship, directly and indirectly, through information access. However, the industry sector in which the women entrepreneurs operate moderates this effect, making it more robust for women in the manufacturing sector than for women in the service sector.

The results of this study have several theoretical and real-world applications. The study theoretically adds to the body of knowledge on government and public policy by presenting empirical data on the regulated mediation mechanism through which government policies and initiatives affect women's entrepreneurship in India. By investigating several types of government policies and initiatives, such as Startup India, Stand Up India, Mudra Yojana, etc., as well as other industry sectors, such as manufacturing and service, which have not been extensively covered in earlier studies, the study also adds to the body of literature. In order to understand the intricate relationships between the factors, the study also incorporates other theoretical viewpoints, including institutional theory, resource-based view, and social cognitive theory.

CONCLUSION

Using a moderated mediation model, this study investigated the effects of various government initiatives and policies on women's entrepreneurship in India. According to the study, both directly and indirectly through access to information, government policies and initiatives have a favourable and considerable effect on women's entrepreneurship. However, the industry sector in which the women entrepreneurs operate moderates this effect, making it less pronounced for manufacturing than for service-based female entrepreneurs. The study provides several theoretical and practical consequences for scholars, policymakers, practitioners, and women entrepreneurs.

Some of the study's limitations offer ideas for future research directions. The study's initial cross-sectional design restrains the application of causal inference. Second, the study employed a self-reported survey methodology that could introduce biases such as standard method variance or social desirability. Third, the study's use of a convenience sample may limit its capacity to generalize. Fourth, the study concentrated on three latent constructs: access to information, women's entrepreneurship, and government policies and initiatives. Fifth, only one moderator variable the industry sector was employed in the study.

REFERENCES

Anderson, J. C., & Gerbing, D. W. (1988). Structural equation modeling in practice: A review and recommended two-step approach. *Psychological Bulletin*, *103*(3), 411–423. doi:10.1037/0033-2909.103.3.411

GEM. (2020). *Global Entrepreneurship Monitor 2019/2020 Global Report*. Retrieved from https://www.gemconsortium.org/report/gem-2019-2020-global-report

Goel, N., & Madan, P. (2019). Benchmarking financial inclusion for women entrepreneurship–a study of Uttarakhand state of India. *Benchmarking*, *26*(1), 160–175. doi:10.1108/BIJ-01-2018-0023

Gupta, V. K., Goktan, A. B., & Gunay, G. (2019). Gender differences in entrepreneurial propensity: Evidence from matriculating students in the United States. *The International Entrepreneurship and Management Journal*, *15*(1), 1–29.

Hair, J. F., Black, W. C., Babin, B. J., & Anderson, R. E. (2019). *Multivariate data analysis* (8th ed.). Cengage Learning.

Ingalagi, S. S., Nawaz, N., Rahiman, H. U., Hariharasudan, A., & Hundekar, V. (2021). Unveiling the crucial factors of women entrepreneurship in the 21st century. *Social Sciences (Basel, Switzerland)*, *10*(5), 153. doi:10.3390ocsci10050153

Kabeer, N., Mahmud, S., & Tasneem, S. (2017). Does paid work provide a pathway to women's empowerment? Empirical findings from Bangladesh. *World Development*, *90*, 225–239.

Kumar, K. (2021). Women Entrepreneurship. In *India: Issues*. Challenges And Ways Forward.

Nair, S. R. (2016). Women entrepreneurship across nations: Opportunities and challenges. Handbook of Research on Entrepreneurship in the Contemporary Knowledge-Based Global Economy, 189–216.

Noor, S., & Isa, F. M. (2020). Contributing factors of women entrepreneurs' business growth and failure in Pakistan. *International Journal of Business and Globalisation*, *25*(4), 503–518. doi:10.1504/IJBG.2020.109115

Sen, A., & Al, M. (2021). Women Entrepreneurship. *PalArch's Journal of Archaeology of Egypt/Egyptology, 18*(9), 69–77.

Sharma, P. (2013). Women entrepreneurship development in India. *Global Journal of Management and Business Studies*, *3*(4), 371–376.

Singh, S., Simpson, R., Mordi, C., & Okafor, C. (2016). Motivation and gender in the informal sector in Nigeria. *Gender in Management*, *31*(4), 250–271.

Srivastava, S., & Agrawal, A. (2020). Women entrepreneurship in India–Problems and prospects. *International Journal of Management Studies*, *7*(2), 1–14.

Chapter 15
Overview of Industry 5.0 on Emerging Technologies and Human and Robot Collaboration

Usha Prabhu
https://orcid.org/0000-0001-6219-5358
Jain University, India

Vasudha Srivatsa
Adarsh Institute of Management and Information Technology, India

P. H. Reshma Sultana
Jain University, India

R. Vennila
https://orcid.org/0000-0002-8849-6295
Jain University, India

B. Manjunath
Jain University, India

ABSTRACT

The mere idea of Industry 5.0 has lately arisen as the hope for a future industry founded on social and environmental sustainability. The proponents of Industry 5.0 argue that Industry 4.0 is not the best framework for ensuring long-term sustainability. Industry 4.0 focuses on technology-driven productivity in all spheres but neglects human intervention in the final production of the product or service; Industry 5.0 emerged by overcoming its fallacy on it. In 2015, the United Nations adopted a set of goals known as the Sustainable Development Goals (SDGs) with the aim of mobilizing all of its member states to take action to protect the environment, address social issues, and build global prosperity. It is a proactive, goal-oriented strategy that re-evaluates social, economic, and environmental expectations. There is synergy between Industry 5.0 and Society 5.0. Industry 5.0 seeks to understand the potential of big data, artificial intelligence, robots, and advanced digitalization in addressing emerging needs in the industrial, societal, and environmental.

DOI: 10.4018/979-8-3693-2193-5.ch015

1. INTRODUCTION

The mere idea of Industry 5.0 has lately arisen as the hope for a future industry founded on social and environmental sustainability. The proponents of Industry 5.0 argue that Industry 4.0 is not the best framework for ensuring long-term sustainability. Industry 4.0 focuses on technology–driven productivity in all spheres but neglects human intervention in the final production of the product or service; thereby, Industry 5.0 emerged by overcoming its fallacy on it (Ghobakhloo, Iranmanesh, Grybauskas, Vilkas, & Petraitė, 2021). Critics say that because it follows neoliberal capitalist norms, Industry 4.0 would exacerbate problems, including economic inequality, environmental devastation, and a fragile global economy, by prioritizing profit and shareholder power (Grabowska & Saniuk, 2022).

The United Nations adopted the Sustainable Development Goals (SDGs) in 2015 to guarantee that all people live in peace and prosperity, put an end to extreme poverty, and safeguard the world. The SDGs were released as a worldwide call to action to all of its member nations. To promote long-term economic growth, SDGs aim to provide more gainful job opportunities through technological advancement. (Prassida & Asfari, 2022).

According to the European Commission, "Industry 5.0" has proposed a blueprint for developing a sector of the economy that prioritizes people and sustainability across Europe. To find an equilibrium between economic progress as well as the elimination of social ills in Japanese society, the Japan Cabinet has proposed Society 5.0. (Amr, 2022). Two similar visions for the future of business and society are Industry 5.0 and Society 5.0. It is possible that when these concepts are discussed simultaneously, there will be some turmoil. (Huang, et al., 2022).

The European Commission (EC) publicly declared the "Fifth Industrial Revolution (Industry 5.0)" in 2021. On January 4th, 2021, the document "Industry 5.0: Towards a Sustainable, Human-centric and Resilient European Industry" was released. Industry 5.0 is moving -looking for ideas that analyze how to change industries into ones that are robust, sustainable, and people-focused (Mao, Wang, Tang, & Qian, 2019)

The emphasis in Industry 5.0 has shifted from monetary value to societal value and from welfare to well-being. When compared to Industry 4.0, the scope of application for the concept of Industry 5.0 is far broader, as it is applicable to every sector and every organization. Therefore, we must take a wide and universal view applicable to all industries when considering the consequences of Industry 5.0 as the approach. The three pillars of Industry 5.0 are a focus on people, resilience, and sustainability. The ramifications of all three for company strategy are substantial.

Analysts predict that 50% of today's jobs will be automated by 2055; however, this date might be as much as 20 years earlier or later, depending on a number of circumstances, including the state of the economy at large. Therefore, it isn't easy to accurately represent the dynamic relationship between worker preferences and organizational reality in a technological context.

- To provide the per capita GDP growth that countries throughout the world require, people will need to continue working alongside robots.
- Businesses can reap significant performance benefits from automation, but only if policymakers see the need to help employees and institutions adjust to the changes brought about by automation (Manyika, et al., 2017)

Industry 5.0 is based on the model, where 3 dimensions are involved- human-centric approach, sustainability & resilience in the economy. The term "Human-centric approach" refers to a method of manufacturing in which people's human wants and needs are prioritized. Reducing energy usage and greenhouse gas emissions, protecting against the exploitation and destruction of natural resources, and avoiding these acts are all part of "sustainability," the practice of meeting the demands of the present without compromising those of future generations. It indicates that through increasing resource efficiency and minimizing waste, emerging technologies like artificial intelligence (AI) can have a big impact on the ecosystem. The concept of "resilience" refers to the ability of industrial production to withstand shocks, protect against disruptions, maintain critical infrastructure during emergencies, especially in the provision of human necessities like security and healthcare, and manage strategic value chains, agile business processes, and adaptable manufacturing capacity.

Creativity and innovation have become one of the main forces behind modern economic development and prosperity, leading to Industry 5.0-customized goods, services, and experiences are the result of a collaborative effort between humans and robots in the "Industry 5.0." (Esben, 2017). There is a new paradigm shift in the industries, and it entails the pervasive use of AI in everyday activities. (Skobelev & Borovik, 2017). Due to the expanding workforce, the advancement of digital technology, and AI-based solutions, companies and their employees face a number of challenges in maintaining a competitive edge. (Nahavandi S., 2019). The technological world, mass customization, and a tremendous shift are taking place in modern manufacturing. Because of advancements in artificial intelligence or the development of brain-machine interfaces, robots have grown increasingly significant. (Nahavandi S., 2019). Industry 5.0 will create links between social and technological systems that will enable mass personalization of goods and services. (Bednar & Welch, 2019)

Businesses started implementing Industry 4.0 as the Fifth Industrial Revolution (Industry 5.0) was starting to take shape. Industry 5.0 is thought to realize that industry's ability to promote social goals beyond employment and growth to become a reliable source of income through ensuring that production is reliable & moral while taking into account the constraints of our present technology. (Breque, De Nul, & Petridis, 2021)

The necessity for new technologies to be built with support for future social values is an urgent priority. Society 5.0 emphasizes that the industry needs to reconsider its place and function in society in light of these changes and questions that are intimately related to technological progress. (Zhong, Xu, Klotz, & Newman, 2017). The groundwork for the introduction of Industry 5.0 can be traced back to Industry 4.0, which prioritized digitalization & AI-driven technologies to increase production flexibility & efficiency over much more fundamental ideals, including social justice and sustainability. It offers a distinct viewpoint and places focus on the value of innovation and research. In Industry 5.0, there have been rumors of the "Age of Augmentation," in which people & machines coexist & cooperate. (Longo F, Padovano, & Umbrello, 2020).

Industries have the potential to contribute to societal concerns, including The theme of society Actively 5.0 is resource conservation, climate change, and societal stability. For businesses, employees, and society as a whole, there is a mutual benefit to integrating these many systems.

Industry must constantly change in order to meet these evolving difficulties; if it is to continue to be the source of prosperity, continuous innovation can enable this sustained adaption. In short,

Industry 5.0's central focus is human-robot collaboration. Human-robot Collaboration is a key component of Industry 5.0, and it will occur whenever & wherever it really is practicable. Robots will perform mundane duties, freeing people to focus on innovation-driven creativity. A different Industry 5.0 concept is the bio-economy, which aims to balance ecological, industry, and economy while judiciously utilizing biological resources for industrial purposes. (Breque, De Nul, & Petridis, 2021).

2. EVOLUTION OF THE INDUSTRIAL REVOLUTION

By the end of the seventeenth century, the Industrial Revolution, which started in England in 1760 & eventually spread to the United States, was well on its way. Mining, textile, agricultural, glass, and other industries were all impacted by the shift from handicrafts to machines that accompanied the introduction of Industry 1.0 (Longo, Padovano, & Umbrello, 2020). The period from 1871 and 1914, known as "Industry 2.0," was a pivotal one for the manufacturing industry, marking a time of increased output and prosperity but also a spike in unemployment as machines gradually supplanted human labor in the workplace. Automation of memory-programmable controllers and computers during The digital revolution and the transition to Industry 3.0 were both initiated in the 1970s of the twentieth century. As a result of this digital revolution, technology has become increasingly digital. The phrase "Industry 4.0" refers to the integration of traditional manufacturing methods with modern technologies such as AI, robotics, the IoT, 3D printing, cloud computing, etc. Businesses that have adopted Industry 4.0 are flexible and prepared to base decisions on data. The term "Industry 4.0" describes the integration of traditional manufacturing methods with modern information and communication technology. Companies that have adopted the practices of Industry 4.0 is agile and prepared to make "data-driven decisions". (Leone, et al., 2020) (Fig. 1).

Figure 1. Evolution of the industrial revolution
Source: Kadir Alpaslan Demir

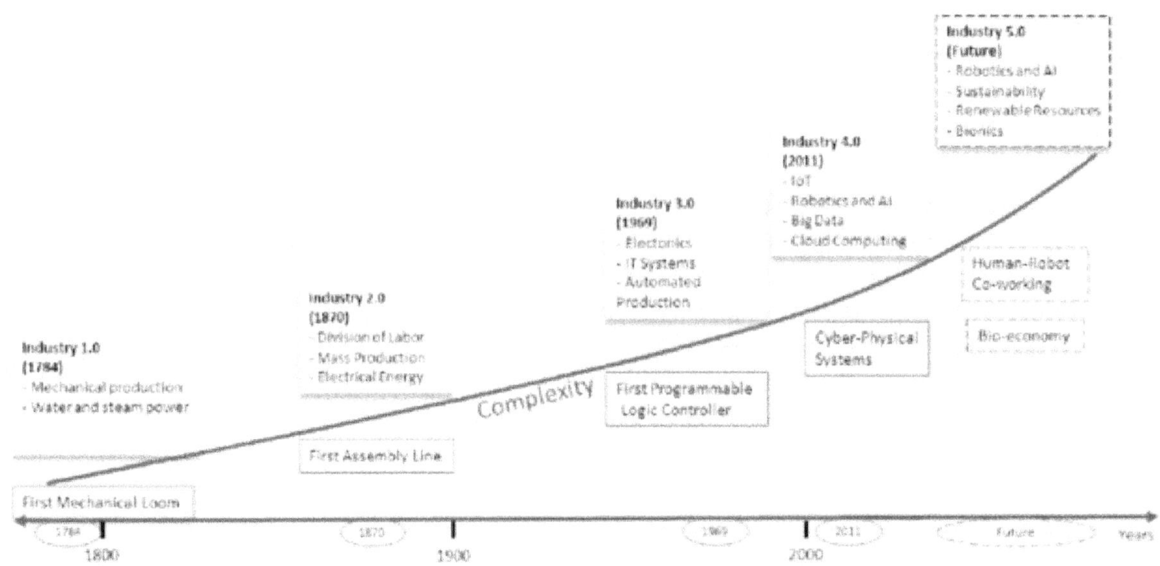

Businesses must invest in breakthroughs and emerging growth areas based on a thorough grasp of long-term developments & create new business models and approaches to reflect those trends in order to remain successful in the future. A competitive skill will be pertinent for market success, making skills development a crucial long-term concern. (Eckhard, Cornelius, Jessica, & Cornelia, 2014)

3. STATEMENT OF THE PROBLEM

Collaborative robots are being developed for natural human interactions. Industry 5.0 is an attempt to move towards smarter manufacturing processes by employing collaboration with humans and robots or cobots (for usage) and the creation of renewable biological resources and recycling of trash to produce high-value products, including food, bio-based products, and bioenergy.

4. REVIEW OF LITERATURE

Transitioning to a bio-economy that ethically exploits biological resources for industrial purposes and upholds a delicate equilibrium between the natural world, industry, and economy is the objective of Industry 5.0 (Demir, Kadir, & Halil, 2018).

Industry 5.0 is the next stage in human evolution when machines and people work in perfect harmony. It will fundamentally alter the division of labor and affect manufacturing work processes (Longo, Francesco, Antonio, & Steven Umbrello, 2020).

The manufacturing sector will become more productive with humans and robotics, and in the future, collaboration with humans and robots (COBOT) will become obligatory in the manufacturing industries (Majumdar, Garq, & Jain, 2021).

Wang (2022) explains the implications of human-centric assembly in the future, and discusses the enhanced human capabilities that will enable a human operator to be more physically and intellectually powerful. The paper focuses on brain robotics, which replicates the human brain to assist human-centric assembly.

Wang highlights that humans help "robots (train, explain, sustain) and robots" helping humans are the foundations of collaborative intelligence, which means, humans must employ their skills not only to teach robots what to do but also to justify their decision-making processes. In a similar vein, robots must enable people to engage in work interactions that fully exploit co-intelligence (both artificial and anthropological) (Wang, Liu, Cooper, Wang, & Gao, 2021).

Gao et al. (2019), Human-Robot Coordination (HRC) creates a more comfortable and productive workplace by fusing strength, and consistency and combining the accuracy of robots with human flexibility, adaptability, and high-level cognition. Future HRC systems must prioritize human-centricity in the interests of long-term viability and resilience.

Industrial output is becoming more efficient as a result of human and machine cooperation, as evidenced by the rise of "Industry 5.0". The future of this phase will involve industrial robots and robot production. Technology developments in artificial intelligence & cognitive computing are boosting the industrial sector and improving corporate efficiency (Chen, et al., 2020).

Demir comes out with two visions in "Industry 5.0." The first vision is "Human-robot" collaboration, combining the strength of humans and robots in the manufacturing sector. Humans will do the creative work, while robots will do the mundane work. The second vision is bio-economy, the optimum utilization of bio-resources (Demir, Kadir, & Halil, 2018)

To implement Industry 5.0, business corporations must ensure that there is a smooth synergy between machines and human peers. It refers to expertise in areas like robotics and artificial intelligence. Training employees in technology becomes pertinent to decrease the cost for businesses (Zhang & Chen, 2020).

Chin (2021) observed, as how Emotional intelligence helped get into Industry 5.0 in the workforce. The survey was conducted among 110 C-suite levels. The results implied that emotional intelligence had a positive effect on workplace productivity. Identifying and expressing emotions has a higher effect on performance than previously thought in the study.

Simoes, Correia, Antonio, and Ana (2020): These studies, which have only been qualitatively done, used a theoretical framework that integrates the "Diffusion of Innovation theory," the "Technology-Organization-Environment Theory," and the "Institutional".

Bi et al. (2021) is of the belief that manufacturing companies need to consider factors like task requirements and design considerations like assurance of safety and trust, ergonomics, and adaptability.

Employee roles will change significantly in a smart factory, and it has been recognized. A cultural approach to organizational structure will give employees a chance to take on more responsibility and advance their personal development (Flores, Xu, & Lu, 2020).

Industry 5.0 It has been established that employees' roles will change significantly in a smart factory. The implementation of a socio-technical method of organizing work will provide workers with the opportunity to take on greater responsibilities and grow as individuals. Employees in the manufacturing sector who wish to further their careers and preserve a work-life balance should always be learning new skills and honing their old ones (Breque, De, & Petrides, 2021).

Abdelmageed & Zayed (2020) is of the opinion that more time and effort from human workers is needed for the adoption of modern technologies. Manufacturing has to adopt technologies like the Internet of Things, collaborative robots, artificial intelligence, real-time data, and software-connected, customized factories.

"Modern technologies, from the Internet of Things" (IoT) to "emerging intelligence," are being made in places where the authors work. They thought that the change from Industry 4.0 to Industry 5.0 would happen when these technologies come together (Skobelev & Borovik, 2017).

5. CONCLUDING PART OF THE REVIEW OF LITERATURE & RESHAPING TO THE FUTURE GOALS

Researchers have highlighted artificial intelligence (AI), supply chain, digital transformation, machine learning, big data, and the Internet of things (IoT) as often utilized buzzwords and key drivers of Industry 5.0. There remains a dearth of literature evaluations pertaining to safety and security concerns, as well as regulatory issues such as standardization and support for legal activities, within the context of Industry 5.0. The realization of Society 5.0 hinges upon the attainment of an equivalent degree of human-centric performance by Industry 5.0. Hence, it is evident that forthcoming systematic literature evaluations have the potential to enhance the foundational elements of Industry 5.0. To illustrate, this study aims to explore strategies for enhancing the resilience of distinct regional economies and manufacturing processes. Additionally, an examination of various technologies that have the potential to facilitate sustainable policies will be conducted (Barata & Kayser, 2023).

From this perspective, Industry 5.0 can be viewed as a supplementary force to the progress achieved in Industry 4.0, with the aim of assisting and reinforcing human capabilities rather than replacing them. This approach enables human intervention as necessary and shifts away from an overreliance on automation in order to integrate critical thinking and adaptability while also using the accuracy and consistency offered by machines.

6. OBJECTIVES

- To understand the concept of Industry 5.0 & its implication on the manufacturing segment
- To examine the dimensions & challenges relating to Industry 5.0.

7. RATIONALE FOR THE PROGRESSION OF INDUSTRY 5.0

The term "Industrial Revolution 5.0" refers to the increasing efficiency of industrial output caused by both people and machines. Industry 5.0 will significantly alter human tasks and will affect industrial work systems (Longo, Francesco, Antonio, & Steven, 2020). By integrating human and robot collaboration (Cobots) and utilizing workers' ability for more complex jobs and flexibility in the tasks. In Industry 5.0, worker tasks add minimal value to the process and optimize the manufacturing processes. (Bednar & Christine, 2019). Future Industry 5.0 will focus on manufacturing industrial robots and other robots. The manufacturing sector has accelerated and become more productive with the advancements in the development of artificial intelligence and cognitive technologies, increasing business efficiency. (Cisneros, et al., 2021).

Companies must have the right employees in place to ensure proper machine-to-person contact in order to implement Industry 5.0. Knowledge of disciplines like robotics and artificial intelligence is required. (Zhang & Chen, A review of research relevant to the emerging industry trends: Industry4.0, IoT, blockchain and business analytics, 2020). It covers sectors of chemical, biotechnology, and energy industries, as well as those related to agriculture, forestry, fisheries, food production, and pulp manufacturing. Due to the use of several life sciences, such as In addition to enabling and industrial technologies like biotechnology, nanotechnology, IT, & engineering, the industries have a large potential for innovation in the fields of agronomy, ecology, food science, and social sciences (Ciervo, 2012).

8. PROPOSED APPROACH

Industry 5.0 is a new paradigm that emphasizes concepts such as human–a human-centered approach, sustainability, organizational resilience, and collaboration between humans and machines. The new trend is defined in the world of business as "neo-industrialization". The goal of Industry 4.0 appears to be technological, specifically the application of digital technologies to boost production output and efficiency. Industry 4.0 will remain important because it facilitates machine-to-machine and the sharing of information.

Four Dimensions of Industry 5.0: Intention to Use Human-Robots Collaboration

People collaborating with intelligent machines and robotic aids is what the term "Industry 5.0" refers to. Robots will help people get more done in using technology because of cutting-edge technologies like big data analytics (Javaid, et al., 2020). In particular, while focusing on the level of organizations, systems, as well as works, it calls for socio-technical roles that examine how people and technology interact. As organizational tools for assessing the design of work systems and making changes to the workplace, particularly in production and manufacturing, a wide range of socio-technical techniques have been created and put into use (Patnayakuni, Ravi, & Cynthia, 2010).

- **Performance Expectations**: defined as how much the organization will profit from utilizing cobots (Human-Robots collaboration) to perform specific tasks.
- **Effort Expectation**: The company believes that using cobots makes tasks easier and requires less work.
- **Social Influence**: the degree to which an organization believes in influencing people to think and should utilize cobots.
- **Facilitation Condition:** The degree to which an organization thinks that a technical and organizational infrastructure facilitates the usage of cobots.

Three Dimensions of Industry 5.0: Actual Use of Human-Robots Collaboration

- **Social Subsystem:** An organization's ability to modify and adjust to the use of cobots is referred to as its social subsystem.
- **Technical Subsystem:** It combines human and robot abilities to achieve the greatest results possible. Manufacturers combine the distinctive cognitive abilities of a human or other skilled human with a robot's capability in the stage of development.
- **Work Design**: Robots and human collaborate on task specialization, which describe the nature of work.

Outcome Of Dimensions: Perceived Work Performance Improvement

Bryant & Allen (2011) surveyed 200 employees in start-up organizations to demonstrate the relationship between technology use and job effectiveness. The use of technology improves job performance and modifies employee behaviour (Lebioda, Laleska, Ivanete, & Anderson, 2019). Yueh, Hsiu-Ping, Ming-Hsin Lu, & Weijane (2016) revealed in the paper that behaviour is a requirement for a sense of enhanced behaviour at work.

New Business Ecosystems

In a globalized society, the costs and benefits of the environment and society are incorrectly accounted for by a narrow concentration on profit. Nations to become true providers of prosperity; instead of merely maximizing efficiency and profit, they must concentrate on the true mission of the organization, which takes social, environmental, and societal considerations into account. This includes responsible innovation that aims to advance prosperity for all of the company's partners, such as shareholders, employees, consumers, society, as well as the environment. It indicates that an industry's human-centric strategy places fundamental human wants and interests at the center of the production process (Maija, Lars, & Athanasios, 2021). Company success depends on managing a network of stakeholders that are involved in the value-creation process. The businesses that are most innovative and adaptable to market changes will win, according to Industry 5.0, which emphasizes a clear move away from mass automation towards the process of increasing human worker capacities (Paschek, Mocan, & Draghici, 2019).

9. ANALYSIS AND DISCUSSIONS

Issues in Human-Robot Co-Working

Industry 5.0, integrating robots into organizations, brings significant changes in the organizations such as organization behavior, structure, ethics, workflow, and work environment. In addition to the adoption of robots in the workplace, many obstacles need to be overcome, including bias towards robots or humans, lack of trust between humans and robots, security concerns, and a lack of training and education programs. Issues are:

- **Legal and regulatory issues:** Co-working with humans and robots would pose a threat if required regulations are absent. Robot has to be clearly and scientifically defined. Laws governing human-robot collaboration should make apparent the differences between robots, drones, and cyborgs (humanoids). Workplace rules should outline the kinds of robots that are permitted, their tasks and responsibilities, the kinds of judgments about robots that robots may make, the kinds of mistakes that robots may commit, and so forth. It requires numerous discussions to be considered, and the rules governing robot development, production, and certification have to be dealt with.
- **Preference for using robots at work:** Every person has a different personal preference regarding whether or not to use a technology. Some employees are eager to work with robots, and some vehemently oppose the idea. Organizations must understand the psychology of the workers regarding working with robots and accordingly bring transition in the organization, as working with robots is not yet a reality.
- **Psychological problems caused by human-robot collaboration:** As technologies get advanced, it pose psychological impact on workers and ushers a wide range of unheard psychological repercussions on many of them.
- **Social effects of human-robot collaboration:** As humans are gregarious, working with peers in the organization is a normal phenomenon for individuals. It's feasible that the human workforce will decrease as the robot workforce in the workplace rises. This might limit the social interactions that people have with one another. Some people believe that social interaction shown by robots is fictitious and that working with a robot is simply the result of computer programming. When robots are at the management level(decision-making), the situations become more difficult. (Barlett, Brendan, Vladimir, & Stuart, 2004), the authors also endorse this view.

- **Shifting functions of HR with technology:** One of the key duties of human resources departments is to carry out work analyses, create job descriptions, and fill open positions with qualified candidates. In the future, HR technology- robots become an integral component of the organization. They need to identify the jobs that robots will take over and distinguish the roles and responsibilities of humans and robots.
- **The changing function of IT departments to robotics departments:** Technology adoption by businesses is inevitable, and co-working with robots is near in the future. Organizations may establish robotics divisions tasked with purchasing and maintaining the organization's robots. Robot updates and maintenance should be carried out safely and securely because robots perform mundane tasks. Working together with robots will probably make it more difficult to protect employee privacy and information.

Ethical Problems Caused by Human-Robot Collaboration

- **Ethical status of robots:** The required ethical behavior among human employees includes being sincere, diligent, empathetic, and cooperative, whereas robots are programmed machines without any emotions nor tire like humans. It's possible that humans cannot compete with robots in this regard in terms of upholding high ethical standards. Hard to predict how the presence of both humans and robots in the workplace might affect work morals. (Briggs, Gordon, & Matthias, 2014), the authors anticipate the same view.
- **Understanding robotics at work:** Co-working with humans and robots will be unacquainted to all office workers. Humans must learn how to interact with robots. There will be robots with various capacities. Manufacturers of robotics will need to figure out how to make devices that can clearly and concisely describe the functions of the organization. Working with various robot types will require training for humans.
- **Reduced human workforce leads to "negative attitude toward robots":** A survey found that the loss of jobs is what people are most concerned about when it comes to robots, both personally and socially. An unfavorable attitude toward robots is likely to develop as they begin to replace humans in certain occupations. Some will contend that the unemployment of humans will be on the rise. This viewpoint will be refuted, and humans will be able to focus on more intellectually stimulating fields like creativity, artistic work, and research but repetitive tasks to be done by robots. Another view is that machines have precision adaptability in tasks, creating apprehension among humans.
- **Robots competing with humans, or humans complementing robots:** Scientists and professionals are debating on the positions and roles that robots take on. An easier solution will be to use robots to supplement human labour. As robots take over more and more mundane duties, humans will be able to focus on more intellectually stimulating pursuits like creativity, art, research, and development. However, many believe robots should be allowed to perform tasks traditionally performed by humans. They all contend that doing this will raise workers' productivity.
- Humans naturally compete with one another for jobs inside companies. The introduction of robots will make management and organizational behavior more challenging. Studies have also been conducted to examine how people would respond to a robotic commander (Cormier, et al., 2013).

10. CONCLUSION AND FUTURE SCOPE FOR RESEARCH

With the rapid pace at which technology is progressing, Manufacturers must modify the production plan by integrating cutting-edge technologies to stay up with customer demand as technology advances at an ever-faster clip. Industry 5.0 is often cited as the solution to the problem (Industry4.0) -as to how to achieve prosperity in the long-term, sustainability, by increasing productivity without eliminating jobs for people. With the introduction of Industry 5.0, repetitive jobs previously performed by humans will be eliminated, radically altering manufacturing processes around the world. Concerns around human-robot interaction were investigated in this research. There is a lot of scope for growth in this area of study, as some of the most pressing issues relating to law, legislation, psychology, society, and ethics need to be tackled. The IT sector frequently uses automation, robotics breakthroughs, AI, and machine learning (ML), but in the "Industry 5.0" era of industrialization, technologies will be used everywhere to increase productivity and efficiency. Because autonomous labours enable more effective and effective production systems by assisting human workers in accomplishing specific tasks, the utilization of human-robot partnerships in manufacturing systems offers several long-term benefits. To perfect the process of human-robot collaboration, research is required.

REFERENCES

Abdelmageed, S., & Zayed, T. (2020). *A study of literature in modular integrated construction-critical review and future directions*. Academic Press.

Amr, A. (2022). Future of Industry 5.0 in society: Human-centric solutions, challenges, and prospective research areas. *Adel Journal of Cloud Computing*, *11*(40), 2–15. PMID:36101900

Barata, J., & Kayser, I. (2023). Industry 5.0–Past, Present, and Near Future. *Procedia Computer Science*, *21*(9), 778–788. doi:10.1016/j.procs.2023.01.351

Barlett, B., Vladimir, E. C., & Stuart, S. (2004). Dogs or robots: why do children see them as robotic pets rather than Canine machines? *Proceedings of the fifth conference on Australasian user interface,* 28, 7-14.

Bednar, P. M., & Welch, C. (2019). Socio-Technical perspectives on Smart Working: Creating meaningful and sustainable systems. *Information Systems Frontiers*, *22*(2), 281–298. doi:10.100710796-019-09921-1

Bi, Z., Mingchao, L., Zhonghua, M., & Zhang, B. (2021). Safety assurance mechanisms of collaborative robotics systems in manufacturing. *Robotics and Computer-integrated Manufacturing*, *67*, 102022. doi:10.1016/j.rcim.2020.102022

Breque, M., De Nul, L., & Petridis, A. (2021). *Industry 5.0: Toward a sustainable, human-centric, and resilient European Industry*. European Commission, Directorate-General for Research and Innovation.

Briggs, G., & Scheutz, M. (2014). How Robots can affect Human Behaviour: Investigating the effects of Robotic displays of Protest and Distress. *International Journal of Social Robotics*, *6*(3), 343–355. doi:10.100712369-014-0235-1

Bryant, P., & Allen, D. (2011). Employment mode choices and late stage start-ups: A preliminary explorations using fsQCA. *American Journal of Entrepreneurship*, *4*(2).

Chen, H., Simoska, O., Lim, K., Grattieri, M., Yuan, M., Dong, F., & Minteer, S. (2020). Fundamentals, applications, and future directions of bioelectrocatalysis. *Chemical Reviews*, *120*(23), 12903–12993. doi:10.1021/acs.chemrev.0c00472 PMID:33050699

Chin, S. T. (2021). Influence of emotional intelligence on the workforce for Industry 5.0. IBIMA Publishing.

Ciervo, M. (2012). *Innovating for Sustainable Growth- A Bioeconomy for Europe*. Academic Press.

Cisneros, S. C., Pishchulov, G., Sampaio, P., Mehandjiev, N., Liu, Z., & Kununka, S. (2021). An approach and decision support tool forming Industry 4.0 supply chain collaborations. *Computers in Industry*, *125*, 103391. doi:10.1016/j.compind.2020.103391

Cormier, D., Gem, N., Nakane, Masayuki, Young, J. E., & Stephane, D. (2013). Would you do as a robot commands? An obedience study for human-robot interaction. *International Conference on Human-Agent Interaction*.

Demir, K. A., & Halil, C. (2018). The next Industrial Revolution: Industry 5.0 and discussions on Industry4.0. *Management Information Systems Perspectives*.

Eckhard, S., Cornelius, P., Jessica, P., & Cornelia, D. Z. (2014). *The Future of Work Jobs and Skills in 2030*. The Foresight Company.

Esben, H. o. (2017, October). *Collaborative Robots Ushering in Industry 5.0*. Academic Press.

Flores, E., Xu, X., & Lu, Y. (2020). Human4.0: A workforce competence typology for Industry 4.0. *Journal of Manufacturing Technology Management*, *31*(4), 687–703. doi:10.1108/JMTM-08-2019-0309

Gao, R., Vaneza, J., Wang, L., Kriiger, J., Wang, X., & Makris, S. (2019). Symbiotic human-robot collaborative assembly. *CIRP Annuals, 68*(2), 701-726.

Ghobakhloo, M., Iranmanesh, M., Grybauskas, A., Vilkas, M., & Petraitė, M. (2021). Industry 4.0, innovation, and sustainable development: A systematic review and a roadmap to sustainable innovation. *Business Strategy and the Environment*, *30*(8), 4237–4257. doi:10.1002/bse.2867

Grabowska, S., & Saniuk, S. (2022). Business models in the industry 4.0 environment-results of web of science bibliometric analysis. *Journal of Open Innovation*, *8*(1), 19. doi:10.3390/joitmc8010019

Huang, S., Wang, B., Li, X., Zheng, P., Mourtzis, D., & Wang, L. (2022). Industry 5.0 and Society 5.0- Comparison, comlementation and Co-evolution. *Journal of Manufacturing Systems*, *64*, 424–428. doi:10.1016/j.jmsy.2022.07.010

Javaid, M., Haleem, A., Singh, R., Haq, M., Raina, A., & Suman, R. (2020). Industry 5.0: Potential applications in COVID-19. *Journal of Industrial Integration and Management*, *5*(04), 507–530. doi:10.1142/S2424862220500220

Lebioda, L., Ivanete, H. S., & Anderson, A. M. (2019). The Influence of Mobile Technology Usage Behavior on Perceived Work Performance. *International Journal of Developmental Research*, *9*(2), 25733–25738.

Leone, L., Fleischhacker, S., Anderson-Steeves, B., Harper, K., Winkler, M., Racine, E., Baquero, B., & Gittelsohn, J. (2020). Healthy food retail during the COVID-19 pandemic: Challenges and future directions. *International Journal of Environmental Research and Public Health*, *17*(20), 7397. doi:10.3390/ijerph17207397 PMID:33050600

Longo, F., Padovano, A., & Umbrello, S. (2020). Value-oriented and ethical technology engineering in industry 5.0: A human-centric perspective for the design of the factory of the future. *Applied Sciences (Basel, Switzerland)*, *10*(12), 4182. doi:10.3390/app10124182

Maija, B., Lars, D. N., & Athanasios, P. (2021). *Industry 5.0- Towards a sustainable, human-centric, and resilient European industry*. European Commission.

Manyika, J., Chui, M., Miremadi, M., Bughin, J., George, K., Willmott, P., & Dewhurst, M. (2017). A future that works: AI, automation, employment, and productivity. *McKinsey Global Institute Research. Tech. Rep*, *60*, 1–135.

Mao, S., Wang, B., Tang, Y., & Qian, F. (2019). Opportunities and challenges of artificial intelligence for green manufacturing in the process industry. *Engineering (Beijing)*, *5*(6), 995–1002. doi:10.1016/j.eng.2019.08.013

Nahavandi, S. (2019). Industry 5.0- A human-centric solution. *Sustainability (Basel)*, *11*(16), 4371. doi:10.3390u11164371

Paschek, D., Mocan, A., & Draghici, A. (2019). Industry 5.0- The expected impact of the next industrial revolution. In *Thriving on future education, industry, business, and society, proceedings of the Make-Learn and TIIM International conference* (pp. 15-17). Piran.

Patnayakuni, R., & Ruppel, C. P. (2010). A soci-technical approach to improving the systems development process. *Information Systems Frontiers*, *12*(2), 219–234. doi:10.100710796-008-9093-4

Prassida, G., & Asfari, U. (2022). A conceptual model for the acceptance of collaborative robots in industry5.0. *Procedia Computer Science*, *197*, 61–67. doi:10.1016/j.procs.2021.12.118

Simoes, A., Correia, Antonio, L. S., & Ana, C. B. (2020). Factors influencing the intention of managers to adopt collaborative robots(cobots)in manufacturing organizations. *Journal of Engineering and Technology Management*.

Skobelev, P., & Borovik, S. (2017). On the way from Industry 4.0 to Industry 5.0: From digital manufacturing to digital society. *Industry 4.0, 2*(6), 307-311.

Wang, L. (2022, January). A futuristic perspective on human-centric assembly. *Journal of Manufacturing Systems*, *62*, 199–201. doi:10.1016/j.jmsy.2021.11.001

Wang, L., Liu, S., Cooper, C., Wang, X., & Gao, R. (2021). Functionblock-based human-robot collaborative assembly driven by brainwaves. *CIRP Annals*, *70*(1), 5–8. doi:10.1016/j.cirp.2021.04.091

Yueh, H.-P., Lu, M.-H., & Lin, W. (2016). Employees'acceptance of mobile technology in a workplace: An empirical study using SEM and fsQCA. *Journal of Business Research*, *69*(6), 2318–2324. doi:10.1016/j.jbusres.2015.12.048

Zhang, C., & Chen, Y. (2020). A review of research relevant to the emerging industry trends: Industry 4.0, IoT, blockchain, and business analytics. *Journal Industrial Integrate Management*, *5*(01), 165–180. doi:10.1142/S2424862219500192

Zhong, R., Xu, X., Klotz, E., & Newman, S. (2017). Intelligent manufacturing in the context of Industry4.0: A Review. *Engineering (Beijing)*, *3*(5), 616–630. doi:10.1016/J.ENG.2017.05.015

Chapter 16
Can Firm Size Moderate Navigating Economic Performance Through Strategic Purchasing?

Uday Inala
University of Hyderabad, India

John Yesudas Valluri
https://orcid.org/0000-0002-3003-7408
Jain University, India

Gunupuru Koteswara Rao
University of Hyderabad, India

Shyamaladevi Balakrishnan
SRM Institute of Science and Technology, Kattankulathur, India

A. S. Kannan
GRT Institute of Engineering and Technology, India

Easwaramoorthy Rangaswamy
Amity Global Institute, Singapore

ABSTRACT

This study empirically investigates the relationship between strategic purchasing, environmental purchasing, and economic performance in the manufacturing industry in India. Employing partial least squares (PLS) analysis guided by the dynamic capability view theory, this study examined the direct and moderating linkages between organizational purchasing practices and economic outcomes. The findings reveal a significant positive association between strategic purchasing and economic performance, with firm size acting as a moderator. Conversely, no moderating effect of firm size is found between environmental purchasing and economic performance. This research underscores the pivotal role of strategic purchasing in maximizing a supplier base, enhancing supplier relations, and influencing expenditures and operations across the supply network. This provides insights into the strategic role of purchasing in maintaining quality standards and enabling international growth.

DOI: 10.4018/979-8-3693-2193-5.ch016

INTRODUCTION

The manufacturing industry is one of the most vital sectors of the economy, as it contributes to the production of goods, the creation of jobs, and the generation of income. However, the manufacturing industry also faces various challenges, such as increasing competition, changing customer demands, environmental regulations, and technological disruptions. Therefore, it is imperative for manufacturing firms to adopt effective strategies and practices that can enhance their performance and competitiveness in the global market (Park et al., 2018).

One of the key areas that can influence the performance of manufacturing firms is purchasing, which refers to the process of acquiring materials, components, services, and equipment from external sources. Purchasing can affect the quality, cost, delivery, and innovation of the products and services offered by the firms, as well as their relationships with the suppliers and customers. Hence, purchasing can be considered as a strategic function that can create value and competitive advantage for the firms (Wagner et al., 2018).

However, not all purchasing practices are equally beneficial for the firms. Some purchasing practices may be more aligned with the strategic goals and objectives of the firms, while others may be more focused on the environmental and social aspects of the purchasing decisions. Therefore, it is important to examine the different types of purchasing practices and their impacts on the economic performance of the firms. In this regard, this study distinguishes between two types of purchasing practices: strategic purchasing and environmental purchasing.

Strategic purchasing refers to the purchasing activities that are aligned with the overall business strategy and objectives of the firm, and that aim to achieve long-term benefits and competitive advantage. Strategic purchasing involves selecting the best suppliers, developing close and collaborative relationships with them, integrating them into the product development and innovation process, and leveraging their capabilities and resources. Strategic purchasing can help the firms to reduce costs, improve quality, enhance delivery, and increase innovation, thereby improving their economic performance (Somjai & Jermsittiparsert, 2019).

Environmental purchasing refers to the purchasing activities that are concerned with the environmental and social impacts of the purchasing decisions, and that aim to minimize the negative effects and maximize the positive effects of the purchasing process on the natural environment and the society. Environmental purchasing involves considering the environmental and social criteria, such as the emissions, waste, energy consumption, and labor standards, of the suppliers and the products, and selecting the suppliers and products that have lower environmental and social footprints. Environmental purchasing can help the firms to comply with the environmental regulations, improve their reputation and image, and meet the expectations of the stakeholders, thereby enhancing their economic performance (Serrano et al., 2020).

However, the relationship between purchasing practices and economic performance may not be direct and simple. There may be other factors that can influence the strength and direction of this relationship. One of such factors is the firm size, which refers to the scale and scope of the firm's operations, resources, and capabilities. Firm size can affect the purchasing practices and the economic performance of the firms in various ways. For instance, larger firms may have more resources and capabilities to implement strategic and environmental purchasing practices, and to achieve economies of scale and scope, than smaller firms. On the other hand, smaller firms may have more flexibility and agility to adapt to the changing market conditions and customer preferences, and to innovate and differentiate themselves, than larger firms. Therefore, firm size can moderate the relationship between purchasing practices and economic performance, either positively or negatively, depending on the context and the situation (Park et al., 2018).

The purpose of this study is to empirically investigate the relationship between strategic purchasing, environmental purchasing, and economic performance in the manufacturing industry in India, and to examine the moderating effect of firm size on this relationship. This study is guided by the dynamic capability view theory, which suggests that firms can achieve superior performance and competitive advantage by developing and deploying their dynamic capabilities, which are the abilities to sense, seize, and transform the opportunities and threats in the external environment. According to this theory, purchasing can be considered as a dynamic capability that can enable the firms to access and utilize the external resources and capabilities of the suppliers, and to adapt and align their purchasing practices with the changing market conditions and customer demands.

This study contributes to the literature on strategic management and supply chain optimization by providing empirical evidence on the linkages between purchasing practices and economic performance in the manufacturing industry, and by exploring the role of firm size as a moderator. This study also offers valuable insights for both academia and industry practitioners on how to design and implement effective purchasing strategies and practices that can enhance the performance and competitiveness of the manufacturing firms in the global market.

LITERATURE REVIEW AND HYPOTHESIS DEVELOPMENT

Strategic Purchasing and Economic Performance

Firm Size and Economic Performance Firm size is a measure of the scale and scope of a firm's operations, resources, and capabilities. Firm size can affect the purchasing practices and the economic performance of the firms in various ways. For instance, larger firms may have more resources and capabilities to implement strategic and environmental purchasing practices, and to achieve economies of scale and scope, than smaller firms. On the other hand, smaller firms may have more flexibility and agility to adapt to the changing market conditions and customer preferences, and to innovate and differentiate themselves, than larger firms. Therefore, firm size can moderate the relationship between purchasing practices and economic performance, either positively or negatively, depending on the context and the situation (Park et al., 2018).

The literature on the relationship between firm size and economic performance is extensive and diverse, but also inconclusive and contradictory. Some studies have found a positive relationship between firm size and economic performance, suggesting that larger firms have higher profitability, productivity, efficiency, and growth than smaller firms (e.g., Majumdar, 1997; Goddard et al., 2005; Lee, 2009; Isik et al., 2017). Other studies have found a negative relationship between firm size and economic performance, implying that smaller firms have higher profitability, productivity, efficiency, and growth than larger firms (e.g., Scherer, 1979; Hall, 1987; Audretsch, 1991; Acs and Audretsch, 1993; Becchetti and Trovato, 2002). Yet other studies have found a non-linear or U-shaped relationship between firm size and economic performance, indicating that medium-sized firms have higher profitability, productivity, efficiency, and growth than both small and large firms (e.g., Smith, 1955; Evans, 1987; Kumar, 1985; Dunne and Hughes, 1994; Mata, 1994).

The mixed results of the literature can be attributed to various factors, such as the different definitions and measures of firm size and economic performance, the different samples and data sources, the different methods and models, the different industries and countries, and the different time periods and contexts. Moreover, the relationship between firm size and economic performance may be influenced by other variables, such as innovation, technology, competition, regulation, governance, and environment. Therefore, it is important to consider the specific characteristics and circumstances of each firm, industry, and country when analyzing the relationship between firm size and economic performance.

H1: Strategic purchasing is positively related to economic performance.

Environmental Purchasing and Economic Performance

In contrast to rival items that fulfil the same function, environmental purchasing is typically characterized by choosing an item with a more negligible or less adverse influence or significant improvement in people's welfare and the ecosystem. Businesses that purchase sustainably are deemed necessary for economic performance and other results (Shafiq et al., 2019).This is because environmental purchasing may significantly reduce wastage of resources, allowing the company to properly handle its assets and improve productivity (Khan &Pillania, 2008).Research has shown that environmentally friendly procurement has a significant impact and protracted sustainability initiatives can assist businesses in increasing savings and improving their ability to predict potential expenses (Talluri and Narasimhan, 2004).Research has shown that corporations may maximize their economic performance when adopting a green procurement strategy (Ambekar et al., 2018; R.Eltantawy et al., 2014; Talluri & Narasimhan, 2004).

Additionally, most consumers now demand that firms behave ethically and protect their environment. Credibility in the marketplace, perceived risk, and commitment to uphold moral standards should all play a significant role in a company's ability to achieve important goals, such as economic success. This prompted us to believe that environmental purchasing might also increase the monetization of sustainable procurement strategies to improve business performance. Consequently, we examined the following:

H2: Environmental purchasing is positively related to economic performance.

H3: Firm size moderates the relationship between strategic purchasing and economic performance.

H4: Firm size moderates the relationship between green procurement and economic performance.

Sampling

The purpose of this study was to examine the relationship between strategic purchasing, environmental purchasing, and economic performance in the manufacturing industry in India, and to explore the moderating effect of firm size on this relationship. To achieve this objective, a survey method was adopted to collect data from the manufacturing firms in India. The target population of this study consisted of the manufacturing firms that were registered with the Confederation of Indian Industry (CII), which is the largest and most representative industry association in India.

Simple random sampling is a sampling method that ensures that each element of the population has an equal and independent chance of being included in the sample. This sampling method is suitable for this study because it can reduce the sampling bias and error, and increase the representativeness and generalizability of the sample. A questionnaire was designed and sent via email to the executives who were deeply engaged in procurement activities in the selected firms. The questionnaire consisted of questions related to strategic purchasing, environmental purchasing, and economic performance, as well as firm size and other demographic variables. The questions were adapted from previous studies and validated by experts and pilot testing. The questions were measured on a five-point Likert scale, ranging from strongly disagree (1) to strongly agree (5).

The response rate of the survey was 43.4%, as 217 completed questionnaires were returned out of the 500 sent. However, after screening the data for missing values, outliers, and inconsistencies, only 203 responses were accepted for the final analysis, and 14 responses were rejected. The final sample size of 203 was considered satisfactory, given the often-low participation ratio for this type of correlational study in India (Rai & Thapa, 2015). The sample size was also adequate for conducting the partial least squares structural equation modeling (PLS-SEM) analysis, which was the main statistical technique used in this study. According to Hair et al. (2019), the minimum sample size required for PLS-SEM analysis is determined by the rule of 10, which states that the sample size should be equal to or larger than 10 times the maximum number of structural paths directed at a latent variable in the structural model. In this study, the maximum number of structural paths directed at a latent variable was four, which implied that the minimum sample size required was 40. Therefore, the sample size of 203 was more than sufficient for the PLS-SEM analysis.

Measurements

The questionnaire used in this study was composed of four sections: the first section collected the demographic information of the respondents, such as their gender, age, education, income, and firm size; the second section measured the strategic purchasing practices of the firms, based on an 8-item scale adapted from previous studies (e.g., Wagner et al., 2018; Somjai and Jermsittiparsert, 2019); the third section measured the environmental purchasing practices of the firms, based on a 6-item scale adapted from previous studies (e.g., Zhu and Sarkis, 2004; Serrano et al., 2020); and the fourth section measured the economic performance of the firms, based on a 5-item scale adapted from previous studies (e.g., Zhu and Sarkis, 2004; Park et al., 2018). All the items were measured on a five-point Likert scale, ranging from strongly disagree (1) to strongly agree (5).

The strategic purchasing scale consisted of eight items that assessed the extent to which the firms adopted strategic purchasing practices, such as selecting the best suppliers, developing long-term relationships with them, integrating them into the product development and innovation process, and leveraging their capabilities and resources. The items were as follows:

- We select our suppliers based on their strategic fit with our business objectives and vision.
- We establish long-term contracts with our suppliers to ensure stability and continuity of supply.
- We involve our suppliers in the early stages of product design and development to enhance quality and innovation.
- We share information and knowledge with our suppliers to improve communication and coordination.
- We provide feedback and incentives to our suppliers to motivate them to improve their performance and capabilities.
- We collaborate with our suppliers to solve problems and implement solutions.
- We evaluate our suppliers regularly and systematically to monitor their performance and satisfaction.
- We seek to reduce the number of suppliers and maintain a lean and efficient supply base.

The environmental purchasing scale consisted of six items that assessed the extent to which the firms adopted environmental purchasing practices, such as considering the environmental and social criteria of the suppliers and the products, and selecting the suppliers and products that have lower environmental and social footprints. The items were as follows:

- We consider the environmental impact of the products we purchase, such as their energy consumption, emissions, waste, and recyclability.
- We consider the social impact of the products we purchase, such as their labor standards, human rights, and ethical practices.
- We prefer to purchase products that have eco-labels or certifications that indicate their environmental and social performance.
- We consider the environmental performance of the suppliers we choose, such as their environmental management systems, policies, and practices.
- We consider the social performance of the suppliers we choose, such as their social responsibility, compliance, and reputation.
- We encourage and support our suppliers to adopt environmental and social practices that reduce their negative impact and increase their positive impact.

The economic performance scale consisted of five items that assessed the extent to which the firms achieved economic benefits from their purchasing practices, such as reducing costs, increasing revenues, improving profitability, and enhancing competitiveness. The items were as follows:

- Our purchasing practices help us to reduce the cost of goods required for our production and operation.
- Our purchasing practices help us to reduce the power utilization costs associated with our production and operation.
- Our purchasing practices help us to reduce the disposal fees related to our production and operation.
- Our purchasing practices help us to increase the return on capital invested in our production and operation.
- Our purchasing practices help us to increase the earnings per share of our firm.

DATA ANALYSIS

The model adopted for this study was subjected to Partial Least squares (PLS) analysis using SmartPLS software (version 3.0) (Ringle et al., 2015). PLS is a statistical technique that allows for the estimation of complex causal models with latent variables (Hair et al., 2014). PLS is suitable for exploratory research and small sample sizes, as it does not impose strict assumptions on the data distribution and measurement scales (Henseler et al., 2009). Evaluation of a small sample size is an advantage of PLS-SEM. After testing the measurement model according to criteria in the literature, the structural model was assessed. According to internal consistency reliability, discriminant validity, and convergent validity were prioritized in the first step of the two-part approach. Internal consistency reliability refers to the extent to which the indicators of a latent variable are consistent in their measurement (Hair et al., 2014). Discriminant validity refers to the extent to which a latent variable is distinct from other latent variables in the model (Fornell and Larcker, 1981). Convergent validity refers to the extent to which the indicators of a latent variable converge or share a high proportion of variance (Hair et al., 2014). The importance of path coefficients was assessed in the second step. Path coefficients represent the hypothesized relationships between the latent variables in the model (Hair et al., 2014). They indicate the direction and strength of the causal effects, and can be tested for statistical significance using bootstrapping (Hair et al., 2014). Bootstrapping is a resampling technique that generates empirical estimates of the standard errors and confidence intervals of the path coefficients (Hair et al., 2014).

Measurement Model

To evaluate the model's psychometric qualities, this research examines the factor loading for every item to establish the reliability of each item. Eminent researchers, agree that loading values greater than or greater to 0.70 are more dependable and, thus, indicate data quality. All item loadings reached the recommended threshold, according to Table 1, except for three strategic purchasing items and one green procurement item, which was left out. To confirm the internal consistency dependability of the model, composite reliability values were examined for all the constructs. The suggested cut-off for CR scores is 0.70 and higher. As shown in Table 1, all constructs had values that were more significant than the recommended level, thus achieving considerable internal consistency reliability. Analyzing the AVE scores, the recommended criterion was 0.50 and above, allowing for the concurrent examination of convergent validity. The research also shows solid convergent validity, as shown in Table 1, with AVE values exceeding the level recommended by researchers to comprehensively evaluate the theoretical model's psychometric features. According to Fornell and Larcker (1981), each construct's AVE value ought to be higher than 0.50, before being evaluated with respect to the square root of those values compared to the reflective loadings of other constructs in the cross-loading table. In this case, the square root scores should be more valuable. According to Table 2, the model also gained considerable discriminant validity, which satisfies the evaluation requirements of the measurement model stage. The results varied from 0.724 to 0.821 (Fig.1).

STRUCTURAL MODEL ASSESSMENT

The latest research proceeded to the following analysis step once the measurement model was verified, at which point the PLS path model was verified. The direct and moderating linkages hypothesised in this research were examined in this investigation, following the claims made by Hair et al. (2017). Table 3 demonstrates that strategic purchasing produced a significant positive association with a firm's economic performance (β= 0.276; t = 3.038) using bootstrapping processes with 5000 bootstraps, supporting Hypothesis 1.

The current research supported the second hypothesis about the connection between environmental purchasing and economic performance and was thus also supported by the current research (β = 0.375; t = 4.45). Interestingly, firm size also moderated the connection between strategic purchasing and economic performance (β= 0.231; t = 3.976), supporting Hypothesis 3, but did not modify the connection between environmental purchasing and economic performance (β= 0.022; t= 0.019), not supporting Hypothesis 5 (Fig.2).

Table 1. Outer loading, VIF, composite reliability, AVE and Cronbach's alpha

Variables and Indicators	Outer Loading	VIF	Composite Reliability	AVE	Cronbach's Alpha
Economic Performance (ECP)			0.832	0.551	0.746
ECP1	0.756	1.475			
ECP2	0.806	2.013			
ECP3	0.755	1.481			
ECP4	0.724	1.578			
ECP5	0.774	1.156			
Environmental Purchasing (ENP)			0.855	0.546	0.788
ENP1	0.737	1.191			
ENP2	0.762	1.552			
ENP3	0.744	1.403			
ENP4	0.801	2.114			
ENP5	0.817	2.146			
Strategic purchasing (STP)			0.884	0.603	0.814
STP1	0.781	1.691			
STP2	0.808	1.867			
STP3	0.821	1.965			
STP4	0.742	1.632			
STP5	0.732	1.558			

Figure 1. Measurement model

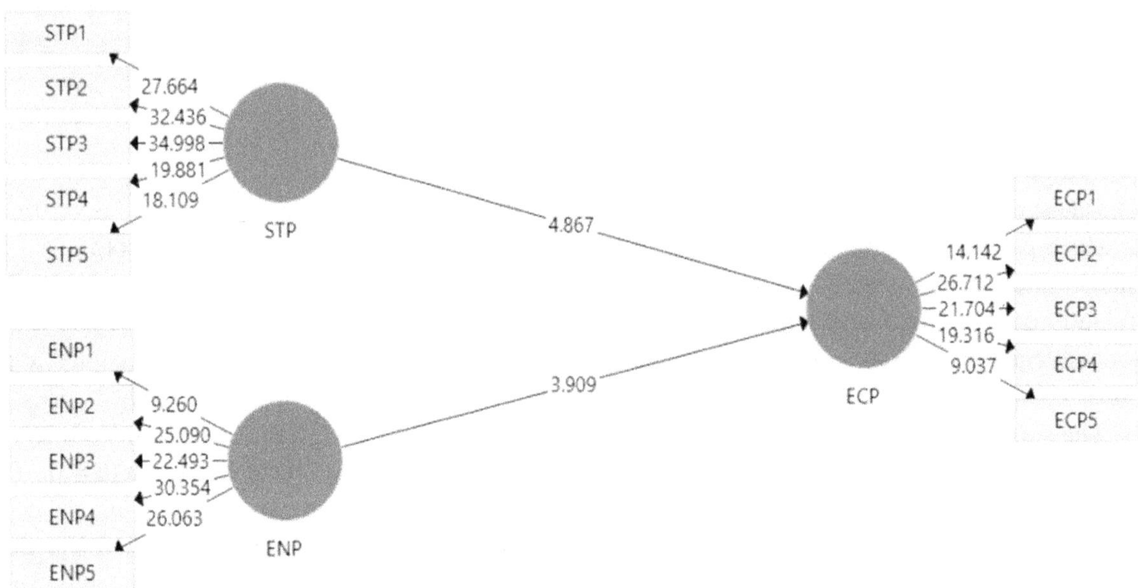

Table 2. Discriminant Validity (Fornell Larcker criterion, Heterotrait-Monotrait ratio [HTMT])

	ECP	ENP	STP
ECP	**0.793**	0.784	0.783
ENP	0.578	**0.740**	0.813
STP	0.631	0.547	**0.823**

Note: The values on either side of the diagonal represent the HTMT ratio and Fornell–Larcker criteria, respectively.

Table 3. Hypothesis results

S. No	Hypothesis	Beta	T Statistics	p Value	Decision
H1	Strategic purchasing -> Economic performance	0.276	3.038	0.001	Supported
H2	Environmental purchasing -> Economic performance	0.375	4.45	0.001	Supported
H3	Strategic purchasing * Firm Size -> Economic Performance	0.231	3.976	0.001	Supported
H4	Environmental purchasing * Firm Size -> Economic Performance	0.022	0.019	0.796	Not supported

Figure 2. Structural model

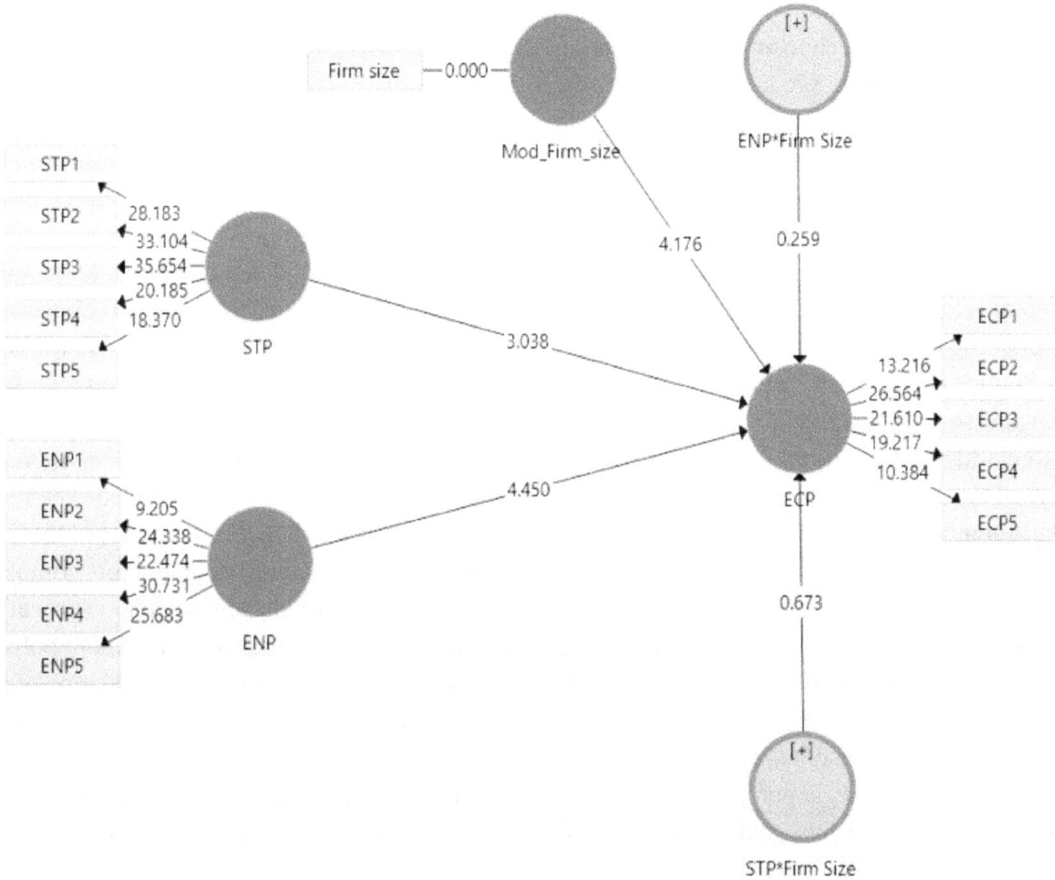

DISCUSSION AND IMPLICATIONS

The objective of this study is to experimentally investigate the significant links between organizational purchasing practices and economic performance. According to previous research by Rafati and Poels (2015), and Zhu and Sarkis (2004), strategic purchasing can improve a company's economic performance. The present research examined and discovered a potential function for strategic purchasing in leveraging an organization's economic performance while bearing these reasons in mind. Thus, strategic purchasing maximizes an organization's supplier base and strengthens its connections with its suppliers. The researchers also discovered that decisions made by one entity in a manufacturing company's supply network affect the expenditures and operations of other companies. When procuring goods, businesses should consider proper client requirements, such as timely delivery and high-quality goods. Strategic purchasing aids supply chains in continuing to grow internationally into emerging nations to cut prices and increase manufacturing capacity. Owing to this development, increasing risks are presented to businesses, and stakeholders' expectations are also raised. Interested parties in a company want to be accountable for its suppliers' moral, ethical, and ecological actions. Strategic purchasing is now included in business sourcing and control of supply chain procedures, which also improves economic performance. In other words, these activities enhance a company's economic performance by lowering the expenses of vendor rationalization and decreasing governance and overall ownership costs.

Considerable research has been conducted on this subject. Our findings suggest that businesses must engage in strategic purchasing approaches to solve all potential cost savings, and base their selections on factual research and market knowledge. As a result of recognizing and minimizing the ecological effects of their supply chains; choosing limited, equitable, or ecologically responsible vendors; utilizing factors of production that were procured ethically; and eliminating waste by repurposing packaging instead of discarding it after use, environmental purchasing can also help a company's economic performance. This finding moves the empirical claims. The findings suggest that creating an environmentally responsible supply chain is one method to future-proof the organization against a future supply problem, comparable to the significant relevance of environmental purchasing towards the remarkable economic performance of the organization. Additionally, this approach will aid in defending against alterations in economic elements, such as fluctuating exchange rates, sociological influences, such as the accessibility of technologies, and environmental influences, such as changing climate. Going forward, there are better opportunities for environmentally friendly purchasing methods to boost the overall economic success of businesses (Aliyu et al., 2019).

Remarkably, the current study discovered a significant research gap and examined the moderating effect of firm size on strategic and environmental purchasing on economic performance. The research found a significant moderating effect of business size on the relationship between strategic purchasing and economic performance. This implies that as an organization grows, sourcing becomes more complex. By implementing strategic purchasing tools, a company can significantly enhance its analytic procurement capacities, rapidly assess different standards at the magnitude, find new vendors to avert monopolization, boost resilience, and make a distinction through supplier-led advancement to the accumulation of earlier unrealized value (Shook et al., 2014).The researchers needed to help locate papers that discussed how firm size might be a moderating factor. Therefore, the current study provides noteworthy findings for those who enjoy strategic purchasing. Large-sized businesses have tremendous opportunities to impact strategic buying decisions and improve firms' financial performance. This suggests that enterprises should consider implementing strategic and environmentally friendly buying practices throughout the supply chain to improve their financial performance.

The results of this study have several practical implications. This research suggests that firms should create environmentally friendly and strategic purchasing methods to achieve economic performance. Here, much has to do with organizational procurement strategies and the creation of strategic sourcing to improve economic performance, such as a drop in the price of materials acquired, a reduction in the price of power consumed, and a drop in the charge for waste discharge. From a more pragmatic perspective, the results suggest that manufacturing companies delve into strategies to enhance and strengthen these connections. Establishing a solid supply chain is crucial from a strategic perspective to maintain strategic and environmental purchasing. It is also necessary for businesses to continue to succeed in the long term.

LIMITATIONS AND THE SCOPE FOR FURTHER STUDIES

There are some things to note for academics to think about in the long term, and the current research was initially conducted in India's manufacturing industry. Therefore, the generalizability of our findings is limited. Consequently, it is advised that additional studies consider examining other areas and industries, including service firms and so forth. The researchers enrolled financial executives for the economic performance variable and representatives of purchasing managerial personnel for the strategic and environmental purchasing variables. The samples and targeted demographics of future research may be expanded to include perspectives of non-managerial staff. This study also examined the mediating impact of environmental collaboration. By contrast, others might consider the viability of various strategic sourcing techniques in various corporate industries.

Some other limitations and suggestions for future research are as follows:

- This study used a cross-sectional design, which limits the ability to infer causal relationships between the variables. Future research could adopt a longitudinal design, which would allow for tracking the changes and effects of the variables over time (Hair et al., 2014).
- This study relied on self-reported data from the respondents, which may introduce biases such as social desirability and common method variance. Future research could use objective data from secondary sources, such as financial reports and environmental audits, to validate the findings and reduce the potential biases (Podsakoff et al., 2003).
- This study focused on the direct and indirect effects of strategic purchasing and environmental purchasing on economic performance. Future research could explore the moderating effects of other factors, such as organizational culture, leadership style, and stakeholder pressure, on the relationships between the variables (Zhu et al., 2013).

REFERENCES

Aliyu, R. M., Ahmad, T., & Nordin, N. B. (2019). The mediating role of innovation on access to finance and business performance of women entrepreneurs. *International Journal of Academic Research in Business & Social Sciences*, *9*(3), 147–159. doi:10.6007/IJARBSS/v9-i3/5644

Ambekar, S., Kapoor, R., Prakash, A., & Patyal, V. S. (2018). Motives, processes and practices of sustainable sourcing: a literature review. *Journal of Global Operations and Strategic Sourcing*.

El Sibaii, S. (2018). *Strategic Sourcing in Construction Companies-A Case Study in Qatar*. Academic Press.

Franke, H., & Foerstl, K. (2020). Goals, conflict, politics, and performance of cross-functional sourcing teams—Results from a social team experiment. *Journal of Business Logistics*, *41*(1), 6–30. doi:10.1111/jbl.12225

Islam, T., Islam, R., Pitafi, A. H., Xiaobei, L., Rehmani, M., Irfan, M., & Mubarak, M. S. (2021). The impact of corporate social responsibility on customer loyalty: The mediating role of corporate reputation, customer satisfaction, and trust. *Sustainable Production and Consumption*, *25*, 123–135. doi:10.1016/j.spc.2020.07.019

Jermsittiparsert, K., & Rungsrisawat, S. (2019). Impact strategic sourcing, supplier innovativeness, and information sharing on supply chain agility. *International Journal of Innovation, Creativity and Change*, *5*(2), 397–415.

Ketchen, D. J. Jr, Crook, T. R., & Craighead, C. W. (2014). From supply chains to supply ecosystems: Implications for strategic sourcing research and practice. *Journal of Business Logistics*, *35*(3), 165–171. doi:10.1111/jbl.12057

Khan, A., & Pillania, R. K. (2008). Strategic sourcing for supply chain agility and firms' performance: A study of Indian manufacturing sector. *Management Decision*.

Medina Serrano, R., González Ramírez, R., Gasco Gasco, J., & Llopis Taverner, J. (2020). Strategic sourcing: Developing a progressive framework for make-or-buy decisions. *Journal of Industrial Engineering and Management*, *13*(1), 133–154. doi:10.3926/jiem.2858

Park, W.-Y., Ro, Y. K., & Kim, N. (2018). Architectural innovation and the emergence of a dominant design: The effects of strategic sourcing on performance. *Research Policy*, *47*(1), 326–341. doi:10.1016/j.respol.2017.11.003

Rafati, L., & Poels, G. (2015). Towards model-based strategic sourcing. *Global Sourcing Workshop 2015*, 29–51.

Rai, N., & Thapa, B. (2015). A study on purposive sampling method in research. Kathmandu: Kathmandu School of Law, 5.

Ringle, C., Da Silva, D., & Bido, D. (2015). Structural equation modeling with the SmartPLS. *Brazilian Journal of Marketing, 13*(2).

Shafiq, A., Johnson, P. F., & Awaysheh, A. (2019). Emerging economy sourcing: Implications of supplier social practices for firm performance. *International Journal of Production Economics*, *218*, 148–158. doi:10.1016/j.ijpe.2019.05.010

Sharma, S. K., Singh, R., & Matai, R. (2018). Force field analysis of Indian automotive strategic sourcing risk management enablers and barriers. *Measuring Business Excellence*, *22*(3), 258–275. doi:10.1108/MBE-09-2017-0062

Somjai, S., & Jermsittiparsert, K. (2019). Mediating Impact of Information Sharing in the Relationship of Supply Chain Capabilities and Business Performance among the Firms of Thailand. *International Journal of Supply Chain Management*, *8*(4), 357–368.

Utami, C. W., Sumaji, Y. M. P., Susanto, H., Septina, F., & Pratama, I. (2019). *Effect of Supply Chain Management Practices on Financial and Economic Sustainable Performance of Indonesian SMEs*. Academic Press.

Vanneste, B. S., & Gulati, R. (2022). Generalized trust, external sourcing, and firm performance in economic downturns. *Organization Science*, *33*(4), 1599–1619. doi:10.1287/orsc.2021.1500

Vogel, R., & Güttel, W. H. (2013). The dynamic capability view in strategic management: A bibliometric review. *International Journal of Management Reviews*, *15*(4), 426–446. doi:10.1111/ijmr.12000

Wagner, S. M., Grosse-Ruyken, P. T., & Erhun, F. (2018). Determinants of sourcing flexibility and its impact on performance. *International Journal of Production Economics*, *205*, 329–341. doi:10.1016/j.ijpe.2018.08.006

Chapter 17
Effect of Crude Oil Price Variations on Stocks With Special Reference to NSE

Shimna Jayaraj
Jain University, India

B.S. Sudha
Jain University, India

T. Shenbagavalli
Jain University, India

Juhi Jain
Jain University, India

V. Vipanchi
Jain University, India

Biswaranjan Senapati
https://orcid.org/0000-0002-0717-5888
Parker Hannifin Corp., USA

ABSTRACT

Crude oil consumption is one of the major economic indicators in the economy. The study examines the interrelation between crude oil prices and the stock market. The stock market indices chosen are Nifty 50, Nifty 100, Nifty 200, Nifty 500, Nifty Auto, Bank, and FMCG. The study has considered only one event, i.e., crude oil for six years, leaving a research gap for analyzing other macroeconomic indicators affecting the Indian stock market. This chapter intends to investigate whether any impact exists on different indices of NSE due to the changes in prices of crude oil globally due to certain internal and external factors. This chapter also helps suggest to the investors their deals in Indian and global markets. This study is done to know the impact of fluctuations in crude oil prices in the global market, which affects the Indian stock market, and also to know the reasons for the fluctuations in crude oil prices. This study also analyzes the dependency level of both variables (crude oil prices globally and the same prices in the Indian stock market).

DOI: 10.4018/979-8-3693-2193-5.ch017

1. INTRODUCTION

National Stock Exchange: NSE is one of the largest stock exchanges in the world, situated in Mumbai. It was set up in 1992. The National Stock Exchange (NSE) was the first exchange in India to provide a fully automated trading platform in the form of a screen-based electronic system available throughout the country. NSE has changed how it functions, considering the latest developments in the Indian economy and technology (Akshaya & Naachimuthu, 2022). NSE has incorporated many financial asset classes and customer segments today. Its multiple roles now include an exchange regulator, Index provider, investor educator, etc. It offers exchanging, clearing, and settlement administrations. It is the only business in India to provide an electronic trading office. As a result, it is the only one that can bring the whole nation's network of financial experts together. Way2Wealth was consolidated as Sivan Web Trading Pvt Ltd in the year 2000 in Bangalore and was rebranded as Way2Wealth Securities Pvt Ltd around the same time. It is a retail-engaged speculation consultative business and provides many other budgetary administrations (Aswathi et al., 2021). As per BSE, It was also positioned among the main ten broking elements in the retail broking section during the budgetary year 2019. It is available crosswise over 21 states in India.

Table 1 gives a clear picture of India's crude oil consumption from 2015 to 2020

Table 1. Consumption of crude oil through imports (%)

Financial Year	Consumption of Crude Oil Through Imports (%)	Amount ($ Million)
2015	77.3	1,43,639
2016	78.3	1,16,443
2017	80.6	65,923
2018	81.7	70,705
2019	83.7	87,372
2020	89	77,000

The positive impact of crude oil prices on the stock market: Energy companies that produce and sell oil tend to see an increase in earnings as crude oil prices rise, which can result in higher stock values for those companies. Reduced gas prices may stimulate consumer spending, which would be advantageous for retailers and manufacturers of consumer goods and the economy as a whole (Gupta, 2022). Positive effects on GDP: In many nations, the energy sector is a major contributor, and rising crude oil prices may indicate more economic activity and expansion (Al-Maaitah et al., 2021a). Increasing investment in oil exploration and production: If crude oil prices rise, businesses might invest more in these activities, which could create jobs and economic expansion (Al-Maaitah et al., 2021b). Crude oil price growth has a positive impact on commodity prices. Prices can indicate a rise in demand for goods, such as metals and minerals, which could result in higher prices and be advantageous for businesses in those sectors (Gupta, 2021a).

Beneficial effects on transportation firms: Oil-dependent transportation firms, like airlines and shipping firms, may profit from higher ticket and freight costs as crude oil prices rise. Positive effect on stock market sentiment: Higher crude oil prices can indicate economic optimism and help to boost the market's good mood (Gupta, 2021b). Higher crude oil prices may result in higher tax collections for governments, which they can utilize to finance public infrastructure initiatives and spur economic growth. The rise in alternative energy production: Higher crude oil prices might result in greater investment in and production of alternative energy sources, which can help businesses in those sectors and stimulate economic growth. Positive effects on emerging market economies: Since many of these nations are net exporters of crude oil, rising oil prices can help them by boosting tax revenues and stimulating economic expansion.

The negative impact of crude oil prices on the stock market: Decreased earnings for non-energy companies: Reduced profits for non-energy firms: If crude oil prices rise, many non-energy firms that use oil as a major input may see their costs rise, hurting profits and stock prices. Increased inflation: Increasing crude oil prices can result in rising inflation, which could force the central bank to boost interest rates to contain inflation. As a result of rising borrowing costs for businesses, higher interest rates may result in decreased stock values. Negative impact on consumer spending: A spike in crude oil prices may leave customers with less discretionary cash on other goods and services, which might hurt consumer spending. This could result in fewer sales and profits for many businesses.

Negative impact on economic growth: High crude oil prices can harm economic growth by reducing economic activity (Kumar & Naachimuthu, 2023). The rising cost of electricity may cause businesses and consumers to cut back on spending. Increased debt levels for countries that import oil: Countries that are net importers of crude oil may have higher debt levels due to having to pay more for imported oil, which might have a detrimental effect on the global economy and stock market. Negative effects on emerging market economies: Many of these economies depend on exporting raw materials, such as crude oil. Dropping oil prices may result in lower tax receipts for the government and slower economic expansion, both of which could harm the stock market (Hana & Naachimuthu, 2023).

High amounts of debt may make it difficult for energy corporations to repay their loans if crude oil prices decline, which could result in bankruptcy or a decline in stock values. Impact on government revenues: If oil prices fall, governments that depend heavily on commodity exports may face a decline in their income, which might result in less expenditure by the government and slower economic growth. Increased turbulence on the stock market: quick fluctuations in crude oil prices lead to higher volatility, which might spook investors and drive down stock prices. Impact of falling crude oil prices on investor sentiment: Lower investor confidence can result from a poorer economy, hurting investor mood and the stock market.

2. REVIEW OF LITERATURE

Awan et al., (2021) performed a complete literature evaluation on the connection between oil fees and stock market indices in the US, Canada, Japan, and the United Kingdom. He observed that most studies show poor dating among oil rate modifications and stock market indices.

According to Bai & Green, (2011) oil fee adjustments are substantial determinants of people's inventory marketplace returns. Certainly, they determined that stock markets tended to rise while oil prices suddenly fell and fell while oil prices suddenly rose. Although the effect of oil costs on the inventory marketplace isn't equal across sectors and industries, it should be noted that the relationship between oil prices and the inventory marketplace is complex and changes through the years. For example, they observed that the electricity industry, which is more dependent on oil, is more tormented by oil fluctuations than the technology zone, which is less dependent on oil. Overall, their findings endorse that even as the connection between the two can be complicated and stimulated by using some of the different elements, changes in oil prices may be an essential driving force of inventory returns.

Bansal & Pasricha, (2009) said that Oil prices appreciably affect inventory returns inside the power and non-strength sectors. However, there is powerful oil rate volatility. Typical, the evidence shows that changes in oil expenses could have a massive effect on inventory marketplace returns, even though the exact courting between oil fees and inventory returns may be complex and vary depending on several circumstances. Stock market.

Liao et al., (2019) investigated the impact of oil costs in the Australian inventory market using a vector autoregressive model. They observed that oil rate adjustments have a sizeable and terrible impact on inventory marketplace returns. Additionally, they discover that the impact of oil fee adjustments on the inventory marketplace is asymmetric, with bad oil price shocks having an extra-sized effect than advantageous shocks.

Özdurak, (2021) explained that the impact of oil costs at the Chinese language stock marketplace changed into investigating the use of a GARCH version. They found that modifications in oil charges greatly impact the stock market's overall performance. In addition, they observed evidence of a non-linear association between oil price adjustments and inventory marketplace returns, with the effect strongest throughout periods of excessive oil fee volatility.

Rajkumar, & Gupta, (2010) investigated the effect of oil prices on the inventory markets of Saudi Arabia and Russia, the most important oil-exporting countries. The results confirmed that oil prices substantially affect those countries' stock markets, with the effect being more potent in Saudi Arabia than in Russia.

Rajput et al., (2012) investigated the impact of oil fees in the Bangladesh stock marketplace. They discover that oil charge changes have a vast, terrible effect on the inventory market's overall performance. In addition, they found proof of massive ripple results from oil charge changes in different financial markets in Bangladesh.

Rao et al., (1999) find a statistically extensive correlation between oil rate modifications and stock market returns in Korea. The findings factor into an uneven impact, wherein terrible oil charge shocks have a greater impact on stock market returns than positive shocks. The authors also discover evidence of large spillover consequences from oil fee changes in different South Korean financial markets. This examines the correlation between Indian stock marketplace returns and oil expenses from 2005 to 2020. The findings display that oil costs considerably affect Indian stock marketplace returns, particularly in the close period (Hana et al., 2022).

Zheng & Du, (2019), from 2002 to 2019, this observation tested the asymmetric dating between oil prices and inventory markets inside the BRICS countries of Brazil, Russia, India, China, and South Africa. The findings suggest that oil fees and stock markets within the BRICS international locations have an uneven courting, with bad shocks having a greater impact on stock markets than tremendous shocks.

Since 2004, the sharp increase and fluctuation in the prices of oil and oil products in world markets have caused concern across all areas (Fig.1). The average price of a basket of Indian crude oil, which hovered around US$23 per barrel (bbl) at the time of the demise of the APM in March 2002 and US$36 per barrel (bbl) in May 2004, rose to an average of US$85.09 per barrel (bbl). In 2010-11. During 2011–12, the average basket price of Indian crude rose further to reach US$111.89 per barrel. After being above $100/barrel for over three years, oil prices began declining significantly in the second half of 2014. Consequently, in 2015–16, 2016–17, 2017–18, and 2018–19, the average price of the basket of Indian crude oil was recorded at $46.17/bbl, $47.56/bbl, $56.43/bbl, and $69.88/bbl respectively. Data from the Petroleum Planning and Analysis Cell shows that on November 4, 2019, the price was $70.68 per barrel (PPAC). Oman, Dubai, and Brent crude are averaged to form the Indian basket. Below is a chart showing the statistics regarding trends in India's crude oil basket from 2002-03 to 2018-19

The RBI uses monetary policy tools such as interest rates, minimum reserve requirements, and open market operations to control inflation, which is subject to changes in the price of oil. For example, the RBI may raise interest rates if oil prices rise significantly to curb inflationary pressures. Rupees in India. For example, if oil prices rise significantly, the RBI may sell dollars to strengthen the rupee and stop it from weakening too much.

Hedging Mechanisms: The RBI has created several hedging mechanisms to assist oil importers in managing their price risks. For example, the RBI has permitted oil marketing companies to use financial products such as futures and options to manage oil price risks. International Cooperation: RBI has also engaged in international cooperation to mitigate the impact of oil price changes. For example, RBI participates in several projects to promote global energy security and stability as a member of the IEA and the International Energy Agency (IEA).

Figure 1. Government and RBI actions

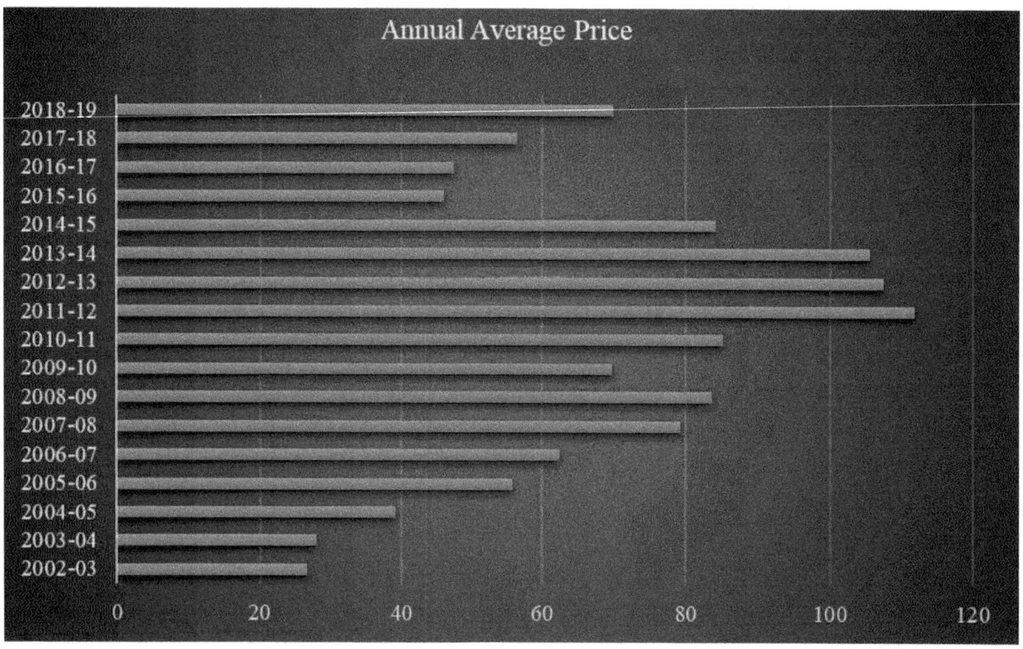

3. RESEARCH METHODOLOGY

3.1 Objectives of the Study

- To study the conceptual mechanism of the Indian commodity market.
- To analyze the correlation between oil prices and the stock market.
- To analyze the effect of crude oil prices on the Indian Stock market.

3.2. Research Design

The design used in this project analysis is analytical. It's a type where the investigation depends on assured critical philosophy to determine details about the subject for the past six years.

3.3. Data, Sources, and Sample Design

Closing date on the S&P CNX Index are collected from the respective website of the national stock exchange, and crude oil closing price data are obtained from Way2Wealth & investing.com

3.4. Framework for Data Analysis

Regression equation: It is a statistical equation used to determine whether a relationship exists between data groups. $y = \alpha + \beta x$

Mean: It is the humble and math normal of a progression of qualities figured by separating the aggregate of all qualities by the number of qualities. Mid-purpose of an arrangement of qualities can likewise be discovered by utilizing mean.

$$X = \frac{\Sigma X}{N}$$

Standard deviation: It is a statistical tool used to measure how much data values vary and spread out.

$$\sigma = \sqrt{\frac{1}{N}\sum_{1}^{N}(X-\bar{X})^2}$$

Beta: Beta is a tool to measure unsystematic risk.

$$\beta = \frac{n\Sigma XY - (\Sigma X)(\Sigma Y)}{n\Sigma X^2 - (\Sigma X)^2}$$

3.5. Hypothesis Framework

It is done to know whether there is any impact on crude oil prices on selected share prices or not.

H_0 – There is no impact of crude oil prices on selected indices.

H_1 – There is an impact of crude oil prices on selected indices.

$$\beta = \frac{n\Sigma XY - (\Sigma X)(\Sigma Y)}{n\Sigma X^2 - (\Sigma X)^2}$$

4. DATA ANALYSIS AND INTERPRETATION

NIFTY 50: Descriptive Statistics

Table 2. Descriptive statistics of NIFTY 50 and crude oil

	N	Min	Max	Mean	S. D	Skewness	Kurtosis
NIFTY-50	2176	2524.20	8996.25	5252.52	1338	.480	.418
CRUDE_OIL	2176	33.87	145.29	84.19	19	-.101	-.028

Regression equation: Nifty 50 = 3584.872+19.806(crude oil)

Model summary: The correlation value R=0.289 indicates a positive correlation between nifty 50 and crude oil price. R square is 0.083, i.e., 8.3% of changes in nifty 50 prices are explainable by crude oil price.

ANOVA:

Table 3. ANOVA of NIFTY 50 and crude oil

Model	Sum of Squares	Df	Mean Square	F	Sig.
Regression equation	324656902.726	1	324656902.726	197.659	.000

The F value is 197.659 significant at a 1% level, so it cannot accept the null hypothesis & indicates that the given regression model explains a major proportion of variance in nifty performance.

Coefficients:

Table 4. Coefficients of NIFTY 50 and crude oil

Model	Unstandardized Coefficients		Standardized Coefficients	T	Sig.
	B	Std. Error	Beta		
(Constant)	3584.872	121.757		29.443	.000
CRUDE_OIL	19.806	1.409	.289	14.059	.000

The P value is less than 0.05, so we cannot accept the null hypothesis. Thus, there is an impact of crude oil prices on nifty 50.

NIFTY 100: Descriptive statistics

Table 5. Descriptive statistics of NIFTY 100 and crude oil

	N	Min	Max	Mean	SD	Skewness	Kurtosis
NIFTY_100	2196	2388.6	8991.4	5146.2	1365	0.487	0.445
CRUDEOIL	2196	33.87	145.29	84.2253	19	-0.105	-0.033

Regression equation: Nifty 100 = 3512.313 + 19.399(crude oil)

Model summary: The correlation value R=0.277 indicates a positive correlation between nifty 100 and crude oil price. R square is 0.077, i.e., 7.7% of changes in nifty 100 prices are explainable by crude oil price.

ANOVA:

Table 6. ANOVA of NIFTY 100 and crude oil

Model	Sum of Squares	Df	Mean Square	F	Sig.
Regression equation	315000000	1	315000000	183.032	0

The F value is 183.032, significant at a 1% level, so it cannot accept the null hypothesis & indicates that the given regression model explains a major proportion of variance in nifty performance.

Coefficients:

Table 7. Coefficients of NIFTY 100 and crude oil

Model	Unstandardized Coefficients		Standardized Coefficients	t	Sig.
	B	Std. Error	Beta		
(Constant)	3512.313	123.971		28.332	0
CRUDEOIL	19.399	1.434	0.277	13.529	0

The P value is less than 0.05, so we cannot accept the null hypothesis. Thus, crude oil prices impact Nifty 100.

NIFTY 200: Descriptive statistics

Table 8. Descriptive statistics of NIFTY 200 and crude oil

	N	Min	Max	Mean	S.D	Skewness	Kurtosis
NIFTY_200	2195	1258.07	4648.3	2698.7	681.8506	0.464	0.588
CRUDEOIL	2195	33.87	145.29	84.1863	19.53928	-0.104	-0.034

Regression equation: Nifty 200 = 1922.389 + 9.221(crude oil)

Model summary: The correlation value R=0.264 indicates a positive correlation between nifty 200 and crude oil price. R square is 0.07, i.e., 7% of changes in nifty 200 prices are explainable by crude oil price.

ANOVA:

Table 9. ANOVA of NIFTY 200 and crude oil

Model	Sum of Squares	df	Mean Square	F	Sig.
Regression equation	71220000	1	71220000	164.615	0

The F value is 164.615, significant at a 1% level, so it cannot accept the null hypothesis & indicates that the given regression model explains a major proportion of variance in nifty performance.

Coefficients:

Table 10. Coefficients of NIFTY 200 and crude oil

Model	Unstandardized Coefficients		Standardized Coefficients	T	Sig.
	B	Std. Error	Beta		
(Constant)	1922.389	62.112		30.95	0
CRUDEOIL	9.221	0.719	0.264	12.83	0

The P value is less than 0.05, so we cannot accept the null hypothesis. Thus, there is an impact of crude oil prices on Nifty 200.

NIFTY 500: Descriptive statistics

Table 11. Descriptive statistics of NIFTY 500 and crude oil

	N	Min	Max	Mean	S.D	Skewness	Kurtosis
NIFTY_500	512	4047.7	7345.55	5487	987.6043	0.393	-1.415
CRUDEOIL	512	43.46	110.53	89.8717	18.47257	-1.417	0.62

Regression equation: Nifty 500 = 9013.003 – 39.234(crude oil)

Model summary: The correlation value R=0.734 indicates a positive correlation between nifty 500 and crude oil price. R square is 0.539, i.e., 53.9% of changes in nifty 500 prices are explainable by crude oil price.

ANOVA:

Table 12. ANOVA of NIFTY 500 and crude oil

Model	Sum of Squares	Df	Mean Square	F	Sig.
Regression equation	268400000	1	268400000	595.192	0

The F value is 595.192, significant at a 1% level, so it cannot accept the null hypothesis & indicates that the given regression model explains a major proportion of variance in nifty performance.

Coefficients:

Table 13. Coefficients of NIFTY 500 and crude oil

Model	Unstandardized Coefficients		Standardized Coefficients	t	Sig.
	B	Std. Error	Beta		
(Constant)	9013.003	147.546		61.086	0
CRUDEOIL	-39.234	1.608	-0.734	24.397	0

The P value is less than 0.05, so we cannot accept the null hypothesis. Thus, there is an impact of crude oil prices on Nifty 500.

NIFTY AUTO: Descriptive statistics

Table 14. Descriptive statistics of NIFTY AUTO and crude oil

	N	Min	Max	Mean	S.D	Skewness	Kurtosis
NIFTY_AUTO	2177	933.07	9099.6	3547.8	1779.915	1.034	0.853
CRUDEOIL	2177	33.87	145.29	84.5423	19.29711	-0.101	0.029

Regression equation: Nifty AUTO = 1887.289 + 19.641(crude oil)

Model summary: The correlation value R=0.213 indicates a positive correlation between nifty AUTO and crude oil price. R square is 0.045, i.e., 4.5% of changes in nifty AUTO prices are explainable by crude oil price.

ANOVA:

The F value is 103.304, significant at a 1% level, so it cannot accept the null hypothesis & indicates that the given regression model explains a major proportion of variance in nifty performance.

Table 15. ANOVA of NIFTY AUTO and crude oil

Model	Sum of Squares	df	Mean Square	F	Sig.
Regression equation	312600000	1	312600000	103.304	0

Coefficients

Table 16. Coefficients of NIFTY AUTO and crude oil

Model	Unstandardized Coefficients		Standardized Coefficients	t	Sig.
	B	Std. Error	Beta		
(Constant)	1887.289	167.571		11.263	0
CRUDEOIL	19.641	1.932	0.213	10.164	0

The P value is less than 0.05, so we cannot accept the null hypothesis. Thus, there is an impact of crude oil prices on nifty AUTO.

NIFTY BANK: Descriptive statistics

Table 17. Descriptive statistics of NIFTY BANK and crude oil

	N	Min	Max	Mean	S.D	Skewness	Kurtosis
NIFTY_BANK	2191	3339.7	20555.25	9539.7	3557.867	0.604	0.345
CRUDEOIL	2191	33.87	145.29	84.1731	19.55607	-0.104	-0.034

Regression equation: Nifty BANK = 6435.856 + 36.875(crude oil)

Model summary: The correlation value R=0.203 indicates a positive correlation between nifty BANK and crude oil price. R square is 0.041, i.e., 4.1% of changes in nifty BANK prices are explainable by crude oil price.

ANOVA:

Table 18. ANOVA of NIFTY BANK and crude oil

Model	Sum of Squares	Df	Mean Square	F	Sig.
Regression equation	1139000000	1	1139000000	93.78	0

The F value is 93.78, significant at a 1% level, so it cannot accept the null hypothesis & indicates that the given regression model explains a major proportion of variance in nifty performance.

Coefficients:

Table 19. Coefficients of NIFTY BANK and crude oil

Model	Unstandardized Coefficients		Standardized Coefficients	t	Sig.
	B	Std. Error	Beta		
(Constant)	6435.856	329.049		19.559	0
CRUDEOIL	36.875	3.808	0.203	9.684	0

The P value is less than 0.05, so we cannot accept the null hypothesis. Thus, there is an impact of crude oil prices on nifty BANK.

NIFTY FMCG: Descriptive statistics

Table 20. Descriptive statistics of NIFTY FMCG and crude oil

	N	Min	Max	Mean	S.D	Skewness	Kurtosis
NIFTY_FMCG	2181	4251.16	22295.15	10203	5121.025	0.667	-0.974
CRUDEOIL	2181	33.87	145.29	84.1778	19.50298	-0.102	-0.027

Regression equation: Nifty FMCG = 4430.462 + 68.574 (crude oil)

Model summary: The correlation value R=0.261 indicates a positive correlation between nifty FMCG and crude oil prices. R square is 0.068, i.e., 6.8% of nifty FMCG price changes are explained by crude oil price.

ANOVA:

Table 21. ANOVA of NIFTY FMCG and crude oil

Model	Sum of Squares	df	Mean Square	F	Sig.
Regression equation	3899000000	1	3899000000	159.494	0

The F value is 159.494, significant at a 1% level, so it cannot accept the null hypothesis & indicates that the given regression model explains a major proportion of variance in nifty performance.

Coefficients:

Table 22. Coefficients of NIFTY FMCG and crude oil

Model	Unstandardized Coefficients		Standardized Coefficients	t	Sig.
	B	Std. Error	Beta		
(Constant)	4430.462	469.174		9.443	0
CRUDEOIL	68.574	5.43	0.261	12.629	0

The P value is less than 0.05, so we cannot accept the null hypothesis. Thus, there is an impact of crude oil prices on nifty FMCG.

Table 23. Consolidated regression analysis

INDEX	N	α	β1	F	R^2
NIFTY 50	2176	3584***	19.806***	197.659***	0.083
		0	0	0	
NIFTY 100	2196	3512***	19.399***	183.032***	0.077
		0	0	0	
NIFTY200	2195	1922***	9.221***	164.615***	0.07
		0	0	0	
NIFTY 500	512	9013***	-39.23***	595.192***	0.539
		0	0	0	
NIFTY AUTO	2177	1887.289***	19.641***	103.304***	0.045
		0	0	0	
NIFTY BANK	2191	6435.856***	36.875***	93.78***	0.041
		0	0	0	
NIFTY FMCG	2181	4430.462***	68.574	159.494	0.068
		0	0	0	

5. FINDINGS IN F VALUE

The F value of regression results for all the selected indices was significant at the 1% level. So, it indicates that the given regression model explained a major proportion of variations in the performance of all the seven selected indices (Tables 2 to 23).

The regression result of all the selected seven indices shows that the coefficient of crude oil is positively significant at 1%. It indicates that the Crude oil prices strongly impact prices of all the selected index values. However, the coefficient of Crude oil prices was found to be negatively significant on prices of Nifty 500. Thus, it indicates that Crude oil prices have a very strong negative impact on prices of Nifty 500.

Further, in the case of the nifty 500, when Crude oil prices increase, the index prices decrease, and when Crude oil prices decrease, the index prices increase. But in the case of all other selected indices, when the Crude oil prices increase, the index prices also increase, and when the crude oil prices decrease, the index prices also decrease; it proves the significance except Nifty 500 because it depends on the impact of selected companies.

6. CONCLUSION

The study has been undertaken to analyze the Impact of Crude oil prices on the Indian stock market. The study considers seven indices of the National Stock Exchange (NSE) and the closing prices of Crude oil from investing.com to analyze whether there is an impact. The study used regression, coefficient, and ANOVA. Overall, the study found a strong impact of crude oil prices on the selected indices of NSE. The result suggests that considering Crude oil prices is also important for the investor investing in selected indices of the National Stock Exchange. The review has been embraced to break down the Impact of Crude oil costs on the Indian securities exchange. The review considered seven lists of National Stock Exchange (NSE) and the end costs of Crude oil from investing.com to analyze the impact. The review utilized relapse, coefficient, and ANOVA. Overall, the review found a solid effect of raw petroleum costs on the given list of NSE indices. The outcome recommends that considering Crude oil costs is likewise imperative when the speculators consider trading in the chosen lists of National Stock Exchange indices. Now that we have found that Crude oil prices impact the movement of stock prices let us try and understand the impact of this phenomenon on our economy. Stated below are some of them:

A hike in crude oil prices will increase current account deficits: India being one of the largest importers of oil globally, an increase in crude oil prices will mean stress on foreign currency outflows, which will lead to rupee depreciation. This would make imports costlier, thus negatively impacting the business of companies that depend on crude oil and other imported raw materials for producing goods and services.

Leads to inflation: A hike in crude oil prices will lead to a hike in prices of all goods and services, thus increasing inflation. Investors perceive inflation negatively, which will negatively impact the movement of the stock market.

Transportation costs: An Increase in transportation costs due to a hike in crude oil prices will lead to an increase in the cost of production and a decrease in the demand of goods and services, which will negatively impact their stock prices.

Portfolio Diversification: The stock prices of Companies heavily dependent on crude oil can certainly be impacted by the fluctuations in crude oil prices. However, a wise decision would be to invest in fundamentally strong companies. Diversifying one's portfolio will also help reduce the impact of crude oil prices on the returns on our investment in the stock markets.

REFERENCES

Akshaya, A., & Naachimuthu, K. P. (2022). Locavorism to Enhance Environmental, Social, & Economic Well-being. *Indian Journal of Agriculture Business*, *8*(1), 25–33.

Al-Maaitah, D. A., Tha'er Majali, M. A., & Almaaitah, T. A. (2021a). The role of leadership styles on staffs job satisfaction in public organizations. *Journal of Contemporary Issues in Business and Government*, *27*(1), 772–783.

Al-Maaitah, T. A., Tha'er Majali, M. A., & Almaaitah, D. A. (2021b). The Impact of COVID-19 on the Electronic Commerce Users Behavior. *Journal of Contemporary Issues in Business and Government*, *27*(1), 772–783.

Aswathi, P., Sangavi, P., Naachimuthu, K. P., & Krishna, T. (2021). *Proceedings of the ICSSR Sponsored Webinar on Human Behavior and Environmental Sustainability*. Academic Press.

Awan, T. M., Khan, M. S., Haq, I. U., & Kazmi, S. (2021). Oil and stock markets volatility during pandemic times: A review of G7 countries. *Green Finance*, *3*(1), 15–27. doi:10.3934/GF.2021002

Bai, Y., & Green, C. J. (2011). Determinants of cross-sectional stock return variations in emerging markets. *Empirical Economics*, *41*(1), 81–102. doi:10.100700181-010-0437-9

Bansal, A., & Pasricha, J. S. (2009). Foreign Institutional Investor's Impact on Stock Prices in India. *Journal of Academic Research in Economics*, *1*(2), 181–189.

Gupta, R. K. (2021a). A study on occupational health hazards among construction workers in India. *International Journal of Enterprise Network Management*, *12*(4), 325–339. doi:10.1504/IJENM.2021.119663

Gupta, R. K. (2021b). Adoption of mobile wallet services: an empirical analysis. *International Journal of Intellectual Property Management, 12*(3), 341 – 353. doi:10.1504/IJIPM.2021.10035526

Gupta, R. K. (2022). Utilization of Digital Network Learning and Healthcare for Verbal Assessment and Counselling During Post COVID-19 Period. Technologies. *Artificial Intelligence and the Future of Learning Post-COVID*, *19*, 117–134.

Hana, M., & Naachimuthu, K. P. (2023). A Comprehensive Model on Rejection Sensitivity. *South India Journal of Social Sciences*, *21*(19), 19–31.

Hana, M., Vishnupriya, S., & Naachimuthu, K. P. (2022). Restorative Effect of Direct and Indirect Nature Exposure - A Systematic Review. *International Journal of Scientific Research*, *11*(5), 10–15.

Kumar, A., & Naachimuthu, K. P. (2023). Market Potential for Shawarma Outlet in Coimbatore - An Analysis. *South India Journal of Social Sciences*, *21*(1), 130–140.

Liao, G., Li, Z., Du, Z., & Liu, Y. (2019). The heterogeneous interconnections between supply or demand side and oil risks. *Energies*, *12*(11), 2226. doi:10.3390/en12112226

Özdurak, C. (2021). Nexus between crude oil prices, clean energy investments, technology companies, and energy democracy. *Green Finance*, *3*(3), 337–350. doi:10.3934/GF.2021017

Rajkumar, & Gupta, H. (2010). FII Flows to India: Economic Indicators. *SCMS Journal of Indian Management*, 104–116.

Rajput, N., Chopra, P., & Rajput, A. (2012). FII and its impact on stock market: A study on lead-lag and volatility spillover. *Asian Journal of Finance & Accounting*, *4*(2). Advance online publication. doi:10.5296/ajfa.v4i2.1874

Rao, K. S., Murhty, M., & Ranganathan, K. V. K. (1999). Foreign Institutional Investments and the Indian Stock Market. *Journal of Indian School of Political Economy*, 623–647.

Zheng, Y., & Du, Z. (2019). A systematic review in crude oil markets: Embarking on the oil price. *Green Finance*, *1*(3), 328–345. doi:10.3934/GF.2019.3.328

Chapter 18
A Study in Rural Areas of Southern Karnataka Districts in Dairy Farming Challenges Faced by the Entrepreneurs

M. S. Naveen Kumar
Jain University, India

S. Ashwini
Government First Grade College, India

G. M. Rajeshwari
REVA University, India

B. G. Guruprasad
Jain University, India

Sheetal V. Hukkeri
Jain University, India

Dilmurod Nasimov
Academy of Public Administration, Uzbekistan

ABSTRACT

The purpose of the study is to shed light on the challenges faced by the current dairy farming entrepreneurs. The study aimed to identify the establishing and operational challenges of dairy farming entrepreneurs. Irrespective of age, gender, financial background, formal education, and experience, people will enter dairy farming. For everyone who is willing to start their farm and who is running their dairy farming, the current study will help them to identify the possible threats to the business. The main purpose is to give a prepared mindset for the potential entrepreneurs to be ready with their strategies to overcome these challenges. The study collected the available research articles on dairy farming. A structured questionnaire was administered and collected the data. Two hundred twenty-eight dairy farmers were taken as the sample, and exploratory factor analysis (EFA) was used to identify the factors with the help of SPSS. The study identified that the land and labor issues are the biggest challenges for dairy farming.

DOI: 10.4018/979-8-3693-2193-5.ch018

INTRODUCTION

In rural India, people are starting their enterprises since they are looking out for their income (Gautam and Mishra, 2016). Dairy entrepreneurship has given life to many people who have started businesses with very little capital and people with high capital, along with differences in their educational backgrounds. Dairy entrepreneurship size is moderate in size in India (Shah. et. al., 2010), But it isn't easy to start an enterprise the rural India (Patel & Chavda, 2013). Some people have tremendous success in their farming at the same time. There are quite a lot of people who have experienced that dairy farming doesn't suit them, and also, it isn't easy to make a profit out of this business. Hence, the study has taken to identify the challenges faced by dairy farming entrepreneurs, which is going to address and throw light on the vital issues of this business. Marketing problems, water supply, finances, and transport were commonly faced by them (Sathya, 2019). The study aimed to bring to the notice the potential dairy farmers hence, they can have different strategies to meet these challenges to run the business successfully. Technological advancement will help rural industries (Barber et al., 2021).

Literacy, less technical knowledge, difficulty in accessing resources and services, lack of communication facilities, risk aversion, and lack of skilled labor (Lavanya et al., 2014). The problems of acquiring the cost of the land or even taking them for lease or rent also is a challenging job. Entering dairy farming without having sufficient capital to meet all expenses and bear them till the business reaches the break-even point (Chaurasiya et al., 2017). Hence, they have to be very careful with respect to the capital they are bringing in the other difficulties like meeting high labor turnover, the threat of health issues for the cattle, housing arrangements, bearing the delayed payment, and having the strength to buy the feeds and other supplements for the cattle in different environmental circumstances makes this business bit difficult. Marketing issues are quite common for rural dairy entrepreneurs (Mohapatra et al.,2012).

Many obstacles prevent the dairy industry in India from expanding and becoming more productive. One of the main problems is the low productivity of cattle ranches, which is caused by the ignorance of farmers and the poor quality of veterinary care. High animal mortality rates, as a result, affect total productivity. These problems are made worse by antiquated farming practices, ineffective supply networks, and difficulties in keeping up with immunization and medical records (Qureshi et al., 2016).

Numerous studies emphasize how livestock farms need to modernize. Productivity can be greatly increased by putting systematic methods and cutting-edge tactics into practice. Farmers use a wide range of diversification tactics, which highlights the significance of customized solutions based on the unique context and expertise of the farmers involved. The unique problems that young farmers inheriting older farms face call for a focus on succession planning and equity creation. The identification of financial planning and smart animal procurement is deemed vital for success in these types of situations.

Furthermore, the examination of both successful and unsuccessful dairy farms highlights how crucial it is to maximize expenses and the use of available infrastructure. When profit margins are shrinking, this optimization becomes essential. An entrepreneurial mindset on farms makes them more capable of overcoming these obstacles. Dairy farming also needs to adjust to climate change while maintaining profitability and sustainability (Khanum et al., 2022). It is crucial to discuss the variations between industrialized and emerging dairy countries' breeds, diets, welfare standards, and technological advancements. For efficient dairy production, a blend of modern and traditional methods tailored to local constraints is advised. In India, the dairy sector is essential to addressing agricultural uncertainty and preventing malnutrition. Its potential is hampered, nonetheless, by farmers' ignorance, restricted access to technology, and difficulties with livestock insurance. Encouraging sustainable growth, enhancing farmers' expertise, and offering reasonably priced technological solutions all depend on government backing. In order to achieve a stable and thriving dairy business in India, it is imperative that insurance issues be resolved and that farmers receive just compensation in the event that cattle is lost.

REVIEW OF LITERATURE

Jadwala and Patel's (2017) study from the Indian Dairy Industry perspective states that even though India is one of the highest milk-producing countries, compared to other high milk-producing countries, its per capita milk production is low and the reason for this is the low efficiency of Indian cattle farms. The farmers involved in cattle breeding lack knowledge and lack of medical history, and the mortality of cattle is too high. The traditional way of rearing cattle, inefficient supply chain, problems in maintaining vaccination as well and the health history of livestock are a few of the challenges of the dairy industry. This study suggested that adaptation of modernization in cattle farms and organized ways of cattle rearing will help in reviving the dairy industry (Kushwah et al., 2020).

Antonio et.al. (2021) study differentiates on-farm diversification procedures adopted by dairy farmers into four distinct groups: ecological, single-product, innovative, and traditional. These tactics are dependent on the outside environment and farmers' entrepreneurial skills. Interestingly, none of these remedies functioned far more effectively than the others. According to the investigation, farmers can successfully adjust to sectoral changes by matching their strategies to their context and skill set. The study emphasizes the importance of system resilience and variety in farming management for both farmers and policymakers. Potential issues are outlined, highlighting areas that require attention for Single-product and Traditional methods (Manivannanan & Tripathi, 2016).

Holden et al. (2021) examine the difficulties faced by young dairy farmers who inherit aging farms, emphasizing equity building and succession planning. To create training programs, senior owners' and new producers' perspectives were obtained through focus groups. Strong financial planning and targeted animal purchases to increase equity are success elements.

Georgia et al. (2022) study analyses 47 dairy farms using Data Envelopment Analysis to determine which ones are the most productive. It compares productive and ineffective farms through the analysis of technical and economic data. The results highlight the importance of optimizing costs and infrastructure utilization to improve intensive dairy farming. The study emphasizes the necessity of having a strong economy in an environment with declining profit margins. Farms with an entrepreneurial mindset are better equipped to handle upcoming difficulties (Patel et al., 2013).

Siddique & Jajja, (2022) study of the dairy industry's dynamics places a focus on farming that is profitable and sustainable while taking climate change into account. It addresses issues and provides recommendations for ethical dairy practices. It is observed that there are differences between developed and developing dairy countries, emphasizing differences in breed, feed, welfare, and technology. For effective dairy production, the study recommends a fusion of traditional and contemporary practices adjusted to regional limits.

Rajeeva et al. (2022) study emphasizes issues with efficiency and sustainability in the global dairy industry. It promotes technical development and environmentally friendly behaviors, such as lowering emissions and improving water management. The report emphasizes the advantages of innovation and growing markets. For a stronger dairy industry, a comprehensive strategy that combines efficiency and sustainability is suggested.

One of the earlier studies states that the Diary Industry in India is helping the farmers tackle agricultural uncertainties and helping them provide their livelihood; dairy products have greatly helped India in reducing the malnutrition and undernourishment levels in the country as well as contributing to employment generation (Dana, 2000). The study also states that the majority of the cattle raisers are unorganized, the landless or small farmers are not the choice of the cooperatives, and the cooperatives generally adopt a fat-based pricing policy, resulting in lower profitability for the farmers. There are many eco-friendly alternatives like soy milk, almond milk, etc, which are turning out as one of the threats for the dairy industry. The dairy industry needs sustainable development, which results in fulfilling the environmental, nutritional, and socio-economic requirements of the nation. The Government of India should take better measures to make diary enterprises more rewarding for minor and marginalized entrepreneurs (Nagrale et al., 2015).

The survey by Khanum et al., (2022) state that the lack of knowledge among the farmers about maintaining the daily data of cows and buffalos to treat sickness is one of the reasons for decreased productivity in dairy farming. The ignorance of calf rearing is also one of the reasons for low productivity. This study also focused on understanding the importance of animal insurance and how the lack of insurance facilities adversely affects dairy enterprises. Lack of veterinary arrangements and lack of knowledge among the farmers regarding deworming with different medications every season is also one of the reasons for the epidemic spreading among the animals, resulting in losses for the dairy enterprises (Dixit et al., 2022).

The technology adaptation in dairy farming helps in increasing the productivity in dairy enterprises, as professional dairy farming facilitates in adaptation of milking machines; TMRs cut the operational cost of the dairy farm and facilitate efficient management (Wanole et al., 2018). The online maintenance of records of each animal is possible with the help of technology, which results in increased productivity, but unfortunately, small and marginalized entrepreneurs cannot afford the same because of lack of funds.

Dairy farming does not get the benefit of livestock insurance through government schemes, and it is very expensive to insure private insurance companies. On the death of the animals, the insurance company suffers a lot in settling the claims, so the representatives of the company try to reject the claim to avoid compensating the farmers, which is one of the triggers for not insuring the animals.

RESEARCH GAP

There are many studies conducted regarding dairy entrepreneurship, and researchers have identified the challenges. But with respect to the southern part of Karnataka, very few studies have been conducted. Dairy entrepreneurship challenges in the rural part of the southern part, too, with Chamarajanagar and Mysore Districts. The current study is taken to throw light on the challenges he dairy entrepreneurs in the same districts.

Objective of the study: To identify the challenges faced by Dairy farmers.

Scope of the study: The study covers the dairy farmers in the southern Karnataka districts of Mysore and Chamarajanagar. Operational and establishing challenges are focused.

Limitations of the study: The study covers only two districts in southern Karnataka, and the personal issues of the dairy farmers are not covered.

RESEARCH METHODOLOGY

The study was conducted in the Mysore and Chamarajanagar districts, which are situated in the southern part of Karnataka. Simple random sampling was applied, and the sample size for the study was 227. A structured questionnaire was administered, and a few farmers were interviewed to collect the data method by using a questionnaire. Exploratory Factor Analysis (EFA) was used to identify the factors. With the help of the SPSS, EFA was conducted, and Microsoft Excel was used (Wakchaure et al., 2015).

The nature of the present research design is descriptive and exploratory. Refined questionnaire questions were asked of the drivers and collected the required data for the study. The questions were asked by interviewing each driver personally at their respective depots and buses. Sources of Data The following is the information about the sources of the data. ¬ Primary data: Research work carried out based on the primary data. The data was collected through the structured questionnaire. Chosen samples from dairy entrepreneurs were interviewed, and answers to the questionnaire were recorded. ¬ Secondary data: Secondary data works as the foundation for any research work. The research work has extracted information from the research journals and websites (Selvakumar & Yoganandan, 2019).

Sampling method A Simple random sampling method was used to select the sample from the sample. Data Suitability Test: The factor analysis process of data factor extraction is the major objective. Before extraction, it must pass through several tests. They are Kaiser-Meyer-Olkin and Bartlett's Test (KMO and Bartlett's Test) measure of sampling adequacy, and the communality values check of the variables. Before doing KMO and Bartlett's test, it is important to decide the number of variables for the factor analysis. KMO and Bartlett's test is conducted before commonality to check sampling adequacy; if it passes, commonalities will be checked. Communalities are the variance of the latent variables, and they should be more than 0.5; the variables must pass through this test by having more than 0.5. KMO and Bartlett's test is conducted after the communality check since the variables deletion having commonality less than 0.5 also affects KMO test results (Obiora & Nwokorie, 2018). Communality is the proportion of each variable's variance that the factors can explain. If the variable's variance values are less than 0.5, they will be deleted from the factors analysis process. Kaiser-Meyer-Olkin measure of sampling adequacy After having the communalities in order to check the sampling adequacy Kaiser-Meyer-Olkin value is considered. The very minimum acceptable value of KMO value is 0.5, and anything above 0.6 is considered a good sampling adequacy value (Raina et al., 2016). The best standard is set to 0.8, and above is the best sampling adequacy value.

The above table 1 shows the commonalities of the variables taken for the study, and all the variables showing more than 0.5 are to be taken for the study. The variables which were not have a lesser value than 0.5 were removed from the study (Table 2).

KAISER-MEYER-OLKIN MEASURE OF SAMPLING ADEQUACY

After having the commonalities to check the sampling adequacy, the Kaiser-Meyer-Olkin value is considered. The very minimum acceptable value of KMO value is 0.5, and anything above 0.6 is considered a good sampling adequacy value. The above table shows the sampling adequacy value of the Kaiser-Meyer-Olkin is 0.762, which is greater than 0.8, proving the best value to process the factor analysis. The sample size for the factor analysis must be decided based on the variables considered for the study. Statisticians agree sample size must be 10 times more than the variables accepted for the factor analysis.

In the present study sample size is 228, which is acceptable by nearly ten times the variables considered for the study.

The following table 3 shows the Eigenvalues, the variance of each factor, cumulative variance, the sum of squared loadings, and rotation sums of the squared loadings.

The above Table 3 shows that the factors are extracted based on the Eigen Values. The factors having more than Eigenvalue 1 have been taken into consideration as components or factors. The initial component has a value of 5.823 second component has a value of 4.408 Third component has a value of 3.855 fourth component has a value of 3.195, and the fifth and final components have a value of 2.296.

Table 1. Data analysis and interpretation

Communalities		
	Initial	**Extraction**
Shortage of land	1.000	0.794
Returning the milk due to quality issues	1.000	0.943
Shortage of water	1.000	0.855
Failure to get on-time feed delivery	1.000	0.763
Weather condition	1.000	0.839
Unable to reach hospital and doctors on time	1.000	0.716
Inconsistent health of cattle	1.000	0.699
Investment on housing	1.000	0.707
Shortage of place to store hay	1.000	0.835
Reduction in payment due to quality	1.000	0.626
Rent payable for land is too high	1.000	0.893
Shortage in feed supply is common	1.000	0.678
High labour charges	1.000	0.494
Unavailability of medicine on time	1.000	0.781
Low quality provided	1.000	0.566
Proper sanitation	1.000	0.584
Cost of the Feeds	1.000	0.809
Delay in payment	1.000	0.795
Chances of the death	1.000	0.704
Claims issue	1.000	0.881
Query response time	1.000	0.927
Durability	1.000	0.828
Disease-causing insects are unavoidable	1.000	0.640
Absenteeism and labor turnover	1.000	0.843
Information about cattle	1.000	0.700
Cleaning labor	1.000	0.678
Extraction Method: Principal Component Analysis.		

Table 2. KMO and Bartlett's test

Kaiser-Meyer-Olkin Measure of Sampling Adequacy.		0.762
Bartlett's Test of Sphericity	Approx. Chi-Square	5639.82
	df	325
	Sig.	0.000

Table 3. The factors are extracted based on the Eigen values

Total Variance Explained									
Component	**Initial Eigenvalues**			**Extraction Sums of Squared Loadings**			**Rotation Sums of Squared Loadings**		
	Total	**% of variance**	**Cumulative %**	**Total**	**% of variance**	**Cumulative %**	**Total**	**% of variance**	**Cumulative %**
1	5.823	22.397	22.397	5.823	22.397	22.397	5.467	21.027	21.027
2	4.408	16.953	39.35	4.408	16.953	39.35	4.01	15.423	36.45
3	3.855	14.826	54.176	3.855	14.826	54.176	3.788	14.568	51.018
4	3.195	12.289	66.466	3.195	12.289	66.466	3.466	13.332	64.35
5	2.296	8.83	75.296	2.296	8.83	75.296	2.846	10.946	75.296
6	0.908	3.49	78.786						
7	0.784	3.015	81.801						
8	0.622	2.394	84.195						
9	0.514	1.976	86.17						
10	0.483	1.856	88.026						
11	0.426	1.638	89.665						
12	0.352	1.355	91.02						
13	0.337	1.296	92.316						
14	0.322	1.239	93.555						
15	0.279	1.073	94.628						
16	0.244	0.939	95.567						
17	0.225	0.864	96.431						
18	0.195	0.749	97.18						
19	0.156	0.599	97.779						
20	0.14	0.538	98.317						
21	0.116	0.446	98.763						
22	0.114	0.44	99.202						
23	0.086	0.331	99.534						
24	0.061	0.234	99.768						
25	0.039	0.15	99.918						
26	0.021	0.082	100						
Extraction Method: Principal Component Analysis.									

Figure 1. The plot exhibits that the eigenvalues

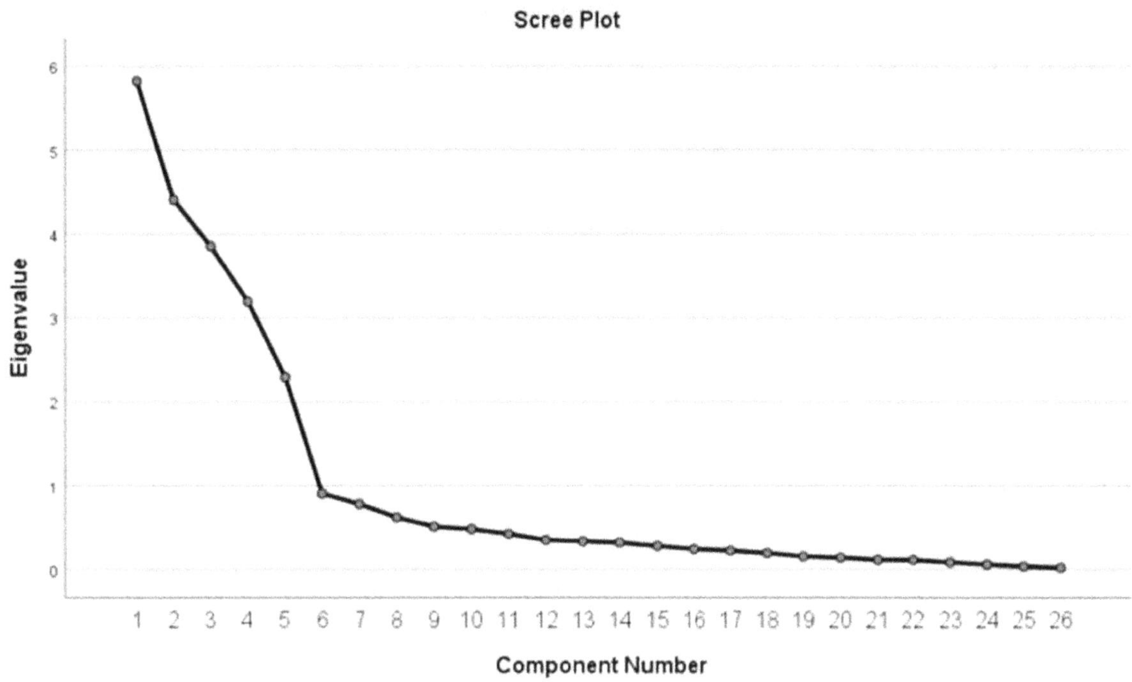

The above Fig. 1 plot exhibits that the Eigen values are more than have been chosen for the study. After the Eigenvalues have been less than one, the line becomes almost straight.

The above table 4 shows the loading of the respective variables, which are all part of the 5 factors that have been chosen for the study. Each variable has considerable loading, which is more than 0.3. However, it can be observed that few variables have cross-loadings to other factors, too. Hence, the variables that can be loaded to one particular factor will be identified by applying rotation to the matrix.

The Bivariate correlation matrix was calculated, and facts of the correlation among the factors of PCA were exhibited. There is no significant correlation between these factors. Hence orthogonal rotation technique must be used to rotate the matrix.

For rotation, the varimax rotation, which is part of orthogonal rotation, was selected. The varimax factor rotation along with the sorting of the data while the factors scores of the components were suppressed to 0.30. Hence, the values below 0.30 were eliminated from the table, and the remaining factors greater than 0.40 as the factor loadings.

The above table shows the loadings of the variables to respective factors clearly without any cross-loading issues. 27 variables have been loaded into five factors. The first factor is having the 7 variables loaded into it. The second, third, and fourth factors have been loaded with 5 variables, and the last factor has been loaded with 4 variables. The first factor loadings have the value of 0.667 to 0.933 as the highest and lowest values. In the second component, the highest and lowest variable loadings are 0.966 to 0.770; in the third variable, 0.934 is the highest and 0.827 is the lowest value; and in the fourth factor, 0.74 is the lowest, and 0.9 is being highest; and the fifth and last factor is having the four variables where the highest is 0.877 and lowest is 0.739 (Table 5).

Table 4. The respective variables, which are all part of the 5 factors

Component Matrix					
	Component				
	1	2	3	4	5
Rent payable for land is too high	0.887				
Absenteeism and labor turnover	0.867				
Shortage of land	0.836				
Shortage of water	0.829	0.308			
Weather condition	0.828	0.313			
Shortage of place to store hay	0.814	0.334			
High labour charges	0.531	0.341			
Returning the milk due to quality issues	-0.380	0.691		0.541	
Query response time	-0.380	0.690		0.531	
Delay in payment		0.676		0.475	
Information about cattle	-0.303	0.658		0.351	
Claims issue		-0.554	0.52632	0.544	
Unavailability of medicine on time		-0.535	0.500	0.484	
Reduction in payment due to quality	-0.3834	0.508		0.461	
Chances of the death		-0.413	0.591	0.428	
Durability	-0.3728		0.568	-0.315	-0.4437
Inconsistent health of cattle		-0.493	0.525	0.414	
Cleaning labor		0.396	0.510	-0.311	
Unable to reach hospital and doctors on time		-0.4941	0.495	0.452	
Proper sanitation	-0.369		0.493		-0.385
Disease-causing insects are unavoidable.			0.474		-0.430
Investment on housing	-0.3361	0.33103	0.463		-0.458
Failure to get on-time feed delivery			0.440	-0.394	0.632
Cost of the Feeds			0.564	-0.385	0.573
Low quality provided			0.379		0.558
Shortage in feed supply is common			0.446	-0.414	0.538
Extraction Method: Principal Component Analysis					
a. 5 components extracted.					

FINDINGS OF THE STUDY

Rent payable for land is too high, Weather conditions, Shortage of water, Shortage of place to store hay, Absenteeism, labor turnover, Shortage of land, and high labor charges have the values 0.933, 0.914, 0.914, 0.907, 0.904, 0.875 and 0.667 respectively. The second factor has five variables loaded onto it they are Returning the milk due to quality issues, Query response time, Delay in payment, Information about cattle, and Reduction in payment due to quality, having values of 0.966, 0.956, 0.886, 0.812, and 0.770 respectively.

Table 5. The loadings of the variables to respective factors

Rotated Component Matrix[a]					
	Component				
	1	2	3	4	5
Rent payable for land is too high	0.933				
Weather condition	0.914				
Shortage of water	0.914				
Shortage of place to store hay	0.907				
Absenteeism and labor turnover	0.904				
Shortage of land	0.875				
High labour charges	0.667				
Returning the milk due to quality issues		0.966			
Query response time		0.956			
Delay in payment		0.886			
Information about cattle		0.812			
Reduction in payment due to quality		0.770			
Claims issue			0.934		
Unavailability of medicine on time			0.877		
Unable to reach hospital and doctors on time			0.831		
Chances of the death			0.831		
Inconsistent health of cattle			0.827		
Durability				0.900	
Investment on housing				0.831	
Disease-causing insects are unavoidable.				0.797	
Cleaning labor				0.781	
Proper sanitation				0.740	
Cost of the Feeds					0.877
Failure to get on-time feed delivery					0.871
Shortage in feed supply is common					0.812
Low quality provided					0.739

Extraction Method: Principal Component Analysis.
Rotation Method: Varimax with Kaiser Normalization.

The third factor has been loaded with 5 variables, i.e., Claims issue, Unavailability of medicine on time, Unable to reach hospital and doctors on time, Chances of death, and Inconsistent health of cattle, have values of 0.934, 0.877, 0.831, 0.831 and 0.827 respectively. The fourth component has 5 variables, and it has the 5 variables loaded into it. They are Durability, Investment in housing, Disease-causing insects are unavoidable, Cleaning labor, and Proper sanitation, having values of 0.9, 0.831, 0.797, 0.781, and 0.740, respectively.

Table 6. Labelling and reliability statistics

Land and labor	
Shortage of land	9.2
The rent payable for land is too high	
Shortage of water	
Absenteeism and labor turnover	
Shortage of place to store hay	
Weather condition	
High labor charges	
Quality and payment issues	
Returning the milk due to quality issues	8.2
Query response time	
Information about cattle	
Delay in payment	
Reduction in payment due to quality	
Medical and Claims issues	
Claims issue	9
Inconsistent health of cattle	
Unavailability of medicine on time	
Unable to reach hospital and doctors on time	
Chances of the death	
Housing for dairy cattle	
Durability	8.8
Investment on housing	
Cleaning labor	
Proper sanitation	
Disease-causing insects are unavoidable.	
External Feed	
Cost of the Feeds	8.3
Failure to get on-time feed delivery	
Shortage in feed supply is common	
Low quality provided	

The fifth and final component of the study has the 4 factors loaded onto it: Cost of the Feeds, Failure to get on-time feed delivery, Shortage in feed supply common, and Low quality provided, which have values of 0.877, 0.871, 0.812, and 0.732.

Support from the people who have the excess land can be utilized for growing cattle feed; also, the rent must be reduced for dairy farming. Weather conditions dry up the land, alternative sources of water must be found, and the plan to drain the excess water from the land must be identified. Keeping the permanent labor or going with a contract would help them to reduce the cost. The payments must be made on exact dates, and information about the right kind of cattle must be given to the farmers. Mediclaim issues must be quick and easy; making the medicine available and quick access to medical facilities will save the lives of cattle and businesses. Housing must be planned at a lower cost, which can be durable and also easy to maintain will be helpful External feed supply must be regularised, and costs must be reduced by providing a discount for the people exclusively dependent on dairy farming.

CONCLUSION

Entrepreneurship always comes up with challenges, and entrepreneurs must be determined to face them. The current paper gives an insight into the challenges that have been faced by the dairy entrepreneurs, like land and labour issues, i.e., the cost of the land is too expensive in many places, the rented or leased lands are long-term commitment which could be another threat to with respect their running cost. These days, the cost of labor cost has skyrocketed, which is creating difficulty in getting the labor and having the labor who can stay for the long run. Meeting the quality requirements all the time is a vital problem for dairy farming. A few times, getting the payment on time is difficult. Medical claims process when things go south and getting on-time treatment is not a possible task very easily. Housing the cattle has to be done in a standardized manner; dairy farming cattle are quite sensitive many times; hence, building and maintaining hygiene is an expensive and fussy factor. Finally, the cost of the external feed is too high; without buying those feeds, it's difficult to get more milk from the cattle.

REFERENCES

Antonio, Beatriz, José, Pérez-Méndez, & Roibás. (2021). Value-Creating Strategies in Dairy Farm Entrepreneurship: A Case Study in Northern Spain. *Animal, 11*(5), 1396. doi:10.3390/ani11051396

Barber, D. III, Harris, M. L., & Jones, J. (2021). An Overview of Rural Entrepreneurship and Future Directions. *Journal of Small Business Strategy*, *31*(4), 1–4. doi:10.53703/001c.29468

Chaurasiya, K. K., Prashant, M., & Badodiya, S. K. (2017). Factors affecting entrepreneurial behaviour of dairy farmers. *Agriculture Update*, *12*(1), 23–30. doi:10.15740/HAS/AU/12.1/23-30

Dana, L. P. (2000). Creating entrepreneurs in India. *Journal of Small Business Management*, *38*(1), 86.

Dixit, A. K., Sirohi, S., Ravishankar, K. M., Cariappa, A. A., Kumar, S., Bhandari, G., & Thakur, A. (2022). Understating emerging value chains and business performance: evidence from dairy industry in India. *Journal of Agribusiness in Developing and Emerging Economies*, (ahead-of-print).

Gautam, R. K., & Mishra, K. (2016). Study on rural women entrepreneurship in India: Issues and challenges. *International Journal of Applied Research*, *2*, 33–36.

Georgia, K. (2022). Entrepreneurship in Dairy Cattle Sector: Key Features of Successful Administration and Management. *Land (Basel)*, *11*(10), 1736–1736. doi:10.3390/land11101736

Jadwala, R., & Patel, S. (2017). Challenges of Indian Dairy Industry. *Indian Journal of Applied Research*, *7*(10), 516–517.

Khanum, R., Mahadi, M. S. A., & Islam, M. S. (2022). Empowering tribal women through entrepreneurship in Sylhet region of Bangladesh. *GeoJournal, 87*(4), 3387–3402. doi:10.100710708-020-10361-7

Kushwah, S. S., Badodiya, S. K., Bhadauria, U. P. S., & Gurjr, R. S. (2020). Impact of entrepreneurial behavioural of farmers for increasing their income through bee keeping activities. *Indian Research Journal of Extension Education, 20*(1), 55–60.

L.A., Jeffrey, Bradley, & Erica. (2011). Challenges and opportunities for new and beginning dairy producers: A Pennsylvania perspective. *Journal of Extension, 49*(3).

Lavanya, M. S., Hemalatha, S., & Indumathi, V. M. (2014). Perspectives of rural entrepreneurship in India. *Journal of Management Research, 3*(1), 95–100.

Manivannanan, C., & Tripathi, H. (2016). Management efficiency of dairy entrepreneurs. *Indian Research Journal of Extension Education, 7*(3), 44–51.

Mohapatra, A. S., Behera, R., & Sahu, U. N. (2012). Constraints faced by tribal entrepreneurs in dairy farming enterprise. *International Journal of Physical and Social Sciences, 2*(7), 171–184.

Nagrale, B. G., Datta, K. K., & Chauhan, A. K. (2015). An analysis of constraints faced by dairy farmers in Vidarbha region of Maharashtra. *Indian Journal of Dairy Science, 68*(4), 390–394.

Obiora, J. N., & Nwokorie, E. C. (2018). Impediments to Rural Youth Entrepreneurship towards the Hospitality Sector in Nigeria: The Case of Ihitte-Uboma, Imo State. *Journal of Tourism and Hospitality Management, 6*(1), 81–91.

Patel, B., & Chavda, K. (2013). Rural entrepreneurship in India: Challenge and problems. *International Journal of Advance Research in Computer Science and Management Studies, 1*(2).

Patel, N. B., Saiyed, L. H., Rao, T. K. S., Ranjeetsingh, R., Modi, R. J., & Sabapara, G. P. (2013). Status and constraints of dairying in the tribal households of Narmada valley of Gujarat-India. *Animal Science (Penicuik, Scotland), 7*(3), 31–37.

Qureshi, M. A., Khan, P. A., & Uprit, S. (2016). Empowerment of rural women through agriculture and dairy sectors in India. *Economic Affairs, 61*(1), 75. doi:10.5958/0976-4666.2016.00011.5

Raina, V., Bhushan, B., Bakshi, P., & Khajuria, S. (2016). Entrepreneurial behaviour of dairy farmers. *Journal of Animal Research, 6*(5), 1–7. doi:10.5958/2277-940X.2016.00123.6

Rajeeva, S. (2022). Global Dairy Sector: Trends, Prospects, and Challenges. *Sustainability (Basel), 14*(7), 4193–4193. doi:10.3390u14074193

Sathya, I. (2019). Rural entrepreneurship in India. *Research Explorer-A Blind Review and Refereed Quarterly International Journal, 7*(2).

Selvakumar, M., & Yoganandan, G. (2019). Problems And Practices Of Micro-Scale Dairy Entrepreneurs In Salem District, Tamilnadu. *International Journal of Scientific & Technology Research, 8*(12), 1485–1489.

Shah, A. K., Malik, B. S., & Yadav, V. K. (2010). Entrepreneurial behaviour and their correlates among dairy entrepreneurs in Northern India. *Indian Journal of Extension Education, 46*(3and4), 53-61.

Siddique, M. I., & Jajja, M. S. S. (2022). Jamal dairy farm: Technology adoption challenges. *Asian Journal of Management Cases*. Advance online publication. doi:10.1177/09728201221107784

Wakchaure, R., Ganguly, S., Para, P. A., Praveen, P. K., Kumar, A., & Sharma, S. (2015). Development of crossbred cattle in India: A review. *International Journal of Emerging Technology and Advanced Engineering*, *5*(10), 75–77.

Wanole, S. N., Bande, K. D., Holkar, S. C., & Mardane, R. G. (2018). Relational analysis of entrepreneurial behavior of banana growers. *International Journal of Chemical Studies*, *6*(3), 2407–2411.

Chapter 19
An Analysis of Credit Management and Bank Lending Practices in Developing Countries

Srinivas Kolachina
https://orcid.org/0000-0002-9310-8218
Koneru Lakshmaiah Education Foundation, India

Lisha Hundia
Koneru Lakshmaiah Education Foundation, India

Kancherla Mounishker
Koneru Lakshmaiah Education Foundation, India

Juluru Venkatesh
Koneru Lakshmaiah Education Foundation, India

Palanivel Rathinasabapathi Velmurugan
https://orcid.org/0000-0002-0395-9060
Berlin School of Business and Innovation, Germany

Ahmed J. Obaid
https://orcid.org/0000-0003-0376-5546
University of Kufa, Iraq

ABSTRACT

The credit system and the banking activities processes increase people's investment practices, enhancing country people's economic condition. The research aims to understand the processes of banking activities and the importance of the credit management system. Concepts and the procedures of the credit management system are the most important things in lending a loan. The theory of banking activities is for understanding the activities of the banned credit system of the banks, including the processes of verification, calculation of loan details, and disbursing of the amount. The primary method has been used for collecting data from the respondents, including quantitative analysis, for a better understanding of all facts. This increases the possibility of earning and promotes developmental activities. Banks' lending practices increase their income, and the credit system increases the scope for developing the economic condition.

DOI: 10.4018/979-8-3693-2193-5.ch019

1. INTRODUCTION

Developing countries denote the countries that are still in the stage of development, and the people are engaging in the good practices of life. Several credit management systems of the financial institutions are demarcated, such as verification of the different customers, providing loans based on different categories of customers, and so on (Olabisi et al. 2019). This research work has prepared to analyse the importance of the role of banking and credit system in developing countries to develop people's economies and increase the number of investments (Tambaip et al., 2023).

Effective credit management is crucial for developing countries' financial stability and economic growth. It involves assessing, monitoring, and controlling credit risks to ensure the soundness of lending activities (Tripathi & Al-Shahri, 2023). Banks in developing countries must employ rigorous credit assessment procedures to evaluate the creditworthiness of borrowers. This includes analyzing financial statements, collateral evaluation, and assessing the borrower's capacity to repay the loan. Risk evaluation helps banks identify potential defaults and make informed lending decisions (Priscila et al., 2023).

Banks in developing countries should diversify their loan portfolios to minimize risk exposure. Concentrating loans in a single sector or borrower increases vulnerability to economic shocks or defaults (Srinivas et al., 2023; Yeruva & Ramu, 2023). Diversification across different industries and borrowers can mitigate risks and enhance overall loan portfolio performance (Said & Tripathi, 2023). Collateral requirements play a significant role in lending practices. Banks should establish appropriate collateral policies to protect their interests in case of default. However, limited access to collateral in many developing countries prevents small businesses and entrepreneurs from accessing credit (Singh et al., 2023).

Microfinance institutions (MFIs) are crucial in providing financial services to the unbanked population. MFIs focus on extending credit to small businesses and low-income individuals who lack access to traditional banking services. These institutions employ unique lending practices, such as group lending and peer monitoring, to mitigate risks. Developing countries need robust regulatory frameworks and effective supervision for prudent lending practices. Regulations should address capital adequacy, loan classification, provisioning, and credit reporting issues. Regulatory oversight promotes transparency, accountability, and stability in the banking sector.

Developing countries can benefit from establishing comprehensive credit information systems. Such systems enable banks to access borrower credit histories, reducing information asymmetry and improving credit decisions (Ramos et al., 2023). Accessible and accurate credit information enhances credit management and reduces default rates. Developing countries should promote financial inclusion to broaden access to credit and banking services. Sustainable lending practices prioritize responsible lending and con projects environmental and social impacts. Incorporating environmental, social, and governance (ESG) factors into lending decisions promotes long-term sustainability (Venkateswaran et al., 2023).

This research has developed to know the facts between the development of the countries, the role of financial organizations, and the suitable credit system behind the development process. According to the views of Muhammad, Alwi & Muhammad (2020), the credit system of any country depends on the nature of customers and the country's interest rate. This means the credit system is to include the people in the financial activities, increasing the banking sector business.

The above Figure 1 represents the number of credit cards and falsifications that have increased from 2016 to 2020 from 4678 to 5998. The number has increased from 201 to 2020 by 1320, which is remarkable (Statista, 2022). This restricts the involvement of the people, which has gradually increased in banking and financial activities from 2016 to 2020 (Saxena et al., 2023).

Figure 1. The number of credit cards increased from 2016 to 2020
Source: Statista (2022)

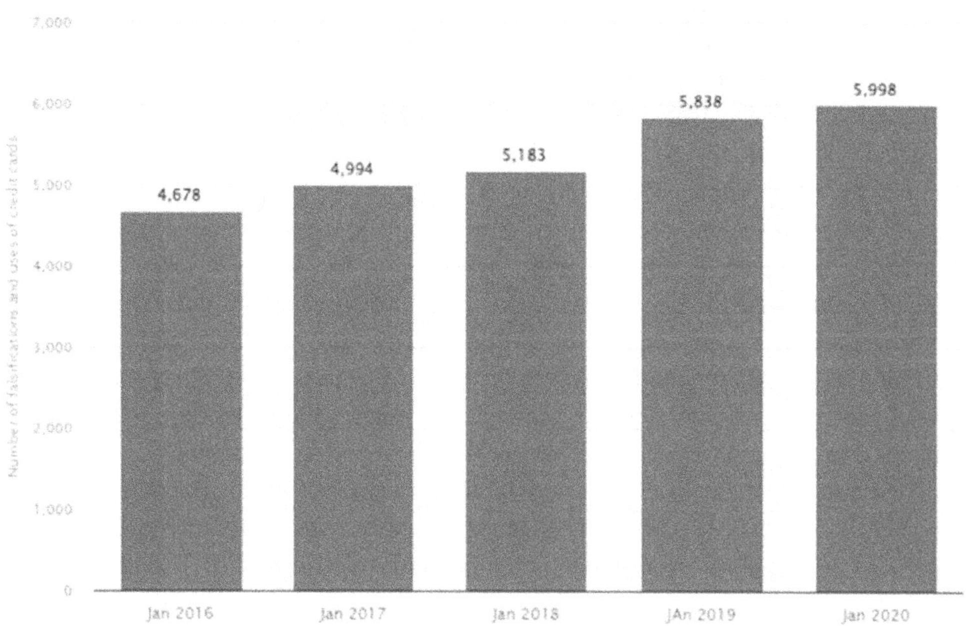

Aim: The research aims to determine the effect of the credit system and the banking processes in developing countries.

Research Objectives

- To know the credit management system in developing countries
- To know the impact of the credit management system among the people and in the developmental economic activities
- To analyse the role of finance and banking sectors and their practices to increase the financial condition of people and country
- To suggest better ways for the best management of customers and services of banks

Research Questions

- What are the important processes of a credit management system?
- What is the importance of the credit system in developing countries?
- How do banks manage the credit management system and analyze the customers?
- What are the bank's processes for the development of the economic condition of the people?

2. LITERATURE REVIEW

2.1. Concepts of the Credit Management System

The credit management system includes many different types of activities to serve credit to the customers with the help of 5C's, as shown in figure 2. According to the views of Zimon & Dankiewicz (2020), credit processes are one of the essential activities of banks and financial organizations. This increases business, one of the banking sector's best earning modes (Sabti et al., 2023). On the other hand, Alphonsus (2019) argued that the credit system of the banks includes the processes of verification, calculation of loan details, disbursing of the amount, and so on (Ramu & Yeruva, 2023). This system includes processes such as checking credit, customer capacity, the purpose of the loan, collateral values, and so on. The 5C's of credit are commonly used in the credit system to assess the borrower's creditworthiness.

Character: Refers to the borrower's credit history and reputation. Lenders evaluate the borrower's past credit behavior, including their payment history, credit utilization, and any defaults or delinquencies. It assesses the borrower's reliability and willingness to repay debts.

Capacity: Focuses on the borrower's ability to repay the loan based on their income, employment stability, cash flow, and existing financial obligations. Lenders analyze the borrower's debt-to-income ratio and evaluate whether their income is sufficient to meet loan repayment requirements.

Figure 2. The 5C's of the credit system
Source: Zimon & Dankiewicz (2020)

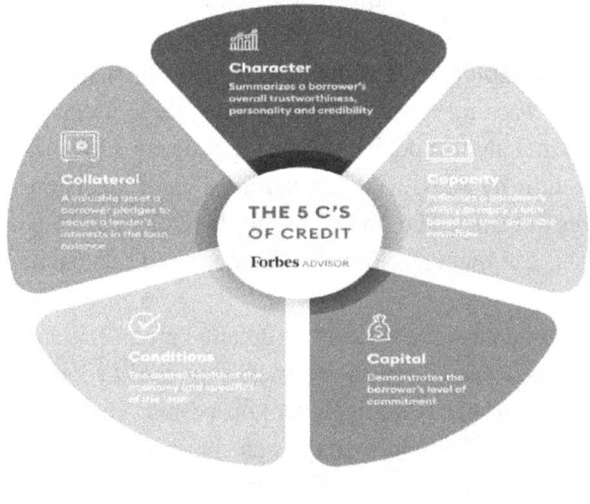

Capital: Relates to the borrower's financial resources and net worth. Lenders assess the borrower's assets, savings, investments, and other sources of capital. A strong capital position cushions financial difficulty and reassures lenders about the borrower's ability to handle financial obligations (Vashishtha & Kapoor, 2023).

Collateral: Involves the assets or property the borrower pledges as security for the loan. Collateral acts as a form of protection for lenders if the borrower defaults. Lenders evaluate the value and quality of the collateral to determine the loan-to-value ratio and the level of risk associated with the loan.

Conditions: Refers to the external factors that may impact the borrower's ability to repay the loan. It considers the overall economic conditions, industry-specific factors, and market trends. Lenders assess the potential risks associated with the borrower's specific circumstances and evaluate how these conditions may affect loan repayment.

The 5C of credit provides a framework for lenders to evaluate borrower's creditworthiness and make informed decisions regarding loan approval, interest rates, and terms. By considering these factors comprehensively, lenders can effectively manage credit risk and ensure responsible lending practices.

Credit management systems focus on assessing and managing credit risk. Research by Abbassy (2020) explores various quantitative models and techniques for credit risk assessment, including statistical models, credit scoring, and machine learning algorithms. The review highlights the importance of accurate risk assessment in credit management to make informed lending decisions and mitigate potential losses.

Credit scoring models are widely used in credit management systems to evaluate the creditworthiness of borrowers. Research by Abbassy & Abo-Alnadr (2019) examines the development and performance of credit-scoring models. The review explores traditional scoring approaches like logistic regression discriminant analysis and newer techniques like ensemble methods and neural networks.

Credit management systems also involve effective portfolio management to optimize risk and return. A review by Abbassy & Ead (2020) discusses portfolio models, diversification strategies, and risk management techniques in credit portfolio management. The review emphasizes balancing risk and returns in credit portfolios to achieve long-term profitability.

Effective credit management systems require ongoing monitoring and control of credit exposures. Research by Alabdullah et al. (2021) examines the role of credit monitoring in preventing loan default and reducing credit risk. The review explores different monitoring mechanisms, including financial covenants, collateral valuation, and early warning systems, and discusses their effectiveness in managing credit risk.

Credit management systems involve decision-making processes for origination, credit limit setting, and pricing. A literature review by Alayli (2023) examines credit decision-making models and factors influencing credit decisions in banks. The review highlights information quality, borrower characteristics, macroeconomic factors, and regulatory environment in credit decision-making (Venkateswaran & Viktor, 2023).

Advancements in technology have significantly impacted credit management systems. Research by Anand et al. (2023) reviews the role of technology, including credit scoring automation, data analytics, and digital platforms, in enhancing credit management processes. The review discusses the benefits and challenges of technology adoption in credit management systems.

A literature review by Ángeles (2022) focuses on credit management practices in developing countries. The review explores institutions' challenges in extending credit to small businesses and low-income individuals. It discusses the role of microfinance institutions, credit guarantee schemes, and financial inclusion initiatives in improving credit access in developing economies.

2.2 Concepts of the Leading Practices of Banks for Developing the People of Developing Countries

The main practice of the bank is to assist people by providing services to save their money in a secure place. Based on the views of Olabisi et al. (2019), banking sectors are interrelated with the financial activities for increasing the financial activities of the people and banks. Another important task of the bank is to enhance their income by providing loans to the customers, which helps to collect the interest against the loan amount. On the other hand, Shiwen et al. (2022) argued that the development of the banking sector has increased to fulfill the objective of the government's small investments and promote the development of the economic base among the people. This helps people's businesses by providing monetary support at the proper time.

Ángeles (2023) has researched Bank lending behavior in developing countries, and they examined the determinants of bank lending behavior in sub-Saharan Africa, including credit management practices. The research also investigates macroeconomic conditions, banking sector characteristics, and regulatory frameworks influencing lending decisions in developing countries.

In research work by Atasever (2023) on Credit risk management practices in commercial banks, credit risk management practices between developing and developed countries are compared. The study also explores various risk management techniques commercial banks employ, such as credit scoring models, collateral requirements, loan loss provisions, and portfolio diversification.

2.3 Challenges Faced by the Banking Sectors to Increase Their Businesses

Several studies highlight the challenges arising from the complex regulatory environment in India's banking sector. Research by Ead & Abbassy (2022) emphasizes the need for regulatory reforms to address issues related to capital adequacy, non-performing assets (NPAs), and governance practices. The review suggests a more conducive regulatory framework can foster growth and attract investment in the banking sector.

Effective credit risk management is essential for the sustainable growth of banks. Research by Ead & Abbassy (2018) and Kanaan-Jebna et al. (2022) examine the challenges in credit risk assessment, loan underwriting, and risk monitoring faced by Indian banks. The reviews emphasize the need for improved credit appraisal techniques, robust credit risk models, and timely identification of early warning signals to mitigate credit risk.

NPAs pose a significant challenge to the Indian banking sector. Studies by Köseoğlu et al. (2022) and Kuragayala (2023) discuss the causes and consequences of NPAs, including issues related to loan recovery, credit risk management, and weak corporate governance. The reviews underscore the importance of effective NPA resolution mechanisms to restore the health of banks and encourage lending.

The inadequate infrastructure and connectivity in certain regions of India pose challenges for expanding banking services. Research by Mert (2022) discusses banks' challenges in establishing and maintaining physical branches in remote areas. The review suggests that leveraging mobile banking, agent banking models, and innovative delivery channels can help overcome infrastructure-related challenges and reach a wider customer base.

Despite efforts to promote financial inclusion in India, challenges persist in expanding banking services to underserved populations. Research by Ocoró et al. (2023) examines the challenges banks face in reaching remote and rural areas, including infrastructure limitations, lack of awareness, and limited access to formal identification documents. The review suggests innovative technologies and partnerships with local stakeholders can help overcome these challenges and enhance financial inclusion.

Adopting technology presents both opportunities and challenges for the banking sector in India. Studies by Pandit (2023) and Phoek et al. (2023) discuss the challenges of implementing digital banking and fintech solutions. These challenges include cybersecurity risks, customer privacy concerns, and the need for upskilling bank employees. The reviews highlight the importance of a robust digital infrastructure and effective risk management practices to harness the benefits of technological advancements.

The banking sector faced challenges through the controlling factors of the higher organizations. According to the views of Sun (2023), the banking sectors are controlled by the interest rate, repo rate, liability holdings, and so on. The government has controlled all these regulations for customers' assets during emergencies.

2.4. Fractional Reserve Theory

The fractional reserve theory in banking and economics suggests that commercial banks hold only a fraction of their customers' deposits as reserves while lending out the remaining portion (Vashishtha & Dhawan, 2023). This allows banks to create new money through the process of credit expansion.

Let us have a glance at some key points related to the fractional reserve theory:

Money Creation and Multiplier Effect: Under the fractional reserve system, when a bank receives a deposit, it must hold a fraction of that deposit as reserves and can lend out the rest. This creates new deposits in the banking system, leading to an expansion of the money supply. The lending and subsequent re-depositing of these funds can result in a multiplier effect, further increasing the money supply.

Reserve Requirements and Regulation: Central banks often set reserve requirements, which determine the minimum fraction of deposits that banks must hold as reserves. These requirements are implemented to ensure financial stability and control the growth of the money supply. Changes in reserve requirements can impact credit creation and the overall functioning of the fractional reserve system.

Money Supply Control and Monetary Policy: Central banks also use open market operations, discount rate changes, and reserve requirements as tools to influence the money supply and implement monetary policy. By adjusting these parameters, central banks can affect economic activity, inflation, and interest rates.

Criticisms and Debates: The fractional reserve theory has been subject to criticism and debates. Some critics argue that the fractional reserve system allows banks to create money, leading to economic instability and inflation. Others question the effectiveness of fractional reserve banking in light of financial crises and argue for alternative monetary systems, such as full-reserve banking or sovereign money.

2.5. Fractional Reserve Theory: Literature Review

This theory describes that the banking sector can create money by using the deposited amount in lending credit to other people against their credit score. According to the views of Murphy (2019), this theory includes the processes of the banking role and the ways they develop the business by gathering money from people and providing loans to the customers, as shown in Figure 3. This enhances the rate of investment in the country and the condition of banks.

Figure 3. Processes of fractional reserve theory of banking activities
Source: Murphy (2019)

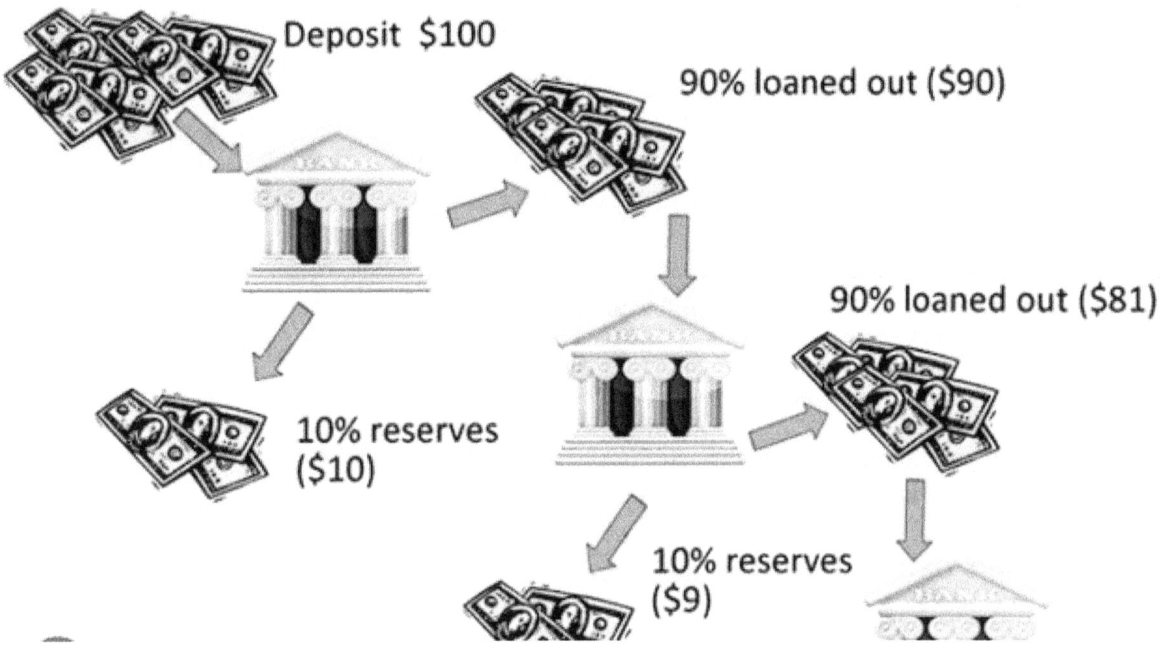

María et al. (2023) provide a comprehensive introduction to economics and include a chapter on money and banking, which covers fractional reserve banking. He explains how the fractional reserve system works and discusses its impact on money supply, credit creation, and monetary policy.

Werner (2014) critically examines the empirical evidence for the fractional reserve theory and discusses alternative theories, such as the credit creation theory. He argues that banks can create money by extending credit, challenging the traditional fractional reserve view.

3. METHODOLOGY

This study has been developed through the use of the primary data collected from the respondents to understand the features of the banking sector and the processes of developing their business. According to Puhl (2020), the primary quantitative processes include the survey, which increases the possibility of acquiring correct data from the respondents. This increases the level of understanding about the matter of the research. Based on the views of Baker et al. (2020), the quantitative analysis is scientific including many statistical and numerical processes. This has developed to increase the research quality and confidence. Using SPSS and the survey of 55 respondents helps to understand everything related to the research topic.

Hypothesis Testing

Hypothesis 1

H1: The Finance system helps the people to grow in life
H0: The financial system does not help people grow in life

Hypothesis 2

H1: The credit management system is based on the character of the borrower
H0: The credit system does not depend on the characteristics of the borrower

Hypothesis 3

H1: The banking sector can manage the activities to meet the needs of customers
H0: Banking sectors not able to maintain the demand of customers

Demographic data

Age

54.55% of respondents are categorized under 30 to 40, and the percentage of respondents between the ages of 40 to 50 is 27.27%. The respondents between 50 to 60 and 20 to 30 are 9.09% each (Figure 4).

Figure 4. Age analysis between 20 to 60
Source: SPSS

What is your age?

		Frequency	Percent	Valid Percent	Cumulative Percent
Valid	20 to 30	5	9.1	9.1	9.1
	30 to 40	30	54.5	54.5	63.6
	40 to 50	15	27.3	27.3	90.9
	50 to 60	5	9.1	9.1	100.0
	Total	55	100.0	100.0	

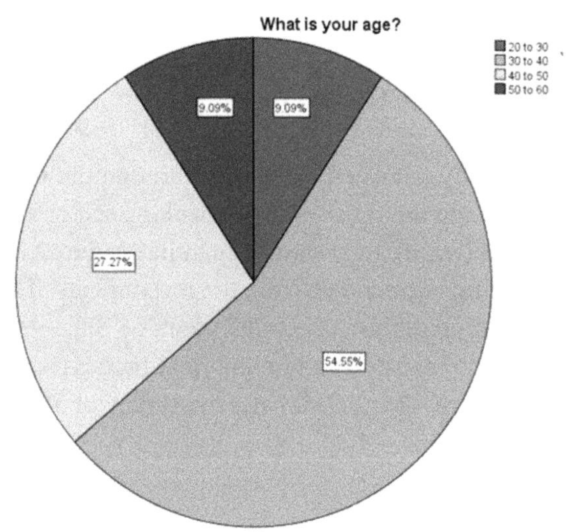

Gender

The percentage of males is 54.55%, females 36.36% among respondents, and the remaining 9.09% others (Figure 5).

Figure 5. Gender analysis
Source: SPSS

What is your gender?

		Frequency	Percent	Valid Percent	Cumulative Percent
Valid	Female	20	36.4	36.4	36.4
	Male	30	54.5	54.5	90.9
	Other	5	9.1	9.1	100.0
	Total	55	100.0	100.0	

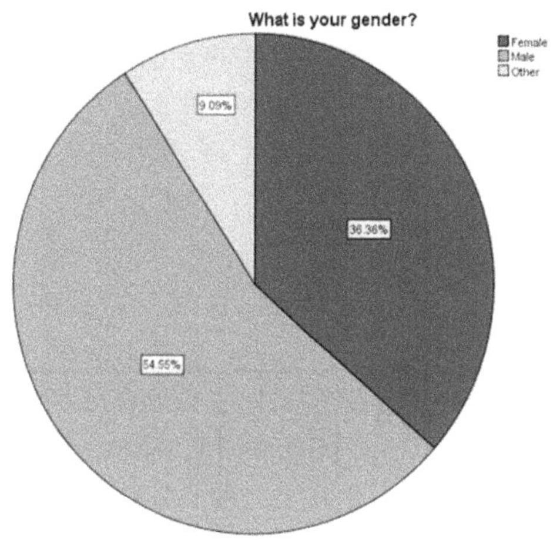

Marital Status

54.55% of respondents are married, and 45.45% of respondents are single (Figure 6)

Figure 6. Status analysis
Source: SPSS

What is your marital status?

		Frequency	Percent	Valid Percent	Cumulative Percent
Valid	Married	30	54.5	54.5	54.5
	Single	25	45.5	45.5	100.0
	Total	55	100.0	100.0	

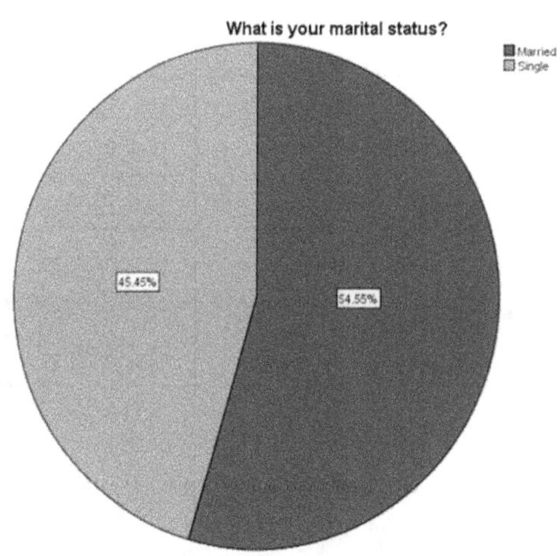

Hypothesis analysis

Hypothesis 1

The regression value of figure 7 is 0.008, greater than the ideal significance value of 0.005, which means the variables of this hypothesis are not strongly correlated. The finance system is crucial in supporting individuals. To detail it more. It is important to note that while it offers significant benefits, it must also operate with proper regulations and oversight to maintain stability and fairness and protect consumers. Striking the right balance between financial innovation, risk management, and consumer protection is vital to ensure that the finance system continues to support individuals' growth and contribute positively to overall societal well-being.

Figure 7. Hypothesis 1
Source: SPSS

Model Summary[b]

Model	R	R Square	Adjusted R Square	Std. Error of the Estimate	Change Statistics					Durbin-Watson
					R Square Change	F Change	df1	df2	Sig. F Change	
1	.357[a]	.127	.111	2.22595	.127	7.730	1	53	.008	1.973

ANOVA[a]

Model		Sum of Squares	df	Mean Square	F	Sig.
1	Regression	38.303	1	38.303	7.730	.008[b]
	Residual	262.606	53	4.955		
	Total	300.909	54			

Coefficients[a]

Model		Unstandardized Coefficients		Standardized Coefficients	t	Sig.
		B	Std. Error	Beta		
1	(Constant)	7.750	.787		9.848	.000
	IV1	-.473	.170	-.357	-2.780	.008

Hypothesis 2

Figure 8 represents the significance values of 0.004, which is within 0.005, and this restricts the variables of this hypothesis from being strongly correlated.

Figure 8. Hypothesis 2
Source: SPSS

Model Summary[b]

Model	R	R Square	Adjusted R Square	Std. Error of the Estimate	Change Statistics					Durbin-Watson
					R Square Change	F Change	df1	df2	Sig. F Change	
1	.379[a]	.144	.127	2.20504	.144	8.887	1	53	.004	2.203

ANOVA[a]

Model		Sum of Squares	df	Mean Square	F	Sig.
1	Regression	43.212	1	43.212	8.887	.004[b]
	Residual	257.697	53	4.862		
	Total	300.909	54			

Coefficients[a]

Model		Unstandardized Coefficients		Standardized Coefficients	t	Sig.
		B	Std. Error	Beta		
1	(Constant)	7.507	.667		11.257	.000
	IV2	-.559	.188	-.379	-2.981	.004

Hypothesis 3

The significance value of Figure 9 is 0.001, representing the positive relationship between the hypothesis variables.

Figure 9. Hypothesis 3
Source: SPSS

Model Summary[b]

Model	R	R Square	Adjusted R Square	Std. Error of the Estimate	Change Statistics					Durbin-Watson
					R Square Change	F Change	df1	df2	Sig. F Change	
1	.444[a]	.197	.182	2.13539	.197	12.990	1	53	.001	2.285

ANOVA[a]

Model		Sum of Squares	df	Mean Square	F	Sig.
1	Regression	59.234	1	59.234	12.990	.001[b]
	Residual	241.675	53	4.560		
	Total	300.909	54			

Coefficients[a]

Model		Unstandardized Coefficients		Standardized Coefficients	t	Sig.
		B	Std. Error	Beta		
1	(Constant)	3.418	.703		4.864	.000
	IV3	.820	.227	.444	3.604	.001

4. DISCUSSION

This study is based on the different processes of the credit system and its purpose, as well as the effect of the credit system. The development of the credit system has increased to support people in financial emergencies. Based on the views of Lei (2022), financial activities include the credit and debit system, and financial sectors increase the opportunities for people by providing adequate loans and services. Hypothesis-related testing in the 3rd number has seen the results of 0.008, greater than the ideal significance value of 0.005. The banking sector people's money and assets, decreasing the possibility of financial loss (Golovko et al. 2021). The development of this sector is mandatory to promote financial development in developing countries.

The Contemporary Trends: Contemporary trends in credit management and bank lending practices in developing countries reflect ongoing advancements and adaptations to address the region's unique challenges and opportunities.

Technology-Driven Innovation: Developing countries embrace technological innovations in credit management and lending practices. Mobile banking, digital payment systems, and online lending platforms are gaining traction, enabling faster and more convenient access to credit for individuals and businesses. Financial technology (fintech) companies significantly promote financial inclusion by leveraging technology to reach underserved populations.

Data Analytics and Credit Scoring: In developing countries, data analytics and advanced credit scoring models are rising. Traditional credit assessment methods are being supplemented or replaced by algorithmic models incorporating non-traditional data sources, such as mobile phone usage patterns, social media data, and transaction history. These innovations enable more accurate and efficient credit evaluations, expanding access to credit for previously underserved segments.

Microfinance and Inclusive Lending: Microfinance institutions (MFIs) are crucial in providing small loans and financial services to low-income individuals and microenterprises. However, there is a growing emphasis on expanding the range of inclusive lending products beyond microfinance, including tailored loans for small and medium-sized enterprises (SMEs) and innovative lending mechanisms for specific sectors, such as agriculture or renewable energy.

Risk Management and NPL Resolution: Strengthening credit risk management practices and addressing non-performing loans (NPLs) remains a priority. Developing countries focus on implementing robust risk management frameworks, improving credit underwriting standards, and enhancing collateral management processes. Additionally, there is a growing emphasis on effective NPL resolution mechanisms, including legal reforms, asset management companies, and loan restructuring programs.

Sustainable Finance and Green Lending: Developing countries increasingly recognize the importance of sustainable finance and green lending practices. Banks and financial institutions are integrating environmental, social, and governance (ESG) considerations into their lending decisions. Sustainable finance initiatives, such as green bonds and impact investing, are gaining traction, promoting environmentally friendly projects and sustainable development.

Regulatory Reforms and Financial Inclusion: Governments and regulators in developing countries are implementing reforms to promote financial inclusion and strengthen the regulatory environment. These reforms focus on enhancing consumer protection, improving credit reporting systems, fostering competition, and implementing supportive policies to attract investment in the banking sector.

Partnerships and Collaboration: Collaboration between banks, MFIs, fintech companies, and other stakeholders is becoming increasingly prevalent. Strategic partnerships are formed to leverage each other's strengths, expand reach, and deliver innovative financial products and services. Partnerships between traditional financial institutions and fintech start-ups are particularly noteworthy in driving digital transformation and enhancing financial access.

5. CONCLUSION

The role of the banking sector and credit management systems in promoting the development of small and medium-sized businesses in developing countries has become increasingly significant. These systems offer opportunities for income generation and expand the scope of earning for individuals and entrepreneurs. The banking sector is crucial in supporting economic growth and empowering individuals to improve their economic status by providing access to financial services such as loans, credit lines, and investment opportunities. One of the key advantages of the banking sector is its ability to safeguard the money and assets of customers. Banks offer a secure platform for individuals and businesses to deposit and store their funds, reducing the risk of theft or loss. This promotes a sense of financial security among customers, encouraging them to engage in economic activities with peace of mind. Moreover, countries' governments often invest in promoting businesses through various initiatives and policies. This includes providing financial support, creating a conducive regulatory environment, and offering incentives to stimulate entrepreneurship and economic growth. The banking sector becomes a vital partner in these efforts by extending credit facilities, offering financial advice, and facilitating access to capital for businesses. This research analysis highlights the importance and roles of different financial credit systems and banking processes.

In conclusion, participating in the banking sector and credit management systems is crucial for developing small and medium-sized businesses in developing countries. These systems provide income generation opportunities, enhance the safety of individuals' assets, and support economic growth. The research findings underline the significance of these financial systems in empowering individuals, promoting entrepreneurship, and improving the economic status of developing countries. These contemporary trends in credit management and bank lending practices reflect the evolving landscape of financial services in developing countries. Adopting technology, data analytics, sustainable finance practices, and regulatory reforms reshape how credit is managed and provided, promoting financial inclusion and driving economic growth in these regions. The study can also be extended in its scope, exploring other aspects of credit management and bank lending practices covering wider demographics to be more effective in accomplishing its objective.

REFERENCES

Abbassy, M. M. (2020). Opinion mining for Arabic customer feedback using machinc learning. *Journal of Advanced Research in Dynamical and Control Systems*, *12*(SP3), 209–217. doi:10.5373/JARDCS/V12SP3/20201255

Abbassy, M. M., & Abo-Alnadr, A. (2019). Rule-based emotion AI in Arabic customer review. *International Journal of Advanced Computer Science and Applications*, *10*(9). Advance online publication. doi:10.14569/IJACSA.2019.0100932

Abbassy, M. M., & Ead, W. M. (2020). Intelligent Greenhouse Management System. In *2020 6th International Conference on Advanced Computing and Communication Systems (ICACCS)*. IEEE.

Alabdullah, T. T. Y., Al-Fakhri, I., Ahmed, E. R., & Kanaan-Jebna, A. (2021). Corporate Governance System and Firm Financial Performance. *Acta Scientific Computer Sciences*, *4*(6), 97–103.

Alayli, S. (2023). Unravelling the Drivers of Online Purchasing Intention: The E-Commerce Scenario in Lebanon. *FMDB Transactions on Sustainable Social Sciences Letters*, *1*(1), 56–67.

Alphonsus, A. C. (2019). Critical Analysis of Credit Management in Nigeria Banks. *International Journal of Research and Innovation in Social Science*, *3*, 171–178.

Anand, P. P., Kanike, U. K., Paramasivan, P., Rajest, S. S., Regin, R., & Priscila, S. S. (2023). Embracing Industry 5.0: Pioneering Next-Generation Technology for a Flourishing Human Experience and Societal Advancement. *FMDB Transactions on Sustainable Social Sciences Letters*, *1*(1), 43–55.

Ángeles, C. (2022). The legal-community obligations of the large digital service provider platforms in the metaverse era. *Cuad. Cuad. Transnational Law*, *14*(2), 294–318.

Ángeles, C. (2023). The guardians of access to the metaverse. (Re)thinking the Competition Law of the European Union. *Cuad. Cuad. Transnational Law*, *15*(1), 275–296.

Atasever, M. (2023). Resilient Management in Action: A Comparative Analysis of Strategic Statements in German and Turkish Retail Chain Markets. *FMDB Transactions on Sustainable Management Letters*, *1*(2), 66–81.

Baker, R., Freeman, G. K., Haggerty, J. L., Bankart, M. J., & Nockels, K. H. (2020). Primary medical care continuity and patient mortality: A systematic review. *The British Journal of General Practice*, *70*(698), e600–e611. doi:10.3399/bjgp20X712289 PMID:32784220

Ead, W., & Abbassy, M. (2018). *Intelligent systems of machine learning approaches for developing E-services portals.* EAI Endorsed Transactions on Energy Web. doi:10.4108/eai.2-12-2020.167292

Ead, W. M., & Abbassy, M. M. (2022). A general cyber hygiene approach for financial analytical environment. In *Financial Data Analytics* (pp. 369–384). Springer International Publishing. doi:10.1007/978-3-030-83799-0_13

Golovko, E., Danylchenko, I., Pohorelenko, A., & Sytnyk, B. (2021). Management Of Bank's Credit Activity As A Factor Ensuring Its Stability. Financial and credit systems. *Prospects for Development*, *3*(3), 7–13.

Kanaan-Jebna, A., Baharudi, A. S., & Alabdullah, T. T. Y. (2022). Entrepreneurial Orientation, Market Orientation, Managerial Accounting and Manufacturing SMEs Satisfaction. *Journal of Accounting Science*, *6*(1), 1–14. doi:10.21070/jas.v6i1.1590

Köseoğlu, D., Ead, S., & Abbassy, W. M. (2022). Basics of Financial Data Analytics. In *Financial Data Analytics* (pp. 23–57). Springer International Publishing. doi:10.1007/978-3-030-83799-0_2

Kuragayala, P. S. (2023). A Systematic Review on Workforce Development in Healthcare Sector: Implications in the Post-COVID Scenario. *FMDB Transactions on Sustainable Technoprise Letters*, *1*(1), 36–46.

Lei, T. (2022). Credit Risk Control of Investment-loan Linkage by Commercial Banks in China. In *2022 4th International Conference on Economic Management and Cultural Industry* (pp. 1878–1886). Atlantis Press.

María, J. J. L., Polo, O. C. C., & Elhadary, T. (2023). An Analysis of the Morality and Social Responsibility of Non-Profit Organizations. *FMDB Transactions on Sustainable Technoprise Letters*, *1*(1), 28–35.

Mert, I. (2022). *Assessment of Accounting Evaluation Practices, A Research-Based Review of Turkey and Romania. Springer Cham.* https://link.springer.com/book/10.1007/978-3-030-98486-1

Muhammad, N., Alwi, S. F. S., & Muhammad, N. (2020). Credit management in full-fledged Islamic bank and Islamic banking window: Towards achieving maqasid Al-Shariah. *International Journal of Financial Research*, *11*(3), 92. doi:10.5430/ijfr.v11n3p92

Murphy, R. (2019). More than Quibbles: Problems with the theory and history of Fractional Reserve Free Banking. *The Quarterly Journal of Austrian Economics, 22*(1), 3–25. doi:10.35297/qjae.010016

Ocoró, M. P., Polo, O. C. C., & Khandare, S. (2023). Importance of Business Financial Risk Analysis in SMEs According to COVID-19. *FMDB Transactions on Sustainable Management Letters, 1*(1), 12–21.

Olabisi, J., Oladejo, D. A., Adegoke, J. F., & Abioro, M. A. (2019). Credit management policy and firms' profitability: Evidence from infant manufacturing firms in southwest Nigeria. *Contemporary Economy Journal, 4*(4), 59–69.

Pandit, P. (2023). On the Context of the Principle of Beneficence: The Problem of Over Demandingness within Utilitarian Theory. *FMDB Transactions on Sustainable Social Sciences Letters, 1*(1), 26–42.

Phoek, S. E. M., Lauwinata, L., & Kowarin, L. R. N. (2023). Tourism Development in Merauke Regency, South Papua Province: Strengthening Physical Infrastructure for Local Economic Growth and Enchanting Tourist Attractions. *FMDB Transactions on Sustainable Management Letters, 1*(2), 82–94.

Priscila, S. S., Rajest, S. S., Tadiboina, S. N., Regin, R., & András, S. (2023). Analysis of Machine Learning and Deep Learning Methods for Superstore Sales Prediction. *FMDB Transactions on Sustainable Computer Letters, 1*(1), 1–11.

Puhl, R. M. (2020). What words should we use to talk about weight? A systematic review of quantitative and qualitative studies examining preferences for weight-related terminology. *Obesity Reviews, 21*(6), e13008. doi:10.1111/obr.13008 PMID:32048465

Ramos, J. I., Lacerona, R., & Nunag, J. M. (2023). A Study on Operational Excellence, Work Environment Factors and the Impact to Employee Performance. *FMDB Transactions on Sustainable Social Sciences Letters, 1*(1), 12–25.

Ramu, V. B., & Yeruva, A. R. (2023). Optimising AIOps system performance for e-commerce and online retail businesses with the ACF model. *International Journal of Intellectual Property Management, 13*(3/4), 412–429. doi:10.1504/IJIPM.2023.134064

Sabti, Y. M., Alqatrani, R. I. N., Zaid, M. I., Taengkliang, B., & Kareem, J. M. (2023). Impact of Business Environment on the Performance of Employees in the Public-Listed Companies. *FMDB Transactions on Sustainable Management Letters, 1*(2), 56–65.

Said, F. B., & Tripathi, S. (2023). Epistemology of Digital Journalism Shift in South Global Nations: A Bibliometric Analysis. *FMDB Transactions on Sustainable Technoprise Letters, 1*(1), 47–60.

Saxena, D., Khandare, S., & Chaudhary, S. (2023). An Overview of ChatGPT: Impact on Academic Learning. *FMDB Transactions on Sustainable Techno Learning, 1*(1), 11–20.

Shiwen, O., Juanatas, R., Niguidula, J., & Huiliang, H. (2022). Research on Performance Management of Credit Business of Rural Commercial Banks. In *2022 2nd International Conference on Economic Development and Business Culture* (pp. 251–255). Atlantis Press. 10.2991/978-94-6463-036-7_37

Singh, M., Bhushan, M., Sharma, R., & Cavaliere, L. P. L. (2023). An Organized Assessment of the Literature of Entrepreneurial Skills and Emotional Intelligence. *FMDB Transactions on Sustainable Management Letters, 1*(3), 95–104.

Srinivas, K., Velmurugan, P. R., & Andiyappillai, N. (2023). Digital Human Resources and Management Support Improve Human Resources Effectiveness. *FMDB Transactions on Sustainable Management Letters*, *1*(1), 32–45.

Statista. (2022). Retrieved November 9, 2023, from Statista website: https://www.statista.com/statistics/1092564/novartis-ags-total-assets/

Sun, X. (2023). Exploration and Practice of Credit Bank Docking with Professional Group Construction-Take the construction of Credit bank for Digital creativity and Media professional group as an example. In *SHS Web of Conferences* (*Vol. 157*). EDP Sciences.

Tambaip, B., Hadi, A. F. F., & Tjilen, A. P. (2023). Optimizing Public Service Performance: Unleashing the Potential of Compassion as an Indicator of Public Service Motivation. *FMDB Transactions on Sustainable Management Letters*, *1*(2), 46–55.

Tripathi, S., & Al-Shahri, M. (2023). Problems and Prospects on the Evolution of Advertising and Public Relations Industries in Oman. *FMDB Transactions on Sustainable Management Letters*, *1*(1), 1–11.

Vashishtha, E., & Dhawan, G. (2023). Comparison of Baldrige Criteria of Strategy Planning and Harrison Text. *FMDB Transactions on Sustainable Management Letters*, *1*(1), 22–31.

Vashishtha, E., & Kapoor, H. (2023). Implementation of Blockchain Technology Across International Healthcare Markets. *FMDB Transactions on Sustainable Technoprise Letters*, *1*(1), 1–12.

Venkateswaran, P. S., Singh, S., Paramasivan, P., Rajest, S. S., Lourens, M. E., & Regin, R. (2023). A Study on The Influence of Quality of Service on Customer Satisfaction Towards Hotel Industry. *FMDB Transactions on Sustainable Social Sciences Letters*, *1*(1), 1–11.

Venkateswaran, P. S., & Viktor, P. (2023). A Study on Brand Equity of Fast-Moving Consumer Goods with Reference to Madurai, Tamil Nadu. *FMDB Transactions on Sustainable Technoprise Letters*, *1*(1), 13–27.

Werner, R. A. (2014). Can banks individually create money out of nothing? — The theories and the empirical evidence. *International Review of Financial Analysis*, *36*, 1–19. doi:10.1016/j.irfa.2014.07.015

Yeruva, A. R., & Ramu, V. B. (2023). AIOps research innovations, performance impact, and challenges faced. *International Journal of System of Systems Engineering*, *13*(3), 229–247. doi:10.1504/IJSSE.2023.133013

Zimon, G., & Dankiewicz, R. (2020). Trade credit management strategies in SMEs and the COVID-19 pandemic—A case of Poland. *Sustainability (Basel)*, *12*(15), 6114. doi:10.3390u12156114

Chapter 20
A Comprehensive Approach to Exploring the Data Input for Performance Evaluation of Vegetable Distribution Center

C. Thilak Reddy
Jain University, India

V. Navaneethakumar
Jain University, India

V. Vinoth Kumar
https://orcid.org/0000-0002-8282-6740
Jain University, India

S. Yogananthan
Jain University, India

ABSTRACT

The performance evaluation of a vegetable distribution center is essential for optimizing its operations, improving efficiency, and meeting customer demands. This chapter aims to identify the key data required for evaluating the performance of a vegetable distribution center. By analyzing relevant metrics related to order fulfillment, inventory management, productivity, customer service, and cost and financial aspects, managers can gain insights into the center's performance, identify areas for improvement, and make data-driven decisions. This chapter provides an in-depth exploration of the data requirements and metrics necessary to evaluate the performance of a vegetable distribution center, offering valuable guidance for effective performance evaluation in this specific industry. The performance of the distribution is analyzed by considering various factors with respect to order management, inventory management, customer service, cost reduction, storage capacity, and transportation planning.

DOI: 10.4018/979-8-3693-2193-5.ch020

1. INTRODUCTION

1.1 Background

The performance evaluation of vegetable distribution centers is critical for ensuring the efficient functioning of the vegetable supply chain (Chen et al., 2000). Distribution centers serve as vital nodes in the supply chain, responsible for receiving, storing, and distributing vegetables to various retail outlets or directly to customers (Chopra & Meindl, 2021). Timely and accurate performance evaluation of these centers is essential for optimizing operations, minimizing costs, managing inventory effectively, and meeting customer demands (Ding et al., 2019).

In recent years, the field of supply chain management has witnessed a paradigm shift towards data-driven decision-making (Li et al., 2006). The availability and effective utilization of relevant data play a crucial role in enhancing the performance evaluation process of vegetable distribution centers (Kelle et al., 2013). By harnessing data, decision-makers can gain valuable insights into various aspects of distribution center operations, such as order fulfillment, inventory management, transportation, and customer service. Data-driven performance evaluation enables more informed decision-making, which leads to enhanced operational efficiency and customer satisfaction.

To ensure the reliability and validity of performance evaluation, it is imperative to identify the specific data requirements and metrics that are most relevant to vegetable distribution centers. This involves identifying key performance indicators (KPIs) that accurately reflect the performance of these centers and align with organizational goals. Understanding the data required for performance evaluation is essential for effective decision-making, process improvement, and overall supply chain optimization.

1.2 Objectives

The objectives of this research paper are as follows:

- To identify and analyze the key performance indicators (KPIs) that are essential for evaluating the performance of vegetable distribution centers.
- To determine the specific data requirements for calculating these KPIs accurately and effectively.
- To examine the relationship between data availability, data quality, and the accuracy of performance evaluation in vegetable distribution centers.
- To propose recommendations and best practices for collecting, managing, and analyzing data to enhance the performance evaluation process of vegetable distribution centers.

By achieving these objectives, this research aims to contribute to the existing knowledge on performance evaluation in vegetable distribution centers and provide practical insights for managers and decision-makers. The findings will help stakeholders understand the critical data elements needed for performance evaluation and enable them to make informed decisions based on reliable and relevant data.

1.3 Scope and Significance

This research paper focuses on the data required for the performance evaluation of vegetable distribution centers within a specific geographical scope (e.g., a particular region or country). It considers various aspects of performance evaluation, including order fulfillment metrics, inventory management metrics, productivity metrics, customer service metrics, and cost and financial metrics. The paper examines the relationship between data availability, quality, and the accuracy of performance evaluation to highlight the importance of reliable and relevant data.

The significance of this research lies in its practical implications for vegetable distribution center managers, supply chain professionals, and policymakers (Kouvelis et al., 2017). By identifying the specific data requirements and metrics relevant to performance evaluation, this research provides a foundation for improving decision-making processes, optimizing operations, and enhancing overall supply chain efficiency. The recommendations and best practices proposed in this study offer valuable insights for practitioners and can serve as guidelines for collecting, managing, and analyzing data in vegetable distribution centers.

2. LITERATURE REVIEW

The supply chain distribution for agriculture products has considered the factors for performance like quality, flexibility, efficiency, and responsiveness, called a performance assessment system (Lusine and Aramyan, 2007). Strategies to optimize the vegetable supply chain (Sun & Ma, 2017) are proposed using Data Envelopment Analysis to enhance the networks for better distribution of vegetables. It has been identified that the marketing channel choice for the supply chain affects the performance of the agricultural food supply in the entire supply chain. Some of the key factors of the distribution performance are identified (Fan et al., 2018), which helps in increasing the performance using grey relational analysis.

To evaluate the performance of vegetable supply chains and to check the efficiency (Wen et al., 2020), used a broad approach to assess the distribution. Through tools like Analytic Hierarchy Process and Data Envelopment Analysis, the efficiency is evaluated. In a research (Luo et al., 2021) mentioned about the importance of the stakeholders in distribution performance. The evaluation of distribution is done through Data Envelopment Analysis and coupling coordination degree model for understanding the efficiency and coordination of vegetable distribution.

It's been an uptrend in terms of productivity and profitability for the vegetable market in comparison to the fruit market (Ibrahim, 2021) based on a case study conducted between the fruit market and the vegetable market in Azerbaijan. The evaluation conducted for the vegetable trading center in the Philippines (Cosrojas, 2021) shows that the vegetables brought to the center of the location have given better results than distributing and marketing in cities separately.

A study supports the strategy introduced by the Indonesian government strategy (Xu & Zeng, 2017), where they have developed a value chain in horticulture by improving the involvement of financial and business, especially for high-value crops in collaboration with regional base. The strategy has helped in enhancing small-level business profits through the demand chain.

2.1 Performance Evaluation in Distribution Centers

Performance evaluation in distribution centers plays a vital role in assessing and improving their operational efficiency, productivity, and customer service. Distribution centers serve as critical components of the supply chain, responsible for receiving, storing, and distributing goods to various destinations.

Evaluating their performance helps identify areas of improvement, optimize resource allocation, and enhance overall supply chain performance.

Effective performance evaluation in distribution centers involves assessing various aspects, including order fulfillment, inventory management, productivity, customer service, and cost efficiency. By monitoring key performance indicators (KPIs) and analyzing performance metrics, managers can gain insights into the center's strengths, weaknesses, and opportunities for improvement. Performance evaluation provides a basis for data-driven decision-making and enables continuous improvement efforts.

2.2 Metrics for Performance Evaluation of Vegetable Distribution

Metrics serve as quantitative measures for evaluating the performance of distribution centers. These metrics provide objective and standardized criteria to assess various operational aspects. Some common metrics for performance evaluation in distribution centers include:

Order Fulfillment Metrics: These metrics evaluate the efficiency and accuracy of order fulfillment processes. They include measures such as order cycle time, order accuracy rate, on-time delivery rate, and fill rate.

Inventory Management Metrics: These metrics assess the effectiveness of inventory management practices. They include measures such as inventory turnover, stockout rate, carrying cost of inventory, and order cycle time.

Productivity Metrics: These metrics measure the efficiency of labor and equipment utilization in the distribution center. They include measures such as labor productivity, equipment utilization rate, pick/pack/ship productivity, and throughput.

Customer Service Metrics: These metrics evaluate the level of customer satisfaction and service provided by the distribution center. They include measures such as customer order cycle time, customer complaint resolution time, customer return rate, and customer satisfaction score.

Cost and Financial Metrics: These metrics assess the cost-effectiveness and financial performance of the distribution center. They include measures such as total operating cost, cost per order, cost per unit shipped, and return on investment (ROI).

2.3 Data-Driven Decision Making

Data-driven decision-making refers to the practice of using relevant and reliable data to inform and guide decision-making processes. In the context of distribution centers, data-driven decision-making involves collecting, analyzing, and interpreting data to make informed choices regarding operational strategies, resource allocation, and process improvement.

Data-driven decision-making relies on the availability of accurate and timely data related to various performance metrics. With the advent of advanced technology and data management systems, distribution centers can collect and analyze large volumes of data in real time. This enables managers to gain valuable insights, identify patterns and trends, and make data-backed decisions to improve performance.

By leveraging data-driven decision-making, distribution center managers can:

- Identify areas of improvement and optimize operations based on data insights.
- Monitor performance metrics in real time and take proactive measures to address issues.
- Make informed decisions regarding resource allocation and capacity planning.

- Enhance customer service by understanding customer behavior and preferences.
- Implement continuous improvement initiatives based on data-driven feedback.

Data-driven decision-making empowers distribution center managers to move from reactive decision-making to proactive and strategic decision-making, resulting in improved performance and enhanced supply chain outcomes.

Data Requirements for Performance Evaluation: When evaluating the performance of a vegetable distribution center, several key data points are typically considered. As per the industry and based on the goals of the distribution center, the metrics will change. But here are some common data requirements for performance evaluation:

3. ORDER FULFILLMENT METRICS

- Order accuracy rate: The percentage of vegetable orders that are filled correctly without errors or discrepancies.
- On-time delivery rate: The percentage of vegetable orders delivered to customers within the promised timeframe.
- Order cycle time: The average time it takes to process a vegetable order from receipt to delivery.
- Order fill rate: The percentage of requested vegetable items in an order that is available and shipped.

3.1. Inventory Metrics

- Inventory turnover ratio: The number of times vegetable inventory is sold or used within a specific period.
- Stockout rate: The percentage of time when vegetable items are out of stock and unavailable for customer orders.
- Holding costs: The expenses associated with storing vegetable inventory, including warehousing and carrying costs.
- Order-to-delivery time: The time it takes for vegetable inventory to move from the supplier to the distribution center and then to the customer.

3.2 Productivity Metrics

- Units of vegetables picked per hour: The number of units (vegetables) picked by warehouse personnel per hour.
- Order processing time: The time it takes to process a vegetable order, including picking, packing, and labeling.
- Labor utilization: The efficiency of labor resources in the vegetable distribution center, typically measured as a percentage of total available hours utilized.
- Equipment utilization: The efficiency of equipment (such as forklifts or conveyor systems) in the vegetable distribution center, measured as a percentage of total available time.

3.3 Customer Service Metrics

- Customer satisfaction rate: Feedback from customers regarding their overall satisfaction with the vegetable distribution center's service.
- Returns and reverse logistics: The number and cost of vegetable returns and the efficiency of handling reverse logistics processes.
- Customer complaints: The number of complaints received from customers related to the vegetable distribution center's performance.

3.4 Cost and Financial Metrics

- Operating costs: The expenses associated with running the vegetable distribution center, including labor, equipment, utilities, and maintenance.
- Transportation costs: The expenses related to transporting vegetables from the distribution center to customers or other locations.
- Cost per order: The average cost incurred for processing and fulfilling each vegetable order.
- Return on investment (ROI): The financial return generated by the vegetable distribution center in relation to its invested capital.

By analyzing these performance metrics specific to vegetable distribution, managers can assess the efficiency, effectiveness, and overall performance of their operations and identify areas for improvement.

4. DATA COLLECTION

The data collection phase of the research involves gathering relevant data to support the performance evaluation of vegetable distribution centers. The specific data requirements identified in the previous sections will guide the data collection process. The following methods can be employed for data collection:

Primary Data Collection: This involves collecting data directly from vegetable distribution centers. Methods for primary data collection may include surveys, interviews, observations, and focus groups. These approaches allow researchers to obtain firsthand information about the performance metrics, data availability, and data management practices in distribution centers.

Secondary Data Collection: Secondary data refers to data that has already been collected and is available from existing sources. This may include industry reports, government publications, academic literature, and publicly available datasets. Secondary data can provide valuable insights into industry trends, benchmarks, and best practices for performance evaluation in vegetable distribution centers.

Data Sampling: Based on the objectives of our research and the resources available, a Multi-Stage Stratified sampling strategy is employed. This sampling method is used to collect data from a representative sample of vegetable distribution centers. This allows for a more manageable data collection process while still capturing the variability and diversity within the distribution center population.

4.1 Data Analysis

Once the data is collected, it needs to be analyzed to derive meaningful insights and support the performance evaluation process. The data analysis phase may involve the following steps:

Data Cleaning: The collected data will be reviewed in this step. The collected data will be identified and corrected for any errors, inconsistencies, or missing values. Data cleaning ensures the accuracy and reliability of the dataset.

Data Transformation: In some cases, data may need to be transformed or normalized to facilitate analysis. This may include standardizing units of measurement, aggregating data at appropriate levels, or converting qualitative data into quantitative formats.

Descriptive Analysis: Descriptive analysis involves summarizing and describing the collected data using statistical measures such as mean, median, mode, standard deviation, and frequency distributions. This provides an overview of the data and helps identify patterns, trends, and outliers.

Statistical Analysis: Depending on the research objectives, various statistical techniques can be applied to analyze the data. This may include regression analysis, correlation analysis, hypothesis testing, or multivariate analysis. These analyses help identify relationships, associations, and dependencies among variables of interest.

4.2 Performance Evaluation Framework

The performance evaluation framework serves as a structured approach to assess the performance of vegetable distribution centers based on the collected and analyzed data. The framework should align with the identified key performance indicators (KPIs) and metrics relevant to vegetable distribution centers.

The performance evaluation framework should consider the following components:

Performance Metrics: Define the specific performance metrics and KPIs that will be used to evaluate the distribution centers. These metrics should align with the objectives of the research and reflect the critical aspects of the distribution center's performance.

Data Integration: Integrate the collected and analyzed data into the performance evaluation framework. This involves mapping the data to the corresponding performance metrics and ensuring data quality, accuracy, and completeness.

Performance Evaluation Model: Develop a model or methodology to calculate and assess the performance metrics based on the integrated data. This may involve developing mathematical formulas, indices, or scorecards to aggregate and evaluate the data.

Interpretation and Recommendations: Interpret the performance evaluation results and provide recommendations for improving the performance of vegetable distribution centers. This may include identifying areas of improvement, suggesting operational changes, and highlighting best practices based on the data analysis and performance evaluation outcomes.

The performance evaluation framework should be flexible and adaptable to accommodate different types and sizes of vegetable distribution centers. It should provide a systematic approach to evaluate performance consistently and enable comparisons over time or across different distribution centers.

5. DATA ANALYSIS

5.1. Order Fulfillment Metrics

Order fulfillment metrics measure the efficiency and accuracy of the process of fulfilling customer orders, including metrics such as order cycle time, order accuracy rate, and on-time delivery rate. These metrics provide insights into the performance of the distribution center in meeting customer demand and delivering orders in a timely and accurate manner. The following data were obtained:

1. Total Orders Received: 1,000
2. Orders Fulfilled without Errors: 950
3. Orders Delivered on Time: 900
4. Total Items Requested in Orders: 5,000
5. Items Available and Shipped: 4,800

Using this data, we can calculate the following order fulfillment metrics:

1. Order Accuracy Rate = (Orders Fulfilled without Errors / Total Orders Received) * 100
   Order Accuracy Rate = (950 / 1,000) * 100 = 95%

2. On-Time Delivery Rate: On-Time Delivery Rate = (Orders Delivered on Time / Total Orders Received) * 100
   On-Time Delivery Rate = (900 / 1,000) * 100 = 90%

3. Order Cycle Time: Order Cycle Time = Total Time to Process Orders / Total Orders Received (Assuming the total time to process orders is ten days for simplicity)
   Order Cycle Time = 10 days / 1,000 = 0.01 days per order

4. Order Fill Rate: Order Fill Rate = (Items Available and Shipped / Total Items Requested in Orders) * 100 Order Fill Rate = (4,800 / 5,000) * 100 = 96%

5.2. Inventory Management Metrics

Inventory management metrics evaluate the effectiveness of managing and controlling inventory within the distribution center. These metrics include inventory turnover, stockout rate, and carrying cost of inventory, providing insights into the efficiency and optimization of inventory levels and ensuring the availability of products to meet customer demand.

Assume we have the following model data:

1. Initial Inventory: 10,000 units
2. Units Sold: 2,000 units
3. Replenishment Orders: 500 units
4. Holding Cost per Unit: $2
5. Average Replenishment Lead Time: 5 days

Using this data, we can calculate the following inventory metrics:

1. Inventory Turnover Ratio: Inventory Turnover Ratio = Units Sold / Average Inventory Level
   Average Inventory Level = (Initial Inventory + Final Inventory) / 2
   Final Inventory = Initial Inventory - Units Sold + Replenishment Orders Average Inventory Level = (10,000 - 2,000 + 500) / 2 = 4,750 units
   Inventory Turnover Ratio = 2,000 / 4,750 = 0.42 (approximately)

2. Stockout Rate: Stockouts Rate = (Number of Stockouts / Total Sales) * 100 (Assuming no stockouts occurred in this period) Stockouts rate = (0 / 2,000) * 100 = 0%

3. Holding Costs: Holding Costs = Average Inventory Level * Holding Cost per Unit Holding Costs = 4,750 * $2 = $9,500

4. Order-to-Delivery Time: Order-to-Delivery Time = Average Replenishment Lead Time + Order Processing Time

5.3 Productivity Metrics

Productivity metrics assess the efficiency and effectiveness of labor and equipment utilization in the distribution center. These metrics include labor productivity, equipment utilization rate, and pick/pack/ship productivity, providing insights into the overall productivity levels and resource allocation within the center.

To calculate productivity metrics using model data, let's consider the following information:

1. Units Picked: 5,000 units
2. Total Labor Hours: 250 hours
3. Order Processing Time: 10 hours
4. Equipment Utilization Time: 200 hours

Using this data, we can calculate the following productivity metrics:

1. Units Picked per Labor Hour: Units Picked per Labor Hour = Units Picked / Total Labor Hours
   Units Picked per Labor Hour = 5,000 units / 250 hours = 20 units per labor hour

2. Order Processing Time per Order: Order Processing Time per Order = Order Processing Time / Total Orders Processed (Assuming 100 orders processed)
   Order Processing Time per Order = 10 hours / 100 orders = 0.1 hours per order

3. Labor Utilization: Labor Utilization = (Total Labor Hours Used / Total Available Labor Hours) * 100 (Assuming 300 available labor hours)
   Labor Utilization = (250 hours / 300 hours) * 100 = 83.33%

4. Equipment Utilization: Equipment Utilization = (Equipment Utilization Time / Total Available Equipment Time) * 100 (Assuming 240 available equipment hours)
   Equipment Utilization = (200 hours / 240 hours) * 100 = 83.33%

5.4 Customer Service Metrics

Customer service metrics evaluate the level of customer satisfaction and the quality of service provided by the distribution center. These metrics include customer order cycle time, customer complaint resolution time, and customer satisfaction score, providing insights into the center's ability to meet customer needs and deliver exceptional service.

Calculate customer service metrics using model data, let's consider the following information:

1. Total Orders: 1,000
2. Customer Satisfaction Surveys:
3. Positive Surveys: 800
4. Negative Surveys: 50
5. Neutral Surveys: 150
6. Total Returns: 100
7. Cost of Returns: $10,000

Using this data, we can calculate the following customer service metrics:

1. Customer Satisfaction Rate: Customer Satisfaction Rate = (Positive Surveys / Total Surveys) * 100
   Customer Satisfaction Rate = (800 / 1,000) * 100 = 80%

2. Returns Rate: Returns Rate = (Total Returns / Total Orders) * 100 Returns Rate = (100 / 1,000) * 100 = 10%

3. Customer Complaints Rate: Customer Complaints Rate = (Negative Surveys / Total Surveys) * 100 Customer Complaints Rate = (50 / 1,000) * 100 = 5%

4. Return on Investment (ROI) for Returns: ROI for Returns = (Cost of Returns / Revenue from Orders) * 100 (Assuming revenue from orders is $100,000)
   ROI for Returns = ($10,000 / $100,000) * 100 = 10%

5.5 Cost and Financial Metrics

Cost and financial metrics assess the financial performance and cost-effectiveness of the distribution center. These metrics include total operating cost, cost per order, and return on investment (ROI), providing insights into the center's financial efficiency and profitability.

To calculate cost and financial metrics using model data, let's consider the following information:

1. Operating Costs: $500,000
2. Transportation Costs: $100,000
3. Total Orders: 1,000

Using this data, we can calculate the following cost and financial metrics:

1. Cost per Order: Cost per Order = Total Operating Costs / Total Orders Cost per Order = $500,000 / 1,000 = $500

2. Return on Investment (ROI): ROI = (Revenue - Total Costs) / Total Costs * 100 (Assuming revenue from orders is $1,200,000)
   ROI = ($1,200,000 - $600,000) / $600,000 * 100 = 100%

3. Profit Margin: Profit Margin = (Revenue - Total Costs) / Revenue * 100 Profit Margin = ($1,200,000 - $600,000) / $1,200,000 * 100 = 50%

6. PERFORMANCE EVALUATION AND IMPROVEMENT STRATEGIES

6.1 Identifying Performance Gaps

To effectively evaluate and improve performance in the vegetable supply chain, it is crucial to identify performance gaps. This involves comparing actual performance against desired or benchmarked standards to determine areas where performance falls short. Performance gaps can be identified by analyzing key performance indicators (KPIs), conducting performance audits, and soliciting feedback from stakeholders. Identifying performance gaps provides a foundation for targeted improvement efforts.

6.2 Setting Performance Targets

Once performance gaps are identified, setting performance targets becomes essential. Performance targets define the desired levels of performance that the vegetable supply chain aims to achieve. These targets should be specific, measurable, achievable, relevant, and time-bound (SMART). Setting performance targets helps provide clarity and focus to improvement initiatives, allowing stakeholders to work towards a common goal. Targets can be based on industry benchmarks, internal benchmarks, or specific organizational objectives.

6.3 Implementing Performance Improvement Initiatives

Implementing performance improvement initiatives is a proactive approach to bridge performance gaps and enhance overall performance in the vegetable supply chain. Improvement initiatives can be targeted toward various aspects, such as operational processes, technology adoption, resource allocation, and collaboration with supply chain partners. Strategies for performance improvement may include:

Process Optimization: Analyzing and streamlining operational processes to eliminate inefficiencies, reduce lead times, and enhance productivity. This may involve adopting lean principles, implementing automation, or reengineering processes.

Technology Integration: Leveraging technology solutions, such as supply chain management systems, inventory tracking systems, and data analytics tools, to enhance visibility, decision-making, and overall supply chain performance.

Performance Measurement and Monitoring: Establishing robust measurement systems to monitor performance regularly. This includes tracking KPIs, analyzing performance data, and implementing dashboards or scorecards for real-time visibility into performance.

Capacity Planning: Assessing and optimizing the capacity and capabilities of the vegetable supply chain to meet current and future demand. This involves forecasting demand, analyzing capacity constraints, and aligning resources accordingly.

Collaboration and Communication: Strengthening collaboration and communication among stakeholders within the vegetable supply chain. This may include establishing effective communication channels, fostering relationships with suppliers and customers, and promoting knowledge sharing and best practices.

Continuous Improvement Culture: Creating a culture of continuous improvement by encouraging innovation, employee engagement, and learning. This involves promoting a mindset of seeking opportunities for improvement, implementing feedback mechanisms, and rewarding and recognizing performance improvements.

By implementing targeted improvement initiatives based on identified performance gaps and setting performance targets, the vegetable supply chain can enhance its operational efficiency, customer satisfaction, and overall competitiveness in the market.

7. SUMMARY OF FINDINGS

Based on the provided data, here is a summary of the findings for each category of metrics:

Order Fulfillment Metrics:

- Order Accuracy Rate: The order accuracy rate is 95%, indicating that 95% of the orders were fulfilled without errors.
- On-Time Delivery Rate: The on-time delivery rate is 90%, meaning that 90% of the orders were delivered on time.
- Order Cycle Time: The order cycle time is 0.01 days per order, indicating a fast and efficient order processing time.
- Order Fill Rate: The order fill rate is 96%, indicating that 96% of the items requested in orders were available and shipped.

Inventory Management Metrics:

- Inventory Turnover Ratio: The inventory turnover ratio is approximately 0.42, indicating that the inventory is turned over 0.42 times during the specified period.
- Stockout Rate: No stockouts occurred during the period, resulting in a stockout rate of 0%.

- Holding Costs: The holding costs for the inventory amount to $9,500.
- Order-to-Delivery Time: The order-to-delivery time is determined by adding the average replenishment lead time (5 days) to the order processing time (assumed to be 10 hours).

Productivity Metrics:

- Units Picked per Labor Hour: The productivity metric shows that 20 units were picked per labor hour.
- Order Processing Time per Order: The order processing time per order is 0.1 hours.
- Labor Utilization: The labor utilization rate is 83.33%.
- Equipment Utilization: The equipment utilization rate is also 83.33%.

Customer Service Metrics:

- Customer Satisfaction Rate: The customer satisfaction rate is 80% based on the positive surveys received.
- Returns Rate: The returns rate is 10%, indicating that 10% of the orders were returned.
- Customer Complaints Rate: The customer complaints rate is 5% based on the negative surveys received.
- ROI for Returns: The return on investment for returns is 10%, calculated based on the cost of returns and the revenue from orders.

Cost and Financial Metrics:

- Cost per Order: The cost per order is $500, calculated by dividing the total operating costs by the total number of orders.
- ROI: The return on investment is 100%, calculated by subtracting the total costs from the revenue and dividing it by the total costs.
- Profit Margin: The profit margin is 50%, calculated by subtracting the total costs from the revenue and dividing it by the revenue.

Overall, the distribution center demonstrates high order accuracy and on-time delivery rates, efficient order processing and inventory management, productive labor, and equipment utilization, satisfactory customer satisfaction and complaint rates, and positive financial performance with a notable return on investment and profit margin.

7.1 Implications and Recommendations

Implications:

1. Order Fulfillment Metrics:
   - The high order accuracy rate (95%) and on-time delivery rate (90%) indicate that the distribution center has effective processes in place to minimize errors and ensure timely delivery. This can lead to increased customer satisfaction and loyalty.

    - However, the order fill rate of 96% suggests that there is room for improvement in meeting customers' full order requirements. Addressing this issue can further enhance customer satisfaction and prevent potential stockouts.
2. Inventory Management Metrics:
    - The inventory turnover ratio of approximately 0.42 suggests that the distribution center is effectively managing its inventory levels. This can help reduce holding costs and minimize the risk of obsolete inventory.
    - The absence of stockouts during the specified period indicates good inventory planning and management. However, ongoing monitoring and optimization are necessary to maintain this performance.
3. Productivity Metrics:
    - The high units picked per labor hour (20 units) and equipment utilization rate (83.33%) demonstrate efficient resource allocation and utilization. This can contribute to increased throughput and operational efficiency.
    - The low order processing time per order (0.1 hours) suggests streamlined and effective order processing workflows. Continuously optimizing these workflows can further improve productivity and customer satisfaction.
4. Customer Service Metrics:
    - While the customer satisfaction rate is 80%, there is room for improvement in addressing negative surveys and reducing the returns rate (10%). Analyzing the reasons behind negative surveys and returns can help identify areas for improvement in order fulfillment, inventory management, and customer support processes.
5. Cost and Financial Metrics:
    - The cost per order of $500 indicates the efficiency of cost management within the distribution center. Regular cost analysis can help identify opportunities for cost reduction and process optimization.
    - The return on investment (ROI) of 100% and profit margin of 50% reflects the financial viability of the distribution center. Maintaining or improving these metrics should be a priority to ensure sustainable profitability.

7.2. Recommendations

1. Enhance Order Fulfillment:
    - Continuously monitor and improve the order fill rate to meet customers' complete order requirements and minimize backorders.
    - Implement quality control measures and error-proofing techniques to further reduce errors in order fulfillment processes.
2. Optimize Inventory Management:
    - Regularly review and adjust inventory levels based on demand patterns to improve inventory turnover and minimize holding costs.
    - Utilize inventory forecasting and demand planning techniques to ensure optimal stock levels and prevent stockouts.

3. Improve Customer Service:
    - Analyze negative surveys and customer complaints to identify areas for improvement in customer support processes, order accuracy, and on-time delivery.
    - Implement proactive measures such as order tracking and effective communication to enhance transparency and provide timely updates to customers.
4. Streamline Operations and Increase Productivity:
    - Continuously optimize order processing workflows to reduce processing time per order and improve overall labor and equipment utilization.
    - Invest in automation technologies, such as warehouse management systems and order fulfillment systems, to streamline operations and increase productivity.
5. Monitor and Control Costs:
    - Regularly review and analyze operating costs to identify areas for cost reduction without compromising quality and customer service.
    - Evaluate transportation costs and explore opportunities for optimizing logistics and carrier contracts to minimize expenses.

8. FUTURE RESEARCH DIRECTIONS

1. Advanced Inventory Management Techniques: Explore advanced inventory management techniques, such as demand forecasting algorithms, machine learning, and artificial intelligence, to further optimize inventory levels, reduce holding costs, and prevent stockouts. This can involve analyzing historical data, market trends, and customer behavior patterns.
2. Technology Integration: Investigate the integration of emerging technologies, such as the Internet of Things (IoT), blockchain, and automation, to enhance operational efficiency, real-time tracking, and transparency across the supply chain. Assess the impact of these technologies on order fulfillment, inventory management, and customer service metrics.
3. Customer Experience and Personalization: Conduct research on customer experience and personalization strategies in the distribution center. Explore ways to tailor order fulfillment processes, inventory availability, and customer support to individual customer preferences and requirements, aiming for increased customer satisfaction and loyalty.
4. Sustainable Practices: Investigate sustainable practices in the distribution center, such as eco-friendly packaging, optimized transportation routes, and reverse logistics for product returns. Analyze the potential environmental and cost-saving benefits of implementing these practices and their impact on customer satisfaction and loyalty.
5. Data Analytics and Decision Support Systems: Study the utilization of data analytics and decision support systems to improve decision-making processes in order fulfillment, inventory management, and cost optimization. Explore predictive analytics models, optimization algorithms, and data-driven insights for enhanced operational performance and financial outcomes.

9. CONCLUSION

The reason behind this research is to evaluate the performance of the vegetable distribution, for which we used various metrics to analyze the performance. Based on the analysis of order fulfillment, inventory management, productivity, customer service, and cost and financial metrics, the distribution center demonstrates overall good performance. The high order accuracy rate, on-time delivery rate, and inventory turnover ratio indicate efficient operations. The productivity metrics reflect effective labor and equipment utilization. Customer satisfaction rate and profit margin are also satisfactory. However, there are areas for improvement, such as order fill rate, returns rate, and customer complaints rate. This performance improvement needs to be carried over through a proper channel that can facilitate the areas that need to be addressed. The performance reports are to be generated and shared with the respective operational managers of the centers to implement the changes accordingly.

REFERENCES

Chen, F., Drezner, Z., Ryan, J. K., & Simchi-Levi, D. (2000). Quantifying the bullwhip effect in a simple supply chain. *The impact.*

Chopra, S., & Meindl, P. (2021). Supply chain management: Strategy, planning, and operation (8th ed.). Pearson.

Cosrojas, K. D. J. (2021). Performance Evaluation of the Vegetable Trading Center in Lantapan, Bukidnon, Philippines. *Agricultural Socio-Economics Journal, 21*(3), 165–174. https://doi.org/ doi:10.21776/ub.agrise.2021.021.3.1

Ding, H., Wu, X., & Ma, Y. (2019). Performance evaluation of vegetable cold chain logistics based on AHP-TOPSIS method. *Nongye Gongcheng Xuebao (Beijing), 35*(13), 251–259.

Fan, Y., Zhang, C., Zhang, X., & Xu, S. (2018). Evaluation of vegetable distribution performance based on grey relational analysis. *Journal of Food Distribution Research, 49*(3), 66–73.

Ibrahim, N. (2021): Performance Evaluation of the Fruit and Vegetable Subsectors in the Azerbaijani Economy: A Combinatorial Analysis Using Regression and Principal Component Analysis. *Proceedings of 12th FEB Zagreb International Odyssey Conference on Economics and Business*, 309-328. https://doi.org/10.22598/odyssey/2021.3

Kelle, P., Akkermans, H., & Voss, C. (2013). The impact of the design of planning and control systems on the performance of integrated supply chains. *International Journal of Production Economics, 145*(1), 192–205.

Kouvelis, P., Chambers, C., & Wang, H. (2017). *Handbook of Integrated Risk Management in Global Supply Chains*. John Wiley & Sons.

Li, S., Ragu-Nathan, B., Ragu-Nathan, T. S., & Rao, S. S. (2006). The impact of supply chain management practices on competitive advantage and organizational performance. *Omega*, *34*(2), 107–124. doi:10.1016/j.omega.2004.08.002 PMID:17876965

Luo, Y., Li, X., & Wang, J. (2021). Evaluation of the efficiency and coordination degree of vegetable distribution channels based on DEA and coupling coordination degree model. *Journal of Food Distribution Research*, *52*(2), 107–118.

Lusine H, & Aramyan. (2007). *Measuring supply chain performance in the Agri-food sector* [PhD thesis]. Wageningen University.

Sun, Z., & Ma, Y. (2017). Evaluation and optimization of vegetable distribution efficiency based on DEA. *Journal of the Saudi Society of Agricultural Sciences*, *16*(1), 84–93.

Wen, Y., Shi, X., Li, Q., & Xu, Q. (2020). Evaluation and analysis of vegetable supply chain performance based on the combination of AHP and DEA. *Journal of Systems Science and Information*, *8*(2), 138–149.

Xu, Y., & Zeng, Q. (2017). Evaluation and optimization of vegetable supply chain performance based on BP neural network. *Proceedings of the 2017 International Conference on Management Science and Industrial Engineering,* 203-209.

Chapter 21
A Study on Total Quality Management (TQM) in Warehouse Management in Logistics Limited

Pooja Kumari
Jain University, India

T. Shenbagavalli
Jain University, India

S. Ashwini
Jain University, India

K. Vidhya
Jain University, India

ABSTRACT

The goal of total quality management (TQM) is to ensure that all customers and users are completely satisfied at all times by preventing defects and equipping employees with the knowledge and attitude necessary to do so. Whether or not total quality management is in place, what TQM techniques have been adopted, how TQM affects warehouse management, and how TQM and warehouse management affect productivity are all questions that were explored in this chapter. This research is based on primary data, which has been collected with the help of questionnaires from the employees in an organization because questionnaires can cover a large population with lower cost and shorter time. A structured questionnaire was formed using Google Forms for the survey and was sent to the respondents for their responses. TQM in warehouse management helps in the effective management of the warehousing system and also has a positive effect on the quality of the warehouse. It provides efficiency to the employee to manage the warehousing system and also upgrade the same.

DOI: 10.4018/979-8-3693-2193-5.ch021

1. INTRODUCTION

Total Quality Management is an important technique that produces an improvement reaction to corporations and to companies. Customer happiness at every stage of the company process is the ultimate goal of this kind of futures planning, which involves much more than simply assuring the quality of products and services (Akshaya & Naachimuthu, 2022). With Total Quality Management, companies do the right thing at the right time at an initial stage. Total Quality Management is an integral aspect of any business, no matter how big or little, for-profit or not (Alabdullah & Ahmed, 2021). TQM, or Total Quality Management, is the strategic management of quality to increase profits and reduce costs while maintaining a competitive edge (Gupta, 2021a). Total quality management (TQM) is a management strategy in which all workers in a company consistently evaluate their operations with the goal of raising both product and service quality and customer satisfaction (Alabdullah et al., 2021a). This process include fixing issues in a company's operations through management training and the use of analytical tools (Alabdullah et al., 2021b). Total quality management (TQM) and quality management strategies are not a "one size fits all" answer when it comes to planning and implementing them in the workplace (Gupta, 2021b; Priscila et al., 2023). Culture, management, and the procedures for developing and distributing goods and services are all distinctive to any individual business (Al-Maaitah et al., 2021a). While the specifics of quality management plans will differ from one business to the next, all will need to have a core set of components (Al-Maaitah et al., 2021b).

Total quality management (TQM) is a strategy for increasing the efficiency and adaptability of a company as a whole (Hana et al., 2022). It's a method for coordinating and enlisting the participation of every member of the organisation, at every level (Kumar & Naachimuthu, 2023). By emphasising prevention over inspection, TQM provides a critical driver for continuous improvement in a business, allowing it to continually enhance its performance (Phoek et al., 2023). Certain TQM proposals produced over the previous few decades by quality gurus like Deming (1986), the field's leading experts, have achieved widespread recognition around the world (Mert, 2020). Their comments shed light on the fundamentals of the Total Quality Management approach. Careful analysis of their writings revealed that the quality gurus hold divergent perspectives on TQM, but with certain commonalities. The Deming Prize (DP), European Quality Award (EQA), Malcolm Baldrige National Quality Award (MBNQA), and Rajiv Gandhi National Quality Award (RGNQA) are just a few of the many quality prizes presented across the world (RGNQA). Each methodology for giving awards is based on a different conception of total quality management. It's important to note that each of these reward structures is unique (Mert, 2021a). Numerous studies have been undertaken on the topic of TQM implementation, with various researchers using varying definitions of the term (Aswathi et al., 2021). The notion is still a subject of controversy and yet a fuzzy and vague concept. To date, TQM has been interpreted in a variety of ways (Mert, 202b).

To improve customer satisfaction and business results, "total quality management" (TQM) programmes have become increasingly popular in recent decades (Kanaan-Jebna et al., 2022). To maximise a company's productivity, total quality management advocates for the involvement of every employee in the management and ongoing refinement of the entire operation (Mert, 2020c). In 1940, during the first international conference on quality control held in Tokyo, the terms "whole quality" and "total quality management" were coined by three Japanese gurus named Deming, Juran, and Feigenbaum. The new phases of quality control and management, also known as total quality management, began in the 1980s and 1990s (Mert, 2022).

TQM was first put into practise in the Japanese automobile and general manufacturing industries (Nagarajan & Naachimuthu, 2022). As a result, the vast majority of published works aim to dispel the widespread misconception that TQM can only be applied in the manufacturing sector (Kuragayala, 2023; Sudheer & Naachimuthu, 2022). Researchers have found that construction companies can benefit from TQM because customer satisfaction is a top priority for every successful business. Past studies have looked at the connection between Total Quality Management and project performance in the Malaysian construction industry, as well as TQM implementation in both the Palestinian and Omani construction sectors (Madhumitha & Naachimuthu, 2023). Despite the similarities in construction processes, the aforementioned studies have focused on countries with distinct characteristics than Pakistan, which is currently experiencing economic troubles (Naachimuthu et al., 2022).

Warehouse Management is essential for all logistics companies. The warehouse is one part of an effective logistics management system for businesses, but without it, businesses are likely to face all sorts of problems (Hana & Naachimuthu, 2023). Thus, to maintain a competitive advantage and to achieve greater customer satisfaction, constant assessment of practices of TQM and warehouse management is essential for logistics organizations Limited.

2. REVIEW OF LITERATURE

According to the research of Ocoró et al. (2023), TQM is "a management strategy that stresses customer satisfaction and continual development in the firm." Each worker in the company contributes to this goal by thinking about how their work will be used. Total quality management's goals include the establishment of quality enhancement as the enterprise's top priority and the enhancement of organisational effectiveness (Tripathi & Al-Shahri, 2023).

According to Fotopoulos and Psomas (2009), quality in the construction business is described as "fulfilling the expectations of owners, regulatory bodies, designers, and builders." TQM is an effective method that integrates quality improvement, quality maintenance, and quality development to provide service at an economic level for reaching complete satisfaction of consumers and clients.

As defined by Ghobadian and Gallear (2001), a project is a time-limited effort to develop a special deliverable. Each project is unique, with well-defined parameters and a fixed completion date. Project-based businesses face delicate and significant issues due to the unpredictability and complexity of the projects themselves. When it comes to building projects, the term "success" might be subjectively defined by various construction companies.

A measure that is deemed successful on one project may be deemed a failure on another, as suggested by Gunasekaran and McGaughey (2003). As a result, construction businesses and organisations may use varying metrics and standards to evaluate the performance of their projects. As a result, the industry as a whole lacks a standard method for gauging project success. Projects vary in location, complexity, distinctiveness, and size, making it challenging to define particular criteria or standard checklists for measuring project success. The iron triangle of cost, schedule, and quality is widely recognised as the standard by which to evaluate the success of a building project (Vashishtha & Dhawan, 2023).

Total Quality Management (TQM) and innovation performance are two topics that Huq and Stolen (1998) address. Its foundation is found mostly in the extensive debate that already exists in the literature on the topic of the connection in question. Questionnaires were produced and sent out to a certain number of employees at the company as part of the research plan. An intriguing approach to settling this debate is presented: a framework established through a theoretical consideration of the TQM's multidimensionality in its application to various organisational settings (Saxena et al., 2023).

For Kanji and Wallace (2000), the paper's overarching goal was to "make management aware of the components of Total Quality Management and so enable the successful implementation of quality management." The significance of this study lies in its identification of crucial TQM elements for its implementation (Srinivas et al., 2023). Tools and methods of Total Quality Management (TQM) include histograms, flowcharts, histogram analysis, and internal audits, among other things. According to the findings, certified businesses can improve their progress toward complete quality with a greater emphasis on people orientation and the application of tools and procedures.

The impact of coworker and organisational support on the relationship between total quality management and performance is investigated by Ahire et al., (1996). The study's author also discovered that the connection between TQM adoption and business success was reflected in the level of backing the initiative received from within the company and among employees (Shifana & Naachimuthu, 2022).

Many different ideas about TQM are presented by Al-Marri et al. (2007), yet they all have the same foundational features. One way in which TQM differs from other management approaches is in its emphasis on the customer. Furthermore, one of the most significant components that ensure the success of TQM techniques is managerial commitment. Other key organisational situations to accomplish TQM performance are organisational culture and modifications. As a result, overall quality management is a management approach that strives to improve business results by raising the bar on the quality of the services and goods produced by the firm (Savya & Naachimuthu, 2022). In the last twenty years, there has been a dramatic uptick in interest in whole quality management strategies. TQM emphasises the importance of the client. Revenue, profit, cash flow, and market share have all increased as a result of the company's attentiveness to, and mastery of, its customers' and clients' needs as well as its dedication to assuring their complete satisfaction (Priyadarshini & Naachimuthu, 2020).

According to I.varado and Kotzab (2001), the first step in any quality programme should be to place the customer in the centre of the business's attention. Their research on TQM in the food industry revealed that the service sector of Spain benefited greatly from a focus on the client. The findings of this research support the idea that putting the needs of customers first can boost productivity and satisfaction at the same time. Improved project outcomes were identified as a result of a focus on customer relationship management (Antony et al., 2002). The following hypothesis is proposed in light of these data concerning the effect of customer satisfaction on project performance.

According to Jasti et al. (2022), TQM has been widely adopted in a variety of service industries as a management method with the overarching goal of improving business output. Moreover, TQM is regarded a full integration between numerous models, procedures, personnel, and communication processes to fulfil all client expectations. Employee involvement refers to people's active participation in the decision-making process at different levels of a business. The concepts of dedication and accountability are also associated with involvement. All levels of staff are essential to a company's success since without them, the business could not function.

Aroef (1999) found that employee participation in quality procedures was the most important factor. Results demonstrated that employee involvement favorably benefited the implementation of the system management technique, process method, ongoing improvement, and decision-making method. The "Components of TQM" model, proposed by Beckford (1998), is a well-known framework for TQM. Top-down support for TQM principles like customer-centricity, employee involvement, supplier management, benchmarking, and information and performance quality are essential. Results include increased output and quality, increased customer happiness, strengthened client loyalty, and punctual delivery. To improve quality, all TQM models agree that managers should plan, implement, and evaluate procedures.

3. OBJECTIVES OF THE STUDY

The main objective of the research is to determine if total quality management is implemented in an organization and the TQM practices adopted by the organization and identify if TQM influences Warehouse management and the impact of TQM and Warehouse Management on productivity.

3.1. Research Methodology

The research study relies on primary data, which has been collected through questionnaires from the employees in the organization because questionnaires can cover a large population with a lower cost and shorter time. A structured questionnaire was formed using Google Forms for the survey and was sent to the respondents for their responses. Data is analyzed with the help of charts, graphs, and tables.

4. ANALYSIS AND INTERPRETATION

TQM works in the organization: According to the survey, we can see that 25% of the employees of the organisation agree that TQM (Total Quality Management) works in the organisation, and 75% of respondents strongly agree on the working of TQM in the organisation. Whereas no employees responded against the topic, i.e., 0 respondents opted for partially disagree or strongly disagree (Table 1).

Table 1. TQM works in the organisation

Options	No. of Respondents	Percentage
Strongly agree	75	75%
Agree	25	25%
Partially Disagree	0	0%
Strongly Disagree	0	0%

According to the survey, we can see that 25% of the employees of the organization agree that TQM (Total Quality Management) works in the organisation, and 75% of respondents strongly agree on the working of TQM in the organisation (Fig.1). Whereas no employees responded against the topic, i.e., 0 respondents opted for partially disagree or strongly disagree.

To what level do you think TQM works in the organisation: This particular question was asked to know the extent to which TQM works in the organisation, and from the above analysis it can be interpreted that 50% of the employees feel that TQM is implemented in the organisation to some extent but not completely, and also 40% of the employees have no issue on the TQM implementation in the organisation (Fig.2).

Figure 1. TQM works in the organization

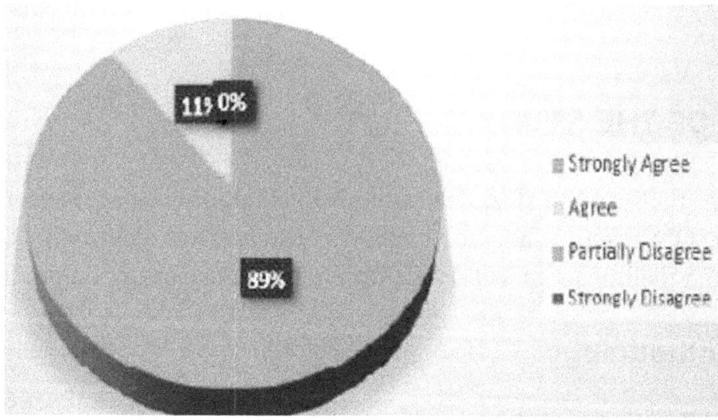

Figure 2. Level to which TQM works in the organisation

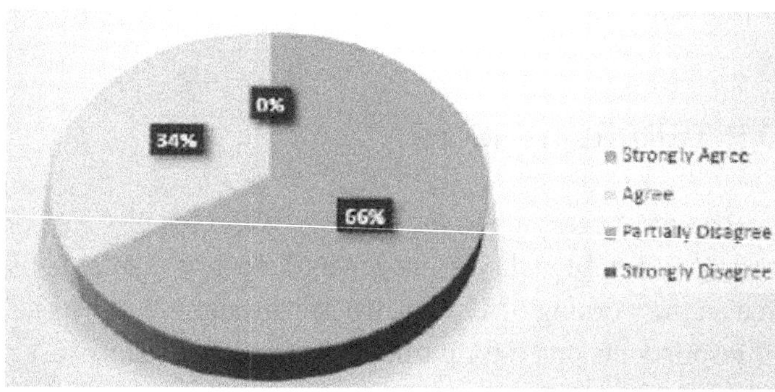

Is TQM beneficial to the organisation? According to the survey, we can see that 85% of the respondent say that TQM is beneficial to the organisation, whereas 15% of the respondent are not sure about it being beneficial to the organisation and thus opting for maybe. None of the respondents opted for TQM not being beneficial to the organisation (Fig.3).

Figure 3. TQM works in the organisation

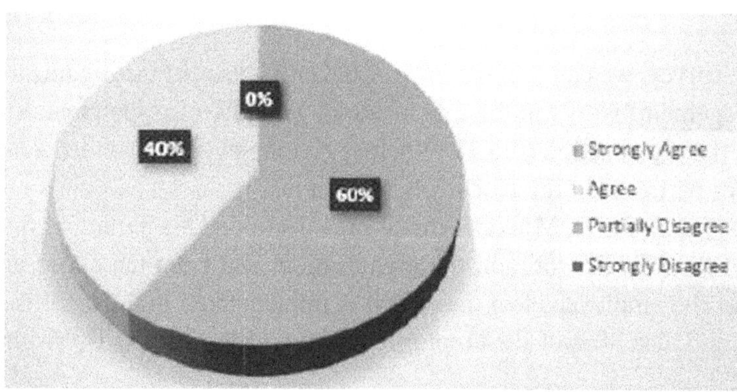

Leadership

Leadership is a TQM practice. Data was collected using survey data from employees, executives, supervisors, and managers who have multiple years of experience.

Top-level manager encourages employee involvement: According to the survey, 80% of the respondents strongly agree that top management encourages employee involvement in decision-making, and 20% of respondents also agree with it. None of the respondents have opted against it (Fig.4).

Figure 4. Top-level management encourages employee involvement

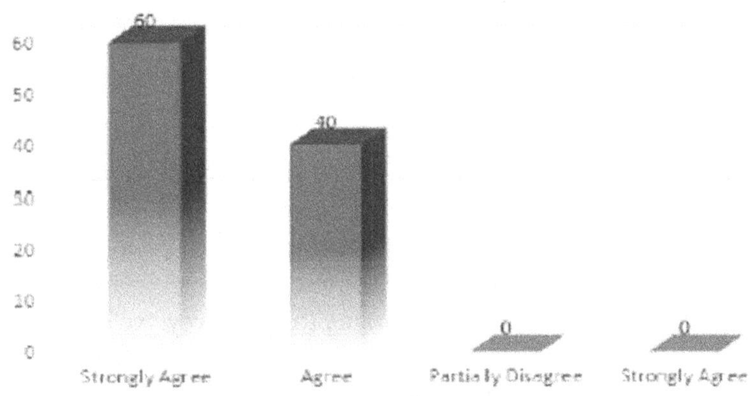

Top-level management allocates adequate resources towards efforts to improve quality. According to the survey, 60% of the respondents say that the top-level management allocates adequate resources towards efforts to improve quality, whereas 40% agree on it too. And none of the respondents disagreed on the same (Fig,5).

Figure 5. Top-level management allocates resources towards Efforts to improve quality

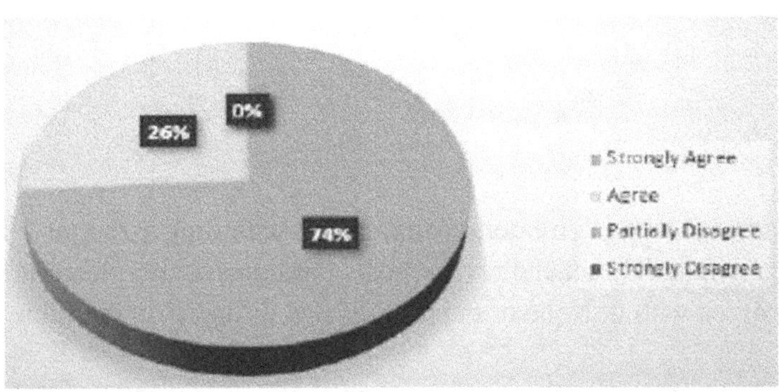

Our Top Management takes responsibility for quality: According to the survey, we can see that 40% of the respondents agree that the Top Management takes responsibility for the quality. Whereas 60% of the respondents strongly agree with it. And none of the respondents disagreed on the same (Fig.6).

Figure 6. Top management takes responsibility for quality

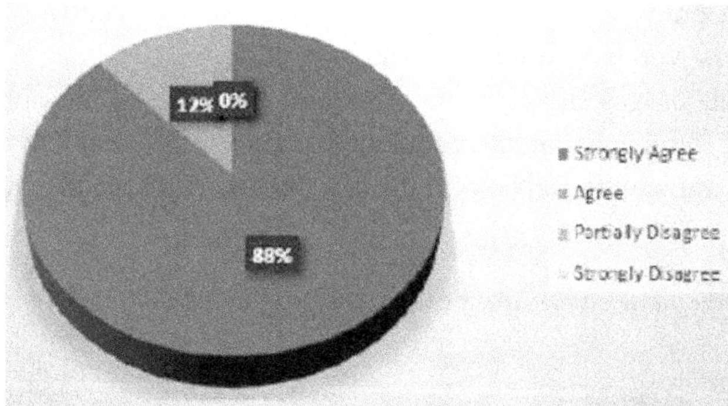

Strategic Planning

Strategic planning has been defined as the process of setting organizational goals, setting a detailed plan, and implementing a strategy to achieve the goal. Strategic planning is another practice of TQM implementation in the organisation. This section of questions was asked to determine the plans of the organisation.

Clear vision on how to achieve our goals: According to the survey, we can see that 40% of the respondents agree that the organisation focuses a clear vision on how to achieve the goals. Whereas 60% of the respondents strongly agree with it. None of the respondents disagree on the same (Fig.7).

Figure 7. Organisation takes an exact long-term view on achieving goals

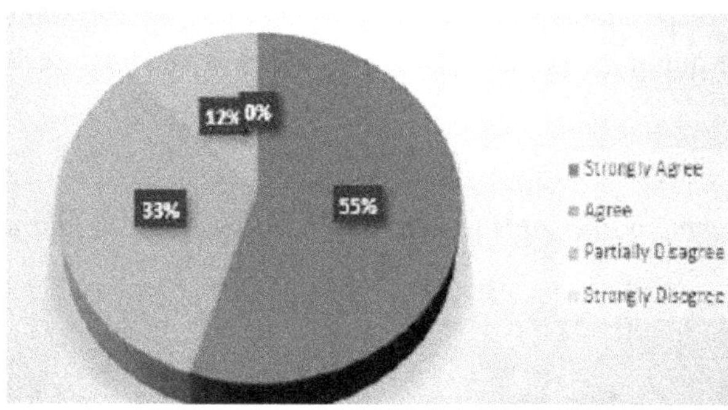

Organizations review goals through extensive planning: According to the survey, we can see that 33% of the respondents agree that they set and review goals through concise planning. Whereas 67% of the respondents strongly agree with it. None of the respondents disagree on the same (Fig.8).

Customer Focus

Customer Focus observes customer complaints and customer expectations and evaluates customer satisfaction. Customer satisfaction is considered to be one of the important elements of the Total Quality of an organisation. In order to achieve Quality in an organization, customer expectations should also be given core importance.

Figure 8. Employees set and review long-term and short-term goals

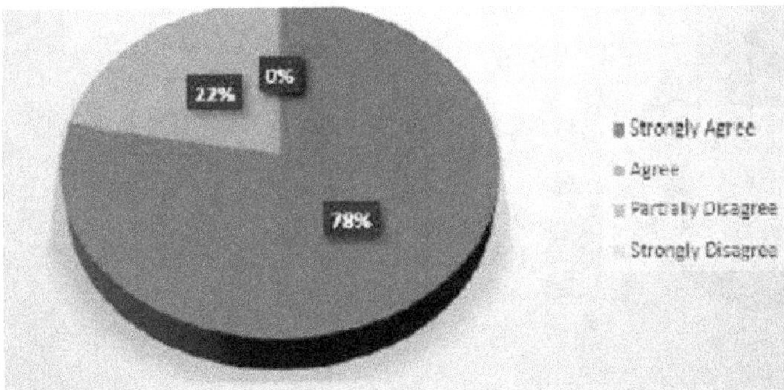

We reset our standards whenever customer needs and expectation changes: According to the survey, we can see that 70% of the respondents strongly agree that an organization reset the standards whenever customer expectation changes, and 30% of the respondents also agree for the same. None of them disagree (Fig.9).

Figure 9. Organisation reset the standards whenever customer needs and expectation changes

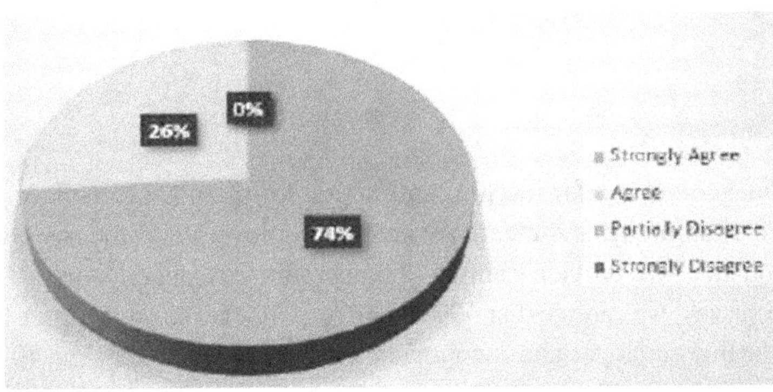

Customer needs are communicated to the employees: According to the survey, we can see that 60% of the respondents strongly agree that customer needs are communicated to the employees. And also 40% of employees also agree on the same. None of the respondents disagreed with it (Fig.10).

Availability of a system for accumulating complaints or suggestions from customers: According to the survey, we can see that 60% of the respondents strongly agree that the organisation has a proper system for collecting complaints and suggestions from the customers. Whereas 40% of respondents also agree on the same. None of the respondents disagree on the same. As per the analysis, we can interpret that the organization has a good system of taking complaints and suggestions into consideration, enabling higher customer satisfaction and customer loyalty (Fig.11).

Figure 10: Customer needs are communicated to employees

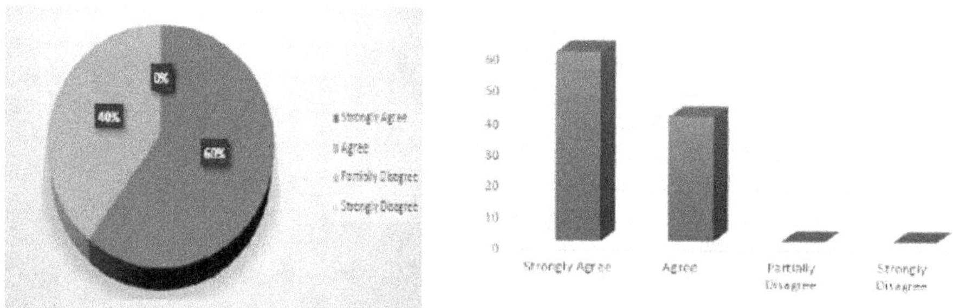

Figure 11. System for collecting complaints and suggestions from customers

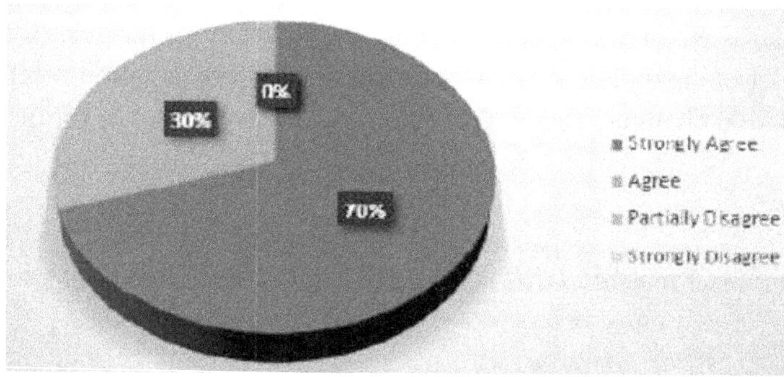

Human Resource

Total Quality Management is a far-reaching intimation for the management of human resources. It highlights self-control, autonomy, and creativity among employees and focuses on active cooperation rather than just compliance. We provide training to line employees and encourage them to perform better: According to the survey, we can see that 60% of the respondents strongly agree that the organisation provides training to the line employee and encourage them to perform better. And 40% of the respondents also agree with the same. None of the respondents disagreed on the same (Fig.12).

Figure 12. Organisation provides training to line employees and encourages them to perform better

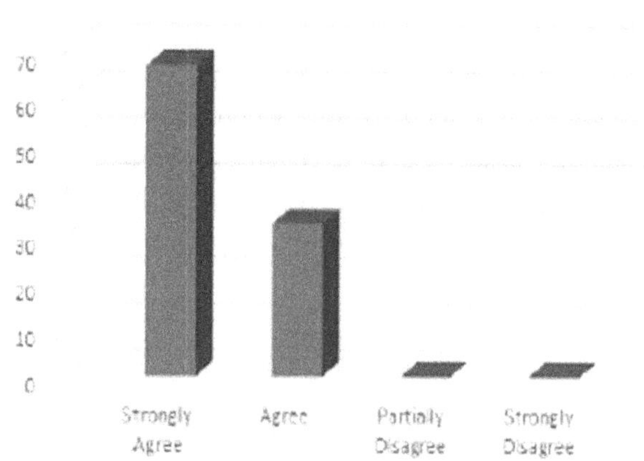

Proper training to the employee keeps the employee upgraded and enhances them to perform better. According to the analysis, we can see that the employees are provided with proper training so as to perform better and take responsibility for their own work. Training in human resources is very well implemented in the organisation (Padmapriya & Naachimuthu, 2023).

Line of employment are responsible for work and inspect the quality of their own work: According to the survey, we can see that 55% strongly agree that the employees are responsible for and inspect the quality of their own work. 33% of respondents also agree on the same. At the same time, 12% of the respondents disagree with the same (Fig.13).

Figure 13. Line of employment is responsible for work and inspects the quality of their own

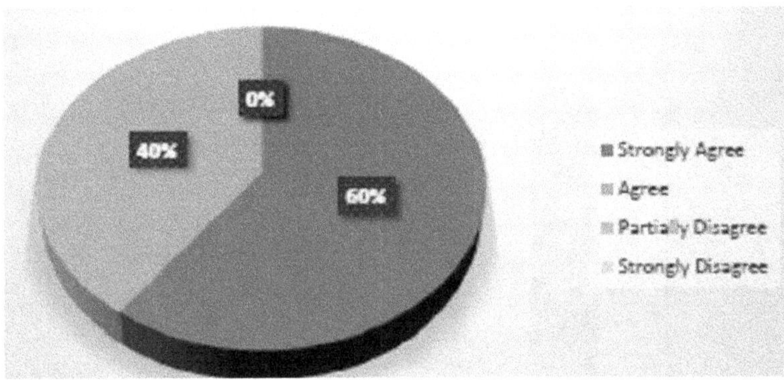

As per the analysis, we can see that most of the employee are efficient enough to review their own work and take responsibility for rectification. The disagreement could be because of their new joining or due to lack of sufficient experience.

Organization assist mechanism (Problem Solving Network) to help employees to solve the problem regarding quality: According to the survey, we can see that 88% of the respondents strongly agree that the organisation has an assisting mechanism to assist line employees in solving quality mechanisms. Also, the rest, 22%, also agree on the same. None of the respondents disagreed with it (Fig.14).

Figure 14. Organisation having quality problem-solving network

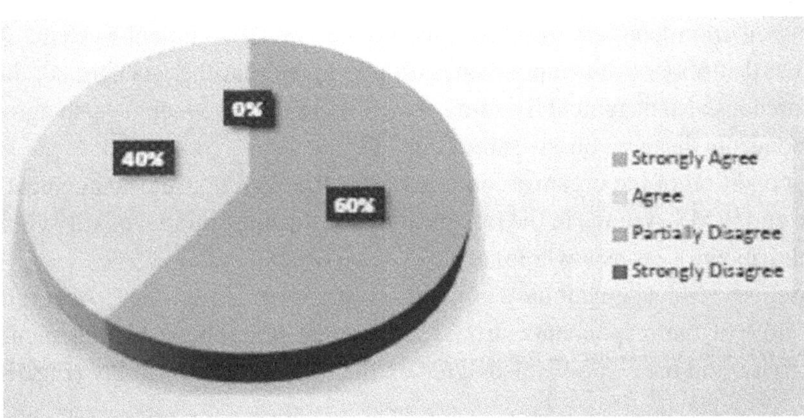

Human resource is the most efficient and effective resource of any organisation. Having an assisting mechanism helps the lone employee to solve some of the basic problems at their level. This increases their responsibility towards work, helps them perform better, and helps improve the quality.

Impact of TQM on Warehouse management

Does the organisation have warehouse performance management system? According to the survey, we can see that 74% of the respondents strongly agree that the organisation has a warehouse performance management system, and also 26% of respondents agree on the same. None of the respondents disagree that the organisation does not have a Warehouse performance management system (Fig.15).

Figure 15. The organisation has a warehouse performance management system

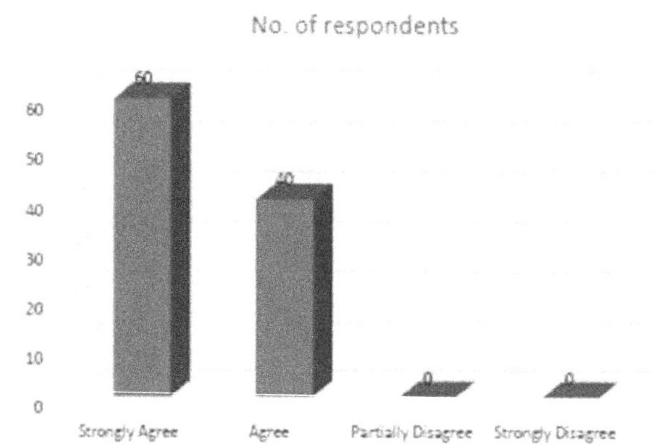

According to this, the organisation has a Warehouse management system to control the activities of the warehouse.

Do level authorities encourage employee's involvement in managing the warehouse? According to the survey, we can see that 60% of the respondents strongly agree that the Top Management encourages employee involvement in warehouse management. Also, 40% of the respondents also agree on the same (Fig.16).

As per the analysis, we can say that the top-level management encourages employee involvement in Warehouse Management by implementing leadership and employee involvement in warehouse Management, hence maintaining quality with the same.

Is the working environment very good for the Warehouse Management System? According to the survey, we can see that 60% of the respondents strongly agree that the working condition is very well suited for the Warehouse Management System. Also, 40% of the respondents also agree with the same. None of the respondents disagree on the same (Fig.17).

The working condition of the organisation is good for the Warehouse Management System as there are separate area and WMS systems in the organisation for receipt, storage, quality check, and dispatch, leading to a systematic process as a whole.

Does the Warehouse Management have continuous improvement activity? According to the survey, we can see that 66% of the respondents strongly agree that Warehouse Management has continuous improvement activity, and the rest 34% also agree on the same but not strongly (Fig.18).

Figure 16. Top management encourages employee involvement in warehouse management

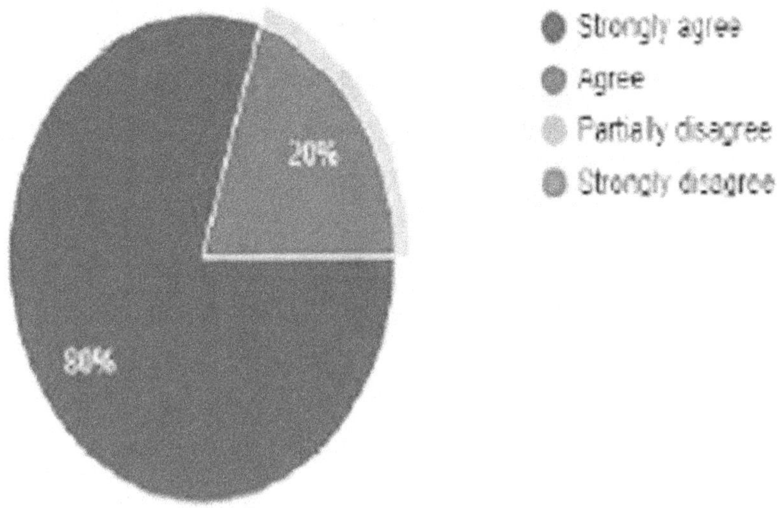

Figure 17. Working condition is good for the warehouse management system

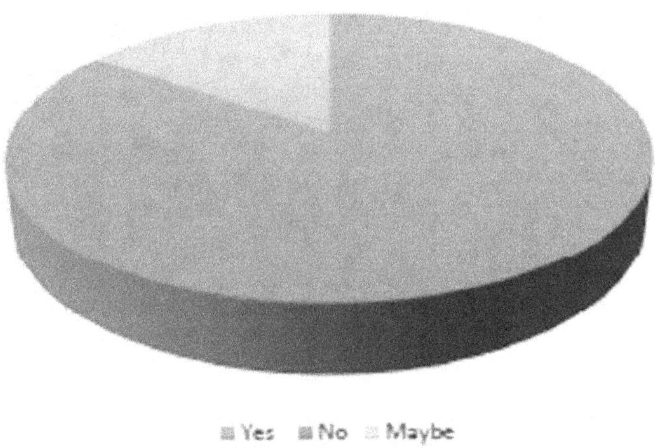

Continuous evaluation and improvement is a part of maintaining quality, whether it is of employees or the Warehouse Management. This shows that to maintain quality, the organization takes continuous improvement steps to manage the Warehousing System.

Does TQM and Warehouse Management help improve quality and production in your organisation: According to the survey, we can see that 89% of the respondents strongly agree that TQM and Warehouse Management help improve quality and production. Also, 11% of the respondents also agree on the same but not strongly as they might feel some scope for improvement in the same (Fig.19).

Figure 18. Warehouse management has continuous improvement activity

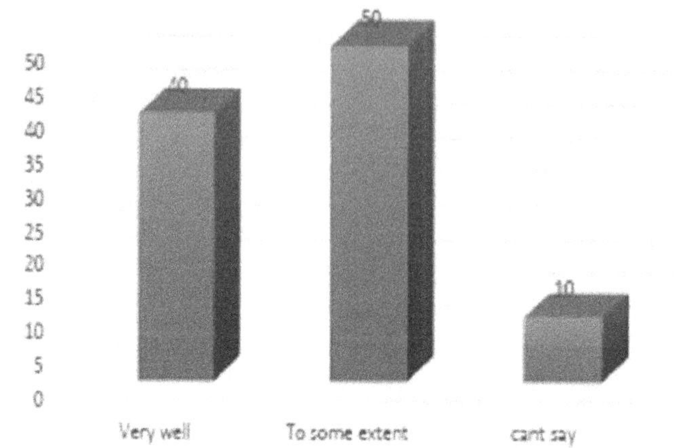

Figure 19. TQM and warehouse management helps improve quality and production

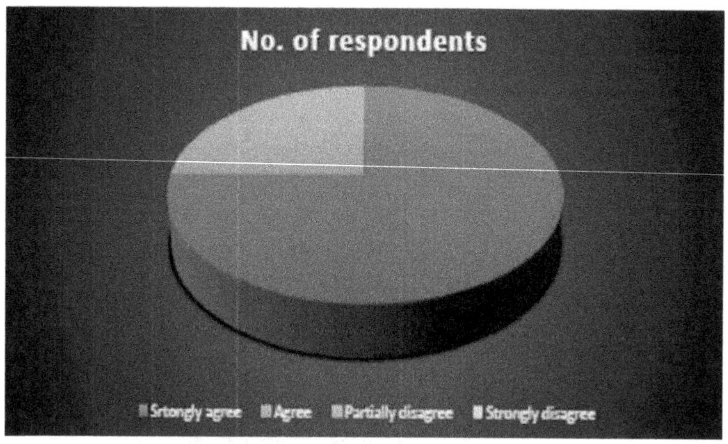

As per the analysis, we can see that TQM and Warehouse Management implemented in the organisation makes it more efficient to perform better and improve quality. Warehouse Management plays a very important role in any logistics company and adding the quality element makes it outperform all the competitors.

Human Resources are the greatest resource of any organisation. Proper training for the employees helps improve quality and production. As per the study, employees in the organisation are trained enough to review their own quality at the ground level and improve efficiency. In this constantly changing market with rapid economic growth, quality has become the major focus of any organisation. The subject of TQM practices and their impact on organizational performance has been addressed to solve quality problems. Due to this, TQM and Warehouse Management both play an increasingly important role in strengthening any logistics company. It is considered to play a crucial role in achieving successful quality performance, which contributes to improving Warehouse Management. It plays a very important role in any logistics company and adding the quality element makes it outperform all the competitors.

5. CONCLUSION

By incorporating everyone in the company, TQM promotes quality as a business strategy and ultimately aims to increase customers' level of happiness. TQM is a method to running a business that aims to maximise an organization's competitiveness by continuous improvement of its products, services, personnel, processes, and environment. When it comes to implementing community development, TQM is a functional management technique that is constantly focused on increasing quality to ensure that its products meet the quality standards of the people served. Work can only be realised as a quality production activity if owned resources are merged with the gradual deployment of management functions. This approach departs from management as a process or set of actions. Customer gratification, creative problem solving, and the relentless pursuit of excellence are at the forefront of a new management paradigm made possible by this idea. The study indicated that TQM works in the organisation, and also from the survey it shows that it works in the organisation to some extent and it is also beneficial to the organisation. Total quality management practices that have been adopted by the organization include leadership, strategic planning, customer focus, and human resources.

REFERENCES

Ahire, S. L., Golhar, D. Y., & Waller, M. A. (1996). Development and validation of TQM implementation constructs. *Decision Sciences*, *27*(1), 23–56. doi:10.1111/j.1540-5915.1996.tb00842.x

Akshaya, A., & Naachimuthu, K. P. (2022). Locavorism to Enhance Environmental, Social, & Economic Well-being. *Indian Journal of Agriculture Business*, *8*(1), 25–33.

Al-Maaitah, D. A., Tha'er Majali, M. A., & Almaaitah, T. A. (2021a). The role of leadership styles on staffs job satisfaction in public organizations. *Journal of Contemporary Issues in Business and Government*, *27*(1), 772–783.

Al-Maaitah, T. A., Tha'er Majali, M. A., & Almaaitah, D. A. (2021b). The Impact of COVID-19 on the Electronic Commerce Users Behavior. *Journal of Contemporary Issues in Business and Government*, *27*(1), 772–783.

Al-Marri, K., Ahmed, A. M. M. B., & Zairi, M. (2007). Excellence in service: An empirical study of the UAE banking sector [A]. *International Journal of Quality & Reliability Management*, *24*(2), 164–176. doi:10.1108/02656710710722275

Alabdullah, T.T.Y., & Ahmed, E.R. (2021). New Insights to Investigate the Impact of Internal Control Mechanisms on Firm Performance: A Study in Oman. *Riset Akuntansi dan Keuangan Indonesia, 6*(2).

Alabdullah, T. T. Y., Al Fakhri, I., Ahmed, E. R., & Jebna, A. K. (2021b). Empirical Study of The Influence of Board of Directors' Feature on Firm Performance. *Russian Journal of Agricultural and Socio-Economic Sciences*, *11*(119), 137–146. doi:10.18551/rjoas.2021-11.16

Alabdullah, T. T. Y., Al-Fakhri, I., Ahmed, E. R., & Kanaan-Jebna, A. (2021a). Corporate Governance System and Firm Financial Performance. *Acta Scientific Computer Sciences*, *4*(6), 97–103.

Antony, J., Leung, K., Knowles, G., & Gosh, S. (2002). Critical success factors of TQM implementation in Hong Kong industries. *International Journal of Quality & Reliability Management, 19*(5), 551–566. doi:10.1108/02656710210427520

Aroef, M. (1999). *Some Observations About Community Efforts to Increase Productivity and Quality.* Working Paper for One Day Seminar on Strategies for Increasing Productivity and Quality Management which are Classified as "World Best Practice", Bandung.

Aswathi, P., Sangavi, P., Naachimuthu, K. P., & Krishna, T. (2021). *Proceedings of the ICSSR Sponsored Webinar on Human Behavior and Environmental Sustainability*. Academic Press.

Beckford, J. (1998). Quality: A Critical Introduction. Psychology Press.

Deming, W. E. (1986). Out of Crisis. MIT Centre for Advanced Engineering Study.

Fotopoulos, C. B., & Psomas, E. L. (2009). The impact of soft and hard TQM elements on quality management results. *International Journal of Quality & Reliability Management, 26*(2), 150–163. doi:10.1108/02656710910928798

Ghobadian, A., & Gallear, D. (2001). TQM implementation: An empirical examination and proposed generic model. *Omega, 29*(4), 343–359. doi:10.1016/S0305-0483(01)00030-5

Gunasekaran, A., & McGaughey, R. E. (2003). TQM in supply chain management. *The TQM Magazine, 15*(6), 361–363. doi:10.1108/09544780310502688

Gupta, R. K. (2021a). A study on occupational health hazards among construction workers in India. *International Journal of Enterprise Network Management, 12*(4), 325–339. doi:10.1504/IJENM.2021.119663

Gupta, R. K. (2021b). Adoption of mobile wallet services: an empirical analysis. *International Journal of Intellectual Property Management, 12*(3), 341 – 353. doi:10.1504/IJIPM.2021.10035526

Hana, M., & Naachimuthu, K. P. (2023). A Comprehensive Model on Rejection Sensitivity. *South India Journal of Social Sciences, 21*(19), 19–31.

Hana, M., Vishnupriya, S., & Naachimuthu, K. P. (2022). Restorative Effect of Direct and Indirect Nature Exposure - A Systematic Review. *International Journal of Scientific Research, 11*(5), 10–15.

Huq, Z., & Stolen, J. D. (1998). Total quality management contrast in manufacturing and service industries. *International Journal of Quality & Reliability Management, 15*(2), 138–161. doi:10.1108/02656719810204757

Jasti, N. V. K., Venkateswaran, V., Kota, S., & Sangwan, K. S. (2022). A literature review on total quality management (models, frameworks, and tools and techniques) in higher education. *The TQM Journal, 34*(5), 1298–1319. doi:10.1108/TQM-04-2021-0113

Jayapriya, J., Poornima, T., & Naachimuthu, K. P. (2022). Hermeneutics of Iniyavai Naarpadhu and Inna Naarpadhu. *Journal of Positive School Psychology, 6*(8), 4358–4368.

Kanaan-Jebna, A., Baharudi, A. S., & Alabdullah, T. T. Y. (2022). Entrepreneurial Orientation, Market Orientation, Managerial Accounting and Manufacturing SMEs Satisfaction. *Journal of Accounting Science, 6*(1), 1–14. doi:10.21070/jas.v6i1.1590

Kanji, G. K., & Wallace, W. (2000). Business excellence through customer satisfaction. *Total Quality Management, 11*(7), 979–998. doi:10.1080/09544120050135515

Kumar, A., & Naachimuthu, K. P. (2023). Market Potential for Shawarma Outlet in Coimbatore - An Analysis. *South India Journal of Social Sciences, 21*(1), 130–140.

Kuragayala, P. S. (2023). A Systematic Review on Workforce Development in Healthcare Sector: Implications in the Post-COVID Scenario. *FMDB Transactions on Sustainable Technoprise Letters, 1*(1), 36–46.

Lvarado, U.Y., & Kotzab, H. (2001). Supply chain management: the integration of logistics in marketing. *Industrial Marketing Management, 30*(2), 183-98.

Madhumitha, D., & Naachimuthu, K. P. (2023). Emotional Regulation among the Members of LGBTQ+ Community. *Education and Society, 47*(2), 34–45.

Mert, I. (2020). Analyzing the Results of Accounting Evaluation Methods Through Practical Applications. *European Business & Management, 6*(4), 95–104. doi:10.11648/j.ebm.20200604.14

Mert, I. (2021a). Analyzing the Sustainability of the Accounting Valuation Practices in Romania during the Adaptation Period to the European Union. *Revista Argentina de Clínica Psicológica, 30*(1), 787–798.

Mert, I. (2021b). The Effects of Collaboration between Internal Auditing and Financial Affairs Departments: A Survey Conducted through the Internal Auditing and Financial Affairs Departments. *Economic Studies, 30*(3), 96–114.

Mert, I. (2021c). The Effects of the Qualitative Parameters of Internal Auditing Works on the Preferences of Investment Funds' Analysts. *Economic Alternatives*, (1), 60–71.

Mert, I. (2022). Investigation Techniques, Methods, Types, and Increasing Impact of Forensic Accounting in Digital Period. *Maliye ve Finans Yazıları*, (118), 13–32. doi:10.33203/mfy.1084274

Naachimuthu, K. P., Ganga, S., & Mathiyoli, P. M. (2022). Psychosocial Impact of COVID-19 Lockdown. *IAHRW International Journal of Social Sciences Review, 10*(1), 52–59.

Nagarajan, G., & Naachimuthu, K. P. (2022). Positive Emotions and Experiences of Trans Men and Trans Women - A Grounded Theory Approach. *International Journal of Early Childhood Special Education, 14*(2), 6430–6447.

Ocoró, M. P., Polo, O. C. C., & Khandare, S. (2023). Importance of Business Financial Risk Analysis in SMEs According to COVID-19. *FMDB Transactions on Sustainable Management Letters, 1*(1), 12–21.

Padmapriya, P., & Naachimuthu, K. P. (2023). Social and Philosophical Construction of Emotions in Bhagavad Gita & Plutchik Wheel of Emotions. *Journal of the Asiatic Society of Mumbai, XCVI*(27), 22–36.

Phoek, S. E. M., Lauwinata, L., & Kowarin, L. R. N. (2023). Tourism Development in Merauke Regency, South Papua Province: Strengthening Physical Infrastructure for Local Economic Growth and Enchanting Tourist Attractions. *FMDB Transactions on Sustainable Management Letters, 1*(2), 82–94.

Priscila, S. S., Rajest, S. S., Tadiboina, S. N., Regin, R., & András, S. (2023). Analysis of Machine Learning and Deep Learning Methods for Superstore Sales Prediction. *FMDB Transactions on Sustainable Computer Letters, 1*(1), 1–11.

Priyadarshini, N. S., & Naachimuthu, K. P. (2020). Ancient and Modern Conception to Virtues: Comparing Naaladiyar and Positive Psychology. In *International Conference on Multi Facets of Sacred Literature* (pp. 1–12). Academic Press.

Savya, N., & Naachimuthu, K. P. (2022). Psychosocial Determinants of Name Dropping: A Conceptual Framework. *Madhya Bharti - Humanities and Social Sciences, 83*(14), 1–12.

Saxena, D., Khandare, S., & Chaudhary, S. (2023). An Overview of ChatGPT: Impact on Academic Learning. *FMDB Transactions on Sustainable Techno Learning*, *1*(1), 11–20.

Shifana, F., & Naachimuthu, K. P. (2022). Elements of Holistic Human Development in Naanmanikkadigai: A Hermeneutic Study. *Journal of Positive School Psychology*, *6*(4), 2218–2231.

Srinivas, K., Velmurugan, P. R., & Andiyappillai, N. (2023). Digital Human Resources and Management Support Improve Human Resources Effectiveness. *FMDB Transactions on Sustainable Management Letters*, *1*(1), 32–45.

Sudheer, V., & Naachimuthu, K. P. (2022). Effect of JPMR on State-Trait Anxiety Among Young Female Adults During COVID-19 Pandemic Lockdown. *International Journal of Health Sciences*, *6*(55), 1192–1202. doi:10.53730/ijhs.v6nS5.8848

Tripathi, S., & Al-Shahri, M. (2023). Problems and Prospects on the Evolution of Advertising and Public Relations Industries in Oman. *FMDB Transactions on Sustainable Management Letters*, *1*(1), 1–11.

Vashishtha, E., & Dhawan, G. (2023). Comparison of Baldrige Criteria of Strategy Planning and Harrison Text. *FMDB Transactions on Sustainable Management Letters*, *1*(1), 22–31.

Chapter 22
A Systematic Study of Central Bank Digital Currency:
Challenges, Limitations, and Its Effects on the Indian Economy

M. S. Nikhil
https://orcid.org/0000-0002-3979-1773
Jain University, India

Nischal V. Atreya
https://orcid.org/0009-0000-3572-2482
Jain University, India

H. Mehul Kumar
Jain University, India

B. Priyadharshini
Jain University, India

S. Ramya
Jain University, India

ABSTRACT

This chapter examines central bank digital currencies (CBDCs) and their possible impact on the Indian economy in an age of digitization. Commercial value, user experience, legal frameworks, and financial stability are crucial to understanding digital currencies. CBDCs are a new payment infrastructure frontier. The chapter emphasizes the significant investments needed to build a large user and merchant network, highlighting the far-reaching effects of digital currencies. This exploration aims to demystify CBDCs as electronic variants of fiat currency. CBDCs, issued by central banks as legal money, are versatile and available to the public, financial institutions, and businesses for savings and transactions. The study describes the rise of digital cash by tracing currency from early barter systems to physical notes and coins. It admits initial skepticism about digital currencies due to their volatility, diversity, and lack of official backing.

DOI: 10.4018/979-8-3693-2193-5.ch022

1. INTRODUCTION

It is crucial to analyze various dimensions to understand digital currencies fully. These dimensions include the commercial relevance of digital currencies, the user interface of digital currencies, the legal structure of digital currencies, and the ramifications for financial stability. Central bank digital currencies (also known as CBDCs) are a revolutionary form of payment infrastructure that requires recognition of the large investments required to build a comprehensive network that includes both consumers and merchants. This is because CBDCs are backed by central banks. Because there hasn't been widespread acceptance of Central Bank Digital Currencies (CBDCs), giving infrastructure the priority, it deserves. Raghava Suresh is currently employed with Tata Consultancy Services (TCS) as an industry advisor for banking, financial services, and insurance (BFSI). Central banks in several countries actively explore and implement their national digital currencies, typically referred to as Central Bank Digital Currency, or CBDC for short. Central Bank Digital Currencies (CBDCs) have the potential to be used in a manner that is equivalent to that of conventional tangible currency, and they can serve a variety of stakeholders, including the general public, financial institutions, and businesses.

The potential of Central Bank Digital Currencies (CBDCs), based on blockchain technology, a decentralized and permission less ledger platform, may be the primary reason for their foundation on blockchain technology. Individuals can use Central Bank Digital Currency (CBDC) for various activities, including saving money and conducting business transactions. These activities are collectively referred to as "transactional activities." The Central Bank Digital Currency (CBDC) can be defined briefly as the electronic embodiment of a country's authorized monetary unit, which exists solely in digital format. This is the most straightforward way to express the meaning of the term. It is of the utmost importance to emphasize that Central Bank Digital Currency (CBDC) is a valid form of payment supported by governmental jurisdiction. Digital currency systems use blockchain technology and operate within centralized networks, incorporating sophisticated procedures for verifying user identities.

Throughout human history, the development of monetary systems has displayed a dynamic and ever-changing nature. This development spans the transition from barter systems, in which physical things functioned as a method of exchange, through the introduction of metallic coins and paper currency as financial instruments and, most recently, the growth of digital currency as a mode of transaction. Barter systems were prevalent in ancient times and included actual objects. At first, the introduction of digital money was met with widespread cynicism. This was mostly due to concerns regarding the existence of many digital currencies, their quick proliferation, significant volatility, and the absence of support from the government. Cryptocurrencies' decentralized and safe nature has raised concerns about their long-term stability, reflected in significant price shifts.

In a budget statement, Nirmala Sitharaman, the Finance Minister of India, stated that the country's central bank wants to launch a Central Bank Digital Currency (CBDC) in the fiscal year 2022-2023. The Indian government has made an important decision in this regard. At the same time, some countries, including China, the United States, South Korea, South Africa, Canada, and Cambodia, are all actively working towards building their centralized digital currencies. The Reserve Bank of India (RBI) has initiated a comprehensive study to evaluate the potential benefits and drawbacks associated with the introduction of a central bank digital currency (CBDC) within the Indian framework. This study intends to determine whether India should implement a CBDC. The major purpose of this study is to determine the fundamental design components that would support the seamless integration of Central Bank Digital Currency (CBDC) with minimal upheaval while also comparing the current system to an idealized system. This study was conducted to determine the essential design components that would facilitate the smooth integration of CBDC.

Private individuals are the only people permitted to own cash that the Central Bank has physically printed. On the other hand, the only organizations permitted to hold reserves of the money held by the central bank are commercial banks, authorized financial institutions, and certain businesses. The increased use of central bank digital currency (CBDC) can potentially improve the safety and efficiency of various financial transactions. These transactions include parties such as wholesalers, homeowners, and financial institutions. The widespread adoption of central bank digital currencies (also known as CBDCs) may result in benefits such as improved operational efficiency and increased safety precautions.

The Bank for International Settlements (BIS) polled central banks worldwide in 2021, and it found that more than 86% of them were actively looking into the possibility of implementing Central Bank Digital Currencies (CBDCs) inside their respective jurisdictions. In addition, a sizeable chunk of sixty percent of these central banks are presently operating in the advanced stages of developing what is known as Central Bank Digital Currency (CBDC). In addition, it is important to point out that a sizeable number, exactly 14 percent, have already begun pilot programs intending to determine the viability and efficiency of Central Bank Digital Currencies (CBDCs) in real-world settings.

Central Bank Digital Currencies (sometimes abbreviated as "CBDCs") are important in the current fast-shifting technological environment and the increasing prevalence of digitalization. These currencies offer a trustworthy and risk-free digital framework for enabling transactions, safeguarding monetary assets, and acting as a unit of value generally accepted worldwide. The primary goal of researching Central Bank Digital Currency (CBDC) in India is to grasp the digitization process and offer scholarly viewpoints on the future direction of India's financial sector. This will be accomplished through primary and secondary sources of information.

2. LITERATURE REVIEW

Thanapackiam et al., (2022) were identified as authors or contributors in a scholarly context. The Digital Rupee is anticipated to serve as India's inaugural Central Bank Digital Currency (CBDC) proposition. If these currencies were under government supervision, they would likely garner significant trust and support. With that being said, the Reserve Bank of India will persist in supporting digital currency, similar to its role in physical banknotes and coins. Per the Reserve Bank of India (RBI), carrying forward losses incurred on cryptocurrencies is not permissible. This implies that alternative revenue streams will not compensate for any financial losses experienced during trading on these platforms and will be carried over to future periods. The work's author is Pratima Ghosh, and the publication year is 2022.

According to Babu & Abraham, (2021) the rise in popularity of private currencies could challenge national currencies with limited responsibility. There is evidence suggesting a decrease in the utilization of paper currency in industrialized nations. Consequently, implementing Central Bank Digital Currency (CBDC) in India requires carefully considering several variables. The successful implementation of the Central Bank Digital Currency (CBDC) architecture holds significant potential for India, as it can effectively address and mitigate the existing digital divide within the country. The potential viability of Central Bank Digital Currency (CBDC) in India appears promising, given the significant advancements in digital literacy and the improvement of payment mechanisms. Implementing a central bank digital currency (CBDC) in India can enhance its economic performance and facilitate its progress. This is evident from the fact that some trading partners of India, including China, Singapore, and the United Kingdom, have already initiated pilot programs for CBDCs within their jurisdictions.

The subject of discussion is the "IAS Gateway (2022)." Experts have proposed many ideas and designs for Central Bank Digital Currency (CBDC) transactions. Ultimately, the Reserve Bank of India (RBI) can determine how transactions involving the Indian rupee are conducted. Implementing Central Bank Digital Currency (CBDC) in India may encounter challenges due to prevailing misconceptions about this digital currency. The efficacy of Central Bank Digital Currency (CBDC) will be contingent upon factors such as its privacy features and user-friendliness.

In the study conducted by Priyadarshini & Kar, (2022) based on recent surveys conducted by the Bank for International Settlements (BIS) about Central Bank Digital Currencies (CBDCs), it has been shown that around 90% of central banks globally are engaged in research activities on CBDCs. Furthermore, nearly half of these central banks have progressed to implementing experimental initiatives in this domain. According to the survey findings, approximately 40 central bank digital currencies (CBDCs) are projected to circulate within six years.

According to Alonso et al., (2021), India is poised to follow suit with other nations in shifting its focus from research and experimentation to the practical implementation of policies. In order to enhance its global competitiveness and provide comprehensive financial and digital security, India must establish a Central Bank Digital Currency (CBDC) expeditiously. Given the potential concerns around disintermediation and financial instability, it is imperative to adopt preventive measures to mitigate and manage these risks.

According to Armelius et al., (2021) are the author of the cited work. There has been a notable surge in the level of interest surrounding Central Bank Digital Currencies (CBDCs), mostly attributed to the perceived value that central banks associated with them to their public policy goals, particularly in terms of offering secure and dependable payment systems. Each individual holds different perspectives on Central Bank Digital Currency (CBDC). An ongoing study is being conducted on the subject, with a limited number of individuals actively testing and applying it systematically and incrementally. This will facilitate the development of a diverse range of payment methods for public use.

Bhowmik (2022) highlights the significance of central banks' analytical frameworks about digital currencies, their considerations about monetary policy alternatives, the issue of central bank digital currencies (CBDCs), the development of blueprints, and the specific application aspects involved.

Padhi (2022) is the author of the text. The general public will be allowed to utilize Central Bank Digital Currencies (CBDCs) to access services facilitating the conversion of cryptocurrencies into traditional fiat currency. Implementing comprehensive data governance and privacy standards in central bank digital currencies (CBDCs) can potentially facilitate the development and establishment highly efficient and effective digital payment systems. Furthermore, it is worth noting that this technology has the potential to contribute to the development of strong data governance and privacy standards.

In a study by Eichengreen et al., (2022), the Reserve Bank looked at retail payment personal living spaces in six different locations from December 2018 to January 2019. The findings, disclosed in the April 2021 edition of the RBI Bulletin, indicate that cash is the prevailing choice for making payments and receiving funds for routine expenditures. Consequently, it possesses distinctive prospects for expediting the expansion of digital payment systems within the nation. Although it is improbable for Central Bank Digital Currency (CBDC) to supplant the utilization of physical currency completely, the inclination for cash usage might be attributed to a certain apprehension about digital payment methods. However, provided anonymity is guaranteed, one may embrace Central Bank Digital Currency (CBDC) if they prioritize the confidentiality aspect of cash transactions. Implementing Central Bank Digital Currency (CBDC) can potentially reduce costs related to the production, transportation, storage, and distribution of physical cash, therefore allowing for a substantial reduction in cash consumption.

According to Kumar (2021), three notable properties of Central Bank Digital Currency (CBDC) are evident. The issuance of the currency would be facilitated by the central bank, with its sole availability being in digital format, thereby conferring legal tender status. According to prevailing beliefs, it is widely anticipated that the initial availability of Central Bank digital currency (CBDC) will be significantly limited.

Singh et al., (2022) conducted a study. Central Bank Digital Currencies (CBDCs) aim to establish a highly secure network that will exclusively grant access to the central bank and a select group of its affiliated financial institutions. Dupuis Gleason and Wang (year) categorized CBDC into three distinct groupings, namely CBDC Wholesale, Central Bank Accounts, and CBDC Popular, based on their comprehensive structural study. The innovative strategies implemented by the government will facilitate broader access to financial services, significantly enhancing the nation's capacity for innovation, technological progress, and entrepreneurial endeavors. Central Bank Digital Currencies (CBDCs) transactions resemble physical currency exchange and do not require financial institutions' involvement to assist and finalize these transactions.

Priyadarshini & Kar, (2021) conducted a study of improvements in cryptocurrency have elicited diverse responses from central banks, with most developed countries either acknowledging their existence or granting them legal recognition through non-regulatory oversight and taxation measures. In recent times, central banks have expressed their support for Central Bank Digital Currencies (CBDCs), partly due to the development of the cryptocurrency industry. The experiences of numerous countries, both large and small, worldwide demonstrate how using technology like Central Bank Digital Currencies (CBDCs) can potentially improve India's payment system.

Chu et al., (2022), stated that ongoing initiatives are being undertaken to establish interconnections between several nations' Central Bank Digital Currency (CBDC) systems to enhance cross-border payment capabilities. As mentioned earlier, the interactions involving Central Bank Digital Currency (CBDC) systems across many nations demonstrate the advancement and enhancement of the domestic CBDC framework. India will proactively exchange and trade information, establish partnerships, and develop procedures to mitigate potential adverse consequences. As the Reserve Bank of India (RBI) aligns with global trends and undertakes research on Central Bank Digital Currencies (CBDCs), India must know the international dangers, problems, and research goals associated with CBDCs. Regarding the legal framework, policymakers should understand the disparate legal structure of payments throughout India and provide a comprehensive framework for regulating and overseeing such payments. Central Bank Digital Currencies (CBDCs) offer enhanced convenience, security, and anonymity. In order to address the potential dangers and issues associated with the implementation of digital bank notes, it is imperative for researchers and policymakers to actively communicate and advocate for the essential design components of this monetary system.

In a study by Tripathi et al., (2022) examined that Central Bank Digital Currency (CBDC) is relatively nascent, presenting significant potential with notable challenges that must be addressed. Central Bank Digital Currency (CBDC) has the potential to enhance financial inclusion and bolster fiscal and monetary policies. The Reserve Bank of India (RBI) and the Government of India are commendably executing the adoption of technology during its nascent phases. This demonstrates the nation's prospective outlook and trajectory while presenting numerous benefits. Despite certain advancements, the available information on decentralized and digital currencies is considerably limited. The development of Central Bank Digital Currency (CBDC) necessitates the involvement of professionals at various levels, from the initial to the latter stages of the process. By employing a well-crafted design and strategic roadmap and implementing a phased approach to task allocation, the likelihood of achieving flawless plan execution is significantly enhanced.

Auer et al., (2022) says that if Central Bank Digital Currencies (CBDCs) are appropriately and effectively designed, they present a potential avenue for enhancing payment and savings mechanisms using technologically advanced digital money issued by central banks. These CBDCs possess unique attributes that can only be provided by central banks and thus have the potential to serve as a foundational element for the future of digital currency. The adoption of cross-border central bank digital currencies (CBDCs) will depend on several key factors, including market acceptance, uniformity in anti-money laundering and combating the financing of terrorism (AML/CFT) measures, and accessibility to payment systems. It is important to note that current payment systems and arrangements possess distinct characteristics and enhancements, such as aligning regulatory, supervisory, and oversight frameworks for cross-border transactions. The individual in question is D. Priyadarshini.

According to Kar (2021), introducing Central Bank Digital Currency (CBDC) in India is an unavoidable development, as it pertains to the timing and manner in which it will be implemented rather than whether it will be implemented. India must implement a Central Bank Digital Currency (CBDC) to preserve global digital and financial security. Nevertheless, there are several apprehensions about fiscal viability. The potential for expedited success is heightened when central bank digital currencies (CBDCs) collaborate with existing and anticipated future payment infrastructure. Central Bank Digital Currencies (CBDCs) present a means by which the central bank can establish a direct communication channel with the wider populace, potentially enhancing the effectiveness of monetary policy transmission.

According to a recent study by Samudrala and Yerchuru (2021), several similarities exist between the issuance of Central Bank Digital Currency (CBDC) and a cask. The introduction of Central Bank Digital Currency (CBDC) necessitates implementing enhanced financial inclusion, improved monetary policy, and adopting a robust and up-to-date payment infrastructure. The Central Bank Digital Currency (CBDC) is subject to limitations that hinder its ability to achieve its intended goals effectively. The identification of an optimal central bank digital currency (CBDC) design has been presented in several domains, considering factors such as the cost of credit and financial stability. This includes striking a balance between limiting the holding of CBDC and enabling consumers to keep as much CBDC as desired.

Abhishek Kumar 2021 states that numerous nations across the globe have initiated investigations into the Central Bank Digital Currency (CBDC) and have also implemented trial initiatives. For instance, Sweden's central bank introduced a digital currency called the e-Krona in response to a noticeable decrease in cash utilization. In 2018, a mere 6% of the aggregate household payments were conducted using physical currency. Similarly, Uruguay has introduced the e-peso, a retail version of the Central Bank Digital Currency (CBDC). Additionally, Ukraine has also developed its digital currency, known as the e-Hryvnia. Implementing a central bank digital currency (CBDC) is expected to yield several benefits for the Reserve Bank of India (RBI), including a cost reduction in cash management and the establishment of a more robust framework for a society that relies less on physical currency. Central Bank Digital Currency (CBDC) has the potential to facilitate the modernization of the payment system, enhance digitization efforts, decrease reliance on foreign currency, and serve as a mechanism for expanding monetary and fiscal policy. Central Bank Digital Currency (CBDC) has the potential to mitigate risks and enhance accessibility by enabling round-the-clock availability and reducing expenses associated with cross-border transactions. This is particularly relevant as cross-border payments involve numerous substantial fees and intricate processes. The implementation of wholesale central bank digital currencies (CBDCs) has the potential to streamline the automation process. If the central bank digital currency (CBDC) is appropriately developed, it can improve financial stability and integrity compared to traditional cash. Implementing an efficient retail central bank digital currency (CBDC) can potentially mitigate the expenses linked to cash utilization. The implementation of Central Bank Digital Currency (CBDC) is expected to have a positive impact not only on the welfare of citizens but also on the growth and development of the digital economy.

According to the study conducted by Auer et al. (2020), considerable emphasis has been devoted to examining the macroeconomic ramifications of monetary policy and the microeconomic utilisation of operational structures, technology, and privacy in developing the Central Bank Digital Currency (CBDC).

Han et al., (2019) have asserted that the Central Bank Digital Currency (CBDC) can yield significant resolutions of financial inclusion and payment systems. The Central Bank Digital Currency (CBDC) is a complex digital infrastructure that can provide global advantages and disruptions. Central Bank Digital Currency (CBDC) is deemed to possess a high level of safety and efficacy, necessitating a significant skill level for its successful implementation.

According to Kumar (2021), the legalisation of Central Bank Digital Currency (CBDC) in India necessitates the change of several laws. The expeditious advancement of numerous legislative measures, such as the Data Protection Bill of 2021 and the Crypto Currency and Regulation of Official Digital Currency Bill of 2021, may necessitate prompt action by the federal government. The Reserve Bank of India (RBI) can temporarily create Central Bank Digital Currency (CBDC). The acceptance of digitization in India necessitates continuous breakthroughs in the process, coupled with establishing a robust regulatory framework. The Reserve Bank of India (RBI) has proactively established the requisite regulatory and monitoring mechanisms for implementing Central Bank Digital Currency (CBDC) in India.

Kumari (2021) Due to the substantial magnitude of the Central Information Centre's (CIC) operations, it is not feasible for the Central Bank Digital Currency (CBDC) to serve as a viable alternative. Consequently, despite the potential implementation of Central Bank Digital Currency (CBDC) in India, a temporary requirement for physical currency would persist. In order to monitor the extent of utilisation during the initial phases of Central Bank Digital Currency (CBDC) implementation, it is possible to impose a limitation on the volume, constraining it within the range of 1% to 2% of the Currency in Circulation (CIC). The expansion of CIC must be driven by technology to enhance its appeal and facilitate frictionless transactions, hence increasing its adoption. The potential efficacy of Central Bank Digital Currency (CBDC) implementation in India is contingent upon using dependable technological infrastructure and establishing a robust security framework.

The Central Bank Digital Currency (CBDC) possesses a heightened susceptibility to cyber threats compared to other platforms inside the nation, primarily due to its status as the largest digital transactions platform in the country. The efficacy of Central Bank Digital Currency (CBDC) hinges on a meticulous and cautious approach to its expansion, including the incorporation of robust safety measures and stringent security protocols. The citation provided is in the format of an academic reference, indicating the author's name and the year of publication. Implementing central bank digital currency (CBDC) will influence the execution of monetary policy, the transmission mechanism, and, at times, the very strategy of monetary policy itself. Interest rates and deposit rates experience substantial influences. Introducing a central bank digital currency (CBDC) is anticipated to have a multifaceted economic impact. On one side, it is expected to provide positive outcomes by diminishing transaction costs fostering increased outputs and welfare. However, it is important to acknowledge that this may also result in inflationary pressures. On the other hand, implementing an account-based CBDC poses potential risks to the financial system's stability.

Morales-Resendiz et al., (2021) conducted a study on the topic. Certain central banks have contemplated providing mechanisms for individuals to engage in financial transactions utilizing currency that the central bank ultimately supports. This initiative aims to enhance safety and stability within the financial system.

3. RESEARCH METHODOLOGY

The data and information interpreted in this research paper are secondary. This data was collected from various other research papers and websites, newsletters, articles, and journals related to the topic of CBCD. Some of the data was also collected from the BIS and RBI websites.

3.1. Objectives

- To study the need for implementation of CBDC in India.
- To study how a big project such as CBDC is implemented.
- To understand the challenges and limitations of CBDC.
- To study the effects on the economy and policies of CBDC in India.

4. DISCUSSIONS AND FINDINGS

In May 2020, a limited number of around 35 countries exhibited a discernible interest in Central Bank Digital Currency (CBDC). Currently, a significant number of nations, around 105, comprising more than 95% of the world's gross domestic product (GDP), are actively researching Central Bank digital currencies (CBDCs). Nearly 50 nations are engaged in the advanced research and development stage of Central Bank Digital Currencies (CBDCs). With that being stated, ten countries have successfully implemented digital currency. Notably, China, at the forefront of digital currency development, is scheduled to commence its pilot program in 2023. Jamaica has just introduced a Central Bank Digital Currency (CBDC) called Jam-DEX. Nigeria, the largest economy in Africa, initiated the rollout of the Central Bank Digital Currency (CBDC) in October 2021. Numerous nations are currently exploring alternative mechanisms for conducting international financial transactions.

The ongoing momentum in the exploration and investigation of Central Bank digital currencies (CBDCs) and digital national currencies is expected to persist, particularly in response to the imposition of financial sanctions on Russia. There are nine ongoing trials of cross-border wholesale central bank digital currency (CBDC) transactions between banks and three cross-border retail CBDC initiatives. According to the Atlantic Council website, it is probable that the global financial network will encounter a substantial challenge to consistency in the foreseeable future. Implementing various Central Bank Digital Currency (CBDC) modules would necessitate the establishment of novel international standards. Central Bank Digital Currency (CBDC) refers to a novel monetary form that is under the control and issuance of a central banking authority. It is intended to replace conventional physical currency, albeit initially on a limited scale.

However, there are plans to expand its use in the future gradually. The implementation and research of CBDC in India are projected to commence during the financial year 2022–23. The implementation of a central bank digital currency (CBDC) is expected to have a substantial impact on the digital economy. This development is anticipated to reduce expenses associated with cash transactions and facilitate the seamless transfer and utilization of funds, including cross-border money transfers. The Society for Worldwide Interbank Financial Telecommunication (SWIFT) is presently utilized as a primary mechanism for conducting overseas transactions, and it is also employed as a means to enforce sanctions on nations, including Russia. The G-10 conducts the oversight of this matter. Two primary Central Bank digital currencies (CBDC) categories are retail CBDC and wholesale CBDC.

The wholesale CBDC primarily facilitates expedited transactions for major financial institutions like banks. By implementing a CBDC, banks can enhance the efficiency of their transactions and streamline cross-border transactions. Retail central bank digital currency (CBDC) primarily replaces conventional physical cash by assuring users that the central government is behind it. Central Bank Digital Currencies (CBDCs) represent a novel and updated iteration of currency, offering numerous advantages and applications, particularly within our swiftly evolving global landscape. If properly conceived and executed, Central Bank Digital Currency (CBDC) can positively impact monetary policy, financial stability, and the effectiveness of payment systems. In addition to the benefits mentioned earlier, Central Bank Digital Currencies (CBDCs) would supplement existing monetary systems and enhance payment modalities.

The user's text does not provide any information to rewrite academically. In order to mitigate illegal activities such as counterfeiting and money laundering, research indicates that the Reserve Bank of India (RBI) recognized approximately 6.9% of counterfeit banknotes, whereas other banks together identified around 91.3%. Using digital currency would yield cost reductions in handling physical cash, including expenses associated with printing and transportation. It would also decrease transaction costs, significantly benefiting the general population. According to a report published in 2022, around 130 million individuals in India and nearly 1.7 billion individuals worldwide lack access to banking services, rendering them unbanked. The introduction of Central Bank Digital Currency (CBDC) presents an opportunity to enhance financial inclusion by facilitating more convenient and cost-effective transactions. While attaining this goal may require significant effort, it is feasible to accomplish it, provided proper design principles are employed.

Implementing Central Bank Digital Currency (CBDC) in India is imperative due to several external factors. This move would benefit the government and the public and serve as a protective measure to safeguard India's digital and financial stability. Many countries, including China, have already initiated the development of their digital currencies, such as the digital Yuan, for both domestic and international trade purposes. If the digital Yuan gains global recognition, there is a possibility of it inundating the Indian market, thereby posing a risk of dollarization. The issuance, control, and regulation of the Central Bank Digital Currency (CBDC) would be entrusted to the Central Bank (RBI). The CBDC would utilize a centralized blockchain system exclusively under the control and supervision of the RBI. Central Bank Digital Currencies (CBDCs) are expected to coexist with traditional currency, given the challenges associated with eliminating currency in circulation (CIS).

CBDCs are likely to be utilized for significant or medium-to-large-scale transactions, while smaller transactions may continue to rely on traditional currency. As per the Reserve Bank of India (RBI), implementing central bank digital currency (CBDC) in India would follow a graded approach. This approach aims to enhance control and mitigate risks by progressing through several stages, including 'Proof of Concept', pilot programs, and the eventual launch. The Proof of Concept (POC) serves as the preliminary phase of implementation, during which the idea is tested to validate if the intended outcomes can be achieved through the proposed implementation. Additionally, it is imperative to ensure that the Central Bank Digital Currency (CBDC) remains by monetary policy and financial stability. During the present fiscal year, the Central Bank Digital Currency (CBDC) would maintain a fixed exchange rate with the Indian rupee, whereby 1 unit of the Indian digital rupee would be equivalent to 1 unit. Implementing Central Bank Digital Currency (CBDC) will commence following thorough research and planning in Tier 1 cities. Subsequently, more steps will be taken based on the outcomes of this initial phase.

However, the total implementation of CBDC in India is anticipated to require significant time. Despite the numerous advantages associated with Central Bank Digital Currency (CBDC), its adoption presents certain challenges. The direct engagement of the central bank with households and businesses would necessitate an expanded role for the Reserve Bank of India (RBI), prompting a redefinition of its functions. This expanded role may burden the RBI, necessitating delegating certain responsibilities to other financial institutions. The Central Bank digital currency (CBDC) may encounter additional obstacles, including the potential for adverse effects on financial stability if its design is inadequate. This might result in bank disintermediation and significant ramifications for the basic operations of banks. Financial literacy is also a pertinent concern, given that one of the primary objectives of implementing Central Bank Digital Currency (CBDC) is to promote financial inclusion. However, the attainment of this goal may be hindered by the prevailing lack of financial literacy among the populace.

Implementing a centralized digital currency, a Central Bank Digital Currency (CBDC), would eliminate transactional anonymity since all financial transactions could be traced. This would have implications for the privacy of the general population, as it would render their financial activities transparent to the Reserve Bank of India (RBI). Introducing a central bank digital currency (CBDC) in India would have significant implications, including various aspects such as economic transformations and the influence on existing policies. Primarily, adopting a CBDC would lead to a transition towards a cashless economy since the digitization of currency would result in a reduction in physical cash circulation. According to the BFSI newsletter, there has been an observed enhancement in monetary transmission due to reduced cash circulation. This is attributed to the central bank's ability to introduce interest-bearing currencies, which improves transmission and leads to more comparable interest rates in the market.

Additionally, the emergence of fintech companies presents an avenue for increased competition in card payments and banking, mitigating the risk of monopolization by payment providers. Moreover, it is imperative to regulate private digital currencies to mitigate potential risks to the nation. These currencies have the potential to facilitate illicit operations and terrorism, as a significant number of transactions remain unnoticed. Central Bank Digital Currencies (CBDCs) are expected to affect many policies. The Reserve Bank of India (RBI) has indicated that the CBDC will incorporate an expiration policy wherein funds held in CBDC accounts may expire if not utilized before the designated expiration date. The concept of "hustle escape" has been addressed in a recent newsletter. Central Bank Digital Currencies (CBDCs) possess the potential to facilitate the distribution of helicopter money directly to individuals, eliminating the reliance on traditional financial institutions. This mechanism allows for the seamless transfer of funds to citizens with a simple push of a button, in contrast to the old method, which necessitated involvement from financial intermediaries. Implementing Central Bank Digital Currency (CBDC) would diminish commercial banks' role, necessitating the Reserve Bank of India (RBI) to assume responsibilities formerly held by these banks, such as providing lending services.

5. CONCLUSION

We have seen the pros and cons of CBDC and the effects it has on the economy and the policies; though all factors suggest and point towards the direction of implementing CBDC, it still is risky and poses many risks to even countries such as the US are struggling with the implementation of Digital Currency. Countries like China have implemented it and are even using it in international trade, and countries such as Singapore, Malaysia, Australia, and South Africa are on the verge of moving forward with one of the world's first cross-border digital currencies. Along with the global competition and the need to protect financial and digital security and stability, India would sooner or later have to implement Digital Currency, but it must be properly designed and must have a properly defined structure to succeed. The conclusion might have limitations because this report is based on secondary data. Even with some of the limitations in India, such as financial illiteracy and such a huge population, India can succeed with CBDC as India is a vast market with people's knowledge evolving and growing rapidly and a huge youngster population, which will help in the spread and success of CBDC.

5.1. Future Scope and Limitations

Considering this report utilizes secondary data as its major source of information, there is a risk that certain hypotheses cannot be represented accurately, which may result in certain constraints. Given that this study uses secondary data as its primary source of information, there is a possibility that certain of the hypotheses cannot be represented exactly. In order to get data that can be relied upon, it is required to conduct targeted surveys on topics such as CBDC and financial literacy in geographically remote areas. In addition, gathering data on the current development status in each nation in real time is essential.

REFERENCES

Alonso, N., Jorge-Vazquez, S. L., & Reier Forradellas, J. (2021). Central banks digital currency: Detection of optimal countries for the implementation of a CBDC and the implication for payment industry open innovation. *Journal of Open Innovation*, *7*(1).

Armelius, H., Claussen, C. A., & Hull, I. (2021). *On the possibility of a cash-like CBDC*. Sveriges Riksbank Staff memo.

Auer, R., Cornelli, G., & Frost, J. (2020). *Rise of the central bank digital currencies: drivers, approaches, and technologies*. Academic Press.

Auer, R., Frost, J., Gambacorta, L., Monnet, C., Rice, T., & Shin, H. S. (2022). Central bank digital currencies: Motives, economic implications, and the research frontier. *Annual Review of Economics*, *14*(1), 697–721. doi:10.1146/annurev-economics-051420-020324

Babu, S., & Abraham, K. M. (2021). Central bank digital currencies: policy and operational perspectives for India. *CSI Transactions on ICT, 9*(2), 85-94.

Bhowmik, D. (2022). Monetary policy implications of central bank digital currency with special reference to India. *Asia-Pacific Journal of Management and Technology*, *2*(3), 1–8.

Chu, Y., Lee, J., Kim, S., Kim, H., Yoon, Y., & Chung, H. (2022). Review of Offline Payment Function of CBDC Considering Security Requirements. *Applied Sciences (Basel, Switzerland)*, *12*(9), 4488. doi:10.3390/app12094488

D, P., & Kar, S. (2022). Assessing the viability of an Indian central bank digital currency (CBDC). *Indian Public Policy Review*, *3*(3), 43–58. doi:10.55763/ippr.2022.03.03.003

Eichengreen, B., Gupta, P., & Marple, T. (2022). A Central Bank Digital Currency For India? *Indian Public Policy Review*, *3*(4), 1–29. doi:10.55763/ippr.2022.03.04.001

Han, X., Yuan, Y., & Wang, F.-Y. (2019). A blockchain-based framework for central bank digital currency. In *2019 IEEE International Conference on Service Operations and Logistics, and Informatics (SOLI)*. IEEE. 10.1109/SOLI48380.2019.8955032

Kumar, A. (2021). Central Bank Digital Currency and its impact on the Indian Financial system. *Asian Journal of Management*, 420–422. Advance online publication. doi:10.52711/2321-5763.2021.00063

Kumari, J. M. (2021). Central Bank Digital Currency (CBDC) Can it Replace Notes and Coins in India. *Management*, *8*(S1), 21–28.

Morales-Resendiz, R., Ponce, J., Picardo, P., Velasco, A., Chen, B., Sanz, L., & Hodge, A. (2021). Implementing a retail CBDC: Lessons learned and key insights. *Latin American Journal of Central Banking*, *2*(1), 100022. doi:10.1016/j.latcb.2021.100022

Padhi, P. K. (2022). *Emergence of Central Bank Digital Currency In Indian Perspective: A Conceptual Analysis*. An Approach Towards Central Bank Digital Currency.

Priyadarshini, D., & Kar, S. (2021). *Central Bank digital currency (CBDC): Critical issues and the Indian perspective*. Academic Press.

Singh, A., John, D. P., & Jacob, A. P. (2022). A Review of Central Bank Digital Currencies. *Ushus Journal of Business Management*, *21*(1), 79–95. doi:10.12725/ujbm.58.5

Thanapackiam, D., Nk, C., & Goudar, K. (2022). The Factors Affecting Implementing Crypto Currencies in India. *Journal of Positive School Psychology*, *6*(7), 771–779.

Tripathi, S., Chaubey, A., & Goel, I. (2022). An empirical analysis of potential Central Bank Digital Currency adoption procedure by Indian government and its implications. *Sachetas*, *1*(1), 32–38. doi:10.55955/110006

Chapter 23
Tourist Behaviour Analysis Using Data Analytics

L. Maria Michael Visuwasam
RMK College of Engineering and Technology, India

M. Srinath
RMK College of Engineering and Technology, India

V. S. Aswin Raj
RMK College of Engineering and Technology, India

A. Sirajudeen
RMK College of Engineering and Technology, India

S. Sudhir Maharaaja
RMK College of Engineering and Technology, India

Dakshin Raja
RMK College of Engineering and Technology, India

ABSTRACT

There has been a lot of hurry in the tourism business in recent years, and the rise of IT technology has had a major impact on vacationers. In recent years, numerous studies of big data have been devoted to analysing tourists' behaviour. Decision-making support from big data analytics has only been shown in a small number of studies. The proliferation of social media's ability to gather massive amounts of data has opened up new avenues for research and improved insights for policymakers. The purpose of this chapter is to gain a deeper comprehension of the motivations behind visitors' actions, as well as the environmental and social influences that shape their experiences. The digital lifestyle pattern outlines the idea of tourist behaviour, bridges the gap between the tourist and the digital world, and allows us to zero in on how that behaviour evolves over time. Using the idea of a digital lifestyle pattern, we may build strategies for the behaviour of tourists.

DOI: 10.4018/979-8-3693-2193-5.ch023

1. INTRODUCTION

Over the past few decades, tourism has been an increasingly significant contributor to national economies around the world. It's one of the biggest industries, and although having a major impact on the environment, it's creating opportunity for national economies to grow and prosper (Dwyer et al., 2020). The economic impact of tourism on the world in 2019 is estimated at €9.5 trillion, or 10.9% of global GDP and 10.8% of total employment. Tourism in Europe is responsible for €2.7 billion ($3.3 billion), 7.1% of GDP, and 37.1 million jobs (Global Economic Impact & Trends 2020, 2020). Over the past ten years, the IT sector has began interacting with other sectors of the economy, including the travel sector. Smart tourism is the genius child of the convergence of data technologies and travel (Kontogianni & Alepis, 2020). Smart tourism, as defined by J, is defined as an approach to travel that makes use of modern information and communication technology to modify visitor experiences in order to make them more efficient and sustainable (Wang & Fesenmaier, 2013). (Lee et al., 2020). According to Li et al. (2017), recent years have seen an uptick in research into various statistical monitoring techniques employed by the tourism industry to keep tabs on customer habits. It can be used as a starting point for formulating a plan to boost tourist hotels' service quality and gain an edge in the market through increased efficiency (Regin et al., 2023).

About 2.7 billion foreign tourists visited the world in 2019, as reported by the UNWTO (United Nations World Tourism Organization, 2019). Between 2010 and 2030, the number of people who travel internationally is projected to grow by 3.3% year. Tourist behaviour analysis is a useful tool for establishing rapport with customers. A company's ability to serve its customers well and enhance their perception of the company depends on the quality of the services they provide to those customers, who are its tourists (Rajest et al., 2023a). Travelers can leverage AI-powered services in the tourist industry to automate tasks like promotion, attraction development, building, and enhancement of the trip experience (Li et al., 2017).

Effective tourist destinations are used and analysed based on a variety of factors that help other tourists make better-informed judgments about where to go (Rajest et al., 2023b). The abundance of information resources across a variety of channels presents a problem for this investigation since it forces vacationers to spend a considerable amount of time deliberating and organising their trips (Ocoró et al., 2023). Organizations in the hospitality industry may learn a great deal about how to keep their guests happy by conducting surveys and doing in-depth analyses of their customers' opinions, requirements, preferences, and experiences. In accordance with Reference (Pearce, 2005), the three main types of users that can profit from this analysis are visitors, government agencies, and private companies (Al Shraah et al., 2013). Improved tourist services allow visitors to immediately use behavioural analysis to their own development or that of their businesses (Al Shraah et al., 2022).

Wi-Fi hotspots and other mobile phone app terminals have enabled new technical means of observation thanks to advancements in network and Internet technologies. The vast majority of tourists now use smartphones while on vacation, and this has a tremendous effect on how they choose which sights to see. Cameras, gateways, Wi-Fi base stations, and other monitoring hardware are necessary for the flow monitoring approaches described by Kashevnik et al. (2019). Not all picturesque locations make it simple to set up and use (Priscila et al., 2023). Most smartphone apps (like Instagram) cater to a younger or middle-aged demographic and so cannot keep tabs on all types of travellers (Khaled Lafi Al-Naif and Ata E. M. Al Shraah, 2018). Thus, social networks are frequently utilised as the foundation for visitor behaviour prediction models based on many sources, such as user-generated material (photos/videos/

reviews). These models are frequently utilised to enhance technologically advanced tourist facilities (Al-maaitah et al., 2021a).

Researchers have investigated visitor traffic and actions at certain tourist attractions through a comprehensive study of tourist behaviour (Vashishtha & Kapoor, 2023).

A tourist behaviour study, data storage and presentation methods, and behaviour analysis tools are presented in this paper.

The authors suggest that we pursue the idea of a digital lifestyle pattern as a representation of the relationship between visitors and various facets of the tourist service industry (Jamal & Habib, 2020).

The digital way of life provides a single interface for all types of data, making it easy to comprehend how the tourist behaviour model was built (Al-maaitah et al., 2021b).

Three examples of behaviour analysis are presented, all of which make use of data collected from people's online activities via GSM (Geo-social media) and ANNs (Artificial Neural Networks) (Basheer & Hajmeer, 2000). (ANN) and User-Generated Maps (VGM) (Abu-Rumman and Qawasmeh, 2021).

These online communities are referred to as "geo-social media" (GSM). Event detection, movement analysis, and user behaviour are just few of the many research areas that have made use of GSM data. Multiple problems with GSM's ability to provide accurate information have been uncovered. The quantity and quality of the available data are the main limitations.

Flexible and data-driven, artificial neural networks (ANNs) may learn from examples and model causal links (Zhang et al., 1998). In recent years, the ANN's primary application has been in the analysis of Big Data (Najafabadi et al., 2015). Based on these data, new models for analysing tourist behaviour will be developed using artificial neural networks (Tripathi & Al-Shahri, 2023).

Social media is the source for Volunteered Geographic Information (VGI). Instagram, Twitter, and Facebook are just a few examples of social media that incorporate a geographical element by letting users tag their present location in posts (Angeline et al., 2023).

The developed system's primary flaw is that it does not account for users' past geo-location information in the affected area (Miah et al., 2017). One way to address the behaviour in question is to put into practise the tourist behaviour analysis system proposed here; the built existing models can make use of the prior geo-locations of the smart tourism system and boost the quality of tourism services for the users.

Therefore, the primary goal of this article is to analyse popular tourism destinations utilising handset GSM and VGI data. The goal of this article is to fully utilise the benefits of big data in order to successfully analyse visitor residence time, dimensional and temporal distribution, and behaviour.

The fundamental contribution of this work is a new general framework for analysing and visualising visitors' behaviour in urban areas based on their mobility patterns, which is achieved through the creative combination and expansion of current methodologies.

The findings of this experiment demonstrate that big data analysis can serve as a technical aid in the administration of tourist regions and significantly enhance the tracking of visitor traffic.

2. LITERATURE REVIEW

Here we will revisit the overview of seminal works, seminal articles, and other essential sources in the subject of Tourist Behaviour Analysis that we covered in the literature review part. In recent years, tourism has expanded at an impressive rate. In 2021, international travel increased by 4.1% from the previous year, as reported by the UNWTO (United Nations World Tourism Organization, 2019). (415 million versus 400 million). The number of overnight overseas visitors was 72% lower than it would have been in a year without a pandemic. This follows a 73 percent drop in overseas visitors in 2020. Travelers, government officials, and business owners are the primary audiences for this study's findings. Several recent studies have examined tourist behaviour from various angles.

In their paper "A Big Data Analytics Method for Tourist Behaviour Analysis" (Hasnat & Hasan, 2018), the authors suggest using Big Data analytics to aid in the decision-making processes of destination management organisations. This technique analyses social unstructured data to help tourism businesses make better long-term plans. Text analysis, spatial data clustering, image processing, and time series modelling are all a part of this approach. For this clustering, we employed the P-DBSCAN algorithm. Seasonal patterns were retrieved using a time series decomposition approach.

A framework for assessing tourist travel is presented in "Identifying visitors and analysing spatial patterns of their destinations from location-based social media data" (Yao et al., 2018). Sixty-seven thousand Floridians who use Twitter provided usable data. K-Means, DBSCAN, Mean-Shift, and other clustering algorithms, as well as a number of classification techniques, have been used by the authors in their examination of the data (Visuwasam & Raj, 2019).

A approach for anticipating both visitor numbers and demand is presented in "A Paired Neural Network Model for Tourist Arrival Forecasting" (Taczanowska et al., 2019). (Visuwasam & Raj, 2020). This new approach uses a paired neural network model in an innovative way (Abu-Rumman, 2021). By applying two low-pass filters to the data on visitor arrivals, we can separate out seasonal patterns and longer-term trends. The trend and seasonal component data were then used to estimate two independent three-layer autoregressive neural networks using an HP filter, a Wavelet transformation, and a moving average neural network, respectively (Saxena et al., 2023).

To paraphrase their article titled "Nature-based Tourism or Mass Tourism in Nature? Using 2,500 interviews with tourists as the primary data source, the authors of "Segmentation of Mountain Protected Area Visitors Using Self-Organizing Maps" (Maria Michael Visuwasam et al., 2020; Phithakkitnukoon et al., 2015) were able to identify four basic categories of tourist profiles.

A framework that makes use of the large-scale opportunistic mobile sensing technique is described in "tourist behaviour utilising large-scale mobile sensing approach: A case study of mobile phone users in Japan" (Nilashi et al., 2017). The behaviour is constructed using the tourists' smartphone GPS data, the number of journeys, and transit type tracks. Clustering of attractions for tourists is accomplished using the DBSCAN technique, and attraction types are determined using random forest classification.

The SOM method of clustering is used by the authors of "A recommender system for the tourism industry combining cluster ensemble and prediction machine learning approaches" (Liu et al., 2018). This model is able to successfully cluster the users' ratings. The SOM model is trained using data from TripAdvisor.

Relationships between popular tourist locations and web queries are described in "Big Data Analytics for Forecasting Tourism Destination Arrivals with the Applied Vector Autoregression Model" (Li & Cao, 2018). The auto-regression vector model established how variables including precipitation, temperature, and days off work affected vacationers' spending habits.

Wang et al., (2018) lay out the methodology used to predict the number of visitors to a destination each month. The authors present the deep network architecture by using time series data on the tourism industry. The LSTM model was enhanced to include a built-in attention mechanism. The interpretability of the provided model is enhanced by the attention mechanism.

The composition of a neural network for time series forecasting is described in "Optimal Forecast Combination Based on Neural Networks for Time Series Forecasting" (Huang et al., 2020). Component forecasting methods chosen by the authors include the back-propagation neural network, the dynamic architecture for artificial neural network, the Elman artificial neural network, and the echo state network. Each neural network's input-hidden neuron combination is calculated with the use of a custom-built heuristic. To get the corresponding combination weights, we investigate a neural network weighting method that uses in-sample training-validation pairs.

In order to analyse visitors' micro-scale spatial-temporal behaviour patterns, the authors of "Tourists' spatial-temporal behaviour patterns in theme Parks" (Bi et al., 2020) attempt to combine numerous data sources. Tourists' temporal-spatial behaviour was analysed using hand-held GPS trackers, and their socio-psychological traits were determined with the help of questionnaires. Density-centre cluster analysis revealed three distinct patterns of spatial-temporal behaviour based on the four parameters of path length, tour time, coverage area, and oval diameter.

Multivariate time series data, such as historical tourist volume data, search engine data, and weather data, are incorporated into LSTM networks by the authors of "Daily Tourism Volume Forecasting for Tourist Attractions" (Mikhailov et al., 2020). This model is recommended for use in estimating the average daily visitor flow to tourist destinations. The findings highlight the importance of search engine data and meteorological data in anticipating tourism volumes.

The following key issues were discovered among the considered solutions that need to be considered while creating a reference model of a tourist behaviour analysis system:

The examined articles only address one data source and one problem at a time, making it impossible to modify or expand the proposed systems. The systems don't think about how to file away the information they get, how to sort it, or how to analyse it.

The considered systems only make limited use of context parameters because of their extreme specialisation. To enhance your ability to forecast visitor behaviour, you can use a number of contextual characteristics to build extra relationships between the data and expose hidden dependencies.

Tourists' inadequate sensor-use of their different electronic devices. The retrieved information will allow for more precise monitoring of tourist hotspots, transportation methods, chance encounters, etc. While several of the examined articles make use of GPS devices, some just use a subset of such devices' capabilities, such as visiting specific landmarks.

3. PROPOSED SYSTEM

The main objective of our tourist behavior analysis is to identify the opinions of common people who travel to a certain place. We do this by analyzing a relatively unstructured and big data set, such as the photos and the comments people post on social media platforms such as Instagram, Facebook, and, in some cases, YouTube. From these comments and photos, we implement a sentiment analysis to find the accurate opinion of the tourists about the place. Various people travel to various places in the world. For each place, we analyze it accordingly and lay down a graphical representation of this data. From this graphical data representation, we can observe each place's tourist attraction and the behaviour and feedback of the tourists from those places.

From this feedback, we will identify the areas of improvement so that we can improve tourism to a large extent in those places. Considering tourist suggestions and requirements, we can make useful changes and introduce new benefits that will be useful for tourists in the future. Using these analysis data… the travel agencies and guides understand what they are doing wrong and improve accordingly to improve customer satisfaction and attract more customers.

The problem that we try to clear out is that some places are not liked by many since the population is increasing; we can clear out some tourist places for shelter or agriculture.

Now, about the unstructured big data set from social media, a lot of unwanted data can be filtered out, and only the required data can be properly extracted and used appropriately for the accuracy of our tourist behaviour analysis model. This is an automated process and never leaves out any unconsidered data. Every comment, every post, and every tweet can contain potential and useful information required by the model.

We use various applications for the working of our model. Some of these applications are:

- Jupyter Notebook
- Anaconda Navigator
- Flickr

Modules used in our model:

- Matplotlib
- Pandas
- OS model

Overall system architecture and explanation:

Figure 1. System architecture

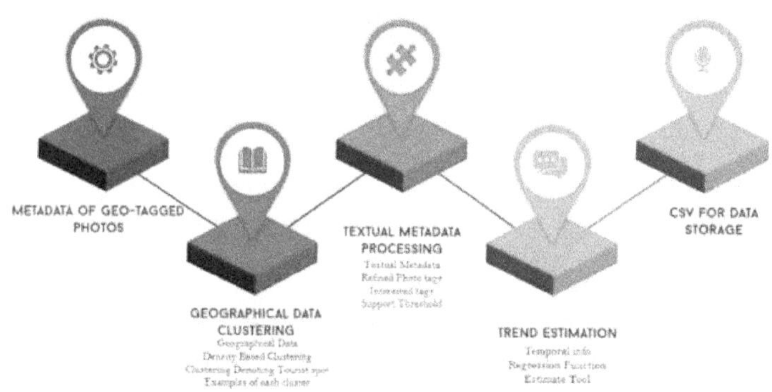

Our approach is to analyse the behaviour of tourists visiting the places (fig.1). To find the people's favorites and the most visited and less visited places, we take the data from social media like Facebook, Instagram, and other sites like Flickr and Twitter. We used k means clustering and random sampling algorithm to find the deviations and find a result; collecting the geo-tagged images, we can use digital pattern life ontology (Miah et al., 2017); geo-tagged images are the images that have the location address of the mobile device or the place where a person currently in. these photos would have been taken by the traveler in the current location using Flickr application interface we can easily take the data from the area which we need to extract data (Collection of domestic tourism statistics for the state of Goa, 2005). The area can be selected by passing the minimum latitude, longitude, and maximum latitude and longitude. The flick provides additional information like time and, date, etc. Our dataset includes name, region, distance, and rating. Surveys are also conducted to find the most and least visited places (Hasnat & Hasan, 2018).

Data Extraction

We extract data from the comments on social media, and by deriving more information from the text, we get more data about the tourist place (Mikhailov & Kashevnik, 2020). Location data are gathered to find the most visited place. Text analysis is a machine-learning approach to retrieve information about a particular source. The text we extract is unstructured and converting it into structured data is important and time-consuming. We classify the text using natural language processing (NLP) (Meob et al., 2021). Once the data is structured, the data will be meaningful. Using sentiment analysis, we can find whether the comment is good or bad by finding the frequency of each word. We can extract more data from the existing data itself; the unseen patterns should be identified and can be used. Web scrapping was done to extract data from sites; to do this, we used beautiful soap to extract data from HTML pages (Abu-Rumman and Qawasmeh, 2021). Geographical data clustering includes finding popular locations. By popular, we mean the most visited locations.

Data Pre-Processing

In data pre-processing, we clean the data set, convert the unstructured raw data to a structured form, and remove the unwanted data (Visuwasam et al., 2021).

Data cleansing:

The dataset is a raw set, and the values of the dataset should be accurate and must be cleaned. Cleaning is a process to convert the data into a structured form. The null values must be removed. Human errors, such as spelling mistakes, should be rectified.

Data transformation:

In data transformation, we change the cleaned data into rows and columns so that it can be meaningful.

Data reduction:

The unwanted part is removed, and when the data is smaller, the data can be handled easily and processed faster.

Now that we have extracted data and processed data. To store the data, we can store it in a CSV file, or we can have a separate database with tables. To process data, we can use Python and R as the language to interact with the data. In Python, we have data science tools and packages with predefined data processing functions.

Firstly, we create a workspace; there are many ways to create a workspace on many platforms like Google Collab. Etc. One famous software is the Anaconda Prompt with Jupyter Notebook with preinstalled libraries. We create a Python kernel and import the necessary mode. To view and process data, we use pandas. It is a library used in data manipulation and processing. Then, we upload the dataset, which is stored in a CSV file. The pandas are imported with a PD alias, and the CSV file is read with the read_csv() function. After that, we set the axis to reset the axis of the dataset. The null values and the empty sets are to be cleared and couldn't be processed. I eliminated extra zeros from the data by dividing it by 100. Using the iloc function, we can select the specific data row or column.

data.iloc[:,1:]=((data.iloc[:,1:])/100).astype('int')

Now that we don't have any null values. We add the Date and Time to keep the data updated and track the time of the data values. Using the describe() method in pandas, we can easily retrieve information like mean, median, standard deviation, count, percentile values, etc.

Data visualization and exploration:

To visualize and explore the data, matplotlib is a good and advanced library that provides methods to plot the graph and form clusters. Plotting, clustering, mapping, and comparisons are done to derive conclusions.

First, let us define the continents

continents = data[['DATE',
'OTHER EUROPE',
'EUROPEAN',
'SUM OF CIS',
'OTHER AMERICA',
'AMERICA',
'OTHER AFRICA',
'AFRICA',
'OTHER ASIA',
'ASIA',]]

To compare the tourist countries in recent years, we use the date time index function to depict the count

finalmonth=monthdata.groupby(['MONTH']).sum().mean(axis=1)
finalmonth=finalmonth.astype('int')
new_order = ['Jan', 'Feb', 'Mar', 'Apr', 'May', 'Jun', 'Jul', 'Aug', 'Sep', 'Oct', 'Nov', 'Dec']
finalmonth = finalmonth.reindex(new_order, axis=0)
set figure size to 10-15
set font size and rotation
plt.yticks(fontsize=17)
plt.title('Average Number of Tourists by Month')
plt.bar(final month.index,final month, color='blue')
display the graph

The locations that the tourists visit are plotted, and monthly plots are also made to analyze the most visited and less visited places.

4. RESULTS AND DISCUSSION

After processing the data, we came to a few conclusions regarding tourism frequency. A large amount of data gives a crucial behaviour of tourists. Analyzing the patterns in the data is very useful, and also, the patterns must be considered to see the deviations and the change; by finding these, we can see how far the tourist people visited and the places which are visited most.

We retrieve information about the total number of visitors by the year, as shown in fig.2.

Figure 2. Average number of tourist per year

YEAR	GERMANY	ALBANIA	AUSTRIA	BELGIUM	BOSNIA AND HERZEGOVINA	BULGARIA	CZECH REPUBLIC	DENMARK	ESTONIA	FINLAND	...	SINGAPORE	SYRIA	SUUDARABIA	THAILAN
2008	4396948	63945	505764	578680	60032	1512243	159224	277997	33686	102634	...	19143	398331	552	
2009	4481571	61247	537721	592651	54137	1623640	166505	296108	36845	138159	...	20070	501016	663	
2010	4370248	50163	497931	544728	47219	1448923	174508	314369	35136	143328	...	18921	891192	849	
2011	4815156	53286	530800	594679	54998	1399434	222228	371195	34809	187079	...	20745	965579	1169	
2012	5025660	59372	504026	612807	61644	1498461	223654	391467	35419	195490	...	22162	333728	1747	

As we can see, the visitor count is increasing in a few countries and decreasing in a few countries. Some of the places have lost their visitors. These places can be changed as some other source or improved according to people's likes. For monthly analysis is shown in fig.3.

Figure 3. Average number of tourist per month

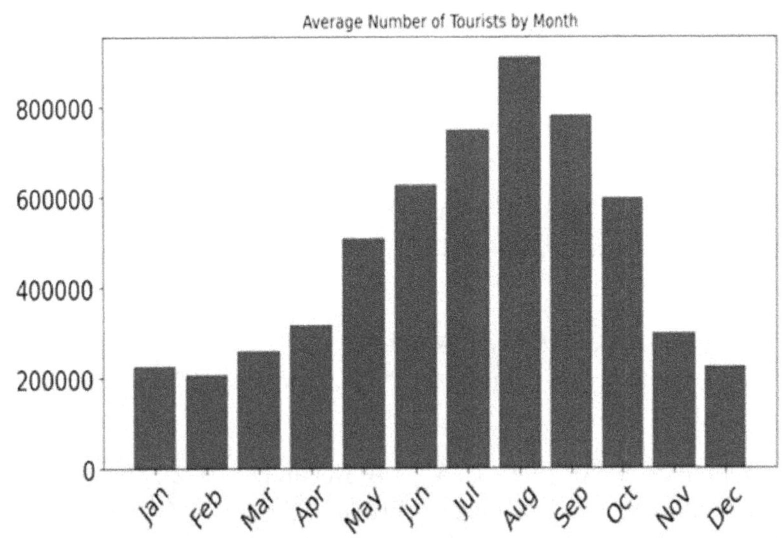

At the time of August, there is a maximum tourist count, and in December was found to be the least.

5. CONCLUSION

This chapter demonstrates the labour involved in collecting tourist datasets and performing preliminary processing on such datasets. We were able to determine the yearly and monthly analysis of tourist visits and tourist preferences with the data that we obtained. This demonstrated how to extract data from a number of different platforms as well as convert unstructured data into structured data. Because of this, we gained several insights, like which nations receive the most and the least visitors. Some of the less used areas can have human-like modifications or improvements made to them, or they can be demolished entirely if they cannot be brought up to date. The area can then be used to build apartments for humans to live in. Because the dataset contains potentially sensitive information, and because many of our decisions were based on the deviations that were found in the dataset, it is important that it be made as precise as possible. In order to obtain results, we carried out a number of different visualisations. In the future, we will make an effort to improve our processes, collect live datasets, and display the outcomes.

REFERENCES

Abu-Rumman, A. (2021). Effective Knowledge Sharing: A Guide to the Key Enablers and Inhibitors. In D. Tessier (Ed.), *Handbook of Research on Organizational Culture Strategies for Effective Knowledge Management and Performance* (pp. 133–156). IGI Global. doi:10.4018/978-1-7998-7422-5.ch008

Abu-Rumman, A., & Qawasmeh, R. (2021). Assessing international students' satisfaction of a Jordanian university using the service quality model. *Journal of Applied Research in Higher Education*. Advance online publication. doi:10.1108/JARHE-05-2021-0166

Al-maaitah, D. A., Tha'er Majali, M. A., & Almaaitah, T. A. (2021a). The role of leadership styles on staffs job satisfaction in public organizations. *Journal of Contemporary Issues in Business and Government*, *27*(1), 772–783.

Al-maaitah, T. A., Tha'er Majali, M. A., & Almaaitah, D. A. (2021b). The Impact of COVID-19 on the Electronic Commerce Users Behavior. *Journal of Contemporary Issues in Business and Government*, *27*(1), 772–783.

Al-Naif, K. L., & Al Shraah, A. E. M. (2018). Working capital management and profitability: Evidence from Jordanian mining and extraction industry sector. *IUG Journal of Economics and Business.*, *2*(1), 42–60.

Al Shraah, A., Abu-Rumman, A., Alqhaiwi, L. A., & AlSha'ar, H. (2022). The impact of sourcing strategies and logistics capabilities on organizational performance during the COVID-19 pandemic: Evidence from Jordanian pharmaceutical industries. *Uncertain Supply Chain Management*, *10*(3), 1077–1090. doi:10.5267/j.uscm.2022.2.004

Al Shraah, A., Irtaimeh, H. J., & Rumman, M. A. (2013). The Strategic Human Resource Management Practices in Implying Total Quality Management (TQM): An Empirical Study on Jordanian Banking Sector. *International Journal of Management*, *4*(5), 179–190.

Angeline, R., Aarthi, S., Regin, R., & Rajest, S. S. (2023). Dynamic intelligence-driven engineering flooding attack prediction using ensemble learning. In *Advances in Artificial and Human Intelligence in the Modern Era* (pp. 109–124). IGI Global. doi:10.4018/979-8-3693-1301-5.ch006

Basheer, I. A., & Hajmeer, M. (2000). Artificial neural networks: Fundamentals, computing, design, and application. *Journal of Microbiological Methods*, *43*(1), 3–31. doi:10.1016/S0167-7012(00)00201-3 PMID:11084225

Bi, J.-W., Liu, Y., & Li, H. (2020). Daily tourism volume forecasting for tourist attractions. *Annals of Tourism Research*, *83*(102923), 102923. doi:10.1016/j.annals.2020.102923

Collection of domestic tourism statistics for the state of Goa. (2005). Retrieved October 27, 2023, from Gov.in website: https://tourism.gov.in/sites/default/files/2020-04/03%20goa.pdf

Hasnat, M. M., & Hasan, S. (2018). Identifying tourists and analyzing spatial patterns of their destinations from location-based social media data. *Transportation Research Part C, Emerging Technologies*, *96*, 38–54. doi:10.1016/j.trc.2018.09.006

Huang, X., Li, M., Zhang, J., Zhang, L., Zhang, H., & Yan, S. (2020). Tourists' spatial-temporal behavior patterns intheme parks: A case study of Ocean Park Hong Kong. *J. Destin. Mark. Manag.*

Jamal, S., & Habib, M. A. (2020). Smartphone and daily travel: How the use of smartphone applications affect travel decisions. *Sustainable Cities and Society*, *53*(101939). doi:10.1016/j.scs.2019.101939

Kashevnik, A., Mikhailov, S., Papadakis, H., & Fragopoulou, P. (2019). Context-driven tour planning service: An approach based on synthetic coordinates recommendation. In *2019 24th Conference of Open Innovations Association (FRUCT)*. IEEE.

Kontogianni, A., & Alepis, E. (2020). Smart tourism: State of the art and literature review for the last six years. *Array (New York, N.Y.)*, *6*(100020). doi:10.1016/j.array.2020.100020

Lee, P., Hunter, W. C., & Chung, N. (2020). Smart tourism city: Developments and transformations. *Sustainability (Basel)*, *12*(10), 3958. doi:10.3390u12103958

Li, Y., & Cao, H. (2018). Prediction for tourism flow based on LSTM neural network. *Procedia Computer Science*, *129*, 277–283. doi:10.1016/j.procs.2018.03.076

Li, Y., Hu, C., Huang, C., & Duan, L. (2017). The concept of smart tourism in the context of tourism information services. *Tourism Management*, *58*, 293–300. doi:10.1016/j.tourman.2016.03.014

Liu, Y.-Y., Tseng, F.-M., & Tseng, Y.-H. (2018). Big Data analytics for forecasting tourism destination arrivals with the applied Vector Autoregression model. *Technological Forecasting and Social Change*, *130*, 123–134. doi:10.1016/j.techfore.2018.01.018

Maria Michael Visuwasam, L., Paulraj, D., Gayathri, G., Divya, K., Hariprasath, S., & Jayaprakashan, A. (2020). Intelligent personal digital assistants and smart destination platform (SDP) for globetrotter. *Journal of Computational and Theoretical Nanoscience*, *17*(5), 2254–2260. doi:10.1166/jctn.2020.8880

Meob, P. D., Fiumarac, G., & Baumgartnerd, R. (2021). *Web Data Extraction, Applications and Techniques: A Survey*. Emilio Ferraraa.

Miah, S. J., Vu, H. Q., Gammack, J., & McGrath, M. (2017). A big data analytics method for tourist behaviour analysis. *Information & Management*, *54*(6), 771–785. doi:10.1016/j.im.2016.11.011

Mikhailov, S., & Kashevnik, A. (2020). Tourist behaviour analysis based on digital pattern of life—An approach and case study. *Future Internet*, *12*(10), 165. doi:10.3390/fi12100165

Mikhailov, S., Kashevnik, A., & Smirnov, A. (2020). Tourist Behaviour Analysis Based on Digital Pattern of Life. *2020 7th International Conference on Control, Decision and Information Technologies (CoDIT)*.

Najafabadi, M. M., Villanustre, F., Khoshgoftaar, T. M., Seliya, N., Wald, R., & Muharemagic, E. (2015). Deep learning applications and challenges in big data analytics. *Journal of Big Data*, *2*(1), 1. doi:10.118640537-014-0007-7

Nilashi, M., Bagherifard, K., Rahmani, M., & Rafe, V. (2017). A recommender system for tourism industry using cluster ensemble and prediction machine learning techniques. *Computers & Industrial Engineering*, *109*, 357–368. doi:10.1016/j.cie.2017.05.016

Ocoró, M. P., Polo, O. C. C., & Khandare, S. (2023). Importance of Business Financial Risk Analysis in SMEs According to COVID-19. *FMDB Transactions on Sustainable Management Letters*, *1*(1), 12–21.

Pearce, P. L. (2005). *Tourist behaviour: Themes and Conceptual Schemes*. Channel View Publications. doi:10.21832/9781845410247

Phithakkitnukoon, S., Horanont, T., Witayangkurn, A., Siri, R., Sekimoto, Y., & Shibasaki, R. (2015). Understandingtourist behavior using large-scale mobile sensing approach: A case study of mobile phone users in Japan. *Pervasive and Mobile Computing*, *18*, 18–39. doi:10.1016/j.pmcj.2014.07.003

Priscila, S. S., Rajest, S. S., Tadiboina, S. N., Regin, R., & András, S. (2023). Analysis of Machine Learning and Deep Learning Methods for Superstore Sales Prediction. *FMDB Transactions on Sustainable Computer Letters*, *1*(1), 1–11.

Rajest, S. S., Singh, B., Obaid, A. J., Regin, R., & Chinnusamy, K. (Eds.). (2023b). Advances in Computational Intelligence and Robotics *Advances in artificial and human intelligence in the modern era*. doi:10.4018/979-8-3693-1301-5

Rajest, S. S., Singh, B., Obaid, J. A., Regin, R., & Chinnusamy, K. (Eds.). (2023a). Recent developments in machine and human intelligence. Advances in Computational Intelligence and Robotics. doi:10.4018/978-1-6684-9189-8

Regin, R., Khanna, A. A., Krishnan, V., Gupta, M., Bose, R. S., & Rajest, S. S. (2023). Information design and unifying approach for secured data sharing using attribute-based access control mechanisms. In Recent Developments in Machine and Human Intelligence (pp. 256–276). IGI Global.

Saxena, D., Khandare, S., & Chaudhary, S. (2023). An Overview of ChatGPT: Impact on Academic Learning. *FMDB Transactions on Sustainable Techno Learning*, *1*(1), 11–20.

Taczanowska, K., González, L., García-Massó, X., Zięba, A., Brandenburg, C., Muhar, A., Pellicer-Chenoll, M., & Toca-Herrera, J.-L. (2019). Nature-based Tourism or Mass Tourism in Nature? Segmentation of Mountain ProtectedArea Visitors Using Self-Organizing Maps (SOM). *Sustainability (Basel)*, *11*(5), 1314. doi:10.3390u11051314

Tripathi, S., & Al-Shahri, M. (2023). Problems and Prospects on the Evolution of Advertising and Public Relations Industries in Oman. *FMDB Transactions on Sustainable Management Letters*, *1*(1), 1–11.

Vashishtha, E., & Kapoor, H. (2023). Implementation of Blockchain Technology Across International Healthcare Markets. *FMDB Transactions on Sustainable Technoprise Letters*, *1*(1), 1–12.

Visuwasam, L. M. M., & Raj, D. P. (2019). NMA: Integrating big data into a novel mobile application using knowledge extraction for big data analytics. *Cluster Computing*, *22*(S6), 14287–14298. doi:10.100710586-018-2287-8

Visuwasam, L. M. M., & Raj, D. P. (2020). A distributed intelligent mobile application for analyzing travel big data analytics. *Peer-to-Peer Networking and Applications*, *13*(6), 2036–2052. doi:10.100712083-019-00799-z

Visuwasam, L. M. M., Swaminathan, S., Rajalakshmi, S., & Kumar, K. P. (2021). A Hotspot Framework for Analyzing Geolocated Travel Data Using Spark. *Annals of RSCB*, 1956–1966.

Wang, D., & Fesenmaier, D. R. (2013). Transforming the travel experience: The use of smartphones for travel. In *Information and Communication Technologies in Tourism 2013* (pp. 58–69). Springer Berlin Heidelberg. doi:10.1007/978-3-642-36309-2_6

Wang, L., Wang, Z., Qu, H., & Liu, S. (2018). Optimal Forecast Combination Based on Neural Networks for TimeSeries Forecasting. *Applied Soft Computing*, *66*, 1–17. doi:10.1016/j.asoc.2018.02.004

World Tourism Organization (UNWTO). (Ed.). (2019). *International Tourism Highlights, 2019 Edition. World Tourism Organization*. UNWTO.

Yao, Y., Cao, Y., Ding, X., Zhai, J., Liu, J., Luo, Y., & Zou, K. (2018). A paired neural network model for tourist arrival forecasting. *Expert Systems with Applications*, *114*, 588–614. doi:10.1016/j.eswa.2018.08.025

Zhang, G., Patuwo, B. E., & Hu, M. Y. (1998). Forecasting with artificial neural networks: The state of the art. *International Journal of Forecasting*, *14*, 35–62. doi:10.1016/S0169-2070(97)00044-7

Chapter 24
A Study on Consumer Preference and Satisfaction Towards Various Brands of Hair Shampoo in Ahmedabad City:
Consumer Preference and Satisfaction Towards Hair Shampoo Brands

Nupur Rawal
GLS University, India

Gurmeet Sikh Singh
GLS University, India

ABSTRACT

Hair shampoo plays a wide role in cosmetic products. Healthy roots and tips, daily shine, stronger hairs are the prime factors among the male and female genders driving the hair care product market globally. In this research, consumer preference and satisfaction towards different brands of hair shampoo in Ahmedabad city is studied. Hence, in this research, 26 brands have been taken both national and international brands to identify consumers' brand preference and factors that consumers consider. A total of 200 respondents' data is collected with the aid of a standardised questionnaire, and exploratory factor analysis and cluster analysis are used to analyse it. The result of the study shows that Dove and L'Oreal Paris are the most preferred brands. Brand image and usage experience, ethical and ecofriendly product, brand preference, product quality, and problem solving ability are the five factors which influence the consumer preference towards hair shampoo through factor analysis. Brand attributes and brand perception are the identified cluster groups through regression factor scores.

DOI: 10.4018/979-8-3693-2193-5.ch024

INTRODUCTION

The Consumer is the King right now. Consumer preference and their satisfaction matters a lot for all organizations whether they are offering any product or services. In India, the market for personal care and cosmetics is anticipated to grow at a 6.5% CAGR between 2022 and 2027 (imarcgroup, 2022). Beauty and personal care products include skin care/sun care, hair care, makeup and colour cosmetics, deodorants and fragrances, oral care and others. Hair Shampoos are included in Hair care segment which includes medicated shampoo, cosmetic shampoo and herbal shampoo out of which Standard shampoo segment in India accounted for market share of 74.3% in 2020 while Anti dandruff accounted for 14.07% of the market share (market research.com, 2021). Hair Shampoo plays a wide role in cosmetic products, It is a simple hair care item under hair care cosmetics representing a viscous liquid created to remove the need for soap when washing your hair and scalp dirt, dust, dandruff and providing intense repair therapy. According to the Reports of Fortune Business Insights, With a predicted CAGR of 3.6% from 2021 to 2028, It is anticipated that the global shampoo market would grow from USD 30.89 billion in 2021 to USD 39.58 billion in 2028.

Consumer brand preference Aaker (1996), towards various hair shampoos varies according to what factors influence them to purchase that particular brand Kapferer (2008). There are in all 26 brands of hair shampoo taken for the study:

L'Oreal Paris, St. Botanica, BBlunt, Schwarzkopf Professional, Dove, Head & Shoulders, Tresemme, Wella Professional, Pantene, Biotique, Matrix, Moroccanoil, Herbal essences, Himalaya, Sunsilk, Garnier, Palmer's, Dabur Vatika, Park Avenue, Nyle, Fiama Di Wills, Patanjali Kesh Kanti, Indulekha, Clinic plus, Palmolive Naturals and Beardo.

The current research is based upon the consumer preference towards hair shampoo brands and factors which influence them to purchase those brands and consumer satisfaction. The study includes the literature review followed by objectives, research methodology, analysis and interpretations, findings, conclusions, limitations, future scope and managerial implications. The study will be focusing upon consumer preferences and satisfaction. Therefore, the study suggested the factors which influence consumer preference towards hair shampoo brands and identified the two cluster groups.

LITERATURE REVIEW

Gohil (2021) focused on the consumer buyer behavior towards personal care products, in this study, the skin care segment is discussed, in which the author has focused upon three cosmeceutical products (Dutta & Nath, 2019). The study also focuses upon consumer preference towards herbal ingredients made from natural origin. Haddad, Awad, Albate, Almashhadani, & Dirani (2020) aimed to investigate female consumers' intention to purchase in Jordon. Brand awareness, brand loyalty and perceived equity are the three selected independent variables for the study to analyze the purchase intention towards eco-friendly products. A total of 107 respondent's data was collected with an online questionnaire and Data analysis was carried out using SPSS software. Multiple regression analysis and descriptive statistics tools were used for finding the results. Lee, Goh, & Mohd Noor (2019) aimed to investigate the factors which affect consumers' intent to purchase skin care products. The four elements that affect a consumer's purchasing intention are brand association, perceived quality, brand loyalty, and brand awareness with perceived quality being the most important factor. In Melaka, Malaysia, local private universities provided a total of 150 responses. Easily accessible sampling was employed to collect the data and analyzed measurement and structural model using SmartPLS. Amberg & Fogarassy (2019) analyzed that For both producers and customers in the market for cosmetics, health and environmental awareness will be popular while the foodstuffs industry will not follow the trend as the range of cosmetics' health effects is much narrower.. In near future, the demand for green cosmetic materials and environment friendly packaging methods will become much wider. The paper focuses on the green consumer behavior in cosmetic market and collected 197 respondent's data through online questionnaire in Hungary. The results are been analyzed through descriptive statistics and cluster analysis which shows that consumers prefer natural cosmetics, traditional ones or both. Jagadeesan & Balaji (2017) focused on the uses of hair care products and brand preferences of male customers in Chennai. Data from 375 respondents in total were gathered through practical non-random sampling. The data were analysed using the percentage analysis, factor analysis, and t-test. The findings of the study includes that enrichment and protection are the two main factors influencing how hair care products are used. The study also identifies how to use hair care products for branded versus unbranded consumer uses. The study concludes that male consumers mostly prefer branded products for their hair in order to enrich and enhance rather than protection and for medical reasons. Khan, Asad, & Mehboob (2017) investigated the purchasing patterns for halal-certified goods in a developing Muslim market. Convenience random sampling was used to select 497 respondents in total. The study focuses on the conceptual framework of the theory of planned behavior. To test the results, We employ structural equation modelling, confirmatory factor analysis, and Pearson correlation. The findings demonstrate that religious commitment, compliance incentive, self identification, and perceived behavioural control have a favourable and significant impact on the intention to buy products with the Halal seal of approval. Ghazalia, Soonb, Mutumc, & Nguyend (2017) aimed to investigate the intention of customers to buy organic personal care goods again. Attitude and product knowledge are the important factors in anticipating future purchases of organic goods, with hedonic value, health value, safety value, and environmental value coming in second and third. Social values and influence of subjective norms on re-purchasing organic products was not supported. Consumers placed attitude as the most crucial aspect in determining whether they would repurchase organic goods, the perception of behavioural control, product knowledge, hedonistic value, environmental value, and safety value come next. Singhal & Malik (2018) aimed to identify female consumers' perceptions on and behaviour towards green marketing in the cosmetics sector. A total of 100 female consumer's responses were collected from the Delhi region, cluster analysis was used to group the respondents according to their attitudes in the direction of green cosmetics. To determine the objectives, tests such the multivariate test, chi-square test, correlation, and factor analysis have been used. The paper highlights that income of the consumers impacts the attitudes of consumers towards green cosmetic products while age and education level has no impact. Yeo, Naina Mohamed, & Muda (2016) focused on the halal cosmetic retail products for Malaysian consumers' purchase motivation through examining the theory of consumption value. The paper explains the relationship between perceived value and customer satisfaction. As the fundamental framework for the theory of consumer value, the study makes use of conditional value, epistemic value, social value, emotional value, and functional value. Matić & Puh (2015) focused on the factors which influence consumer's intention towards purchasing natural cosmetics. The data was collected through questionnaire and 204 consumers from Dubrovnik – Neretva Country data was analyzed through binary correlation analysis with logistic regression. According to the findings of binary logistic regression, customer purchase intentions are influenced by gender, a consumer's propensity to buy organic food, and a consumer's propensity to buy new natural cosmetics brands. However, consumers' propensity for health consciousness has no bearing on their intentions to purchase natural cosmetics. The correlation analysis's findings show a high positive link between consumers' references to natural cosmetics and purchase intentions for those products. Wei, Lee, Chen, & Wu (2013) focuses on the hairdressing industry's client relationship management. In order to determine client preferences and better satisfy their needs, data mining techniques were applied. The RFM Model was used to analyse four different consumer kinds in a hair salon: devoted clients, prospective clients, brand-new clients, and lost clients. The study was conducted in hair salon at Taiwan, SOM and K means methods were applied to apply the RFM Model using the two stage clustering method. Kim & Chung (2011) focused on the consumer purchase intention for organic personal care products (skin & hair care products) using the theory of planned behavior. The study examined how attitudes towards buying organic items are influenced by environmental consciousness and appearance consciousness, with past experiences serving as a moderator of the attitude-purchase intention link. A total of 207 respondents' data was collected in the USA through an online survey and to examine the association between the variables, multiple regression analysis was employed. Jensen (2011) aimed to evaluate the applicability of Dick and Basu's theory of client loyalty on the market for grocery products. Five grocery product categories including coffee, shampoo, tooth paste, washing powder and toilet paper are included in the study to investigate brand loyalty. A total of 348 household's respondent's data was collected to test the hypothesised relationships. The results show the expected difference between product categories and loyalty categories and resulting in women being more loyal customers than men (Hossain & Shila, 2020). The study is concerned with the variables affecting consumers' decisions on personal care items. A total of 300 respondents' data was collected from Dhaka city, Bangladesh with 5 point Likert scale. The paper analyzed that specialization and the most critical component for personal care products is product attributes. Mean Rank of variables depending on personal preference and One tailed t- test are used for testing the data collected.

Vyas (2014) carried out an empirical study to evaluate the Indian hair care products market by contrasting myths with facts and client satisfaction with fictions. The study aims at identifying brand preference among the users. The findings show a substantial correlation between brand choice and anticipated purchases (Bass & Talarzyk, 1972). The research identifies the correlation between brand preference and attitude evaluations based on perceptions of and important rankings for particular product characteristics. The findings of the study states that results firmly establish the relationship between brand choice and attitude measures (Singh, Hansen, & Gupta, 2005). The study contributes by providing a dependence model based on associated preferences for characteristics shared by categories. According to the study's findings, there is a strong correlation between consumers' preferences for various product attributes within and across categories. As a result, model estimates can be used to forecast preferences for a given attribute in a new category, and potential customers for a new product within an existing category can be ranked according to how likely they are to buy it.

OBJECTIVES

The main objectives of the study are:

1. To study the brand preference of consumers towards hair shampoo.
2. To research factors influencing consumer preference for hair shampoo

3. To analyze the purpose of consumers towards usage of hair shampoo.
4. To analyze the satisfaction level of consumers using hair shampoo.

RESEARCH METHODOLOGY

Sources of data: Both primary and secondary data are used in the investigation. A questionnaire is used to obtain the primary data. The secondary data is gathered from books, articles, websites, reports, and journals.

Type of study: The research design used for the study is descriptive and exploratory in nature.

Area of study: The research is done in Ahmedabad city only.

Sample size: 200 respondents both male and female consumers data is collected. For data collection, a non – probability convenience sampling method is used.

Tools for analysis: SPSS has been utilised to employ statistics. For analyzing the collected data, Frequency analysis has been performed to determine the hair shampoo brand that consumers prefer, to analyze the purpose of consumers towards usage of hair shampoo and to analyze the satisfaction level of consumers using hair shampoo. Factor analysis is used to identify the factors influencing the preference of consumers towards hair shampoo. Cluster analysis is used to identify cluster groups through regression factor scores.

ANALYSIS AND FINDINGS

Descriptive Analysis

The descriptive analysis is performed on 200 responses collected. The results are presented in Table 1.

Table 1. Profiles of respondents' population

Characteristics	Sub Categories	Frequency	Percentage
Gender	Male	111	55.5
	Female	89	44.5
	TOTAL	200	100.0
Age	15 – 30	75	37.5
	31 – 45	67	33.5
	46 – 60	36	18.0
	61 and above	22	11.0
	TOTAL	200	100.0

continues on following page

Table 1. Continued

Characteristics	Sub Categories	Frequency	Percentage
Educational Qualification	10th	4	2.0
	12th	3	1.5
	Graduate	86	43.0
	Post Graduate	88	44.0
	Professional	19	9.5
	TOTAL	200	100.0
Occupation	Students	43	21.5
	Employee	84	42.0
	Self Employed	37	18.0
	Homemaker	15	7.5
	Other	21	10.5
	TOTAL	200	100.0
Income (Monthly) (Rs.)	Below 10000	19	9.5
	10001 – 30000	45	22.5
	30001 – 50000	55	27.5
	50001 and above	81	40.5
	TOTAL	200	100.0
Marital Status	Married	127	63.5
	Unmarried	71	35.5
	Divorced	2	1.0
	Widow	-	-
	TOTAL	200	100.0
Family Type	Nuclear Family	104	52.0
	Joint Family	96	48.0
	TOTAL	200	100.0
Family Members Using Shampoo	1	5	2.5
	2	31	15.5
	3	45	22.5
	More than 3	119	59.5
	TOTAL	200	100.0

The results presented in Table 1 show the demographic nature of the respondents. Out of the 200 respondents, 111 are male and 89 are female. 75 respondents are falling under the age group of 15-30 years, 88 respondents have post graduate degree while 86 respondents are graduate. 84 respondents are employed, 81 respondents income is above Rs. 50000. 127 respondents are married and 104 respondents belong to nuclear families. 119 respondents have more than 3 family members, who are using shampoo.

The results presented in Table 2 shows Consumer brand preference towards hair shampoo. Study includes 26 National and international brands out of which 31 respondents preferred Dove while 30 respondents preferred L'Oreal Paris hair shampoo. Therefore, there is only 0.5% of difference between these two brands as preference by consumers for hair shampoo. 23 respondents have preferred Wella Professional while 18 respondents have preferred the Tresemme brand.

Table 2. Consumer brand preference

Brands	Frequency	Percent
L'Oreal Paris	30	15
St.Botanica	2	1
BBlunt	1	0.5
Schwarzkopf Professional	3	1.5
Dove	31	15.5
Head & Shoulders	18	9
Tresemme	23	11.5
Wella Professional	5	2.5
Pantene	12	6
Biotique	7	3.5
Matrix	-	-
Moroccanoil	1	0.5
Herbalessences	2	1
Himalaya	9	4.5
Sunsilk	12	6
Garnier	5	2.5
Palmer's	-	-
Dabur Vatika	4	2
Park Avenue	1	0.5
Nyle	3	1.5
Fiama Di Wills	4	2
Patanjali kesh Kanti	11	5.5
Indulekha	4	2
Clinic Plus	11	5.5
Palmolive Naturals	-	-
Beardo	1	0.5
Total	200	100

Table 3. Purpose of usage of hair shampoo

S. No.	Purpose	Opinion of the Respondents					
		Strongly Disagree	Disagree	Neutral	Agree	Strongly Agree	Total
	Daily Shine	1 (0.5)	5 (2.5)	34 (17.0)	70 (35.0)	90 (45.0)	200 (100.0)
	Dryness Care	2 (1.0)	3 (1.5)	17 (8.5)	85 (42.5)	93 (46.5)	200 (100.0)
	Dandruff Care	2 (1.0)	4 (2.0)	20 (10.0)	70 (35.0)	104 (52.0)	200 (100.0)
	Hair Fall Rescue	-	4 (2.0)	25 (12.5)	78 (39.0)	93 (46.5)	200 (100.0)
	Intense Repair Therapy	2 (1.0)	6 (3.0)	38 (19.0)	76 (38.0)	78 (39.0)	200 (100.0)
	Nourishing Oil Care	3 (1.5)	2 (1.0)	29 (14.5)	90 (45.0)	76 (38.0)	200 (100.0)
	Colour Rescue	9 (4.5)	10 (5.0)	66 (33.0)	75 (37.5)	40 (20.0)	200 (100.0)
	Smells fresh and long lasting	5 (2.5)	2 (1.0)	38 (19.0)	79 (39.5)	76 (38.0)	200 (100.0)
	Damaged scalp and hair	4 (2.0)	3 (1.5)	30 (15.0)	74 (37.0)	89 (44.5)	200 (100.0)
	Herbal in Nature	2 (1.0)	3 (1.5)	31 (15.5)	90 (45.0)	74 (37.0)	200 (100.0)
	Avoid Unpleasant odour	2 (1.0)	1 (0.5)	29 (14.5)	84 (42.0)	84 (42.0)	200 (100.0)
	Fragrance	3 (1.5)	4 (2.0)	31 (15.5)	109 (54.5)	53 (26.5)	200 (100.0)
	Healthy roots and tips	1 (0.5)	2 (1.0)	19 (9.5)	89 (44.5)	89 (44.5)	200 (100.0)
	Graying of hair	4 (2.0)	6 (3.0)	30 (15.0)	81 (40.5)	79 (39.5)	200 (100.0)

Figures in bracket are shown percentages

The results presented in Table 3 shows the purpose of consumers towards usage of hair shampoo. Majority of the respondents strongly agree that daily shine, dryness care, dandruff care, hair fall rescue, damaged scalp and hair, healthy roots and tips and to avoid unpleasant odour are the main purpose for usage of hair shampoo while some respondents agree that Nourishing oil care, color rescue, smells fresh and long lasting, herbal in nature, fragrance, are the main reason for usage of hair shampoo. 81 respondents agree that graying of hair is also the main purpose of usage of hair shampoo.

The results presented in Table 4 shows that 133 respondents are satisfied with their hair shampoo while there are 43 respondents who are highly satisfied with usage of hair shampoo.

Table 4. Level of satisfaction

Level of Satisfaction	Frequency	Percentage
Highly Dissatisfied	1	0.5
Dissatisfied	1	0.5
Neutral	22	11.0
Satisfied	133	66.5
Highly Satisfied	43	21.5
TOTAL	200	100.0

Table 5. level of satisfaction respondents obtained from purchase and consumption

S. No.	Factors	Opinion of the Respondents					
		Highly Dissatisfied	Dissatisfied	Neutral	Satisfied	Highly Satisfied	Total
	Price	1 (0.5)	1 (0.5)	18 (9.0)	105 (52.5)	75 (37.5)	200 (100.0)
	Quality	1 (0.5)	-	14 (7.0)	102 (51.0)	83 (41.5)	200 (100.0)
	Packaging	1 (0.5)	1 (0.5)	44 (22.0)	83 (41.5)	71 (35.5)	200 (100.0)
	Advertising	1 (0.5)	5 (2.5)	63 (31.5)	87 (43.5)	44 (22.0)	200 (100.0)
	Naturalness	1 (0.5)	3 (1.5)	34 (17.0)	99 (49.5)	63 (31.5)	200 (100.0)
	Hair Type	1 (0.5)	1 (0.5)	27 (13.5)	106 (53.0)	65 (32.5)	200 (100.0)
	Hair Problem	1 (0.5)	1 (0.5)	35 (17.5)	98 (49.0)	65 (32.5)	200 (100.0)
	Fragrance	1 (0.5)	2 (1.0)	38 (19.0)	103 (51.5)	56 (28.0)	200 (100.0)
	Usage of the product	1 (0.5)	-	31 (15.5)	109 (54.5)	59 (29.5)	200 (100.0)

Figures in bracket are shown percentages

The results presented in table 5 shows that respondents are satisfied with the factors which influence them for purchase and consumption of hair shampoo. Majority of the respondents have answered satisfied with all the factors while there are 0.5% respondents who are highly dissatisfied with the factors.

Table 6. Factor analysis

KMO and Bartlett's Test		
Kaiser-Meyer-Olkin Measure of Sampling Adequacy.		.884
Bartlett's Test of Sphericity	Approx. Chi-Square	3259.218
	df	435
	Sig.	.000

Figure 1. Scree plot

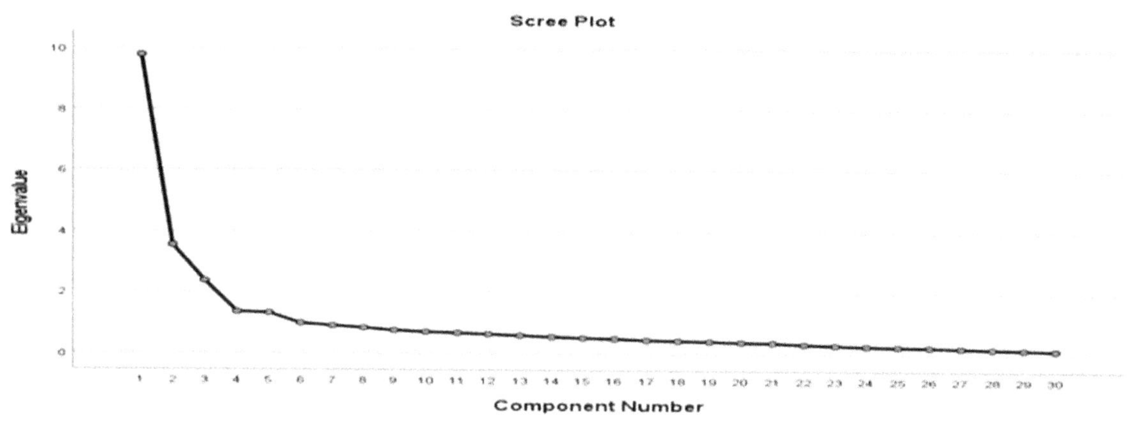

Table 6 shows the results of an exploratory factor analysis that was done to determine and look into the correlations between the variables. To evaluate sample adequacy, the Kaiser-Meyer-Olkin (KMO) measure of sampling adequacy is computed, 0.884 is the KMO which indicates sample is excellent for sampling. The Barlett test of sphericity is used to determine the overall significance of correlation matrices (Chi-square = 3259.218 approximately and significance at 0.000) provided as well as proof that the data set's factor analysis was accurate..

The Rotated Component Matrix was used for extracting factors. Factors influencing consumers towards hair shampoo is a five dimensional construct. These factors are grouped into five groups.

Factor 1 (Brand image and usage experience) This factor is loaded by six variables (0.839, 0.824, 0.689, 0.672, 0.593, 0.568) that briefly describes the brand image among the consumers mind and their experience related to the hair shampoo.

Factor 2 (Ethical and eco friendly product) the second factor is loaded by six variables (0.829, 0.786, 0.760, 0.684, 0.616, 0.611) that describes the negative side of using hair shampoo which may cause harmful damage to hairs due to various reasons.

Factor 3 (Brand Preference) the third factor is loaded by four variables (0.723, 0.722, 0.595, 0.571) that describe the consumers priority towards brands, consumers taste and preferences towards brands.

Factor 4 (Product Quality) the fourth factor is loaded by five variables (0.765, 0.669, 0.662, 0.636, 0.614) that describes the quality of the shampoo, and reasons behind the usage of shampoo by the consumers to add moisture to the hair.

Factor 5 (Problem solving ability) The fifth factor is loaded by three variables (0.725, 0.674, 0.661) that describe the purpose of using shampoo to solve hair related problems.

Cluster Analysis

Cluster analysis is used to classify the group objects based on the characteristics. In this study, factor scores are taken as inputs to the cluster analysis instead of raw data. In order to determine whether consumer preferences for hair shampoo are similar or different, cluster analysis is employed to examine the number of respondents that are organised into clusters.

There are two clusters, with 121 respondents in cluster 1 and 79 respondents in cluster 2, according to Table No. 7.2.

Table 7. Final cluster centers

Final Cluster Centers		
	Cluster	
	1	2
REGR factor score: Brand image and usage experience	.43736	-.66988
REGR factor score: Ethical and eco friendly product	-.13991	.21430
REGR factor score: Brand Preference	-.06153	.09424
REGR factor score: Product Quality	.19325	-.29600
REGR factor score: Problem solving ability	.38695	-.59267

Cluster 1

There are 121 respondents in Cluster 1 making up this cluster. The respondents majorly agree with brand image and usage experience, product quality and problem solving ability. Cluster 1 can be defined as Brand attributes.

Cluster 2 has 79 respondents forming a part of this cluster. The respondents have favorable behavior towards ethical and eco friendly product and brand preference. Cluster 2 can be defined as Brand perception.

Table 8. Number of cases in each cluster

Number of Cases in Each Cluster		
Cluster	1	121.000
	2	79.000
Valid		200.000
Missing		.000

CONCLUSION

From the study it can be concluded that the majority of the consumers preferred Dove and L'Oreal Paris brand for hair shampoo. On the basis of factor analysis, it can be concluded that there are five factors which influence the consumers preference towards hair shampoo i.e. Brand image and usage experience, Ethical and eco friendly product, Brand preference, Product quality and Problem solving ability. Cluster analysis was conducted by taking regression factor scores as inputs to identify the cluster groups. The findings included two types of clusters which were named as Brand attributes and Brand perception. Thus, the marketer has a huge opportunity to change the perception of consumers from ruinous effects of shampoo to the advantageousness of hair shampoo consumption. Respondents strongly agree that daily shine, dryness care, dandruff care, hair fall rescue, damaged scalp and hair, healthy roots and tips and to avoid unpleasant odour are the main purpose for usage of hair shampoo while some respondents agree that Nourishing oil care, color rescue, smells fresh and long lasting, herbal in nature, fragrance, are the main reason for usage of hair shampoo. The study also concludes that the majority of the respondents are satisfied with their hair shampoo.

LIMITATIONS OF THE STUDY

Data for this study were gathered exclusively from respondents who lived in Ahmedabad, both male and female. As a result, it cannot be generalised to other cities, states, or nations. Due to time and resource limitations, the study limited the number of participants to 200. This study includes non-probability convenience sampling method. The consumers had the restriction to choose the brand from the given list of 26 national and international brands of hair shampoo.

FUTURE SCOPE

The current status of the research includes various factors which leads to consumer preference and satisfaction, however, nowadays consuemrs are more inclined towards sustainable products, green products and organix products. Even consumer prefer customized products especially as per their hair scalp and hair growth. Therefore, researchers can study upon those factors in future. Variables could be added to the study like purchase intention, social media influence on purchase decision, brand awareness, consumer attitude, etc. As far as future scope is concerned, researchers can increase the sample size and target other cities, states or countries. Researchers can also take some more shampoo brands which are not included in this study.

MANAGERIAL IMPLICATIONS

As per the above study, Hair shampoo plays a wide role for cleansing scalp, making hair shine, smooth and dust free. Consumers prefer shampoo for various purposes which will help the companies to invent different variants among shampoo and provide them importance towards branding decisions to introduce products through latest marketing techniques such as artificial intelligence.

REFERENCES

Amberg, N., & Fogarassy, C. (2019). Green Consumer Behavior in the Cosmetics Market. *Resources*, *137*(8), 1–19. doi:10.3390/resources8030137

Baskaran, E., & Arulalan, M. V. (2017). *Determinants of Personal Care Products Usage Purposes (A Study with Special Reference to Male Consumers in Chennai City)* [Doctoral Thesis]. University of Madras.

Bass, F. M., & Talarzyk, W. W. (1972, February). An Attitude Model for the Study of Brand Preference. *JMR, Journal of Marketing Research*, *9*(1), 93–96. doi:10.1177/002224377200900121

Fortune Business Insights. (2021). *Shampoo market size, share & COVID 19 impact Analysis, By Product type (Medicated and non medicated), Form (Liquid, solid, and others), Application (Household and commercial), Distribution channel, and Regional Forecast, 2021-2028*. Available at: https://www.fortunebusinessinsights.com/shampoo-market-103432

Ghazalia, E., Soonb, P. C., Mutumc, D. S., & Nguyend, B. (2017). Health and cosmetics: Investigating consumers' values for buying organic personal care products. *Journal of Retailing and Consumer Services*, *39*, 154–163. doi:10.1016/j.jretconser.2017.08.002

Gohil, V. (2021). Consumer Buying Behavior of Personal Care Product: A Comparative Study of Male and Female Users. *Aegaeum Journal*, *9*(1), 466–471.

Haddad, S. A., Awad, A., Albate, D., Almashhadani, I., & Dirani, W. (2020). Factors affecting green cosmetics purchase intention. *Journal of Management Information and Decision Sciences*, *23*(4), 332–342.

Hossain, M. S., & Shila, N. S. (2020). Factors influencing consumer decision making for personal care products. *Dhaka University Journal of Biological Sciences, 29*(1), 53-59.

Imarcgroup. (2022). *India Beauty and Personal Care Market: Industry Trends, Share, Size, Growth, Opportunity and Forecast 2022-2027*. Available at: https://www.imarcgroup.com/india-beauty-personal-care-market

Jagadeesan, P., & Balaji, P. (2017). Hair Care Product Usage Purposes and Brand Predilection of Male Consumers. *Indian Journal of Public Health Research & Development, 8*(4), 367–371. doi:10.5958/0976-5506.2017.00371.0

Jensen, J. M. (2011). Consumer loyalty on the grocery product market: An empirical application of Dick and Basu's framework. *Journal of Consumer Marketing, 28*(5), 333–343. doi:10.1108/07363761111149983

Khan, M. M., Asad, H., & Mehboob, I. (2017). Investigating the consumer behavior for Halal endorsed products: Case of an emerging Muslim market. *Journal of Islamic Marketing, 8*(4), 1–21. doi:10.1108/JIMA-09-2015-0068

Kim, H. Y., & Chung, J. E. (2011). Consumer purchase intention for organic personal care products. *Journal of Consumer Marketing, 28*(1), 40–47. doi:10.1108/07363761111101930

Lee, J. E., Goh, M. L., & Mohd Noor, M. N. (2019). Understanding purchase intention of university students towards skin care products. *PSU Research Review, 3*(3), 161–178. doi:10.1108/PRR-11-2018-0031

Market research.com. (2021). *Shampoo (Haircare) Market in India - Outlook to 2025; Market Size, Growth and Forecast Analytics*. Available at: https://www.marketresearch.com

Matić, M., & Puh, B. (2015). Consumer's purchase intention towards natural cosmetics. *Ekonomski Vjesnik/Econviews – Review of Contemporary Entrepreneurship, Business, and Economic Issues*, 53-64.

Singh, V. P., Hansen, K. T., & Gupta, S. (2005, May). Modeling Preferences for Common Attributes in Multicategory Brand Choice. *JMR, Journal of Marketing Research, 42*(2), 195–209. doi:10.1509/jmkr.42.2.195.62282

Singhal, A., & Malik, G. (2018). The attitude and purchasing of female consumers towards green marketing related to cosmetic industry. *Journal of Science and Technology Policy Management*, 1-19.

Vyas, M. (2014). An Analysis of Hair care Products with reference to Indian market (Myths Facts Vs Fictions and consumer satisfaction). *International Journal of Research and Development in Technology and Management Science- Kailash, 21*(2), 1-12.

Wei, J. T., Lee, M. C., Chen, H. K., & Wu, H. H. (2013). Customer relationship management in the hairdressing industry: An application of data mining techniques. *Expert Systems with Applications, 40*(18), 7513–7518. doi:10.1016/j.eswa.2013.07.053

Yeo, B. L., Naina Mohamed, R. H., & Muda, M. (2016). A Study of Malaysian Customers Purchase Motivation of Halal Cosmetics Retail Products: Examining Theory of Consumption Value and Customer Satisfaction. *Procedia Economics and Finance, 37*, 176–182. doi:10.1016/S2212-5671(16)30110-1

Chapter 25
Data-Driven Talent Management Practices for Eco-Innovation in State-Owned Enterprises

Sulaiman Olusegun Atiku
https://orcid.org/0000-0001-9364-3774
Namibia University of Science and Technology, Namibia & Walter Sisulu University, South Africa

Doreen K. Menjengua
Namibia University of Science and Technology, Namibia

Andrew Jeremiah
Namibia University of Science and Technology, Namibia

Hylton James Villet
Namibia University of Science and Technology, Namibia

ABSTRACT

This study explores the influence of data-driven talent management practices on eco-innovation in state-owned enterprises. A literature review was conducted to examine the role of people data, HR metrics, and people analytics in enhancing talent management practices and eco-innovation in state-owned enterprises. Findings revealed that people data is essential for making talent decisions and developing effective talent retention strategies. Additionally, two key drivers of eco-innovations were identified and grouped into external and internal drivers. External drivers include environmental regulations, competition pressures, and customers' demands for eco-friendly products and services. Internal drivers are organizational capabilities, technological capabilities, and corporate social responsibility. Therefore, data-driven talent development interventions are necessary for advancing organizational and technological capabilities to boost eco-innovation performance in state-owned enterprises.

DOI: 10.4018/979-8-3693-2193-5.ch025

INTRODUCTION

The qualitative nature of human resources (HR), as opposed to other management functions such as finance, operations, marketing, and sales, has led managers to make people-oriented decisions based on intuition, feelings, and instincts (Shrivastava, Nagdev & Rajesh, 2018). The HR function produces a vast amount of people data while undertaking regular activities, such as recruitment data, demographic data, talent development data, performance management data, employee survey data (employee engagement survey), training needs analysis (TNA) data, and exit interview data. HR departments recognise the importance of leveraging data effectively for effective decision-making but fail to do so. The non-application of people data in people-oriented decisions by the HR departments in State-Owned Enterprises (SOEs) can be attributed to a lack of knowledge, experience, or even the foresight to appreciate the enormous possibilities presented by HR analytics modelling (Edwards & Edwards, 2019).

The human resources functions in SOEs collect and analyse a vast amount of data, which could be channelled into making informed policy decisions in Namibia. This raises the question of whether SOEs use people data when making strategic decisions, particularly around talent management practices (talent attraction, development, and retention) to improve the creativity, eco-innovation, and sustainability (economic, social, and environmental) of SOEs. Economic sustainability can be referred to as business activities that support long-term returns on investment without compromising environmental and social sustainability (Carroll & Shabana, 2010). Social sustainability is a process for creating sustainable successful places that promote wellbeing, by understanding what people need from the places they live and work (Palich & Edmonds, 2013). Environmental sustainability is the ability to maintain an ecological balance in the natural environment and conserve natural resources to support the wellbeing of current and future generations (Duran et al., 2015). Therefore, there is a need for informed talent management practices to promote workforce creativity and support the long-term economic sustainability of SOEs without compromising environmental and social sustainability.

Talent management decisions to enhance workplace creativity and innovation are not only difficult to implement, but they may also be expensive if handled incorrectly. Making effective talent management decisions is challenging because decision-makers generally have little or inadequate data from which to reliably conclude which individual is best suited for any opportunity. When organisations invest in the wrong people or wrong programmes, they create teams that are doomed to fail, and their talent management efforts are ultimately eroded (Russell & Bennett, 2015). Investment in the wrong people will impact the economic sustainability of SOEs. Therefore, this chapter examines the influence of data-driven talent management practices on eco-innovation in SOEs.

The following sections of this chapter provide adequate background on data-driven business intelligence and the role of people data in talent management practices for eco-innovation to enhance sustainability of SOEs. The background is followed by a literature review on talent management approaches and practices, talent management challenges, people data as well as its influence on talent analytics and decisions. Subsequently,

BACKGROUND

Globalisation has ushered in a talent war, driving organisations to re-direct their attention from focusing on increasing productivity and differentiating their products and services to concentrating on their inimitable resources, namely their human asset or particularly their talent, which offers them a competitive advantage (Al Aina & Atan, 2020). The latter, according to Ibrahim and Daniel (2018), is that resource which the organisation possesses, which their competitors cannot imitate or substitute, thereby necessitating the organisation's focus on such an intangible asset.

Multinational firms are engaging in a constant war for talent in a globalised world. Big data analytics, which is, gathering data electronically, analysing it, and transforming it into actionable intelligence, is one of the most obvious new tools to bring talent management to the next level (Dahlbom et al., 2019). The key to successful talent identification is the ability to spawn a host of number-crunching insights that can help to identify true talent, personalise the development process, and even foresee future capability requirements with unprecedented precision and depth. The world of HR is fast-changing by the day, with key areas of a notice being talent identification, employee performance predictions leading to retention of critical talent within the organisation, and observation of the proper career path for development. However, according to Meena and Janani (2016), human capital can only be a competitive advantage if they are satisfied with their jobs, which subsequently leads to their high performance.

The significance of talent and its management is emphasised in both business and academia. Talent management may come within the purview of the human resource function; however, its influence is seen throughout the business. Hiring accuracy, minimising time-to-fill, and retaining talent is critical to an organisation's bottom line and they speak to a company's overall health (Mondal, 2021).

There are several reports (Deloitte, 2020) contending that talent management is currently a priority issue for companies as it can be a source of competitive advantages in their dynamic and competitive environments, by providing strategic opportunities for sustainable advantage (De La Calle-Duran et al., 2021). According to PricewaterhouseCoopers (PWC, July 2020), some organisations have well-crafted strategies which, however, ultimately fail since there is no alignment between the strategy, the workforce, and talent management. The truth holds that people drive the business strategy and ultimately the business success. Organisations should adopt systems thinking holistic approach when implementing strategies, such that any hidden loops such as failure in strategy alignment to workforce capabilities are identified and rectified well in advance. Talent management in the world of work has become critical for workforce creativity and sustainable competitive advantage (Atiku, 2020).

Globally, competition for a skilled workforce has become fierce among organisations. According to Alhajjar et al. (2018), globalisation and issues of Industry 4.0 have enabled talented employees not to limit the marketing of their skills within one region, but they can look for jobs in firms across the world. A creative workforce has become the major asset of all successful organisations globally, thus necessitating the need for increased focus on attracting and retaining a competent workforce whilst simultaneously increasing employee efficiency and sustainable business solutions (Fields & Atiku, 2017). Organisations such as Starbucks, Southwest Airlines, and Google have over the years embraced and implemented this notion, thereby making them highly competitive from a global perspective in their respective sectors. Nasril et al. (2021) buoy this notion, stating that the focus on human resources should be more on increasing productivity and efficiency as the competition among nations lately has gotten tougher hence requiring talent of high quality who can manage and implement innovative and creative ideas within organisations. In Africa, albeit at a slow pace, organisations are focusing on the recruitment, development, and retention of skilled and talented local employees to match their corporate culture and drive success (Talent Agenda Series, 2017).

To perform competitively in this changing landscape, the technological shifts brought about by Industry 4.0 require equally significant changes in talent management practices (Whysall et al., 2019). Current approaches appear to be falling short in terms of equipping organisations with the talent they need to operate effectively within this rapidly changing environment. Bakre (2019) compared the changes happening in HR with the evolution that changed the professional practice of accounting to finance decision science and sales to marketing decision science. Both finance and marketing serve as frameworks for improving decisions about customers and money, which occur both within and outside the marketing and finance departments. The evolution of HR and HR measures will require a sound decision science for human resources wherever they are made. Hence, the HR department is under immense pressure to align its initiatives and obligations to the new paradigm. The department needs to embrace various tools brought about by the new technological developments in executing their strategic objectives such as attracting, developing, and retention of key talent. This aligns with the findings and suggestions by CIPD (2018) that HR should embrace and implement analytics as a continuous transformational project which is made successful by people analytics and data-driven approaches, with the executive team assuming full ownership of the project. With talent retention at the forefront of organisational agendas, Albinus (2021) suggests that organisations take a different approach, one that focuses on finding the right role for the employees in their chosen career path. This can be accomplished through an in-depth critical analysis of the organisation's HR function and the business data.

The HR department, like other departments in state-owned enterprises, reports on important HR indicators quarterly to the Board, the HR & Remuneration Committee, and the Executive Management Committee (EXCO), to contribute to effective decision-making regarding HR management (Namibia Statistics Agency, 2018-2019). However, the HR Quarterly report, which is descriptive, does not aid the executive management in decision-making. The pressure to gain deeper insights into the workforce always starts at the top. A survey by Deloitte revealed that 53% of respondents highlighted their leaders' interest in workforce data has arisen in the last 18 months (Deloitte, 2020). Better workforce metrics are desired for a variety of reasons, most of which are focused on the future, with details on the workforce's readiness to meet new demands taking precedence (Deloitte, 2020). Therefore, this study examines the critical role of people data in advancing talent management practices and eco-innovation in SOEs.

TALENT

The quest for talent is a never-ending saga and investing in high-potential employees translates to lower operational costs (Mihalcea, 2017). The term talent in business has several definitions. In some organisations, talent is referred to as individuals with high potential. This is in line with Tafti et al.'s (2017) definition, which states that talented people are those that possess outstanding talents and are successful in a variety of activities or fields. Another definition of talent within an organisation, speaks to talent as being all individuals within the organisation that just need to be trained, coached, mentored, and engaged to their optimal levels (Anlesinya & Amponsah-Tawiah, 2020).

Contrary to the notion that talent is linked to the individual's abilities or training, De La Calle-Duran et al. (2021) have a second approach of considering talent, which specifically focuses on the position and not the individual employee. De La Calle-Duran et al. (2021) further proffer that talent resides in the key position within the organisation, meaning that only the employee who holds that key strategic position is classified as talent. The Namibia Statistics Agency's Succession and Talent Management Policy and Procedures (2017) define talent as employees who meet or exceed performance expectations as well as demonstrate the potential to perform at the next level of work. According to Vaiman et al. (2012), the identification, attraction, and retention of talented and high valued employees have increased in importance in recent years. Talent management has undoubtedly elevated concerns related to human resource management to the CEO's agenda to a considerably larger degree than in the past. When implemented correctly, talent management has a beneficial influence on an organisation's production and profitability (Jyoti & Rani, 2014). The working definition of talent for this study is the one by NSA's Succession and Talent Management Policy and Procedures (2017), as cited above. With this understanding talent needs to be adequately managed in SOEs to improve service delivery and enhance their sustainability in the post-pandemic world.

TALENT MANAGEMENT

There are numerous talent management definitions which are available, each of which examines talent management through a different lens. Vladescu (2012, as cited in Pyszka & Gajda, 2015), defines talent management as an integrated set of activities that ensure an organisation's ability to attract, retain, and develop the talented individuals it needs for future purposes. While Collings and Mellahi (2009, as cited in Sivathanu & Pillai, 2019, p. 457) define talent management as:

Activities and processes that involve the systematic identification of key positions that differentially contribute to the organisation's sustainable competitive advantage, the development of a talent pool of high-potential and high-performing incumbents to fill these roles, and the development of a differentiated human resource architecture to facilitate filling these positions with competent incumbents, and to ensure their continued commitment to the organisation.

According to the Namibia Statistics Agency's Succession and Talent Management Policy and Procedures (2017), talent management is a set of integrated organisational HR processes that are designed to attract, develop, motivate, and retain productive and engaged employees. The goal of talent management is to create a high-performance and sustainable organisation that meets its strategic and operational goals and objectives.

The majority of the definitions in literature have similar notions since they all refer to identifying talented, high-potential, or high-performing workers, or identifying critical positions that must be managed for an organisation to succeed. Talent management is the act of improving and enhancing employee talent within an organisation through the use of resources, policies, and procedures. According to Orlova et al. (2015), it involves the practice of continuously discovering, developing, using, and retaining those people, who are especially valuable either in terms of having a great potential for the future of the organisation, or because they are capable of resolving business and operational issues which are critical for sustainability. Hence, talent management's key focus is the attraction of personnel who are highly skilled, skills development, and retention of employees which comprises a committed and differentiated competitive workforce. In this current volatile business environment, SOEs should develop HR strategies that embrace new technological developments associated with Industry 4.0. This is in agreement with concerns raised by Thomas (2016) who asked the following question: "In the era of big data, how is the world of HR changing?" There are three main areas where these changes are at the edge of glory: identifying talent, identifying the right career and development path and, more crucially, predicting employee performance and maintaining a competent workforce (Atiku & Fields, 2018; Atiku et al., 2022).

Just as in the past, when HR evolved from personnel management to strategic human resource management and subsequently talent management, an industrial revolution is again disrupting the current talent management practices. The 4th industrial revolution is paving the way for a more progressive talent management in the future, provided HR, can respond to the disruptive challenges in a timely and appropriate fashion. It is noted from the preceding overviews that it is imperative for organisations in this new and challenging business era to effectively adopt talent management practices, which focus on employee engagement among other variables impacting top-line revenue and in turn profit maximisation.

Discussions by Fegley (2006) compliment the above analysis on focusing on talent management as a tool of engaging employees in the current business environment. These discussions do not only emphasise the practice of recruitment and development, but they further highlight the aligning and strategic positioning of human capital with the organisation's goals such as increased sustenance and profit maximisation. In addition to that, the organisation will be simultaneously decreasing organisational costs and key staff turnover. Furthermore, through talent management, organisations can implement succession planning, career and retention planning, and leadership development. Hence, through advanced technologies and increased availability of voluminous people data which can be processed into smart data for people analytics, the HR function is busy transiting to more of a continuous organisational practice with a strategic aim of driving the outcomes of an organisation.

The subject of talent management has been developing over the years, however, with not much evidence of its impact on the SOEs' bottom-line, thus leaving a lot of gaps in the literature. This view has been corroborated by Gallardo-Gallardo et al. (2015) that knowledge and the notion of talent management have over the years gained the attention of academics and HR practitioners. However, the subject matter still lacks in terms of practical literature. This aligns with the findings of a study conducted by Thunnissen et al. (2013), which found that publications on talent management in SOEs lacked evidence and that they are scarce regarding empirical studies. The studies, according to Gallardo-Gallardo et al. (2015), revealed that the data collected regarding the subject matter was limited to only 35 countries which included mainly the US, UK, Ireland, Netherlands, and Australia, with a few studies having been done in countries from the Middle East where data from India and China were collected. Thus, conclusions from the studies were not entirely conclusive from a global perspective as these left gaps regarding other regions in the world and mostly developing nations such as those from Africa since the element of differing cultures plays a significant role in talent management practices. In support, studies conducted by the Dutta and Mia (2011), exposed that the global issue of talent management is lacking. This in turn affects key positions of most organisations worldwide, thereby encouraging leading organisations such as Walmart, Google and Starbucks to bring about talent management (Price & Toye, 2017) at the top of their agendas.

Talent Management Approaches

Different organisations have different conceptions about what talent and talent management is and how it is realised. It is from this perspective that there are two broad talent management approaches namely inclusive and exclusive approaches. Organisations can follow either an inclusive (also known as a humanistic approach or egalitarian approach) or an exclusive approach (which is the elitist approach) to talent management. The point of departure of the humanistic approach is that all employees can add value to ensure high-performance delivery. It is for this reason that all employees should be included in the talent management process (Cappelli & Keller, 2014). The inclusive or humanistic approach acknowledges that each person possesses some level of skills, and all employees are regarded as talented. The premise that talent may be developed rather than born is central to this approach. Organisations that use this approach stress the effort of "creating" talent, so all employees, regardless of their professional experience, are offered opportunities (Ibrahim & Daniel, 2018).

Contrary to the inclusive approach is the exclusive or elitist approach. This approach recognises that only a small percentage of employees has the skills that distinguish them as talented. This group of employees would have exceptional performance and high potential, which set them apart from other employees. Employers who concentrate on this approach focus more on attracting brilliant individuals rather than creating them (Ibrahim & Daniel, 2018).

The entrepreneurial approach which is more recent regarding talent as an emphasis on motivation and drive and experience playing a major role in developing talent. According to Bolander et al. (2017), organisations practicing entrepreneurial practices in attracting talent have an inclusive view regarding talent, as all employees have the likelihood of being talents if they are placed in environments where each is able to excel. The authors further highlight that the entrepreneurial practice is more of an inclusive approach, though organisations practicing it do not claim that all employees are talents. In addition, these organisations tend to define talent from an attitude of employee perspective rather than the performance perspective. The emphasis is on the individual employee's desire of seeking out and welcoming challenges and their preparedness to assume new responsibilities. It is from these new challenges and responsibilities that the identified incumbents attain experience and learning from it, thereby leading them to be progressively talented. Another issue worth noting from this perspective is that a talented individual in one organisation may not be talented under another organisation due to the approach's prominence on cultural fit. The approach to talent management that an organisation adopts depends on the type of the organisation, with the humanistic approach tending to be favoured by non-hierarchical and mainly flat organisations as compared to the hierarchical approach (elitist) such as in accounting and law firms and other specialised organisations that place more emphasis on individual performance that is robust.

Talent Management Practices

There are three main predominant practices in talent management: talent attraction, talent development, and talent retention, with career management and succession planning at times being added as the fourth practice:

Talent Attraction

This practice is the first in the talent management process, with organisations being expected to use appropriate methods and techniques in the attraction and selection of the right talent that is competitive and has the ability and potential to drive the company towards sustainable and competitive performance. Talent attraction, according to Stroud (2020), is a term that is used in the field of human resources to describe how organisations go about attracting the best talent through implied and envisioned incentives. Similarly, Osburg et al. (2020) proffer that talent attraction involves recruiting the most capable talents through measures such as financial incentives, career development programmes and or flexible working hours. Organisations also use factors such as company ethicality, i.e., the extent to which job seekers perceive a company as acting responsibly towards the environment and society (Osburg et al., 2020). Another technique used in the recruitment of the right candidate is the psychometric assessments.

The latter is commonly used by organisations to assess the satisfaction of a job vacancy and a potential employee. This assists the organisation in determining an applicant's eligibility by evaluating attributes such as their abilities, talents and motivation. The knowledge obtained from the assessment provides useful guidance in deciding on the right candidate for the position (Saha, 2020). The organisation needs to decide whether the valuable people data collected through the psychometric assessment, such as their behavioural drives and needs will be shared with the direct supervisor. Alternatively, whether it will be used to personalise the on boarding process or will the data be used to help the new hireling to fit within the new team they are joining. The author further states that the organisation may have good people data, but it just needs to put it to good use.

In today's global environment, location has not stopped employers from attracting and hiring the right talent beyond the borderlines. This argument is confirmed by the African Association for Public Administration and Management (2008, as cited in Schlechter et al., 2014), that talent scarcity in Africa can be attributed to the developed countries' employers having a good talent acquisition strategy that promotes an attractive employer brand and also offers foreign nationals with opportunities to become permanent residents. The positive organisational image and benefits serve as effective attraction tools for hiring talent globally (African Association for Public Administration and Management, 2008 as cited in Schlechter et al., 2014).

One of the factors that entice prospective employees to apply for any opening as stated above is the employer's brand. In Namibia, Deloitte Namibia conducted a survey called "the best company survey" which has been a Deloitte endeavour for almost a decade. The Best Company survey continues to be a reliable source of comparable data for businesses. The survey provides the chance to discover how employees perceive the current workplace environment in order to decide where changes can be made and, conversely, what attributes can be celebrated. The survey acknowledges that attraction and engagement are intrinsically linked and that they are required in gaining a complete picture of what attracts and retains an employee. The Attraction Index measures the overall attraction of employees to the organisation. It is an expression of the employees' alignment to the brand and an indicator of retention. In 2019, Trustco Group Holdings took first place as the best company to work for, while FirstRand Namibia took second place (Deloitte, 2019). Participation in such a survey provides the employer with vital data for decision making around the attraction and retention of employees.

Employers are now using recruitment data to attract new talent, and according to Gleeson (2020), by analysing the data of the organisation's current employees, the employer can learn about what to look for or what to look out for in prospective employees. This concurs with Talentlyft (2018), who states that people and business data can be utilised to draw insights about how to identify the right candidate for a position or even what makes an organisation appealing to prospective future employees. This means that using data for talent acquisition benefits both the prospective candidate and the HR team in locating the talent they are looking for. An example of such data is the recruitment data, which is used to attract the best candidate for the job (Gleeson, 2020).

Talent Development

The purpose of talent development is to ensure that organisations carry out activities that nurture talent. Thus, when talent has been identified, organisations do not stop there but go further to ensure that the identified talent is developed. Tarique and Schuler (2010), define talent development as the identification and implementation of development strategies that can address the current and future needs of an organisation. In Williamson (2011), talent development is defined as a process that is in place and is meant for skills and attitude improvement of employees. This definition is further enhanced by Ibrahim and Daniel (2018), that talent development is a process where talented employees are assisted in skills and knowledge acquisition, which are critical to their success and performance in their successive current and future roles. The preceding definition aligns with the suggestions by Mendez and Stander (2011, as cited in Ibrahim & Daniel (2018), that organisations ought to constantly develop their talent in line with environmental changes such as the current technological advances. Thus, the employees are equipped with relevant skills and knowledge befitting the organisation's evolving strategic goals. Tafti et al. (2017) corroborate this notion by stating that after identifying potential talents, training programmes are presented to develop their competencies. Hence, the organisation should put in place a development plan which ensures that the existing or acquired talent is prepared for current and future needs. The acquired talent, during the recruitment process, undergoes a psychometric assessment/psychological testing. The latter, according to Wilsher (2015), has long been used in the recruitment process, emphasising that the cost of a bad hiring decision is a significant incentive for pre-employment screening, as most people involved in the recruitment process are well aware.

Given the increasingly competitive and potentially contentious nature of the job market, many will rely on cognitive and personality tests to provide adequate evidence to hire or not to hire an applicant. Once the employee joins the organisation, talent development is achieved through formalised learning models which are programme and experience-based, with activities like job rotations, challenging assignments and internal courses with certificates being awarded upon completion. Furthermore, organisations also utilise performance review to examine an employee's effectiveness and decide appropriate next steps in terms of training and development. For example, performance evaluations can also provide useful information about the employee's experience and contributions. If a high-performing employee starts to underperform, it could signal a problem with the organisation's culture, which may lead to disengagement.

Career Management and Succession Planning

Due to people's hierarchy of needs as discussed by Michael Porter, employees also tend to go through the same process whereby, in this instance, when their talent has been developed, they further look forward to being offered better opportunities within the organisation where their newly acquired skills can be applied, and if not, they look outwards for better opportunities. Hence, organisations must practice career management and succession planning. According to Bolander et al. (2017), these activities are designed and intended to ensure that talented employees are optimally utilized by placing them in relevant jobs that match their acquired skills and knowledge. Career management is going through rapid change as much as organisations are changing due to the current volatility, uncertainty, complexity, and ambiguity of the global business environment. This has been long identified by Baruch (2006, as cited in Cappelli & Keller, 2014) as happening due to the lack of expected returns from employers. As such, employees have the liberty to go elsewhere where they are appreciated and recognised, thereby forcing employers to gradually shift from their traditional command and control model for employee management, which focuses only on the achievement of organisational goals.

The above citations from Baruch are further confirmed by Cappelli and Keller (2014), who found that organisations in the past, and some currently, focusing on the traditional organisational careers approach, tended to be authoritarian and bound by employees while advocating for the organisation's needs through formalised career practices. However, new conceptual models have come into play, which promote placing the career burden on employees as individuals rather than employers. This is a self-managed career approach that is centred on employees' needs and responsibilities, not those of the organisation as in the past. Therefore, careers become more self-directed and boundary-less (Bolander et al., 2017). Organisations should focus on drawing up career paths either vertically or horizontally within the organisation, thereby resulting in upward mobility or skills development within the same role or a complete rotation of the job (Meyers et al., 2013).

Cappelli and Keller (2014) vouch for the new system of career management where employers and employees continuously seek opportunities that align talent and organisational needs within the firm through two models, namely: career lattice and internal job boards. The lattice model offers employees manifold advancement and development paths emanating from upward and lateral links in the midst of jobs found in the organisation. Thus, the multidirectional theoretical model is fulfilled through promoting succession planning. According to Van der Heijde and Van der Heijden (2006, as cited in Cappelli & Keller, 2014), rather than developing employees to fit narrow jobs at a specific time in the future, this model develops broad competencies in employees as lateral moves increasingly replace vertical moves as a form of development. Thus, there is an increased likelihood of meeting impending strategic jobs, which are demanded by the ever-increasingly changing business environment, since the internal pool of talent has been continuously developing extensive competencies.

Internal job boards are really more of an extension of the lattice model, which supports multiple career paths for existing employees in an organisation. Their main agenda is to necessitate information exchange, which is vital to both employers and employees in short-term career matching decisions, and to create a competitive market for talent within the organisation.

Talent Retention

Talent retention has been defined by Ibrahim and Daniel (2018) as the process of retaining employees who are talented for a longer time within an organisation. Once talent has been identified and developed through career enhancement, what is left is for the organisation to make sure that such talent is retained. The intense competition for skilled labour forces organisations to develop talent retention strategies in order to maintain a competent workforce and drive eco-innovation (Fields & Atiku, 2017). HR departments in SOEs should develop strategies or interventions such as reward schemes, recognition plans, and work-life balance strategies, which are common practices at some of the most successful first-world enterprises like Starbucks and Southwest Airlines. High turnover of talented staff is perilous for an organisation to the extent that it lowers productivity and increases costs through the constant attraction of a new talent pool to replace the ones leaving (Echols, 2015).

Cappelli and Keller (2014) assert that retention challenges are mainly self-inflicted, although employers attribute such concerns to changes in attitude by employees. According to Bidwell et al. (2013), employers are changing preferences rather than employees' preferences changing, which is central to the increase in external mobility. The authors further highlight that, owing to reluctance or the inability to assure employees of continued employment, employers have encouraged employees to take full responsibility of their careers, thus creating external mobility as an alternative path for them in the quest for better opportunities. As a result, talent retention strategies are one of the most important components of a talent management system (Tafti et al., 2017). Essential for the development of talent retention strategies, organisations should use data to better understand what candidates want and discover the benefits and types of organizational culture that ideal candidates seek. By offering the candidates what they want from the onset, organisations would be able to retain more talent (Gleeson, 2020). In cases where employees exit the organisation, exit interviews can be used to gather data. Exit interviews provide insights into the employee's experiences as well as the possible reasons for turnover. The idea is to figure out if an employee's departure is linked to engagement problems. Likewise, Amushila and Bussin (2021) emphasises that through the examination of people data such as exit interviews, the organisation will be able to understand its retention challenges.

Through people data, HR leaders can observe which employees are set to leave the organisation, or which employees are not engaged in their current roles, or even find out which employees within the organisation are better suited for a different role (Albinus, 2021). The majority of employees resign as a result of low engagement, when they feel they have more to offer and they are not challenged enough, or because they simply do not enjoy working for that organisation. To avoid high turnover, employers need to conduct employee engagement surveys. This is a market research tool that provides organisations with critical information on their employees, such as if they are likely to leave the organisation. The finding of the survey can be used to make informed decisions to ensure that employees are engaged and, as a result, remain with the employer (Lorman, 2020).

HR Metrics and Talent Retention

The concept of HR metrics was discussed by Boudreau and Ramstad (2007), whereby metrics are defined as the tools of accountability that facilitate the evaluation of results of a particular function. HR metrics are key performance indicators (KPI) as these are metrics that indicate the gradient of HR practices and outcomes (Pillai & Sivathanu, 2021). There are three types of metrics that organisations collect in order to evaluate HR activities and their impact on the business strategy (efficiency, effectiveness and impact). According to Levenson and Fink, (2017), a potentially meaningful set of effectiveness metrics for the HR function concerns talent and talent management. In most organisations, human resources are in charge of acquiring, developing, and deploying talent. In order to determine how effectively organisations are carrying out this responsibility, measures of talent quality, talent development, and talent deployment are needed. A compelling argument may be made that talent metrics should be regularly revised, so that organisations have ongoing data with respect to the condition of their human resources.

Talent Management Challenges

Talent management in Africa, as well as the rest of the world, faces a variety of challenges. Organisations in Africa have a shortage of experienced professionals to develop effective talent retention strategy design and execution (Anlesinya et al., 2019). Organisations in Africa need to put an effective talent retention strategy in place as a way of addressing the issue of professional brain drain in Africa. For example, the African Union estimates that about 70,000 skilled professionals emigrate from Africa annually (Clemens & Pettersson, 2008). Talent management is one of the competencies with the poorest application in South African workplaces (Mwila & Turay, 2018). Ineffective talent management is a big challenge that different African nations face in the knowledge economy. For example, in Ghana, cultural factors influence the successful execution of talent management initiatives owing to foreign managers' failure to train and manage indigenous managers. In South Africa, leaders lack of the will to execute talent retention strategies. Talent management challenges include a lack of performance management, talent development, talent retention, remuneration challenges, complex governmental legislation and red tape, and a lack of leadership on the part of talent management practitioners (Filippus & Schultz, 2019; Jeremiah et al., 2023).

From a global perspective, some of the following talent management decision-making challenges were also highlighted by Vaiman et al. (2012):

- *Talent shortages—internationally:* There has been an increasing concern over the shortage of talent in specific areas such as the health sector owing to the current COVID-19 global pandemic. Both locally based and international companies are faced with intensified global competition for talent, which has become one of the major key success factors, amounting to increased competitive advantage.
- *Demographics and societal trends:* The authors opine that the decline in the birth rate, accompanied by increasing longevity, are critical demographic trends impacting the management of talent decisions, and they are a huge source of challenges in talent management. There has been an alarming concern over the supply of talented labour resulting from shifting demographic profiles, thus leading to new and innovative talent practices such as advanced technologies and people analytics in recruitment.
- *Diversity:* Lately, due to globalisation, diverse employment groups have become the norm, with organisations being made up of a workforce coming from different backgrounds and having different cultures. This has a strong bearing on how talent is managed in organisations.
- *Permanent shift to a knowledge-based economy:* developed economies like the US and UK are experiencing rapid growth in the service sector, resulting in increased demand by companies for highly skilled value-adding workers to fill the growing complex roles that warrant higher cognitive abilities.

PEOPLE DATA

People data (also referred to as employee data, HR data, and workforce data) is defined as datasets describing people in organisations (Morrison, 2013). People data, often referred to as "employee data," is the essential key information on the organisation's employees. It often contains datasets that describe the employees' strengths and limitations, as well as how well they think, communicate, interact with others, and generally how they work (Kim, n.d.). Fallon (2022) defines employee data as all the details that an organisation collects about its employees. Employee data includes both basic information such as the date of birth or ethnicity and specific information such as workplace performance, which would inform decisions around promotions and training programmes. Executives appear to be using people data more extensively in their strategic plans and decision-making than in the past. People data is being collected in greater quantities and tracked more closely in order to improve the human experience, talent recruitment, retention, and productivity (Almaaitah et al., 2020).

According to Huus (2015), when management asks the right questions and actively requests people data, it has the potential to greatly enhance talent management capabilities and make decisions for employees across the business more data-driven and future-proof. The insurgence of new advanced technologies coupled with the increasing volatility, uncertainty, complexity, and ambiguity of the business environment has forced organisations to evolve, resulting in the changing of business models and even the adoption of new strategies, with organisational functions changing their roles accordingly. The world of HRM has not been spared by this either. The organisation and configuration of all global economies have been continuously altered by these new technologies, affecting labour markets, financial markets, and many more, leaving most organisations vulnerable (Sumer, 2018). The emergence of Industry 4.0 and increased technological innovations influenced people management, workplace environments, and other domains in the business world. There has been an emergence of many different terms in the HR world, such as eHRM, digital HRM, HR analytics, Big data analytics, People analytics, People/Employee data, and HRIS, with all of them, in their own way, contributing to the current and future technology-based talent management practices in the new era (CIPD, 2018).

People analytics is derived from the use of the vast data made available by ever-innovating internet technologies. Employees have become an asset and key success factor in HR activities, resulting in competitive advantages for organizations. Data flows through every organisation, across various departments, and it is at the heart of success for some of the world's most successful companies, such as Google, Amazon, and Facebook. Data without context or reference point analysis has no significance, yet it is required for information generation. Humans provide contexts and reference points that are relevant and meaningful to data before communicating new information to a receiver. The receiver's interpretations allow them to decide if the information is valuable. Individuals then mix and synthesise multiple pieces of knowledge to develop a deeper understanding that offers value through action (Bumblauskas et al., 2017).

According to experts in numerous sectors, data-driven decision-making is positively associated with profitability, productivity, and market value (Heijden, 2019). Mountains of new data are suddenly available to help organisations answer key questions about their workforce and its needs. According to Harris et al. (2011), HR executives must use data to ask the hard questions that are vital for the organisation, instead of just reporting on the past performance of the organisation. The rise of digital collaboration platforms and news methods for harvesting data, along with new technologies and novel approaches for finding and managing talent, are redefining how organisations will build their workforces going forward (Leong, 2021).

Capturing and managing workforce data takes a lot of effort and money for organisations. However, having this data is not sufficient. The HR manager should be able to analyse the data to understand trends and get valuable insights. This is easier said than done. Workforce (people) analytics may assist HR managers in analysing and understanding changes throughout an employee's career, as well as predicting them (Lal, 2015). This data may be present in organisations in different applications and in different formats. The integration of data from silos is essential for transforming it into relevant, timely, and actionable insights. This creates a single source of data that is clean and easy to analyse and visualise (Lal, 2015). However, there is currently a lack of knowledge about what HR data is being used for, how it is being applied, and what factors affect the application outcomes. There is also a dearth of research in this field, with academic literature only beginning to emerge (Angrave et al., 2016). A report by the CIPD (2018), reveals that a global analysis shows that the most collected data on people is related to employee pay and benefits and employee turnover rates. Employee and productivity performance rates, revenue per employee data, and workforce return on investment are the least likely people data to be collected in the United Kingdom. In contrast, data on the gender pay gap ratio is unlikely to be collected in the United States of America. The report concluded by recommending that measures such as return on investment should be collected and calculated more regularly by the HR functions. Moreover, HR should improve the extent to which it collects and reports on different types of data to both its internal and external stakeholders. According to the Unit (2016), there must always be a decent chance that the information the organisation is trying to collect and analyse will correct or improve a costly business error.

Though leading organisations in various sectors such as retail (Walmart, Targat, Amazon, and Tesco), IT (Microsoft, IBM, and Tata Consultancy Service), and Telecommunications Services (Vodacom Group, Telefonica, and AT and T Inc) are busy implementing new technologies such as using Big Data and People data in various functions of their organisations, most companies globally are yet to catch up and are worlds behind those that have already implemented this.

In today's data-rich environments, the risk is that organisations will become clogged by hundreds, if not thousands of transactional or tactical metrics, missing important signals that should be conveyed by the "critical few" scorecard metrics. Metrics should help provide evidence that authenticates or invalidates hypotheses regarding the effects of data driven decision on eco-innovations in organisations. Focusing on what information is required to inform business decisions helps measure what has more impact (Schiemann & Ulrich, 2017).

What has happened to make a data revolution possible in talent management? Over the past several years, vast improvements have occurred in how we understand, measure, and categorise both personality traits and cognitive abilities. Since these individual characteristics do not appreciably change with training, coaching, or incentives, it is critical to identify and understand them when making decisions about whom to hire, train, or promote. Over the past several years, it has become important to identify and understand individuals before making the decision to hire, train, or promote them. This has seen the rise of the data revolution in talent management, which aids in the understanding, measuring, and categorising of an individual's personality traits and cognitive abilities (Russell & Bennett, 2015).

Importance of People Data

Houghton and Green (2018) assert that in HR, like in so many other areas of business today, data and technology are at the vanguard of innovation. Many new possibilities to use people data to better understand who our employees are, how they work, and what work means to them are developing as many organisations incorporate data and technology into their workforce practices. Houghton and Green (2018) further argue that people-data insights may help organisations to move away from making decisions based on just instincts or habits and towards decisions that are evidence-based and focused on developing long-term positive results. Fernandez and Gallardo-Gallardo (2020) concur that in recent years, the use of workforce data has grown in popularity and relevance. The data is being regarded as a form of evidence, which is important for improving decision-making by executives, HR professionals, and line managers. There is an increasing demand for the use of HR data. However, Duane and Bartholin (2019) maintain that there is currently a lack of knowledge about what HR data is being used for, how it is being applied, and what factors affect the application outcomes. As a result, it is critical that HR consider and engage numbers and metrics in its activities by asking meaningful questions about data and harnessing it for their own profound and rich acumen, preventing analytics from becoming skills silos. There is also a dearth of research in this field, with academic literature only beginning to emerge (Angrave et al., 2016). There are several barriers to using employee data (Isson & Harriott, 2016). For example, massive amounts of internal and externally siloed information are stored using disparate, incompatible technologies. Even if the data is available, it must be culled to optimise the stages of the talent management life cycle. Aside from reporting, most organisations lack the specialised personnel required to generate and convert data stores into business outcomes. This view is in accord with Deloitte's (2019) report, which states that many executives interviewed believed that the HR department lacks the expertise to use HR data to forecast workforce performance and improvement. The report further states that new-style HR professionals should have two extremely important skills: firstly, they should have a head for analytics together with the ability to present findings, and secondly, the capacity to persuade executives (Unit, 2016).

Literature emphasizes the importance of people's data to stakeholders such as investors in making informed investment decisions, not just businesses. According to the literature, combining people data with other business data provides investors with a complete picture of how the business is performing. CIPD (2019), argues that HR leaders have an important role to play in helping investors understand both the value of the workforce and people-related risks through the collection and reporting of data so as to uncover how people add value in organisations and inform better business decision-making. This notion is supported by Houghton and Green (2018), who proffer that external stakeholders such as investors, regulators, and prospective employees are continuously seeking people and organisational data to shape their understanding of organisations.

When it comes to the definition and implementation of talent management, there appears to be no unanimity. Sparrow (2019) states that in the area of talent management, there is a fragmented body of knowledge and definitions of talent and talent management remain ambiguous. For this research, the definition by Orlova et al. (2015) is adopted, which states that talent management involves the practice of continuously discovering, developing, using, and retaining those people in an organisation, who are especially valuable either in terms of having great potential for the future of the organisation, or because they are capable of resolving business and operational issues that are critical for the company. While most businesses realise the need for talent management, they often fail to manage it effectively. Contrary to most literature advocating for a move from operational reporting to analytics, Minbaeva (2017) states that for some companies, basic analytics of HR and business data is sufficient.

Many SOEs have struggled to turn their large amounts of data into usable, thoughtful, and effective knowledge. The demand for increased worker reporting and analytics skills has almost certainly never been greater. Several companies have reported that descriptive statistics added the most value to their organisations (Van der Togt & Rasmussen, 2017). However, organisations have often not tested whether the concepts that they report on truly have a relationship with important performance indicators. Thus, it can be debated whether decision-makers are truly receiving the information they require to make the best decision possible. It therefore seems important to test the strategic relevance of the information contained in the reports so as to add the most value to an organisation through this type of service (Peeters et al., 2020).

People Data and Talent Analytics

With the recognition that human talent leads to a competitive advantage, the utilisation of workforce analytics has become a trend as all functions have started seeing the importance of data. Through the analysis of the data, organisation can attract and retain the right people, and this information has become important to the executive management (Unit, 2016). This notion was also alluded to by Davenport et al. (2010) by posing the following questions regarding the use of employee data for talent analytics:

- "Do you *think* you know how to get the best from your people?"
- "How do investments in your employees actually affect workforce performance?"
- "Who are your top performers?"
- "How can you empower and motivate other employees to excel?"

Answers to these questions are most likely to be based on gut feelings and, in most cases, are not accurate for organisations not adopting people analytics. However, radical innovative companies such as Google, Amazon, and Walmart, have since incorporated this phenomenon in their HR systems, thereby enhancing their competitive advantage and, in the process, achieving high productivity levels, increased employee engagement, and top talent retention.

Leading-edge companies such as Harra's Entertainment, a US-based hotel and casino group, have been using analytics for different purposes such as customer selection, and it has done well for itself. The company expanded its use of analytics to its people decisions by applying insights gained from people data analytics, assisting them with decisions regarding appropriate position staffing of its employees and enhancing personalized customer service by computing the optimal number of staff members needed for manning all service points of customer interaction (Davenport et al., 2010).This means that organisations have increased their data collection regarding their workforce and this has also elevated the weight and importance of such workforce data to both internal and external stakeholders (CIPD, 2019). Taking Harrar's Entertainment into this context, it is noted that the organisation used employee metrics in the evaluation of its workforce's health and wellness programmes to influence engagement and the Triple P Bottom-line (profit, people, and planet).

Contemporary management approaches relying on guesswork to make people decisions. For example, managing talent has been revised by the introduction of data analytics. Companies like Google and AT and T have since discarded traditional approaches of measuring performance by managerial perceptions (which is more of a gut feeling) by moving to quantitative analysis as a tool for predicting high performance at the workplace. Evans (2012) indicates that there are numerous tools and systems available in the new technological era that allow for the provision of mass outputs ranging from talent metrics reporting and descriptive analytics to predictive and prescriptive analytics. Hence, according to the author:

Descriptive analytics, such as HR metrics, talent reporting, talent benchmarking, and talent scorecards, are used to condense raw data and convert it into meaningful information by analysing it through mediums such as bar charts, line graphs, and reports revealing trends over time.

Predictive analytics: This includes metrics on employees intending to leave and sick day predictions per week, month, year, or cycle. According to Evans (2012), this is when an organisation uses past data to forecast future outcomes by modelling relationships between variables and then extrapolating these relationships forward in time. Predictive analytics helps to highlight relationships that are otherwise undetectable through standard descriptive methods. It is able to offer trend analysis and forecasting as well as a combination of lagging data and leading indicators.

Prescriptive analytics are used when an organization's objectives regarding employees are reduced or maximized using the best alternatives method of optimisation, and when combined with arithmetic and mathematical predictive analytics techniques to assist organisations in making decisions that incorporate uncertainty in raw data. Examples of such analytics include pricing strategies, worker roster or schedules designed for optimising worker successful sales opportunities.

People Data and Talent Decisions

The success of an organisation may be measured by the success of its decisions. Decisions should be founded on a solid foundation of historical experiments. One of the most essential foundations is to rely on HR systems and use historical data to make judgments. The HR manager's decisions are influenced by a variety of variables, ranging from judgment and human experience to knowledge preferences, all of which might cause inaccurate, unforeseen, and inconsistent decisions (Hamoud et al., 2020).

According to Minbaeva and Collings (2013), talent decisions are assumed to be fair since they are based on performance management systems. Nevertheless, talent decisions are frequently based on inadequate information, which contributes to the failure of talent management strategies. They proffer that not only is the information utilised for decision-making incorrect, but the managers making the decisions also have limited cognitive capabilities to make a judgment using all the pertinent information. Similarly, Makela et al. (2010, as cited in Vaiman & Collings, 2012), point out that talent decisions are based on bounded rationality based on available performance data and anticipations of future potential.

In coping with their limited ability to process such complex and incomplete information, managers often make decisions based on a subset of the information available, thereby leading to biases in decision making (Vaiman & Collings, 2012). HR managers can no longer afford to make judgments based on gut instincts or a sense of the surroundings and unique scenarios. Being able to answer such questions accurately and on a timely basis will assist the HR managers in making informed decisions. One essential component of making well-informed decisions is having the proper data about the workforce (Lal, 2015). Evidence-based talent management decisions require more and more data on an individual basis in real-time to find out what employees care about right now. Tapping into this ambient people data to make predictive statements about the workforce is becoming an integral part of the new talent management order (Claus, 2019). Hence, data driven talent management practices is essential in promoting eco-innovation and achieving sustainable development in the SOEs.

Eco-Innovation

Eco-innovation could be referred to as an organisational response to the United Nations Sustainable Development Goals. Eco-innovation is a business strategy that promotes green creativity and the development of products and services that are eco-friendly. Eco-innovation is a strategy that provides customer and business values in order to reduce the negative impact of industrial activities on the environment and promote sustainable development (Cai & Zhou, 2014). Accordingly, the key drivers of eco-innovations can be grouped into external and internal drivers. The external drivers of eco-innovation in organisations include environmental regulations, competition pressures, and customers' demands for products and services that are eco-friendly. The internal drivers of eco-innovation in organisations include organisational capabilities, technological capabilities, and corporate social responsibility. Effective knowledge management is essential in building organisational capabilities and enhancing workforce creativity for the development of products and services that are eco-friendly (Atiku, 2020). Data-driven talent management practices can be adopted to develop technological capabilities and ensure continuous business process improvement for eco-innovation performance. The corporate social responsibility strategy to promote eco-innovations in organisations is channelled through building employee green consciousness exhibited through employee green behaviour, managerial environmental awareness reflected through pro-environmental behaviour at the organisational level (Atiku, 2019; Peng & Liu, 2016). The HR intervention to drive eco-innovation and sustainable development in contemporary organisations is illustrated in Figure 1.

Figure 1.

RECOMMENDATIONS

The managerial implications put forward in this paper were derived from the findings of the literature review conducted. The findings were systematically illustrated in Figure 1. Application of data-driven talent management practices suggests the need for HR practitioners to ask the right questions and actively request and collect people's data. This is dependent on developing reliable and/or valid HR metrics for the collection of employee data in SOEs. Employee engagement surveys, for example, and employee culture surveys, among others, have proven to be reliable tools for gathering accurate and complete people data.

The use of HR analytics, which requires expertise in statistical analysis and the development of talent management capabilities, is essential in making effective talent decisions across the business units (Huus, 2015). With the use of people data in making strategic decisions about talent attraction, employers are now using recruitment data to attract new talent (Gleeson, 2020). The employer can then learn what to look for or what to watch out for in prospective employees. Some conclusions reached by Talentflyft (2018) showed that people and business data can be used to gain insights into how to find the right candidate for a position or even what makes an organisation appealing to prospective future employees. In recent times, the use of artificial intelligence for accurate prediction has improved hiring quality and efficiency (Mahmood, 2017).

Talent data enables organisations to constantly develop their talent in line with environmental changes such as the current technological advances (Ibrahim & Daniel, 2018). It becomes imperative to note that talent development without a sound talent retention strategy is a waste of time and resources. Therefore, SOEs should utilise data to better understand what candidates or existing employees want before developing talent retention strategies.

Career management and succession planning activities are designed to ensure that talent are optimally utilised by placing them in relevant jobs matching their acquired skills and knowledge (Bolander et al., 2017). Furthermore, SOEs should focus on drawing up career paths, either vertically or horizontally, within the organisation, thus allowing for upward mobility or skills development within the same role or a complete rotation of the job (Meyers et al., 2013).

HR managers can no longer afford to make judgments based on gut instincts or a sense of the surroundings and unique scenarios. Managers should be able to conduct a proper talent analytics on a timely basis, this will assist them in making informed decisions. One essential component of making well-informed decisions is having a set of credible data about the workforce (Lal, 2015). Therefore, tapping into this ambient people data to make predictive statements about the workforce is becoming an integral part of the new talent management model to promote eco-innovation in contemporary workplaces (Claus, 2019).

FUTURE AREAS OF RESEARCH

Future research could adopt an explanatory research design to examine the conceptual framework proposed in this study. The proposed framework is a research model on data-driven talent management practices for eco-innovation in SOEs. This provides an opportunity for future research to test the research model using structural equation modelling. The quantitative studies in this area of research will contribute to the literature on data-driven talent management practices, eco-innovation, and SOEs' sustainability, which is a major concern in many developing countries in Africa.

CONCLUSION

The aim of this chapter was to explore the influence of data-driven talent management practices on eco-innovation in SOEs. Through a literature review approach, this study holds that the use of HR metrics and people data will enhance talent management practices and improve eco-innovation performance in SOEs. People data is effective in assisting organisations in making informed decisions about talent attraction, with such data assisting the organisation in drawing insights about how to identify the right candidate for various positions. Talent development interventions will provide meaningful outcomes to SOEs when people's data such as performance data is the central source of information in developing learning and development activities. In addition, SOEs should put in place policies that encourage career growth and development opportunities in line with the current and future relevant skill sets in the industry, including the utilisation of performance data in the determination of the training required by employees. If people data is effectively utilised, HR metrics such as employee turnover rates and productivity per employee will be enhanced, with most of the metrics being considered as sources of information for talent development and retention strategies in SOEs.

REFERENCES

Al Aina, R., & Atan, T. (2020). The impact of implementing talent management practices on sustainable organisational performance. *Sustainability (Basel)*, *12*(20), 8372. doi:10.3390u12208372

Albinus, P. (2021). *How data is driving the exploding internal talent marketplace*. https://hrexecutive.com/how-data-is-driving-the-exploding-internal-talent-marketplace/

Alhajjar, A. A., Kassim, R. N. M., Raju, V., & Alnachef, T. (2018). Driving industry 4. 0 business through talent management of human resource system: The conceptual framework for banking industry. *World Journal of Research and Review*, *7*(3), 53–57.

Almaaitah, M., Alsafadi, Y., Altahat, S., & Yousfi, A. (2020). The effect of talent management on organizational performance improvement: The mediating role of organizational commitment. *Management Science Letters*, *10*(12), 2937–2944. doi:10.5267/j.msl.2020.4.012

Amushila, J., & Bussin, M. H. (2021). The effect of talent management practices on employee retention at the Namibia University of Science and Technology: Administration middle-level staff. *SA Journal of Human Resource Management*, *19*, 11. doi:10.4102ajhrm.v19i0.1485

Angrave, D., Charlwood, A., Kirkpatrick, I., Lawrence, M., & Stuart, M. (2016). HR and analytics: Why HR is set to fail the big data challenge. *Human Resource Management Journal*, *26*(1), 1–11. doi:10.1111/1748-8583.12090

Anlesinya, A., Amponsah-Tawiah, K., & Dartey-Baah, K. (2019). Talent management research in Africa: Towards multilevel model and research agenda. *African Journal of Economic and Management Studies*, *10*(4), 440–457. doi:10.1108/AJEMS-12-2018-0371

Annual Report 2018-2019. (2021). *Namibia Statistics Agency*. https://d3rp5jatom3eyn.cloudfront.net/cms/assets/documents/Annual_Report_2018-2019

Atiku, S., Kaisara, G., Kaupa, S., & Villet, H. (2022). Dimensions of learning organization: Implications for human resources effectiveness in commercial banks. *Management Science Letters*, *12*(2), 117–124. doi:10.5267/j.msl.2021.10.002

Atiku, S. O. (2019). Institutionalizing Social Responsibility Through Workplace Green Behavior. In S. Atiku (Ed.), *Contemporary Multicultural Orientations and Practices for Global Leadership* (pp. 183–199). IGI Global. doi:10.4018/978-1-5225-6286-3.ch010

Atiku, S. O. (2020). Knowledge Management for the Circular Economy. In N. Baporikar (Ed.), *Handbook of Research on Entrepreneurship Development and Opportunities in Circular Economy* (pp. 520–537). IGI Global. doi:10.4018/978-1-7998-5116-5.ch027

Atiku, S. O., & Fields, Z. (2018). Organisational learning dimensions and talent retention strategies for the service industries. In Disruptive Technology: Concepts, Methodologies, Tools, and Applications (pp. 1145-1168). IGI Global. doi:10.4018/978-1-5225-3009-1.ch017

Bakre, P. (2019). The role of HR analytics in the Global village. *International Journal of Trend in Scientific Research and Development*, *3*(2), 411–414. doi:10.31142/ijtsrd21340

Bolander, P., Werr, A., & Asplund, K. (2017). The practice of talent management: A framework and typology. *Personnel Review*. https://www.emerald.com/insight/content/doi/10.1108/PR-02-2016-0037/full/pdf?title=the-practice-of-talent-management-a-framework-and-typology

Boudreau, J. W., & Ramstad, P. M. (2007). *Beyond HR: The new science of human capital*. Harvard Business Press.

Bumblauskas, D., Nold, H., Bumblauskas, P., & Igou, A. (2017). Big data analytics: Transforming data to action. *Business Process Management Journal*, *23*(3), 703–720. doi:10.1108/BPMJ-03-2016-0056

Cai, W. G., & Zhou, X. L. (2014). On the drivers of eco-innovation: Empirical evidence from China. *Journal of Cleaner Production*, *79*, 239–248. doi:10.1016/j.jclepro.2014.05.035

Cappelli, P., & Keller, J. R. (2014). Talent management: Conceptual approaches and practical challenges. *Annual Review of Organizational Psychology and Organizational Behavior*, *1*(1), 305–331. doi:10.1146/annurev-orgpsych-031413-091314

Carroll, A. B., & Shabana, K. M. (2010). The business case for corporate social responsibility: A review of concepts, research and practice. *International Journal of Management Reviews*, *12*(1), 85–105. doi:10.1111/j.1468-2370.2009.00275.x

CIPD. (2018). *People analytics: Driving business performance with people data*. Chartered Institute of Personnel and Development. https://www.cipd.co.uk/Images/investor-perspectives-on-workforce-data_tcm18-55499.pdf

CIPD. (2019). *The intangible workforce investors perspective on workforce data. London: chartered institute of personnel and development*. https://www.cipd.co.uk/Images/investor-perspectives-on-workforce-data_tcm18-55499.pdf

Claus, L. (2019). HR disruption: Time already to reinvent talent management. *Business Research Quarterly*, *22*(3), 207–215. doi:10.1016/j.brq.2019.04.002

Clemens, M. A., & Pettersson, G. (2008). New data on African health professionals abroad. *Human Resources for Health*, *6*(1), 1–11. doi:10.1186/1478-4491-6-1 PMID:18186916

Dahlbom, P., Siikanen, N., Sajasalo, P., & Jarvenpää, M. (2019). Big data and HR analytics in the digital era. *Baltic Journal of Management*, *15*(1), 120–138. doi:10.1108/BJM-11-2018-0393

Dahlbom, P., Siikanen, N., Sajasalo, P., & Jarvenpää, M. (2020). Big data and HR analytics in the digital era. *Baltic Journal of Management*, *15*(1), 120–138. doi:10.1108/BJM-11-2018-0393

Davenport, H. T., Harris, J., & Shapiro, J. (2010). *Competing on talent analytics*. https://hbr.org/2010/10/competing-on-talent-analytics

De La Calle-Duran, M. C., de la Luz Fernandez-Alles, M., & Valle-Cabrera, R. (2021). Talent identification and location: A configurational approach to talent pools. *Intangible Capital*, *17*(1), 17–32. doi:10.3926/ic.1440

Deloitte. (2019). *Deloitte Namibia best company survey 2019 winners*. https://www2.deloitte.com/za/en/namibia/pages/human-capital/articles/Deloitte-Namibia-Best-Company-Survey-Awards-2019.html

Deloitte. (2020). 2020 global human capital trends. *The social enterprise at work: Paradox as a path forward*. https://www2.deloitte.com/content/dam/Deloitte/at/Documents/human-capital/at-hc-trends-2020

Deloitte. (2021). *The social enterprise in a world disrupted: Leading the shift from survive to thrive*. Retrieved from June 2022 from https://www2.deloitte.com/content/dam/Deloitte/lu/Documents/human-capital/lu-hc-trends-2021.pdf

Duane, A., & Bartholin, T. (2019). *Human resources data analytics – Evidence from an Irish manufacturing perspective. Human Resources Division International Conference (HRIC).*

Duran, D. C., Gogan, L. M., Artene, A., & Duran, V. (2015). The components of sustainable development-a possible approach. *Procedia Economics and Finance*, *26*, 806–811. doi:10.1016/S2212-5671(15)00849-7

Dutta, S., & Mia, I. (2011, April). The global information technology report 2010–2011. In *World Economic Forum* (Vol. 24, pp. 331-391). Academic Press.

Echols, M. (2015). *Winning the Turnover War*. Retrieved on 20th July 2015 from: http//: www.talentmgt.com

Edwards, M. R., & Edwards, K. (2019). *Predictive HR analytics: Mastering the HR*. Kogan Page Publishers.

Evans, R. J. (2012). *Business Analytics: The Next Frontier for Decision Sciences.* Carl H. Lindner College of Business, University of Cincinnati, http://faculty.cbpp.uaa.alaska.edu/afef/business_analytics.htm

Fallon, N. (2022, July 1). *The Importance of Employee Data*. Https://Www.Business.Com/Hr-Software/Employee-Data/

Fegley, S. (2006). *2006 talent management survey report - Society for human resource management*. managementw.shrm.org/hr-today/trends-and-forecasting/research-and-surveys/pages/2006_20talent_20management_20survey_20report.aspx

Fernandez, V., & Gallardo-Gallardo, E. (2020). Tackling the HR digitalization challenge: Key factors and barriers to HR analytics adoption. *Competitiveness Review*. Advance online publication. doi:10.1108/CR-12-2019-0163

Fields, Z., & Atiku, S. O. (2017). Collective Green Creativity and Eco-Innovation as Key Drivers of Sustainable Business Solutions in Organizations. In Z. Fields (Ed.), *Collective Creativity for Responsible and Sustainable Business Practice* (pp. 1–25). IGI Global. doi:10.4018/978-1-5225-1823-5.ch001

Filippus, K., & Schultz, C. M. (2019). Exploring talent management execution in the Ministry of Justice in the Namibian public sector. *SA Journal of Human Resource Management*, *17*(1), 1–9. doi:10.4102ajhrm.v17i0.1162

Gallardo-Gallardo, E., Nijs, S., Dries, N., & Gallo, P. (2015). Towards an understanding of talent management as a phenomenon-driven field using bibliometric and content analysis. *Human Resource Management Review*, *25*(3), 264–279. doi:10.1016/j.hrmr.2015.04.003

Gleeson, C. (2020). *How to use recruitment data to attract talent*. Retrieved April 2021, from: https://www.occupop.com/blog/how-to-use-recruitment-data-to-attract-talent

Hamoud, A. K., Abd Ulkareem, M., Hussain, H. N., Mohammed, Z. A., & Salih, G. M. (2020, May). Improve HR decision-making based on data Mart and OLAP. *Journal of Physics: Conference Series*, *1530*(1), 012058. doi:10.1088/1742-6596/1530/1/012058

Harris, J. G., Craig, E., & Light, D. A. (2011). Talent and analytics: New approaches, higher ROI. *The Journal of Business Strategy*, *32*(6), 4–13. doi:10.1108/02756661111180087

Heijden, L. M. A. (2019). *Exploring the effects of HR analytics on strategic decision making* [Master's thesis]. University of Twente. https://purl.utwente.nl/essays/79817

Houghton, E., & Green, M. (2018). *People analytics: Driving business performance with people data.* https://search.proquest.com/docview/2043508044?accountid=130472

Huus, T. (2015). *People Data: how to use and apply human capital metrics in your company*. Springer. doi:10.1057/9781137466969

Ibrahim, A. U., & Daniel, C. O. (2018). Talent management and its effects on the competitive advantage in organisations. *International Journal of recent advances in Multidisciplinary Research, 5*(11), 4247-4253.

Isson, J. P., & Harriott, J. S. (2016). *People analytics in the era of big data: Changing the way you attract, acquire, develop, and retain talent*. John Wiley and Sons. doi:10.1002/9781119083856

Jeremiah, A., Atiku, S. O., & Villet, H. J. (2023). Leadership effectiveness and sustainability of State-Owned Enterprises. In N. Baporikar (Ed.), *Leadership and Governance for Sustainability* (pp. 55–80). IGI Global. doi:10.4018/978-1-6684-9711-1.ch004

Jyoti, J., & Rani, R. (2014). Exploring talent management practices: Antecedents and consequences. *International Journal of Management Concepts and Philosophy, 8*(4), 220–248. doi:10.1504/IJMCP.2014.066903

Kim, H. (n.d.). *3 analytics tools that measure people data*. Academic Press.

Lal, P. (2015). Transforming HR in the digital era: Workforce analytics can move people specialists to the center of decision-making. *Human Resource Management International Digest, 23*(3), 1–4. doi:10.1108/HRMID-03-2015-0051

Leong, K. (2021). *A data-driven approach to identifying-and retaining - Top employees*. https://hbr.org/2021/05/a-data-driven-approach-to-identifying-and-retaining-top-employees

Levenson, A., & Fink, A. (2017). Human capital analytics: Too much data and analysis, not enough models and business insights. *Journal of Organisational Effectiveness: People and Performance, 4*(2), 145–156. doi:10.1108/JOEPP-03-2017-0029

Lorman. (2020). *10 benefits of employee engagement survey*. https://www.lorman.com/blog/post/10-benefits-of-employee-engagement-surveys

Mahmood, S. (2017). *21st century staffing: The wave of artificial intelligence in recruitment*. https://search.proquest.com/docview/2043508044?accountid=130472

Meena, K., & Janani, S. J. (2016). Issues and challenges in gaining competitive advantage in human resource. *International Conference on "Research Avenues in Social Science, 1*(3), 230–234. https://ijariie.com/AdminUploadPdf/Issues_and_challenges_in_gaining_competitive_advantage_through_human_resource_c_1224

Meyers, C., Van Woerkom, M., & Dries, N. (2013). Talent – innate or acquired? Theoretical considerations and their implications for talent management. *Human Resource Management Review, 23*(4), 305–321. doi:10.1016/j.hrmr.2013.05.003

Mihalcca, A. (2017). Employer branding and talent management in the digital age. *Management Dynamics in the Knowledge Economy, 5*(2), 289–306. doi:10.25019/MDKE/5.2.07

Minbaeva, D. (2017). Human capital analytics: Why aren't we there? Introduction to the special issue. *Journal of Organizational Effectiveness: People and Performance*, *4*(2), 110–118. doi:10.1108/JOEPP-04-2017-0035

Minbaeva, D., & Collings, D. G. (2013). Seven myths of global talent management. *International Journal of Human Resource Management*, *24*(9), 1762–1776. doi:10.1080/09585192.2013.777539

Mondal, S. (2021). *The rise of talent intelligence in 2022*. https://ideal.com/rise-of-talent-intelligence-feature/

Morrison, R. (2013). *What is big data and what is people data*. https://www.orgvue.com/resources/articles/the-key-to-challenge-in-organisation-design-isnt-big-data-its-people-data-part-3/

Mwila, N. K., & Turay, M. I. S. (2018). Augmenting talent management for sustainable development in Africa. *World Journal of Entrepreneurship, Management and Sustainable Development*, *14*(1), 41–49. doi:10.1108/WJEMSD-03-2017-0012

Namibia Labour Force Survey 2018 Report. (2018). https://d3rp5jatom3eyn.cloudfront.net/cms/assets/documents/Labour_Force_Survey_final_-_2018.pdf

Nasril, F., Indiyati, D., & Ramantoko, G. (2021). Talent performance analysis using people analytics approach. Budapest International Research and Critics Institute (BIRCI-Journal): Humanities and Social Sciences, 4(1), 216-230.

Orlova, L. V., Afonin, Y. A., & Voronin, V. V. (2015). Talent management and knowledge: Theory, methodology, models. *Review of European Studies*, *7*(9), 75. doi:10.5539/res.v7n9p75

Osburg, V. S., Yoganathan, V., Bartikowski, B., Liu, H., & Strack, M. (2020). Effects of ethical certification and ethical eWoM on talent attraction. *Journal of Business Ethics*, *164*(3), 535–548. doi:10.100710551-018-4018-8

Palich, N., & Edmonds, A. (2013). Social sustainability: creating places and participatory processes that perform well for people. *Environment Design Guide*, 1–13.

Peeters, T., Paauwe, J., & Van De Voorde, K. (2020). People analytics effectiveness: Developing a framework. *Journal of Organizational Effectiveness: People and Performance*, *7*(2), 203–2019. doi:10.1108/JOEPP-04-2020-0071

Peng, X., & Liu, Y. (2016). Behind eco-innovation: Managerial environmental awareness and external resource acquisition. *Journal of Cleaner Production*, *139*, 347–360. doi:10.1016/j.jclepro.2016.08.051

Pillai, R., & Sivathanu, B. (2021). Measure what matters: Descriptive and predictive metrics of HRM-pathway toward organisational performance. *International Journal of Productivity and Performance Management*. Advance online publication. doi:10.1108/IJPPM-10-2020-0509

Price, C., & Toye, S. (2017). *Accelerating performance: how organizations can mobilize, execute, and transform with agility*. John Wiley & Sons.

Pricewaterhousecopper (PWC). (2020). *HR Matters Namibia Newsletter* (3rd ed.). https://www.pwc.com/na/en/assets/pdf/hr-matters-july-edition-2020.pdf

Pyszka, A., & Gajda, D. (2015). Successful talent management through positive CSR-driven transactions. *Journal of Positive Management*, *6*(2), 3–19. doi:10.12775/JPM.2015.007

Russell, C., & Bennett, N. (2015). Big data and talent management: Using hard data to make the soft stuff easy. *Business Horizons*, *58*(3), 237–242. doi:10.1016/j.bushor.2014.08.001

Saha, B. (2020). The significance of psychometric tests in the recruitment process for an organization to induce its effectivity. *International Journal of Research in Engineering, Science and Management*, *3*(8), 268–273.

Schiemann, W. A., & Ulrich, D. (2017). Rise of HR - New mandates for IO. *Industrial and Organizational Psychology: Perspectives on Science and Practice*, *10*(1), 3–25. doi:10.1017/iop.2016.76

Schlechter, A., Hung, A., & Bussin, M. (2014). Understanding talent attraction: The influence of financial rewards elements on perceived job attractiveness. *SA Journal of Human Resource Management*, *12*(1), 1–13. doi:10.4102ajhrm.v12i1.647

Shrivastava, S., Nagdev, K., & Rajesh, A. (2018). Redefining HR using people analytics: The case of Google. *Human Resource Management International Digest*, *26*(2), 3–6. doi:10.1108/HRMID-06-2017-0112

Sivathanu, B., & Pillai, R. (2019). Technology and talent analytics for talent management - A game-changer for organisational performance. *The International Journal of Organizational Analysis*, *28*(2), 457–473. doi:10.1108/IJOA-01-2019-1634

Sparrow, P. (2019). A historical analysis of critiques in the talent management debate. *Business Research Quarterly*, *22*(3), 160–170. doi:10.1016/j.brq.2019.05.001

Stroud, J. (2020, May 22). *Talent attraction: what it is and things to think about.* Https://Blog.Proactivetalent.Com/Talent-Attraction-What-It-Is-and-Things-to-Think-About

Sumer, B. (2018). Impact of Industry 4.0 on Occupations and Employment in Turkey. *European Scientific Journal, 14*(10).

Tafti, M. M., Mahmoudsalehi, M., & Amiri, M. (2017). Critical success factors, challenges and obstacles in talent management. *Industrial and Commercial Training*, *49*(1), 5–21. doi:10.1108/ICT-05-2016-0036

Talent Agenda Series. (2017). *Talent management in Africa and the challenges involved.* https://www.talentagendaseries.com/hr-insight-blog/2017/7/26/talent-management-inafrica-and-the-challenges-involved

Talentlyft. (2018). *Talent Acquisition Analytics: What it is & Why it Matters.* Retrieved from https://www.talentlyft.com/en/blog/article/233/talentacquisition-analytics-what-it-is-why-it-matters

Tarique, I., & Schuler, R. S. (2010). Global talent management: Literature review, integrative framework, and suggestions for further research. *Journal of World Business*, *45*(2), 122–133. doi:10.1016/j.jwb.2009.09.019

Thoma, C. (2016). *Big data in talent management - The next challenge.* https://www.linkedin.com/pulse/big-data-talent-management-next-challenge-christoph-thoma

Thunnissen, M., Boselie, P., & Fruytier, B. (2013). Talent management and the relevance of context: Towards a pluralistic approach. *Human Resource Management Review*, *23*(4), 326–336. doi:10.1016/j.hrmr.2013.05.004

Unit, E. I. (2016). *Use of workforce analytics for competitive advantage.* SHRM Foundation.

Vaiman, V., Scullion, H., & Collings, D. (2012). Talent management decision making. *Management Decision*, *50*(5), 25–941. doi:10.1108/00251741211227663

Van der Togt, J., & Rasmussen, T. H. (2017). Toward evidence-based HR. *Journal of Organizational Effectiveness: People and Performance*.

Whysall, Z., Owtram, M., & Brittain, S. (2019). The new talent management challenges of Industry 4.0. *Journal of Management Development*, *38*(2), 118–129. doi:10.1108/JMD-06-2018-0181

Williamson, D. (2011). Talent management in the new business world: How organizations can create the future and not be consumed by it. *Human Resource Management International Digest*, *19*(6), 33–36. doi:10.1108/09670731111163518

Wilsher, S. (2015). Behaviour profiling: Implications for recruitment and team building. *Strategic Direction*, *31*(9), 1–5. doi:10.1108/SD-02-2015-0023

Chapter 26
Data-Driven Decision Making for Achieving Sustainability in Apparel Business Value Chain

Kamalendu Pal
https://orcid.org/0000-0001-7158-6481
University of London, UK

ABSTRACT

Data-supported decision-making and understanding the customer's behaviour has become an essential and challenging problem for apparel businesses to sustain their position in competitive markets. Current information communication technologies (ICT) are ushering hope to mitigate this challenge, particularly the blockchain with internet of things (IoT)-based enterprise information system framework providing relevant services in global networks that mediate effective and sustainable supply chain operations. Data collection and interpretation of collected data (known as data analytics) on business-specific value creation process is most important in this architecture. This chapter reviews recent literature on technology-driven supply chain automation and related data analytics-related issues for managing sustainability. Lastly, the chapter presents an application area of 'market basket analysis' technique that focuses on discovering patterns in retail transaction data with the help of an algorithmic data mining method.

INTRODUCTION

Apparel products are essential commodities for human society. The apparel industry's operational practices have been changing rapidly in recent decades, and its business activities are considered responsible for their day-to-day work that affects society directly or indirectly. The increase in human population has demanded approaches that are more adaptable to the sustainability and ecology of the apparel industry. In addition, trends in apparel product development are influenced by the globalization of manufacturing networks, digitization of business operations, and multifaceted consumer expectations related to operational sustainability. Consequently, industry experts seek detailed information regarding apparel products' constituent elements, products, and production processes' environmental impact. Besides,

DOI: 10.4018/979-8-3693-2193-5.ch026

apparel product manufacturing has often fragmented, and a globally dispersed production network acts as a significant stimulus in industry-specific supply chain network deployment and value creation for the entire business operations. Historically, the concept of supply chain operations (or *value chain network* for business prosperity) and management practice is getting much more complex due to business processes outsourcing and their product traceability monitoring for regulatory purposes and quality assurance management. Supply chain operation managers appreciate the importance of enforcing assessment through achievement by using data-driven decision metrics. At the same time, enterprise operation management activities in the apparel industry have been evolving in recent decades. The whole industry relies on a new form of knowledge and network-based intelligent response to any issues related to enterprise sustainability (e.g., environmental, financial, quality assurance, customer satisfaction, and human resource utilization). In this way, traceability is essential to managing and mitigating unprecedented social, economic, and environmental sustainability in regular business operations. Industrial sectors often use technology-driven traceability systems to secure their '*band name*' and revenue protection (Eryilmaz et al., 2020). The crucial ingredients of traceability management are business process-related data gathering, data processing, data-driven decision-making, and secure information-sharing system architecture (Pal, 2023). In this way, it creates an essential ingredient for an attractive industrial operation management using technologies.

Rresearchers (Sneddon et al., 2006) described the idea of an industrial world where challenges exist to maintain sustainability for controlling environmental pollution inequality in global environmental policies and organizational approaches. The same research group also highlighted ways that need to be used in implementing industrial sustainable development practices. These approaches deal with the issues related to challenges in social integration, economic and environmental management, global policies, and disparities in industrial applications deployment. In this way, industrial sustainability is highlighting new research agenda by which it tries to understand, review, and improve the fundamental characteristic interactions among nature and society. Sustainability cares about meeting the requirements of the present and coming generations of human lead society. Academics and practitioners are introducing new business models with an emphasis on resource waste prevention and putting focus on work practice efficiency. In a simplistic apparel business model consists of procurement of textile fiber, fiber colouring, yarn preparation, knitting and finishing the products, and sending them to sales outlets, as shown in Figure 1.

The growing population and increased consumption of apparel products are causing higher environmental burdens on air, water, and soil associated with producing raw materials, manufacturing ingredients, and ultimate items of interest. Besides, the disposal of apparel products at the use end-life requires to be considered in more account. For example, apparel products are usually made from various materials and ingredients chosen by considering the design, purpose of the item, and performance needed for use. The adequate selection of materials, components, and constituent ingredients provides an immense opportunity for the overall sustainability of the apparel products through their life cycle. To develop more ecological and sustainable products, in what concerns the materials and components selection process and incorporation in the ultimate product design.

In this way, materials and constituent ingredients to develop more sustainable apparel products are: (i) type of material and components (e.g., recycled, recyclable, and/or biodegradable), (ii) origin and transportation methods associated, (iii) materials (e.g., textiles, polymers, leather) produced by ecofriendly processes and the use the minimum amount of chemicals and energy in their production process, (iv) water-based solvents and glues, (v) minimization of hazards and restricted substances, (vi) the renewable material ingredients, (vii) produced by simplified manufacturing production processes,

(viii) produced with innovative manufacturing technology with sustainability at the center of creation, and (xi) consciousness of environmental related issues in every steps of these new products life cycle.

Many apparel companies have successfully changed their business operational activities to be more sustainable and have embedded sustainability into their regular functions. In other words, these companies have motivated their employees with a sense of sustainable corporate steward that helps them to engage in more sustainable-supporting corporate activities. When employees integrate environmental and societal sustainable-related issues in corporate decisions, sustainability progress manifests in individual business goals, decisions, and actions. Business process-generated data drives these decisions and actions. In this way, the use available data for analytics design has also started to get immense value for handling business operations. However, estimates of the data value are required to calculate an appropriate understanding of how data can contribute value to the apparel's regular business operations and how to manage the collection and use of various data types.

This chapter's main objective is to highlight a systemic approach for the apparel industry, the value of data, and data analytics in day-to-day operations. In order to understand the broad sources of data in the apparel industry, the chapter uses Professor Michael Porter's value chain model to identify the data sources in the apparel industry. Data collection and processing power provide the information system architecture for any industry, and this chapter provides a new technology-based approach to provide a solid foundation. Given the rapid evolutions and the enlargement of secure data processing and transferring ability, this chapter mainly describes two critical technologies, the IoT and blockchain-based concepts, which are essential in today's industrial data processing environment. Next, the chapter provides an example of the apparel industry's sales data processing. In the last section, the chapter concludes with future research directions and concluding remarks.

Figure 1. Apparel business activities from production to consumption

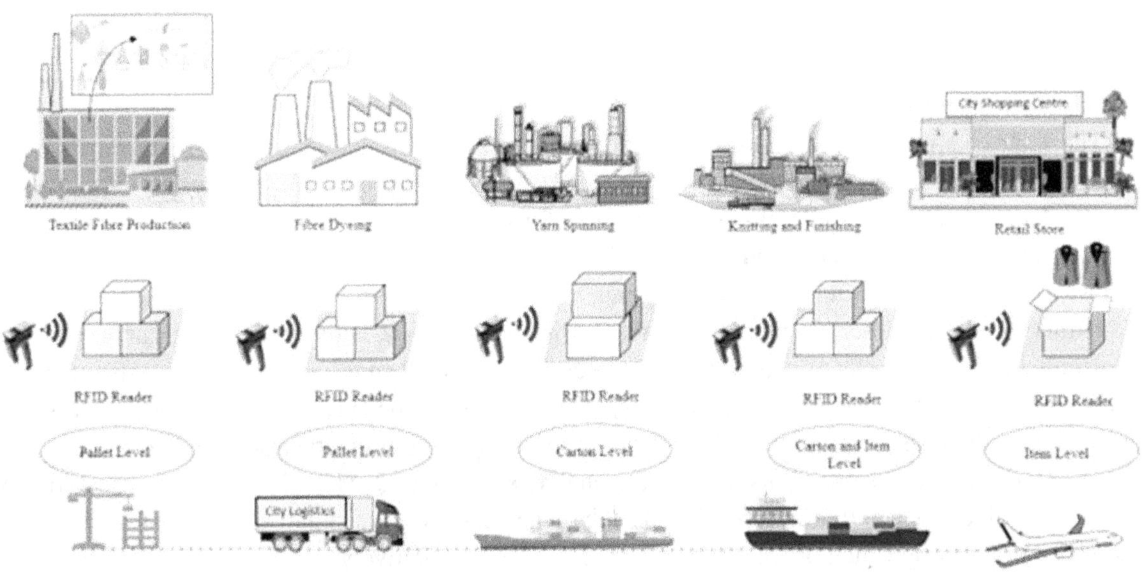

BACKGROUND AND RELATED LITERATURE REVIEW

The apparel manufacturing and retailing activities have changed in recent decades due to business process automation, and disruptive technologies play an important role. The influences of these activities include environmental, economic, societal, and as well as those of their supply chain operations. Moreover, sustainability is all around apparel industries and manufacturing activities and has become a significant challenge and crucial topic of investigation. The inclusion of sustainability-related business activities enhances the operational green agenda-related performance of the enterprises, and it also presents a way for businesses to accumulate a new set of advantages that provide them attain competitiveness by using sustainability agendas around regular operations.

In order to assess the organizational completive advantage of operations, strategic management techniques to assess the business performance and *value chain analysis* (Porter, 1986) play an essential role. Professor Michael Porter introduced the value chain analysis concept and application steps. The term "value chain" describes a set of business operational functionalities of the company that brings value to the enterprise's consumers through products and services. The business benefits usher in revenue generation when consumers are happy to offer the costs over the break-event cost in providing those products and related services.

Figure 2 diagrammatically describes the value chain model that helps to identify and assess those value-creating activities comprising an industrial business operation (e.g., apparel manufacturing and sales). The value chain analysis model consists of business activities that an apparel company can use to analyse deliver a product or a service. n this analysis, it is considered a series of business activities that are related to raw materials procurement and sales of finished products. The series of activities consists of (i) coming materials and putting them in temporary storage and warehouses around manufacturing plants for material management purposes, (ii) logistical production management that involves in the transformation of raw materials into semi-finished or finished materials, and calculating the expenditure for the final outputs (e.g., goods and services), (iii) next, it consider the business storage and transportation costs from manufacturing plants to the sales shops for ultimate consumers, (iv) product market-based identity or banding and sales related communication, and finally (v) sales of the products to consumers and after-sales service plan.

The value chain analysis also considers four operational support functionalities: (i) the administration and management part of the planning activities that includes the procurement of materials and services, (ii) the deployment of technological infrastructures for processing raw materials to finished products, (iii) required staffs recruitment and training related strategic actions, and (iv) manufacturing business infrastructures that look after the financial, legal, and public service-related issues.

In this way, Porter describes breaking down a business operational activity that represent the primary constituent building blocks of competitive advantage. Operational supervisors can then assess how individual business operation adds some enhancement of value to the final product or service. It is also evident from the research that industrial business process operations can be rewarded and create added value to the revenue streams by using big data analytics (Deloitte & MHI, 2016). The critical idea of this added value is generating insightful data analysis and using the data analysis's ultimate results with industrial partners by which operation managers can act collaboratively.

The recent types of data analytics require sophisticated and robust information and communication technology provision and modern data structures utilization and management ability to enhance day-to-day activities operational efficiency (Kohl & Grover, 2008) (Shapiro, 2010) quickly and promptly

(Mithras et al., 2011). Moreover, researchers urged industrial manufacturing companies to deploy new data-acquiring methods (e.g., Radio Frequency Identification (RFID) tags, nanotechnology-based techniques, and Sensors) and data storage repositories supported by the new generation of package software systems (e.g., enterprise resource planning (ERP), supplier relationship management (SRM)) to improve industrial operations scheduling (Davenport & O'Dea, 2011) (Dwyer & Renner, 2011).

Sustainability-related issues are the other important factor that plays an essential role in new industrial value chain operational activities. Sustainability practices provide the safest route to governmental regulations and customer satisfaction (Pal, 2023) (Lee & Zhang, 2019). Industrial data analytics are providing a way to accomplish social issues (Widmann & Hoeyer, 2018) and create value-added economic revenue (Pal, 2023) at the same time, optimize the operating environment green environment effects (Pal, 2021) (Hazen et al., 2016).

Moreover, the ramifications of massive-collected data analyses on Lean, Agile, Resilient, Green, and Economical (LARGE) issues outcome are providing some guidelines for different categories of supply chain operations (Chun Wu, 2003) (Dora et al., 2016) (Baramichai et al., 2007) (Cabral et al., 2012) (Srivastava, 2007) in present years. Some researchers put forward the panacea of the LARGE ideas of industrial operations as a value-added manifestation. The following section briefly presents a selection of LARGE concepts based on recent research.

Figure 2. Value chain analysis model

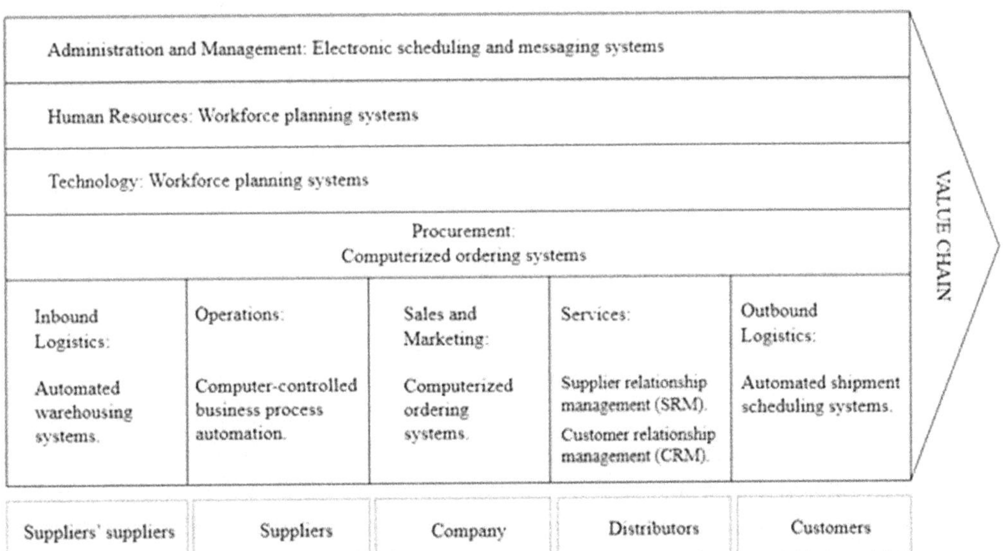

Recent Supply Chain Data Analytics Research

Industrial manufacturing businesses require to place sustainable work practices to comply with international institution guided regulations. Big data analytics are helping businesses to achieve social dimensions and improve economic values while optimizing the green effects related to corporate sustainability.

In addition, the research articles reviews of the researcher-works realised that some western countries (e.g., United Kingdom, United States of America, and Germany) are using vast business operation related data collection and analyses for supply chain management. Developing countries (e.g., India, China) are also under the microscope of industrial manufacturing sustainability related research works. Figure 3 presents a diagrammatic visualization of sustainability related research for few countries.

This research works described various application areas in various manufacturing industries and the utilization of big data processing-related issues. The main agenda is to show that business operational practices that in the past were carried out on speculative or time-consuming complex mathematical modelling of reality can now be done by exploiting heavy duty data-driven computation methods. Such huge business operations related data analysis currently drives nearly all aspects of the manufacturing industry. The industry Supply Chain Operations Reference (SCOR) model, which uses a complex industry specific operational functionalities coordination method to the supply chain community, has often been used in research work design and analysis. The SCOR model considers customer engagement information, regular business transactions, and market economic indicators related issues. In this analysis, the SCOR model uses a standardized multi-level business operation with Key Performance Indicators (KPIs) over various levels of activities. The SCOR method uses five-elements based operational strategy: Plan (P), Source (S), Make (M), Deliver (D), and Return (R) – from the suppliers' supplier to customers' customers, and all aligned with leading enterprise's operational strategy, material, work, and information flow. Figure 4. presents the SCOR model's operations.

In this way, every process metric uses aspects of a performance characteristic for operational, tactical, and strategic performance measurements across the whole business operations. For instance, any process's performance characteristics are either customer-facing (reliability, responsiveness, and flexibility) or internal-facing (expenditure and infrastructural issues) metrics. Level 1 related performance measurement metrics are primary, high-level measures that may cross multiple SCOR processes. These performance metrics present measure the business intelligence (BI) for critical key performance indicators (KPIs). Each Level 1 metric can be disintegrated to the lower Level 2 and Level 3 metrics, thus presenting standardized operational, tactical, and strategic performance measurements across the industrial apparel supply chain operations. Consequently, data driven decision making plays an essential role in regular business operations.

Significant technological advancements have been achieved in apparel product production, transportation, and sales-related activities, in recent years. Often this achievement relates to a new generation of industrial businesses processes data capture, storage, and processing methods. Apparel industry-specific data is uploaded daily in massive quantity to different storage platforms in the form of text, image, audio and video, through various media such as blogs, emails, social networks, photo and advertising hosting services. Besides, apparel industries business operational data are stored on individual corporation data storages. Many companies (e.g., Google, Microsoft, Facebook, and Twitter) are also collecting a large amount of data about the web users, their related interaction activities with the social media, and this data is commonly termed as Big Data (Pal, 2018).

Figure 3. Recent research on manufacturing industry and supply chain

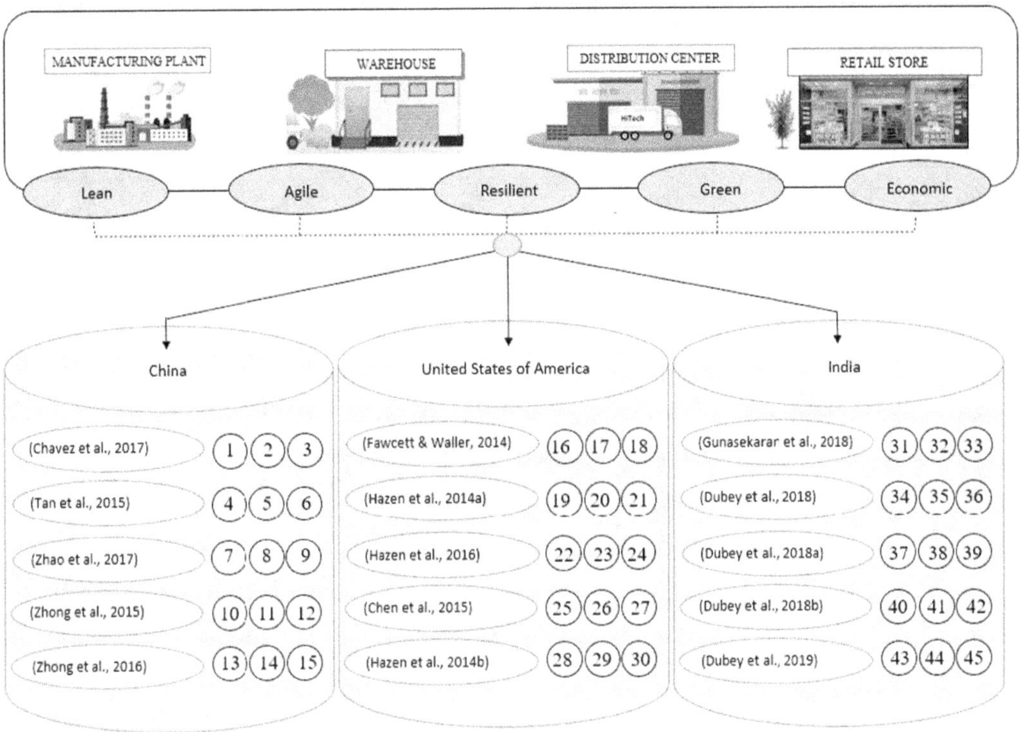

LEGENDS

1. Delivery Flexibility
2. Cost and Quality
3. Customer Satisfactions
4. Manager Competence Skills
5. Case of Optimal Decision
6. Analytic Infrastructure Model
7. Green Supply Chain
8. Inherent Risk
9. Total Cost Management
10. Manufacturing with Sensor Networks
11. Business Case Study
12. RFID Technology
13. Big Data Processing Technologies
14. Decision Make Model
15. Big Data Interpretation
16. Supply Chain Agility
17. Capacity Analysis
18. Operational Dynamics
19. Correlational Decision Analysis
20. Prediction Through Profiling
21. Collaborative Supply Chain
22. Manufacturing Organizations
23. Senior-Level Supply Chain Managers
24. Big Data Based Decisions
25. Factor Analysis
26. Senior Executive Managers
27. Technological Capabilities
28. Big Data Framework for Supply Chain
29. Structural Equation Modelling
30. Operational Dynamics Analysis
31. Big Data Processing Technologies
32. Supply Chain Performance
33. Top Management Commitment
34. Big Data Processing Technologies
35. Decision Make Model
36. Organizational Flexibility
37. Resource Complementarity
38. Organizational Compatibility
39. Temporal Orientation
40. Big Data Based Business Operations
41. Decision Make Model
42. Collaborative Performance
43. Senior-Level Supply Chain Managers
44. Supply Chain Resilience
45. Big Data Analytics

Figure 4. An organizational overview of the SCOR model

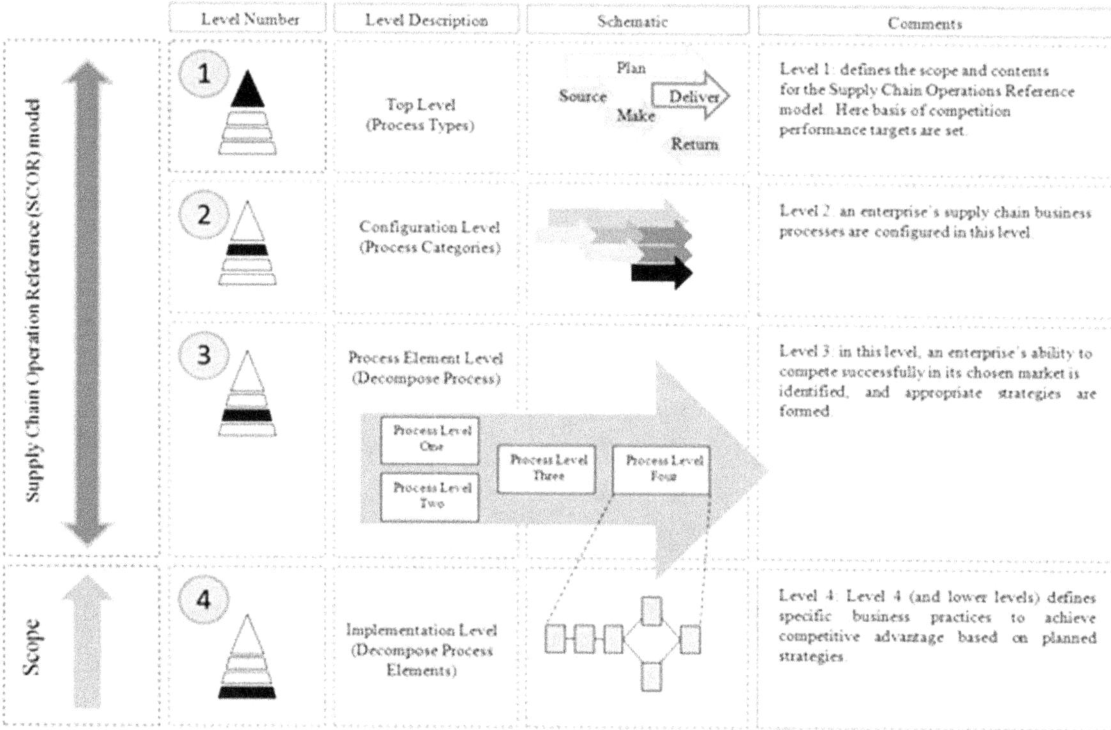

BIG DATA SIGNIFICANCE AND DATA ANALYTICS

Big Data is a common technical phrase that describes a significant volume of structured and unstructured data produced by various industrial business processes. For ordinary people's understanding, it is often presented with different numbers of Vs. (e.g., 4V – that is, Volume, Velocity, Variety, Veracity, and 5Vs or 6Vs), moreover, it describes the challenge the business world needs to address. Figure 5 presents a brief overview of big data for industrial use and some relevant socio-technical issues for business application development. For example, consumer behavioural characteristics to design and develop recommendation systems.

Academics and practitioners are assessing bottlenecks in various industrial applications. These bottlenecks have been tackled by various categories of data management models and algorithms. The following section discusses various databases developed to store significant data for analysis.

DATA PROCESSING AND MANUFACTURING INDUSTRY

Historically, data processing systems have been inseparable technological means for regular manufacturing and distribution operations. In the 1970s, manufacturing business operations were coordinated with the help of third generation programming (i.e., COBOL) applications (e.g., material management, raw material procurement, human resource management, and transportation). The early 1980s gifted relational data management systems for industrial applications development.

Figure 5. A conceptual view of big data for industrial use

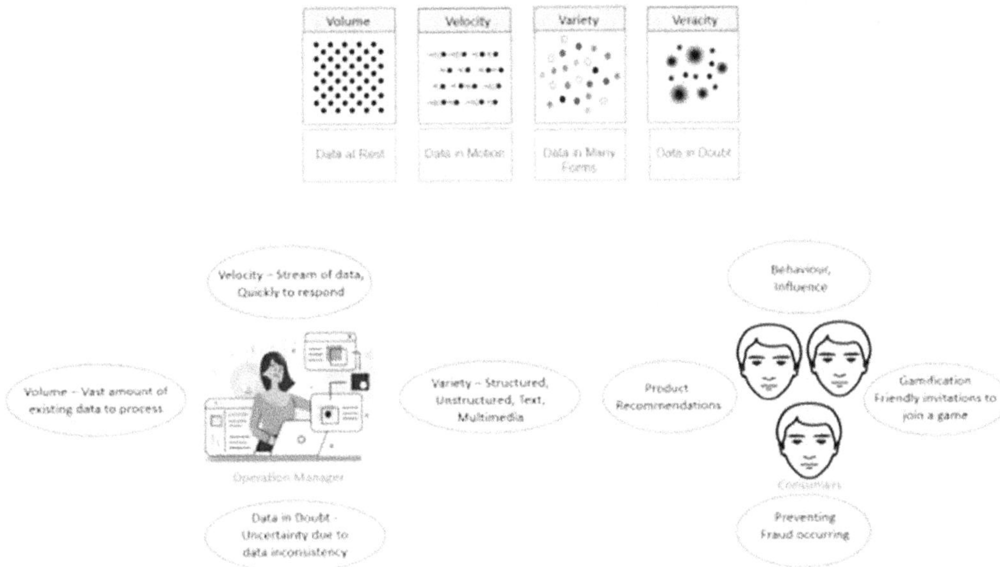

However, with the increased volume of semi- or unstructured and interconnected data, storing data in relational databases has become tedious and inefficient since these information processing systems have constrained data models and deal poorly with relationships. The drawbacks of traditional database systems, particularly the relational data model, to mitigate the needs of industrial applications have led to the development of new-generation database technologies. Among them, Graph Databases are calling the attention of the database community because, in trendy projects where a database is needed, the extraction of worthy information relies on processing the graph-like structure of the data. Activity around graph databases flourished in today's industrial applications.

One of the most essential elements conforming to a database is its 'database model' or simply 'data model.' In the most general sense, a data model needs a collection of conceptual tools to model representations of real-world entities and the relations among these entities. From a database point of view, a data model consists of three components: a set of data structure types, operators or inference rules, and a set of integrity rules. Graph databases (e.g., Neo4j) are good at storing relationship-oriented data naturally and efficiently using nodes and edges.

THE ERA OF BIG DATA ANALYTICS

The main objective of processing Big Data is to generate differentiated value which can be trusted. This is done by applying *advanced analytics* against the complete data collection regardless of scale. To understand the critical issues of Big Data, one needs to understand the *data sources* of business processes within industrial applications.

Graph database models are used in present days for their advantages in data analytics design purposes. The advantages of using a graph data model are introducing a level of abstraction that allows more natural modelling of graph data, query languages, operations, and algorithms for storing and querying graphs. Graph databases store data in the form of *nodes*, *edges*, and *relationships* that provide index-free adjacency. Figure 6. Few basic preliminaries of graph database are described in Table -1.

Table 1. Some main characteristics of graph database

A graph is a pair G = (V, E) of sets such that E ⊆ (V x V). The elements of V are vertices or nodes of the graph G, and the element of E are its *edges* or *relationships*. Because academic literature on graph theory typically talks about vertices and edges, which available graph database and its APIs operate on nodes and relationships respectively, these terms are used interchangeably in this chapter.

Order – The order of a graph G, denoted by |G|, is the number of vertices of G. Its number of edges is denoted by ||G||.

Incident Vertex – A vertex v is incident with an edge e if $v \in$ e; then e is an edge at v. An edge $\{x, y\}$ can be written as xy.

Vertex Degree – The set of all edges in E at a vertex v is denoted E(v). The degree of a vertex v, denoted as d(v), is the number |E(v)| of edges at v.

Subgraph – Given two graphs G = (V, E) and G' = (V', E'), G' is a subgraph of G, written as G' ⊆ G and G' contains all the edges $xy \in$ E with x, y ∈ V', then G' is an induced subgraph of G.

Path – A path is a non-empty graph P = (V, E) of the form $V=\{x_0,x_1,\ldots,x_k\}$, $E= x_0x_1,x_2,\ldots,x_{k-1}x_k\}$. The number of edges in a path is its length.

Centrality – One of the reasons for the success of graph databases has been the lack of the capability of relational databases to process the highly connected data efficiently. Various details in the data can also be stored as properties of nodes and edges. It is well-suited for storing complex relationships between attributes. In this way, the centrality property plays an essential role.

Centrality is defined as the relative importance of a node in a graph based on how well they "*connect*" the graph. For example, in a social network, it is important to know how connected each person is with other people. People who are more connected in a graph are more central to the network and thus they have more influence or importance in the community represented by that network. There are different types of centrality measures that have been proposed in recent decades. Three of the most discussed are degree centrality, closeness centrality, and betweenness centrality.

Degree centrality – It is defined as the number of edges incident upon a node (i.e., the degree of the node). If the network is directed, then degree centrality uses two measures. If the network is directed, then degree centrality uses two measures. One is in-degree, and it is the number of incoming links. The other is out-degree and it is the number of outgoing links. For a graph G (V, E) with n nodes, the degree centrality, *CD (v)* is defined as -

$$CD(v)=\frac{degree(v)}{n-1}$$

It takes certain number of operations to calculate degree centrality for all nodes in a graph in a dense adjacency matrix representation of the graph.

Closeness centrality – Closeness of a node is the average length of the shortest path between the node and all other nodes in the graph. Closeness can be regarded as a measure of how long it will take to spread information from a node to all other nodes sequentially.

Based on the above concepts, different data clustering algorithms and community detection algorithms (e.g., Louvain algorithm) have been developed. In the latter part of this chapter presents a community detection experimental result.

Figure 6. Characteristics of relational and graph database

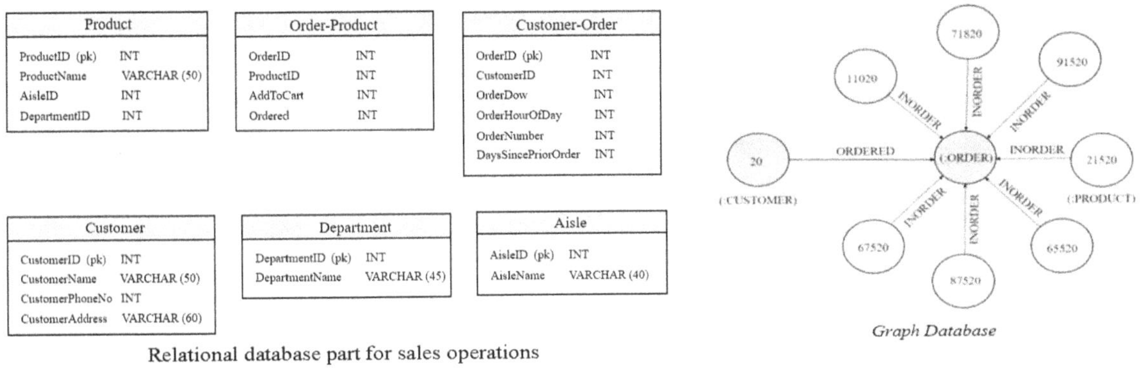

Big Data Analytics

A simple definition is that "BI is a wider group of software applications, technologies, infrastructure, and processes for gathering, storing, accessing, and analyzing data to help business users make operational decisions" (Watson, 2009). The methodology used in this chapter's research is based on the cross-industry standard process for the data mining model conceived initially by IBM research in the mid-1990s. The model consists of six phases for conducting a data mining project. The six phases are (i) understanding business, (ii) data understanding which deals with the initial data collection and analysis, (iii) data preparation, (iv) modelling, (v) evaluation, and (vi) deployment. Figure 8 (b) represents the model.

The research of the current chapter is evaluated by clustering algorithm on a graph shown in Figure 8(a). That graph is known as the connected caveman graph, and it was initially proposed by Duncan J Watts (Watts, 1999). Structurally, it is formed by modifying a set of isolated k-cliques by removing one edge from each clique and connecting it to a neighbouring clique. However, the graph in Figure 8(a) does not resemble a real network, but the current research project of this chapter chose it as it will help evaluate the implemented algorithm. Such a graph contains communities that can be used to verify the proposed Algorithm 1. The result of the community detection is satisfied by the verification method.

Techniques for Analytics

Most techniques used to analyze big data analytics are based on applied mathematical computation and machine learning paradigms. However, big data analytics techniques are widespread and context specific. These techniques can be classified and discussed according to the data under investigation.

Depending on the type of data, four central big data analytics can be defined: (i) text analytics: this technique is used to find out relevant information from textual data, (ii) audio analytics: techniques deployed to extract information from unstructured audio data. Customer service telephone conversations with customers are the primary source of audio analytics. Some of the main techniques used for audio analytics include large vocabulary, continuous speech recognition and phonetics-based systems, (iii) video analytics: methods used to monitor and analyze video streams. Video analytics has been mainly used as a replacement for labor-intensive observation.

Figure 7. Typical types of big data application systems

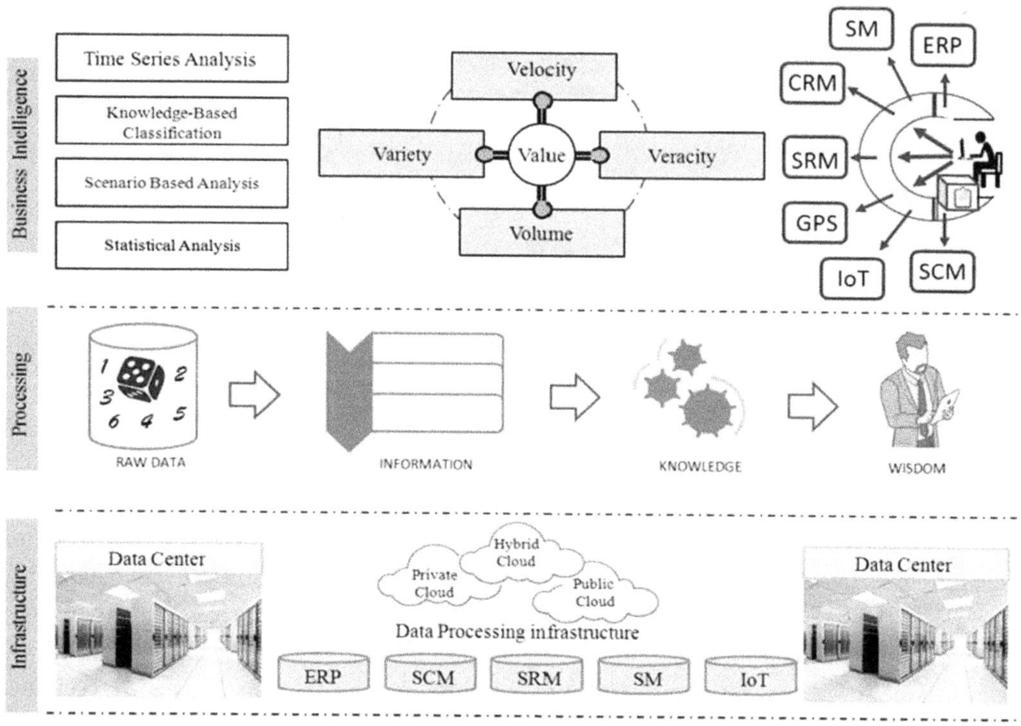

In addition, many business applications of video analytics are being used in manufacturing to collect data on customer demographics and preferences, and (iv) social media analytics: techniques used to analyze structured and non-structured data from social media channels (e.g., Twitter, Facebook). Some exciting techniques used to analyze social media data are community detection, social influence analysis and link prediction. Many successful enterprises have invested large sums of money in business intelligence and data warehousing tools and technologies. These enterprises believe that up-to-date, accurate and integrated information about their supply chain, products and customers is critical for their survival.

In order to solve a problem, the Big Data-based application uses intelligent reasoning in automated software that helps users apply analytical and scientific methods to business decision-making. The software applications that focus on the industrial decision support systems, providing Big Data-based tools to support a user's global supply chain reasoning process to develop a solution to the problem.

Once the industrial business process data is collected, it needs to be stored for processing purposes. In the data processing phase, the collected data is analyzed for business operational decision making. Data analysis is broadly classified into two different categories: (i) exploratory, and (ii) confirmatory. The main objective of exploratory analysis is to discover patterns and model the data. Exploratory data analysis is usually followed by a phase of confirmatory data analysis which aims at model validation. Many mathematical techniques have been proposed to perform data analysis. Statistical pattern recognition and machine learning is often used with predicative analysis that consists of finding relationships among objects in consideration and predicting future events, based on the knowledge obtained. Pattern recognition comprises of three phases: data representation, learning and inference.

Data Representation

In order to analyze the collected data, the analysis process needs an appropriate representation scheme to represent the data. Again, this representation involves picking a set of properties to identify the objects of interest in the data set. A d-dimensional vector $x=(x_1,x_2,\ldots,x_d)^T$ represents each object, where $x_p, p\in[d]$ denotes a feature. The features may be *numerical, categorical* or *ordinal*. For example, a written textual artifact may be represented using the words in the artifact; in which case each x_p denotes a word in the artifact. An image may be presented by the pixel intensity values. In this case, x_p is the numerical intensity value at the p^{th}pixel.

Data Clustering Algorithms

In general, two types of data clustering algorithms (i.e., hierarchical, partitional) have been used in data science historically. As the name suggests, hierarchical clustering algorithms build a hierarchy of clusters where the root of the tree contains all the n points in the data set, and the leaves contain the individual points. Figure 8(a) shows a set of points in two-dimensional space, containing three clusters. Hierarchical clustering generates a dendrogram for the collected data. Figure 8(b) presents a dendrogram generated using the complete-link agglomerative hierarchical clustering algorithm. Partitional clustering algorithms, directly partition the collected data into different clusters, as shown in Figure 8(c). There are different types of clustering algorithms are available for data clustering. For example, Figure 8(c) depicts the three clusters, represented by the red, blue and green points, and obtained using the *k*-means algorithm.

Figure 8. Various categories of data clustering

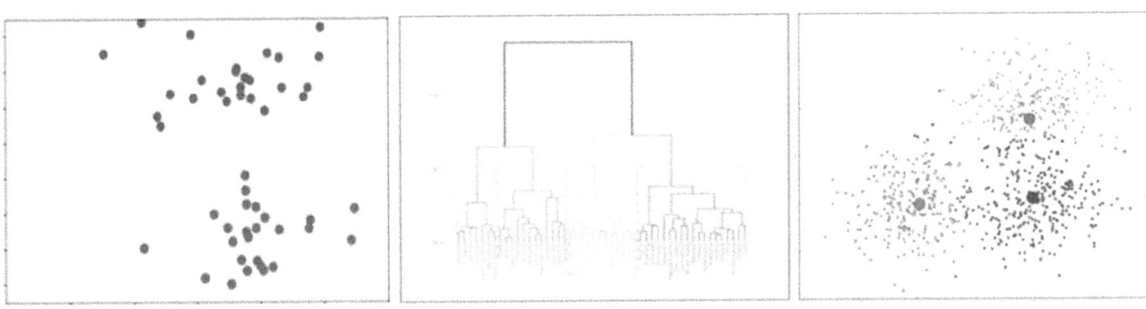

(a) (b) (c)

The methodology used in this chapter's research is inspired by the cross-industry standard process for the data mining model conceived initially by IBM research in the mid-1990s. The model consists of six phases for conducting a data mining project. The six phases are (i) understanding business, (ii) data understanding which deals with the initial data collection and analysis, (iii) data preparation, (iv) modelling, (v) evaluation, and (vi) deployment. Figure 8 (b) represents the model.

Figure 9. Connected caveman graph of six cliques

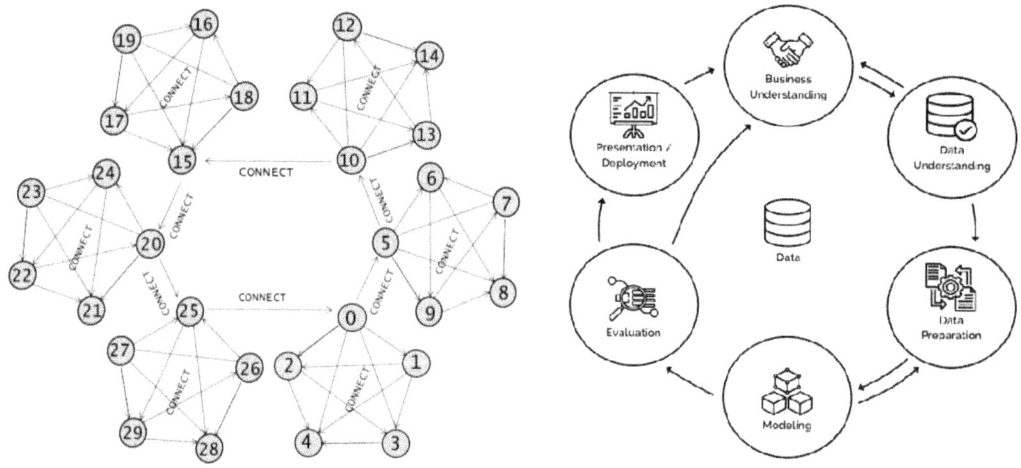

(a) (b)

The research of the current chapter is evaluated by clustering algorithm on a graph shown in Figure 8(a). That graph is known as the connected caveman graph, and it was initially proposed by Duncan J Watts (Watts, 1999). However, the graph in Figure 8(a) does not resemble a real network, but the current research project of this chapter chose it as it will help evaluate the implemented algorithm. Such a graph contains communities that can be used to verify the proposed Algorithm 1. The result of the community detection is satisfied by the verification method.

Algorithm 1: *Louvain community detection algorithm*

```
G be the initial network;
while Put each node of G in its own community do
    while some nodes are moved do
        foreach Node in the network do
            place n in its neighboring community including its own which maximizes
            the modularity gain;
        end
    end
    if the new modularity is higher than the previous modularity then
        G = the network between communities of G;
    else
        Terminate;
    end
end
```

RETAIL SALES DATA ANALYTIC EXAMPLE

Big data analytics are playing an essential role in today's apparel business. It is geared towards storing, processing, and visualizing many real-time business process-related data. In order to do these data-related activities, industrial analytics applications require the appropriate tools and create an operating work area, which helps to get meaningful strategic information from the gathered data. Apparel business retail operation is one area that collects vast amounts of business-processes operational data regularly. Retail operation managers must understand their consumer's purchasing patterns and behaviour to make better business decisions.

Big data analytics are playing an essential role in today's apparel business. It is geared towards storing, processing, and visualizing many real-time business process-related data. In order to do these data-related activities, industrial analytics applications require the appropriate tools and create an operating environment. Retail operation managers must understand their consumer's purchasing patterns (as shown in Figure 11) and behaviour to make better business decisions.

Figure 10. Graph data model used for database design and information generated

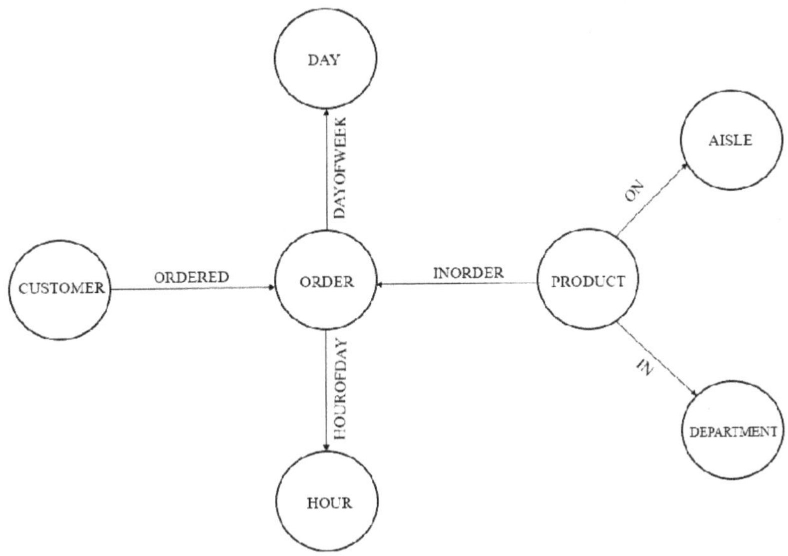

Figure 11. Number of orders placed at various hours of a particular day

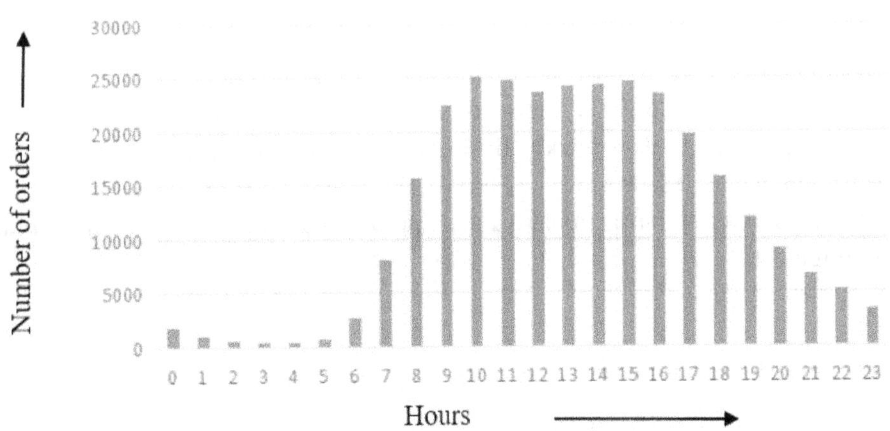

FUTURE RESEARCH DIRECTIONS

As big data-based apparel sales analytics are getting prominence, their implementations use different techniques for regular operation management. Researchers are using artificial intelligence-based network technologies to solve different types of operational issues, and one of the prominent issues is algorithmic recommendation systems. This chapter presented the Louvain clustering algorithm to produce non-overlapping clusters of products and evaluate the influence of an overlapping community clustering algorithm. In the future, the current research will consider more detailed information regarding apparel retailing data (e.g., order timestamp, customer demographics, and other relevant geographic details) to enhance the recommendation system. Another important characteristic of future projects is applying the service-oriented processing capability of analytics. Besides, the current project wants to include seasonal variations of products from customers' requirements, and it needs to include the organizational capability to deploy new information and communication technologies (e.g., augmented reality (AR), virtual reality (VR) and inclusion of new technologies to capture real-time data streams (i.e., IoT, RFID technology).

CONCLUSION

This chapter presents the essential need of data-driven business decisions for operational efficiency. Even when facing a straightforward decision, the number of problem characteristics that need to be considered can exceed business operation managers' ability of imagination. However, business managers have used different tools and techniques to minimize the complexity of business decision-making. One of the prominent techniques is business operational modelling by using spreadsheets. It helps data-driven business decisions based on business operational information. However, the reality is that business decision-making is much more complex than the mathematical models-based reasoning mechanisms would lead managers to believe.

In the 1970s, Frederic Vester's ideas influenced the formation of Germany's environmentally friendly Green Party. At the same time, he popularized the structured reasoning mechanism of network thinking. Since then, there have been a few well-known books for operational managers (e.g., managing complex systems, out of control in the 1990s, and the black swan). All these books highlight how to handle complex situations, systematic thinking, chaos theory, and self-organization theory for business decisions.

This chapter presents a graph-based framework for data analytics for apparel product sales management. Apparel product sales business processes collect vast amounts of retail data regularly. These data are interlinked as a network of activities, and traditional methods are not promising for identifying existing relationships between products. The central objective of this chapter is to present a way that can be used for getting insights into the data quickly. Besides, it is realized that graph database is easy to deploy for high-dimensional data in real-world applications. The chapter uses the 'Louvain Algorithm' to find network communities in retail transactional data and produces a customer recommendation system using the Neo4j graph database.

REFERENCES

Akter, S., Wamba, S. F., Gunasekaran, A., Dubey, R., & Childe, S. J. (2016). How to improve firm performance using big data analytics capability and business strategy alignment? *International Journal of Production Economics*, *182*, 113–131. doi:10.1016/j.ijpe.2016.08.018

Alqudah, S., Shrouf, H., Suifan, T., & Alhyari, S. (2020). A Moderated Mediation Model of Lean, Agile, Resilient, and Green Paradigms in the Supply Chain. Int. J Sup. Chain. *Mgt.*, *9*(4), 1.

Arunachalam, D., Kumar, N., & Kawalek, J. P. (2018). Understanding big data analytics capabilities in supply chain management: Unravelling the issues, challenges and implications for practice. *Transportation Research Part E, Logistics and Transportation Review*, *114*, 416–436. doi:10.1016/j.tre.2017.04.001

Baesens, A. (2014). *Analytics in a big data world: The essential guide to data science and its applications*. John Wiley & Sons.

Coyle, D. (2023). *Cogs and Monsters: What Economics Is, and What It Should Be, United State of America*. Princeton University Press.

Davenport, T. H. (2006). *Competing on analytics, Harvard Business Review*. Harvard Business Press.

Davenport, T. H., & Harris, J. G. (2007). *Competing on analytics – the new science of winning*. Harvard Business School Publishing Corporation.

Davenport, T. H., & O'dwyer, J (2011). Tap into the Power of Analytics. *Supply Chain Quarterly*, 28-31.

Davis-Sramek, B., Germain, R., & Iyer, K. (2010). Supply Chain Technology: The Role of Environment in Predicting Performance. *Journal of the Academy of Marketing Science*, *38*(1), 42–55. doi:10.100711747-009-0137-1

Deloitte & MHI. (2014). *The 2014 MHI Annual Industry Report – Innovation the driven supply chain*. MHI.

Deloitte & MHI. (2016). *The 2016 MHI Annual Industry Report – Accelerating change: How innovation is driving digital, always-on Supply Chains*. MHI.

Dietrich, B., Plachy, E. C., & Norton, M. F. (2014). *Analytics across the enterprise: How IBM realize business value from big data and analytics*. IBM Press Books.

Dubey, R., Gunasekaran, A., & Childe, S. J. (2018a). Big data analytics capability in supply chain agility: The moderating effect of organizational flexibility. *Management Decision*.

Dubey, R., Gunasekaran, A., Childe, S. J., Fosso Wamba, S., Roubaud, D., & Foropon, C. (2019a). Empirical investigation of data analytics capability and organizational flexibility as complements to supply chain resilience. *International Journal of Production Research*, 1–19.

Dubey, R., Gunasekaran, A., Childe, S. J., Luo, Z., Wamba, S. F., Roubaud, D., & Foropon, C. (2018b). Examining the role of big data and predictive analytics on collaborative performance in context to sustainable consumption and production behaviour. *Journal of Cleaner Production*, *196*, 1508–1521. doi:10.1016/j.jclepro.2018.06.097

Dubey, R., Gunasekaran, A., Childe, S. J., Roubaud, D., Wamba, S. F., Giannakis, M., & Foropon, C. (2019b). Big data analytics and organizational culture as complements to swift trust and collaborative performance in the humanitarian supply chain. *International Journal of Production Economics*, *210*, 120–136. doi:10.1016/j.ijpe.2019.01.023

Dubey, R., Gunasekaran, A., Childe, S. J., Wamba, S. F., & Papadopoulos, T. (2016). The impact of big data on world-class sustainable manufacturing. *International Journal of Advanced Manufacturing Technology*, *84*(1–4), 631–645. doi:10.100700170-015-7674-1

Fawcett, S. E., & Waller, M. A. (2014). Supply chain game changers—mega, nano, and virtual trends—and forces that impede supply chain design (ie, building a winning team). *Journal of Business Logistics*, *35*(3), 157–164. doi:10.1111/jbl.12058

Fosso Wamba, S., Gunasekaran, A., Papadopoulos, T., & Ngai, E. (2018). Big data analytics in logistics and supply chain management. *International Journal of Logistics Management*, *29*(2), 478–484. doi:10.1108/IJLM-02-2018-0026

Giannakis, M., & Louis, M. (2016). A multi-agent based system with big data processing for enhanced supply chain agility. *Journal of Enterprise Information Management*, *29*(5), 706–727. doi:10.1108/JEIM-06-2015-0050

Govindan, K., Cheng, T. C. E., Mishra, N., & Shukla, N. (2018). Big data analytics and application for logistics and supply chain management. *Transportation Research Part E, Logistics and Transportation Review*, *114*, 343–349. doi:10.1016/j.tre.2018.03.011

Gunasekaran, A., Papadopoulos, T., Dubey, R., Wamba, S. F., Childe, S. J., Hazen, B., & Akter, S. (2017). Big data and predictive analytics for supply chain and organizational performance. *Journal of Business Research*, *70*, 308–317. doi:10.1016/j.jbusres.2016.08.004

Handfield, R. (2006). *Supply Market Intelligence: A Managerial Handbook for Building Sourcing Strategies*. Taylor & Francis. doi:10.4324/9780203339527

Handfield, R., & Nichols, E. Jr. (2004). Key Issues in Global Supply Base Management. *Industrial Marketing Management*, *33*(1), 29–35. doi:10.1016/j.indmarman.2003.08.007

Hazen, B. T., Boone, C. A., Ezell, J. D., & Jones-Farmer, L. A. (2014). Data quality for data science, predictive analytics, and big data in supply chain management: An introduction to the problem and suggestions for research and applications. *International Journal of Production Economics*, *154*, 72–80. doi:10.1016/j.ijpe.2014.04.018

Hazen, B. T., Skipper, J. B., Ezell, J. D., & Boone, C. A. (2016). Big Data and predictive analytics for supply chain sustainability: A theory-driven research agenda. *Computers & Industrial Engineering*, *101*, 592–598. doi:10.1016/j.cie.2016.06.030

Lavalle, S., Lesser, E., Shockey, R. H., & Crosthwait, N. M. (2011). Big Data, Analytics and the Path from Insight to Value. *MIT Sloan Management Review*, *52*(2), 21–32.

Liberatore, M., & Luo, W. (2010). The Analytics Movement. *Interfaces*, *40*(4), 313–324. doi:10.1287/inte.1100.0502

Mayika, J. M., Chui, B., Brown, J., Bughin, R., Dobbs, Roxburgh, C., & Byers, A. (2011). *Big Data: The Next Frontier for Innovation, Competition, and Productivity*. McKinsey Report.

O'dwyer, J., & Renner, R. (2011). The Promise of Advanced Supply Chain Analytics, Supply Chain. *Management Review*, *15*, 32–37.

Pal, K. (2016). *Supply Chain Coordination Based on Web Service, Supply Chain Management in the Big Data Era*. IGI Publication.

Pal, K. (2017). Supply Chain Coordination Based on Web Services. In Supply Chain Management in the Big Data Era. IGI Global.

Pal, K. (2018). A Big Data Framework for Decision Making in Supply Chain. In Predictive Intelligence Using Big Data and the Internet of Things. IGI Global.

Pal, K. (2019). Quality Assurance Issues for Big Data Applications in Supply Chain Management. In Predictive Intelligence Using Big Data and the Internet of Things. IGI Global.

Pal, K. (2020). Information sharing for manufacturing supply chain management based on blockchain technology. In Cross-Industry Use of Blockchain Technology and Opportunities for the Future. IGI Global.

Pal, K. (2021a). Applications of Secured Blockchain Technology in Manufacturing Industry. In Blockchain and AI Technology in the Industrial Internet of Things. IGI Global.

Pal, K. (2021b). Privacy, Security and Policies: A Review of Problems and Solutions with Blockchain-Based Internet of Things Applications in Manufacturing Industry. *Procedia Computer Science*, *191*, 176–183. doi:10.1016/j.procs.2021.07.022

Pal, K. (2022). A Decentralized Privacy-Preserving Healthcare Blockchain for IoT, Challenges, and Solutions. In Prospects of Blockchain Technology for Accelerating Scientific Advancement in Healthcare. IGI Global.

Pal, K. (2023a). Security Issues and Solutions for Resource-Constrained IoT Applications Using Lightweight Cryptography. In Cybersecurity Issues, Challenges, and Solutions in the Business World. IGI Global.

Pal, K. (2023b). Drivers of Sustainable Supply Chain Management Using Internet of Things-Based Blockchain Technology. In Government Impact on Sustainable and Responsible Supply Chain. IGI Global.

Pal, K., & Yasar, A. (2020). Internet of Things and blockchain technology in apparel manufacturing supply chain data management. *Procedia Computer Science*, *170*, 450–457. doi:10.1016/j.procs.2020.03.088

Poluha, R. G. (2007). *Application of the SCOR Model in Supply Chain Management*. Youngstown.

Sathi, A. (2012). Big data analytics: Disruptive technologies for changing the game. MC Press.

Shapiro, J. (2010). Advanced Analytics for Sales & Operations Planning. *Analytics Magazine*, (May-June), 20–26.

Siegel, E. (2013). *Predictive analytics: The power to predict who will click, buy, lie or die*. John Wiley & Sons Inc.

Stern, N. (2007). *The Economics of Climate Change: The Stern Review*. Cambridge University Press. doi:10.1017/CBO9780511817434

Stock, J. R. (2013). Supply chain management: A look back, a look ahead. *Supply Chain Quarterly*, *2*, 22–26.

Supply Chain Council. (2010). http://supply-chain.org/f/down-load/726710733/SCOR10.pdf

Svilvar, M., Charkraborty, A. & Kanioura, A. (2013). Big data analytics in marketing. *OR/MS Today*.

Trkman, P., McCormack, K., de Oliveira, M. P. V., & Ladeira, M. B. (2010). The Impact of Business Analytics on Supply Chain Performance. *Decision Support Systems*, *49*(3), 318–327. doi:10.1016/j.dss.2010.03.007

Zhao, R., Liu, Y., Zhang, N., & Huang, T. (2017). An optimization model for green supply chain management by using a big data analytic approach. *Journal of Cleaner Production*, *142*, 1085–1097. doi:10.1016/j.jclepro.2016.03.006

Zhong, R. Y., Huang, G. Q., Lan, S., Dai, Q. Y., Chen, X., & Zhang, T. (2015). A big data approach for logistics trajectory discovery from RFID-enabled production data. *International Journal of Production Economics*, *165*, 260–272. doi:10.1016/j.ijpe.2015.02.014

Zhong, R. Y., Lan, S., Xu, C., Dai, Q., & Huang, G. Q. (2016). Visualization of RFID-enabled shopfloor logistics Big Data in Cloud Manufacturing. *International Journal of Advanced Manufacturing Technology*, *84*(1–4), 5–16. doi:10.100700170-015-7702-1

Chapter 27
Impact of Intangible Capital, Organisational Culture, and Innovative Capabilities on the Organisational Performance of the Indian IT Industry

Asuri Simhakutty Kannan
GRT Institute of Engineering and Technology, India

P. Aranganathan
Gnanam School of Business, India

B. Elamurugan
Sri Manakula Vinayagar Engineering College, India

Christina Sheela
Gnanam School of Business, India

V. Anandavel
Sakthi Institute of Management and Information Studies, India

K. Ravichandran
New York Institute of Technology, UAE

ABSTRACT

There is well-researched evidence for the linkages among intellectual capital, innovation capability, and organisational performance. However, no concrete evidence of such a relationship can be identified in knowledge-based industries such as the information technology (IT) sector. This study examined how organisational performance, organizational culture, and intellectual capital (human capital and organizational capital) are interconnected in the Indian IT sector and explored further how innovation capability can play a mediating role. In Bangalore, Hyderabad, and Chennai, 486 middle-level employees of selected IT companies were randomly selected for data collection. The authors used Smart PLS 3. A positive substantial impact is demonstrated by human capital, organizational capital, and culture on innovation capability, and an equally favorable substantial impact is demonstrated by innovation capability, human capital, and organizational capital on organizational performance.

DOI: 10.4018/979-8-3693-2193-5.ch027

1. INTRODUCTION

In Uncertainty, Complexity, Ambiguity (VUCA) world, Intellectual capital has become an engine of the economic, social and cultural development (Radjenovic, et al., 2021). emphasized its significance on the enterprise survival, growth, innovativeness, competitiveness and performance, which was validated by Zander (1996) and (1999). Stewart (1997) categorized the elements of intellectual capital into 3 broad dimensions including human Investing in capital, organizing capital, and investing in relationships capital. The act, a process capital, and a process capital in a classification system based on Edvinsson and Malone (1997).

Several studies found that the firm's intellectual capital (IC) is strongly connected to its capability to innovate new products or services (Xiaobo & Sivalogathasan, 2013). The focus on the intellectual capital in India has seen a significant improvement. During the year 2015, India stood at 81th rank as per the report by "World Intellectual Property Organisation (WIPO)" in 2020. However, India has witnessed an improvement in the ranking on Innovation and Human Capital where it is ranked 46th among 132 economics featured in Global Innovation Index (GII), 2021 and hence there is a scope for further improvement across the various sectors.

The present study has been carried out in the Indian Information and Technology sector, as it is evident from the NASSCOM- "Resilience to Resurgence -22" report that Indian IT sector revenue touched US $ 227 billion in FY 22 and sector is growing at 15.5% YoY., and Gartner 2021 report reveals the Indian IT spending is expected to increase to US $101.8 billion by 2025. In order to continue on the growth trajectory and retain the competitive advantage over neighbors, investment in Innovation Capability is of paramount importance (Edvinsson and Malone, 1997). The culture within an organization ability (Lam, et al., 2021). Research ability is closely (Al-kalouti et al., 2020; Azmi et al., 2019).

But on the contrary, it was observed that there is minimum reporting of Intellectual Capital in IT enterprises (Madan, 2011). Despite the fact that there is no attempt to assess how innovation capability influences organizational performance in the Indian IT sector, it is A literature review found that organizational culture has no connection to intellectual capital. An analysis of how innovation capability influences An analysis of organizational culture, human capital, and structural capital is presented in this dissertation.

Following are the research questions that will be addressed by the prevailing study:

- Whether human capital, organizational Organizational culture and capital have a positive relationship with performance?
- Whether The above relationship is mediated by innovation capability?

Present research work will provide a framework for managers to foster innovation capability by effectively managing the components of intellectual capital within their firms to ensure their firm's expected performance. Literature reviews, theoretical frameworks, and hypotheses are presented in the second section of the paper, followed by discussions of methodology, results, results, and findings. A discussion of future directions and management implications is discussed in the sixth section, following the discussions in the fourth, fifth, and sixth sections.

2. HYPOTHESIS AND THEORIES

Several studies have demonstrated how resources can predict both offerings and performance of firms. The theory of resource-based competition is developed in this study to address the issue of how firms can compete with one another in terms of performance. Managing resources, competence, and adaptive capabilities effectively will lead to better performance by firms (Krizandl & Bontis, 2007). Numerous researchers have examined the effects of intangible resources that include intellectual capital (human resources, organizational structures, social networks, and technical resources) Bontis and colleagues (2000) discuss organizational performance. Intellect and Resource-based theory can be used to describe organizational performance. Denison and Mishra, (1995) shown that organizational culture influences a firm's performance significantly. Several studies have found that organizational culture influences innovation substantially, including Saydi (2016) and Lam et al. (2021). An organization's culture, innovation capability, and performance all affect intellectual capital value, according to this conceptual model.

2.1 Capacity for Innovation and Intellectual Capital

Intellectus Model

During the year 2002, the Intellectus Knowledge Forum of Central Investigation on the Society of Knowledge developed a new model of measurement and management of intangibles. This new model assumed an advance from the previous and most recent Jurczak (2008) describes intellectual capital as all connected knowledge resources (material or nonmaterial, tangible, or intangible) that the organization disposes of in creating value needed to gain competitive advantage in the long-term period. The main components of intellectual capital are human capital (competence capital, attitude and intellectual agility of all members of the organization and their ability to make decisions, solve the problems); organizational capital (intellectual property, organizational structure, databases, computer equipment, management style, organizational culture); relational capital (relationship with a customer, strategic partners, investors etc.)

A worker's overall abilities, experience, talents, and tacit knowledge are described as their human capital (Edvinsson & Malone, 1997). According to growing literature, "human capital" (Smith et al., 2012; D'Este et al., 2014; Oliveira et al., 2017; Dhar et al., 2020). Sullivan & Edvinsson (1996) define structural capital as the infrastructure built by firms to Knowledge can be produced and used more efficiently. As a means of increasing value creation for an organization, organizational capital aims to empower human capital. Based on findings from earlier research, Hypotheses were developed as follows:

Hypothesis-1 Human capital positively impacts innovation capability.
Hypothesis-2 Capital plays a positive role in innovation capability

2.2 Innovating Within an Organization Capability

Organizational culture is the only form of intellectual capital that the company directly owns and remains within the company even when employees (human and social capital) leave the organization (Delgado-Verde et al., 2013;Subramaniam and Youndt, 2005).

An organization's intellectual capital can only come from tends to own altogether and sustain even after its people leave the firm is organizational culture. It is also one of the elements in the literature that is assumed to most efficaciously stimulate innovative behavior among members of the organization. The capability to innovate has also been linked to organizational culture as a key driver (Martins & Terblanche, 2003). Regardless of the fact, that several literature reviews argue that organizational culture is a component of structure capital (Kaul & Singh, 2019), the following hypothesis was formulated due to the high influence of "organizational culture" on innovative capability based on the majority of the studies.

Hypothesis-3 Innovation capability is positively influenced by organizational culture.

2.3 Organizational Performance and Innovation Capability

A significant correlation exists between organization performance and innovation capability (Beltramino et al., 2020). Developing new products and services to improve. (Yang, 2012). Hence it is hypothesized as follows:

Hypothesis-4 Innovation capability has a positive influence on organizational performance.

2.4 Organizational Performance and Intellectual Capital

Human capital relates to the process of strengthening an employee's skills, talents, capacities, beliefs, and social assets through training, education, and other professional efforts, leading to employee satisfaction and performance, and subsequently corporate performance (Marimuthu, et al., 2009). Bontis et al., (2000) successfully demonstrated the firms belonging to service and non-service sectors across Malaysia. The following hypothesis is therefore made out in light of the literature mentioned above.

Hypothesis-5 Organizational performance is positively influenced by human capital.
Hypothesis-6 Organizational capital has a positive influence on the organizational performance.

2.5 Performance and Culture in Organizations

Organizational culture is directly linked to performance, according to many studies (Polychroniou and Trivellas, 2017; Gorondutse & Hilman, 2019). However, several studies argue that there is no significant link between the two (Leithy, 2017; Rashid & Shah, 2016).

Hypothesis-7 The organization's culture Influences the performance of an organization in a positive way.

2.6 Mediation Impact of Innovative Capability on Human Capital, Structural Capital: The Culture of an Organization Affects Its Performance

Citrasari et al. (2022) developed a model to illustrate how social Possesses a positive impact on an organization's performance affects its innovation capability and performance leads to higher competitive advantages (Ali et al.,2021). This in turn could lead to better performance by firms (Ali et al.,2021). Organizational performance is strongly influenced by innovation capability, according to a number of studies (Wu, X., & Sivalogathasan, V., 2013; Mutalib et al.,2020).

Abdirahman, & Tarique, R. M., (2020) identified that the independent and dependent variables demonstrated a favorable link, indicating that "structural capital and innovation capability" have a substantial influence over company performance (Figure 1).

There is evidence that organization culture has a beneficial effect on innovation capability as well as on a favorable impact on an organization's Performance measures have been measured (O'Cass & Sok, 2014; Alkalouti et al., 2020). Despite this, Indian research has not focused heavily on the relationship between organizational culture and innovation capability. Organizational culture and innovation capability are not clearly outlined in the Indian IT sector. A comprehensive literature review led to the following hypothesis:

Hypothesis 8: Innovation capability mediates organizational performance.
Hypothesis 9: A mediating role is played by innovation capability organizational capital and performance.
Hypothesis 10: Organizational performance and innovation capability are interconnected.

Figure 1. Conceptual model

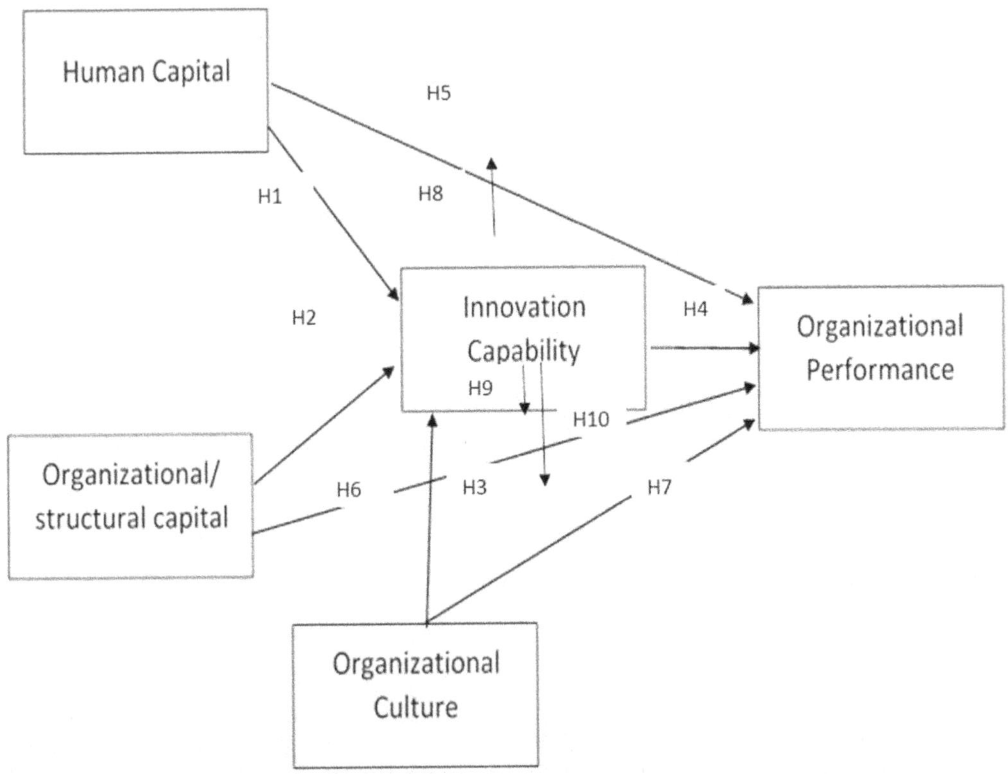

3. THEORY

3.1. Collection of Samples and Data

The study adopted a quantitative research design using a survey method to collect primary data from the respondents. The target population for the study was the middle-level employees working in the top five Indian IT organizations, namely TCS, Infosys, HCL Technologies, Wipro Limited, and Tech Mahindra Limited. These organizations were selected based on their ranking in the NASSCOM Top 20 IT-BPM Employers in India (2022). The study focused on the middle-level employees because they play a crucial role in bridging the gap between the top management and the lower-level employees, and they are expected to exhibit high levels of engagement and performance in their work. The study also considered the geographical location of the respondents, as the IT industry in India is concentrated in three major cities: Bangalore, Hyderabad, and Chennai. These cities account for more than 60% of the total IT exports from India.

The study used a convenience sampling technique to select the respondents from the target population. The study aimed to achieve a minimum sample size of 384, which was calculated using the formula for large populations (>50000) given by Krejcie and Morgan (1970). The study distributed 560 questionnaires to the potential respondents through online platforms such as email and social media. Out of the 560 questionnaires, 486 were returned with complete responses, resulting in a response rate of 86.8%. The study used SPSS 20.0 software for data analysis.

3.2 Measurement

The data collection was done using the tool 'structured questionnaire' which was constructed using previous literature and related survey instruments. In order to analyze the constructs, a "five-point Likert scale" type was used to score them, with a 1 being a strongly disagreeing answer and a 5 being a strongly agreeing answer. Bontis et al., (2000) developed the scale to measure "human capital" and "structural capital". The dependent variable "organizational performance" was measured using a scale. A set of questions was developed for evaluating the impact of "organizational culture" on "innovation capability" based on research by Maher (2014). Lastly, Atuahene-Gima (1995) developed a scale for measuring innovation capability & Hogan et al., (2011).

4. ANALYSIS AND RESULTS OF THE DATA

4.1 Reliability of Data Validity

"Reliability and validity" were analyzed using measurement model (refer to Table 1). Components acquiring "outer loadings" from '0.40 to 0.70' should be normally deleted enhance "composite reliability or average variance extracted (AVE)" significantly acceptable levels (Hair et al., 2016). Removal of the items HC 4, HC 5, HC 6, HC 8, HC 9, HC10, HCA 1, HCA 3, HCA 7, HCA 8, and OP 1 had increased "composite reliability and AVE" significantly, even though the construct's values already were well above the recommended limit. After 11 indicators were eliminated from the conceptual framework, analysis of the 'confidence interval' of the loadings indicated that neither of the component's outer loadings had a zero (Figures 2 and 3).

" a minimum reliability value was determined as 0.70 based on Cronbach's alpha, rho a, and composite reliability. To have returned a rho a value of greater than 0.70, which indicates stronger reliability. 'AVE' exceeded 0.5, leading to convergent validity. Heseler and Larcker (2015) use the heterotrait-monotrait correlation ratio and Square Root of the AVE in their analysis of correlations among latent variables. In which the value is lower than the (conservative) limit of 0.85. As shown in Tables 2 and 3, this implies discriminant validity.

4.2 Structural Model

The hypothesized channels of the investigation framework are represented in the "structural model." It is examined using the "R^2, Q^2, and significance" of routes. The dependent variable's 'R^2' value is employed to calculate the intensity of each structural route (Hair et al., 2017). The 'R^2' value must be higher than or equal to '0.1' and all 'R^2' values shown in Table 3 are higher than '0.1'. The conclusions suggest that the constructs' "predictive ability" is substantial (Refer to Table 4). "Standardised root mean square residual" was also used to evaluate "model fit". The "standardized root mean square residual" was estimated to be 0.112, which is marginally higher than the specified limit of 0.10, but well underneath the PLS-SEM threshold. The reason for this is that in "covariance-based SEM and PLS-SEM," the gap between "observed and model-implied correlations" performs various roles. (Hair et al., 2016). The formulated hypotheses were evaluated to determine the link's significance in terms of improving "goodness of fit."

The results reveal that, H_1 was accepted and according to the results, human Innovation capability was found to be significantly impacted by capital ($\beta = .450$, $t = 8.160$, $p < .001$). Similarly, H_2 and H_3 were accepted and according to the results, organizational A favorable correlation ($\beta = .194$, $t = 5.449$, $p < .001$) and ($\beta = .358$, $t = 6.462$, $p < .001$) respectively. Based on the results of the study, "innovation capability" has a positively substantial impact on "organizational performance" (t = 5.748, p - 0.000). Furthermore, H5 and H6 were accepted with indicating that "human capital" and "organizational capital" had a substantial "organizational performance" (score = .032, coefficient = 6.784, significance .011). "organizational culture" on "organizational performance" was not found by the results of H7 ($\beta = .083$, $t = 1.138$, $p = .255$). The seven hypotheses analysed were accepted in six cases, while one (H7) which investigated was rejected. From the 5,000 resamples used in this study, table 3 represents the 95 percent confidence intervals. A confidence interval that is not 'zero' indicates that there is a substantial relationship. Table 4 summarises the outcomes of the hypothesis testing.

4.2.1 Analysis Mediation

According to tables 5 and 6, the results of mediation analysis were not accepted. H8 was not accepted where both direct relationship ($\beta = 0.355$, $t = 6.673$, $p < 0.06$) and indirect relationship ($\beta = 0.168$, $t = 4.173$, $p < 0.02$) was revealed to be "significant. The results indicate that "human capital" influences "organizational performance" partially through "innovation capability".

Table 1. Results of analysis of reliability and validity

'Construct'	Item	'Loading'	'Alpha'	'rho_A'	'CR'	'AVE'
Human Capital	HC1	0.802	0.848	0.852	0.892	0.623
	HC2	0.810				
	HC7	0.768				
	HC8	0.736				
	HC3	0.826				
Organizational Capital	OC1	0.783	0.848	0.909	0.886	0.609
	OC2	0.810				
	OC4	0.772				
	OC6	0.766				
	OC7	0.771				
Organizational Culture	OCU3	0.800	0.836	0.838	0.884	0.605
	OCU4	0.712				
	OCU5	0.743				
	OCU6	0.817				
	OCU7	0.810				
Innovation Capability	ICA2	0.793	0.820	0.822	0.881	0.65
	ICA4	0.741				
	ICA5	0.841				
	ICA6	0.847				
Organizational Performance	OP2	0.692	0.839	0.846	0.882	0.557
	OP3	0.796				
	OP5	0.797				
	OP6	0.819				
	OP7	0.716				
	OP8	0.644				

Abbreviations: "AVE" - "Average variance extracted"; "CR"- "Composite reliability".

Table 2. Fornell–Larcker criterion of correlations

Construct	Innovation Capability	Human Capital	Organizational Capital	Organizational Culture	Organizational Performance
Innovation Capability (IC)	0.807				
Human capital (HC)	0.703	0.789			
Organizational Capital (OC)	0.238	0.073	0.780		
Organizational Culture (OCU)	0.665	0.669	0.033	0.778	
Organizational Performance (OP)	0.713	0.736	0.093	0.607	0.746

Table 3. Heterotrait–Monotrait ratio of correlations

Construct	Innovation Capability	Human Capital	Organizational Capital	Organizational Culture	Organizational Performance
Capability to innovate	-				
Capital human	0.838				
Organizational Capital	0.255	0.150			
Organizational Culture	0.799	0.789	0.117		
Organizational Performance	0.859	0.865	0.135	0.729	-

Table 4. Direct relationship testing

Hypotheses	'Path Coefficients'	'SD'	't' Value (Bootstrap)	'p' Values	'BI'	
					2.50%	97.50%
H1: HC → IC	0.45	0.055	8.160	0.000	0.342	0.566
H2: OC → IC	0.194	0.036	5.449	0.000	0.130	0.265
H3: OCU → IC	0.358	0.055	6.462	0.000	0.233	0.461
H4: IC → OP	0.355	0.062	5.748	0.000	0.230	0.480
H5: HC → OP	0.432	0.064	6.784	0.000	0.314	0.568
H6: OC → OP	0.132	0.036	4.080	0.000	0.094	0.232
H7: OCU → OP	0.083	0.073	1.138	0.255	-0.066	0.217
R^2 Innovation Capability = 0.600						
R^2 Organizational Performance = 0.621						
Q^2 Innovation Capability = 0.325						
Q^2 Organizational Performance = 0.329						

Abbreviations: BI- bias corrected confidence interval; HC- "Human Capital"; OC- "Organizational Capital"; OCU- "Organizational Culture"; IC- "Innovation Capability"; OP- "Organizational Performance".

H9 was not accepted where direct relationship ($\beta = 0.132$, $t = 4.080$, $p < 0.05$) and indirect relationship ($\beta = 0.159$, $t = 4.180$, $p < 0.01$) was considered to be "significant". The results indicates that "organizational capital" impacts "organizational performance" partially through "innovation capability."

H10 was accepted where the direct relationship was shown to be 'insignificant' ($\beta = 0.083$, $t = 1.138$, $p > 0.05$), and the indirect effect was found to be 'significant' ($\beta = 0.127$, $t = 4.569$, $p < 0.01$). The results indicate a "whole mediation" and this reveals that "organizational culture" influences "organizational performance" completely through "innovation capability."

Table 5. The indirect effect of mediation (mediation analysis)

Indirect Effect	'Coefficient'	'SD'	'T' Value (Bootstrap)	'P' Values	'BI'	
					2.50%	97.50%
H8; An organization's ability to innovate is impacted by its human capital	0.168	0.038	4.173	0.000	0.092	0.242
H9: Innovation capability leads to organizational performance through organizational capital	0.159	0.016	4.180	0.000	0.039	0.104
H10: Performance of an organization depends on its culture and innovation capabilities	0.127	0.028	4.569	0.000	0.073	0.184

Table 6. A study of mediation's direct effects

Effects Directly Related To	'Coefficient'	'p' Values
Performance of organizations is influenced by human capital	0.432	0.000
Capital Organizational → Organizational Performance	0.132	0.000
Organizational Culture → Organizational Performance	0.083	0.255

Figure 2. Final path model

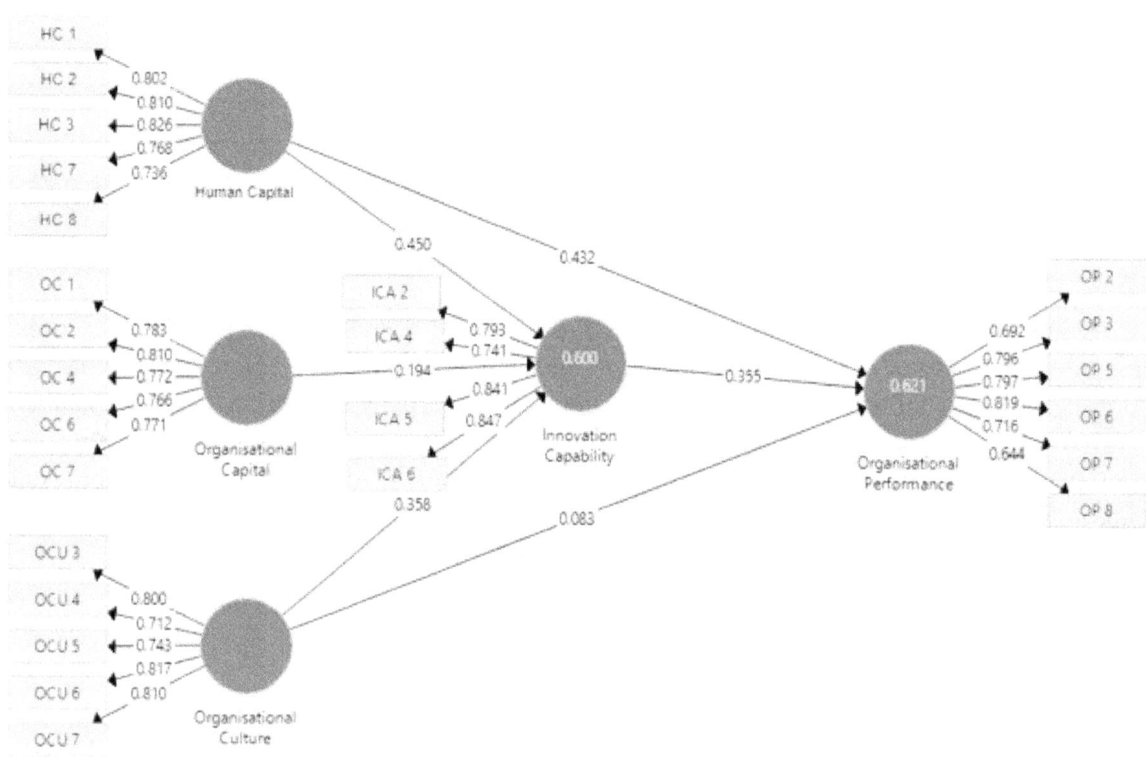

Figure 3. Model post bootstrapping

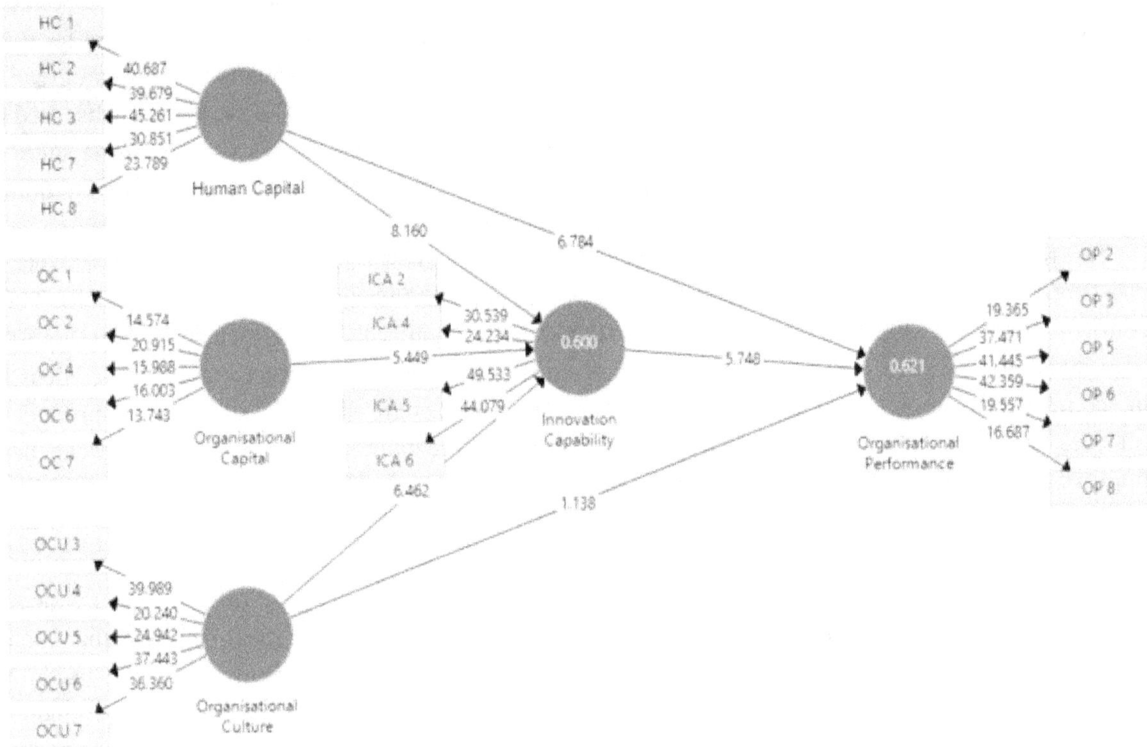

5. DISCUSSION AND CONCLUSION

The main purpose of this study was to explore the impact of intangible capital, organisational culture, and innovative capabilities on organisational performance in the Indian IT industry. The study used a quantitative approach and collected data from 486 middle-level employees of selected IT companies in Bangalore, Hyderabad, and Chennai. The data was analysed using Smart PLS 3 software and the results revealed some interesting findings that have both theoretical and practical implications.

The finding that "human capital has a considerable impact on innovation capability" was consistent with previous studies (Dakhli & Clercq, 2004). This suggests that employees who are intelligent, creative, and skilled can generate new ideas and knowledge that can lead to innovation. Human capital can also help firms to cope with any kind of challenging situation by applying their innovation skills (Zahra et al., 2000). Therefore, IT firms should invest in developing and retaining their human capital by providing them with adequate training, motivation, and rewards.

"Organisational capital" also had a significant effect on "innovation capability", which was in line with prior literature (Beltramino et al., 2020). This indicates that the organisational structures, systems, and processes that support innovation are crucial for enhancing the innovation capability of IT firms. Organisational capital includes aspects such as knowledge management, information technology, and intellectual property rights that can facilitate the creation, dissemination, and protection of innovation. The effectiveness and progress of every firm will be influenced by "organisational capital" and "innovation capability" (Edvinsson & Malone, 1997).

The finding that "organisational culture" had a significant impact on "innovation capability" was in accordance with previous research findings (Kenny & Reedy, 2006). This implies that the values, beliefs, and norms that shape the behaviour and attitude of employees towards innovation are important for fostering a culture of innovation. The result-driven firms that employ "organisational culture" can greatly enhance their chances of becoming a powerhouse of innovation capabilities. The study also observed a significant relationship between "organisational culture and performance", as reported by earlier studies (Kotter, 2012; Martinez et al., 2015). This shows that a positive and supportive organisational culture can motivate employees to perform better and achieve higher levels of satisfaction and loyalty.

The result that "innovation capability" had a significant effect on "organisational performance" was supported by previous studies' findings (Eisingerich et al., 2009; YuSheng & Ibrahim, 2020). This confirms that innovation capability is a key determinant of organisational performance, as it enables firms to create and deliver value to their customers and stakeholders. Innovation capability can enhance the competitiveness and profitability of IT firms by enabling them to offer new or improved products, services, or processes that meet the needs and expectations of the market. Innovation capability can also improve the efficiency and effectiveness of IT firms by enabling them to reduce costs, increase quality, and optimise resources.

In the final analysis, this study argues that the three variables of human capital, organisational capital, and organisational culture influence organisational performance critically. Two relationships are mediated by "innovation capability", namely "human capital and organisational capital" on "organisational performance". However, "organisational culture and organisational performance" are only partially mediated by "innovation capability". This means that organisational culture has both a direct and an indirect effect on organisational performance, through innovation capability. These findings have important implications for theory and practice, as they provide a comprehensive and integrated model of the factors that affect the innovation capability and performance of IT firms.

6. RESEARCH IMPLICATIONS

The significance of "intellectual capital" in the Indian IT industry was proved by this investigation and the growth of "intellectual capital" can fruitfully boost. The results analysis revealed that both theoretical and practical contributions had helped the specified domain. Theoretically, establishing the postulated linkages explicates the significance of "human capital, organizational capital, organizational culture, and innovation capability" in improving "organizational performance". Also, this research contributes literature linking "human capital, organizational capital, and organizational culture" to "innovation capability", and also it strengthens the relationship established in the literature that "innovation capability" highly contributes to increased "organizational performance". This study has firmly contributed to addressing a gap "intellectual capital, innovation capability, and organizational performance", and also stimulating more investigation into the relevant topic. The study revealed that the IT sector has to place more emphasis on "innovation and intellectual capital". It did, however, highlight some important combining "intellectual capital and innovation capability", the causal link between the two concepts. The main outcome of the study is that enhanced "intellectual capital" brought on by the enhancement of "innovation capabilities" might significantly affect firm performance and have important practical implications.

The study also highlights the impact of "innovation capabilities on organizational performance" especially in the IT sector. The validation of the suggested model emphasized the need of developing "human capital, organizational capital, organizational culture", and improve "innovation capability" in the quest for greater "organizational performance" for executives and decision-makers of the IT sector. The results also recommended that "organizational performance" can be linked to a firm's spirit of innovation, enabling the IT firms to generate better results and productivity and achieve a competitive advantage. Considering the significance of "human capital, organizational capital, and organizational culture on innovation capability" and "innovation capability on organizational performance", executives and decision-makers of IT firms must focus on improving them to continuously improve the performance of their firms. This study can very well guide the policymakers of the IT firms to formulate human capital development strategies on par with the information age that can enhance their firms' innovation capability, which is vital for improved organizational performance.

7. FUTURE SCOPE

The current study has taken into consideration dimensions such as "human capital, structural capital, organizational culture, and innovation capability" to analyse the performance of the IT firms since they are characterised by "knowledge-intensive tasks and intellectual property-based competition". As a result, the findings showed a greater link between firms' performance and intellectual capital, organisational culture, and innovation capabilities. However, in order to conduct future research in the IT sector and other technology-based sectors, additional factors that influence the success of such firms, including "relational capital, environmental uncertainty, and knowledge sharing," can also be taken into consideration in addition to the dimension used for this study.

Relational capital refers to the value of the relationships that a firm has with its customers, suppliers, partners, and other stakeholders. It is an important source of competitive advantage and innovation, as it enables the firm to access external resources, information, and opportunities. Relational capital can be measured by indicators such as customer satisfaction, loyalty, retention, referrals, and reputation. Future research can explore how relational capital affects the innovation capability and performance of IT firms, and how it can be enhanced by effective communication, collaboration, and trust-building strategies.

Environmental uncertainty refers to the degree of unpredictability and complexity in the external environment that a firm operates in. It is a challenge for IT firms, as it affects their ability to plan, adapt, and innovate. Environmental uncertainty can be influenced by factors such as technological changes, market dynamics, customer preferences, regulatory policies, and social trends. Future research can examine how environmental uncertainty affects the innovation capability and performance of IT firms, and how it can be mitigated by proactive scanning, forecasting, and learning mechanisms.

Knowledge sharing refers to the process of exchanging and transferring knowledge within and across the firm. It is a key driver of innovation, as it enables the firm to leverage its human and organisational capital, and create new knowledge. Knowledge sharing can be facilitated by factors such as organisational culture, structure, systems, and incentives. Future research can investigate how knowledge sharing affects the innovation capability and performance of IT firms, and how it can be promoted by creating a supportive culture, a flexible structure, an efficient system, and a rewarding incentive scheme.

REFERENCES

Abdirahman, M. D., & Tarique, R. (2020). Impact of structural capital and innovation capability on firm performance, (Case study of Pharma industry in Karachi-Pakistan). *The Strategic Journal of Business & Change Management*, *7*(1), 736–748.

Atuahene-Gima, K. (1995). An exploratory analysis of the impact of market orientation on new product performance: A contingency approach. *Journal of Product Innovation Management*, *12*(4), 275–293. doi:10.1111/1540-5885.1240275

Azmi, R., Suradi, M., & Riza, N. (2019). Innovation capability and organization performance in Malaysian public sector: A conceptual framework. *AIP Conference Proceedings*, *2111*, 020016. doi:10.1063/1.5111223

Bablu, Mutalib, & Sobhani. (2020). Innovation Capability on Human Capital and Organizational Performance. *International Journal of Advanced Science and Technology*, *29*(14).

Beltramino, N. S., García-Perez-de-Lema, D., & Valdez-Juárez, L. E. (2020). The structural capital, the innovation and the performance of the industrial SMES. *Journal of Intellectual Capital*, *21*(6), 913–945. doi:10.1108/JIC-01-2019-0020

Bontis, N., Keow, W. C. C., & Richardson, S. (2000). Intellectual capital and business performance in Malaysian industries. *Journal of Intellectual Capital*, *1*(1), 85–100. doi:10.1108/14691930010324188

D'Este, P., Rentocchini, F., & Vega-Jurado, J. (2014). The Role of Human Capital in Lowering the Barriers to Engaging in Innovation: Evidence from the Spanish Innovation Survey. *Industry and Innovation*, *21*(1), 1–19. doi:10.1080/13662716.2014.879252

Eisingerich, A. B., Rubera, G., & Seifert, M. (2009). Managing service innovation and inter-organizational relationships for firm performance: To or commit diversity? *Journal of Service Research*, *11*(4), 344–356. doi:10.1177/1094670508329223

Fornell, C., & Larcker, D. F. (1981). Structural Equation Models with Unobservable Variables and Measurement Error: Algebra and Statistics. *JMR, Journal of Marketing Research*, *18*(3), 382–388. doi:10.1177/002224378101800313

Hair, J. F., Hult, G. T. M., Ringle, C. M., & Sarstedt, M. (2017). *A Primer on Partial Least Squares Structural Equation Modeling (PLS-SEM)* (2nd ed.). Sage Publications Inc.

Henseler, J., Ringle, C. M., & Sarstedt, M. (2015). A New Criterion for Assessing Discriminant Validity in Variance-Based Structural Equation Modeling. *Journal of the Academy of Marketing Science*, *43*(1), 115–135. doi:10.100711747-014-0403-8

Kenny, B., & Reedy, E. (2006). The Impact of Organizational Culture Factors on Innovation Levels in SMEs: An Empirical Investigation. *Irish Journal of Management*, *27*(2), 119–142.

Lam, L., Nguyen, P., Le, N., & Tran, K. (2021). The Relation among Organizational Culture, Knowledge Management, and Innovation Capability: Its Implication for Open Innovation. *Journal of Open Innovation*, *7*(1), 66. doi:10.3390/joitmc7010066

Leithy, W. (2017). Organizational Culture and Organizational Performance. *International Journal of Economics & Management Sciences.*, *06*(4). Advance online publication. doi:10.4172/2162-6359.1000442

Martinez, E., Beaulieu, N., Gibbons, R., Pronovost, P., & Wang, T. (2015). Organizational Culture and Performance. *The American Economic Review*, *105*(5), 331–335. doi:10.1257/aer.p20151001

Martins, E., & Terblanche, F. (2003). Building Organisational Culture That Stimulates Creativity and Innovation. *European Journal of Innovation Management*, *6*(1), 64–74. doi:10.1108/14601060310456337

Rashid, H., & Shah, A. B. A. (2016). Impact of Organizational Culture on Organizational Performance: Evidence from Education Sector. *Journal of Business Management and Economic Studies*, *1*(1), 16–30.

Smith, M. B., Bryan, L. K., & Vodanovich, S. J. (2012). The counter-intuitive effects of flow on positive leadership and employee attitudes: Incorporating positive psychology into the management of organizations. *The Psychologist Manager Journal*, *15*(3), 174–198. doi:10.1080/10887156.2012.701129

Stewart, T. A. (1997). *Intellectual Capital: The New Wealth of Organizations*. Doubleday.

Yang, J. (2012). Innovation capability and corporate growth: An empirical investigation in China. *Journal of Engineering and Technology Management, 29*(1), 34-46. . doi:10.1016/j.jengtecman.2011.09.004

Zahra, S. A., Ireland, R. D., & Hitt, M. A. (2000). International expansion by new venture firms: International diversity, mode of market entry, technological learning and performance. *Academy of Management Journal*, *43*(5), 925–950. doi:10.2307/1556420

Compilation of References

Abbassy, M. M., & Ead, W. M. (2020). Intelligent Greenhouse Management System. In *2020 6th International Conference on Advanced Computing and Communication Systems (ICACCS)*. IEEE.

Abbassy, M. M. (2020). Opinion mining for Arabic customer feedback using machine learning. *Journal of Advanced Research in Dynamical and Control Systems*, *12*(SP3), 209–217. doi:10.5373/JARDCS/V12SP3/20201255

Abbassy, M. M., & Abo-Alnadr, A. (2019). Rule-based emotion AI in Arabic customer review. *International Journal of Advanced Computer Science and Applications*, *10*(9). Advance online publication. doi:10.14569/IJACSA.2019.0100932

Abdel Azeem, H. A. H., & Al-Abyadh, M. H. A. (2021). Self-compassion: The influences on the university students' life satisfaction during the COVID-19 outbreak. *International Journal of Human Rights in Healthcare*. Advance online publication. doi:10.1108/IJHRH-08-2021-0153

Abdelmageed, S., & Zayed, T. (2020). *A study of literature in modular integrated construction-critical review and future directions*. Academic Press.

Abdirahman, M. D., & Tarique, R. (2020). Impact of structural capital and innovation capability on firm performance, (Case study of Pharma industry in Karachi-Pakistan). *The Strategic Journal of Business & Change Management*, *7*(1), 736–748.

Abu-Rumman, A. (2021). Effective Knowledge Sharing: A Guide to the Key Enablers and Inhibitors. In D. Tessier (Ed.), *Handbook of Research on Organizational Culture Strategies for Effective Knowledge Management and Performance* (pp. 133–156). IGI Global. doi:10.4018/978-1-7998-7422-5.ch008

Abu-Rumman, A., & Qawasmeh, R. (2021). Assessing international students' satisfaction of a Jordanian university using the service quality model. *Journal of Applied Research in Higher Education*. Advance online publication. doi:10.1108/JARHE-05-2021-0166

Adnan, M., & Anwar, K. (2020). Online learning amid the COVID-19 pandemic: Students' perspectives. *Journal of Pedagogical Sociology and Psychology*, *2*(1), 45–51. doi:10.33902/JPSP.2020261309

Adolph, S., Tisch, M., & Metternich, J. (2014). Challenges and approaches to competency development for future production. *Journal of International Scientific Publications – Educational Alternatives, 12*(8), 1001-1010.

Agarwal, R., & Helfat, C. E. (2009). Strategic renewal of organizations. *Organization Science*, *20*(2), 281–293. doi:10.1287/orsc.1090.0423

Ahire, S. L., Golhar, D. Y., & Waller, M. A. (1996). Development and validation of TQM implementation constructs. *Decision Sciences*, *27*(1), 23–56. doi:10.1111/j.1540-5915.1996.tb00842.x

Akshaya, A., & Naachimuthu, K. P. (2022). Locavorism to Enhance Environmental, Social, & Economic Well-being. *Indian Journal of Agriculture Business*, *8*(1), 25–33.

Akter, S., Wamba, S. F., Gunasekaran, A., Dubey, R., & Childe, S. J. (2016). How to improve firm performance using big data analytics capability and business strategy alignment? *International Journal of Production Economics*, *182*, 113–131. doi:10.1016/j.ijpe.2016.08.018

Al Aina, R., & Atan, T. (2020). The impact of implementing talent management practices on sustainable organisational performance. *Sustainability (Basel)*, *12*(20), 8372. doi:10.3390u12208372

Al Khawaldeh, S., Alawneh, Y., & Alzboun, M. (2022). The availability of quality standards for the construction of science achievement tests from the point of view of the examination committees. *Hunan Daxue Xuebao. Shehui Kexue Ban*, *49*(9), 1233–1247.

Al Shehri, M., McLaughlin, P., Al-Ashaab, A., & Hamad, R. (2017). The impact of organizational culture on employee engagement in Saudi banks. *Journal of Human Resources Management Research*, *2017*, 761672. Advance online publication. doi:10.5171/2017.761672

Al Shraah, A., Abu-Rumman, A., Alqhaiwi, L. A., & AlSha'ar, H. (2022). The impact of sourcing strategies and logistics capabilities on organizational performance during the COVID-19 pandemic: Evidence from Jordanian pharmaceutical industries. *Uncertain Supply Chain Management*, *10*(3), 1077–1090. doi:10.5267/j.uscm.2022.2.004

Al Shraah, A., Irtaimeh, H. J., & Rumman, M. A. (2013). The Strategic Human Resource Management Practices in Implying Total Quality Management (TQM): An Empirical Study on Jordanian Banking Sector. *International Journal of Management*, *4*(5), 179–190.

Alabdullah, T.T.Y., & Ahmed, E.R. (2021). New Insights to Investigate the Impact of Internal Control Mechanisms on Firm Performance: A Study in Oman. *Riset Akuntansi dan Keuangan Indonesia, 6*(2).

Alabdullah, T.T.Y., Ahmed, E.R. (2021). New Insights to Investigate the Impact of Internal Control Mechanisms on Firm Performance: A Study in Oman. *Riset Akuntansi dan Keuangan Indonesia, 6*(2).

Alabdullah, T. T. Y., Al Fakhri, I., Ahmed, E. R., & Jebna, A. K. (2021b). Empirical Study of The Influence of Board of Directors' Feature on Firm Performance. *Russian Journal of Agricultural and Socio-Economic Sciences*, *11*(119), 137–146. doi:10.18551/rjoas.2021-11.16

Alabdullah, T. T. Y., Al-Fakhri, I., Ahmed, E. R., & Kanaan-Jebna, A. (2021a). Corporate Governance System and Firm Financial Performance. *Acta Scientific Computer Sciences*, *4*(6), 97–103.

Al-Abrat, N. A. S., & Alabyad, M. H. A. (2021). The Extent of Awareness of Faculty Members at Al-bayda University About the Concept of Educational Technology and Their Attitudes Towards It. In A. M. Al-Bakry (Ed.), *New Trends in Information and Communications Technology Applications. NTICT 2021* (Vol. 1511). Springer. doi:10.1007/978-3-030-93417-0_13

Al-Abyadh, M. H. A., & Abdel Azeem, H. A. H. (2022). Academic achievement: Influences of university students' self-management and perceived self-efficacy. *Journal of Intelligence*, *10*(3), 55. doi:10.3390/jintelligence10030055 PMID:35997411

Alawneh, Y. (2022). Role of Kindergarten Curriculum in Instilling Ethical Values among Children in Governorates of Northern West Bank, Palestine, Dirasat. *Education in Science*, *49*(3), 360–375.

Alawneh, Y., Ashamali, M., Abdel-Hassan, R., & Al-khawaldeh, S., & Engestroom, Y. (2022). Degree Of Use Of E-Learning Science Teachers In Public High Schools In During The Corona-Covid 19 Pandemic. *Journal of Positive School Psychology*, *6*(2), 1060–1070.

Alayli, S. (2023). Unravelling the Drivers of Online Purchasing Intention: The E-Commerce Scenario in Lebanon. *FMDB Transactions on Sustainable Social Sciences Letters*, *1*(1), 56–67.

Albinus, P. (2021). *How data is driving the exploding internal talent marketplace*. https://hrexecutive.com/how-data-is-driving-the-exploding-internal-talent-marketplace/

Alexis, A. a. (2017). HR Metrics and Talent Analytics. In D. G. Collings (Ed.), *Oxford Handbook of Talent Management*. Oxford University Press.

Alhajjar, A. A., Kassim, R. N. M., Raju, V., & Alnachef, T. (2018). Driving industry 4. 0 business through talent management of human resource system: The conceptual framework for banking industry. *World Journal of Research and Review*, *7*(3), 53–57.

Aliyu, R. M., Ahmad, T., & Nordin, N. B. (2019). The mediating role of innovation on access to finance and business performance of women entrepreneurs. *International Journal of Academic Research in Business & Social Sciences*, *9*(3), 147–159. doi:10.6007/IJARBSS/v9-i3/5644

Al-maaitah, D. A., Tha'er Majali, M. A., & Almaaitah, T. A. (2021). The role of leadership styles on staffs job satisfaction in public organizations. *Journal of Contemporary Issues in Business and Government*, *27*(1), 772–783.

Al-Maaitah, D. A., Tha'er Majali, M. A., & Almaaitah, T. A. (2021a). The role of leadership styles on staffs' job satisfaction in public organizations. *Journal of Contemporary Issues in Business and Government*, *27*(1), 772–783.

Almaaitah, M., Alsafadi, Y., Altahat, S., & Yousfi, A. (2020). The effect of talent management on organizational performance improvement: The mediating role of organizational commitment. *Management Science Letters*, *10*(12), 2937–2944. doi:10.5267/j.msl.2020.4.012

Al-maaitah, T. A., Tha'er Majali, M. A., & Almaaitah, D. A. (2021). The Impact of COVID-19 on the Electronic Commerce Users Behavior. *Journal of Contemporary Issues in Business and Government*, *27*(1), 772–783.

Al-Marri, K., Ahmed, A. M. M. B., & Zairi, M. (2007). Excellence in service: An empirical study of the UAE banking sector [A]. *International Journal of Quality & Reliability Management*, *24*(2), 164–176. doi:10.1108/02656710710722275

Al-Naif, K. L., & Al Shraah, A. E. M. (2018). Working capital management and profitability: Evidence from Jordanian mining and extraction industry sector. *IUG Journal of Economics and Business.*, *2*(1), 42–60.

Alonso, N., Jorge-Vazquez, S. L., & Reier Forradellas, J. (2021). Central banks digital currency: Detection of optimal countries for the implementation of a CBDC and the implication for payment industry open innovation. *Journal of Open Innovation*, *7*(1).

Alphonsus, A. C. (2019). Critical Analysis of Credit Management in Nigeria Banks. *International Journal of Research and Innovation in Social Science*, *3*, 171–178.

Alqudah, S., Shrouf, H., Suifan, T., & Alhyari, S. (2020). A Moderated Mediation Model of Lean, Agile, Resilient, and Green Paradigms in the Supply Chain. Int. J Sup. Chain. *Mgt.*, *9*(4), 1.

Ambekar, S., Kapoor, R., Prakash, A., & Patyal, V. S. (2018). Motives, processes and practices of sustainable sourcing: a literature review. *Journal of Global Operations and Strategic Sourcing*.

Amberg, N., & Fogarassy, C. (2019). Green Consumer Behavior in the Cosmetics Market. *Resources, 137*(8), 1–19. doi:10.3390/resources8030137

Ameisen, E. (2019). *Building machine learning-powered applications*. O'Reilly Media.

Amr, A. (2022). Future of Industry 5.0 in society: Human-centric solutions, challenges, and prospective research areas. *Adel Journal of Cloud Computing, 11*(40), 2–15. PMID:36101900

Amushila, J., & Bussin, M. H. (2021). The effect of talent management practices on employee retention at the Namibia University of Science and Technology: Administration middle-level staff. *SA Journal of Human Resource Management, 19*, 11. doi:10.4102ajhrm.v19i0.1485

Anand, P. P., Kanike, U. K., Paramasivan, P., Rajest, S. S., Regin, R., & Priscila, S. S. (2023). Embracing Industry 5.0: Pioneering Next-Generation Technology for a Flourishing Human Experience and Societal Advancement. *FMDB Transactions on Sustainable Social Sciences Letters, 1*(1), 43–55.

Anderson, J. C., & Gerbing, D. W. (1988). Structural equation modeling in practice: A review and recommended two-step approach. *Psychological Bulletin, 103*(3), 411–423. doi:10.1037/0033-2909.103.3.411

Ángeles, C. (2022). The legal-community obligations of the large digital service provider platforms in the metaverse era. *Cuad. Cuad. Transnational Law, 14*(2), 294–318.

Ángeles, C. (2023). The guardians of access to the metaverse. (Re)thinking the Competition Law of the European Union. *Cuad. Cuad. Transnational Law, 15*(1), 275–296.

Angeline, R., Aarthi, S., Regin, R., & Rajest, S. S. (2023). Dynamic intelligence-driven engineering flooding attack prediction using ensemble learning. In *Advances in Artificial and Human Intelligence in the Modern Era* (pp. 109–124). IGI Global. doi:10.4018/979-8-3693-1301-5.ch006

Angrave, D., Charlwood, A., Kirkpatrick, I., Lawrence, M., & Stuart, M. (2016). HR and analytics: Why HR is set to fail the big data challenge. *Human Resource Management Journal, 26*(1), 1–11. doi:10.1111/1748-8583.12090

Anlesinya, A., Amponsah-Tawiah, K., & Dartey-Baah, K. (2019). Talent management research in Africa: Towards multilevel model and research agenda. *African Journal of Economic and Management Studies, 10*(4), 440–457. doi:10.1108/AJEMS-12-2018-0371

Annual Report 2018-2019. (2021). *Namibia Statistics Agency*. https://d3rp5jatom3eyn.cloudfront.net/cms/assets/documents/Annual_Report_2018-2019

An, Q., Hong, W. C. H., Xu, X., Zhang, Y., & Kolletar-Zhu, K. (2023). How Education Level Influences Internet Security Knowledge, Behaviour, and Attitude: A Comparison among Undergraduates, Postgraduates and Working Graduates. *International Journal of Information Security, 22*(2), 305–317. doi:10.100710207-022-00637-z PMID:36466362

Antonio, Beatriz, José, Pérez-Méndez, & Roibás. (2021). Value-Creating Strategies in Dairy Farm Entrepreneurship: A Case Study in Northern Spain. *Animal, 11*(5), 1396. doi:10.3390/ani11051396

Antony, J., Leung, K., Knowles, G., & Gosh, S. (2002). Critical success factors of TQM implementation in Hong Kong industries. *International Journal of Quality & Reliability Management, 19*(5), 551–566. doi:10.1108/02656710210427520

Armelius, H., Claussen, C. A., & Hull, I. (2021). *On the possibility of a cash-like CBDC*. Sveriges Riksbank Staff memo.

Armstrong, M., & Taylor, S. (2016). *Armstrong's Handbook of Human Resource Management Practice* (13th ed.). Kogan.

Aroef, M. (1999). *Some Observations About Community Efforts to Increase Productivity and Quality.* Working Paper for One Day Seminar on Strategies for Increasing Productivity and Quality Management which are Classified as "World Best Practice", Bandung.

Arslan, F., Singh, B., Sharma, D. K., Regin, R., Steffi, R., & Rajest, S. S. (2021). Optimization technique approach to resolve food sustainability problems. In *2021 International Conference on Computational Intelligence and Knowledge Economy (ICCIKE).* IEEE. 10.1109/ICCIKE51210.2021.9410735

Arunachalam, D., Kumar, N., & Kawalek, J. P. (2018). Understanding big data analytics capabilities in supply chain management: Unravelling the issues, challenges and implications for practice. *Transportation Research Part E, Logistics and Transportation Review, 114*, 416–436. doi:10.1016/j.tre.2017.04.001

Aswathi, P., Sangavi, P., Naachimuthu, K. P., & Krishna, T. (2021). *Proceedings of the ICSSR Sponsored Webinar on Human Behavior and Environmental Sustainability.* Academic Press.

Atasever, M. (2023). Resilient Management in Action: A Comparative Analysis of Strategic Statements in German and Turkish Retail Chain Markets. *FMDB Transactions on Sustainable Management Letters, 1*(2), 66–81.

Atiku, S. O., & Fields, Z. (2018). Organisational learning dimensions and talent retention strategies for the service industries. In Disruptive Technology: Concepts, Methodologies, Tools, and Applications (pp. 1145-1168). IGI Global. doi:10.4018/978-1-5225-3009-1.ch017

Atiku, S. O. (2019). Institutionalizing Social Responsibility Through Workplace Green Behavior. In S. Atiku (Ed.), *Contemporary Multicultural Orientations and Practices for Global Leadership* (pp. 183–199). IGI Global. doi:10.4018/978-1-5225-6286-3.ch010

Atiku, S. O. (2020). Knowledge Management for the Circular Economy. In N. Baporikar (Ed.), *Handbook of Research on Entrepreneurship Development and Opportunities in Circular Economy* (pp. 520–537). IGI Global. doi:10.4018/978-1-7998-5116-5.ch027

Atiku, S., Kaisara, G., Kaupa, S., & Villet, H. (2022). Dimensions of learning organization: Implications for human resources effectiveness in commercial banks. *Management Science Letters, 12*(2), 117–124. doi:10.5267/j.msl.2021.10.002

Atuahene-Gima, K. (1995). An exploratory analysis of the impact of market orientation on new product performance: A contingency approach. *Journal of Product Innovation Management, 12*(4), 275–293. doi:10.1111/1540-5885.1240275

Auer, R., Cornelli, G., & Frost, J. (2020). *Rise of the central bank digital currencies: drivers, approaches, and technologies.* Academic Press.

Auer, R., Frost, J., Gambacorta, L., Monnet, C., Rice, T., & Shin, H. S. (2022). Central bank digital currencies: Motives, economic implications, and the research frontier. *Annual Review of Economics, 14*(1), 697–721. doi:10.1146/annurev-economics-051420-020324

Awan, T. M., Khan, M. S., Haq, I. U., & Kazmi, S. (2021). Oil and stock markets volatility during pandemic times: A review of G7 countries. *Green Finance, 3*(1), 15–27. doi:10.3934/GF.2021002

Azmi, R., Suradi, M., & Riza, N. (2019). Innovation capability and organization performance in Malaysian public sector: A conceptual framework. *AIP Conference Proceedings, 2111*, 020016. doi:10.1063/1.5111223

Bablu, Mutalib, & Sobhani. (2020). Innovation Capability on Human Capital and Organizational Performance. *International Journal of Advanced Science and Technology, 29*(14).

Babu, S., & Abraham, K. M. (2021). Central bank digital currencies: policy and operational perspectives for India. *CSI Transactions on ICT, 9*(2), 85-94.

Bacq, S., & Lumpkin, G. T. (2020). Social Entrepreneurship and COVID-19. *Journal of Management Studies*, *58*(1), 285–288. doi:10.1111/joms.12641 PMID:32398883

Baesens, A. (2014). *Analytics in a big data world: The essential guide to data science and its applications*. John Wiley & Sons.

Bag, S., Gupta, S., & Luo, Z. (2020). Examining the role of logistics 4.0 enabled dynamic capabilities on firm performance. *International Journal of Logistics Management*, *31*(3), 607–628. doi:10.1108/IJLM-11-2019-0311

Bai, Y., & Green, C. J. (2011). Determinants of cross-sectional stock return variations in emerging markets. *Empirical Economics*, *41*(1), 81–102. doi:10.100700181-010-0437-9

Baker, T., & Smith, L. (2019). *Educ-AI-tion rebooted? Exploring the future of artificial intelligence in schools and colleges*. Academic Press.

Baker, R., Freeman, G. K., Haggerty, J. L., Bankart, M. J., & Nockels, K. H. (2020). Primary medical care continuity and patient mortality: A systematic review. *The British Journal of General Practice*, *70*(698), e600–e611. doi:10.3399/bjgp20X712289 PMID:32784220

Bakker, A. B., & Demerouti, E. (2008). Towards a model of work engagement. *Career Development International*, *13*(3), 209–223. doi:10.1108/13620430810870476

Bakre, P. (2019). The role of HR analytics in the Global village. *International Journal of Trend in Scientific Research and Development*, *3*(2), 411–414. doi:10.31142/ijtsrd21340

Balas-Timar, D. (2015). Relationship between job performance and job satisfaction viewed from the chaos theory perspective. *International Journal of Education and Research*, *3*(3), 517–534.

Balas-Timar, D., & Ignat, S. (2015). Conceptual applicant screening model with fuzzy logic in industrial organizational contexts. *Procedia: Social and Behavioral Sciences*, *203*, 257–263. doi:10.1016/j.sbspro.2015.08.291

Bansal, A., & Pasricha, J. S. (2009). Foreign Institutional Investor's Impact on Stock Prices in India. *Journal of Academic Research in Economics*, *1*(2), 181–189.

Barata, J., & Kayser, I. (2023). Industry 5.0–Past, Present, and Near Future. *Procedia Computer Science*, *21*(9), 778–788. doi:10.1016/j.procs.2023.01.351

Barber, D. III, Harris, M. L., & Jones, J. (2021). An Overview of Rural Entrepreneurship and Future Directions. *Journal of Small Business Strategy*, *31*(4), 1–4. doi:10.53703/001c.29468

Bari, A., Chaouchi, M., & Jung, T. (2016). *Predictive analytics for dummies*. Wiley.

Barlett, B., Vladimir, E. C., & Stuart, S. (2004). Dogs or robots: why do children see them as robotic pets rather than Canine machines? *Proceedings of the fifth conference on Australasian user interface,* 28, 7-14.

Barney, J. (1991). Firm resources and sustained competitive advantage. *Journal of Management*, *17*(1), 99–120. doi:10.1177/014920639101700108

Basheer, I. A., & Hajmeer, M. (2000). Artificial neural networks: Fundamentals, computing, design, and application. *Journal of Microbiological Methods*, *43*(1), 3–31. doi:10.1016/S0167-7012(00)00201-3 PMID:11084225

Baskaran, E., & Arulalan, M. V. (2017). *Determinants of Personal Care Products Usage Purposes (A Study with Special Reference to Male Consumers in Chennai City)* [Doctoral Thesis]. University of Madras.

Bass, F. M., & Talarzyk, W. W. (1972, February). An Attitude Model for the Study of Brand Preference. *JMR, Journal of Marketing Research*, *9*(1), 93–96. doi:10.1177/002224377200900121

Batool, K., Zhao, Z.-Y., Irfan, M., & Żywiołek, J. (2023). Assessing the role of sustainable strategies in alleviating energy poverty: An environmental sustainability paradigm. *Environmental Science and Pollution Research International*, *30*(25), 67109–67130. doi:10.100711356-023-27076-0 PMID:37103699

Batth, V. (2018). The study of financial performance of Indian public sector undertakings. *Global Journal of Finance and Management*, *10*(1), 21–43.

Beaunoyer, E., Dupéré, S., & Guitton, M. J. (2020). COVID-19 and digital inequalities: Reciprocal impacts and mitigation strategies. *Computers in Human Behavior*, *111*, 106424. doi:10.1016/j.chb.2020.106424 PMID:32398890

Beckford, J. (1998). Quality: A Critical Introduction. Psychology Press.

Bednar, P. M., & Welch, C. (2019). Socio-Technical perspectives on Smart Working: Creating meaningful and sustainable systems. *Information Systems Frontiers*, *22*(2), 281–298. doi:10.100710796-019-09921-1

Behera, M., Mishra, S., Mohapatra, N., & Behera, A. R. (2020). COVID-19 pandemic and micro, small and medium Enterprises (MSMEs): Policy response for revival. *SEDME (Small Enterprises Development, Management & Extension Journal): A Worldwide Window on MSME Studies*, *47*(3), 213–228. doi:10.1177/09708464211037485

Beltramino, N. S., García-Perez-de-Lema, D., & Valdez-Juárez, L. E. (2020). The structural capital, the innovation and the performance of the industrial SMES. *Journal of Intellectual Capital*, *21*(6), 913–945. doi:10.1108/JIC-01-2019-0020

Bhowmik, D. (2022). Monetary policy implications of central bank digital currency with special reference to India. *Asia-Pacific Journal of Management and Technology*, *2*(3), 1–8.

Bi, J.-W., Liu, Y., & Li, H. (2020). Daily tourism volume forecasting for tourist attractions. *Annals of Tourism Research*, *83*(102923), 102923. doi:10.1016/j.annals.2020.102923

Bisht, R. K., Jasola, S., & Bisht, I. P. (2020). Acceptability and challenges of online higher education in the era of COVID-19: A study of students' perspective. *Asian Journal of Education and E-Learning*. doi:10.1108/AEDS-05-2020-0119

Bisoyi, B., Das, D., Subbarao, P. S., & Das, B. (2019). An evaluation on green manufacturing: It's technique, significance and rationality. *IOP Conf. IOP Conf. Ser. Mater. Sci. Eng*, *653*(1).

Biswas, A. (2021). The impact of Industry 4.0 on HR. *The Journal of Business Strategy*, *42*(1), 44–53.

Bi, Z., Mingchao, L., Zhonghua, M., & Zhang, B. (2021). Safety assurance mechanisms of collaborative robotics systems in manufacturing. *Robotics and Computer-integrated Manufacturing*, *67*, 102022. doi:10.1016/j.rcim.2020.102022

Bolander, P., Werr, A., & Asplund, K. (2017). The practice of talent management: A framework and typology. *Personnel Review*. https://www.emerald.com/insight/content/doi/10.1108/PR-02-2016-0037/full/pdf?title=the-practice-of-talent-management-a-framework-and-typology

Bontis, N., Keow, W. C. C., & Richardson, S. (2000). Intellectual capital and business performance in Malaysian industries. *Journal of Intellectual Capital*, *1*(1), 85–100. doi:10.1108/14691930010324188

Boström, M. (2017). The Fourth Industrial Revolution: How digitization is transforming human resources. *Human Resource Management Review*, *27*(4), 600–612.

Boudreau, J. W., & Ramstad, P. M. (2007). *Beyond HR: The new science of human capital*. Harvard Business Press.

Brad, S. (2021). *6 Tips for Maximum API Security*. DuoCircle Blog. https://www.duocircle.com/email-security/6-tips-for-maximum-api-security

Breier, M., Kallmuenzer, A., Clauss, T., Gast, J., Kraus, S., & Tiberius, V. (2021). The role of business model innovation in the hospitality industry during the COVID-19 crisis. *International Journal of Hospitality Management*, *92*, 102723. doi:10.1016/j.ijhm.2020.102723 PMID:36919038

Breque, M., De Nul, L., & Petridis, A. (2021). *Industry 5.0: Toward a sustainable, human-centric, and resilient European Industry*. European Commission, Directorate-General for Research and Innovation.

Briggs, G., & Scheutz, M. (2014). How Robots can affect Human Behaviour: Investigating the effects of Robotic displays of Protest and Distress. *International Journal of Social Robotics*, *6*(3), 343–355. doi:10.100712369-014-0235-1

Brown, R., & Rocha, A. (2020). Entrepreneurial uncertainty during the Covid-19 crisis: Mapping the temporal dynamics of entrepreneurial finance. *Journal of Business Venturing Insights*, *14*, e00174. doi:10.1016/j.jbvi.2020.e00174

Brozzi, R., Forti, D., Rauch, E., & Matt, D. T. (2020). The advantages of Industry 4.0 applications for sustainability: Results from a sample of manufacturing companies. *Sustainability (Basel)*, *12*(9), 3647. doi:10.3390u12093647

Bryant, P., & Allen, D. (2011). Employment mode choices and late stage start-ups: A preliminary explorations using fsQCA. *American Journal of Entrepreneurship*, *4*(2).

Bumblauskas, D., Nold, H., Bumblauskas, P., & Igou, A. (2017). Big data analytics: Transforming data to action. *Business Process Management Journal*, *23*(3), 703–720. doi:10.1108/BPMJ-03-2016-0056

Burkov, A. (2019). *The hundred-page machine learning book*. Andriy Burkov.

Burmeister, C., Luettgens, D., & Piller, F. T. (2015). Business model innovation for industry 4.0: Why the "how connections, sensors, and data are revolutionizing business". *Harvard Business Review*.

Buttle, F. (2016). *Customer relationship management: Concepts and tools*. Routledge.

Cai, W. G., & Zhou, X. L. (2014). On the drivers of eco-innovation: Empirical evidence from China. *Journal of Cleaner Production*, *79*, 239–248. doi:10.1016/j.jclepro.2014.05.035

Capelli, P., Neely, A., & Stiehl, B. (2018). *Strategic human capital: A new approach to talent management in the age of uncertainty*. Harvard Business Review Press.

Cappelli, P., & Keller, J. R. (2014). Talent management: Conceptual approaches and practical challenges. *Annual Review of Organizational Psychology and Organizational Behavior*, *1*(1), 305–331. doi:10.1146/annurev-orgpsych-031413-091314

Carroll, A. B., & Shabana, K. M. (2010). The business case for corporate social responsibility: A review of concepts, research and practice. *International Journal of Management Reviews*, *12*(1), 85–105. doi:10.1111/j.1468-2370.2009.00275.x

Cascio, W. F. (2016). *Managing human resources: Productivity, quality of work life, profits* (7th ed.). McGraw-Hill/Irwin.

Casino, F., Dasaklis, T. K., & Patsakis, C. (2019). A systematic literature review of blockchain-based applications: Current status, classification, and open issues. *Telematics and Informatics*, *36*, 55–81. doi:10.1016/j.tele.2018.11.006

CFI Report. (2022). Retrieved November 6, 2023, from Ctif-cfi.be website: https://www.ctif-cfi.be/index.php/en/news-quick-links/252-annual-report-2022

Chapman, B., Swainston, J., Grunfeld, E. A., & Derakshan, N. (2020). COVID-19 outbreak effects on job security and emotional functioning amongst women living with breast cancer. *Frontiers in Psychology*, *11*, 582014. doi:10.3389/fpsyg.2020.582014 PMID:33192902

Chaurasiya, K. K., Prashant, M., & Badodiya, S. K. (2017). Factors affecting entrepreneurial behaviour of dairy farmers. *Agriculture Update*, *12*(1), 23–30. doi:10.15740/HAS/AU/12.1/23-30

Chen, F., Drezner, Z., Ryan, J. K., & Simchi-Levi, D. (2000). Quantifying the bullwhip effect in a simple supply chain. *The impact.*

Chen, H., & Eyoun, K. (2021). Do mindfulness and perceived organizational support work? Fear of COVID-19 on restaurant frontline employees' job insecurity and emotional exhaustion. *International Journal of Hospitality Management*, *94*, 102850. doi:10.1016/j.ijhm.2020.102850 PMID:34785844

Chen, H., Simoska, O., Lim, K., Grattieri, M., Yuan, M., Dong, F., & Minteer, S. (2020). Fundamentals, applications, and future directions of bioelectrocatalysis. *Chemical Reviews*, *120*(23), 12903–12993. doi:10.1021/acs.chemrev.0c00472 PMID:33050699

Chin, S. T. (2021). Influence of emotional intelligence on the workforce for Industry 5.0. IBIMA Publishing.

Chopra, S., & Meindl, P. (2019). *Supply chain management: Strategy, planning, and operation*. Pearson.

Chopra, S., & Meindl, P. (2021). Supply chain management: Strategy, planning, and operation (8th ed.). Pearson.

Chorna, I. (2022, October 11). *HR forecast*. Retrieved from Big data for HR: Everything you need to know: https://hrforecast.com/how-will-big-data-transform-your-hr-practices/

Chu, Y., Lee, J., Kim, S., Kim, H., Yoon, Y., & Chung, H. (2022). Review of Offline Payment Function of CBDC Considering Security Requirements. *Applied Sciences (Basel, Switzerland)*, *12*(9), 4488. doi:10.3390/app12094488

Ciervo, M. (2012). *Innovating for Sustainable Growth- A Bioeconomy for Europe*. Academic Press.

CIPD. (2018). *People analytics: Driving business performance with people data*. Chartered Institute of Personnel and Development. https://www.cipd.co.uk/Images/investor-perspectives-on-workforce-data_tcm18-55499.pdf

CIPD. (2019). *The intangible workforce investors perspective on workforce data. London: chartered institute of personnel and development*. https://www.cipd.co.uk/Images/investor-perspectives-on-workforce-data_tcm18-55499.pdf

Cirillo, S., Polese, G., Salerno, D., Simone, B., & Solimando, G. (2023). Towards Flexible Voice Assistants: Evaluating Privacy and Security Needs in IoT-enabled Smart Homes. *FMDB Transactions on Sustainable Computer Letters*, *1*(1), 25–32.

Cisneros, S. C., Pishchulov, G., Sampaio, P., Mehandjiev, N., Liu, Z., & Kununka, S. (2021). An approach and decision support tool forming Industry 4.0 supply chain collaborations. *Computers in Industry*, *125*, 103391. doi:10.1016/j.compind.2020.103391

Claus, L. (2019). HR disruption: Time already to reinvent talent management. *Business Research Quarterly*, *22*(3), 207–215. doi:10.1016/j.brq.2019.04.002

Cleland, K., & Williamson, A. (2017). Digital legacies: Personal artifacts in an augmented reality. In *Proceedings of the 2017 CHI Conference on Human Factors in Computing Systems* (pp. 1731-1744). ACM.

Clemens, M. A., & Pettersson, G. (2008). New data on African health professionals abroad. *Human Resources for Health*, *6*(1), 1–11. doi:10.1186/1478-4491-6-1 PMID:18186916

Colclough, S. N., Moen, Ø., Hovd, N. S., & Chan, A. (2019). SME innovation orientation: Evidence from Norwegian exporting SMEs. *International Small Business Journal*, *37*(8), 780–803. doi:10.1177/0266242619870731

Collection of domestic tourism statistics for the state of Goa. (2005). Retrieved October 27, 2023, from Gov.in website: https://tourism.gov.in/sites/default/files/2020-04/03%20goa.pdf

Cooper, H. D., Paterson, N. L., Stadler, M. J., & Saks, A. M. (2014). The relative importance of proactive behaviors and outcomes for predicting newcomer learning, well-being, and work engagement. *Journal of Vocational Behavior, 84*(3), 318–331. doi:10.1016/j.jvb.2014.02.007

Cormier, D., Gem, N., Nakane, Masayuki, Young, J. E., & Stephane, D. (2013). Would you do as a robot commands? An obedience study for human-robot interaction. *International Conference on Human-Agent Interaction.*

Cosrojas, K. D. J. (2021). Performance Evaluation of the Vegetable Trading Center in Lantapan, Bukidnon, Philippines. *Agricultural Socio-Economics Journal, 21*(3), 165–174. https://doi.org/ doi:10.21776/ub.agrise.2021.021.3.1

Council, F. H. (2020, January 2). *Nine Benefits Of Embracing Big Data In Human Resources.* Retrieved from Forbes Human Resources Council: https://www.forbes.com/sites/forbeshumanresourcescouncil/2020/01/02/nine-benefits-of-embracing-big-data-in-human-resources/?sh=42edc12b6582

Coyle, D. (2023). *Cogs and Monsters: What Economics Is, and What It Should Be, United State of America.* Princeton University Press.

D'Este, P., Rentocchini, F., & Vega-Jurado, J. (2014). The Role of Human Capital in Lowering the Barriers to Engaging in Innovation: Evidence from the Spanish Innovation Survey. *Industry and Innovation, 21*(1), 1–19. doi:10.1080/13662716.2014.879252

Dahlbom, P., Siikanen, N., Sajasalo, P., & Jarvenpää, M. (2019). Big data and HR analytics in the digital era. *Baltic Journal of Management, 15*(1), 120–138. doi:10.1108/BJM-11-2018-0393

Dajani, D., & Zaki, M. A. (2015). *The impact of employee engagement on job performance and organisational commitment in the Egyptian banking sector.* Academic Press.

Dam, N. A. K., Le Dinh, T., & Menvielle, W. (2019). Marketing Intelligence from Data Mining Perspective. *International Journal of Innovation, Management and Technology, 10*(5), 184–190. doi:10.18178/ijimt.2019.10.5.859

Dana, L. P. (2000). Creating entrepreneurs in India. *Journal of Small Business Management, 38*(1), 86.

Davenport, H. T., Harris, J., & Shapiro, J. (2010). *Competing on talent analytics.* https://hbr.org/2010/10/competing-on-talent-analytics

Davenport, T. H., & O'dwyer, J (2011). Tap into the Power of Analytics. *Supply Chain Quarterly*, 28-31.

Davenport, T. H. (2006). *Competing on analytics, Harvard Business Review.* Harvard Business Press.

Davenport, T. H., & Harris, J. G. (2007). *Competing on analytics – the new science of winning.* Harvard Business School Publishing Corporation.

Davenport, T. H., & Harris, J. G. (2007). *Competing on Analytics: The New Science of Winning.* Harvard Business Review Press.

Davenport, T., Guha, A., Grewal, D., & Bressgott, T. (2020). How artificial intelligence will change the future of marketing. *Journal of the Academy of Marketing Science, 48*(1), 24–42. doi:10.100711747-019-00696-0

David Rajesh, Manimaran, & Venkateswaran. (2015). A study on the linkage between service quality, service loyalty and customer satisfaction in commercial banks in Madurai, Tamil Nadu, India. *International Journal of Contemporary Research in Humanities and Social Sciences, 2*(1), 89-103.

Davis-Sramek, B., Germain, R., & Iyer, K. (2010). Supply Chain Technology: The Role of Environment in Predicting Performance. *Journal of the Academy of Marketing Science*, *38*(1), 42–55. doi:10.100711747-009-0137-1

De La Calle-Duran, M. C., de la Luz Fernandez-Alles, M., & Valle-Cabrera, R. (2021). Talent identification and location: A configurational approach to talent pools. *Intangible Capital*, *17*(1), 17–32. doi:10.3926/ic.1440

Deloitte & MHI. (2014). *The 2014 MHI Annual Industry Report – Innovation the driven supply chain.* MHI.

Deloitte & MHI. (2016). *The 2016 MHI Annual Industry Report – Accelerating change: How innovation is driving digital, always-on Supply Chains.* MHI.

Deloitte. (2017, February 27). *People Analytics: Recalculating The Route*. Retrieved from Deloitte: https://www.deloitte.com/global/en/our-thinking/insights/topics/talent/human-capital-trends/people-analytics-in-hr.html

Deloitte. (2019). *Deloitte Namibia best company survey 2019 winners.* https://www2.deloitte.com/za/en/namibia/pages/human-capital/articles/Deloitte-Namibia-Best-Company-Survey-Awards-2019.html

Deloitte. (2019). *HR Transformation: Accelerating Change with a Human Focus*. Deloitte.

Deloitte. (2019). *Industry 4.0 and the future of work.* https://www2.deloitte.com/content/dam/Deloitte/lu/Documents/technology/lu-en-industry-4-0-future-work.pdf

Deloitte. (2020). 2020 global human capital trends. *The social enterprise at work: Paradox as a path forward.* https://www2.deloitte.com/content/dam/Deloitte/at/Documents/human-capital/at-hc-trends-2020

Deloitte. (2021). *The social enterprise in a world disrupted: Leading the shift from survive to thrive*. Retrieved from June 2022 from https://www2.deloitte.com/content/dam/Deloitte/lu/Documents/human-capital/lu-hc-trends-2021.pdf

Demeter, E., Rad, D., & Balas, E. (2021). Schadenfreude and General Anti-Social Behaviours: The Role of Violent Content Preferences and Life Satisfaction. BRAIN. *Broad Research in Artificial Intelligence and Neuroscience*, *12*(2), 98–111. doi:10.18662/brain/12.2/194

Deming, W. E. (1986). Out of Crisis. MIT Centre for Advanced Engineering Study.

Demir, K. A., & Halil, C. (2018). The next Industrial Revolution: Industry 5.0 and discussions on Industry4.0. *Management Information Systems Perspectives*.

Devi, B. T., & Rajasekaran, R. (2023). A Comprehensive Review on Deepfake Detection on Social Media Data. *FMDB Transactions on Sustainable Computing Systems*, *1*(1), 11–20.

Dexit, A., & Pandey, A. K. (2011). SMEs and Economic Growth in India: Cointegration Analysis. *The IUP Journal of Financial Economics*, *IX*(2), 41–57.

Díaz-Chao, Á., Ficapal-Cusí, P., & Torrent-Sellens, J. (2021). Environmental assets, Industry 4.0 technologies and firm performance in Spain: A dynamic capabilities path to reward sustainability. *Journal of Cleaner Production*, *281*, 125264. doi:10.1016/j.jclepro.2020.125264

Dietrich, B., Plachy, E. C., & Norton, M. F. (2014). *Analytics across the enterprise: How IBM realize business value from big data and analytics*. IBM Press Books.

Ding, H., Wu, X., & Ma, Y. (2019). Performance evaluation of vegetable cold chain logistics based on AHP-TOPSIS method. *Nongye Gongcheng Xuebao (Beijing)*, *35*(13), 251–259.

Dixit, A. K., Sirohi, S., Ravishankar, K. M., Cariappa, A. A., Kumar, S., Bhandari, G., & Thakur, A. (2022). Understating emerging value chains and business performance: evidence from dairy industry in India. *Journal of Agribusiness in Developing and Emerging Economies*, (ahead-of-print).

D, P., & Kar, S. (2022). Assessing the viability of an Indian central bank digital currency (CBDC). *Indian Public Policy Review*, *3*(3), 43–58. doi:10.55763/ippr.2022.03.03.003

Duane, A., & Bartholin, T. (2019). *Human resources data analytics – Evidence from an Irish manufacturing perspective. Human Resources Division International Conference (HRIC).*

Dubey, R., Gunasekaran, A., & Childe, S. J. (2018a). Big data analytics capability in supply chain agility: The moderating effect of organizational flexibility. *Management Decision.*

Dubey, R., Gunasekaran, A., Childe, S. J., Fosso Wamba, S., Roubaud, D., & Foropon, C. (2019a). Empirical investigation of data analytics capability and organizational flexibility as complements to supply chain resilience. *International Journal of Production Research*, 1–19.

Dubey, R., Gunasekaran, A., Childe, S. J., Luo, Z., Wamba, S. F., Roubaud, D., & Foropon, C. (2018b). Examining the role of big data and predictive analytics on collaborative performance in context to sustainable consumption and production behaviour. *Journal of Cleaner Production*, *196*, 1508–1521. doi:10.1016/j.jclepro.2018.06.097

Dubey, R., Gunasekaran, A., Childe, S. J., Roubaud, D., Wamba, S. F., Giannakis, M., & Foropon, C. (2019b). Big data analytics and organizational culture as complements to swift trust and collaborative performance in the humanitarian supply chain. *International Journal of Production Economics*, *210*, 120–136. doi:10.1016/j.ijpe.2019.01.023

Dubey, R., Gunasekaran, A., Childe, S. J., Wamba, S. F., & Papadopoulos, T. (2016). The impact of big data on world-class sustainable manufacturing. *International Journal of Advanced Manufacturing Technology*, *84*(1–4), 631–645. doi:10.100700170-015-7674-1

Dumas, M., La Rosa, M., Mendling, J., & Reijers, H. A. (2018). *Fundamentals of Business Process Management.* Springer. doi:10.1007/978-3-662-56509-4

Duran, D. C., Gogan, L. M., Artene, A., & Duran, V. (2015). The components of sustainable development-a possible approach. *Procedia Economics and Finance*, *26*, 806–811. doi:10.1016/S2212-5671(15)00849-7

Dutta, S., & Mia, I. (2011, April). The global information technology report 2010–2011. In *World Economic Forum* (Vol. 24, pp. 331-391). Academic Press.

Ead, W. M., & Abbassy, M. M. (2022). A general cyber hygiene approach for financial analytical environment. In *Financial Data Analytics* (pp. 369–384). Springer International Publishing. doi:10.1007/978-3-030-83799-0_13

Ead, W., & Abbassy, M. (2018). *Intelligent systems of machine learning approaches for developing E-services portals.* EAI Endorsed Transactions on Energy Web. doi:10.4108/eai.2-12-2020.167292

Echols, M. (2015). *Winning the Turnover War.* Retrieved on 20th July 2015 from: http//: www.talentmgt.com

Echols, M. E. (2005). Engaging employees to impact performance. *Chief Learning Officer*, *4*(2), 44–48.

Eckhard, S., Cornelius, P., Jessica, P., & Cornelia, D. Z. (2014). *The Future of Work Jobs and Skills in 2030.* The Foresight Company.

Edwards, M. R., & Edwards, K. (2019). *Predictive HR analytics: Mastering the HR.* Kogan Page Publishers.

Efrat, K., Gilboa, S., & Yonatany, M. (2017). When marketing and innovation interact: The case of born-global firms. *International Business Review*, *26*(2), 380–390. doi:10.1016/j.ibusrev.2016.09.006

Eichengreen, B., Gupta, P., & Marple, T. (2022). A Central Bank Digital Currency For India? *Indian Public Policy Review*, *3*(4), 1–29. doi:10.55763/ippr.2022.03.04.001

Eisingerich, A. B., Rubera, G., & Seifert, M. (2009). Managing service innovation and inter-organizational relationships for firm performance: To or commit diversity? *Journal of Service Research*, *11*(4), 344–356. doi:10.1177/1094670508329223

El Sibaii, S. (2018). *Strategic Sourcing in Construction Companies-A Case Study in Qatar*. Academic Press.

Emrouznejad, A., Anouze, A. L., & Thanassoulis, E. (2010). A semi-oriented radial measure for measuring the efficiency of decision making units with negative data, using DEA. *European Journal of Operational Research*, *200*(1), 297–304. doi:10.1016/j.ejor.2009.01.001

Engagedly. (2014). Retrieved from Engagedly: https://engagedly.com/

Enterprise Resource Planning. (2021). Retrieved October 20, 2023, from indiamart.com website: https://m.indiamart.com/proddetail/enterprise-resource-planning-21681980191.html

ERP Management System. (2020, June 19). Retrieved October 20, 2023, from PT. Centra Rekayasa Enviro website: https://cr-enviro.com/new/?page_id=284

Esben, H. o. (2017, October). *Collaborative Robots Ushering in Industry 5.0*. Academic Press.

Evans, R. J. (2012). *Business Analytics: The Next Frontier for Decision Sciences.* Carl H. Lindner College of Business, University of Cincinnati, http://faculty.cbpp.uaa.alaska.edu/afef/business_analytics.htm

Evans, W. R., & Davis, W. D. (2005). High-performance work systems and organizational performance: The mediating role of internal social structure. *Journal of Management*, *31*(5), 758–775. doi:10.1177/0149206305279370

Fallon, N. (2022, July 1). *The Importance of Employee Data*. Https://Www.Business.Com/Hr-Software/Employee-Data/

Fan, Y., Zhang, C., Zhang, X., & Xu, S. (2018). Evaluation of vegetable distribution performance based on grey relational analysis. *Journal of Food Distribution Research*, *49*(3), 66–73.

Fatma, I. (2020). *The effects of COVID-19 pandemic on the workforce in Turkey*. Academic Press.

Fawcett, S. E., & Waller, M. A. (2014). Supply chain game changers—mega, nano, and virtual trends—and forces that impede supply chain design (ie, building a winning team). *Journal of Business Logistics*, *35*(3), 157–164. doi:10.1111/jbl.12058

Fegley, S. (2006). *2006 talent management survey report - Society for human resource management*. managementw.shrm.org/hr-today/trends-and-forecasting/research-and-surveys/pages/2006_20talent_20management_20survey_20report.aspx

Felsberger, A., Qaiser, F. H., Choudhary, A., & Reiner, G. (2022). The impact of Industry 4.0 on the reconciliation of dynamic capabilities: Evidence from the European manufacturing industries. *Production Planning and Control*, *33*(2-3), 277–300. doi:10.1080/09537287.2020.1810765

Fernández-Aráoz, C. (2019). The future of work: Building a people-centered organization. *MIT Sloan Management Review*, *60*(2), 12–16.

Fernandez, V., & Gallardo-Gallardo, E. (2020). Tackling the HR digitalization challenge: Key factors and barriers to HR analytics adoption. *Competitiveness Review*. Advance online publication. doi:10.1108/CR-12-2019-0163

Festervand, T. A., Grove, S. J., & Eric Reidenbach, R. (1988). The sales force as a marketing intelligence system. *Journal of Business and Industrial Marketing*, *3*(1), 53–59. doi:10.1108/eb006051

Fields, Z., & Atiku, S. O. (2017). Collective Green Creativity and Eco-Innovation as Key Drivers of Sustainable Business Solutions in Organizations. In Z. Fields (Ed.), *Collective Creativity for Responsible and Sustainable Business Practice* (pp. 1–25). IGI Global. doi:10.4018/978-1-5225-1823-5.ch001

Filippus, K., & Schultz, C. M. (2019). Exploring talent management execution in the Ministry of Justice in the Namibian public sector. *SA Journal of Human Resource Management*, *17*(1), 1–9. doi:10.4102ajhrm.v17i0.1162

Fiore, J. a. (2014). *Workforce Analytics: The Three-Minute Guide*. Deloitte.

Fleck, A. (2023, February 2). *Microsoft*. Retrieved from Enabling advanced HR analytics and AI with Microsoft Azure Data Lake: https://www.microsoft.com/insidetrack/blog/enabling-advanced-hr-analytics-and-ai-with-microsoft-azure-data-lake/

Flores, E., Xu, X., & Lu, Y. (2020). Human4.0: A workforce competence typology for Industry 4.0. *Journal of Manufacturing Technology Management*, *31*(4), 687–703. doi:10.1108/JMTM-08-2019-0309

Fornell, C., & Larcker, D. F. (1981). Structural Equation Models with Unobservable Variables and Measurement Error: Algebra and Statistics. *JMR, Journal of Marketing Research*, *18*(3), 382–388. doi:10.1177/002224378101800313

Fortune Business Insights. (2021). *Shampoo market size, share & COVID 19 impact Analysis, By Product type (Medicated and non medicated), Form (Liquid, solid, and others), Application (Household and commercial), Distribution channel, and Regional Forecast, 2021-2028*. Available at: https://www.fortunebusinessinsights.com/shampoo-market-103432

Fosso Wamba, S., Gunasekaran, A., Papadopoulos, T., & Ngai, E. (2018). Big data analytics in logistics and supply chain management. *International Journal of Logistics Management*, *29*(2), 478–484. doi:10.1108/IJLM-02-2018-0026

Fotopoulos, C. B., & Psomas, E. L. (2009). The impact of soft and hard TQM elements on quality management results. *International Journal of Quality & Reliability Management*, *26*(2), 150–163. doi:10.1108/02656710910928798

Frank, F., Finnegan, R., & Taylor, C. (2004). The Race for Talent: Retaining and Engaging Workers in the 21st Century. *Human Resource Planning, 27.*

Franke, H., & Foerstl, K. (2020). Goals, conflict, politics, and performance of cross-functional sourcing teams—Results from a social team experiment. *Journal of Business Logistics*, *41*(1), 6–30. doi:10.1111/jbl.12225

Frauenthaler, P., Sigwart, M., Spanring, C., Sober, M., & Schulte, S. (2020). ETH relay: A cost-efficient relay for ethereum-based blockchains. In *2020 IEEE International Conference on Blockchain (Blockchain).* IEEE. 10.1109/Blockchain50366.2020.00032

Fry, R., & Cilluffo, A. (2019). A rising share of undergraduates are from poor families, especially at less selective colleges. Pew Research Center.

Gaayathri, R. S., Rajest, S. S., Nomula, V. K., & Regin, R. (2023). Bud-D: Enabling Bidirectional Communication with ChatGPT by adding Listening and Speaking Capabilities. *FMDB Transactions on Sustainable Computer Letters*, *1*(1), 49–63.

Gallardo-Gallardo, E., Nijs, S., Dries, N., & Gallo, P. (2015). Towards an understanding of talent management as a phenomenon-driven field using bibliometric and content analysis. *Human Resource Management Review*, *25*(3), 264–279. doi:10.1016/j.hrmr.2015.04.003

Gallup, Inc. (2013). *The benefits of employee engagement*. Retrieved November 11, 2023, from Gallup.com website: https://www.gallup.com/workplace/236927/employee-engagement-drives-growth.aspx

Gans, J. (2018). Strategy for Start-ups. Competitive Strategy Magazine. *Harvard Business Review*, 44–51.

Gao, R., Vaneza, J., Wang, L., Kriiger, J., Wang, X., & Makris, S. (2019). Symbiotic human-robot collaborative assembly. *CIRP Annuals, 68*(2), 701-726.

Gautam, R. K., & Mishra, K. (2016). Study on rural women entrepreneurship in India: Issues and challenges. *International Journal of Applied Research, 2*, 33–36.

Gedenk, K., Neslin, S. A., & Ailawadi, K. L. (2006). Sales Promotion. In *Retailing in the 21st Century* (pp. 345–359). Springer Berlin Heidelberg. doi:10.1007/3-540-28433-8_22

GEM. (2020). *Global Entrepreneurship Monitor 2019/2020 Global Report*. Retrieved from https://www.gemconsortium.org/report/gem-2019-2020-global-report

Georgia, K. (2022). Entrepreneurship in Dairy Cattle Sector: Key Features of Successful Administration and Management. *Land (Basel), 11*(10), 1736–1736. doi:10.3390/land11101736

Ghazalia, E., Soonb, P. C., Mutumc, D. S., & Nguyend, B. (2017). Health and cosmetics: Investigating consumers' values for buying organic personal care products. *Journal of Retailing and Consumer Services, 39*, 154–163. doi:10.1016/j.jretconser.2017.08.002

Ghobadian, A., & Gallear, D. (2001). TQM implementation: An empirical examination and proposed generic model. *Omega, 29*(4), 343–359. doi:10.1016/S0305-0483(01)00030-5

Ghobakhloo, M., Iranmanesh, M., Grybauskas, A., Vilkas, M., & Petraitė, M. (2021). Industry 4.0, innovation, and sustainable development: A systematic review and a roadmap to sustainable innovation. *Business Strategy and the Environment, 30*(8), 4237–4257. doi:10.1002/bse.2867

Ghosh, S. (2020). Examining the COVID-19 relief package for MSMEs. *Economic and Political Weekly, 55*(22), 10–12.

Giannakis, M., & Louis, M. (2016). A multi-agent based system with big data processing for enhanced supply chain agility. *Journal of Enterprise Information Management, 29*(5), 706–727. doi:10.1108/JEIM-06-2015-0050

Giri, Y. (2021, August 17). Big Data in HR: 4 Key Applications. *HR Trends*, p. 1. Retrieved from https://www.randstad.in/hr-news/hr-trends/big-data-hr-4-key-applications/

Gleeson, C. (2020). *How to use recruitment data to attract talent.* Retrieved April 2021, from: https://www.occupop.com/blog/how-to-use-recruitment-data-to-attract-talent

Gloor, P. A. (2015, November 17). *What Email Reveals About Your Organization.* Retrieved from Massachusetts Institute of Technology Sloan Management Review: https://sloanreview.mit.edu/article/what-email-reveals-about-your-organization/

Goasduff, L. (2021, June 9). *Information Technology.* Retrieved from Digital Workers Say Flexibility Is Key to Their Productivity: https://www.gartner.com/smarterwithgartner/digital-workers-say-flexibility-is-key-to-their-productivity

Goel, N., & Madan, P. (2019). Benchmarking financial inclusion for women entrepreneurship–a study of Uttarakhand state of India. *Benchmarking, 26*(1), 160–175. doi:10.1108/BIJ-01-2018-0023

Gohil, V. (2021). Consumer Buying Behavior of Personal Care Product: A Comparative Study of Male and Female Users. *Aegaeum Journal, 9*(1), 466–471.

Golovko, E., Danylchenko, I., Pohorelenko, A., & Sytnyk, B. (2021). Management Of Bank's Credit Activity As A Factor Ensuring Its Stability. Financial and credit systems. *Prospects for Development, 3*(3), 7–13.

Govindan, K., Cheng, T. C. E., Mishra, N., & Shukla, N. (2018). Big data analytics and application for logistics and supply chain management. *Transportation Research Part E, Logistics and Transportation Review, 114*, 343–349. doi:10.1016/j.tre.2018.03.011

Grabowska, S., & Saniuk, S. (2022). Business models in the industry 4.0 environment-results of web of science bibliometric analysis. *Journal of Open Innovation, 8*(1), 19. doi:10.3390/joitmc8010019

Grooms, B. T. F. (2001). *Marketing Intelligence: Executive Management Perceptions of Value* [Doctoral thesis]. Brunel University.

Gunasekaran, A., & McGaughey, R. E. (2003). TQM in supply chain management. *The TQM Magazine, 15*(6), 361–363. doi:10.1108/09544780310502688

Gunasekaran, A., Papadopoulos, T., Dubey, R., Wamba, S. F., Childe, S. J., Hazen, B., & Akter, S. (2017). Big data and predictive analytics for supply chain and organizational performance. *Journal of Business Research, 70*, 308–317. doi:10.1016/j.jbusres.2016.08.004

Gupta, R. K. (2021b). Adoption of mobile wallet services: an empirical analysis. *International Journal of Intellectual Property Management, 12*(3), 341 – 353. doi:10.1504/IJIPM.2021.10035526

Gupta, R. K. (2019). *HRMS (Human Resource Management System)*. Concepts, Applications, and Challenges. Excel Books.

Gupta, R. K. (2021a). A study on occupational health hazards among construction workers in India. *International Journal of Enterprise Network Management, 12*(4), 325–339. doi:10.1504/IJENM.2021.119663

Gupta, R. K. (2021b). Adoption of mobile wallet services: An empirical analysis. *International Journal of Intellectual Property Management, 12*(3), 341–353. doi:10.1504/IJIPM.2022.124634

Gupta, R. K. (2022). Utilization of Digital Network Learning and Healthcare for Verbal Assessment and Counselling During Post COVID-19 Period. Technologies. *Artificial Intelligence and the Future of Learning Post-COVID, 19*, 117–134.

Gupta, S., Qian, X., Bhushan, B., & Luo, Z. (2019). Role of cloud ERP and big data on firm performance: A dynamic capability view theory perspective. *Management Decision, 57*(8), 1857–1882. doi:10.1108/MD-06-2018-0633

Gupta, V. K., Goktan, A. B., & Gunay, G. (2019). Gender differences in entrepreneurial propensity: Evidence from matriculating students in the United States. *The International Entrepreneurship and Management Journal, 15*(1), 1–29.

Haddad, S. A., Awad, A., Albate, D., Almashhadani, I., & Dirani, W. (2020). Factors affecting green cosmetics purchase intention. *Journal of Management Information and Decision Sciences, 23*(4), 332–342.

Hair, J. F., Black, W. C., Babin, B. J., & Anderson, R. E. (2019). *Multivariate data analysis* (8th ed.). Cengage Learning.

Hair, J. F., Hult, G. T. M., Ringle, C. M., & Sarstedt, M. (2017). *A Primer on Partial Least Squares Structural Equation Modeling (PLS-SEM)* (2nd ed.). Sage Publications Inc.

Hamid, M., Wahab, S. A., Hosna, A. U., Hasanat, M. W., & Kamruzzaman, M. (2020). Impact of coronavirus (COVID-19) and employees' reaction to changes on employee performance of Bangladesh. *International Journal of Business and Management, 8*(8). Advance online publication. doi:10.24940/theijbm/2020/v8/i8/BM2008-013

Hamoud, A. K., Abd Ulkareem, M., Hussain, H. N., Mohammed, Z. A., & Salih, G. M. (2020, May). Improve HR decision-making based on data Mart and OLAP. *Journal of Physics: Conference Series, 1530*(1), 012058. doi:10.1088/1742-6596/1530/1/012058

Hana, M., & Naachimuthu, K. P. (2023). A Comprehensive Model on Rejection Sensitivity. *South India Journal of Social Sciences, 21*(19), 19–31.

Hana, M., Vishnupriya, S., & Naachimuthu, K. P. (2022). Restorative Effect of Direct and Indirect Nature Exposure - A Systematic Review. *International Journal of Scientific Research, 11*(5), 10–15.

Hanaysha, J. (2016). Improving employee productivity through work engagement: Evidence from higher education sector. *Management Science Letters*, *6*(1), 61–70. doi:10.5267/j.msl.2015.11.006

Handfield, R. (2006). *Supply Market Intelligence: A Managerial Handbook for Building Sourcing Strategies*. Taylor & Francis. doi:10.4324/9780203339527

Handfield, R., & Nichols, E. Jr. (2004). Key Issues in Global Supply Base Management. *Industrial Marketing Management*, *33*(1), 29–35. doi:10.1016/j.indmarman.2003.08.007

Han, X., Yuan, Y., & Wang, F.-Y. (2019). A blockchain-based framework for central bank digital currency. In *2019 IEEE International Conference on Service Operations and Logistics, and Informatics (SOLI)*. IEEE. 10.1109/SOLI48380.2019.8955032

Harris, J. G., Craig, E., & Light, D. A. (2011). Talent and analytics: New approaches, higher ROI. *The Journal of Business Strategy*, *32*(6), 4–13. doi:10.1108/02756661111180087

Harter, J. K., Schmidt, F. L., & Hayes, T. L. (2002). Business-unit-level relationship between employee satisfaction, employee engagement, and business outcomes: A meta-analysis. *The Journal of Applied Psychology*, *87*(2), 268–279. doi:10.1037/0021-9010.87.2.268 PMID:12002955

Hasan, N., & Bao, Y. (2020). Impact of "e-Learning crack-up" perception on psychological distress among college students during COVID-19 pandemic: A mediating role of "fear of academic year loss. *Children and Youth Services Review*, *118*, 105355. doi:10.1016/j.childyouth.2020.105355 PMID:32834276

Hasnat, M. M., & Hasan, S. (2018). Identifying tourists and analyzing spatial patterns of their destinations from location-based social media data. *Transportation Research Part C, Emerging Technologies*, *96*, 38–54. doi:10.1016/j.trc.2018.09.006

Hazen, B. T., Boone, C. A., Ezell, J. D., & Jones-Farmer, L. A. (2014). Data quality for data science, predictive analytics, and big data in supply chain management: An introduction to the problem and suggestions for research and applications. *International Journal of Production Economics*, *154*, 72–80. doi:10.1016/j.ijpe.2014.04.018

Hazen, B. T., Skipper, J. B., Ezell, J. D., & Boone, C. A. (2016). Big Data and predictive analytics for supply chain sustainability: A theory-driven research agenda. *Computers & Industrial Engineering*, *101*, 592–598. doi:10.1016/j.cie.2016.06.030

Heath, S. (2020). *The digital hereafter: Exploring death and the afterlife in the digital age*. Cambridge Scholars Publishing.

Hecklau, F., Galeitzke, M., Flachs, S., & Kohl, H. (2016). Holistic approach for human resource management in industry 4.0. *Procedia CIRP*, *54*, 1–6. doi:10.1016/j.procir.2016.05.102

Heijden, L. M. A. (2019). *Exploring the effects of HR analytics on strategic decision making* [Master's thesis]. University of Twente. https://purl.utwente.nl/essays/79817

Henseler, J., Ringle, C. M., & Sarstedt, M. (2015). A New Criterion for Assessing Discriminant Validity in Variance-Based Structural Equation Modeling. *Journal of the Academy of Marketing Science*, *43*(1), 115–135. doi:10.100711747-014-0403-8

Herhausen, D., Miočević, D., Morgan, R. E., & Kleijnen, M. H. P. (2020). The digital marketing capabilities gap. *Industrial Marketing Management*, *90*, 276–290. doi:10.1016/j.indmarman.2020.07.022

Homburg, C., & Wielgos, D. M. (2022). The value relevance of digital marketing capabilities to firm performance. *Journal of the Academy of Marketing Science*, *50*(4), 666–688. doi:10.100711747-022-00858-7 PMID:35463184

Hong, W. C. H. (2018). The Effect of Absence of Explicit Knowledge on ESL/EFL Stress-Placement Accuracy: A quasi-experiment. *Asian EFL Journal*, *20*(2), 262–279.

Hong, W. C. H. (2021a). Improving English as a foreign language learners' writing using a minimal grammar approach of teaching dependent clauses: A case study of Macao secondary school students. In B. L. Reynolds & M. F. Teng (Eds.), *Innovative Approaches in Teaching English Writing to Chinese Speakers* (pp. 67–90). De Gruyter Mouton. doi:10.1515/9781501512643-004

Hong, W. C. H. (2021b). Macao Secondary School EFL Teachers' Perspectives on Written Corrective Feedback: Rationales and Constraints. *Journal of Educational Technology and Innovation*, *1*(04), 1–13.

Hong, W. C. H. (2023). The impact of ChatGPT on foreign language teaching and learning: Opportunities in education and research. *Journal of Education Technology and Innovation*, *5*(1).

Hong, W. C. H., Chi, C.-Y., Liu, J., Zhang, Y.-F., Lei, N.-L., & Xu, X.-S. (2022). The influence of social education level on cybersecurity awareness and behaviour: A comparative study of university students and working graduates. *Education and Information Technologies*. PMID:35791319

Hossain, M. S., & Shila, N. S. (2020). Factors influencing consumer decision making for personal care products. *Dhaka University Journal of Biological Sciences*, *29*(1), 53-59.

Houghton, E., & Green, M. (2018). *People analytics: Driving business performance with people data.* https://search.proquest.com/docview/2043508044?accountid=130472

Huang, X., Li, M., Zhang, J., Zhang, L., Zhang, H., & Yan, S. (2020). Tourists' spatial-temporal behavior patterns intheme parks: A case study of Ocean Park Hong Kong. *J. Destin. Mark. Manag.*

Huang, M.-H., & Rust, R. T. (2021). A strategic framework for artificial intelligence in marketing. *Journal of the Academy of Marketing Science*, *49*(1), 30–50. doi:10.100711747-020-00749-9

Huang, S., Wang, B., Li, X., Zheng, P., Mourtzis, D., & Wang, L. (2022). Industry 5.0 and Society 5.0- Comparison, comlementation and Co-evolution. *Journal of Manufacturing Systems*, *64*, 424–428. doi:10.1016/j.jmsy.2022.07.010

Huq, Z., & Stolen, J. D. (1998). Total quality management contrast in manufacturing and service industries. *International Journal of Quality & Reliability Management*, *15*(2), 138–161. doi:10.1108/02656719810204757

Hussain, S., & Alam, F. (2023). Willingness to Pay for Tourism Services: A Case Study from Harappa, Sahiwal. *FMDB Transactions on Sustainable Management Letters*, *1*(3), 105–113.

Huster M. (2005). *Marketing Intelligence: A First Mover Advantage*. Academic Press.

Huus, T. (2015). *People Data: how to use and apply human capital metrics in your company*. Springer. doi:10.1057/9781137466969

Ibáñez, M. J., Guerrero, M., Yáñez-Valdés, C., & Barros-Celume, S. (2022). Digital social entrepreneurship: The N-Helix response to stakeholders' COVID-19 needs. *The Journal of Technology Transfer*, *47*(2), 556–579. doi:10.100710961-021-09855-4 PMID:33814697

Ibrahim, A. U., & Daniel, C. O. (2018). Talent management and its effects on the competitive advantage in organisations. *International Journal of recent advances in Multidisciplinary Research*, *5*(11), 4247-4253.

Ibrahim, N. (2021): Performance Evaluation of the Fruit and Vegetable Subsectors in the Azerbaijani Economy: A Combinatorial Analysis Using Regression and Principal Component Analysis. *Proceedings of 12th FEB Zagreb International Odyssey Conference on Economics and Business*, 309-328. https://doi.org/10.22598/odyssey/2021.3

Imarcgroup. (2022). *India Beauty and Personal Care Market: Industry Trends, Share, Size, Growth, Opportunity and Forecast 2022-2027*. Available at: https://www.imarcgroup.com/india-beauty-personal-care-market

Ingalagi, S. S., Nawaz, N., Rahiman, H. U., Hariharasudan, A., & Hundekar, V. (2021). Unveiling the crucial factors of women entrepreneurship in the 21st century. *Social Sciences (Basel, Switzerland)*, *10*(5), 153. doi:10.3390ocsci10050153

International Chamber of Shipping. (n.d.). *Shamika Sirimanne*. Retrieved March 31, 2023, from https://www.ics-shipping.org/person/shamika-sirimanne/

Islam, T., Islam, R., Pitafi, A. H., Xiaobei, L., Rehmani, M., Irfan, M., & Mubarak, M. S. (2021). The impact of corporate social responsibility on customer loyalty: The mediating role of corporate reputation, customer satisfaction, and trust. *Sustainable Production and Consumption*, *25*, 123–135. doi:10.1016/j.spc.2020.07.019

Isson, J. P., & Harriott, J. S. (2016). *People analytics in the era of big data: Changing the way you attract, acquire, develop, and retain talent*. John Wiley and Sons. doi:10.1002/9781119083856

Jadwala, R., & Patel, S. (2017). Challenges of Indian Dairy Industry. *Indian Journal of Applied Research*, *7*(10), 516–517.

Jagadeesan, P., & Balaji, P. (2017). Hair Care Product Usage Purposes and Brand Predilection of Male Consumers. *Indian Journal of Public Health Research & Development*, *8*(4), 367–371. doi:10.5958/0976-5506.2017.00371.0

Jamal, S., & Habib, M. A. (2020). Smartphone and daily travel: How the use of smartphone applications affect travel decisions. *Sustainable Cities and Society*, *53*(101939). doi:10.1016/j.scs.2019.101939

Jamous, T. (2023, February 22). *Forbes Councils Member*. Retrieved from Remote And Flexible Working Remain The Biggest Opportunities For Inclusive Workplaces: https://www.forbes.com/sites/forbesbusinesscouncil/2023/02/22/remote-and-flexible-working-remain-the-biggest-opportunities-for-inclusive-workplaces/?sh=342c79503ccd

Jasti, N. V. K., Venkateswaran, V., Kota, S., & Sangwan, K. S. (2022). A literature review on total quality management (models, frameworks, and tools and techniques) in higher education. *The TQM Journal*, *34*(5), 1298–1319. doi:10.1108/TQM-04-2021-0113

Javaid, M., Haleem, A., Singh, R., Haq, M., Raina, A., & Suman, R. (2020). Industry 5.0: Potential applications in COVID-19. *Journal of Industrial Integration and Management*, *5*(04), 507–530. doi:10.1142/S2424862220500220

Jayapriya, J., Poornima, T., & Naachimuthu, K. P. (2022). Hermeneutics of Iniyavai Naarpadhu and Inna Naarpadhu. *Journal of Positive School Psychology*, *6*(8), 4358–4368.

Jeba, J. A., Bose, S. R., & Boina, R. (2023). Exploring Hybrid Multi-View Multimodal for Natural Language Emotion Recognition Using Multi-Source Information Learning Model. *FMDB Transactions on Sustainable Computer Letters*, *1*(1), 12–24.

Jensen, J. M. (2011). Consumer loyalty on the grocery product market: An empirical application of Dick and Basu's framework. *Journal of Consumer Marketing*, *28*(5), 333–343. doi:10.1108/07363761111149983

Jeremiah, A., Atiku, S. O., & Villet, H. J. (2023). Leadership effectiveness and sustainability of State-Owned Enterprises. In N. Baporikar (Ed.), *Leadership and Governance for Sustainability* (pp. 55–80). IGI Global. doi:10.4018/978-1-6684-9711-1.ch004

Jerman, A., Pejić Bach, M., & Aleksić, A. (2019). Transformation towards smart factory system: Examining new job profiles and competencies. *Systems Research and Behavioral Science*, *37*(2), 388–402. doi:10.1002res.2657

Jermsittiparsert, K., & Rungsrisawat, S. (2019). Impact strategic sourcing, supplier innovativeness, and information sharing on supply chain agility. *International Journal of Innovation, Creativity and Change*, *5*(2), 397–415.

Jin, G., Sperandio, S., & Girard, P. (2017). Management of the design process: Human resource allocation in factories of the future. *Insight - International Council on Systems Engineering*, *20*(4), 19–22. doi:10.1002/inst.12175

Jyoti, J., & Rani, R. (2014). Exploring talent management practices: Antecedents and consequences. *International Journal of Management Concepts and Philosophy*, *8*(4), 220–248. doi:10.1504/IJMCP.2014.066903

Kabeer, N., Mahmud, S., & Tasneem, S. (2017). Does paid work provide a pathway to women's empowerment? Empirical findings from Bangladesh. *World Development*, *90*, 225–239.

Kahn, W. A. (1990). Psychological conditions of personal engagement and disengagement at work. *Academy of Management Journal*, *33*(4), 692–724. doi:10.2307/256287

Kambur, E., & Yildirim, T. (2022). From traditional to smart human resources management. *International Journal of Manpower*. Advance online publication. doi:10.1108/IJM-10-2021-0622

Kanaan-Jebna, A., Baharudi, A. S., & Alabdullah, T. T. Y. (2022). Entrepreneurial Orientation, Market Orientation, Managerial Accounting and Manufacturing SMEs Satisfaction. *Journal of Accounting Science*, *6*(1), 1–14. doi:10.21070/jas.v6i1.1590

Kang, J., Kim, H., Kim, H., & Kim, S. (2019). The impact of Industry 4.0 on human resource management: A literature review. *Sustainability*, *11*(13), 3.

Kanji, G. K., & Wallace, W. (2000). Business excellence through customer satisfaction. *Total Quality Management*, *11*(7), 979–998. doi:10.1080/09544120050135515

Karthik, R. a. (2022, January 31). *SAP News Center*. Retrieved from HR Transformation Is Changing in a New Hybrid Era: https://news.sap.com/2022/01/hr-transformation-is-changing-in-new-hybrid-era/

Kashevnik, A., Mikhailov, S., Papadakis, H., & Fragopoulou, P. (2019). Context-driven tour planning service: An approach based on synthetic coordinates recommendation. In *2019 24th Conference of Open Innovations Association (FRUCT)*. IEEE.

Kasket, E. (2019). *All the Ghosts in the Machine: Illusions of Immortality in the Digital Age*. Robinson.

Kaur, R., & Singh, D. (2021). Industry 4.0 and HRD: Reimagining the future of workplace learning and development. In Redesigning Work in the Fourth Industrial Revolution (pp. 147-159). Springer.

Kavanagh, M. J., Thite, M., & Johnson, R. D. (2017). *Human Resource Information Systems: Basics, Applications, and Future Directions*. SAGE Publications.

Kelle, P., Akkermans, H., & Voss, C. (2013). The impact of the design of planning and control systems on the performance of integrated supply chains. *International Journal of Production Economics*, *145*(1), 192–205.

Kenny, B., & Reedy, E. (2006). The Impact of Organizational Culture Factors on Innovation Levels in SMEs: An Empirical Investigation. *Irish Journal of Management*, *27*(2), 119–142.

Ketchen, D. J. Jr, Crook, T. R., & Craighead, C. W. (2014). From supply chains to supply ecosystems: Implications for strategic sourcing research and practice. *Journal of Business Logistics*, *35*(3), 165–171. doi:10.1111/jbl.12057

Khan, A., & Pillania, R. K. (2008). Strategic sourcing for supply chain agility and firms' performance: A study of Indian manufacturing sector. *Management Decision*.

Khan, M. A., Kumar, N., Mohsan, S. A. H., Khan, W. U., Nasralla, M. M., Alsharif, M. H., Żywiołek, J., & Ullah, I. (2023). Swarm of UAVs for network management in 6G: A technical review. *IEEE Transactions on Network and Service Management*, *20*(1), 741–761. doi:10.1109/TNSM.2022.3213370

Khan, M. M., Asad, H., & Mehboob, I. (2017). Investigating the consumer behavior for Halal endorsed products: Case of an emerging Muslim market. *Journal of Islamic Marketing*, *8*(4), 1–21. doi:10.1108/JIMA-09-2015-0068

Khanum, R., Mahadi, M. S. A., & Islam, M. S. (2022). Empowering tribal women through entrepreneurship in Sylhet region of Bangladesh. *GeoJournal*, *87*(4), 3387–3402. doi:10.100710708-020-10361-7

Kharlantseva, M. (2023, July 4). *Everhour*. Retrieved from Workforce Optimization: Benefits and Strategies to Boost Productivity: https://everhour.com/blog/workforce-optimization/#:~:text=Workforce%20optimization%2C%20also%20known%20as,satisfaction%20to%20meet%20business%20goals

Kim, H. (n.d.). *3 analytics tools that measure people data*. Academic Press.

Kim, H. Y., & Chung, J. E. (2011). Consumer purchase intention for organic personal care products. *Journal of Consumer Marketing*, *28*(1), 40–47. doi:10.1108/07363761111101930

Kontogianni, A., & Alepis, E. (2020). Smart tourism: State of the art and literature review for the last six years. *Array (New York, N.Y.)*, *6*(100020). doi:10.1016/j.array.2020.100020

Köseoğlu, D., Ead, S., & Abbassy, W. M. (2022). Basics of Financial Data Analytics. In *Financial Data Analytics* (pp. 23–57). Springer International Publishing. doi:10.1007/978-3-030-83799-0_2

Kosuru, V. S. R., & Venkitaraman, A. K. (2022). Developing a Deep Q-Learning and Neural Network Framework for Trajectory Planning. *European Journal of Engineering and Technology Research*, *7*(6), 148–157. doi:10.24018/ejeng.2022.7.6.2944

Kotler, P. (1999). *Marketing Management: Analysis, Planning, Implementation and Control* (9th ed.). Prentice Hall College Inc.

Kouvelis, P., Chambers, C., & Wang, H. (2017). *Handbook of Integrated Risk Management in Global Supply Chains*. John Wiley & Sons.

Kozlenkova, I. V., Samaha, S. A., & Palmatier, R. W. (2014). Resource-based theory in marketing. *Journal of the Academy of Marketing Science*, *42*(1), 1–21. doi:10.100711747-013-0336-7

KPMG. (2023). *The future of HR*. Retrieved from Workforce Insights and Analytics: https://advisory.kpmg.us/insights/future-hr/future-hr-workforce-insights-analytics.html

Kumar, V. (2018, December 20). *The Role of Big Data in Human Resource Management*. Retrieved from Association for Intelligent Information Management: https://info.aiim.org/aiim-blog/role-of-big-data-in-human-resource-management

Kumar, A. (2021). Central Bank Digital Currency and its impact on the Indian Financial system. *Asian Journal of Management*, 420–422. Advance online publication. doi:10.52711/2321-5763.2021.00063

Kumar, A., & Naachimuthu, K. P. (2023). Market Potential for Shawarma Outlet in Coimbatore - An Analysis. *South India Journal of Social Sciences*, *21*(1), 130–140.

Kumari, J. M. (2021). Central Bank Digital Currency (CBDC) Can it Replace Notes and Coins in India. *Management*, *8*(S1), 21–28.

Kumar, K. (2021). Women Entrepreneurship. In *India: Issues*. Challenges And Ways Forward.

Kumar, V., & Reinartz, W. (2016). *Customer relationship management: Concept, strategy, and tools*. Springer.

Kundariya, H. (2023, March 3). *Workpay Technologies, Inc.* Retrieved from How Big Data and Analytics Is Transforming Human Resources in the 21st Century: https://www.myworkpay.com/blogs/how-big-data-and-analytics-is-transforming-human-resources-in-the-21st-century#:~:text=Data%20analytics%20can%20provide%20HR%20with%20a%20clear,attrition%20issues%20in%20real-time%20and%20improve%20employee%20retention

Kuragayala, P. S. (2023). A Systematic Review on Workforce Development in Healthcare Sector: Implications in the Post-COVID Scenario. *FMDB Transactions on Sustainable Technoprise Letters*, *1*(1), 36–46.

Kushwah, S. S., Badodiya, S. K., Bhadauria, U. P. S., & Gurjr, R. S. (2020). Impact of entrepreneurial behavioural of farmers for increasing their income through bee keeping activities. *Indian Research Journal of Extension Education*, *20*(1), 55–60.

L.A., Jeffrey, Bradley, & Erica. (2011). Challenges and opportunities for new and beginning dairy producers: A Pennsylvania perspective. *Journal of Extension*, *49*(3).

Lal, P. (2015). Transforming HR in the digital era: Workforce analytics can move people specialists to the center of decision-making. *Human Resource Management International Digest*, *23*(3), 1–4. doi:10.1108/HRMID-03-2015-0051

Lam, L., Nguyen, P., Le, N., & Tran, K. (2021). The Relation among Organizational Culture, Knowledge Management, and Innovation Capability: Its Implication for Open Innovation. *Journal of Open Innovation*, *7*(1), 66. doi:10.3390/joitmc7010066

Lasi, H., Fettke, P., Kemper, H., Feld, T., & Hoffmann, M. (2014). Industry 4.0. *Business & Information Systems Engineering*, *6*(4), 239–242. doi:10.100712599-014-0334-4

Laudon, K. C., & Laudon, J. P. (2020). *Management information systems: Managing the digital firm*. Pearson.

Lavalle, S., Lesser, E., Shockey, R. H., & Crosthwait, N. M. (2011). Big Data, Analytics and the Path from Insight to Value. *MIT Sloan Management Review*, *52*(2), 21–32.

Lavanya, M. S., Hemalatha, S., & Indumathi, V. M. (2014). Perspectives of rural entrepreneurship in India. *Journal of Management Research*, *3*(1), 95–100.

Ldbyani, A., & Al-Abyadh, M. H. A. (2022). Relationship between Dark Triad, Mental Health, and Subjective Well-being Moderated by Mindfulness: A Study on Atheists and Muslim Students. *Islamic Guidance and Counseling Journal*, *5*(1), 71–87. doi:10.25217/igcj.v5i1.2642

Lebioda, L., Ivanete, H. S., & Anderson, A. M. (2019). The Influence of Mobile Technology Usage Behavior on Perceived Work Performance. *International Journal of Developmental Research*, *9*(2), 25733–25738.

Lee, J. E., Goh, M. L., & Mohd Noor, M. N. (2019). Understanding purchase intention of university students towards skin care products. *PSU Research Review*, *3*(3), 161–178. doi:10.1108/PRR-11-2018-0031

Lee, P., Hunter, W. C., & Chung, N. (2020). Smart tourism city: Developments and transformations. *Sustainability (Basel)*, *12*(10), 3958. doi:10.3390u12103958

Lei, T. (2022). Credit Risk Control of Investment-loan Linkage by Commercial Banks in China. In *2022 4th International Conference on Economic Management and Cultural Industry* (pp. 1878–1886). Atlantis Press.

Leithy, W. (2017). Organizational Culture and Organizational Performance. *International Journal of Economics & Management Sciences.*, *06*(4). Advance online publication. doi:10.4172/2162-6359.1000442

Leone, L., Fleischhacker, S., Anderson-Steeves, B., Harper, K., Winkler, M., Racine, E., Baquero, B., & Gittelsohn, J. (2020). Healthy food retail during the COVID-19 pandemic: Challenges and future directions. *International Journal of Environmental Research and Public Health*, *17*(20), 7397. doi:10.3390/ijerph17207397 PMID:33050600

Leong, K. (2021). *A data-driven approach to identifying-and retaining - Top employees*. https://hbr.org/2021/05/a-data-driven-approach-to-identifying-and-retaining-top-employees

Levenson, A., & Fink, A. (2017). Human capital analytics: Too much data and analysis, not enough models and business insights. *Journal of Organisational Effectiveness: People and Performance*, *4*(2), 145–156. doi:10.1108/JOEPP-03-2017-0029

Lian, X., Hong, W. C. H., Xu, X., Kimberly, K. Z., & Wang, Z. (2022). The influence of picture book design on visual attention of children with autism: A pilot study. *International Journal of Developmental Disabilities*, 1–11. PMID:37885844

Liao, G., Li, Z., Du, Z., & Liu, Y. (2019). The heterogeneous interconnections between supply or demand side and oil risks. *Energies*, *12*(11), 2226. doi:10.3390/en12112226

Liberatore, M., & Luo, W. (2010). The Analytics Movement. *Interfaces*, *40*(4), 313–324. doi:10.1287/inte.1100.0502

Lies, J. (2019). Marketing intelligence and big data: Digital marketing techniques on their way to becoming social engineering techniques in marketing. *International Journal of Interactive Multimedia and Artificial Intelligence*, *5*(5), 134. doi:10.9781/ijimai.2019.05.002

Li, L., Lin, J., Ouyang, Y., & Luo, X. (2022). Evaluating the impact of big data analytics usage on the decision-making quality of organizations. *Technological Forecasting and Social Change*, *175*(121355), 121355. doi:10.1016/j.techfore.2021.121355

Li, S., Ragu-Nathan, B., Ragu-Nathan, T. S., & Rao, S. S. (2006). The impact of supply chain management practices on competitive advantage and organizational performance. *Omega*, *34*(2), 107–124. doi:10.1016/j.omega.2004.08.002 PMID:17876965

Littman, J. (2015). Digital legacy and death: Practical and ethical aspects of digital inheritance. *International Journal of Law and Information Technology*, *23*(4), 349–370.

Liu, H., Lv, Z., Song, Z., Zhou, S., Liu, W., & Fang, M. (2022). Application of blockchain technology in electric vehicle charging piles based on electricity Internet of Things. *Wireless Communications and Mobile Computing*, *2022*, 1–10. doi:10.1155/2022/8533219

Liu, Y.-Y., Tseng, F.-M., & Tseng, Y.-H. (2018). Big Data analytics for forecasting tourism destination arrivals with the applied Vector Autoregression model. *Technological Forecasting and Social Change*, *130*, 123–134. doi:10.1016/j.techfore.2018.01.018

Li, Y., & Cao, H. (2018). Prediction for tourism flow based on LSTM neural network. *Procedia Computer Science*, *129*, 277–283. doi:10.1016/j.procs.2018.03.076

Li, Y., Hu, C., Huang, C., & Duan, L. (2017). The concept of smart tourism in the context of tourism information services. *Tourism Management*, *58*, 293–300. doi:10.1016/j.tourman.2016.03.014

Lodha, S., Malani, H., & Bhardwaj, A. K. (2023). Performance Evaluation of Vision Transformers for Diagnosis of Pneumonia. *FMDB Transactions on Sustainable Computing Systems*, *1*(1), 21–31.

Longo, F., Padovano, A., & Umbrello, S. (2020). Value-oriented and ethical technology engineering in industry 5.0: A human-centric perspective for the design of the factory of the future. *Applied Sciences (Basel, Switzerland)*, *10*(12), 4182. doi:10.3390/app10124182

Lorman. (2020). *10 benefits of employee engagement survey*. https://www.lorman.com/blog/post/10-benefits-of-employee-engagement-surveys

Lucey, J. J. (2009). The impact of a communications strategy and five step survey process on the improvement of employee engagement. *Management Services*, 9–15.

Luckin, R., Holmes, W., Griffiths, M., & Forcier, L. B. (2016). *Intelligence unleashed - an argument for AI in education*. Academic Press.

Luo, Y., Li, X., & Wang, J. (2021). Evaluation of the efficiency and coordination degree of vegetable distribution channels based on DEA and coupling coordination degree model. *Journal of Food Distribution Research*, *52*(2), 107–118.

Lusine H, & Aramyan. (2007). *Measuring supply chain performance in the Agri-food sector* [PhD thesis]. Wageningen University.

Luthans, F., & Peterson, S. J. (2002). Employee engagement and manager self-efficacy. *Journal of Management Development*, *21*(5), 376–387. doi:10.1108/02621710210426864

Lvarado, U.Y., & Kotzab, H. (2001). Supply chain management: the integration of logistics in marketing. *Industrial Marketing Management, 30*(2), 183-98.

MacLeod, D., & Clarke, N. (2011). *Engaging for success: Enhancing performance through employee engagement, a report to Government*. Academic Press.

Madhumitha, D., & Naachimuthu, K. P. (2023). Emotional Regulation among the Members of LGBTQ+ Community. *Education and Society*, *47*(2), 34–45.

Mahmood, S. (2017). *21st century staffing: The wave of artificial intelligence in recruitment*. https://search.proquest.com/docview/2043508044?accountid=130472

Maija, B., Lars, D. N., & Athanasios, P. (2021). *Industry 5.0- Towards a sustainable, human-centric, and resilient European industry*. European Commission.

Ma, L., & Sun, B. (2020). Machine learning and AI in marketing – Connecting computing power to human insights. *International Journal of Research in Marketing*, *37*(3), 481–504. doi:10.1016/j.ijresmar.2020.04.005

Malik, H. (2013). Relationship between leader behaviors and employees'jobsatisfaction:a path-goal approach. *Pakistan Journal of Commerce and Social Sciences*, *7*(1), 209–222.

Manivannanan, C., & Tripathi, H. (2016). Management efficiency of dairy entrepreneurs. *Indian Research Journal of Extension Education*, *7*(3), 44–51.

Manyika, J., Chui, M., Miremadi, M., Bughin, J., George, K., Willmott, P., & Dewhurst, M. (2017). A future that works: AI, automation, employment, and productivity. *McKinsey Global Institute Research. Tech. Rep*, *60*, 1–135.

Mao, S., Wang, B., Tang, Y., & Qian, F. (2019). Opportunities and challenges of artificial intelligence for green manufacturing in the process industry. *Engineering (Beijing)*, *5*(6), 995–1002. doi:10.1016/j.eng.2019.08.013

Marchesi, L., Marchesi, M., Tonelli, R., & Lunesu, M. I. (2022). A blockchain architecture for industrial applications. Blockchain. *Research and Applications*, *3*(4), 100088. doi:10.1016/j.bcra.2022.100088

Maria Michael Visuwasam, L., Paulraj, D., Gayathri, G., Divya, K., Hariprasath, S., & Jayaprakashan, A. (2020). Intelligent personal digital assistants and smart destination platform (SDP) for globetrotter. *Journal of Computational and Theoretical Nanoscience*, *17*(5), 2254–2260. doi:10.1166/jctn.2020.8880

María, J. J. L., Polo, O. C. C., & Elhadary, T. (2023). An Analysis of the Morality and Social Responsibility of Non-Profit Organizations. *FMDB Transactions on Sustainable Technoprise Letters*, *1*(1), 28–35.

Market research.com. (2021). *Shampoo (Haircare) Market in India - Outlook to 2025; Market Size, Growth and Forecast Analytics*. Available at: https://www.marketresearch.com

Marler, J. a. (2016). An Evidence-based Review of HR Analytics. *The International Journal of Human Resource Management, 28*(1), 3-26.

Martinez, E., Beaulieu, N., Gibbons, R., Pronovost, P., & Wang, T. (2015). Organizational Culture and Performance. *The American Economic Review*, *105*(5), 331–335. doi:10.1257/aer.p20151001

Martins, E., & Terblanche, F. (2003). Building Organisational Culture That Stimulates Creativity and Innovation. *European Journal of Innovation Management*, *6*(1), 64–74. doi:10.1108/14601060310456337

Maseleno, A., Patimah, S., Syafril, S., & Huda, M. (2023). Learning Preferences Diagnostic using Mathematical Theory of Evidence. *FMDB Transactions on Sustainable Techno Learning*, *1*(2), 60–77.

Matarazzo, M., Penco, L., Profumo, G., & Quaglia, R. (2021). Digital transformation and customer value creation in Made in Italy SMEs: A dynamic capabilities perspective. *Journal of Business Research*, *123*, 642–656. doi:10.1016/j.jbusres.2020.10.033

Mathurajothi, S., Subramani, S., & Venkateswaran, P. S. (2018). A Study on the Impact of Service Quality on Student Satisfaction towards the University Libraries in Dindigul District, Tamil Nadu, India. *Asian Journal of Information Science and Technology*, *8*(3), 63–66. doi:10.51983/ajist-2018.8.3.200

Matić, M., & Puh, B. (2015). Consumer's purchase intention towards natural cosmetics. *Ekonomski Vjesnik / Econviews – Review of Contemporary Entrepreneurship, Business, and Economic Issues*, 53-64.

Mayika, J. M., Chui, B., Brown, J., Bughin, R., Dobbs, Roxburgh, C., & Byers, A. (2011). *Big Data: The Next Frontier for Innovation, Competition, and Productivity.* McKinsey Report.

Mazor, A. H. (2018). *Deloitte*. Retrieved from Talent acquisition analytics: Using analytics for smarter sourcing and hiring decisions: https://www2.deloitte.com/us/en/pages/human-capital/articles/talent-acquisition-analytics.html

McAfee. (2019, June 19). *McAfee*. Retrieved from Expanding Our Vision to Expand the Cybersecurity Workforce: https://www.mcafee.com/blogs/other-blogs/executive-perspectives/expanding-our-vision-to-expand-the-cybersecurity-workforce/

McAfee, A. B. (2012). Big Data: The Management Revolution. *Harvard Business Review*, *90*(10), 60–68. PMID:23074865

McGee, J. (2015). *Market-based view*. Wiley Encyclopedia of Management., doi:10.1002/9781118785317.weom120075

Medina Serrano, R., González Ramírez, R., Gasco Gasco, J., & Llopis Taverner, J. (2020). Strategic sourcing: Developing a progressive framework for make-or-buy decisions. *Journal of Industrial Engineering and Management*, *13*(1), 133–154. doi:10.3926/jiem.2858

Meena, K., & Janani, S. J. (2016). Issues and challenges in gaining competitive advantage in human resource. *International Conference on "Research Avenues in Social Science, 1*(3), 230–234. https://ijariie.com/AdminUploadPdf/Issues_and_challenges_in_gaining_competitive_advantage_through_human_resource_c_1224

Mendenhall, M. E., Lee, J., & Yasin, M. M. (2018). Talent management in the context of Industry 4.0. *Journal of World Business*, *53*(4), 410–417.

Meob, P. D., Fiumarac, G., & Baumgartnerd, R. (2021). *Web Data Extraction, Applications and Techniques: A Survey*. Emilio Ferraraa.

Mert, I. (2020). Analyzing the Results of Accounting Evaluation Methods Through Practical Applications. *European Business & Management*, *6*(4), 95–104. doi:10.11648/j.ebm.20200604.14

Mert, I. (2021a). Analyzing the Sustainability of the Accounting Valuation Practices in Romania during the Adaptation Period to the European Union. *Revista Argentina de Clínica Psicológica*, *30*(1), 787–798.

Mert, I. (2021b). The Effects of Collaboration between Internal Auditing and Financial Affairs Departments: A Survey Conducted through the Internal Auditing and Financial Affairs Departments. *Economic Studies*, *30*(3), 96–114.

Mert, I. (2021c). The Effects of the Qualitative Parameters of Internal Auditing Works on the Preferences of Investment Funds' Analysts. *Economic Alternatives*, (1), 60–71.

Mert, I. (2022). *Assessment of Accounting Evaluation Practices, A Research-Based Review of Turkey and Romania. Springer Cham.*

Mert, I. (2022). Investigation Techniques, Methods, Types, and Increasing Impact of Forensic Accounting in Digital Period. *Maliye ve Finans Yazıları*, (118), 13–32. doi:10.33203/mfy.1084274

Meyers, C., Van Woerkom, M., & Dries, N. (2013). Talent – innate or acquired? Theoretical considerations and their implications for talent management. *Human Resource Management Review*, *23*(4), 305–321. doi:10.1016/j.hrmr.2013.05.003

Miah, S. J., Vu, H. Q., Gammack, J., & McGrath, M. (2017). A big data analytics method for tourist behaviour analysis. *Information & Management*, *54*(6), 771–785. doi:10.1016/j.im.2016.11.011

Mihalcea, A. (2017). Employer branding and talent management in the digital age. *Management Dynamics in the Knowledge Economy*, *5*(2), 289–306. doi:10.25019/MDKE/5.2.07

Mikhailov, S., Kashevnik, A., & Smirnov, A. (2020). Tourist Behaviour Analysis Based on Digital Pattern of Life. *2020 7th International Conference on Control, Decision and Information Technologies (CoDIT).*

Mikhailov, S., & Kashevnik, A. (2020). Tourist behaviour analysis based on digital pattern of life—An approach and case study. *Future Internet*, *12*(10), 165. doi:10.3390/fi12100165

Minbaeva, D. (2017). Human capital analytics: Why aren't we there? Introduction to the special issue. *Journal of Organizational Effectiveness: People and Performance*, *4*(2), 110–118. doi:10.1108/JOEPP-04-2017-0035

Minbaeva, D., & Collings, D. G. (2013). Seven myths of global talent management. *International Journal of Human Resource Management*, *24*(9), 1762–1776. doi:10.1080/09585192.2013.777539

Modi, S., Braniff, L., El-Zoghbi, M., Emig, A., Michaels, L., & Stark, E. (2022). *Digital Adoption of MSMEs During COVID-19*. Retrieved November 6, 2023, from Centerforfinancialinclusion.org website: https://content.centerforfinancialinclusion.org/wp-content/uploads/sites/2/2022/09/Digital-adoption-of-Msmes-During-covid19-1.pdf

Mohapatra, A. S., Behera, R., & Sahu, U. N. (2012). Constraints faced by tribal entrepreneurs in dairy farming enterprise. *International Journal of Physical and Social Sciences*, *2*(7), 171–184.

Mohsan, S. A. H., Othman, N. Q. H., Khan, M. A., Amjad, H., & Żywiołek, J. (2022). A comprehensive review of micro UAV charging techniques. *Micromachines*, *13*(6), 977. doi:10.3390/mi13060977 PMID:35744592

Mondal, S. (2021). *The rise of talent intelligence in 2022*. https://ideal.com/rise-of-talent-intelligence-feature/

Morales-Resendiz, R., Ponce, J., Picardo, P., Velasco, A., Chen, B., Sanz, L., & Hodge, A. (2021). Implementing a retail CBDC: Lessons learned and key insights. *Latin American Journal of Central Banking*, *2*(1), 100022. doi:10.1016/j.latcb.2021.100022

Morrison, R. (2013). *What is big data and what is people data.* https://www.orgvue.com/resources/articles/the-key-to-challenge-in-organisation-design-isnt-big-data-its-people-data-part-3/

MSME annual report 2022-23. (2022). Retrieved November 6, 2023, from Gov.in website: https://msme.gov.in/msme-annual-report-2022-23

MSMEs risk build-up amid COVID-19 pandemic, says the report. (2021). *Business Standard News.* Retrieved November 6, 2023, from Business-standard.com website: https://www.business-standard.com/article/economy-policy/watch-out-for-msme-risk-build-up-amid-covid-19-pandemic-says-report-121021801579_1.html

Muangkammuen, P., Intiruk, N., & Saikaew, K. R. (2018). Automated Thai-FAQ Chatbot using RNN-LSTM. In *2018 22nd International Computer Science and Engineering Conference (ICSEC).* IEEE.

Muhammad, N., Alwi, S. F. S., & Muhammad, N. (2020). Credit management in full-fledged Islamic bank and Islamic banking window: Towards achieving maqasid Al-Shariah. *International Journal of Financial Research, 11*(3), 92. doi:10.5430/ijfr.v11n3p92

Mukhuty, S., Upadhyay, A., & Rothwell, H. (2022). Strategic sustainable development of Industry 4.0 through the lens of social responsibility: The role of human resource practices. *Business Strategy and the Environment, 31*(5), 2068–2081. doi:10.1002/bse.3008

Munsamy, M., & Telukdarie, A. (2019). Digital HRM model for process optimization by adoption of Industry 4.0 technologies. *Proceedings of the IEEE International Conference on Industrial Engineering and Engineering Management,* 374-378. 10.1109/IEEM44572.2019.8978726

Murphy, K. P. (2012). *Machine learning: A probabilistic perspective.* MIT Press.

Murphy, R. (2019). More than Quibbles: Problems with the theory and history of Fractional Reserve Free Banking. *The Quarterly Journal of Austrian Economics, 22*(1), 3–25. doi:10.35297/qjae.010016

Mwila, N. K., & Turay, M. I. S. (2018). Augmenting talent management for sustainable development in Africa. *World Journal of Entrepreneurship, Management and Sustainable Development, 14*(1), 41–49. doi:10.1108/WJEMSD-03-2017-0012

Naachimuthu, K. P., Ganga, S., & Mathiyoli, P. M. (2022). Psychosocial Impact of COVID-19 Lockdown. *IAHRW International Journal of Social Sciences Review, 10*(1), 52–59.

Nagarajan, G., & Naachimuthu, K. P. (2022). Positive Emotions and Experiences of Trans Men and Trans Women - A Grounded Theory Approach. *International Journal of Early Childhood Special Education, 14*(2), 6430–6447.

Nagrale, B. G., Datta, K. K., & Chauhan, A. K. (2015). An analysis of constraints faced by dairy farmers in Vidarbha region of Maharashtra. *Indian Journal of Dairy Science, 68*(4), 390–394.

Nahavandi, S. (2019). Industry 5.0- A human-centric solution. *Sustainability (Basel), 11*(16), 4371. doi:10.3390u11164371

Nair, S. R. (2016). Women entrepreneurship across nations: Opportunities and challenges. Handbook of Research on Entrepreneurship in the Contemporary Knowledge-Based Global Economy, 189–216.

Najafabadi, M. M., Villanustre, F., Khoshgoftaar, T. M., Seliya, N., Wald, R., & Muharemagic, E. (2015). Deep learning applications and challenges in big data analytics. *Journal of Big Data, 2*(1), 1. doi:10.118640537-014-0007-7

Namibia Labour Force Survey 2018 Report. (2018). https://d3rp5jatom3eyn.cloudfront.net/cms/assets/documents/Labour_Force_Survey_final_-_2018.pdf

Nasril, F., Indiyati, D., & Ramantoko, G. (2021). Talent performance analysis using people analytics approach. Budapest International Research and Critics Institute (BIRCI-Journal): Humanities and Social Sciences, 4(1), 216-230.

Nathan, M. M. (2013). *Knowledge defines the growth strategy.* www.exceljockey.com

Networks, J. (2012). *Introduction to Big Data: Infrastructure And Networking Considerations.* Juniper Networks.

Ngai, E. W. T., & Cheng, T. C. E. (2019). Employee well-being in Industry 4.0: A review of literature. *International Journal of Human Resource Management, 30*(16), 2265–2282.

Nilashi, M., Bagherifard, K., Rahmani, M., & Rafe, V. (2017). A recommender system for tourism industry using cluster ensemble and prediction machine learning techniques. *Computers & Industrial Engineering, 109*, 357–368. doi:10.1016/j.cie.2017.05.016

Niraj, R., & Kashyap, G. (2019). Scenario planning: A tool for strategic thinking. *Business Horizons, 62*(4), 563–573.

Nithyanantham, V. (2023). Study Examines the Connection Between Students' Various Intelligence and Their Levels of Mathematical Success in School. *FMDB Transactions on Sustainable Techno Learning, 1*(1), 32–59.

Nocker, M. a. (2019). Big Data and Human Resources Management: The Rise of Talent Analytics. *Big Data and Employee Wellbeing, Social Sciences, 8*(10), 273.

Noor, S., & Isa, F. M. (2020). Contributing factors of women entrepreneurs' business growth and failure in Pakistan. *International Journal of Business and Globalisation, 25*(4), 503–518. doi:10.1504/IJBG.2020.109115

O'dwyer, J., & Renner, R. (2011). The Promise of Advanced Supply Chain Analytics, Supply Chain. *Management Review, 15*, 32–37.

O'Neil, K., & Achter, T. (2018). Disruptive trends in workforce development. *Journal of Workforce Development, 12*(1), 1–1.

Obiora, J. N., & Nwokorie, E. C. (2018). Impediments to Rural Youth Entrepreneurship towards the Hospitality Sector in Nigeria: The Case of Ihitte-Uboma, Imo State. *Journal of Tourism and Hospitality Management, 6*(1), 81–91.

Ocoró, M. P., Polo, O. C. C., & Khandare, S. (2023). Importance of Business Financial Risk Analysis in SMEs According to COVID-19. *FMDB Transactions on Sustainable Management Letters, 1*(1), 12–21.

Ogunmola, G. A., Singh, B., Sharma, D. K., Regin, R., Rajest, S. S., & Singh, N. (2021). Involvement of distance measure in assessing and resolving efficiency environmental obstacles. In *2021 International Conference on Computational Intelligence and Knowledge Economy (ICCIKE).* IEEE. 10.1109/ICCIKE51210.2021.9410765

Olabisi, J., Oladejo, D. A., Adegoke, J. F., & Abioro, M. A. (2019). Credit management policy and firms' profitability: Evidence from infant manufacturing firms in southwest Nigeria. *Contemporary Economy Journal, 4*(4), 59–69.

Oosterman, J. M., Drossaert, C. H., Eysenbach, G., & Graafland, M. (2016). Towards a new paradigm for patient-web communication: Seeking to address the pitfalls of health 1.0. *Journal of Medical Internet Research, 18*(6), e110.

Oran, O. (2016, June 7). *Wall Street Hopes Artificial Intelligence Software Helps It Hire Loyal Bankers.* Retrieved from Reuters: https://www.reuters.com/article/us-banks-hiring-ai-idUSKCN0YT163

Orlova, L. V., Afonin, Y. A., & Voronin, V. V. (2015). Talent management and knowledge: Theory, methodology, models. *Review of European Studies, 7*(9), 75. doi:10.5539/res.v7n9p75

Osburg, V. S., Yoganathan, V., Bartikowski, B., Liu, H., & Strack, M. (2020). Effects of ethical certification and ethical eWoM on talent attraction. *Journal of Business Ethics, 164*(3), 535–548. doi:10.100710551-018-4018-8

Otomeyt. (2022, July 7). AI. *Big Data is Redefining HR Practices*, p. 1.

Otto, S. S. (2016, December 5). *Chief Learning Officer.* Retrieved from Corporate Learning's Transformation in the Digital Age: https://www.chieflearningofficer.com/2016/12/05/corporate-learnings-transformation-digital-age/

Özdurak, C. (2021). Nexus between crude oil prices, clean energy investments, technology companies, and energy democracy. *Green Finance*, *3*(3), 337–350. doi:10.3934/GF.2021017

Padhi, P. K. (2022). *Emergence of Central Bank Digital Currency In Indian Perspective: A Conceptual Analysis.* An Approach Towards Central Bank Digital Currency.

Padmapriya, P., & Naachimuthu, K. P. (2023). Social and Philosophical Construction of Emotions in Bhagavad Gita & Plutchik Wheel of Emotions. *Journal of the Asiatic Society of Mumbai*, *XCVI*(27), 22–36.

Pal, K. (2017). Supply Chain Coordination Based on Web Services. In Supply Chain Management in the Big Data Era. IGI Global.

Pal, K. (2018). A Big Data Framework for Decision Making in Supply Chain. In Predictive Intelligence Using Big Data and the Internet of Things. IGI Global.

Pal, K. (2019). Quality Assurance Issues for Big Data Applications in Supply Chain Management. In Predictive Intelligence Using Big Data and the Internet of Things. IGI Global.

Pal, K. (2020). Information sharing for manufacturing supply chain management based on blockchain technology. In Cross-Industry Use of Blockchain Technology and Opportunities for the Future. IGI Global.

Pal, K. (2021a). Applications of Secured Blockchain Technology in Manufacturing Industry. In Blockchain and AI Technology in the Industrial Internet of Things. IGI Global.

Pal, K. (2022). A Decentralized Privacy-Preserving Healthcare Blockchain for IoT, Challenges, and Solutions. In Prospects of Blockchain Technology for Accelerating Scientific Advancement in Healthcare. IGI Global.

Pal, K. (2023a). Security Issues and Solutions for Resource-Constrained IoT Applications Using Lightweight Cryptography. In Cybersecurity Issues, Challenges, and Solutions in the Business World. IGI Global.

Pal, K. (2023b). Drivers of Sustainable Supply Chain Management Using Internet of Things-Based Blockchain Technology. In Government Impact on Sustainable and Responsible Supply Chain. IGI Global.

Palich, N., & Edmonds, A. (2013). Social sustainability: creating places and participatory processes that perform well for people. *Environment Design Guide*, 1–13.

Pal, K. (2016). *Supply Chain Coordination Based on Web Service, Supply Chain Management in the Big Data Era.* IGI Publication.

Pal, K. (2021b). Privacy, Security and Policies: A Review of Problems and Solutions with Blockchain-Based Internet of Things Applications in Manufacturing Industry. *Procedia Computer Science*, *191*, 176–183. doi:10.1016/j.procs.2021.07.022

Pal, K., & Yasar, A. (2020). Internet of Things and blockchain technology in apparel manufacturing supply chain data management. *Procedia Computer Science*, *170*, 450–457. doi:10.1016/j.procs.2020.03.088

Pande, S. D., & Chetty, M. S. R. (2021). Fast medicinal leaf retrieval using CapsNet. In *Advances in Intelligent Systems and Computing* (pp. 149–155). Springer Singapore.

Pande, S., & Chetty, M. S. R. (2018). Analysis of Capsule Network (Capsnet) Architectures and Applications. *Journal of Advanced Research in Dynamical and Control Systems*, *10*(10), 2765–2771.

Pande, S., & Chetty, M. S. R. (2019). Bezier Curve Based Medicinal Leaf Classification using Capsule Network. *International Journal of Advanced Trends in Computer Science and Engineering*, *8*(6), 2735–2742. doi:10.30534/ijatcse/2019/09862019

Pandit, P. (2023). On the Context of the Principle of Beneficence: The Problem of Over Demandingness within Utilitarian Theory. *FMDB Transactions on Sustainable Social Sciences Letters*, *1*(1), 26–42.

Park, W.-Y., Ro, Y. K., & Kim, N. (2018). Architectural innovation and the emergence of a dominant design: The effects of strategic sourcing on performance. *Research Policy*, *47*(1), 326–341. doi:10.1016/j.respol.2017.11.003

Paschek, D., Mocan, A., & Draghici, A. (2019). Industry 5.0- The expected impact of the next industrial revolution. In *Thriving on future education, industry, business, and society, proceedings of the MakeLearn and TIIM International conference* (pp. 15-17). Piran.

Pasumarti, S. S., & Pasumarti, S. S. (2019). Work life balance: A challenge for employees in Indian IT and ITES industry. *Rupkatha Journal on Interdisciplinary Studies in Humanities*, *11*(2). Advance online publication. doi:10.21659/rupkatha.v11n2.15

Patel, B., & Chavda, K. (2013). Rural entrepreneurship in India: Challenge and problems. *International Journal of Advance Research in Computer Science and Management Studies*, *1*(2).

Patel, N. B., Saiyed, L. H., Rao, T. K. S., Ranjeetsingh, R., Modi, R. J., & Sabapara, G. P. (2013). Status and constraints of dairying in the tribal households of Narmada valley of Gujarat-India. *Animal Science (Penicuik, Scotland)*, *7*(3), 31–37.

Patnayakuni, R., & Ruppel, C. P. (2010). A soci-technical approach to improving the systems development process. *Information Systems Frontiers*, *12*(2), 219–234. doi:10.100710796-008-9093-4

Payne, A., & Frow, P. (2013). *Strategic customer management: Integrating relationship marketing and CRM*. Cambridge University Press. doi:10.1017/CBO9781139057417

Pearce, P. L. (2005). *Tourist behaviour: Themes and Conceptual Schemes*. Channel View Publications. doi:10.21832/9781845410247

Peeters, T., Paauwe, J., & Van De Voorde, K. (2020). People analytics effectiveness: Developing a framework. *Journal of Organizational Effectiveness: People and Performance*, *7*(2), 203–2019. doi:10.1108/JOEPP-04-2020-0071

Peng, X., & Liu, Y. (2016). Behind eco-innovation: Managerial environmental awareness and external resource acquisition. *Journal of Cleaner Production*, *139*, 347–360. doi:10.1016/j.jclepro.2016.08.051

Perera, S. (2020). Digital legacy: Legal and ethical considerations in the post-mortem management of online accounts. *Information & Communications Technology Law*, *29*(1), 34–58.

Phillips-Wren, G., & Hoskisson, A. (2015). An analytical journey towards big data. *Journal of Decision Systems*, *24*(1), 87–102. doi:10.1080/12460125.2015.994333

Phithakkitnukoon, S., Horanont, T., Witayangkurn, A., Siri, R., Sekimoto, Y., & Shibasaki, R. (2015). Understanding-tourist behavior using large-scale mobile sensing approach: A case study of mobile phone users in Japan. *Pervasive and Mobile Computing*, *18*, 18–39. doi:10.1016/j.pmcj.2014.07.003

Phoek, S. E. M., Lauwinata, L., & Kowarin, L. R. N. (2023). Tourism Development in Merauke Regency, South Papua Province: Strengthening Physical Infrastructure for Local Economic Growth and Enchanting Tourist Attractions. *FMDB Transactions on Sustainable Management Letters*, *1*(2), 82–94.

Pillai, R., & Sivathanu, B. (2021). Measure what matters: Descriptive and predictive metrics of HRM-pathway toward organisational performance. *International Journal of Productivity and Performance Management*. Advance online publication. doi:10.1108/IJPPM-10-2020-0509

Pillai, R., & Srivastava, K. B. L. (2022). Smart HRM 4.0 for achieving organizational performance: A dynamic capability view perspective. *International Journal of Productivity and Performance Management*. Advance online publication. doi:10.1108/IJPPM-04-2022-0174

Pillai, R., Yadav, S., Sivathanu, B., Kaushik, N., & Goel, P. (2022). Use of 4.0 (I4.0) technology in HRM: A pathway toward SHRM 4.0 and HR performance. *Foresight*, *24*(6), 708–727. doi:10.1108/FS-06-2021-0128

Pio, L., Cavaliere, L., Mangalasserri, K., Venkateswaran, P. S., Byloppilly, R., & Effendy, F. (2021). The Impact Of Brand Counterfieting on Consumer Behavior In the Fashion Sector. *Turkish Journal of Physiotherapy and Rehabilitation*, *32*(3), 19831–19847.

Poluha, R. G. (2007). *Application of the SCOR Model in Supply Chain Management*. Youngstown.

Popenici, S., & Kerr, S. (2017). Exploring the impact of artificial intelligence on teaching and learning in higher education. *Research and Practice in Technology Enhanced Learning*, *12*(1), 22. Advance online publication. doi:10.118641039-017-0062-8 PMID:30595727

Prasad, R., & Mondal, A. (2020). Impact of COVID-19 pandemic on Indian economy with special reference to Indian MSMEs sector. *Research Gate*, (7), 16–21.

Prassida, G., & Asfari, U. (2022). A conceptual model for the acceptance of collaborative robots in industry5.0. *Procedia Computer Science*, *197*, 61–67. doi:10.1016/j.procs.2021.12.118

Price, C., & Toye, S. (2017). *Accelerating performance: how organizations can mobilize, execute, and transform with agility*. John Wiley & Sons.

Pricewaterhousecopper (PWC). (2020). *HR Matters Namibia Newsletter* (3rd ed.). https://www.pwc.com/na/en/assets/pdf/hr-matters-july-edition-2020.pdf

Priscila, S. S., Rajest, S. S., Tadiboina, S. N., Regin, R., & András, S. (2023). Analysis of Machine Learning and Deep Learning Methods for Superstore Sales Prediction. *FMDB Transactions on Sustainable Computer Letters*, *1*(1), 1–11.

Priyadarshini, D., & Kar, S. (2021). *Central Bank digital currency (CBDC): Critical issues and the Indian perspective*. Academic Press.

Priyadarshini, N. S., & Naachimuthu, K. P. (2020). Ancient and Modern Conception to Virtues: Comparing Naaladiyar and Positive Psychology. In *International Conference on Multi Facets of Sacred Literature* (pp. 1–12). Academic Press.

Provost, F., & Fawcett, T. (2013). *Data science for business*. O'Reilly Media.

Puhl, R. M. (2020). What words should we use to talk about weight? A systematic review of quantitative and qualitative studies examining preferences for weight-related terminology. *Obesity Reviews*, *21*(6), e13008. doi:10.1111/obr.13008 PMID:32048465

Puhovichova, D., & Jankelova, N. (2022). *Changes of human resource management in the context of the impact of the fourth industrial revolution*. Retrieved from https://stumejournals.com/journals/i4/2020/3/138.full.pdf

Pyszka, A., & Gajda, D. (2015). Successful talent management through positive CSR-driven transactions. *Journal of Positive Management*, *6*(2), 3–19. doi:10.12775/JPM.2015.007

Quinn, L., Dibb, S., Simkin, L., Canhoto, A., & Analogbei, M. (2016). Troubled waters: The transformation of marketing in a digital world. *European Journal of Marketing*, *50*(12), 2103–2133. doi:10.1108/EJM-08-2015-0537

Qureshi, M. A., Khan, P. A., & Uprit, S. (2016). Empowerment of rural women through agriculture and dairy sectors in India. *Economic Affairs*, *61*(1), 75. doi:10.5958/0976-4666.2016.00011.5

Rabindran, R., & Bozic, D. (2015). A study of privacy and data security in human resource management. *International Journal of Information Management*, *35*(6), 586–595.

Rad, D., Balas, E., Ignat, S., Rad, G., & Dixon, D. (2020). A Predictive Model of Youth Bystanders' Helping Attitudes. *Revista romaneasca pentru educatie multidimensionala-Journal for Multidimensional Education, 12*(1Sup2), 136-150.

Rad, D., Balas, E., Ignat, S., Rad, G., & Dixon, D. (2020). A Predictive Model of Youth Bystanders' Helping Attitudes. *Revista Romanesco pentru educatie multidimensionala-Journal for Multidimensional Education, 12*(1Sup2), 136-150.

Rad, D., Balas, E., Ignat, S., Rad, G., & Dixon, D. (2020a). A Predictive Model of Youth Bystanders' Helping Attitudes. *Revista romaneasca pentru educatie multidimensionala-Journal for Multidimensional Education, 12*(1Sup2), 136-150.

Rad, D., Balas, E., Ignat, S., Rad, G., & Dixon, D. (2020b). A Predictive Model of Youth Bystanders' Helping Attitudes. *Revista romaneasca pentru educatie multidimensionala-Journal for Multidimensional Education, 12*(1Sup2), 136-150.

Rad, D., Dughi, T., & Demeter, E. (2019). The Dynamics of the Relationship between Humor and Benevolence as Values. *Revista romaneasca pentru educatie multidimensionala-Journal for Multidimensional Education, 11*(3), 201-212.

Rad, D., Dughi, T., & Demeter, E. (2019). The Dynamics of the Relationship between Humor and Benevolence as Values. *Revista romaneasca pentru educatie multidimensional-Journal for Multidimensional Education, 11*(3), 201-212.

Rad, D., & Balas, V. E. (2020). A Novel Fuzzy Scoring Approach of Behavioural Interviews in Personnel Selection. BRAIN. *Broad Research in Artificial Intelligence and Neuroscience*, *11*(2), 178–188. doi:10.18662/brain/11.2/81

Rad, D., Balas, V., Lile, R., Demeter, E., Dughi, T., & Rad, G. (2020b). Statistical Properties of a New Social Media Context Awareness Scale (SMCA)-A Preliminary Investigation. *Sustainability (Basel)*, *12*(12), 5201. doi:10.3390u12125201

Rad, D., & Demeter, E. (2020). A Moderated Mediation Effect of Online Time Spent on Internet Content Awareness, Perceived Online Hate Speech and Helping Attitudes Disposal of Bystanders. *Postmodern Openings*, *11*(2, Supl 1), 107–124. doi:10.18662/po/11.2Sup1/182

Rad, D., Egerau, A., Roman, A., Dughi, T., Balas, E., Maier, R., & Rad, G. (2022). A Preliminary Investigation of the Technology Acceptance Model (TAM) in Early Childhood Education and Care. BRAIN. *Broad Research in Artificial Intelligence and Neuroscience*, *13*(1), 518–533. doi:10.18662/brain/13.1/297

Rafati, L., & Poels, G. (2015). Towards model-based strategic sourcing. *Global Sourcing Workshop 2015*, 29–51.

Rai, N., & Thapa, B. (2015). A study on purposive sampling method in research. Kathmandu: Kathmandu School of Law, 5.

Raina, V., Bhushan, B., Bakshi, P., & Khajuria, S. (2016). Entrepreneurial behaviour of dairy farmers. *Journal of Animal Research*, *6*(5), 1–7. doi:10.5958/2277-940X.2016.00123.6

Rajeeva, S. (2022). Global Dairy Sector: Trends, Prospects, and Challenges. *Sustainability (Basel)*, *14*(7), 4193–4193. doi:10.3390u14074193

Rajest, S. S., Singh, B., Obaid, J. A., Regin, R., & Chinnusamy, K. (Eds.). (2023a). Recent developments in machine and human intelligence. Advances in Computational Intelligence and Robotics. doi:10.4018/978-1-6684-9189-8

Rajest, S. S., & Regin, R., T, S., & R, S. (2022). Strategic Leadership And Alignment Affect Organisation Performance. *Central Asian Journal Of Mathematical Theory And Computer Sciences*, *3*(12), 248–266.

Rajest, S. S., Singh, B., Obaid, A. J., Regin, R., & Chinnusamy, K. (Eds.). (2023b). Advances in Computational Intelligence and Robotics *Advances in artificial and human intelligence in the modern era.*, doi:10.4018/979-8-3693-1301-5

Rajkumar, & Gupta, H. (2010). FII Flows to India: Economic Indicators. *SCMS Journal of Indian Management*, 104–116.

Rajput, N., Chopra, P., & Rajput, A. (2012). FII and its impact on stock market: A study on lead-lag and volatility spillover. *Asian Journal of Finance & Accounting*, *4*(2). Advance online publication. doi:10.5296/ajfa.v4i2.1874

Rakesh, S. (2023). *What is Multi-Factor Authentication (MFA)?* LoginRadius Blog. https://www.loginradius.com/blog/identity/what-is-multi-factor-authentication/

Ramos, J. I., Lacerona, R., & Nunag, J. M. (2023). A Study on Operational Excellence, Work Environment Factors and the Impact to Employee Performance. *FMDB Transactions on Sustainable Social Sciences Letters*, *1*(1), 12–25.

Ramu, V. B., & Yeruva, A. R. (2023). Optimising AIOps system performance for e-commerce and online retail businesses with the ACF model. *International Journal of Intellectual Property Management*, *13*(3/4), 412–429. doi:10.1504/IJIPM.2023.134064

Rana, G., & Sharma, R. (2019). Emerging human resource management practices in Industry 4.0. *Strategic HR Review*, *18*(4), 18. doi:10.1108/SHR-01-2019-0003

Rao, K. S., Murhty, M., & Ranganathan, K. V. K. (1999). Foreign Institutional Investments and the Indian Stock Market. *Journal of Indian School of Political Economy*, 623–647.

Rashid, H., & Shah, A. B. A. (2016). Impact of Organizational Culture on Organizational Performance: Evidence from Education Sector. *Journal of Business Management and Economic Studies*, *1*(1), 16–30.

Rathore, M., & Mehrotra, D. (2021). Smart HR 4.0: Enabling Industry 4.0 through HRM. In *Industry 4.0 and Smart Manufacturing* (pp. 133–144). Springer.

RathoreU. (2020). From slowdown to lockdown: Effects of the COVID-19 crisis on small firms in India. Oxford Policy Management, 1–32. doi:10.2139/ssrn.3615339

Ravindra, S. (2019, September 17). *Data Science*. Retrieved from 4 Applications of Big Data in HR (With Real-World Examples): https://www.kolabtree.com/blog/4-applications-of-big-data-in-hr-with-real-world-examples/

Razvan. (2022, September 6). *hranalyticslibrary.com*. Retrieved from HR Analytics Challenges & How to Overcome Them: https://hranalyticslibrary.com/hr-analytics-challenges-overcome/

Reddy, M. K. (2016, February 7). *1.IIB introduction*. Retrieved October 20, 2023, from IIB Developer website: https://iibdeveloper.wordpress.com/2016/02/07/how-to-learn-ibm-integration-bus/

Regin, R., Khanna, A. A., Krishnan, V., Gupta, M., & Bose, R. S., & Rajest, S. S. (2023). Information design and unifying approach for secured data sharing using attribute-based access control mechanisms. In Recent Developments in Machine and Human Intelligence (pp. 256–276). IGI Global.

Regin, R., Khanna, A. A., Krishnan, V., Gupta, M., Bose, R. S., & Rajest, S. S. (2023). Information design and unifying approach for secured data sharing using attribute-based access control mechanisms. In Recent Developments in Machine and Human Intelligence (pp. 256–276). IGI Global.

Regin, R., & Rajest, S. S., T, S., & R, S. (2023a). A Review of Secure Neural Networks and Big Data Mining Applications in Financial Risk Assessment. *Central Asian Journal of Innovations on Tourism Management and Finance*, *4*(2), 73–90.

Regin, R., & Rajest, S. S., T, S., & R, S. (2023b). An Analytical Study of Development in Response to the COVID-19 Pandemic. *Central Asian Journal of Medical and Natural Science*, *4*(1), 199–216.

Regin, R., & Rajest, S. S., T, S., & R, S. (2023c). Human Resource Perspective and Pitfalls at Work. *Central Asian Journal of Innovations on Tourism Management and Finance*, *4*(1), 31–49.

Regin, R., Rajest, S. S., Shynu, T., & Steffi, R. (2023). Audit Committee and the Overall Performance of Companies. International Journal on Economics. *Finance and Sustainable Development*, *5*(3), 18–31.

Regin, R., Suman Rajest, S., Shynu, T., & Steffi, R. (2023). Electronic Tourism as A Destination Marketing Strategy for World Travellers. *Central Asian Journal of Mathematical Theory and Computer Sciences.*, *4*(5), 9–28.

Rialti, R., Marzi, G., Ciappei, C., & Busso, D. (2019). Big data and dynamic capabilities: A bibliometric analysis and systematic literature review. *Management Decision*, *57*(8), 2052–2068. doi:10.1108/MD-07-2018-0821

Ringle, C., Da Silva, D., & Bido, D. (2015). Structural equation modeling with the SmartPLS. *Brazilian Journal of Marketing, 13*(2).

Rojko, A. (2017). Industry 4.0 concept: Background and overview. *International Journal of Interactive Mobile Technologies, 11*(5), 77–89. doi:10.3991/ijim.v11i5.7072

Roman, A., Rad, D., Egerau, A., Dixon, D., Dughi, T., Kelemen, G., & Rad, G. (2020). Physical Self-Schema Acceptance and Perceived Severity of Online Aggressiveness in Cyberbullying Incidents. *Journal of Interdisciplinary Studies in Education*, *9*(1), 100–116. doi:10.32674/jise.v9i1.1961

Rostami, P., Ramezani, M., & Sabri, M. (2020). Smart human resource management: A review of literature. *International Journal of Information Management*, *52*, 101653.

Rothmann, S., & Rothmann, S. Jr. (2010). Factors associated with employee engagement in South Africa. *SA Journal of Industrial Psychology*, *36*(2), 1–12. doi:10.4102ajip.v36i2.925

Rurkkhum, S., & Bartlett, K. R. (2012). The relationship between employee engagement and organizational citizenship behaviour in Thailand. *Human Resource Development International*, *15*(2), 157–174. doi:10.1080/13678868.2012.664693

Russell, C., & Bennett, N. (2015). Big data and talent management: Using hard data to make the soft stuff easy. *Business Horizons*, *58*(3), 237–242. doi:10.1016/j.bushor.2014.08.001

Sabarirajan, A., & Geethanjali. (2011). A study on quality of work life and organizational performance among the employees of public and private banks in Dindigul. *International Journal of Economics and Research, 2*(6), 38-45.

Sabti, Y. M., Alqatrani, R. I. N., Zaid, M. I., Taengkliang, B., & Kareem, J. M. (2023). Impact of Business Environment on the Performance of Employees in the Public-Listed Companies. *FMDB Transactions on Sustainable Management Letters*, *1*(2), 56–65.

Saha, B. (2020). The significance of psychometric tests in the recruitment process for an organization to induce its effectivity. *International Journal of Research in Engineering, Science and Management*, *3*(8), 268–273.

Sahasranamam, S., Stephan, U., & Zbierowski, P. (2021, July 29). *What can Indian entrepreneurs tell us about surviving COVID?* Retrieved November 6, 2023, from World Economic Forum website: https://www.weforum.org/agenda/2021/07/five-post-covid-trends-among-indias-entrepreneurs/

Sahut, J.-M., Iandoli, L., & Teulon, F. (2021). The age of digital entrepreneurship. *Small Business Economics*, *56*(3), 1159–1169. doi:10.100711187-019-00260-8

Said, F. B., & Tripathi, S. (2023). Epistemology of Digital Journalism Shift in South Global Nations: A Bibliometric Analysis. *FMDB Transactions on Sustainable Technoprise Letters*, *1*(1), 47–60.

Sajini, S., Reddi, L. T., Regin, R., & Rajest, S. S. (2023). A Comparative Analysis of Routing Protocols for Efficient Data Transmission in Vehicular Ad Hoc Networks (VANETs). *FMDB Transactions on Sustainable Computing Systems*, *1*(1), 1–10.

Sanghera, T. (2020, December 23). *Surviving COVID: The challenges facing India's small businesses.* Retrieved November 6, 2023, from Al Jazeera website: https://www.aljazeera.com/economy/2020/12/23/surviving-covid-the-challenges-facing-indias-small-businesses

Sathi, A. (2012). Big data analytics: Disruptive technologies for changing the game. MC Press.

Sathya, I. (2019). Rural entrepreneurship in India. *Research Explorer-A Blind Review and Refereed Quarterly International Journal, 7*(2).

Savya, N., & Naachimuthu, K. P. (2022). Psychosocial Determinants of Name Dropping: A Conceptual Framework. *Madhya Bharti - Humanities and Social Sciences, 83*(14), 1–12.

Saxena, D., & Chaudhary, S. (2023). Predicting Brain Diseases from FMRI-Functional Magnetic Resonance Imaging with Machine Learning Techniques for Early Diagnosis and Treatment. *FMDB Transactions on Sustainable Computer Letters*, *1*(1), 33–48.

Saxena, D., Khandare, S., & Chaudhary, S. (2023). An Overview of ChatGPT: Impact on Academic Learning. *FMDB Transactions on Sustainable Techno Learning*, *1*(1), 11–20.

Schiemann, W. A., & Ulrich, D. (2017). Rise of HR - New mandates for IO. *Industrial and Organizational Psychology: Perspectives on Science and Practice*, *10*(1), 3–25. doi:10.1017/iop.2016.76

Schilder, J., & Clark, D. (2018). Digital legacy planning: A new way to talk about and plan for digital death and the digital afterlife. *Omega*.

Schlechter, A., Hung, A., & Bussin, M. (2014). Understanding talent attraction: The influence of financial rewards elements on perceived job attractiveness. *SA Journal of Human Resource Management*, *12*(1), 1–13. doi:10.4102ajhrm.v12i1.647

Schmelzer, R. (2023, January 5). TechTarget. *Top Trends in Big Data for 2023 and Beyond*, p. 1.

Schooley, S. (2023, March 23). *How to Utilize Big Data for Human Resources.* Retrieved from Business.com: https://www.business.com/articles/how-to-utilize-big-data-for-human-resources/

Scott, A. (2021, August 24). *Data Science Central.* Retrieved from Big Data Technology Importance in Human Resource Management: https://www.datasciencecentral.com/big-data-technology-importance-in-human-resource-management/

Sels, L., De Winne, S., Delmotte, J., Maes, J., Faems, D., & Forrier, A. (2006). Linking HRM and small business performance: An examination of the impact of HRM intensity on the productivity and financial performance of small businesses. *Small Business Economics*, *26*(1), 83–101. doi:10.100711187-004-6488-6

Selvakumar, M., & Yoganandan, G. (2019). Problems And Practices Of Micro-Scale Dairy Entrepreneurs In Salem District, Tamilnadu. *International Journal of Scientific & Technology Research*, *8*(12), 1485–1489.

Sen, A., & Al, M. (2021). Women Entrepreneurship. *PalArch's Journal of Archaeology of Egypt/Egyptology, 18*(9), 69–77.

Sepúlveda, M. J., & Parra-Arnau, J. (2021). Digital Death: A Critical Review of the Literature and the Challenges Ahead. In *International Conference on Human-Computer Interaction* (pp. 564-580). Springer.

Shafiq, A., Johnson, P. F., & Awaysheh, A. (2019). Emerging economy sourcing: Implications of supplier social practices for firm performance. *International Journal of Production Economics*, *218*, 148–158. doi:10.1016/j.ijpe.2019.05.010

Shah, A. K., Malik, B. S., & Yadav, V. K. (2010). Entrepreneurial behaviour and their correlates among dairy entrepreneurs in Northern India. *Indian Journal of Extension Education, 46*(3and4), 53-61.

Shamim, S., Cang, S., Yu, H., & Li, Y. (2016). Management approaches for industry 4.0: A human resource management perspective. In *2016 IEEE Congress on Evolutionary Computation (CEC)* (pp. 5309-5316). IEEE. 10.1109/CEC.2016.7748365

Shanks, G., Seddon, P. B., & Willcocks, L. (Eds.). (2018). *Enterprise resource planning: Concepts and practice*. Routledge.

Shapiro, J. (2010). Advanced Analytics for Sales & Operations Planning. *Analytics Magazine*, (May-June), 20–26.

Sharda, R., Delen, D., Turban, E., & King, D. (2017). *Business Intelligence, Analytics, and Data Science: A Managerial Perspective*. Pearson.

Sharma, D. K., Jalil, N. A., Regin, R., Rajest, S. S., Tummala, R. K., & Thangadurai. (2021). Predicting network congestion with machine learning. In *2021 2nd International Conference on Smart Electronics and Communication (ICOSEC)*. IEEE.

Sharma, D. K., Jalil, N. A., Regin, R., Rajest, S. S., Tummala, R. K., & Thangadurai. (2021a). Predicting network congestion with machine learning. In *2021 2nd International Conference on Smart Electronics and Communication (ICOSEC)*. IEEE.

Sharma, D. K., Singh, B., Raja, M., Regin, R., & Rajest, S. S. (2021b). An Efficient Python Approach for Simulation of Poisson Distribution. In *2021 7th International Conference on Advanced Computing and Communication Systems (ICACCS)*. IEEE.

Sharma, D. K., Singh, B., Regin, R., Steffi, R., & Chakravarthi, M. K. (2021c). Efficient Classification for Neural Machines Interpretations based on Mathematical models. In *2021 7th International Conference on Advanced Computing and Communication Systems (ICACCS)*. IEEE.

Sharma, T. (2019, September 26). *Top 5 Big Data Use Cases in the HR Department*. Retrieved from Global Tech Council: https://www.globaltechcouncil.org/big-data/top-5-big-data-use-cases-in-the-hr-department/

Sharma, D. K., Singh, B., Herman, E., Regine, R., Rajest, S. S., & Mishra, V. P. (2021d). Maximum information measure policies in reinforcement learning with deep energy-based model. In *2021 International Conference on Computational Intelligence and Knowledge Economy (ICCIKE)*. IEEE. 10.1109/ICCIKE51210.2021.9410756

Sharma, M. S., & Sharma, M. V. (2014). Employee engagement to enhance productivity in current scenario. *International Journal of Commerce and Business Management*, *3*(4), 595–604.

Sharma, P. (2013). Women entrepreneurship development in India. *Global Journal of Management and Business Studies*, *3*(4), 371–376.

Sharma, S. K., Singh, R., & Matai, R. (2018). Force field analysis of Indian automotive strategic sourcing risk management enablers and barriers. *Measuring Business Excellence*, *22*(3), 258–275. doi:10.1108/MBE-09-2017-0062

Shaw, P., & Varghese, R. M. (2018). Industry 4.0 and future of HR. *Journal of Management*, *5*(6), 96–103.

Sherman, R. (2014). *Business Intelligence Guidebook: From Data Integration to Analytics*. Morgan Kaufmann.

Shifana, F., & Naachimuthu, K. P. (2022). Elements of Holistic Human Development in Naanmanikkadigai: A Hermeneutic Study. *Journal of Positive School Psychology*, *6*(4), 2218–2231.

Shiwen, O., Juanatas, R., Niguidula, J., & Huiliang, H. (2022). Research on Performance Management of Credit Business of Rural Commercial Banks. In *2022 2nd International Conference on Economic Development and Business Culture* (pp. 251–255). Atlantis Press. 10.2991/978-94-6463-036-7_37

Shrivastava, S., Nagdev, K., & Rajesh, A. (2018). Redefining HR using people analytics: The case of Google. *Human Resource Management International Digest, 26*(2), 3–6. doi:10.1108/HRMID-06-2017-0112

Shruthi, S., & Aravind, B. R. (2023). Engaging ESL Learning on Mastering Present Tense with Nearpod and Learningapps.org for Engineering Students. *FMDB Transactions on Sustainable Techno Learning, 1*(1), 21–31.

Shuck, M. B., Rocco, T. S., & Albornoz, C. A. (2011). Exploring employee engagement from the employee perspective: Implications for HRD. *Journal of European Industrial Training, 35*(4), 300–325. doi:10.1108/03090591111128306

Shynu, T., Rajest, S. S., Regin, R., & Steffi, R. (2023). Analysis of the Impact of Employee Training and Development on Performance. *Central Asian Journal of Innovations on Tourism Management and Finance, 4*(6), 1–25.

Shynu, T., Rajest, S. S., Regin, R., & Steffi, R. (2023). Data Mining-Based Point of Sale with Auto-Source Triggering and Business Reports. *Central Asian Journal Of Mathematical Theory And Computer Sciences, 4*(2), 116–141.

Siddhesh, S. (2022). *What is Data Encryption?* Geeksforgeeks Blog. https://www.geeksforgeeks.org/what-is-data-encryption/

Siddique, M. I., & Jajja, M. S. S. (2022). Jamal dairy farm: Technology adoption challenges. *Asian Journal of Management Cases*. Advance online publication. doi:10.1177/09728201221107784

Siegel, E. (2013). *Predictive analytics: The power to predict who will click, buy, lie or die*. John Wiley & Sons Inc.

Siegel, E. (2013). *Predictive analytics: The power to predict who will click, buy, lie, or die*. Wiley.

Simchi-Levi, D., Kaminsky, P., & Simchi-Levi, E. (2019). *Designing and managing the supply chain: Concepts, strategies, and case studies.* McGraw-Hill Education.

Simoes, A., Correia, Antonio, L. S., & Ana, C. B. (2020). Factors influencing the intention of managers to adopt collaborative robots(cobots)in manufacturing organizations. *Journal of Engineering and Technology Management.*

Singh, A., John, D. P., & Jacob, A. P. (2022). A Review of Central Bank Digital Currencies. *Ushus Journal of Business Management, 21*(1), 79–95. doi:10.12725/ujbm.58.5

Singhal, A., & Malik, G. (2018). The attitude and purchasing of female consumers towards green marketing related to cosmetic industry. *Journal of Science and Technology Policy Management*, 1-19.

Singh, M., Bhushan, M., Sharma, R., & Cavaliere, L. P. L. (2023). An Organized Assessment of the Literature of Entrepreneurial Skills and Emotional Intelligence. *FMDB Transactions on Sustainable Management Letters, 1*(3), 95–104.

Singh, S., Simpson, R., Mordi, C., & Okafor, C. (2016). Motivation and gender in the informal sector in Nigeria. *Gender in Management, 31*(4), 250–271.

Singh, V. P., Hansen, K. T., & Gupta, S. (2005, May). Modeling Preferences for Common Attributes in Multicategory Brand Choice. *JMR, Journal of Marketing Research, 42*(2), 195–209. doi:10.1509/jmkr.42.2.195.62282

Sivathanu, B. B., & Pillai, B. (2018). Smart HR 4.0: How industry 4.0 is disrupting HR. *Human Resource Management International Digest, 26*(4), 7–11. doi:10.1108/HRMID-04-2018-0059

Sivathanu, B., & Pillai, R. (2020). Technology and talent analytics for talent management: A game changer for organizational performance. *The International Journal of Organizational Analysis, 28*(2), 457–473. doi:10.1108/IJOA-01-2019-1634

Skobelev, P., & Borovik, S. (2017). On the way from Industry 4.0 to Industry 5.0: From digital manufacturing to digital society. *Industry 4.0, 2*(6), 307-311.

Smith, C. M., Shanks, G., & Smith, A. D. (2017). My loved one's Facebook account: Deceased user practices on social networking sites. *Information Technology & People*, *30*(2), 443–466.

Smith, J. D., & Johnson, A. B. (2018). *Human Resource Management Systems: Strategy, Implementation, and Effectiveness*. Pearson.

Smith, M. B., Bryan, L. K., & Vodanovich, S. J. (2012). The counter-intuitive effects of flow on positive leadership and employee attitudes: Incorporating positive psychology into the management of organizations. *The Psychologist Manager Journal*, *15*(3), 174–198. doi:10.1080/10887156.2012.701129

Somjai, S., & Jermsittiparsert, K. (2019). Mediating Impact of Information Sharing in the Relationship of Supply Chain Capabilities and Business Performance among the Firms of Thailand. *International Journal of Supply Chain Management*, *8*(4), 357–368.

Soni, S. (2019). Impact of organizational culture on employee engagement and effectiveness in Indian manufacturing company. *IITM Journal of Management and IT*, *10*(2), 42–52.

Sparrow, P. (2019). A historical analysis of critiques in the talent management debate. *Business Research Quarterly*, *22*(3), 160–170. doi:10.1016/j.brq.2019.05.001

Srinivas, K., Velmurugan, P. R., & Andiyappillai, N. (2023). Digital Human Resources and Management Support Improve Human Resources Effectiveness. *FMDB Transactions on Sustainable Management Letters*, *1*(1), 32–45.

Srivastava, D. K., & Roychoudhury, B. (2020). Words are important: A textual content based identity resolution scheme across multiple online social networks. *Knowledge-Based Systems*, *195*, 105624. doi:10.1016/j.knosys.2020.105624

Srivastava, D. K., & Roychoudhury, B. (2021). Understanding the Factors that Influence Adoption of Privacy Protection Features in Online Social Networks. *Journal of Global Information Technology Management*, *24*(3), 164–182. doi:10.1080/1097198X.2021.1954416

Srivastava, S., & Agrawal, A. (2020). Women entrepreneurship in India–Problems and prospects. *International Journal of Management Studies*, *7*(2), 1–14.

Stalin, G., Meharajan, T., & Venkateswaran, P. S. (2019). Impact of HRM practices on select IT companies' performance in Madurai. *International Journal of Scientific & Technology Research*, *8*(12), 169–172.

Statista. (2022). Retrieved November 9, 2023, from Statista website: https://www.statista.com/statistics/1092564/novartis-ags-total-assets/

Steffi, R., Rajest, S. S., Regin, R., & Shynu, T. (2023). An Examination of the Effects That Marketing Methods Have on Non-Governmental Organizations. *Middle European Scientific Bulletin*, *34*(3), 189–207.

Steffi, R., Rajest, S. S., Regin, R., & Shynu, T. (2023). Developing Banking Sector Strategies Amid Economic Turmoil. International Journal on Economics. *Finance and Sustainable Development*, *5*(4), 78–100.

Stern, N. (2007). *The Economics of Climate Change: The Stern Review*. Cambridge University Press. doi:10.1017/CBO9780511817434

Stewart, T. A. (1997). *Intellectual Capital: The New Wealth of Organizations*. Doubleday.

Stock, J. R. (2013). Supply chain management: A look back, a look ahead. *Supply Chain Quarterly*, *2*, 22–26.

Storey, J., Ulrich, D., & Wright, P. (2019). *Strategic Human Resource Management: A Research Overview.* . doi:10.4324/9780429490217

Strickland, J. (2015). *Predictive analytics using R.* CreateSpace Independent Publishing Platform.

Stroud, J. (2020, May 22). *Talent attraction: what it is and things to think about.* Https://Blog.Proactivetalent.Com/Talent-Attraction-What-It-Is-and-Things-to-Think-About

Subbarao, S. (2019). Influence of Demographic Factors on Recruitment and Selection of Employees in IT & ITES Industry. *Journal of Advanced Research in Dynamical & Control Systems, 11*(6), 52–61.

Subbarao, S. (2020). CSR and Socio-Economic Development-A case study of selected PSU's in the State of Odisha. *Journal of Critical Reviews, 7*(13), 1407–1415.

Sudheer, V., & Naachimuthu, K. P. (2022). Effect of JPMR on State-Trait Anxiety Among Young Female Adults During COVID-19 Pandemic Lockdown. *International Journal of Health Sciences, 6*(55), 1192–1202. doi:10.53730/ijhs.v6nS5.8848

Sumer, B. (2018). Impact of Industry 4.0 on Occupations and Employment in Turkey. *European Scientific Journal, 14*(10).

Sumner, M. (2018). *Enterprise resource planning.* Pearson.

Sun, X. (2023). Exploration and Practice of Credit Bank Docking with Professional Group Construction-Take the construction of Credit bank for Digital creativity and Media professional group as an example. In *SHS Web of Conferences (Vol. 157).* EDP Sciences.

Sundaray, B. K. (2011). Employee engagement: A driver of organizational effectiveness. *European Journal of Business and Management, 3*(8), 53–59.

Sun, Z., & Ma, Y. (2017). Evaluation and optimization of vegetable distribution efficiency based on DEA. *Journal of the Saudi Society of Agricultural Sciences, 16*(1), 84–93.

Supply Chain Council. (2010). http://supply-chain.org/f/down-load/726710733/SCOR10.pdf

Susmitha, M. M. (2014). *Growth and Performance of Small-size Industries in India with special reference to Kerala.* www.ffymag.com

Svilvar, M., Charkraborty, A. & Kanioura, A. (2013). Big data analytics in marketing. *OR/MS Today.*

Taczanowska, K., González, L., García-Massó, X., Zięba, A., Brandenburg, C., Muhar, A., Pellicer-Chenoll, M., & Toca-Herrera, J.-L. (2019). Nature-based Tourism or Mass Tourism in Nature? Segmentation of Mountain ProtectedArea Visitors Using Self-Organizing Maps (SOM). *Sustainability (Basel), 11*(5), 1314. doi:10.3390u11051314

Tafti, M. M., Mahmoudsalehi, M., & Amiri, M. (2017). Critical success factors, challenges and obstacles in talent management. *Industrial and Commercial Training, 49*(1), 5–21. doi:10.1108/ICT-05-2016-0036

Talend. (n.d.). *How Does Big Data Work for HR Analytics?* Retrieved from Talend: https://www.talend.com/resources/big-data-hr-analytics/#:~:text=Without%20the%20use%20of%20big%20data%2C%20recruiting%20top,delivering%20results%20and%20which%20ones%20aren%E2%80%99t%20very%20effective

Talent Agenda Series. (2017). *Talent management in Africa and the challenges involved.* https://www.talentagendaseries.com/hr-insight-blog/2017/7/26/talent-management-inafrica-and-the-challenges-involved

Talentlyft. (2018). *Talent Acquisition Analytics: What it is & Why it Matters.* Retrieved from https://www.talentlyft.com/en/blog/article/233/talentacquisition-analytics-what-it-is-why-it-matters

Tambaip, B., Hadi, A. F. F., & Tjilen, A. P. (2023). Optimizing Public Service Performance: Unleashing the Potential of Compassion as an Indicator of Public Service Motivation. *FMDB Transactions on Sustainable Management Letters*, *1*(2), 46–55.

Tarique, I., & Schuler, R. S. (2010). Global talent management: Literature review, integrative framework, and suggestions for further research. *Journal of World Business*, *45*(2), 122–133. doi:10.1016/j.jwb.2009.09.019

Thanapackiam, D., Nk, C., & Goudar, K. (2022). The Factors Affecting Implementing Crypto Currencies in India. *Journal of Positive School Psychology*, *6*(7), 771–779.

The Hindu. (2020). *MSMEs will be the biggest casualty of COVID-19 in India*. https://www.thehindu.com/business/msmes-will-be-the-biggest-casualty-of-covid-19-in-india-study/article31084751.ece

Thoma, C. (2016). *Big data in talent management - The next challenge*. https://www.linkedin.com/pulse/big-data-talent-management-next-challenge-christoph-thoma

Thunnissen, M., Boselie, P., & Fruytier, B. (2013). Talent management and the relevance of context: Towards a pluralistic approach. *Human Resource Management Review*, *23*(4), 326–336. doi:10.1016/j.hrmr.2013.05.004

Tripathi, S., & Al-Zubaidi, A. (2023). A Study within Salalah's Higher Education Institutions on Online Learning Motivation and Engagement Challenges during Covid-19. *FMDB Transactions on Sustainable Techno Learning*, *1*(1), 1–10.

Tripathi, S., & Al-Shahri, M. (2023). Problems and Prospects on the Evolution of Advertising and Public Relations Industries in Oman. *FMDB Transactions on Sustainable Management Letters*, *1*(1), 1–11.

Tripathi, S., Chaubey, A., & Goel, I. (2022). An empirical analysis of potential Central Bank Digital Currency adoption procedure by Indian government and its implications. *Sachetas*, *1*(1), 32–38. doi:10.55955/110006

Tristan Boutros. (2023). *The Process Improvement Handbook*. McGraw–Hill Education.

Trkman, P., McCormack, K., de Oliveira, M. P. V., & Ladeira, M. B. (2010). The Impact of Business Analytics on Supply Chain Performance. *Decision Support Systems*, *49*(3), 318–327. doi:10.1016/j.dss.2010.03.007

Tucmeanu, E. R., Tucmeanu, A. I., Iliescu, M. G., Żywiołek, J., & Yousaf, Z. (2022). Successful management of IT projects in healthcare institutions after COVID-19: Role of digital orientation and innovation adaption. *Healthcare (Basel)*, *10*(10), 2005. doi:10.3390/healthcare10102005 PMID:36292452

Tupper, H. a. (2022, July 4). *Harvard Business Review*. Retrieved from Employee Retention: It's Time to Reimagine Employee Retention: https://hbr.org/2022/07/its-time-to-reimagine-employee-retention

Unit, E. I. (2016). *Use of workforce analytics for competitive advantage*. SHRM Foundation.

Utami, C. W., Sumaji, Y. M. P., Susanto, H., Septina, F., & Pratama, I. (2019). *Effect of Supply Chain Management Practices on Financial and Economic Sustainable Performance of Indonesian SMEs*. Academic Press.

Vaiman, V., Scullion, H., & Collings, D. (2012). Talent management decision making. *Management Decision*, *50*(5), 25–941. doi:10.1108/00251741211227663

Vairam, T., Sarathambekai, S., & Balaji, R. (2021). Blockchain-based Voting System in Local Network. In *2021 7th International Conference on Advanced Computing and Communication Systems (ICACCS)*. IEEE.

Valdez-Juárez, L. E., Castillo-Vergara, M., & Ramos-Escobar, E. A. (2022). Innovative business strategies in the face of COVID-19: An approach to open innovation of SMEs in the Sonora region of Mexico. *Journal of Open Innovation*, *8*(1), 47. doi:10.3390/joitmc8010047

Van der Togt, J., & Rasmussen, T. H. (2017). Toward evidence-based HR. *Journal of Organizational Effectiveness: People and Performance.*

Vanneste, B. S., & Gulati, R. (2022). Generalized trust, external sourcing, and firm performance in economic downturns. *Organization Science*, *33*(4), 1599–1619. doi:10.1287/orsc.2021.1500

Vashishtha, E., & Dhawan, G. (2023). Comparison of Baldrige Criteria of Strategy Planning and Harrison Text. *FMDB Transactions on Sustainable Management Letters*, *1*(1), 22–31.

Vashishtha, E., & Kapoor, H. (2023). Implementation of Blockchain Technology Across International Healthcare Markets. *FMDB Transactions on Sustainable Technoprise Letters*, *1*(1), 1–12.

Vasu, M. S., & Jayachandra, K. (2014). Growth and Development of MSMEs in India: Prospects and problems. *Indian Journal of Applied Research*, *4*(5), 125–127. doi:10.15373/2249555X/MAY2014/40

Vazakidis, A., Kitsantas, T., & Chytis, E. (2019). A Review of Blockchain Technology and Its Applications in the Business Environment. *International Conference on Enterprise, Systems, Accounting, Logistics & Management.*

Venkatasubramanian, S., Gomathy, V., & Saleem, M. (2023). Investigating the Relationship Between Student Motivation and Academic Performance. *FMDB Transactions on Sustainable Techno Learning*, *1*(2), 111–124.

Venkateswaran, P. S., Sabarirajan, A., & Arun, B. (2018). Impact of customer satisfaction on brand loyalty towards e-home appliances in Madurai. *International Journal of Exclusive Management Research*, 162–165.

Venkateswaran. P.S. (2023). Industry 5 - Challenges and Opportunities for business and industries. In *Transition from Industry 4.0 to Industry 5.0: Radical changes in Indian Business Environment* (pp. 233-245). Infinite Learning Solutions.

Venkateswaran, D. R. P. S., Sabarirajan, D. R. A., Rajest, S. S., & Regin, R. (2019). The theory of the postmodernism in consumerism, mass culture and globalization. *Journal of Research on the Lepidoptera*, *50*(4), 97–113. doi:10.36872/LEPI/V50I4/201075

Venkateswaran, P. S. (2015). Influence of information systems in Engineering Institutions at Madurai District, Tamil Nadu, India. *International Journal of Applied Engineering Research: IJAER*, *9*(21), 10513–10528.

Venkateswaran, P. S., Sabarirajan, A., Arun, B., Muthupandian, T., & Manimaran, D. S. (2018). Technology Acceptance Model for Making Decision to Purchase Automobile in Coimbatore District. *International Journal of Mechanical Engineering and Technology*, *9*(11), 1608–1613.

Venkateswaran, P. S., Singh, S., Paramasivan, P., Rajest, S. S., Lourens, M. E., & Regin, R. (2023). A Study on The Influence of Quality of Service on Customer Satisfaction Towards Hotel Industry. *FMDB Transactions on Sustainable Social Sciences Letters*, *1*(1), 1–11.

Venkateswaran, P. S., Sundar, S., Chandrasekar, K., Manju, E., & Geetha, U. (2020). The Role of University Faculties in Sustainable Development in Higher Education in Tamil Nadu, India. *International Journal of Advanced Science and Technology*, *29*(1), 1206–1219.

Venkateswaran, P. S., & Viktor, P. (2023). A Study on Brand Equity of Fast-Moving Consumer Goods with Reference to Madurai, Tamil Nadu. *FMDB Transactions on Sustainable Technoprise Letters*, *1*(1), 13–27.

Venkitaraman, A. K., & Kosuru, V. S. R. (2023). Hybrid deep learning mechanism for charging control and management of Electric Vehicles. *European Journal of Electrical Engineering and Computer Science*, *7*(1), 38–46. doi:10.24018/ejece.2023.7.1.485

Verevka, T. V. (2019). *Development of industry 4.0 in the hotel and restaurant business.* IBIMA Business Review. doi:10.5171/2019.324071

Verma, A., Bansal, M., & Verma, J. (2020). *Industry 4.0: Reshaping the future of HR.* Strategic Direction., doi:10.1108/SD-12-2019-0235

Vermeer, S. A., Araujo, T., Bernritter, S. F., & van Noort, G. (2019). Seeing the wood for the trees: How machine learning can help firms in identifying relevant electronic word-of-mouth in social media. *International Journal of Research in Marketing, 36*(3), 492–508. doi:10.1016/j.ijresmar.2019.01.010

Vidhya, A. (2022). Retrieved October 22, 2023, from Analyticsvidhya.com website: https://www.analyticsvidhya.com/

Vijayarani, K., Nithyanantham, V., Christabel, A., & Marupaka, D. (2023). A Study on Relationship Between Self-Regulated Learning Habit and Achievement Among High School Students. *FMDB Transactions on Sustainable Techno Learning, 1*(2), 92–110.

Vishal, B. (2012). *Log Management as a Service.* SitePoint Blog. https://www.sitepoint.com/log-management-as-a-service/

Visuwasam, L. M. M., Swaminathan, S., Rajalakshmi, S., & Kumar, K. P. (2021). A Hotspot Framework for Analyzing Geolocated Travel Data Using Spark. *Annals of RSCB*, 1956–1966.

Visuwasam, L. M. M., & Raj, D. P. (2019). NMA: Integrating big data into a novel mobile application using knowledge extraction for big data analytics. *Cluster Computing, 22*(S6), 14287–14298. doi:10.100710586-018-2287-8

Visuwasam, L. M. M., & Raj, D. P. (2020). A distributed intelligent mobile application for analyzing travel big data analytics. *Peer-to-Peer Networking and Applications, 13*(6), 2036–2052. doi:10.100712083-019-00799-z

Vocations, V. (2007). Retrieved from Virtual Vocations: https://www.virtualvocations.com/aboutus

Vogel, R., & Güttel, W. H. (2013). The dynamic capability view in strategic management: A bibliometric review. *International Journal of Management Reviews, 15*(4), 426–446. doi:10.1111/ijmr.12000

Vyas, M. (2014). An Analysis of Hair care Products with reference to Indian market (Myths Facts Vs Fictions and consumer satisfaction). *International Journal of Research and Development in Technology and Management Science-Kailash, 21*(2), 1-12.

Wagner, S. M., Grosse-Ruyken, P. T., & Erhun, F. (2018). Determinants of sourcing flexibility and its impact on performance. *International Journal of Production Economics, 205*, 329–341. doi:10.1016/j.ijpe.2018.08.006

Wakchaure, R., Ganguly, S., Para, P. A., Praveen, P. K., Kumar, A., & Sharma, S. (2015). Development of crossbred cattle in India: A review. *International Journal of Emerging Technology and Advanced Engineering, 5*(10), 75–77.

Walker, J. (2012, September 20). Meet the New Boss: Big Data. *The Wall Street Journal.*

Wallarm. (2021). *What is RBAC (Role-Based Access Control)?* Wallarm Blog. https://www.wallarm.com/what/what-exactly-is-role-based-access-control-rbac

Walton, R. E. (1985). From control to commitment in the workplace. *Harvard Business Review, 63*(2), 77–84.

Wang, D., & Fesenmaier, D. R. (2013). Transforming the travel experience: The use of smartphones for travel. In *Information and Communication Technologies in Tourism 2013* (pp. 58–69). Springer Berlin Heidelberg. doi:10.1007/978-3-642-36309-2_6

Wang, L. (2022, January). A futuristic perspective on human-centric assembly. *Journal of Manufacturing Systems, 62*, 199–201. doi:10.1016/j.jmsy.2021.11.001

Wang, L., Liu, S., Cooper, C., Wang, X., & Gao, R. (2021). Functionblock-based human-robot collaborative assembly driven by brainwaves. *CIRP Annals*, *70*(1), 5–8. doi:10.1016/j.cirp.2021.04.091

Wang, L., Wang, Z., Qu, H., & Liu, S. (2018). Optimal Forecast Combination Based on Neural Networks for TimeSeries Forecasting. *Applied Soft Computing*, *66*, 1–17. doi:10.1016/j.asoc.2018.02.004

Wanole, S. N., Bande, K. D., Holkar, S. C., & Mardane, R. G. (2018). Relational analysis of entrepreneurial behavior of banana growers. *International Journal of Chemical Studies*, *6*(3), 2407–2411.

Warner, K. S. R., & Wäger, M. (2019). Building dynamic capabilities for digital transformation: An ongoing process of strategic renewal. *Long Range Planning*, *52*(3), 326–349. doi:10.1016/j.lrp.2018.12.001

Watson, D., & Taylor, S. (2020). Diversity and inclusion in Industry 4.0: The role of technology. *Human Resource Management Review*, *30*(2), 181–192.

Weerasinghe, K., Scahill, S. L., Pauleen, D. J., & Taskin, N. (2022). Big data analytics for clinical decision-making: Understanding health sector perceptions of policy and practice. *Technological Forecasting and Social Change*, *174*(121222), 121222. doi:10.1016/j.techfore.2021.121222

Wei, J. T., Lee, M. C., Chen, H. K., & Wu, H. H. (2013). Customer relationship management in the hairdressing industry: An application of data mining techniques. *Expert Systems with Applications*, *40*(18), 7513–7518. doi:10.1016/j.eswa.2013.07.053

Wen, Y., Shi, X., Li, Q., & Xu, Q. (2020). Evaluation and analysis of vegetable supply chain performance based on the combination of AHP and DEA. *Journal of Systems Science and Information*, *8*(2), 138–149.

Werner, R. A. (2014). Can banks individually create money out of nothing? — The theories and the empirical evidence. *International Review of Financial Analysis*, *36*, 1–19. doi:10.1016/j.irfa.2014.07.015

What's MSME. (n.d.). Retrieved November 6, 2023, from Gov.in website: https://msme.gov.in/know-about-msme

Whysall, Z., Owtram, M., & Brittain, S. (2019). The new talent management challenges of Industry 4.0. *Journal of Management Development*, *38*(2), 118–129. doi:10.1108/JMD-06-2018-0181

Wijesundara, I., & Fernando, A. (2020). Digital Legacy: Challenges and Opportunities in Estate Planning. In *Proceedings of the 2020 2nd International Conference on Computer Science and Software Engineering* (pp. 93-97). ACM.

Wiliandri, R. (2020). A Conceptual Approach to Identify Factors Affecting the Digital Transformation of Micro, Small and Mediumsized Enterprises (MSMEs) during Covid-19 Pandemic in Indonesia. *Ekonomi Bisnis*, *25*(2), 66–85. doi:10.17977/um042v25i2p66-85

Williamson, D. (2011). Talent management in the new business world: How organizations can create the future and not be consumed by it. *Human Resource Management International Digest*, *19*(6), 33–36. doi:10.1108/09670731111163518

Wilsher, S. (2015). Behaviour profiling: Implications for recruitment and team building. *Strategic Direction*, *31*(9), 1–5. doi:10.1108/SD-02-2015-0023

Winters, R., & Hummel, M. (2014). *Practical predictive analytics*. Pearson.

Wislon, H. C. G. (2023). Retrieved from WislonHCG: https://www.wilsonhcg.com/

Wisner, J. D., Tan, K. C., & Leong, G. K. (2019). *Principles of supply chain management: A balanced approach*. Cengage Learning, UK.

Wolor, C. W., Solikhah, S., Fidhyallah, N. F., & Lestari, D. P. (2020). Effectiveness of E-training, E-leadership, and work life balance on employee performance during COVID-19. *Journal of Asian Finance. Economics and Business*, *7*(10), 443–450. doi:10.13106/jafeb.2020.vol7.no10.443

Wong, Y. C., Ho, K. M., Chen, H., Gu, D., & Zeng, Q. (2015). Digital divide challenges of children in low-income families: The case of Shanghai. *Journal of Technology in Human Services*, *33*(1), 53–71. doi:10.1080/15228835.2014.998576

World Tourism Organization (UNWTO). (Ed.). (2019). *International Tourism Highlights, 2019 Edition. World Tourism Organization*. UNWTO.

Wright, P. M., & Ulrich, M. D. (2017). A road well-traveled: The past, present, and future journey of strategic human resource management. *Annual Review of Organizational Psychology and Organizational Behavior*, *4*(1), 45–65. doi:10.1146/annurev-orgpsych-032516-113052

Xero. (2006). Retrieved from Xero Limited: https://www.xero.com/about/

Xu, X., Hong, W. C. H., Zhang, Y., Jiang, H., & Liu, J. (2023). Learning Paths Design in Personal Learning Environments: The Impact on Postgraduates' Cognitive Achievements and Satisfaction. *Innovations in Education and Teaching International*, 1–16. doi:10.1080/14703297.2023.2189603

Xu, Y., & Zeng, Q. (2017). Evaluation and optimization of vegetable supply chain performance based on BP neural network. *Proceedings of the 2017 International Conference on Management Science and Industrial Engineering*, 203-209.

Yang, J. (2012). Innovation capability and corporate growth: An empirical investigation in China. *Journal of Engineering and Technology Management, 29*(1), 34-46. . doi:10.1016/j.jengtecman.2011.09.004

Yao, Y., Cao, Y., Ding, X., Zhai, J., Liu, J., Luo, Y., & Zou, K. (2018). A paired neural network model for tourist arrival forecasting. *Expert Systems with Applications*, *114*, 588–614. doi:10.1016/j.eswa.2018.08.025

Yeo, B. L., Naina Mohamed, R. H., & Muda, M. (2016). A Study of Malaysian Customers Purchase Motivation of Halal Cosmetics Retail Products: Examining Theory of Consumption Value and Customer Satisfaction. *Procedia Economics and Finance*, *37*, 176–182. doi:10.1016/S2212-5671(16)30110-1

Yeruva, A. R., & Ramu, V. B. (2023). AIOps research innovations, performance impact, and challenges faced. *International Journal of System of Systems Engineering*, *13*(3), 229–247. doi:10.1504/IJSSE.2023.133013

Yueh, H.-P., Lu, M.-H., & Lin, W. (2016). Employees' acceptance of mobile technology in a workplace: An empirical study using SEM and fsQCA. *Journal of Business Research*, *69*(6), 2318–2324. doi:10.1016/j.jbusres.2015.12.048

Zahra, S. A., Ireland, R. D., & Hitt, M. A. (2000). International expansion by new venture firms: International diversity, mode of market entry, technological learning and performance. *Academy of Management Journal*, *43*(5), 925–950. doi:10.2307/1556420

Zhang, C., & Chen, Y. (2020). A review of research relevant to the emerging industry trends: Industry 4.0, IoT, blockchain, and business analytics. *Journal Industrial Integrate Management*, *5*(01), 165–180. doi:10.1142/S2424862219500192

Zhang, G., Patuwo, B. E., & Hu, M. Y. (1998). Forecasting with artificial neural networks: The state of the art. *International Journal of Forecasting*, *14*, 35–62. doi:10.1016/S0169-2070(97)00044-7

Zhang, Y. X., Xu, S., Zhang, L., & Yang, M. (2021). Big Data and Human Resource Management Research: An Integrative Review and New Directions for Future Research. *Journal of Business Research*, *133*, 34–50. doi:10.1016/j.jbusres.2021.04.019

Zhao, R., Liu, Y., Zhang, N., & Huang, T. (2017). An optimization model for green supply chain management by using a big data analytic approach. *Journal of Cleaner Production, 142*, 1085–1097. doi:10.1016/j.jclepro.2016.03.006

Zheng, Y., & Du, Z. (2019). A systematic review in crude oil markets: Embarking on the oil price. *Green Finance, 1*(3), 328–345. doi:10.3934/GF.2019.3.328

Zhong, R. Y., Huang, G. Q., Lan, S., Dai, Q. Y., Chen, X., & Zhang, T. (2015). A big data approach for logistics trajectory discovery from RFID-enabled production data. *International Journal of Production Economics, 165*, 260–272. doi:10.1016/j.ijpe.2015.02.014

Zhong, R. Y., Lan, S., Xu, C., Dai, Q., & Huang, G. Q. (2016). Visualization of RFID-enabled shopfloor logistics Big Data in Cloud Manufacturing. *International Journal of Advanced Manufacturing Technology, 84*(1–4), 5–16. doi:10.100700170-015-7702-1

Zhong, R., Xu, X., Klotz, E., & Newman, S. (2017). Intelligent manufacturing in the context of Industry4.0: A Review. *Engineering (Beijing), 3*(5), 616–630. doi:10.1016/J.ENG.2017.05.015

Zimmermann, S. (n.d.). *Labor Market 5.0: Enhance strategic HR planning through Big Data Skills Analysis*. Retrieved from WifOR: https://www.wifor.com/en/enhance-strategic-hr-planning-through-big-data-skills-analysis/#:~:text=Big%20Data%20Skills%20Analysis%20supports%20companies%20in%20preparing,in%20order%20to%20counteract%20shortages%20of%20skilled%20labor

Zimon, G., & Dankiewicz, R. (2020). Trade credit management strategies in SMEs and the COVID-19 pandemic—A case of Poland. *Sustainability (Basel), 12*(15), 6114. doi:10.3390u12156114

Żywiołek, J., Tucmeanu, E. R., Tucmeanu, A. I., Isac, N., & Yousaf, Z. (2022). Nexus of transformational leadership, employee adaptiveness, knowledge sharing, and employee creativity. *Sustainability (Basel), 14*(18), 11607. doi:10.3390u141811607

About the Contributors

Sonia Singh, Director of Toss Global Management and Human Resource, Education and Management consultancy company with operations in India, UAE and UK is a Researcher, Educator, Human Resource, Administrator and Corporate leader. She is also assessor for different quality awards of UAE. For over 22 years she served in India and abroad in different capacities and areas of expertise. Previously, Dr. Sonia Singh served as Group HR Director at LIN SCAN, one of the leading Oil and Gas companies with 8 offices around the world including UAE, Russia, India, Canada, Egypt, Minsk, Singapore and Malaysia, operations in 56 countries and more than 800 employees on board. She is a prominent speaker at different Universities and Government offices across UAE. She has been invited as Guest Speaker by SEWA (Sharjah Electricity and Water Authority). She was also a guest speaker for Emirates Canadian University College, (Umm Al Quwain), First Forum of "Year of Tolerance" under the patronage of Ruler of Umm Al Quwain. She is Recipient of the "Education Excellence Award" and honored by Hon. Penisimani Epenisa Fiftia, Minister of Education and Training, the Kingdom of Tonga for the support to African Community for Higher Education. She is the Editor, Guest editor of Scopus Indexed, ABDC and Web of science Journals. She is Board Member of GBRS (Research Forum of St. John University, USA, a collaboration between St. John's University's, Tobin College of Business and a diverse group of international scholars and Universities. She is an Advisory board member Gulf American University. Recognized for her excellent work in academics and corporate outside India and appeared in Coffee Book Tables launched in India, UK, and UAE.

S. Suman Rajest is currently working as Dean of Research and Development (R&D) & International Student Affairs (ISA) at Dhaanish Ahmed College of Engineering, Chennai, Tamil Nadu, India. He is an Editor in Chief of the International Journal of Human Computing Studies and The International Journal of Social Sciences World, He is the Chief Executive Editor of the International Journal of Advanced Engineering Research and Science, International Journal of Advanced Engineering, Management and Science, The International Journal of Health and Medicines, The International Journal of Management Economy and Accounting Fields and The International Journal of Technology Information and Computer and also he is an Editorial Board Member in International Journal of Management in Education, Scopus, Inderscience, EAI Endorsed Transactions on e-Learning, and Bulletin of the Karaganda university Pedagogy series. He is also a Book Series Editor in IGI Global Publisher, Springer, etc. All of his writing, including his research, involves elements of creative nonfiction in the Human Computing learning system. He is also interested in creative writing and digital media, Learning, AI, student health learning, etc. He has published 155 papers in peer-reviewed international journals. He has authored and co-authored several scientific book publications in journals and conferences and is a frequent reviewer of international journals and international conferences and also, he is also a reviewer in Inderscience, EAI Journals, IGI Global, Science Publications, etc.

Slim Hadoussa is a Professor of Management Information System and Dean of the Faculty at Brest Business School France. He obtained his PhD in Management Information System from University of Toulouse I Capitole France in 2009 awarded by the Ministry of Foreign and European Affairs France. He has an international teaching experience as an Associate Professor at MENA and Gulf Region Universities especially at Saudi Electronic University, Saudi Arabia and University of Carthage Tunisia. He contributes to diverse research, cooperation and visiting programs at MENA Region (Saudi Arabia, Morocco, Egypt, Tunisia, etc.). His research and teaching interest focus on MIS and organizational change, performance in different sectors such health care, education, commerce, tourism, etc. His publications focus on digitalization process and organizational consequences. His research projects treat subjects dealing with social media, e-learning experiences at universities, e-commerce and e-marketing, e-health and decision-making process, etc. He has several publications at peer reviewed international journal indexed FNEGE France, ABS, Web of Science and Scopus.

Ahmed J. Obaid is a Asst. Professor at the Department of Computer Science, Faculty of Computer Science and Mathematics, University of Kufa, Iraq. Dr. Ahmed holds a Bachelor in Computer Science, degree in – Information Systems from College of Computers, University of Anbar, Iraq (2001-2005), and a Master Degree (M. TECH) of Computer Science Engineering (CSE) from School of Information Technology, Jawaharlal Nehru Technological University, Hyderabad, India (2010-2013), and a Doctor of Philosophy (PhD) in Web Mining from College of Information Technology, University of University of Babylon, Iraq (2013-2017). He is a Certified Web Mining Consultant with over 14 years of experience in working as Faculty Member in University of Kufa, Iraq. He has taught courses in Web Designing, Web Scripting, JavaScript, VB.Net, MATLAB Toolbox's, and other courses on PHP, CMC, and DHTML from more than 10 international organizations and institutes from USA, and India. Dr. Ahmed is a member of Statistical and Information Consultation Center (SICC), University of Kufa, Iraq.

R. Regin is currently working as an Assistant Professor in the Department of Computer Science and Engineering at the SRM Institute of Science and Technology, Ramapuram, Chennai, Tamil Nadu, India. He has a specialization in the branch of information and communication. He holds experience of 10+ years in teaching faculty and research. He has also published papers in 55 reputed international journals, 40 international conferences, and 15 national conferences. He is a member of professional bodies like IE and IETE. He is also a Book Series Editor for IGI Global Publisher, Springer, etc. He is the Editor-in-Chief of the International Journal of Technology Information and Computers, Growing Scholar USA, and a member of the Journal Ilmiah Teunuleh's Editorial Advisory Board. He does research work in the fields of VANET, WSN, MANET, Cloud Computing, Network Security, and Information Security. He is a reviewer for many reputed journals like Springer, Inderscience, etc.

* * *

Shashank Agarwal is an analytics expert who has channeled his expertise within the healthcare space over the years. His experience cuts across various areas in market access, artificial intelligence, brand analytics, predictive modeling, launch strategy, and multi-channel marketing in several Fortune 500 companies such as CVS Health, AbbVie, and IQVIA.

K. M. Ashifa holds a doctorate in social work and is currently employed as an assistant professor in the department of social work at Istanbul Gelisim University in Turkey. She has 16 years of experience, including 9 years as an academician, 4 years as a researcher, and 3 years as a human rights educator in the development sector. Additionally, she collaborated with Kalasalingam Academy of Research and Education in Tamil Nadu and Istanbul Nisantasi University in Turkey. From 2008 to 2011, she also served as the state coordinator for Kerala's Human Rights Education under the UN World Programme. She has two books on the subject of human rights education to her credit, along with 151 research papers to her credit that have been published in peer-reviewed, highly indexed journals as chapters in edited books. At national and international seminars and conferences, she has participated and delivered 35 research articles. Icon of India 2023 Icon of India 2023 for the contribution in Research and Development in Academic by Institute of Social Reforms and Higher Education Charitable trust and Savitha School of Management Indiances., The ASDF Global Research Award 2021, the Dr. APJ Abdul Kalam Lifetime Achievement National Award2021 for Teaching, Research, and Publication, given by the International Institute for Social and Economic Reforms, and the Innovative Academic Research and Dedicated Teaching Faculty Award given by the Society of Engineers & Technicians, Malaysia, in 2017 are just a few of the accolades she has received for her dedication to research.

Sulaiman Olusegun Atiku is a Professor of Human Resources, and Director of Research at Harold Pupkewitz Graduate School of Business (HP-GSB), Namibia University of Science and Technology, Namibia. He is a pragmatic researcher specializing in Strategic Human Resource Management. His current research area of interest includes Human Capital Formation for the Fourth Industrial Revolution, and Human Resource Management Practices for Promoting Sustainability. He has over 15 years' experience in Higher Education. A native of Lagos, Sulaiman graduated from the University of KwaZulu-Natal with a PhD degree in Human Resource Management. His Master of Science degree was awarded in Human Resources and Industrial Relations at Lagos State University, Nigeria. His Bachelor of Science (Honours) degree was also awarded at Lagos State University in the field of Industrial Relations and Personnel Management. He has lectured several courses in his field home/abroad and published many scholarly articles in international journals. He is a member of International Labour and Employment Relations Association (ILERA), Nigerian Institute of Management (NIM), and Institute of People Management (IPM) South Africa.

Amit Bhanushali is an exceptionally accomplished Quality Assurance Manager with an impressive career spanning over 22 years in the dynamic IT industry. He holds a Master's degree in Business Data Analytics from West Virginia University, solidifying his academic foundation in addition to his extensive practical experience. Amit is firmly rooted in West Virginia, USA, and proudly holds the status of a Senior IEEE Member, reflecting his enduring commitment to innovation and excellence. His significant contributions to software testing research and practice leave an indelible mark on the industry, testifying to the depth of his knowledge and the value of his insights. Amit's exceptional expertise encompasses a wide spectrum, from automation and performance testing to the strategic implementation of DevOps and CI/CD processes. His ability to navigate and lead testing efforts in complex cloud environments sets him apart as a true industry luminary. Moreover, he lends his insightful voice to several thought-provoking articles on cutting-edge topics such as artificial intelligence and machine learning, underscoring his thought leadership and impact on software quality engineer.

Andrew Jeremiah, PhD, leads the Human Resources Management Section in the Department of Governance and Management Sciences, in the Faculty of Commerce, Human Sciences, and Education at the Namibia University of Science and Technology (NUST). He oversees the section's teaching and learning, and research activities of the section. Andrew has served NUST for the past 11 years as a Human Resource Management lecturer and doubles up as a researcher and research coordinator. He has been actively involved in the crafting, designing and implementation of new programmes such as Honours degrees in Human Resource Management and Employment Relations, and the master's degree in human resource management at NUST. Before joining NUST, Andrew served as a Programme Manager in the Department of Higher Education – TVET Section in South Africa, in Cape Town. He also served as a Training and Development Manager at Olivine Industries and Cairns Foods Limited respectively, in Harare in Zimbabwe. Before this, he had served as a Training Officer in the Department of National Parks and Wildlife Management in Harare, and as a High School Teacher under the Ministry of Education and Culture, where he also served as a National Chief Examiner for African languages at Ordinary Level. Andrew holds a Doctorate in Human Resource Management from the Cape Peninsula University of Technology (CPUT), a Master of Business Administration (MBA) from the University of Zimbabwe (UZ), Diplomas in High School Teaching and Human Resource Management from the University of Zimbabwe (UZ) and the Institute People Management of Zimbabwe (IPMZ) respectively.

Sankalp Mahesh Kokse is a student of VIT Pune currently pursuing BTech degree in computer engineering.

Dilmurod Nasimov is a professor of the Academy of Public Administration of the Republic of Uzbekistan.

Kamalendu Pal is with the Department of Computer Science, School of Science and Technology, City, University of London. Kamalendu received his BSc (Hons) degree in Physics from Calcutta University, India, Postgraduate Diploma in Computer Science from Pune, India, MSc degree in Software Systems Technology from the University of Sheffield, Postgraduate Diploma in Artificial Intelligence from Kingston University, MPhil degree in Computer Science from the University College London, and MBA degree from the University of Hull, United Kingdom. He has published over hundred international research articles (including book chapters) widely in the scientific community with research papers in the ACM SIGMIS Database, Expert Systems with Applications, Decision Support Systems, and conferences. His research interests include knowledge-based systems, decision support systems, teaching and learning practice, blockchain technology, software engineering, service-oriented computing, sensor network simulation, and supply chain management. He is on the editorial board of an international computer science journal and is a member of the British Computer Society, the Institution of Engineering and Technology, and the IEEE Computer Society.

Sachin Parate is a Principal Product Manager at Twilio where he leads Twilio's international tech expansion. Sachin has 12 years of progressive experience across Tech Product Management and Data Science. Sachin has built great products that he is extremely proud of, which include building and launching a multi-billion dollar credit card product and building a successful start-up. He also has an undergrad degree in technology from one of the top technology college in India known as the Indian Institute of Technology (IIT), Bombay.

Usha Prabhu holds four Master degrees- MA, M. Phil, MBA, UGC- NET, Ph.D. She has more than 22 Years of teaching experience at the graduate and post-graduate levels. She was one of the member in the syllabus revision committee for the PG- MBA at Bangalore University. She is currently a Faculty at Jain (Deemed-to be University, Bangalore Karnataka, India. She co-authored the book- Organization Behaviour for PG Students.

Easwaramoorthy Rangaswamy, Principal & Provost, Amity Global Institute, Singapore is a distinguished management professional and recipient of various awards including the "Award for 12 Most Influential Business Professors Under 40" by Singapore Business Review. He holds a PhD in Management and is Associate Fellow of Higher Education Academy, United Kingdom. He has taught for University of London, London School of Economics, University of Northampton, Anglia Ruskin University, UK; Victoria University, Australia and Bharathiar University & Visveswaraiah Technological University, India.

Sandeep Rangineni is a Data Test Engineer at Pluto TV, with over 12 plus years of experience in the IT industry, primarily within the streaming media industry. He holds a Master's degree in Engineering Management and Master's degree in Information Technology. Sandeep has a diverse skill set, working with technologies such as PL/SQL, Azure Databricks, Salesforce, Informatica, and Snowflake. Currently, he is actively engaged in researching Data Engineering and Data Quality topics. Sandeep has professional certifications in Salesforce admin, AWS Data Analytics and Safe 5 practitioner. Sandeep is a senior member of IEEE, professional member of BCS and fellow of IETE, three esteemed technology organizations, and has served as a judge for reputable award organizations in Technology which including Globee Awards, Stevie Awards, NCWIT Aspirations, and Brandon Hall Group.

Palanivel Rathinasabapathi Velmurugan is associated with BSBI, Berlin, as a professor in the Human Resource Management and Finance Stream. Prior to joining BSBI, he held the designation "Head" Faculty of Management at Sharda University, Uzbekistan, Central Asia, and "Dean of Arts" assignments at DMI St. John the Baptist University, Malawi, Central Africa. Also, he has been associated earlier with DMI St. Eugene University in Zambia, MAM Business School and various Engineering Colleges in India. He has a Ph.D. in Management from Mannonmanium Sundaranar University in India. Besides this, he holds an MBA Degree from SRM University in India and a BE Chemical Engineering degree from Annamalai University in India. Also, he completed six NPTEL Certificate Programs conducted by various IITs in India. He brings with him 14 years of rich working experience in teaching and research. Furthermore, he has a keen interest in the Case Method of teaching and research. He is an academic out of passion. Not only that, but he also takes a keen interest in guiding Ph.D. students. He has supervised three Ph.D. research scholars under his supervision at DMI St. Eugene University in Zambia.

Latha Thamma Reddi is a Principal Product Manager with two decades of IT industry experience in ERP, Digital Transformation, Software Engineering Development, Cloud Migration, Risk Management, Product, Portfolio & Program Management, Consulting & Presales. Latha is a seasoned leader with experience in managing larger teams, successfully led Global multi- disciplinary engineering teams for complex projects delivery in Hewlett Packard Inc, Hewlett Packard Enterprise and DXC Technology for HP, HPE, SABRE & Philips Clients. Latha is an IEEE Senior member and Fellow member. She is a Board Director for PMI Fort Worth Chapter as volunteer. Also, an "Advisory Committee" Member for Contact center world. Latha served as a judge for reputable award organizations in Technology and

Business which include Globee Awards, Brandon Hall Group and Stevie Awards. Latha has published several research papers in major research publications and other major media Latha has strong track record of working with C-suite and senior executives on developing business strategy and execution. Latha also helps startups and corporations with insights on small-to-medium-large proposals that might not be visible through regular sources. Latha is a globally recognized, award-winning product coach, known for motivating and training young professionals across over 15 countries. Her expertise in product management transforms novices into competent professionals, elevating their careers.

Biswan Senapati is a Platinum-level ERP-SAP Consultant with 20+ years of industry experience in domain consulting, business consulting, and solution architecture for large-scale ERP systems design, development, implementation, rollout, support, and business process re-engineering capacity in supply chain, chemicals, hi-tech, CPG, pharmaceuticals, wholesale, fashion retail, health care, and manufacturing domains.

Muhammed Shafi M. K. is working as Assistant Professor at VIT Business School, VIT University, Chennai Campus. He was working as Assistant professor and Adhoc Faculty at MITS Madanapalle and NIT Warangal respectively. He was awarded Ph.D from National Institute of Technology, Warangal and completed M.Phil and MBA from a central university named 'MANUU-Hyderabad'. Apart from qualifying UGC NET, he was selected for the UGC Fellowship called 'Maulana Azad National Fellowship' during his doctoral research period. His papers have been published in ABDC-B ranked, Scopus indexed and other peer reviewed journals. He has presented fifteen research papers at various doctoral, international and national conferences. He is the editorial board members of various international journals like Indian Journal of Finance and Banking, International Journal of Recent Research in Commerce Economics and Management etc and review member of BOHR International Journal of Advances in Management Research and United International Journal for Research & Technology.

P. S. Venkateswaran is currently working as a Professor in the Department of Management Studies, PSNA College of Engineering & Technology, Dindigul affiliated to Anna University, Chennai where he teaches courses in Advertising, marketing and Research Methods. He has served in various faculty positions from Assistant Professor to Professor in leading Arts & Colleges such as Cherran Arts and Science College, Kangeyam and Sree Saraswathi Thyagaraja College, Pollachi. He received MSc in Physics, an M.B.A., from Bharathiar University and MPhil from Alagappa University Karaikudi. He received his Ph.D in Business Administration from Madurai Kamaraj University, Madurai. He is having twenty two years of teaching and nine years of research & consultancy experience. His research activities include on Branding, Advertising and Digital marketing He conducted more than 90 Entrepreneurship Awareness Camps and trained around 8000 Engineering, Arts and Science College students and motivated them towards entrepreneurship. He also conducted 10 Faculty Development programmes, 10 EDP/WEDP programmes and 7 TEDP programmes. He trained more the 200 women entrepreneurs in Dindigul District.

R. Vennila, M.Com., M.Phil., MBA., PGDCA., Ph.D., is currently working as an Associate Professor, School of Commerce and Management in Jain (Deemed to be) University, Bangalore. She serves as a guide for UG, PG and Ph.D scholars. Her area of interest in Finance. She is having 15 years of experience in Teaching and 2 years in Industry. She has attended more than 10 FDPs in India. She acted as a Guest Lecture and Speaker for more than 10 Seminars and Webinars. She published more than 50 articles in various International and National Journals. She has presented more than 100 papers in various national and international Conferences.

Hylton James Villet holds a PhD in organization communication. He has vast experience as a senior manager in the IT industry in Namibia. He is the Director of the Harold Pupkewitz Graduate School of Business at Namibia University of Science and Technology. He has published several articles on organizational behaviour, leadership, strategic management and human resource management. 03ff5b65-9c6a-4a55-be69-ef7ed48011c0)

Doreen Zaaaruka is an HR professional with over 15 years' experience working in manufacturing industry, education industry, non-governmental organisations and state-owned-enterprises (SOEs). She holds a Masters of Leadership and Change Management, as well as a Bachelor of Human Resource Management Honours from the Namibia University of Science and Technology (NUST). She further holds a Bachelors of Arts Psychology from the University of Namibia (UNAM). Her areas of expertise include recruitment & selection, organisational development, talent management, performance management, employee wellness and compensation & payroll management. Doreen is currently the Manager: Administration and Compensation at the Namibia Postal limited (NamPost).

Index

A

Access to Information 209-211, 213, 215-216, 218-219
AI Tools 27, 125-133
Apparel Industry 395-397
Artificial Intelligence 20-23, 26, 35, 105, 112, 116, 118, 124-125, 173, 175, 221, 223, 225-227, 367, 386
Attribution Modeling 35, 38, 56

B

Big Data 20-21, 25, 27, 30, 37, 51, 109-116, 118-121, 164, 173, 182, 221, 226, 228, 343, 345-348, 371, 373, 381-382, 398-400, 402-403, 405-406, 408-409
Blockchain 179-186, 188-189, 191, 227, 332, 339, 395
Blockchain Technology 179-185, 191, 332
Brand Preference 356-357, 359, 362, 365-366
Business Intelligence 34, 37-44, 111, 152, 157-158, 370, 400, 406
Business Process Management 158-159
Business Sustainability 164

C

Central Bank Digital Currency (CBDC) 331-340
Challenges for BI 42
Clustering Models 51
Communication Technology 224, 344, 398
Competitor Intelligence 167
Consumer Preference 356-357, 367
Consumer Satisfaction 37, 357
Cost and Financial Aspects 296
COVID-19 137-139, 141, 143-146, 193, 195-197, 199-200, 202-206
COVID-19 Crises 146
Cross-Selling and Upselling Model 53
Cryptocurrency 179-181, 186, 335
Customer intelligence 167
Customer Relationship Management 37, 55-57, 149-150, 152, 154, 167, 173, 175, 316
Customer Segmentation 38-40, 51, 53, 57-59
Customer Service 36, 50, 83, 91, 154, 156, 158, 296-299, 301, 305, 308, 311, 384, 405

D

Dairy Farming 264-267, 274-275
Data Analytics 2, 5, 21-25, 27-28, 30, 53, 89, 100, 105, 109-111, 113-115, 118-120, 132, 157, 228, 282, 291-292, 307, 343, 346, 371, 381, 384, 395, 397-399, 402-403, 405, 408-410
Data Integration 38-39, 156, 302
Data Mining 157, 164-165, 168, 175, 198, 359, 395, 405, 407
Data Requirements 296-298, 300-301
Data Visualization 38-40, 350
Data Warehousing 38-39, 406
Decision Tree Model 58
Digital Legacy 64-65, 67-68, 70-74, 83-85

E

Economic Performance 235-241, 244-245, 333
Employee Engagement 4-5, 24, 27-28, 30, 87-96, 102-104, 115, 137-145, 157, 307, 370, 374, 379, 384, 386
Employee Performance 15, 25, 27-28, 102, 110, 140-143, 145, 157, 371, 373
Enterprise Business Solution 150
Enterprise Resource Planning 37, 149, 151-153, 399
Entrepreneurs 193, 195-202, 206, 209-211, 213-216, 218-219, 264-265, 267-268, 275, 279, 291
Environmental Purchasing 235-241, 244-245
EVM 183, 186

F

Firm Size 235-237, 239, 241, 244
Frequently Asked Questions (FAQ) 179-180

G

Government Initiatives 198, 209-211, 218-219
Government Policies and Initiatives 209-211, 213-216, 218-219

H

Hair Care 356-359
Hair Shampoo 356-357, 360, 362-367
Hardhat 186
Higher Education 120, 124-126
HR Metrics 157, 369, 379, 384, 386-387
Human Resource Management 1-2, 5-6, 10-11, 14-15, 21-23, 109, 111, 118, 120, 140, 156-157, 373-374, 402
Human Resources 1-2, 14-15, 20-22, 24, 27-28, 30, 109-120, 152, 156, 322-323, 326-327, 370-372, 375, 379, 417

I

Indian IT Industry 415, 425-426
Industry 4.0 20-26, 28-30, 221-224, 226-227, 371, 373, 381
Industry 5.0 35, 221-229, 231
Industry Sector 209, 211, 213, 215-216, 218-219
Innovative Capabilities 415, 425
Innovative strategies 199, 335
Internet of Things 20-21, 23, 172, 182, 226, 395
Inventory Management 53, 150, 153, 155-156, 170, 296-299, 303, 307-308, 311
Investments 2, 43-44, 110, 279, 281, 283, 331-332

L

Land and Labor 264
Lending 205, 278-279, 282-284, 290-292, 340
Lockdown 137-138, 143-144, 195, 197, 199, 205

M

Marketing Campaigns 38, 40-41, 52, 54, 58-59, 154
Marketing Intelligence 164-169, 172-175
Metrics 4-5, 14, 38-40, 83, 89, 91, 101, 110, 117, 157-159, 216, 296-308, 311, 315, 369, 372, 379, 382, 384, 386-387, 396, 400
Moderated Mediation 209, 215, 218-219
MSMEs 193-200, 202-206

N

National Stock Exchange (NSE) 249, 253, 261
Nifty 248, 254-259, 261

O

Order Fulfillment 156, 296-300, 303, 307, 311
Organisational Culture 316, 415, 425-427
Organizational Performance 1-3, 10, 14, 21, 30, 39, 90, 110, 139-140, 157, 326, 415-418, 420-421, 423, 426-427

P

Paper Currency 332-333
Performance Evaluation 24, 39, 296-302, 306
Personal Heritage Preservation 64
Predictive Analytics 21, 25-27, 35, 39, 41, 43, 49-51, 57-59, 158, 384
Product Intelligence 167
Productivity 15, 20-22, 27-28, 30, 35, 91-92, 95-96, 100, 103, 105, 113, 115, 117-118, 120, 131, 140-146, 153-154, 159, 202, 221-222, 226, 231, 237-238, 265, 267, 296, 298-300, 304, 307-308, 311, 313-314, 316-317, 370-371, 378, 380-381, 384, 387, 427
Propensity Model 57
Purchase Intention 357, 359, 367

R

RFM Model 57, 359

S

Sales Forecasting Model 52
Sales Pipeline Analysis 54
Sentiment Analysis 35, 55, 347, 349
Smart HR 4.0 20-22, 24-30
Smart Tourism 344-345
Society 5.0 221-223, 226
Strategic Purchasing 235-239, 241, 244-245

Strategic Sourcing 245
Supply Chain 43-44, 150, 152, 155-156, 170, 180-182, 184, 197, 200, 226, 237, 244-245, 266, 297-300, 306-307, 395-396, 398-401, 406
Supply Chain Management 150, 152, 170, 180-181, 184, 297, 307, 400
Supply Chain Planning 155-156
Sustainable Development 126, 165, 221-222, 267, 291, 385, 396
Sustainable Development Goals 221-222, 385

T

Talent Attraction 370, 375, 386-387
Talent Development 2-3, 12, 23, 369-370, 375-377, 379, 386-387
Talent Identification 371
Talent Retention Strategy 379, 386
Technology Advancements 20, 26
Total Quality Management (TQM) 313-317, 322, 327
Tourist Behaviour 343-348

V

Value Chain Network 396
Vegetable Distribution Center 296, 298, 300

W

Women Entrepreneurship 210-211, 213
Work Efficiency 140-145

www.ingramcontent.com/pod-product-compliance
Lightning Source LLC
LaVergne TN
LVHW060350300926
849162LV00006B/1241
9798369321935